Sent to Mrs Bingham Jy 4 199? 1992

Kiss, Mrs Beky and Mary Tibbs

THE HISTORY OF
THE WORLD SERIES

THE HISTORY OF

THE WORLD SERIES

THE COMPLETE CHRONOLOGY
OF AMERICA'S GREATEST
SPORTS TRADITION

GENE SCHOOR

William Morrow and Company, Inc.
New York

Recognizing the importance of preserving what has been written, it is the policy of William Morrow and Company, Inc., and its imprints and affiliates to have the books it publishes printed on acid-free paper, and we exert our best efforts to that end.

Library of Congress Cataloging-in-Publication Data

Schoor, Gene.
    The history of the World Series : the complete chronology of
America's greatest sports tradition / Gene Schoor.
        p.   cm.
    Includes bibliographical references (p.).
    ISBN 0-688-07995-4
    1. World Series (Baseball)—History—Chronology.   2. Baseball—
United States—Records.   I. Title.
GV878.4.S35   1990
796.357′646—dc20
                                                90-34210
                                                CIP

Printed in the United States of America

First Edition

1 2 3 4 5 6 7 8 9 10

BOOK DESIGN BY PATRICE FODERO

To my mentor, Dr. Ed Haislet, an unforgettable professor at the University of Minnesota, now in his eightieth season, whose lectures and personal one-on-one sessions inspired me to start writing. Now after fifty books, Ed and I still talk and he still has the old spirit and fire, much like the great Vince Lombardi. God bless, Ed.

And to my lifelong friend, Max Kanter, who edited my Passaic High School term papers, and still painstakingly edits every paragraph, every page, through all these years. Thanks, Max.

Acknowledgments

No history of the World Series that stretches from the early 1880s to the present day, with a scope as wide as that of the national pastime, is possible without the help and cooperation of hundreds of people. To all of them I am grateful. Many of the former great stars, coaches, managers, and sportswriters took time from their busy daily routine to answer questions and to supply material pertinent to the most stirring World Series moments. First and foremost, a grateful thank-you to Pat Kelly of the National Baseball Hall of Fame, who cheerfully collated and gathered hundreds of the photographs for this book; to Bill Guilfoyle, associate director of the Hall of Fame; and to Tom Heitz, librarian at the Hall of Fame, and to all the assistants for their marvelous aid in this project.

I also want to express my appreciation to the many World Series heroes who aided me: to Bob Feller, Stan Musial, Sandy Koufax, Grover Cleveland Alexander, Dizzy Dean, Pepper Martin, Leo Durocher, Johnny Sain, Lou Boudreau, Ty Cobb, Pee Wee Reese, Willie Mays, Roy Campanella, Mickey Mantle, Billy Martin, Casey Stengel, Yogi Berra, Phil Rizzuto, Lefty Gomez, Joe McCarthy, Ralph Houk, Larry Sherry, Don Larsen, Whitey Ford, Tom Lasorda, Rogers Hornsby, Tris Speaker, Mel Ott, Carl Hubbell, Lew Burdette, and many others.

A special thank-you goes to the public relations directors of a number of major league teams: to Harvey Greene and Anne Mileo of the Yankees; Dan Ewald of the Tigers, Tom Mee of the Minnesota Twins; Mickey Morabito of the Oakland Athletics; Kip Ingle of the Cardinals; and Roland Hemond, general manager of the Orioles.

And a very special thank-you goes to Jimmy Breslin, Dick Schaap, Red Smith, Jimmy Powers, Dick Young, Jimmy Cannon, Al Buck, Lenord Cohen, Lee Allen, Warren Brown, Joe Durso, Milt Gross, Jerry Mitchell, Bob Farrell, Arch Murray, Joe King, Dan Parker, and so many others. . . .

I am deeply indebted to my great editor at William Morrow, Adrian Zackheim, whose surgical editing helped make this a very special project; to my special editor at Morrow, Pam Altschul, who constantly handled my every query with great ability and charm: and to that hall-of-fame literary agent Julian Bach, the greatest.

Additional photographs are from Jay Horowitz, public relations manager, New York Mets, the New York *Daily News*, the *Brooklyn Eagle*, *Minneapolis Star*, Wide World Photos.

SELECTED BIBLIOGRAPHY

Allen, Lee. *100 Years of Baseball*. New York: Bartholomew House, 1953.

———. *Hot Stove League*. New York: A.S. Barnes, 1955.

Berra, Yogi, and Ed Fitzgerald. *Yogi*. New York: Doubleday, 1960.

Cannon, Jimmy. *Who Struck John?* New York: Dial Press, 1958.

Durocher, Leo. *The Dodgers and Me*. New York: Ziff-Davis, 1948.

Durso, Joe. *Amazing: The Miracle of the Mets*. Boston: Houghton Mifflin, 1970.

Einstein, Charles. *Willie Mays*. New York: Putnam, 1964.

Feller, Bob. *Strikeout Story*. New York: A.S. Barnes, 1947.

Ford, Whitey, Mickey Mantle, and Joe Durso. *Whitey and Mickey*. New York: Viking Press, 1977.

Gies, Joe, and Robert Shoemaker. *Stars of the World Series*. New York: Thomas Y. Crowell, 1964.

Golenbock, Peter. *Dynasty: The New York Yankees*. Englewood Cliffs, N.J.: Prentice-Hall, 1975.

Graham, Frank Jr. *Casey Stengel*. New York: John Day, 1958.

———. *The New York Yankees*. New York: Putnam, 1958.

Holmes, Tommy. *Dodger Daze and Knights*. New York: David McKay, 1953.

Hornsby, Rogers. *My Kind of Baseball*. New York: David McKay, 1953.

Koppett, Leonard. *The New York Mets*. New York: Collier Books, 1970.

Koufax, Sandy. *Sandy Koufax*. New York: Viking Press, 1966.

Lieb, Fred. *The Story of World Series*. New York: Putnam, 1950.

———. *Baseball as I Have Known It*. New York: Coward, McCann, and Geoghegan, 1977.

MacLean, Norman. *Casey Stengel*. New York: Drake Publishers, 1976.

Mann, Arthur. *Baseball Confidential*. New York: David McKay, 1951.

Meany, Tom. *Colliers Greatest Sport Stories*. New York: A.S. Barnes, 1955.

———. *Mostly Baseball*. New York: A.S. Barnes, 1958.

Musial, Stan. *Stan Musial*. New York: Doubleday, 1964.

Objoski, Robert. *The All Stars*. New York: Stein and Day, 1980

Pepe, Phil. *The Wit and Wisdom of Yogi Berra*. New York: Hawthorne Books, 1974.

Robinson, Jackie. *The Jackie Robinson Story*. New York: Doubleday, 1972.

Schoor, Gene. *Billy Martin*. New York: Doubleday, 1981.

Shoemaker, Robert, and Joseph Gies. *Stars of the Series*. New York: Thomas Y. Crowell, 1965.

Smith, Ira. *Baseball's Greatest Outfielders*. New York: A.S. Barnes, 1954.

Trimble, Joe. *Yogi Berra, MVP*. New York: A.S. Barnes, 1956.

Vecsey, George. *Joy in Mudville: A History of the Mets*. New York: McCall Publishing Co., 1970.

Wind, Herbert Warren. *The Gilded Age of Sport*. New York: Simon and Schuster, 1964.

See also: *Sport, Sports Illustrated, Sporting News, Inside Baseball, Inside Sports, Brooklyn Eagle,* and *U.S.A. Today.*

Contents

The World Series:
The Early Skirmishes

Imagine, if you will, the arrogance of manager Leo Durocher, decreeing that there would be no World Series just because he would not permit his Giants, National League champs, to be on the same field with the Cleveland Indians, American League winners. Leo, in refusing to play, called the Indians "a fumbling bunch of bushers playing in a two-bit league."

Sounds impossible?

Yet it did happen.

Another famous New York manager of an earlier era had done just that, and with the identical words, and made his edict stick.

It happened just eighty-six years ago, when the great John McGraw stunned the baseball fraternity by scornfully giving the back of his hand to a postseason challenge from the Boston Puritans, the 1904 American League champs. McGraw's stubborn refusal to play Boston touched off one of the most acrimonious arguments in the turbulent history of baseball.

When this happened on a day in 1904, New York bartenders busily pulled half-maddened Giants fans off tormenting American League supporters who had been sneering that the hated McGraw and his boss, owner John Brush, were actually afraid that the upstart Puritans would run the Giants out of the ballpark. But the Boston team was turned down by the Giants' owner, John J. Brush. (From that period on, this sort of rude refusal was termed a "brush-off.")

Newspapers echoed the taunts, and one sportswriter gloomily predicted that the Giants' manager's stand would cause harm to his ball club from which it might never recover.

Instead of a World Series battle with the Puritans, McGraw and John Brush arranged a rollicking party for the champions at the swank Erlanger Theatre in the heart of Broadway. Stage performers, political bigwigs, and prize fight champions paid as much as $100 per person to attend the affair, which lasted throughout the night. The party was the most exciting, extravagant affair of the year. Brush purchased some $5,000 worth of tickets for friends. Among those who attended were the incomparable Lillian Russell, Diamond Jim Brady, "Bet a Million" Gates, jockey Tod Sloan, heavyweight champ Jim Jeffries. Harry Stevens, who had begun his catering empire ten years earlier, presented diamond cuff links to the Giant players. The emcee of this fabulous evening was none other than the manager of the Giants, John J. McGraw.

When it became known that McGraw would not play Boston, Puritan fans held mass meetings all over downtown Boston and burned a doll-like form of the Giant manager in effigy. They called McGraw a coward and thousands of crazed Boston fans assailed John J. in letters to the press.

Meanwhile, McGraw calmly sat in his offices at the Polo Grounds, unwilling to dignify the Boston team with any sort of reply.

1

Doubleday Field, Cooperstown, N.Y. It was on this site in 1839 that Cadet Abner Doubleday originated baseball.

In those early days, baseball was loosely organized and still poorly regulated. There was no all-powerful baseball czar to order McGraw to play the Puritans. A series between the two leagues, which was clamored for each year by the fans, had not become the inviolate tradition of the game, as it is today.

Surely, baseball is America's national pastime. From April to October as many as fifty million spectators cheerfully pay admission to sit in ballparks across the country. Many millions of additional fans watch the games on television and listen to the daily radio broadcasts. Another fifteen million adults and young boys and girls participate in baseball programs organized by their local communities.

When one thinks about the enormous popularity of baseball, a pertinent question often comes to mind: Where, and how, was this great national game born?

Actually, the origins of baseball are somewhat hazy. Except for box scores, very little about the game was recorded before 1890. A great many people insist that baseball is purely an American invention, designed by Abner Doubleday, a West Point cadet who lived in Cooperstown, New York. Others argue that baseball slowly evolved as a combination of two British games, rounders and cricket. And the controversy reached bitter heights during the early twentieth century.

One of the earliest champions of the rounders theory was an Englishman, Henry Chadwick. In 1837 he began a remarkable career in America, writing about baseball and covering individual games for the biggest newspapers and magazines published at the time. He also wrote several books about baseball, originated the scoring system, compiled the first rule book, and developed numerous other ideas for the game. Because he was such an outstanding authority on the game, many people refer to Chadwick as "the father of baseball." But Chadwick strongly believed that baseball had evolved from the British game of rounders, which had already been played for nearly two centuries.

Albert Spalding, one of the game's early stars as a player, then a manager and club owner, and the greatest propagandist and missionary that baseball has ever known, found the rounders theory to be sheer nonsense and formed a Na-

Gen. Abner Doubleday

Henry Chadwick developed the first shorthand method of scoring baseball games and also published baseball's first guidebooks.

tional Committee composed of the game's notables, to settle the matter of baseball's origin in 1905. The committee, chaired by Abraham Mills, a former president of the National League, studied the question for two years and in 1907 concluded that Abner Doubleday should indeed be credited with the initiation of baseball in Cooperstown, New York, in 1839. To prove his point, Spalding and the committee demonstrated that baseball had evolved out of the old Colonial game of one ole cat, played by three boys, which had then become two ole cat, played by four boys; then, three ole cat, played by six boys; and, finally, four ole cat, played by eight boys, was played in the early nineteenth century. Then, according to Spalding, "some ingenious American boy figured out how to change the players into competing teams," and so developed town ball.

In 1839, Abner Doubleday first outlined the diamond-shaped baseball field, including the location of players on the field, and then drew up a crude draft of the rules of the game, which he named "baseball."

"And that," said chairman Mills, "proved beyond doubt that baseball is an American game and has no connection with the British version."

However, baseball as we know it has gone through a gradual evolution. Young American men of the early nineteenth century were surely just as inventive as today's young players, and, starting with the game of rounders, they no doubt changed the official rules to suit the conditions under which their game was played. Early players first developed one ole cat and two ole cat, which used one and two bases, and then town ball, which used four bases and a batter's box between home plate and first base. All of the early variations were based on the same principle: A ball was tossed to a batter who hit the ball and ran to a base or bases. But the equipment and methods of scoring and putting out runners varied.

Town ball, with its many variations, reached the height of its popularity in the early nineteenth century. It proved to be an excellent source of mass recreation in a world where automobiles, radios, and television sets were not

Captain Harry Wright, former English cricket star, organized the first professional baseball team, the Cincinnati Red Stockings, in 1869.

even dreamed of. There was plenty of space in which to play, and whatever equipment was used was either handmade or very inexpensive. Within a few years, town ball players began to form clubs, and those clubs represented the first step toward the game of professional baseball.

The most famous ballplaying group of the early nineteenth century was the Knickerbocker Club of New York City, organized in 1845. Membership in the Knickerbockers was restricted to the socially prominent gentlemen of New York, who had been playing the game among themselves on the site of the original Madison Square Garden on Madison Avenue and Twenty-sixth Street.

One day the Knickerbockers received a challenge from another team in New York, called the New York Nine, and the Knicks readily accepted the challenge. The date for the game was set for June 19, 1846, at a favorite field for cricket, the Elysian Fields in Hoboken, New Jersey.

The Knicks were so confident of beating their rivals that they didn't bother to practice and were soundly defeated by a 23–1 score. Though the Knickerbockers lost the game, the wonderful dinner and champagne at McCarty's Hotel in Hoboken more than made up for the defeat.

The New York Nine team either went back to playing cricket or disbanded, for they never played another game. The Knickerbockers were unable to find another opponent for five years.

Then suddenly, in the 1850s, organized baseball clubs began to spring up everywhere, in

Al Spalding, remembered today as the founder of the well-known sporting-goods company. In the 1870s he was the greatest pitcher in baseball, leading Boston to four successive titles. He was the nation's most celebrated athlete.

virtually every large city, including Manhattan, Brooklyn, Boston, Baltimore, Philadelphia, and Washington. As the years went by, the makeup of the teams changed. The clubs were no longer limited to "gentlemen." Clerks, shopkeepers, lawyers, almost any young man who had the time, could and did join the "nines." By the late 1850s, well over two hundred clubs had been organized.

In 1857 sixteen clubs formed a National Organization of Baseball Players in order to establish a uniform code of rules and conduct for the game. One important rule that was adopted stated: "Members may not accept money for playing baseball."

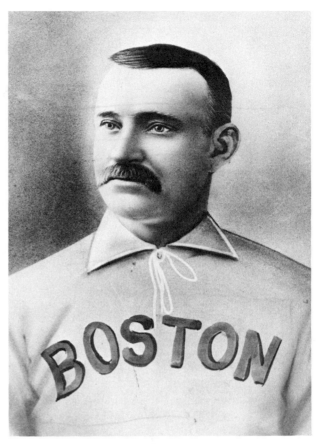

In 1894 Charles "Hoss" Radbourne won 26 of his team's final 27 games and the championship for the Providence Greys.

His name was Adrian Anson, but he was known as Cap to everyone, a great player of the nineteenth century and the game's greatest manager. Cap managed the White Sox for nineteen years and won five championships. He was the first player to garner 3,000 or more hits.

Baseball really came into its own in the decade following the Civil War. It became America's foremost pastime, and was regarded as the national game. Record attendance at the important games of 1865 was followed by a tenfold increase in the number of clubs, and by 1866 it was estimated that more than 200,000 spectators attended the games yearly.

Professionalism slowly began to develop as star players received and accepted offers of money. Their sole responsibility was to play ball for the organization that employed them.

In 1869 baseball-minded Cincinnatians were determined that they would have a winning team and decided to pay all their players. The 1868 Red Stockings had four paid players in their ranks but decided they could not really establish themselves unless the amateur element was completely eliminated. So they turned to Harry

Wright, who had come to Cincinnati as an instructor for the Union Cricket Club at a salary of $1,200 a year. In November 1867 he was hired to play and manage the Cincinnati Red Stockings team at the same salary. This was the beginning of professional baseball in America.

Ignoring local players, Wright searched the East and the Midwest and selected a ten-man squad with three substitutes. The total payroll for the season, which lasted from March 15 to November 15, was $9,300.

With Harry Wright and his brother George as the nucleus of the team, the Red Stockings outclassed every team they played that first season. Crowds of more than six thousand would attend the games, paying an admission price of ten and twenty-five cents.

The success of the Red Stockings so stimulated interest in baseball that clubs became numerous enough and strong enough to form an all-professional league.

In the spring of 1871 the representatives of ten professional teams met in New York City and formed the National Association of Professional Baseball Players. The teams in the newly formed league included the Philadelphia Athletics, Rockford Forest Citys, Chicago White Stockings, Fort Wayne Kekiongas, New York Mutuals, Washington Nationals, Washington Olympics, Brooklyn Eckfords, Cleveland Forest Citys, and Boston Red Stockings.

The rules of the new league provided that every member club play five games with every other club within the league. The team that won the most number of games would be considered the national champions. The first recognized champions were the Philadelphia Athletics.

The launching of an all-professional league and the establishment of a national champion look wonderfully simple on paper, but those first professional years were full of problems. Players moved from one team to another when offered more money, for there was no legal way for the association to force a player to stay with one club. The owners also had financial problems. They had to make money to survive. That meant they had to have a winning team that fans would want to pay money to see. As a result, the owners ruthlessly outbid each other for the better players.

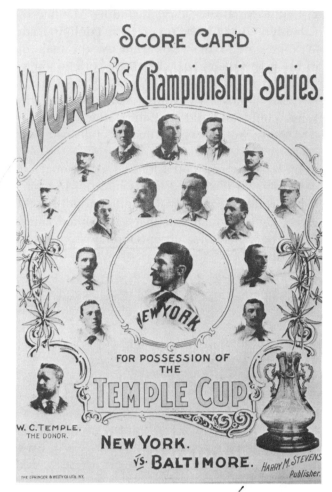

Col. William Temple, a Pittsburgh sportsman, donated this ornate silver trophy, the Temple Cup, in 1893. For the next four years it was the first prize for winning the National League Championship.

The first professional organization collapsed as a result of the bribing of a number of players, open gambling, rowdiness, and drinking among the fans at games. A second organization, called the National Association of Professional Baseball Clubs, grew from the wreckage in 1875. William Hulbert, principal owner of the Chicago White Stockings, organized the new association. In essence, Hulbert proposed that the league would be an organization of clubs not players. The clubs would pay a membership fee of one hundred dollars; players' contracts with clubs were to be written, not oral; players could not jump teams; any player found guilty of a dishonest act in a game would be barred for life.

N.L 1875

The association selected Morgan Bulkeley, the former Connecticut governor, as the league president. The new league, the National League, would play a seventy-game schedule. Each team would play every other team five times at home and five times away.

For the first few years that the two leagues coexisted, each prospered from its own intra-league competition. Then in 1884, as the two leagues straightened out their differences over territorial and player rights, the first World Series was arranged by officials of both leagues.

The Series involved the Providence Grays, champions of the National League, and the Metropolitans of New York, pennant winners of the American Association, in a three-game postseason classic.

Charlie Radbourne, Providence's star pitcher, wasn't a big man as were most of the great fastball pitchers who followed him—Amos Rusie, Walter Johnson, Rube Waddell, Bob Feller. He was only five feet nine and weighed 165 pounds but threw with terrific speed and by winning 35 of his team's last 37 games, he literally carried the Grays to the pennant. In the first game, Radbourne outpitched the Mets' great hurler Tim Keefe, allowing the Mets just 2 hits as Providence won the game, 6–0. Radbourne again outpitched Keefe to win the second game by a 3–1 margin, and the very next day, Radbourne, pitching his third game in three days, coasted to an easy 11–2 victory in a game that was called after the sixth inning.

Thus the first World Series ended with the Providence Grays defeating the highly regarded Mets in baseball's first big upset.

Prior to 1885, baseball was quite different from the scientific, fast-moving action game that is shown on prime-time television today.

During that period the distance between the bases was 90 feet (which it still is) but the pitcher stood facing the batter from a distance of 50 feet. Today that distance is 60 feet, 6 inches.

Before a pitcher delivered the ball, the batter could call for the kind of pitch he wanted. He could call for the ball to be thrown low or high. And if the pitch was not in that specified area, it was called a ball.

The pitcher had to deliver the ball to the batter underhand and with a stiff arm, and the ball had to be released from below the pitcher's waist. If the ball was thrown in any other way, it was called a ball.

Three strikes constituted an out. But it took six balls for a batter to receive a walk.

Some fielders wore thin gloves that were cut off at the fingers.

In 1893 the pitching mound was moved back to where it is today and in the fall of 1884, the rules committee changed the rule to allow pitchers to throw the ball overhand to the batter.

Cap Anson's Chicago White Stockings captured the championship in the National League in 1885, while the St. Louis Browns of the American Association won the first of their four consecutive championships.

Constantine Adrian "Cap" Anson, was the first white child born among the Pottawattomi Indian tribe in Iowa. As a youngster, Anson played baseball every moment he could spare from his daily chores, and by the time he was nineteen, he had received offers from a number of professional teams. He finally accepted an offer to play for Rockford, an outstanding team in Illinois, for the then amazing salary of sixty-six dollars per week. Cap Anson was the first major league player to attain the 3,000-hit total. A right-handed hitter, Cap led all National League batters four times.

In a career that began in 1876 with Chicago, Anson dominated the game with his uncanny ability to hit the ball. His twenty-two-year batting average of .334 places Anson alongside such all-time greats as Ty Cobb, Rogers Hornsby, and Tris Speaker.

As manager of the Chicago team, Anson won five championships in his first nine years. Then he went twelve years without ever winning another title. Yet his popularity with fans never diminished. When he was finally eased out of his post with Chicago in 1897, Cap took over as the manager of the Giants, but he left the Giants after handling the club for only twenty-two games and retired from the game.

Charles Comiskey, the St. Louis manager, was such a versatile player as a youngster that he could pitch, play second or third, and even catch if the regular catcher was injured. By the time he was eighteen, young Comiskey had played with teams in Elgin, Illinois; Milwaukee, and Dubuque, Iowa.

When the Browns offered Comiskey the princely sum of $125 per month, he jumped at the opportunity and became the team's best first baseman. Until Comiskey played first base for the Browns, it was common practice for the first baseman to keep his foot anchored to the base. Comiskey, however, moved back from the base and roamed over into the territory between himself and the second baseman. This radical move created a sensation, and within a few weeks all of the professional first basemen had copied Comiskey's style of play.

Comiskey's great style caught the fancy of the St. Louis Browns and at the end of the 1883 season, the twenty-three-year-old youngster was named manager of the team. By the end of the 1885 season, Comiskey's second year as manager, the Browns won the pennant in the American Association and Comiskey issued a challenge to Cap Anson for a seven-game series to decide the championship. Anson accepted.

That Series should actually be called the Series of Big Boots, for the players of both clubs made a total of 100 errors. The final game was one of the most ragged ever played; the two teams were charged with 27 errors. The second game was a riotous one, as thousands of fans erupted and fought each other when Comiskey angrily objected to umpire Dan Sullivan's decision on a play.

"If you don't reverse your decision," Comiskey screamed, "I'll take my players off the field. Anyway, all of your people are horse thieves."

"You can't take your players off the field, Comy," said Cap Anson. "The people in this ballpark paid good money to see the game. And they're your fans; you can't just walk out on them."

With the crowd chanting, jeering, screaming, Comiskey called his players together and led them from the field, heaping more abuse on the umpire.

Of course umpire Joe Sullivan had no other alternative than to order the game forfeited and award it to the Chicago White Stockings. The forfeited game left much bitterness in its wake and there was doubt that the Series would continue. However, the next day play was resumed and continued until the finish.

Officials of the two leagues met after the Series ended, and after hours of wrangling, decided that the second game had been properly forfeited to Chicago; then they decided that the Series

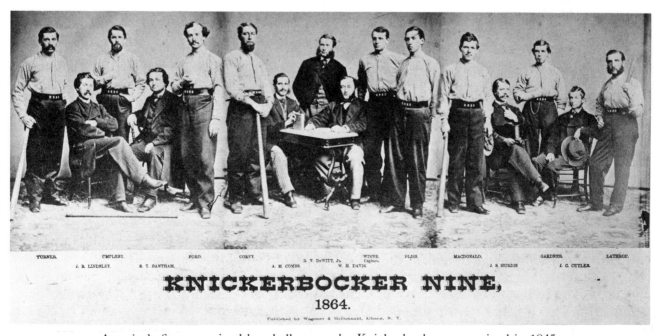

KNICKERBOCKER NINE,
1864.

America's first organized baseball team, the Knickerbockers, organized in 1845

had led to so much bitterness it would be best to call the entire Series a draw.

Following the rhubarb of 1885, there seemed to be a strong possibility that the World Series between the major league champions would be discontinued. Al Spalding, then president of the Chicago team and later founder of the Spalding sporting goods firm, said after the final game of the 1885 Series that he wanted nothing further to do with the Association, especially "with that terrible man Von der Ahe."

But St. Louis owner Chris Von der Ahe, proprietor of a prosperous saloon and grocery in St. Louis, sent his manager, Charlie Comiskey, to Chicago to call on Spalding and Cap Anson with a surprising offer for another Series in 1886.

"We'll take the challenge, and will play your team only on one condition," said Anson, "and that is *winner take all*. And by all, I mean every dime that comes through the gate."

To the surprise of the entire baseball world, Von der Ahe accepted the terms and the Series was on. With an anticipated gate of about $15,000, it loomed as the biggest sporting event in history.

The Browns and White Stockings met again in 1886 with the result that the Brownies once again defeated Cap Anson's White Stockings, 4 games to 2.

In the Series opener, Chicago pitcher John Clarkson shut out the Browns, 6–0; but St. Louis came back the very next day to bury the Browns, 12–0. The third game went to Chicago as King Kelly, the White Stockings' star, smashed out 3 singles and a home run to give his team an 11–4 victory. The Browns then spurted and took the next two games to give the Browns a 3 games to 2 edge in the Series. The final game of the Series, on October 23, was a tense, bitterly fought engagement that went into the tenth inning with the teams tied 3–3.

In the Browns' half of the tenth inning, Curt Welch, the center fielder, singled and dashed to third on a couple of groundouts. The next hitter was Hugh Nicol, the Brownies' poorest hitter. So Welch decided he would try to steal home for the winning run.

King Kelly, Chicago's catcher, was one of the stars of the era and had a great throwing arm. He never thought that Welch would try to steal.

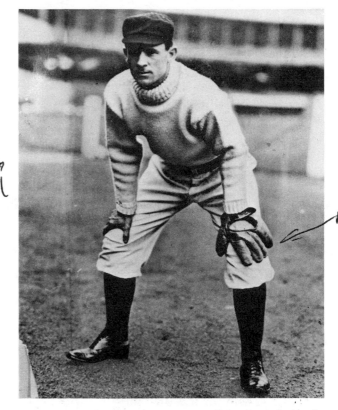

John J. McGraw at twenty was the acknowledged leader of the championship Baltimore Orioles.

Curt suddenly took a long lead off third. Kelly noted the long lead and signaled for a pitchout. The pitch came in to Kelly, but Welch, speeding toward home with the pitch, slid underneath Kelly's foot as Kelly juggled the ball and desperately tried for the tag. The umpire ruled Welch safe and the Brownies had won the World Series on Welch's daring gamble.

Fred Stearns, president of the Detroit team, issued a formal challenge to Von der Ahe and the Browns in 1887 after the Tigers had won the American Association championship. Stearns felt that there had not been enough games in the 1886 Series to determine a real champion, and he suggested a fifteen-game Series, with each player on the winning team receiving $100, and the Series champions also receiving $200 with which to buy an "appropriate championship banner." Stearns also suggested a test whereby two umpires would handle the games: One would be stationed behind the plate, to call balls and strikes; the other, near second base to decide all putouts made on the bases and in the field.

Games were scheduled in St. Louis, Detroit, Pittsburgh, Brooklyn, New York City, Philadelphia, Boston, Washington, Baltimore, and Chicago.

The Series began in Sportsman's Park in St. Louis, and the Browns easily took the opener, 6–1. The Tigers fought back the next day and evened the Series as Pete Conway outpitched Dave Foutz to win 5–3.

The third game, in Detroit, played on a cold, blustery mid-October afternoon, was one of the epic games of World Series play. Detroit eked out a thrilling 2–1 struggle that saw 29-game winner Charlie Getzein outpitch Bob Caruthers, another 29-game winner, in a marvelous duel that had the crowd standing and screaming throughout the game. The Browns outhit the Detroit team 13 to 7, but outstanding infield play by Detroit saved the day for them.

In Pittsburgh, pitcher Lady Baldwin shut out the Browns the next afternoon for an 8–0 Detroit win. In the next game at Brooklyn, Bob Caruthers took a 5–2 win for the Brownies. But from then on, it was all Detroit, as they won in New York, 9–0; 3–1 in Philadelphia; in Boston, 9–2; and again in Philadelphia, 4–2. The Browns succumbed in Washington, and in the final game in Detroit, before an excited crowd of more than five thousand boisterous fans, Detroit pounded out a 6–3 victory over the Browns. The joyous fans tore across the field after the final out to hoist their heroes onto their shoulders and parade them all around the field.

The city of Detroit prepared a heroes' welcome for its new champions. Manager Bill Watkins, captain Ned Hanlon, and the players were given gold keys to the city and then both teams paraded down Woodward Avenue to the old Russell Hotel for a roast beef dinner and champagne.

Receipts for the fifteen-game Series amounted to over $45,000, but expenses totaled $33,000. It was no wonder that the winning players were rewarded with only $100 each. Chris Von der Ahe was so angry at losing the Series to Detroit in 1887 that he sold five of his star players—Bob Caruthers, Dave Foutz, Doc Bushong, Curt Welch, and Bill Gleason—to Brooklyn for a total of $15,000. But the new

Pitcher Deacon Phillippe of the Pittsburgh team pitched 5 complete games in the 1903 World Series, winning 3 games and losing 2. He is the only hurler in baseball history ever to pitch 5 complete Series games.

players that the crafty Von der Ahe obtained—pitchers Silver King, Koenig, Icebox Chamberlain, and Jim Devlin; catcher Big Milligan; shortstop Shorty Fuller; and outfielder Tom McCarthy—proved just as formidable, and the Browns won their fourth straight pennant in 1888.

The 1888 Series was the first of many interleague series played on the historic Polo Grounds in the Bronx and was the first of some eighteen championships won by the New York Giants before they moved to San Francisco.

The Series got under way and Von der Ahe chartered a special train to transport the Browns and their fans to New York. The Brownie rooters on the World Series Special brought fistfuls of money to bet on their favorite team, and the New York gamblers rushed forward to cover the St. Louis bettors. It was one of the biggest sports events ever held on the East Coast, and hundreds of thousands of dollars were bet on the two teams.

The most interesting outcome of the Series was that, even after the seventh game, when the Giants were assured of victory, the two remaining games were played. Both club owners wanted the dollars from admission sales. The Giants played the last two games casually and carelessly and lost both to the Browns by unusually high scores: 14–11 and 18–7.

Enhancing the Giants' popularity was Jim Mutrie, their colorful field manager, who basked in the glory of his champions. Mutrie would arrive at the ballpark every day dressed formally in high hat and tails, and would parade about the field shouting, "Who are the people?" Without waiting for a reply he would scream at the top of his voice, "The Giants fans are the people!"

The Giants repeated as pennant winners in 1889 and took on their most bitter cross-river opponents, the Brooklyns. That Series preceded the first modern New York-Brooklyn Series by some fifty-two years, but the rivalry between the two clubs was just as bitter then.

Manager Bill McGunnigle's team lifted the fans of the "Brooklyn Bridegrooms" (six Brooklyn players were newly wedded) to the heights as the Brooks won 3 of the first 4 games played. But in a sudden reversal of fortune, Brooklyn dropped 5 games in a row to the hated Giants, and the Giants won their second straight World Series, 6 games to 3.

The American Association collapsed in 1890 because a number of its top players jumped their teams in order to play in the new Players' League. Some players doubled their salaries by doing so. The 1890 season saw the three leagues fighting one another for attendance, with the result that the season proved a financial disaster for all concerned.

In 1894 a wealthy Pittsburgh sportsman, William Temple, a minority owner of the Pirates, donated an ornate trophy, later called the Temple Cup, as the prize for a series between the first- and second-place teams in the National League. There were four Temple Cup Series between 1894 and 1897, but interest waned quickly after the Baltimore Orioles finished first or second and participated in all of them. The series was abandoned after 1897, for it never attracted national attention.

At the end of the 1898 season, Harry Von der Horst, owner of both the Orioles and the Brooklyn team, transferred manager Ned Hanlon and several Oriole stars to Brooklyn, for he felt there was more money to be made with a successful team in the New York area.

Intrigued by the Brooklyn example, the Robison brothers, who owned the Cleveland Spiders, bought the St. Louis franchise and transferred all of their stars to St. Louis just in time for the 1899 season.

Still searching for further angles that would make additional dollars to give them an edge over rivals in the league, the National League club owners missed seeing the specter of competition that loomed just outside their league.

Ban Johnson, a feisty ex-sportswriter, now president of the minor league Western Association, joined Charlie Comiskey in 1900 to expand

The immortal Denton "Cy" Young won 2 games for the Red Sox in the 1903 Series. Young won an incredible total of 511 major league games in a twenty-two-year career.

the western loop to a major league. Johnson, who had been denied major league status by the National League owners a year earlier, proceeded to move a team into Cleveland. He then moved the St. Paul franchise to Chicago and announced his intention to change the Western Association's name to the American League in 1901 and to make it a major league enterprise.

John Brush, the wealthy owner of the New York Giants, then persuaded John McGraw to leave his post as manager of the Orioles and come to the Giants. As soon as McGraw left the Orioles, taking some of their top players, Ban Johnson quickly assembled a makeshift team in Baltimore to complete the schedule. That move protected the Baltimore franchise and permitted Johnson in 1900 to move the team to New York, where it became the progenitor of today's New York Yankees. Now Johnson had teams in Boston, Philadelphia, Detroit, Cleveland, Baltimore, Washington, Milwaukee, and New York. The assembling of the American League was complete.

In 1903 a committee of National League officials, led by president Harry Pulliam, met with Ban Johnson and Charles Somers of the new American League and, after several days of acrimonious arguments and discussion, arrived at a peaceful solution to the many problems. Johnson agreed not to invade Pittsburgh with a new team, and the National League declared that it would officially recognize a second major league.

A National Commission was to be created to settle all the game's administrative problems and Garry Herrmann of the Cincinnati team was elected chairman of the new commission. That commission laid the foundation of the rules and regulations that have guided organized baseball to this very day.

It was also decided that the American League an the National League were going to play competitive ball. Even though various club owners in both leagues hated and fought one another, they would try to forget their differences in the interest of baseball.

One of the first to forgive and forget was Barney Dreyfuss, president and chief owner of the Pittsburgh team. Dreyfuss had won the National League's most important concession of

peace: the pledge of the American League to "stay out of Pittsburgh" and not to raid any of their players. Barney fared very well, and his anger toward the American League officials subsided. Besides, Dreyfuss was sitting on top of the world, as his Pirates had beaten feisty John McGraw's New York Giants by 7 games to win their first National League pennant.

In the American League, the flashy Boston Pilgrims, led by third baseman Jim Collins, had wrapped up the pennant by the end of August, and thus the stage was set for the first postseason World Series between the fledgling American League and the National League.

Dreyfuss sought out the Pilgrims' owner, Henry Killilea, and challenged him to a postseason series. Killilea accepted the challenge. Both teams agreed to play a best-of-nine-games series, and to split the box-office receipts between them. The two owners also agreed that neither club could use a player who had been signed after September 1, a restriction that remains in the World Series rules today.

Although the Pittsburgh pitchers had established a glamorous shutout record during the regular season, the team's pitching performances fell short in the Series. Sam Leever, a 25-game winner, came up with a lame arm. Ed Doheny, who had won 16 games, suddenly went berserk; he almost killed a faith-healer doctor and a male nurse and wound up in an insane asylum. That placed Pittsburgh's pitching burden on the husky shoulders of one man, Deacon Phillippe, a 24-game winner. The Deacon made a heroic and brilliant effort; he pitched 5 complete games in a little less than two weeks, and won 3 of them. However, it wasn't quite enough, for the Pilgrims had the immortal Cy Young, a 28-game winner, and Bill Dinneen, a 21-game winner, and they were primed for the Series.

Two umpires officiated at the games. Grim-visaged Hank O'Day, who in 1889 had pitched and won two Series games for the Giants against Brooklyn, and Tom Connolly, who became chief of umpires in the American League.

The Series opened in Boston as a crowd of more than sixteen thousand wild-eyed Pilgrim fans jammed every inch of the ballpark. But the frenzied joy of the local fans was quickly stilled

The World Champion Boston Red Sox, 1903

as the Pirates jolted Cy Young for 4 big runs in the very first inning. Jimmy Sebring, the Pirates' right fielder, hit the first home run in a World Series in the very first inning, and the Pirates took an easy 7–3 victory. The Pirate pitcher, Deacon Phillippe, limited the Pilgrims to 6 base hits and fanned 10 Pilgrims.

In the second game, husky Bill Dinneen struck out 11 Pirates and allowed Pittsburgh just 3 hits, while a pair of home runs by left fielder Patsy Dougherty enabled Dinneen to win by a 3–0 score.

Despite a massive crowd of some eighteen thousand fans, filling the park and often disrupting the third game, the Pirates, behind the effective hurling of Deacon Phillippe, again took the measure of Cy Young, by a 4–2 score.

After several rain delays in Pittsburgh, play was resumed on October 6. The rubber-armed Deacon Phillippe chalked up his third successive win in a close, intense 5–4 battle. Bill Dinneen of the Pilgrims was hit freely as Honus Wagner drove out 3 base hits to wrap up the game for Pittsburgh.

In the fifth game, manager Fred Clarke selected Bill Kennedy to oppose Cy Young. Kennedy was equal to the herculean task, as he battled Young on every pitch. It was a marvelously tense 0–0 duel going into the sixth inning, when suddenly all hell broke loose. The Pirates' great defense fell apart. They committed 4 errors in that inning as the Pilgrims smashed out 6 big runs. In the seventh inning, Boston continued their attack with 4 more runs, to win a lopsided 11–2 game.

The Pilgrims evened the Series when they won the sixth game, as Bill Dinneen outpitched Sam Leever to win 6–3.

Game seven was a wild affair, as more than seventeen thousand fans packed the small ballpark. And in that game the Deacon, arm-weary, was pounded for a 7–3 defeat. But win or lose, the Pirate fans, in a ceremony before the start of the game, called Phillippe to home plate, where he was wildly cheered and then awarded an expensive diamond stickpin.

The eighth game, delayed by several days of continuous rain, enabled the dog-tired Phillippe to get a couple of extra days' rest, but it was not enough.

"You're the only pitcher I've got," lamented manager Clarke to the Deacon. "You can beat those Pilgrims."

"I'll give it everything I've got," said Phillippe.

The Deacon gave it his best shot, but the better-rested Bill Dinneen was too good that day. He allowed the Pirates just 4 hits, while the Pilgrims took a 3–0 shutout victory and the Series.

Pittsburgh lost that Series in spite of Deacon Phillippe winning 3 games. But the Deacon still wrote two immortal records into World Series history: He was the first pitcher to pitch and win 3 World Series games, and the only pitcher in baseball history to pitch 5 complete World Series games.

The baseball-mad Boston fans, led by the famous Royal Rooters, a group of fans who traveled with the team, paraded far into the night. They carried Jimmy Collins, Bill Dinneen, Cy Young, Patsy Dougherty, and the other Boston players around the park on their shoulders and reveled long after the ball park shut down for the night.

Yet the Series left a sour taste with Boston fans, despite the Pilgrims' victory. Charges were leveled against Joe Smart, the business manager of the team, and Killilea, stating that they were both involved with ticket speculators and that prices paid for hundreds of tickets were as high as five dollars. Sportswriters and even several of the team owners had to pay their way into the Series, and the press blasted Smart and Killilea every day for weeks after the Series had ended.

The Series drew 100,429 customers, which produced a gate of $55,500. Pirate owner Barney Dreyfuss threw his Series share into the pot, so that each Pirate got a loser's share of $1,316. Killilea kept his owner's share of $6,700 so that each Boston player's share, which amounted to $1,182, was less than the amount each Pirate received.

New York Giants Refuse to Play Boston Red Sox

Pilgrim?

The New York Giants captured their first pennant in 1904 with a record of 106 wins and 47 losses. Chicago was second, with a won-lost record of 93-60, and even the local papers acknowledged that the Giants' runaway race to the pennant had robbed the season of real interest.

"It [the season] was a failure artistically and financially," one writer editorialized, "except Chicago and New York." The Philadelphia franchise was up for sale and all the other teams in the league were in deep financial trouble. Baseball was surely doomed, people were saying, unless somebody did something immediately.

Meanwhile, the young American League was embroiled in a red-hot race, with the New York Highlanders battling right down to the final day of the season against the 1903 champions, the Boston Pilgrims.

New York fans eagerly looked forward to their first subway Series (at a time when the subway cost only a nickel), and were absolutely pop-eyed at the prospect of a dream pitching duel between the Giants' incomparable Christy Mathewson and the Highlanders' great hurler, John Chesbro. Joe Gordon, president of the Highlanders, was so sure that his team would win the pennant that he sent a formal note challenging the Giants. The note went to Giant president John T. Brush, who replied that his club "was content to rest on its laurels."

Brush hated Ban Johnson and the entire New York American League crowd—which included Frank Farrell, Bill Devery, Joe Gordon, and Clark Griffith—and he still thought of the Highlanders as the latest "invaders" of New York City. Brush resented the stipulation in the 1903 peace treaty that permitted the Highlanders of the American League to come into New York, and he had even taken legal steps to restrain the enforcement of the peace compact. He felt that if he permitted his Giants to compete, he would be extending a glad hand to Farrell and Devery of the Highlanders, and that that would mean accepting them as equals of his Giants, which he would never agree to.

$1

Yankee

The Highlanders reduced the argument to mere rhetoric by succumbing to Boston on the final game of the year, but John Brush continued to refuse to participate in a Series with the American League. The Giant players did not take kindly to passing up a chance to make about $1,500 per man for a Series between the two teams, for it was as much as most of the players earned for an entire season. They held a meeting and requested permission to play the Boston team, but Brush remained adamant.

The failure of the Giants to play the Pilgrims was sharply criticized by the nation's press and their fans, and the widely read *Sporting News* said in a front-page story: "The 1904 Boston Pilgrims are the World Champions by default."

1905

New York Giants Versus
Philadelphia Athletics

In August 1891, a train pulled into Baltimore from the North, carrying an eighteen-year-old country lad named John Joseph McGraw. He jauntily bounced down from the day coach and stepped into a new and tumultuous world. He had come from Truxton, New York, and was carrying all his worldly goods, including his baseball glove, in a cardboard suitcase.

A graduate of the Iron and Oil Baseball League, McGraw had played with Cedar Rapids in Iowa after playing ball in such nondescript towns as Wellsville, Ocala, and Gainesville, Florida, and in Havana, Cuba. He was moving fast now, rapidly developing the skills that made him an excellent third baseman and a fine hitter.

He had played just thirty-one games at Cedar Rapids when the manager of the Orioles (of the American Association) offered him a contract, and John J. jumped at the opportunity to play with the great Oriole team for they had a marvelous tradition and had been one of the great early championship clubs.

Then an unbelievable thing happened to McGraw. He did not play in his best form—he hit only .245 for the year. But during the winter the National League expanded to twelve teams and absorbed Baltimore. Now John McGraw was a big leaguer.

Through the next few years, McGraw developed into one of the great stars of baseball, and the Orioles won pennants in 1895 and again in 1896. In 1897 the Orioles won the Temple Cup from the Boston Pilgrims.

In the winter of 1899, Louisville, Washington, Cleveland, and Baltimore were dropped from the National League as the league officials realized that a twelve-team league was unwieldy and, more important, unprofitable. McGraw and his bosom pal Wilbert Robinson were shipped off to St. Louis to play for that club.

The summer of 1900 was not a happy one for John J. and Robinson. They didn't like St. Louis, and often they would deliberately provoke an umpire into expelling them from a game when the team played at home. There was a racetrack across the street from the ballpark, and McGraw and Robbie would tear off their baseball suits and dash over there in time for the first race. As soon as the season ended, they were back in Baltimore checking out the business in a bar and grill they owned.

The National League was in a death struggle with the newly formed American League, and John McGraw jumped into the battle with both heart and hands. He was summoned to meetings by both leagues and was urged to join both.

When Ban Johnson finally announced his American League lineup in 1901, Baltimore had a brand-new team in the league, and its chief stockholder and manager was McGraw. Johnson and McGraw simply could not stand each other.

"A real baseball war was on," McGraw re-

16

called. "And we immediately started a raid on the National League and I managed to grab most of the players that I wanted from my former Baltimore club." McGraw began to listen to new overtures from the National League, and before the season was over, he had completed a deal with the new owner of the New York Giants, John Brush; by the beginning of the 1902 season he was in New York as manager of the Giants.

At age twenty-nine, McGraw left Baltimore a famous star, with twelve years behind him as a major leaguer, two and a half years as a successful manager, and a reputation as one of the smartest, toughest, roughest men in the game. He was a formidable-looking man, with big, broad shoulders. He wore high starched collars, and four-in-hand ties with a fleur-de-lis pin daintily stuck in the center. His shirts and shoes were made in Havana. He was only five feet seven, but his sinister look and wide shoulders made him seem a foot taller. He created an immediate sensation after two weeks in New York City by raiding his former Baltimore team and luring away such stars as Joe McGinnity, Steve Brodie, Jack Cronin, and Dan McGann.

After watching his Giants work out for a few days, McGraw was certain that the tall, good-looking, soft-spoken first baseman with the rifle arm would be better as a pitcher than as a first baseman. He quickly switched Christy Mathewson to the mound, where he became the greatest pitcher in Giant history and one of the greatest pitchers of all time.

Like most of the ballplayers of his day, Christy Mathewson grew up on a farm. The Mathewson family farm was outside Factoryville, Pennsylvania, where he was born on August 12, 1880, one of five children. Factoryville, sixteen miles from Scranton, was named for a cotton factory that had failed.

Young Christy began playing ball at the age of eleven because it was a new and exciting game that had recently been taken up by the men of the town. He was a tall, muscular, powerful boy, and was playing with boys aged seventeen to nineteen. Almost from the very beginning he was something special. He could throw an "in-curve" and an "out-curve." He had invented those pitches himself.

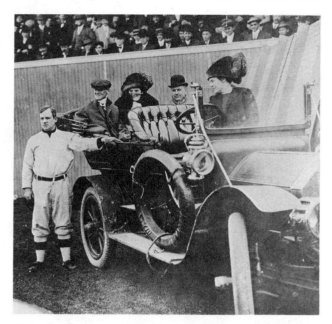

John J. McGraw stands beside the new car, with team owner John Brush, Mrs. Brush, caterer Harry Stevens, and Mrs. McGraw. The car was a gift to McGraw by Giant fans for winning the 1905 Series.

To most would-be pitchers today, trying to throw a curveball is nothing unusual. But in those days, the curveball was not as prevalent. The early pitchers just reared back and fired the ball, as straight and hard as they could. Once he found he could actually curve a ball, Christy kept practicing it constantly. It was the curve that fooled all the batters when they gave him the now famous tryout in the town square.

One summer when he was sixteen Christy was sitting in the stands in Scranton, watching the Scranton professional team play. A player spotted Christy and came over to him as he sat munching a bag of peanuts.

"Aren't you the kid who pitched for Factoryville?" the player asked.

Christy said that he was. The player told him that their regular pitcher had failed to show up, and asked Matty if he would care to pitch. Christy put the peanuts down and followed the player onto the field. That day he struck out 15 professional ballplayers.

In 1908, at age seventeen, Matty entered Bucknell University in Lewisburg, Pennsylvania. While attending school he pitched for

Christy Mathewson (*left*) posted 3 stunning shutout wins in the 1905 Series, while Joe "Iron" McGinnity (*right*) shut out the Athletics in the fourth game. The two great Giants stars stand with manager John McGraw (*center*) prior to the fifth and final game of the Series.

Honesdale, a town near the school. His contract called for him to be paid $200 per month, plus room and board. At the very same time he played with the Honesdale team, he was playing with the Bucknell football, baseball, and basketball teams, and was president of his class, a leading member of the glee club, and head of two literary societies.

Matty's first organized team was the Taunton, Massachusetts, club, in the New England League. He signed with Taunton in 1899 for the then princely sum of ninety dollars per month, and it was there that Matty first saw the incredible "fadeaway" pitch that Taunton pitcher Eddie Williams threw. (Similar to today's slider, but a much sharper drop.)

When Williams showed the mechanics of the pitch to Matty, the youngster wondered if a right-handed pitcher could master the delivery.

He began to practice throwing the pitch an hour a day, then increased the time to two hours each day, day after day. It was a difficult and painful delivery and it was a miracle that Matty didn't ruin his arm. Finally, after months of experimenting, Matty was able to control the pitch and it became the keystone of his incredible career. In a tight spot, when he needed that one pitch, he used the fadeaway. It was a pitch that even the great batters couldn't hit.

Bucknell University's football team traveled to Philadelphia in the fall of 1899 for a game against a heavily favored University of Pennsylvania team. Bucknell's star was the triple-threat halfback, eighteen-year-old Christy Mathewson, who would run, pass, and drop-kick with the best in the nation.

On the morning before the big game against Penn, Matty was "lobby-sitting" in the Warwick Hotel when a man named "Phenom" John Smith walked up to him.

"Son, I saw you pitch for Taunton last season," he said. "I'm going to manage the Norfolk team next season. That's in the Virginia League. I'll give you eighty dollars a month to play for us and you'll get your money every month."

Matty looked carefully at the man, liked his seemingly honest, rugged face, and signed the contract then and there. That afternoon Smith and thousands of football fans watched Matty kick two long-distance field goals against Pennsylvania, one of the best teams in the East.

When the baseball season began, Matty traveled to Norfolk where he joined the team, and by midsummer Mathewson was the sensation of the minor leagues as he won 21 of the 23 games he pitched and received a raise from eighty dollars a month to ninety dollars.

Late in July 1890, manager Phenom John Smith talked with his young pitcher and told him that he had offers from the Philadelphia Athletics and the New York Giants.

"Which team do you want to play for?" Smith asked.

Matty said he would think it over.

"I began to study the list of pitchers with each team," said Matty in his autobiography. "The Giants were usually near the bottom of the league and they needed pitchers. So I told Smith I'd like to go to New York."

When John McGraw took over as manager of the Giants and switched Matty from first base to the pitching mound, the team was ready to roll. In 1904 the Giants won the National League pennant, but that was the famous year McGraw and John Brush ignored the Boston Pilgrims' request for a World Series.

In 1905 the Giants, the toast of New York, were ready. All of New York was now talking about the magnificent new fire engine called Big Six. And it was Sam Crane, a fine sportswriter for the *New York Sun,* who called Matty, who had won 31 games that season, "the Big Six" of pitchers. The nickname stuck for the rest of Matty's life.

In 1905 the Philadelphia Athletics, led by Connie Mack, won the American League flag. On October 9, at the Athletics' park in the Brewerytown section of Philadelphia, *the first official World Series began.*

Connie Mack, né Cornelius McGillicuddy, was born during the Civil War on December 22, 1862, in East Brookfield, Massachusetts, a boomtown that produced shoes for the Union soldiers. As a youngster, Connie had to work in a shoe factory, but at lunchtime and immediately after work the boys and young men began to play baseball. They played Saturday and Sunday and every spare minute they could. By the time Connie was fifteen years old, he had grown to an incredible six-foot-one-inch youngster, weighing only 150 pounds.

By 1884, Connie Mack was talented enough to sign a contract with the New York Mets for ninety dollars a month.

A pillar of sobriety in an arena where there was constant drinking, Connie nevertheless commanded respect and admiration as he climbed the ladder in the world of baseball. He became one of the smartest, shrewdest players, and his strategy and uncanny ability to "hit in the pinches" made him one of the most valuable. By 1895, during the heyday of John McGraw's Orioles, Connie Mack was named manager of the Milwaukee team.

Once the Spanish-American War ended in 1898, Mack and McGraw and Ban Johnson all converged on a collision course. While McGraw was skipping to the National League in New York, Johnson was bestowing the Philadelphia franchise in the American League to his buddy Connie Mack. And Mack, in turn, offered the public three sizable attractions: an admission price of twenty-five cents, half that of the rival Nationals; Mack's brand-new ballpark; and the opportunity to see new heroes such as the immortal Rube Waddell, Mack's greatest pitcher and McGraw's greatest nemesis.

John McGraw called his 1905 team his greatest, perhaps because they were his first pennant-winning team. The Giants of 1905 had an infield consisting of Art Devlin, another collegian, at third base; Bill Dahlen at shortstop; Bill Gilbert, second base; and Dan McGann, first base. The outfield was made up of Sam Mertes in left field; Mike Donlin in center; and George Browne in right field. Roger Bresnahan and Frank Bowerman were the Giant catchers. The pitching staff, dominated by Mathewson, also included Iron Man McGinnity, Leon Ames, Dummy Taylor, and a very fine southpaw relief hurler named George Wiltse.

The Athletics had one of the most picturesque clubs ever assembled. In left field they had Topsy Hartsel; Bris Lord was in center; and roly-poly Socks Seybold was the right fielder. Two Crosses, Lave and Monte, played third and short (they were not related); Dan Murphy was at second base; and the home-run-hitting star, Harry Davis, with 8 during the regular season, was at first base; Ossee Schreckengost was the

Shibe Park, Philadelphia, home field of the Athletics

Giants star Christy Mathewson allowed the A's just 14 hits in 3 Series games within a span of six days to spark the Giants to the championship.

catcher, though Mike Powers, a doctor in the off-season, caught Eddie Plank. Pitchers included Rube Waddell, Eddie Plank, and right-handers Chief Bender, Andy Coakley (who later coached at Columbia University for years), and Weldon Henley. (One of Coakley's Columbia stars was Lou Gehrig.)

An interesting off-the-field financial arrangement was made by a number of Giant and Athletic players. John Brush's rules adopted by the National Commission called for a great discrepancy in the money that went to the winning and losing players, and the players did not care to risk coming away with only 25 percent of the pot. Therefore, individual Giants and A's agreed to pool winning and losing shares and split them fifty-fifty.

Only McGraw and Mathewson of the Giants and Connie Mack ignored such side agreements.

(One can imagine what today's sportswriters and commentators would say about such an arrangement.)

On September 1, the Athletics were returning from Boston after a series there when they picked up Andy Coakley in the Providence railroad station. Andy was wearing his summer straw hat and big Rube Waddell tried to flip it off. Coakley warded him off, tossing his uniform bag at Big Rube, and during the scuffle, Waddell fell on his million-dollar left shoulder. The resulting injury was serious enough to sideline him for the rest of the season. Losing Waddell meant as much to the A's as losing Mathewson would have to the Giants, and it just about shattered the morale of the Athletics as they prepared for the opening game of the Series at Shibe Park in Philadelphia on October 9.

With Waddell injured, Connie Mack called on his other ace, the great Eddie Plank, a 26-game winner during the season, while all of New York waited with bated breath for the appearance of Big Six Mathewson.

In the first game, Matty and Plank battled tooth and nail through four scoreless innings, as the crowd of more than seventeen thousand who jammed the Athletics' park roared with every pitch, every hit, every move of the players. Then, Matty led off the fifth inning and lined Plank's first pitch into center field for a base hit. Roger Bresnahan forced Matty, but that hit decided the game. Plank forgot there was a runner on base, went into his long windup, and the fleet-footed Bresnahan stole second. Dan McGann, the Giant first baseman, doubled off the left field wall, and Bresnahan came in for the first World Series run in history. Another two-base hit, by the second baseman, Billy Gilbert, brought in another Giant run. It was more than enough for Mathewson, who shut out the Athletics for the rest of the game. In the top of the ninth inning, Matty came up to hit with a Giant runner on first base and caught the A's flat-footed as he bunted beautifully down the third-base line. Bresnahan then singled up the middle for another Giant run. The game ended as Matty blanked the Athletics in the last half of the ninth inning with his remarkable fadeaway pitch and came away with his first World Series victory, 3–0. Matty was magnificent as he allowed the

A's but 4 hits, struck out 5, and did not walk a single Philadelphia batter.

The next day, October 10, in New York's Polo Grounds, a crowd of more than twenty-four thousand sat in utter dismay as their great Giants in their new solid-black uniforms were clearly outplayed by the cool, crafty twenty-two-year-old Chippewa Indian, Chief Bender, who held the vaunted Giant batters at his mercy. He fanned 8 New Yorkers and completely outpitched Iron Man McGinnity to win by a 3–0 score. McGinnity pitched well for the Giants, but 2 Giant errors allowed the A's their runs, and now the Series was tied at 1 game each.

Nobody knew it at the time, but those 3 runs were the only runs that Connie Mack's team would score during the entire Series. It rained on the third day, so the National Commission ruled that the third game would be played in Philadelphia, and the next two games in New York, which would give the Giants a Saturday date at home.

The Athletics took a 9–0 drubbing in the third game, as the Giants simply overpowered them. The Athletics were their own worst enemy; they made 5 errors, 3 by second baseman Dan Murphy.

The game clearly showed how the loss of Waddell affected the Athletics. "If we had Rube available the Series would be different," said Connie Mack.

The New York Times saluted Matty with its lead story, which said: "In the aggregate, a eulogy of today's game would point without discrimination to the 9 men who did the work, but individually only that professor of occult speed and unbelievable curveball, Christy Mathewson."

The fans flocked back to New York for game four, crowding the hotels, jamming Broadway with baseball arguments, bets, and hoopla.

The fourth game was a pitchers' battle between Iron Joe McGinnity, who gave up but 5 hits to the A's, and Eddie Plank, who allowed the Giants only 4 hits. But the Giants scored on

Champions of 1905 – McGraw's Giants. On the Club Roster Were Such Names as Bresnahan, Wiltse, "Dummy" Taylor, George Brown, Devlin, McCormick, McGinnity, McGann, Ames, Bowerman, Gilbert and Marshall

NEW YORK GIANTS
1905

BRESNAHAN   WILTSE   TAYLOR   BROWN   DEVLIN   DUNN   McCORMICK   ELLIOTT

MATHEWSON   DAHLEN

MERTES   McGINNITY   McGANN   WARNER   McGRAW   AMES   BOWERMAN   GILBERT   MARSHALL

The 1905 World Champion Giants

2 costly errors by the Mackmen and snatched a win by a 1–0 score. When the Series ended, Connie Mack promptly fired Lave Cross, captain of the team, who was responsible for one of the errors that had given the game to New York.

As Matty walked to the mound for the fifth game, the crowd of twenty-seven thousand set up a chant: "Take off your cap, Matty!" It was a tribute to the two successive shutouts Matty had pitched. But instead of doffing his own cap, Matty reached over and took off that of Joe McGinnity, hero of the previous day's game. The crowd cheered for a full minute, while the band played an enthusiastic and confident overture: "We'll All Get Stone Blind."

The fifth game was a Homeric struggle between two of the all-time-great pitching stars of baseball. Mathewson, pitching with one day's rest, allowed the A's 3 scattered hits in the first five innings. Chief Bender matched Matty's performance, but the incomparable Mathewson was just a shade better. No other pitching performance in World Series history compares to the exhibition of pitching artistry displayed by Christy Mathewson. Christy ran his collection of scoreless Athletic innings to twenty-seven as he completely shut down the vaunted Athletic hitters with only 6 hits for a brilliant 2–0 victory.

In the fifth inning, the Chief momentarily weakened and walked the first 2 Giant batters, Sam Mertes and Bill Dahlen. And both men advanced on a bunt. Billy Gilbert then drove a long fly to center field and Mertes scored after the catch to give the Giants a 1–0 lead.

That was the only run of the game until the eighth inning, when Matty walked and scored on Bresnahan's long two-base drive to make it 2–0 in favor of the Giants.

When Matty struck out the last batter to end the game, New York City erupted in a wild celebration. The entire city lionized every Giant player, from the batboy to John McGraw.

When the fans spied Matty coming out of the clubhouse, they hoisted him onto their shoulders and paraded about the area singing and shouting his name.

Even though the Series played to three overflow crowds and the attendance peaked at a combined total of 91,723 fans, the total gate receipt was just $68,436. Of course, some tickets had cost as little as fifty cents. Nevertheless, the players received almost as much money for the Series as they received in their annual salary. Each Giant player was paid $1,142, while the losing Athletics received only $370 each. Connie Mack and the Athletics' owner contributed an additional $500 to every member of the Athletics. However, when the Philadelphia players settled their side agreement with the Giant players, they fared as well as the Giants.

John McGraw, writing about his life in *Baseball* magazine back in the 1940s, said:

Of all the World Series in which I have taken part, I think the picture of the 1905 Series stands out most vividly in my memory as my greatest baseball thrill.

To begin with, we decided to do the thing up in some spectacular way and I had some special all-black uniforms made for the Giants. I will never forget the impression created in Philadelphia and the thrill that I personally got when the Giants suddenly trotted out from their dugout resplendent in uniforms of black flannel, trimmed with white. The letters in white spelled out GIANTS in large block letters.

I have heard many Army officers say that the snappiest dressed outfit is usually made up of the best fighters. I can well understand that. The psychological effect of being togged out in snappy uniforms was immediately noticeable upon the players. The Athletics in their regular season uniforms appeared dull alongside our champions.

The only setback to that Series was when I discovered the financial arrangement set between many of the Giant and Athletic players. I was disgusted at their unwillingness to take a gambling chance.

Bresnahan, Matty, and I, however, refused to do any pairing. After getting the big share of the receipts we had the last laugh on the others. Several of them, I understand afterwards, tried to run out on their agreements.

1906

Chicago White Sox Versus Chicago Cubs

If the American League suffered a crushing defeat in the first World Series in 1905, the junior loop had quick, sweet revenge in an unexpected victory in 1906, when the Chicago White Sox upset the heavily favored Chicago Cubs, 4 games to 2, in the first intracity World Series. The result was so surprising that it was no wonder the former enemies, Ban Johnson and Charlie Comiskey, unashamedly hugged and kissed each other after the fourth White Sox victory.

The Cubs became known as baseball's Wonder Team after they romped off with the National League pennant by 20 games over the Giants. They won 116 games and lost a scant 36, for a .763 percentage. It stands as one of the most remarkable seasons in baseball's long history.

That was the great Cub team that featured Tinker and Evers and Chance, who were famous for their many double plays. Yet the catalyst of the Cub infield, and a player who has never received proper acclaim, was third baseman Harry Steinfeldt, the club's leading hitter during the regular season. It was the "Tinker to Evers to Chance" combination (immortalized in a poem by noted writer Franklin P. Adams) that received the acclaim, but it was Steinfeldt who was the glue of the champion Cubs.

The White Sox, known as the Hitless Wonders for their anemic team batting average of .230, won 93 games while losing 58 to clinch the pennant by 4½ games over the New York Highlanders.

The first game was played at the old West Side Park of the Cubs on October 9, and the rest of the games alternated between the two Chicago ballparks. October 9 was a cold, rainy day, and only thirteen thousand fans braved the freezing weather to witness a marvelous pitching duel between Mordecai "Three Finger" Brown, the ace of the Cubs, and the droll White Sox southpaw, Nick Altrock. Brown began the game by striking out 3 White Sox hitters in the first inning, then fanned 2 more in the second. He did not allow a hit until a sub third baseman, George Rohe, tripled in the fifth inning and scored on an easy grounder by Patsy Dougherty. In the sixth inning the Sox scored again to go ahead 2–0.

In their half of the sixth inning, the Cubs finally scored. Johnny Kling walked and advanced to third on a wild pitch, and a sacrifice fly brought him home.

That was all the scoring as the Sox went on to a 2–1 victory.

The next afternoon Harry Steinfeldt led the Cub attack with 3 hits in a 7–1 shellacking of the White Sox. Cub pitcher Ed Reulbach was magnificent as he allowed the White Sox just 1 solitary hit while fanning 6 Sox hitters.

Twenty-one-year-old Chief Bender defeats the Giants with a brilliant 4-hit shutout in game two of the Series. It was the lone Athletic victory in the Series.

Back in the Cubs' ballpark on October 11 for the third game, George Rohe once again became the Cub Killer as he tripled off pitcher Jack Pfiester with the bases full, and the White Sox again took the ball game, this time by a 3–0 score. Ed Walsh, the handsome White Sox ace, allowed the Cubs just 3 hits while striking out 12.

In the fourth game, Three Finger Brown allowed the Sox but 2 hits as he dazzled their hitters with his elusive forkball, served from the three fingers of his right hand. Brown struck out 5 White Sox players and came away with a stunning 1–0 victory.

With the Series tied at 2 games each, and an overflow crowd of more than twenty-seven thousand fans on hand, the Sox cracked out 12 base hits off three Cub pitchers to outslug the Cubs, 8–6. Second baseman Frank Isbell sparked the attack with a record 4 doubles, while the un-

known George Rohe kept up his tremendous slugging, driving out 3 base hits as the Sox took a 3 games to 2 advantage in the Series.

In the sixth game on Sunday, October 14, police ordered the gates to the ballpark closed as nearly twenty thousand jammed the Cubs' West Side Park.

Three Finger Brown was cuffed around like a rookie, yielding 8 hits in one and one-third innings as the incredible White Sox belted him from pillar to post and then jumped reliever Orvie Overall for 4 more runs. The White Sox closed the six-day Series with a stunning 8–3 win to capture the World Championship.

Charles Comiskey was so delighted with his team's win that he threw his share of the first four games, a total of about $15,000, into the players' pot, so that each Sox player received $1,874, while the losing Cubs each received 25 percent of the players' pool, or about $438.

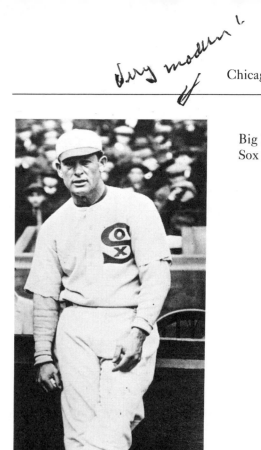

Big Ed Walsh won 2 crucial games for the White Sox in the Series.

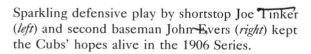

Sparkling defensive play by shortstop Joe Tinker (*left*) and second baseman John Evers (*right*) kept the Cubs' hopes alive in the 1906 Series.

Chicago Cubs Versus Detroit Tigers

In the American League the Detroit Tigers and the Philadelphia Athletics battled each other throughout the season, with the Tigers finally capturing the pennant in the final ten days by 4½ games. In the National League the Chicago Cubs once again took the pennant, having romped away from the second-place Pittsburgh Pirates by 17 games.

The Tigers, led by young Tyrus Raymond Cobb, displayed a fresh, cocky, aggressive brand of baseball.

The first game of the Series was held at Chicago on October 8. The Tigers led 3–1 going into the ninth inning. Suddenly, the roof caved in as the battling Cubbies scored 2 runs to tie the game at 3–3. Then, when the teams played on even terms through the twelfth inning, still tied, the umpires called the game because of darkness. The game was declared a tie, to be replayed the following day.

The Tigers seemed to enter a state of shock over having had a certain win in their hands and seeing it slip away. They never recovered.

In the second game, on October 9, Cub hurler Jack Pfiester, a 15-game winner during the season, outpitched the Tigers' George Mullin, a 21-game winner, in a tense game that ended with the Cubs winning, 3–1. Each team collected 9 hits, but the Cubs stole 5 bases, which proved to be the edge they needed to win.

The third game, played in the record time of one hour, thirty-five minutes, resulted in another victory for the Cubs by a 5–1 margin. But the Tigers still wouldn't quit, and jumped out to a 1–0 lead in game four, on a cold, blustery day in Detroit on October 11.

Pitcher Bill Donovan seemingly had the Cubs at bay, as he allowed only 3 hits in the first four innings. Then it began to rain and the game was halted for fifteen to twenty minutes. During the interval, Donovan's arm stiffened, and the Cubs came back to pound him for 7 hits and 6 runs, and a 6–1 win.

The fifth and final game on Saturday, October 12, at Tiger Stadium, turned into a magnificent pitching duel between two of baseball's greatest pitchers, Three Finger Brown and George Mullin. Both teams garnered 7 hits, but the Cubs bunched their blows in the first two innings to score 2 runs, and that was enough for a 2–0 shutout over the Tigers, and a sweep of the Series.

In the 1907 World Series the contending players divided the spoils on a 60-40 basis, and the players did quite well. Owner Murphy threw in an additional $10,000 for the Cubs' shares, and, not to be outdone, Bill Yawkey of the Tigers tossed in $15,000 for the Tiger players. As a result, Cub players got $2,143, while the Tigers each received $1,946.

The Cubs clearly deserved their World Series victory as they outhit the Tigers .257 to .209, while Harry Steinfeldt, the Cubs' great third baseman, captured batting honors with a stunning .471 average. Johnny Evers, the team's fine second baseman, hit for a .350 average. Claude Rossman of the Tigers was the leading Tiger batter, with a .400 average.

The big surprise was the horrible batting of the American League batting champion, Ty Cobb, who had hit .350 during the season but was held to a .200 average during the Series.

The Cubs really won the Series on the base paths as they ran almost at will against the Tiger catchers. The Cubs stole a record number of 18 bases, 6 of them by their fleet center fielder, Jim Slagle.

Ty Cobb in his first World Series in 1907 hit for a meager .200. However, he did win the first of his batting titles with a .350 average for the season.

Mordecai "Three Finger" Brown shut out the Tigers in the fifth and final game of the 1907 Series.

Chicago Cubs Versus Detroit Tigers

The 1908 American League pennant race was a thriller, with the Tigers, the Cleveland Indians, and the White Sox battling each other to the final day of the season. When the Tigers defeated the White Sox on the final day, 7–0, it meant a pennant for the winner and third place for the loser.

In the National League the Cubs won their third straight pennant by defeating Pittsburgh and the Giants in the last two games of the season. That led to a second meeting between the two midwestern champions.

The opening game of the Series, in Detroit, was played in rain, sleet, and snow. The Cubs, behind 1–0 going into the fourth inning, routed Tiger pitcher Ed Killian by blasting out 4 runs to take a 5–1 lead. They held on to the lead until the last half of the seventh inning, when the Tigers finally bared their fangs. Led by Ty Cobb, who finally began to hit the ball, the Tigers ripped into pitcher Ed Reulbach for 3 runs and then chased Orvie Overall during a 2-run rally in the eighth inning to take the lead over the Cubs, 6–5. Seemingly on the ropes, the Cubs came to life with 6 consecutive base hits off Ed Summers, and scored 5 times to take a thrilling 10–6 victory.

In the second game, at Chicago on October 11, Billy Donovan of the Tigers pitched almost perfect ball for seven and a third innings as he set down 22 Cub batters in order. But in the eighth inning, Solly Hofman got a scratch hit. Joe Tinker then drove a pitch into the crowd that lined left field, and, after a fifteen-minute argument between the Tigers, who claimed the hit should have been a ground-rule double, and the Cubs, who said that it was a home run, umpire Bill Klem agreed with the Cubs.

When play was resumed, the Cubs batted around, scored 6 more runs, and posted another come-from-behind win by a 6–1 score.

The Tigers finally showed their vaunted slugging prowess in the third game as they ripped the Cubs apart with an 11-hit attack led by the irascible Ty Cobb. Cobb drove out a triple, a double, and 2 singles to spark an 8–3 win for the Tigers.

That wound up the Tigers' scoring for the balance of the Series as Three Finger Brown and Orvie Overall wrapped it up for the Cubs with shutout victories. Brown hurled a magnificent 4-hit win, 3–0, and then Overall came back the next day and, allowing the Tigers 3 hits, posted a 2–0 win to clinch the Series once again for the Chicago Cubs.

Many years later, in an article in the *Los Angeles Times*, Orvie Overall, then a successful banker in California, talked about that World Series:

In the two Series I pitched against Bill Donovan, I pitched four games and got out with three wins and a tie. But that Donovan was a truly great pitcher. A real artist out there on the mound and he was a grand fellow.

While I am proud of those Series wins of so long ago, I don't hesitate to say that if Donovan had had the Cub hitters behind him, and I had pitched for the Tigers, the verdict could easily have been reversed.

Second baseman Johnny Evers sparked the Cubs' defense in the Series and hit for a gaudy .350 average.

Pitcher Orvie Overall won 2 games for the Cubs, including a sensational 3-hit shutout in the final game of the Series.

1909

Pittsburgh Pirates Versus Detroit Tigers

The National League continued to ride high, wide, and handsome in 1909, winning its third straight World Series. A new wonder team, the Pittsburgh Pirates, had appeared on the National League horizon. Though the Cubs, without their great catcher Johnny Kling, a season-long hold-out, won 104 games in their effort to make it four straight championships, Fred Clarke's Pirates shot by them with 110 victories and a percentage of .724 to win their first pennant.

In the American League, the Tigers, with a remodeled infield, won the pennant again, this time in a bitter fight against their stubborn foes of 1907, the Athletics. Donie Bush had taken over for O'Leary at shortstop; George Moriarty unseated Captain Coughlin at third; and mid-season deals in 1909 brought Jim Delahanty to play second base and Tommy Jones to play first base, replacing Claude Rossman. While the brilliant Hughie Jennings, the Tiger manager, was wheeling and dealing, the incredible Ty Cobb led all Tiger, and other, batters with a .377 average to win the American League batting crown.

As the Tigers took batting practice on Friday afternoon, October 8, at spanking-new Forbes Field in Pittsburgh, a quartet of Pirate pitchers watched the Tigers slam ball after ball out of the park.

As the two Tiger stars and their hard-hitting teammates took their turns lacing the ball into every corner of the park, the four Pirate pitchers started to kid each other.

"Gee, I wish Clarke would let me pitch to those guys," said twenty-seven-year-old Babe Adams, who had just completed his first season in the major leagues. "I'd stand those big guys on their ears. Cobb looks like a sucker to me, and Crawford don't look so hot."

"Sure, they're a bunch of overrated bums," another of the young pitchers chirped up.

"It won't happen," said Sam Leever. "You only won twelve games and I only got eight wins this year. It'll be the more seasoned guys again. We'll see the Series from our dugout."

Just at that moment, manager Fred Clarke walked over to the dugout, rubbing up a new baseball. As he approached the rookies, he tossed the sphere to Adams, who almost fell down in surprise. "What's this, Skipper?"

Then, before Clarke could answer his rookie star, George Gibson, the Pirates' fine catcher said, "Come on, Adams. Warmup."

Babe Adams was another farm boy who had learned to play baseball after the day's chores were done. A stocky, good-looking youngster with jet-black hair, he was easygoing, modest, and very popular with the fans and his teammates. Yet Clarke's decision to start him in the Pirates' first World Series opener astonished everybody.

The Pirates had captured the pennant on the

strength of their three big pitching stars: Howie Camnitz, with a 25-6 record; Vic Willis, with a 22-11 record; and Lefty Leifield, with a 19-8 record. It was thought that they would be all the pitching that the Pirates would need to win.

But manager Fred Clarke had been considering Adams for several days, for he had received a tip from John Heydler, the new president of the National League. Heydler had visited Clarke a few days before the Series started. "Fred," he had said, "I don't know who you're going to pitch in your first game, but I saw Detroit play a game a couple of weeks ago and they could not hit pitcher Dolly Gray. Dolly pitches very much like Adams; and I think Adams is even faster. He's a winner for you."

The first inning of the first game was in many ways the turning point of the entire Series. Tiger leadoff man Davey Jones walked and Donie Bush, the number two hitter, bunted, advancing

Cubs manager, the brilliant Frank Chance, led all hitters with a marvelous .421 average for the Series.

Ty Cobb drove out 4 hits in the third game of the Series to spark the lone Detroit win in the Series.

Jones to second base. Ty Cobb came up to hit and Adams, trying to work the corners on Cobb, walked him. Sam Crawford, the next batter, took a terrific cut at the pitch and topped the ball straight to the mound. Adams scooped up the ball and in the same motion fired to third base to get Jones sliding in. Jim Delahanty, the Tigers' number 5 hitter, drove the first pitch on a line to Fred Clarke in left field and Cobb tore in after the catch for the first run of the Series. A base hit would score 2 runs, and would probably finish Adams.

Babe pitched carefully to George Moriarty, who smashed a grounder toward the hole between short and third, but Lady Luck was riding with Babe Adams: The ball hit Jim Delahanty on the leg as he was racing for third base, causing an automatic out, and the dangerous inning was over with only 1 run for the Tigers.

Adams was in complete control of Detroit after that first inning. Although the Tigers did threaten on several occasions, the superb defensive play

The 1909 World Champion Pittsburgh Pirates

of the Pirate infield and outfield cut off several Tiger drives as Babe Adams mowed his opponents down in the eighth and ninth innings to capture the first Pittsburgh victory by a 14–1 score.

It was a marvelous victory for the rookie pitcher, and for manager Fred Clarke, a magnificent bit of strategy had worked well. Now he had himself three ace pitchers fresh and ready to handle the tough Tigers. It could mean a Pirate sweep of the Series.

But the Tigers clawed back the very next day behind the brilliant slants of Bill Donovan, who shut down the Pirates with but 5 base hits while striking out 7, with a 7–2 win. In the fifth inning, Cobb electrified the large crowd as he stole home on pitcher Vic Willis.

For loyal Tiger fans, the third game was a heartbreaker. The Pirates got off to an early 6–0 lead with 5 runs in the first inning, but the Tigers fought back with 4 runs in the seventh. In a furious ninth-inning finish, each team scored twice, but the Pirates had a 2-run lead and eked out an 8–6 win.

For the fourth game, on October 12 in Detroit, Tiger manager Jennings started his ace George Mullin, and George pitched a brilliant 5-hit shutout as the Tigers won the game, 5–0 and tied the Series at 2 games each. In the fifth inning, Pirate pitcher Deacon Phillippe, hero of the 1903 Series, brought a roar from the Pirate rooters as he walked to the mound to relieve Lefty Leifield. He was cheered for fully five minutes, and then proceeded to blank the Tigers in the remaining four innings.

The teams returned to Pittsburgh for the fifth game. The weather was miserable. Once again manager Clarke decided to utilize his freshman pitcher, Babe Adams, and the Babe once more came through with a brilliant performance for an 8–4 win over the Tigers. Babe was in trouble in the very first inning when he was clubbed for a home run by left fielder Jones, but Adams regained his composure and retired Bush, Cobb, and Crawford in order, and then proceeded to shut down the Tigers until the sixth inning, when he weakened, allowing the Tigers to tie the score with 2 runs. In the Pirates' seventh inning, playing manager Fred Clarke slammed a 3-run homer into the bleachers, and that was the decisive blow, giving the Pirates a 6–3 lead. Honus Wagner was hit by a pitch, then stole second and third and came home on a wild pitch for the Pirates' fourth run of the inning. In the Tigers' eighth inning, Crawford slammed one of the longest home runs ever seen, but it was the Tigers' last gasp, as Adams shut down the Detroit club in the ninth inning and took his second Series victory.

In many respects, the sixth game was the best of the Series. The teams moved back to Detroit on October 14, and although the weather was again cold and windy, the two-hour thriller provided enough fire to warm the hearts and minds of the slim crowd of some ten thousand fans.

The Pirates, needing only one victory to clinch the championship, seemed to have the game well in hand as they jumped on George Mullin for 3 runs in the first inning. Bobby Byrne opened with a single. Tom Jones allowed Tommy Leach's sharp ground ball to roll through him, and Byrne came in to score. Clarke singled up the middle. Honus Wagner doubled, allowing Clarke and Leach to score, then Mullin bore down and got the Pirates out without further damage.

Vic Willis started on the mound for Pittsburgh, and the Tigers gradually began to claw back. They scored a run in the first inning. In the fourth, Sam Crawford walked, and Jim Delahanty and Tom Jones singled to load the bases.

The Pirates' great shortstop Honus Wagner was the Series hitting star as he pounded out a lusty .333 average.

Talk of the 1909 Series was the phenomenal pitching of the Pirates' freshman hurler Babe Adams, who won 3 games in the Series.

Clarke then fumbled Davey Jones's hit and 2 runs came in, enabling the Tigers to tie the game at 3–3. In the fifth inning, the Tigers moved out in front. Bush singled, Cobb advanced him with a groundout, and Crawford smashed a liner at Wagner, who just made the play at first base. Delahanty doubled, scoring Bush, to give the Tigers a 4–3 edge. In the sixth inning the Tigers added to their lead as Davey Jones singled, stole second, and came in to score following a double by Ty Cobb. It was now 5–3, Detroit.

The ninth was an inning of explosive action, of hits sprayed all over the field, line drives, wild throws, arguments, and actual fistfights that brought the huge crowd to their feet time after time, with cheers that could be heard all over town.

Dots Miller opened the inning for Pittsburgh with a base hit. The Pirates' first baseman, Bill Abstein, followed with another base hit. Then Owen Wilson stepped up to hit, and the Tiger infield, expecting a bunt, moved in for the play. Wilson bunted the ball right in front of the plate. Catcher Crazy Schmit pounced on the rolling ball like a big cat, and in one motion fired it to first base. Wilson and the ball reached first base together, and Wilson crashed into first baseman Tom Jones, knocking him ten feet into the air. The ball rolled away from the unconscious Jones, and Miller scored from third base on the play, while the other runners advanced.

At that point, with Jones still on the ground, fights broke out all over the diamond. Fifteen minutes passed before the umpires took control and play was resumed. Sam Crawford came in to replace the injured Tom Jones for the Tigers.

The Pirate runners on second and third represented the tying and winning runs. The next batter, George Gibson, hit a short fly ball to center for an easy out, and Bill Abstein, the runner on third, disregarding his coach's advice, set sail for home. The Tigers had been riding and jeering Abstein throughout the game, and he was determined to reach home safely. Catcher Schmit had the plate blocked and set himself for the play. He took the throw from his pitcher, and as he set himself to tag Abstein, Bill drove in with his spikes high, right at Schmit, who made the tag as both men went flying through the air. They were up immediately throwing punches, unleashing a wild melée, until rookie umpire Bill Evans separated the two players. Ed Abbaticchio batted for pitcher Phillippe, and as he swung for a third strike, Wilson tried to steal third base. He was out on a very close play, as Moriarty, the Tiger third baseman, was spiked badly. The game ended with Wilson and Moriarty on the ground, bleeding, fighting, and kicking at each other with their spikes. That wild half-inning gave the Pirates 1 run, but that was not enough as the Tigers retained a 5–4 edge. The teams were now deadlocked at 3 games each.

The following account was written by Honus Wagner, the great shortstop for the Pittsburgh Pirates:

When a fellow has played 2,785 games over a span of 21 years it's not the easiest thing in the world to pick out a single game and say it was his best or that it gave him his biggest thrill. But I was never sharper than in our last game of the World Series in 1909 against the Detroit Tigers.

I'm still willing to testify that the club of Hughie Jennings, Ty Cobb, Sam Crawford, Donie Bush, Davy Jones, and George Moriarty was a holy terror. And it tickled me no end to think that the Pirates outbattled and outfought and then beat them.

Cobb stole two bases in the series, but I was lucky and got six. Cobb made six hits. I made eight.

Ask Ty what happened the day he stood on first and yelled at me, "Hey, Kraut Head, I'm comin' down on the next pitch. I told him to come ahead and, by golly, he did. But George Gibson, our catcher, laid the ball right in my glove and I stuck it on Ty as he came in. I guess I wasn't too easy about it, 'cause it took three stitches to sew up his lip. That was the kind of series it was from start to finish.

Fred Clarke, our manager, told us we'd better sharpen our spikes since the Tigers would be sure to, and we took him at his word. We were sorta rough, too, I guess.

Trouble started in the first game. The Tigers let us have it and we gave it back to 'em with interest. There was a jawing match on nearly every pitch, and it was a good thing we had two of the greatest umpires, Bill Klem and Silk O'Loughlin. They knew their business and there weren't any riots.

In that first game, Fred Clarke hit a home run off George Mullin, who was the Tigers' best pitcher that year. I followed Clarke at the plate and I could see that Mullin was boiling, and anxious to get back at us. I always stood pretty far back from the plate, but this time I took every inch I could, figuring Mullin would throw at me. I wasn't wrong. He laid his fastball right into my ribs. Of course you can't say a thing like that was deliberate, but our boys reckoned it was, and from that minute the roughhousing was on.

We came into the final game tied at three apiece. The game was played in Detroit and the night before the Tiger rooters hired two or three bands to play in front of our hotel and they played all night trying to keep us from getting any sleep. But Clarke fooled 'em by taking us to another hotel, near the lake, where it was peaceful.

Our pitcher in the game was Babe Adams, the kid who had two of our three victories. Babe was hardly old enough to shave, but Clarke had a hunch on him all along. I guess I don't have to tell you what the feeling was the last day. Wild Bill Donovan, who started for the Tigers, lived up to his reputation and we got two runs off him in the second. Mullin came in to pitch in the fourth and couldn't find the plate either. There were two walks, two singles, giving us two more runs. In the sixth I got my only hit, but it was a three-bagger that drove in Clarke and Tom Leach, and I kept coming and scored when Jones made a bad throw from the outfield. We picked up another run in the seventh inning, and with Adams pitching perfect ball, that was the score, 8 to 0. There were close plays all day long, and guys would be spiking each other as they slid into the bases, and there were fights with the umpires, and fans and the Tiger players. It was unbelievable, but true, and we beat 'em badly.

Philadelphia Athletics Versus Chicago Cubs

In the first five World Series, the new American League pennant winners went down to defeat four times, its sole win thanks to the White Sox (the Hitless Wonders) of 1906. In each contest except the 1909 Series, the American League team did not put up much of a fight, losing quickly and decisively.

In 1910, however, there was a sudden change. Connie Mack's Philadelphia Athletics were a team of budding superstars, and they whipped Frank Chance's Chicago Cubs, knocking the daylights out of the much heralded Cub pitching staff. Two Philadelphia players in particular shone brightly in that World Series. Eddie Collins and Frank Baker were, in fact, the outstanding batting stars of Series competition in an otherwise dead-ball era.

Second baseman Eddie Collins, brilliant base runner, remarkable infielder, and great left-handed hitter, remains one of the two or three greatest stars ever to play that position.

Collins started his professional career while still at Columbia University in New York, sneaking off the campus to play ball under the name of Sullivan. He played one year for Connie Mack as Sullivan, then went back and used his real name. Always a great World Series player, Collins set a number of Series records in addition to finishing his twenty-five-year career with a lifetime batting average of .333.

Third baseman Frank Baker was a solidly built, muscular country boy, whose thick-handled fifty-two-ounce bat would have felt like a telephone pole in the hands of today's players. Baker was another farm boy, from Trappe, Maryland, a town that still boasts of his prowess. A born slugger who came along a dozen years too early for the jackrabbit ball, Baker differed from many long-ball hitters of later days in that he very rarely struck out. "I never saw any reason why a man with a bat in his hand should be unable to hit a ball thrown past him," he once told sportswriter Terry Shore.

In the 1910 Series, Collins and Baker sparked the Athletics' attack as each man drove out 9 hits. Collins hit for a gaudy .429 Series average, while Baker slugged the ball for a .409 average.

In the early twentieth century, Connie Mack introduced three Philadelphia youngsters who would develop into three of the most remarkable pitchers in baseball history. In 1901 there was the spectacular Eddie Plank, a Gettysburg College star, who won 17 games in his first season, and the unbelievable George Edward "Rube" Waddell. A year or so later, the great Indian, Charles Albert "Chief" Bender, made his debut in 1903 as a twenty-year-old kid by winning 17 games in his first full season.

Although Bender's features were those of an Indian, and in his heyday as a pitcher he had all

The 1910 World Series champs, the Philadelphia Athletics

the coolness under fire of the traditional aborigine, the Chief actually was only one-quarter Indian. His father was of Dutch descent, and his mother was half Chippewa. Born in Brainerd, Minnesota, Bender was educated, with the great Jim Thorpe, at the old Carlisle Indian School, where Pop Warner coached baseball as well as football. Warner discovered Bender as a fifteen-year-old kid throwing stones along the sidelines at a Carlisle football game. He promptly ordered him to report for the varsity baseball team. Within a few weeks Bender became the school's top pitcher.

It was the custom back in the early twentieth century for the young Indians to leave school in the spring, work on farms until the fall semester, and then return to school. The Chief was pitching hay when he received an offer to pitch for the Dillsburg, Pennsylvania, team for $5 dollars. The team was quartered about eighteen miles from Carlisle. Then he went to Dickinson College for a year and pitched for the Harrisburg team. One day while pitching for Harrisburg, he

beat the Chicago Cubs in an exhibition game, 3–1. Connie Mack happened to be at the game and signed him on the spot to play with the Athletics for the then princely sum of $1,800.

From 1903 until the World Series of 1910, Bender was one of Philadelphia's pitching stars. During the next ten years he was one of Connie Mack's most consistent hurlers, winning a total of 191 games before he was traded in 1914.

Connie Mack's second World Series opened in Shibe Park on October 17, a cold, crisp fall day. The Athletics were eager and excited at the opportunity to challenge the Chicago Cubs, easy victors over the Tigers in 1904 and the 1908 Series.

One of the nation's leading sportswriters flatly predicted that "the Mackmen [would be] no match for the experienced and battle-scarred Cubs."

A day before the Series opened, Mack sought out the Chief. "I'm looking for you to take charge of the Cubs in this important first game, Albert," he said.

Frank Baker, the A's' great third baseman, was one of the leading hitters in the Series with a marvelous .409 average.

"Don't worry, Mr. Mack. I'm ready for them," said Bender.

A crowd of more than twenty-six thousand excited fans sat spellbound as Chief Bender worked his magic on the hapless Cubs and held them to 3 scattered singles. The Chief struck out 8 Cub batters, holding the hard-hitting Chicago team scoreless until the ninth inning, when the suddenly jittery Mackmen made 2 errors, allowing the Cubs to score their lone run. Final score: 4–1, Athletics.

In the second game, Jack Coombs, a 31-game winner during the regular season, was Mack's pitching selection and he too was outstanding, allowing the Cubs 8 scattered hits and 3 runs, while the A's fell upon the offerings of Three Finger Brown for 14 blows and came away with their second straight win, 9–3.

Although hit freely and often, Brown was behind by only a 3–2 margin until the seventh inning. Then the Athletics opened up with a 6-run barrage that wrapped up the game.

Eddie Collins, who had already collected 2 doubles, a single, and 2 stolen bases, led off the seventh inning with a walk. Frank Baker singled, and then both Harry Davis and Dan Murphy doubled, and a deluge of base hits rattled off the fences as Brown left the mound in tears. Lew Richie finished the game for the A's.

October 9 was an off-day used for traveling from Philadelphia to Chicago. On the train, reporters asked Connie Mack about his pitcher for the third game. Sportswriters had noted in their stories that Plank would be the Athletics' pitcher, but Mack said, "Coombs did such a great job in Philadelphia for us yesterday, I think I'll come back with him again."

Jack Coombs started in wobbly fashion and was hit hard in the first inning. The Cubs scored 1 run in the first, and 2 more in the second. But the Athletics tied the score with 1 run in the first and 2 more in the second, to even the game at 3–3.

Then manager Frank Chance removed starting pitcher, Ed Reulbach, and inserted Harry McIntire. McIntire, in turn, was driven out quickly, with 3 successive base hits, and then Jack Pfiester came in to pitch. However, the A's continued their assault by pounding Jack for 9 hits, including a 3-run homer by Dan Murphy. Murphy's drive hit the top of a sign in right field. Manager Chance argued that the hit should be limited to two bases. He continued to argue so ardently that he was thrown out of the game. He was the first player to be ejected from a World Series game.

To make the day even drearier, the A's continued their assault by scoring 4 additional runs off Pfiester in the seventh inning, to give the A's an easy 12–5 victory.

The fourth game, delayed by rain for one day, gave the Cubs an opportunity to rest and to redeploy their shattered forces. Manager Chance selected a brilliant twenty-four-year-old pitcher, King Cole, who in his rookie year posted a spectacular 20-4 record.

Connie Mack selected his ace, Chief Bender,

who was good but not as effective as he was in the first game. The Cubs hit the Chief hard throughout the game for 11 hits and a 4–3 win.

On Sunday, October 23, more than twenty-seven thousand fans jammed every inch in the Cubs' ballpark hoping to root their team on to another victory. They felt that a Saturday win for the Cubs was a spark that might ignite the once mighty team.

It was true that the magnificent Cub infield of Tinker, Evers, and Chance, and the marvelous Harry Steinfeldt on third base, was getting on in years. Joe Tinker was now thirty years old, Evers was twenty-nine, Frank Chance was thirty-three, and Steinfeldt was thirty-three. In five years they had won four National League championships and two World Series, and despite their ages Cub fans and manager Chance felt certain that they could pull this Series out for the team and their fans.

For this crucial game, Connie Mack once more called on his tall ex-Colby College star, Jack Coombs, and manager Frank Chance called on Three Finger Brown as his last hope.

The A's picked up a run in the first inning, but the Cubs matched it in their half of the second, and it was a 1–1 game into the fourth inning, when the A's went ahead with another run.

The Cubs rallied and filled the bases with 1 out in the fourth inning, and the Cub fans became absolutely nutty with excitement as Connie Mack called time-out to talk to his pitcher Jack Coombs. "Just take your time, Jack," said Mack. "Nice and easy. Just don't walk anybody. Don't give 'em a run. Let 'em work for it."

"Don't worry, Mr. Mack, I'll take care of this situation," said Coombs.

Coombs fired his fastball in to Tinker, and then struck him out with a curveball. Then Jack fired three fastballs in to Jim Archer, and Archer went down swinging as Cub fans groaned in dismay.

The score was 2–1 into the eighth inning, when the A's exploded another bomb off pitcher Brown. Coombs singled but was forced by Hartsel, who then stole both second and third. Bris Lord doubled, scoring Hartsel, and then Eddie Collins smashed out his third hit, a long double,

scoring Lord. Now the score was 4–1, Athletics. Before the fatal eighth inning ended, the Athletics had pounded out 3 more runs for a 7–1 lead.

In a final but futile effort, the Cubs managed 1 run in their half of the eighth inning to make it a 7–2 game, but Jack Coombs held them scoreless in the ninth.

As the game ended, the Athletics on the bench and thousands of fans rushed onto the field to mob their heroes.

When Connie Mack brought his new world-champions back home from Chicago, they were given a tumultuous reception. A crowd estimated at more than fifty thousand packed Broad and Market streets. One of the fans in the reception line was a lantern-jawed, square-shouldered youngster, a ballplayer from the Germantown section of Philadelphia. He had played some

Popular Larry Dole, the classy Giants infielder, was the leading Giants batter with a .304 average for the Series.

professional baseball, was a great fan of the
Athletics, and worshiped Connie Mack.

Nineteen years later, that same youngster led
his Chicago Cubs against his idol, Connie Mack.
It was the World Series of 1929 and the youngster was now the manager of the pennant-winning Chicago Cubs. His name was Joe McCarthy.

Jack Combs, the A's' pitcher, outdueled the great
Christy Mathewson to win the third game of the
Series.

1911

38,281[?]

Philadelphia Athletics Versus New York Giants

The Philadelphia Athletics brought more joy to the American League in 1911 when they bowled over the heavily favored New York Giants. Their victory was especially sweet for Ban Johnson, Connie Mack, and Ben Shibe, the Athletics' owner, as it was achieved against their bitter rivals, John McGraw and John Brush. In this Series, the Athletics avenged their 1905 disaster by defeating the Giants, 4 games to 2.

The road to the Series came somewhat harder. The Athletics lost 6 of their first 8 games and were in the cellar of the American League, while the Tigers blasted away all opposition, winning 21 of their first 23 games. It looked like a runaway for the Tigers.

Gradually the A's, sparked by their young stars, Eddie Collins, Home Run Baker, and Jack Barry, plus the effective pitching of Jack Coombs, Chief Bender, and Eddie Plank, plugged away and by July Fourth had moved into first place. Over the next few weeks they dropped back again, but on August 4 they again vaulted into first place and remained there, breezing home in front of the Tigers by 13½ games to win another pennant for Connie Mack.

The Giants, on the other hand, virtually ran their rivals in the National League out of the pennant race as the team stole a record 347 bases during the season. McGraw had rebuilt the Giants with several classy newcomers: Buck Herzog at third base; Art Fletcher at shortstop; Larry Doyle at second base; the unfortunate Fred Merkle at first base; and four speedy youngsters, Josh Devore, Fred Snodgrass, Red Murray, and Beals Becker, in the outfield. Chief Meyers was the catcher. Christy Mathewson, with a 26-13 record, was the star of a fine pitching staff, which included Rube Marquard, Leon Ames, Otis Crandall, and George Wiltse.

By 1911, the World Series had developed from a postseason event of interest mainly to the cities whose teams were playing to something closer to the great national spectacle that it is today. The nation virtually closed up shop to await the result of the crucial battles between Mack and "Mac," Connie Mack and John McGraw.

No Series has ever been covered as extensively as were the games of the 1911 Series, as newspapers throughout the nation featured the minutest details of every game played.

The first game was held at the Polo Grounds before a crowd of 38,281, the largest World Series audience thus far.

The Giants won that game, a marvelous duel between two of the game's greatest stars, Christy Mathewson and Chief Bender. The final score was 2–1 as Matty gave up 6 hits while striking out 6 batters. But the Indian Chief was a mite better; he struck out 11 Giants and allowed but 5 hits.

Frank Baker's tremendous home runs won 2 games in the Series for the Athletics and earned him the nickname Home Run Baker, which he used to sign his checks and letters for the rest of his life.

Game two featured a pitching duel between two left-handed stars, Eddie Plank and Rube Marquard. Plank was brilliant in this matchup allowing the Giants just 5 hits while striking out 8. Frank Baker slammed out the first of his 2 home runs in the Series, both of which came at crucial moments. Those 2 home runs earned him the nickname Home Run Baker, which stuck with him for the rest of his life.

At the top of the sixth inning, with the score tied 1–1, Collins stroked a double down the left field line. Then Franklin Baker, the Maryland farm boy, caught one of Marquard's fastballs and drove it far and wide over the right field fence; the gleeful Collins danced in ahead of Baker, giving the A's an exciting 3–1 victory.

The third game again featured some brilliant pitching, between the Colby College kid, Jack Coombs, and Christy Mathewson. Matty had the edge, as he continually outsmarted the Athletics' hitters; he had them popping up and hitting ground balls to the infield for easy outs. But Coombs matched Matty's superb performance and the two teams began the ninth inning with the Giants in front by a score of 1–0.

Matty got the first batter out on a fly ball. Then up to the plate stepped Frank Baker. Matty fired in a vicious fastball. Baker swung and missed. Then, another pitch for a ball, and then another fastball missed the corner. The count was 2 balls and 1 strike when Matty came in with his great fadeaway pitch. Baker took a tremendous swing, caught the ball on the fat part of his big bat, and the ball rocketed high and far over the right field fence for another Baker four-bagger.

Baker's home run only tied the score, but it had an odd psychological effect on the crowd, and on both teams.

The Giants' defense cracked wide open in the eleventh inning as Collins and the pesky Baker slapped singles in rapid succession. Shortstop Art Fletcher then fumbled Dan Murphy's ground ball and Collins scored. Then Harry Davis singled and Baker came in, and it was 3–1, Philadelphia.

In the Giants' half of the eleventh inning, Buck Herzog singled, went to second on Chief Meyers's grounder, then scored the final Giants' run when Collins booted Becker's ground ball. Attempting to steal second, Becker was thrown out and the Giants' threat was ended with the A's on top by a 3–2 score.

The Series was postponed for six successive days because of rains that flooded Philadelphia. Finally, the fourth game took place on October 24, and when play commenced, the first-game pitchers, Christy Mathewson and Chief Bender, were on the mound again.

"I think you're going to win this one, Albert," said Connie Mack as he told the tall Indian he would pitch. "I don't think we'll find Matty as effective as in the first game. He's very tired."

The Giants gave Matty a lift with a 2-run lead as Josh Devore singled, then scored on Larry

Doyle's triple. Fred Snodgrass scored Doyle with a sacrifice fly, and it was 2–0, Giants.

But in the fourth inning, Matty's magic fade-away pitch deserted him as Baker, Davis, and Murphy drove out successive two-base hits. Two runs came in and then Murphy scored, to make it 3–2, Philadelphia.

In the fifth inning, Collins singled and came all the way home when Baker slammed a long drive that was good for two bases, to give the Athletics a 4–2 win.

The Giants, however, won a reprieve the next day, when they entered the last half of the ninth inning on the short end of a 3–1 score, and with 2 outs rallied for 2 big runs to tie the game, 3–3.

The roar from the crowd at the Polo Grounds rolled across Coogan's Bluff for ten minutes. It rose to a shattering level in the last half of the tenth when the Giants came up to bat.

Doyle opened the inning with a ringing double, and slid safely into third on a bunt by Snodgrass. Then Fred Merkle drove a long fly ball to the wall that Murphy chased down and caught. Meanwhile, Doyle tagged up at third and then barreled into home plate with a beautiful fadeaway slide. The only trouble was that he fell away from the plate and never touched it.

Umpire Bill Klem, behind the plate, watched the play in amazement and said later that if any Philadelphia player had tagged Doyle before he left the field, he would have been called out. None of them did and the Giants walked off with a 4–3 victory.

The next day, though, the A's literally tore the Giants apart in the seventh inning with 7 big runs as the Giants' defense collapsed. The Athletics simply outfought and outhit the Giants with a 13-hit barrage, and took the World Series with a shattering 13–2 victory.

Connie Mack, manager of the World Champion Athletics

The World Series had now reached the big-money stage. Even though grandstand admission was only $2, the total gate was $342,364. The players' shares were well beyond the previous payouts, with the winning Athletics each receiving $3,654 and the losing Giants receiving more than $2,400 each. The two club presidents, John Brush and Ben Shibe, each received checks for $90,118.

1912

Boston Red Sox Versus
New York Giants

There were momentous events occurring in the world outside the sports pages in 1912, as the New York Giants won the National League flag by 10 games over the Pittsburgh Pirates, and the Boston Red Sox beat Connie Mack's "greatest team." The White Star liner *Titanic* disastrously sank after hitting an iceberg during her maiden voyage from Southampton, England, to New York, with a loss of some fifteen hundred lives. China became a republic in 1912 and elected its first president. Captain Robert Scott and four companions reached the South Pole, only to perish on their attempted return to civilization. Teddy Roosevelt, saying, "I feel like a bull moose," broke away from the Republican party and fought both President Taft and Woodrow Wilson for the White House. A highly decorated police lieutenant, Charles Becker, of the New York City Police Department, was going on trial for masterminding the murder of big-time gambler Herman Rosenthal, who had said that Becker was his silent partner. Then at two o'clock one morning as he left the posh Hotel Metropole, Rosenthal was gunned down by four well-known triggermen, and the story pushed all other news off the front pages for weeks at a time.

But as the World Series approached, the staid *New York Times* announced: "Who will doubt that public interest will center on the game of baseball at our Polo Grounds and in Boston?"

In 1912 the Giants took over first place on May 15 and remained there for the rest of the pennant race. The Giants were a running, fighting, hard-hitting team, with Buck Herzog at third; Art Fletcher at short; Laughing Larry Doyle, captain, at second; Fred Merkle at first; and four flashy speedsters, Josh Devore, Fred Snodgrass, Red Murray, and Beals Becker, in the outfield. A burly California Indian, Chief Jack Meyers, did most of the catching. The incredible Christy Mathewson, who won 23 games during the season, still was New York's pitching ace, but the club's pennant had been made possible by the acquisition of the great left-hander Rube Marquard, an $11,000 lemon in 1909, but an $11,000 ace in 1912. Giant hurlers Leon Ames, George Wiltse, and Otis Crandall rounded out the pitching staff.

The Giants were also joined in mid-season by the man the king of Sweden had described as "the greatest athlete in the world": Indian Jim Thorpe. Jim had gone from the tiny Indian school in Carlisle, Pennsylvania, to become world famous after winning the prestigious decathlon and pentathlon events in the 1912 Olympics, a feat no one has been able to equal to this date.

Later, when Jim was stripped of his Olympic crown for playing a few professional baseball games, John McGraw phoned him with an offer to play with the Giants. "Jim, I'll give you forty-five hundred dollars to play for the Giants." "Sounds okay, Mr. McGraw, but I'd like you to talk to Pop Warner. He's my coach." Warner took the phone and said, "Mr. McGraw, every big-league team has been in touch with us. I think he's worth more than your forty-five-hundred-dollar offer."

"Okay," said McGraw, "I don't even know if he can play major league ball, but I know he's fast and he's a great athlete. Look, Pop," said McGraw, "I'll make it five thousand dollars and I'll give him a three-year contract. I think a lot of people would pay to see Jim with the Giants."

He was right. People did pay to see Jim, even though he did not play during the 1912 season, but was kept on the sidelines by McGraw and carefully tutored until the 1913 season, when he was inserted into the Giants' lineup.

The 1912 Red Sox had one of their greatest teams, with a star at every position. But if one star had to be singled out, it was Tristram Speaker, "the Gray Eagle." Called "Spoke" by his teammates, Tris was a former rodeo rider and telegraph lineman from Hubbard, Texas.

Tris was an all-around athlete in high school, and developed into a star pitcher at Forth Worth Polytechnic Institute. He began his professional baseball career with the Cleburne, Texas, team in 1906, but he failed to win a single game. Then an injury to a Cleburne outfielder enabled Tris to find his niche. Pressed into service in the outfield, Tris immediately displayed indications of his potential greatness. Once on base, Tris would be off and running. He stole 33 bases in 84 games, and that performance was enough to move him up to Houston in 1907, where he led the Texas League in hitting, with a .315 average and 39 stolen bases.

George Huff, who managed the Red Sox that season, for only fourteen days, scouted Speaker and purchased his contract for $750. It was to be one of the greatest bargains in baseball history.

It took several years for Speaker actually to break into the regular lineup. He was shunted back down to the Texas League in 1907 and 1908, and literally had to beg several managers for another opportunity when the Red Sox failed to pick up his contract. Even John McGraw shrugged off Speaker during spring training in

Rube Marquard was the greatest pitcher in baseball as he won 19 games in a row during the season to lead his team to the pennant. Then in the Series, Rube won 2 games for the Giants.

1908, reporting that his roster was filled.

Finally, in 1909, Tris hit .350 for Little Rock and was promptly sold to the Red Sox, for $500.

In 1910, Tris became the center fielder in a Red Sox outfield that included Harry Hooper in right field and George "Duffy" Lewis in left field. By 1912 the Boston outfield had developed into the one most brilliant defensive unit in the major leagues. Speaker's batting had improved tremendously and his average zoomed to an amazing .383, leading the Sox to another American League pennant.

The Red Sox pitching staff was far and away the finest in the league, with Smokey Joe Wood,

Red Sox manager Jake Stahl (*left*) and Giants manager John McGraw (*right*) prior to the Series opener

Buck O'Brien, Hugh Bedient, Ray Collins, and Charlie Hall all contributing to the 105 Red Sox victories.

In the infield, the combination of Heinie Wagner at shortstop and Steve Yerkes at second base was outstanding, especially when player-manager Jake Stahl perched himself at first base and Larry Gardner at third.

The night before the first game of the World Series, the sky over Manhattan was lit up by a torchlight parade down Broadway by the Royal Rooters, a boisterous mob of wild and frantic Boston fans led by the mayor of Boston, Honey Fitzgerald. They marched, danced, and sang in anticipation of a victory over the Giants.

The front page of *The New York Times* carried this description: "If the air around Times Square was supercharged with suspense of the approaching contest, there was no word to describe the excitement in the atmosphere around the Polo Grounds where the general admission line began to form 24 hours before game time."

Before the game, the Royal Rooters marched around the diamond singing "Tessie" and "When I Get You Alone Tonight," while the New York fans hissed and booed and fighting broke out throughout the stands. Honey Fitz presented Tris Speaker and manager Jake Stahl with new cars, gifts from the Boston fans.

As the game began, Giant fans were stunned as McGraw started the twenty-two-year-old rookie Jeff Tesreau against Joe Wood. "What's the matter with Matty?" they shouted. McGraw had decided that Tesreau's spitball would give the Red Sox so much trouble that the Giants might take the first game and then he could come back with Matty in the second game.

The Giants belabored Smokey Joe Wood in the third inning and scored 2 runs on a walk, a single, a texas leaguer that fell for a double, and another single by Red Murray.

The Red Sox got a couple of breaks in the sixth inning and scored 1 run. Devore ran in front of Snodgrass just as Fred was about to handle Speaker's line drive. Snodgrass got his glove on the ball, but it bounced away for a triple, and Tris scored on Duffy Lewis's out.

The seventh inning was lucky for Boston, as they iced the game with 3 big runs to take a 4–2 lead. Honus Wagner and Hick Cady singled with 1 out. Then Wood hit a grounder straight at Doyle, which should have resulted in a double play. Doyle booted the ball, but did get Cady at second base. Then Harry Hooper doubled, Steve Yerkes singled, and 3 runs were in for the Red Sox.

The Giants threatened in the ninth when, with 1 out, Merkle, Herzog, and Meyers singled for 1 run. But as the Giant fans screamed with excitement, Smokey Joe Wood bore down and struck out Art Fletcher and pesky Doc Crandall on six steaming pitches that tore into catcher Bill Carrigan's glove with an explosive force and the Red Sox won, 4–3.

Boston fans had a brief opportunity to gloat when their team cuffed the great Mathewson for 3 big runs in the very first inning of game two, in Boston.

But the Giants kept plugging away, with 1 run in the second inning and another in the fourth, to keep within striking distance of the Sox. In the eighth inning, with Boston still leading, 4–2, the Giants made their bid. Snodgrass drove a pitch into the air and Lewis muffed the catch. Doyle singled, and then doubles by Murray and Herzog gave the Giants 3 big runs and a 5–4 edge. But the Sox tied it at 5–5 when Lewis doubled and Gardner's drive whizzed through Fletcher's legs for a base hit and Duffy scored the tying run.

In the tenth inning, Merkle tripled and scored on a sacrifice fly, and the Giants had a 6–5 lead. But the Red Sox came back fighting mad. Speaker slugged a tremendous drive to left field for a triple. Tris was trying to score on his long drive, but as he rounded third base, Herzog gave him a shove with his hip, and he had to slow down momentarily. But Tris, who had never stopped running, turned the corner and headed for home and scored when catcher Meyers dropped the relay throw. After Tris was called safe at home, he got up and charged Herzog at third base and the two men fought until the umpires pulled them apart.

When peace was restored, the umpires decided it was too dark to continue to play and called the game with the score 6–6.

The tie game gave the wearied sportswriters a chance to get a night's rest, as the World Series Commission ruled that it should be played off immediately in Boston.

The third game, on October 10, was one of the wildest, screwiest in World Series history. Half of the nearly thirty-five thousand spectators left the ballpark thinking the Red Sox had won by a 3–2 score, but the Giants had actually won the game, 2–1.

The World Series games began at three o'clock, and by the ninth inning of game three, the field was in semidarkness. Marquard, pitching with all the artistry at his command, had blanked the Red Sox for eight innings, and as the ninth inning began, the Giants held a 1–0 lead.

But, in the Red Sox' half of the ninth inning, a mist had blown across the field and hung over right field. Speaker led off with a long fly ball for an easy out. Duffy Lewis singled, and Gard-

Center fielder Tris Speaker led the Red Sox's batters with an even .300 batting average for the 8-game Series.

ner sent a scorching hit to left field for a double, scoring Lewis. Stahl hit to Marquard for another out. Fletcher threw the ball away after fielding Wagner's grounder, and Stahl went to third base. A few moments later, Wagner stole second base.

Then all hell broke loose. Red Sox catcher Forrest Cady came up to hit. He boomed a long, low drive deep into right field. Josh Devore, looking like an elf in the darkening mist, sprinted in after the ball and caught it at his shoe tops on a dead run. Without changing his stride, he continued running, right into the clubhouse. Only the fans along the right field stands were in position to see the catch. The others believed the ball had gone past little Josh, and, seeing Stahl and Wagner cross the plate, thought the pair had scored the runs to give Boston a sensational victory, 3–2. But it was a Giant victory by a 2–1 margin, and Red Sox fans screamed in agony about the Giants "stealing" a game from them.

Smokey Joe Wood and Hugh Bedient won the next two games for the Red Sox, by scores of 3–1 and 2–1. Hughie Bedient was the hero in the Red Sox 2–1 victory as he outpitched the great Christy Mathewson.

Jake Stahl wanted to pitch Wood again in the fifth game, to wrap up the Series for the Red Sox, but club owner Jim McAleer had other ideas. He visited his manager in his hotel room in New York and asked, "Who are you pitching tomorrow?"

"Wood, of course," replied the surprised manager.

"Is that smart?" countered McAleer. "We're ahead, three games to one. Why not give Joe Wood another day of rest and use O'Brien instead?"

Stahl tried to argue, but McAleer reminded him who the boss was. O'Brien pitched the next day.

In the very first inning, the game was over as the Giants slammed O'Brien for 5 runs. The Giants battered O'Brien and Collins for 11 hits and a 5–2 victory.

The following day in Boston was another riotous one at the ballpark. Very few people expected more than three games in Boston, and the Royal Rooters had bought out a section of the left field stands for those games and assumed that those seats would be available for this game. However, Bob McRoy, in charge of ticket sales, had placed the seats on sale for this game at the regular windows, and they were sold out quickly.

A view from behind first base at the Polo Grounds, home of the New York Giants in the 1912 Series

BOSTON-AMERICAN LEAGUE CHAMPIONS—1912

1912

O'BRIEN P | CARRIGAN C | WOOD P | NUNAMAKER C | SPEAKER C.F. | HENRIKSON R.F. | HALL P | CICOTTE | GARDNER 3d B. | WAGNER S.S. | THOMAS C | HOOPER R.F. | LEWIS L.F. | HAGERMAN P | LEONARD P | Dr. QUIRK | PAPE U | ENGLE U | YERKES 2d B. | BRADLEY S.S. | KRUG P | BEDIENT P | BUSHELMAN P | CADY C | McCARTHY Mascot | STAHL 1st B.

The 1912 World Champion Boston Red Sox

When the one thousand or so Royal Rooters marched out onto the field before the game they found their seats occupied. And there was hell to pay, as tempers flared. The umpires couldn't get the Rooters off the field, and finally, after more than a half hour of pushing, shoving, and actual fighting, mounted police drove the Rooters behind the bleachers.

The net result was harmful to Joe Wood and Boston. Joe had tried to warm up, but he couldn't get onto the field, as the Royal Rooters were scrambling all over the diamond. When play was finally started, his arm had stiffened; he was hit hard for half a dozen runs in the first inning as the Giants ran the Red Sox ragged on their way to a one-sided 11–4 victory.

In the dugout before the eighth and final game, manager Stahl talked to Hugh Bedient. "Kid, you've got to win this one for us. It's the biggest game of your life. Just pitch the way you did your last time out and you can beat Mathewson again."

It was a tremendously exciting game. The Giants scored once in the third inning, with only Harry Hooper's marvelous catch preventing a second run. Little Josh Devore clubbed a tremendous drive to right field, and Hooper dived for the ball just as it reached the bleachers. He caught it in his bare hand just before he crashed into the second row of the stands. Actually, the catch was illegal, since Hooper was entirely out of the playing field when he caught the ball. But no Red Sox official protested the remarkable catch.

The score was 1–0 going into the seventh inning, with the great Matty in control of the Red Sox. Then Jake Stahl popped a fly ball into short left field as three Giants, Devore, Snodgrass, and Fletcher, stood around and watched. Nobody made a move, and the ball dropped in for a hit. A walk moved Stahl to second base; then Olaf Henriksen pinch-hit for Bedient and doubled to left, and Stahl came in with the tying run.

Joe Wood came in to pitch in the tenth inning. Red Murray whacked his second double of the game and scored on Fred Merkle's single, and the Giants went ahead, 2–1.

With Matty needing only one inning to hold this slim lead, it looked like a cinch for the Giants. Then Clyde Engle, hitting for Wood, raised an easy, lazy fly ball to Snodgrass in center field. Fred had to move only ten feet to get the ball, and then suddenly, a tremendous, sorrowful "O-O-Oh" issued from the crowd when the ball trickled right through Snodgrass's hands, and Engle was on second base.

The unhappy Snodgrass tried to atone for the horrible error and made a diving catch of Harry Hooper's line smash, but there was something eerie in the air now as Matty, possibly unnerved by the costly error, walked Yerkes. Tris Speaker came up to bat. Once again the fates were unkind to Matty. Speaker raised an easy foul just a few feet outside the coaching box at first base, and the ball dropped between Merkle and catcher Chief Meyers. Merkle should have caught the ball in his hip pocket, but he did not.

Speaker was given another chance to hit and made the most of the situation. Tris promptly belted the first pitch for a single that brought in Engle with the tying run as Yerkes took third base. Then Larry Gardner drove a long fly ball to deep right field, and Yerkes sped home with the winning run. And the Red Sox were the world champions by a 3–2 score.

The 1912 World Series bounty was large. Each winning Boston player received $4,025 while each Giant player got $2,566. The 1912 World Series has since been dubbed as "Snodgrass's $30,000 error."

1913

Philadelphia Athletics Versus New York Giants

In the last half of August 1913, the Giants started a drive that brought them their third straight pennant and their fifth in ten years. And for the third time, they faced their bitter rivals, the Athletics, who coasted to the American League championship, 9½ games ahead of Washington. Each team had taken one World Series, and this would be the deciding one, and the last, between the two most celebrated managers in the game.

Just before the first game, Connie Mack sat in the Philadelphia dugout and listened to the sage advice of a friendly fortune-teller, who said, "You will win the Series, Mr. Mack."

Connie grinned. "Yes, but my men will have to fight for it all the way. The Giants are very strong."

"You will win it easier than you did two years ago; all signs are most favorable," she insisted.

Mack had made a number of changes in his all-star lineup; he moved Ed Murphy into right field and then brought up Wally Schang from Buffalo as his regular catcher. It was the beginning of a marvelous nineteen-year career for Schang. Mack also strengthened his pitching staff, with Joe Bush, Bob Shawkey, Herb Pennock, and Carroll Brown, to back up his two great stars, Chief Bender and Eddie Plank.

John McGraw also added a few new faces to his team. George Burns, a former catcher, now an outfielder, pushed Josh Devore out of left field; and pitcher Al Demaree, who had joined the team in 1912 but seen little action, won 13 games during the season and joined the great stars, Mathewson, Marquard, and Tesreau, to give the Giants an almost unbeatable quartet of pitchers.

"It's the same old act," wrote sportswriter Fred Lieb as the Athletics overpowered the Giants to win the opening game of the Series at the Polo Grounds. Before a crowd of more than thirty-six thousand frantic Giant fans, each team powered 11 hits, with the Athletics' stars Home Run Baker and Eddie Collins each driving out 3 apiece. Baker lived up to his nickname as he smashed a terrific home run with Collins on base in the fifth inning and the A's jumped out to a 5–4 lead. The big blow by Baker drove pitcher Rube Marquard out of the game. The Giants fought back gamely, urged on by their shouting, half-crazed fans, and scored 3 runs in their half of the fifth inning, but that was not enough as Chief Bender bore down and stifled the Giant rally. In the eighth and ninth innings, the skies darkened and the weather turned black and threatening; Bender simply overpowered the hapless Giants and the A's took the first game, 6–4.

In the second game, those pitching immortals Christy Mathewson and Ed Plank renewed a rivalry that had begun in 1899 when both pitch-

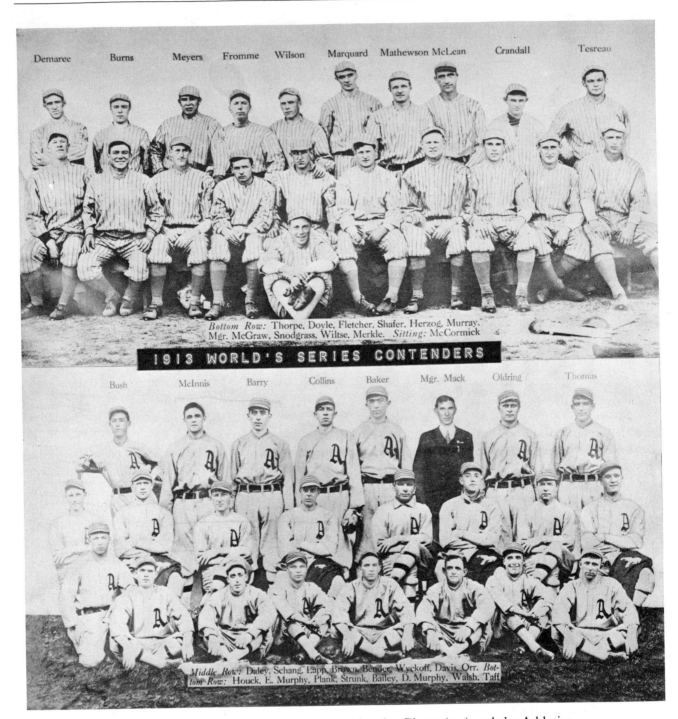

Demaree   Burns   Meyers   Fromme   Wilson   Marquard   Mathewson McLean   Crandall   Tesreau

Bottom Row: Thorpe, Doyle, Fletcher, Shafer, Herzog, Murray, Mgr. McGraw, Snodgrass, Wiltse, Merkle. *Sitting:* McCormick

1913 WORLD'S SERIES CONTENDERS

Bush   McInnis   Barry   Collins   Baker   Mgr. Mack   Oldring   Thomas

Middle Row: Daley, Schang, Lapp, Brown, Bender, Wyckoff, Davis, Orr. *Bottom Row:* Houck, E. Murphy, Plank, Strunk, Bailey, D. Murphy, Walsh, Taff

The rival contenders for the championship, the Giants (*top*) and the Athletics (*bottom*)

ers were collegians: Matty, the Bucknell star; and Plank, the ace of the Gettysburg team. And though Plank, a stylish southpaw, came within an eyelash of victory, it was the great Giant right-hander who again wore the hero's mantle. For

eight and a half innings, Plank and Matty fought each other in a scoreless duel. Suddenly Matty called for a time-out, beckoned his infield to the mound, and said, "I'm going to give them nothing but fastballs, so be on your toes. They'll

Manager McGraw watches his team take batting practice while Christy Mathewson waits for his turn at bat.

scoring McLean, to give the Giants a 1–0 edge. A fielder's choice on Herzog, a walk to Doyle, and a single by Fletcher gave the Giants 2 more runs and the ball game, by a 3–0 score.

When the Series resumed for the third game, at the Polo Grounds on October 9, each team had won 1 game. McGraw had Jeff Tesreau, his third pitching ace, ready, while Connie Mack was forced to utilize his "kid pitcher," Leslie Bush, better known as Bullet Joe.

"I knew if the kid could conquer his wildness, he would beat the Giants," said Mack.

Bullet Joe held the Giants to 5 hits while the A's pounded Tesreau and Crandall for 12 safeties. Eddie Collins once again was the batting star for the A's, with a triple and 2 singles, and young Wally Schang belted out a home run to give the Athletics the third game by an 8–2 margin.

probably hit nothing but grounders. Let's go."

Whether Matty's words were the encouragement the Giants needed, we'll never know. For then began one of the most amazing defensive stands in World Series play. Strunk, the Athletics' leadoff hitter, singled to center. Jack Barry, the A's' shortstop, then scratched a lazy grounder between Matty and first baseman Wiltse. Doyle, the Giants' second baseman, got his hands on the ball, but he threw wildly and the runners advanced to second and third base, with nobody out.

Then came the Giants' Thermopylae, with George Wiltse in the lead. Jack Lapp smashed a ground ball to Wiltse, George fired the ball in to the plate, and Strunk was called out on a very close play. Then Ed Plank slapped Matty's first pitch to Wiltse, and once again Wiltse's great throw to the Giants' catcher got the runner, Barry, on another close play. Saved by those two plays at the plate by Wiltse, Matty closed out a scary ninth inning.

The marvelous defensive plays did something for the Giants' morale and they came back to play inspired ball in the tenth inning. Larry McLean singled and Wiltse sacrificed him to second. Then the great Mathewson broke the scoreless tie by singling sharply to center field,

Chief Bender won 2 games in the Series, bringing his career total in Series play to 6 games.

Fred Merkle, Giants first baseman, slides in to score in the seventh inning of game four of the Series.

The fourth game, back in Philadelphia, was won by Chief Bender, his sixth World Series win, a record that endured for twenty-nine years. But the Chief almost frittered away a 6–0 lead and had to use all of his skill and cunning to finish ahead, 6–5.

Faithful Eddie Plank finally defeated his nemesis, Christy Mathewson, in the fifth and final game of the Series, at the Polo Grounds on October 11, as he allowed the Giants only 2 hits.

The A's quickly jumped on Matty for a run in the first inning and 2 more in the third for a

3–0 lead as Plank mowed down the Giants as fast as they came up to bat. It wasn't until the fifth inning that the Giants got their first man on base.

Tillie Shafer walked with 1 out to open the Giants' fifth inning and promptly stole second base on the first pitch. Then, on a hit-and-run play, Red Murray hit a high fly over the pitching box. Shafer, on second, ran off the base, then seemed bewildered as the Giant coaches screamed at him to get back. As this was going on, the entire Athletics' infield gathered around the fly ball, undecided as to who should make the catch. Finally, Baker lunged for the ball, knocked into Plank, jolted the ball out of Eddie's hands, and all runners were safe. McLean then singled for the Giants' lone run. The only other man to reach base for the Giants was Matty, who led off the sixth inning with a scorching single, but was left stranded as Plank retired the side without any further trouble, giving the A's the Series by a 3–1 margin. Not only were the Athletics once again world champions, they had won the final set of their three Series match with the Giants.

An unfortunate aftermath of this Series was the bitter dispute over a misunderstood signal that occurred between McGraw and his best friend, Wilbert Robinson, his chief coach at third base. It ended in turning their lifelong friendship into one of the most intense rivalries in baseball, as Robinson later became manager of the Brooklyn Dodgers and the two teams became bitter enemies for the rest of their days.

1914

Boston Braves Versus Philadelphia Athletics

Johnny Gaffney grew up on New York's East Side, where he watched some of his boyhood pals become famous as burglars, kidnappers, and killers. A few became firemen. John became a first-rate cop. After a few exciting years on the police force, John turned to politics and was quickly elected district captain of the election board. Shortly thereafter he became involved in the construction business, and his contacts brought him business worth millions. He became so powerful he was selected chief of Tammany Hall, New York's Democratic organization and the city's most powerful political stronghold. It was Gaffney's firm that handled the huge excavation jobs for both the Penn Station and Grand Central Station projects.

In 1911, a syndicate headed by Gaffney and John Montgomery Ward, a former manager of Brooklyn and the Giants, now a noted New York lawyer, purchased control of the Boston baseball team. But it was Gaffney who wielded the control of the team, even though Ward was a noted baseball man and knew the game. Gaffney indirectly named the team after Tammany Hall. Tammany was the name of an Indian tribe and Gaffney's team became the Boston Braves.

Gaffney sought out and hired George Stallings to manage the team. A graduate of the Virginia Military Institute, his dedication to baseball was proved when he gave up the study of medicine to play baseball.

Near the end of the 1912 season, John Gaffney sat in a private box seat at the Polo Grounds with his new manager and watched his pitiful Braves lose to the pennant-winning Giants.

"This club is a horror," Stallings replied when Gaffney asked him what he thought of his Braves.

"Well, you're the new boss," answered Gaffney. "Make whatever changes you wish. Remember, I want a winner."

"I've been stuck with some terrible teams in my time," mused Stallings aloud, "but this one beats 'em all."

Two years from that day, John Gaffney had his winner. The 1914 Boston Braves were hailed as the greatest of all baseball teams. Stallings became known throughout the land as the Miracle Man.

George Tweedy Stallings was one of baseball's first bona fide split personalities. Away from the ballpark, he was dignified, fastidious, and meticulous in every way. Chesterfieldian in his dress and manners, courtly to ladies. Swarthy, moon-faced, and bright-eyed, he would have been a cinch for today's men-of-distinction ads.

But on the bench during a ball game, Stallings was a different person. No man, not even John McGraw or Leo Durocher, ever reached the heights of invective hurled by George. He could and did fly into a schizophrenic rage at the drop of a pop fly. Sputtering with a fury that invited apoplexy, George told off his ballplayers as they

55

had never been told off before. And, curiously enough, nobody minded the tongue lashings of Stallings. "It was an art with him," Hank Gowdy, one of his star players, remarked years later.

It was Stallings's habit to sit on the same spot on the bench day after day during the season, his knees and his feet close together. As he grew agitated, he would slide his feet, still close together, back and forth over the floor of the dugout. Sometimes he would slide his entire body. He wore the seat of a pair of pants clean through during the second game of the 1914 World Series.

Years after George had left baseball behind, the legend of Stallings persisted. Perhaps the best of all the stories concerns his retirement to his plantation in Haddock, Georgia, named The Meadows, which was brought on by his poor health and disgust with baseball. He was ill, suffering from a serious cardiac disturbance.

"Mr. Stallings," said the specialist at the completion of an examination, "you have an unusually bad heart. Is there any way you can account for it?"

Stallings hesitated, looking at the doctor.

"Bases on balls, all those bases on balls, you son of a bitch. Bases on balls," cursed Stallings softly, turning his face to the wall.

On one occasion Stallings bawled out a pitcher who had given up a succession of walks and had been taken out of the game.

"You bases-on-balls bonehead," roared George. "G'wan to the clubhouse and burn up your uniform."

The pitcher trudged into the clubhouse beyond center field. A few minutes later, smoke was seen rising from the chimney of the clubhouse. A player on the field pointed it out to Stallings.

"What? Is he really burning up his uniform?" shouted George. "My God, what a bonehead. Somebody go and stop him before he burns up the clubhouse."

Stallings set a high value on morale. He was way ahead of the immortal Bill Roper, Princeton's football coach, with the team-that-won't-be-beaten-can't-be-beaten theory. He felt that if his players believed they could win, they would win.

But most important, Stallings was a baseball wizard. Asked what his system was, he always replied, "Play the percentages." He had an incredible baseball mind, and when he discussed various plays at his daily morning team meetings, even hardened veterans knew they were listening to a master.

Stallings brought up a couple of baseball's most prized characters to play their first big-league games with the Boston Braves. One was Mike Gonzalez, a catcher from Cuba who was to win more attention for his catch-as-catch-can wrestling with the English language than he ever would as a player or a coach. Gonzalez was brought up from the Havana Reds and caught one game for the Braves against the Giants. He went hitless in 3 times at bat, and the Giants stole 5 bases on him in seven innings. He later shrugged his performance off, saying, "She run. I throw. She safe."

But the Braves introduced a more colorful performer than Gonzalez to big-league baseball. He came from the New Bedford League. He was small (weighing only 150 pounds at the time), but had one of the biggest hearts and one of the longest names: Walter James Vincent "Rabbit" Maranville. They called him Rabbit because a little girl once watching him bounce around in a practice pepper game at New Bedford had giggled at his antics and said, "You jump around just like a rabbit." Until then he had been known as Stumpy.

Maranville was an imp. He was baseball's Peter Pan. His body aged during the twenty-three years he played, but his spirits always remained young. He stood just five feet five and had the physique of a small boy, but on the field, at shortstop, he was a heavyweight. A mischievous sprite, he was to become a darling of the fans, a worrier of managers, and one of the great umpire baiters in history.

Although a brilliant fielder whether playing short or second base, nothing Maranville ever did tickled fans as much as his vest-pocket catches. No matter how high the fly, Rabbit would always catch the ball with his hands cupped under his belt buckle.

Almost every story of the Boston Braves of 1914 deals mainly with the three-man pitching

staff of Lefty Tyler, Bill James, and Dick Rudolph. Those were the pitchers who would appear in the World Series, and among them they
won 69 of the 94 games the Braves won that
season.

Bill James was tall and rugged and could throw
a ball as hard as anyone in the league, and he
could throw a wet ball. He was a spitball pitcher,
and, while he lasted, one of the best. Beside
James, Dick Rudolph looked like Jeff of the
Mutt and Jeff comic strip. He was a little fellow,
but a smart and crafty hurler. Lefty Tyler also
won some crucial games in 1914 and finished the
season with 16 victories.

Johnny Evers was a star when the Braves
bought him from the Cubs in 1914. While a part
of the Cubs' infield, famous for its Evers-Tinker-
Chance trio, Evers had become the best second
baseman in the National League. On the diamond, he was a wildcat, snarling at umpires and
opposing players and clawing and fighting all the
way. After he had been angered by roommate
Joe Tinker, he didn't speak to Tinker again for
more than fifteen years, even though the two
played side by side with the Cubs for
eleven years.

Rabbit Maranville got his
nickname because of his
hippety-hop moves at
shortstop in the Series.

The double-play combination that Stallings
put together, Maranville to Evers to Schmidt,
was a good one that figured prominently in the
team's success. Charlie Deal was the third baseman, but in mid-season Stallings bought Red
Smith from Brooklyn, and he turned out to be
the Braves' best extra-base hitter.

The weakest part of the Braves was their
outfield, and Stallings juggled eleven players
during the season in an attempt to round out the
team. The only outfielder who played regularly
was Joe Connolly in center field. George Whitted, Larry Gilbert, Les Mann, Herb Moran, Josh
Devore, and Ted Cather were among the Braves'
outfielders that season. Their catcher was the
powerful but mild Hank Gowdy, whose fiercest
invective was "Holy cow."

The years have grown into decades since the
"miracle" of the 1914 Braves, and still baseball
historians argue whether George Stallings's team
was the luckiest, the weakest, or just the gamest
club ever to win a pennant and a World Series.

The Braves got off to a dismal start as the

season opened. They won only 1 of their first 22
games. But manager Stallings never gave up. He
raved and ranted like a maniac, sliding up and
down on the bench, moving his players around,
fining them recklessly every time they made a
"bonehead play."

The Braves lost games, but they never lost
their spirit and as Stallings predicted, the team
began to hit its stride and began to win. They
gradually picked up games on the leaders and a
winning streak moved them into sixth place.
Then they were in fifth place and by the middle
of August, they spurted into second place and
were now being called the Miracle Team.

It became a brawling pennant race, as tight
races always were in those days. They were
fighting and scratching and clawing for those
extra-base hits, a walk, and even getting on base
by allowing opposing pitchers to hit them. Anything to get on base and get moving.

On Labor Day they returned to Boston after
a most successful road trip for a crucial series
with the Giants. It is doubtful if any single day

of baseball in Boston ever will attract more paid admissions than were collected for the pre- and postluncheon games with New York that Labor Day. Owner Gaffney announced a total of 74,163 for the doubleheader.

Cecil B. De Mille couldn't have improved on the script for the morning game, when the Braves beat the great Christy Mathewson, scoring twice in the ninth inning with 1 out.

The double win for the Braves catapulted them into first place, and from that day on the Braves were unbeatable. On September 29 they clinched the pennant by defeating the Cubs.

Meanwhile, in the American League, the Philadelphia Athletics had won another pennant, by 13½ games over the second-place Boston Red Sox. The A's, with their incredible $100,000 infield, which consisted of Stuffy McInnis at first base, the sure-handed Ed Collins at second, Jack Barry at shortstop, and Home Run Baker at third, were considered practically unbeatable. The outfield, featuring Eddie Murphy, Amos Strunk, and Rube Oldring, were solid and dependable. And the pitching staff was the talk of the league with the sensational Chief Bender, Ed Plank, Bullet Joe Bush, Herb Pennock, and Bob Shawkey. Wally Schang was the mainstay of the catching crew.

Just before the Series began, Stallings opened up a war of nerves against the A's. He accused Connie Mack of closing Shibe Park to the Braves for pre-Series practice, and he warned his players not to speak to the A's under penalty of a stiff fine unless it was to insult them. He refused to use the visitors' dressing room in the clubhouse, and had the team dress a few blocks away at the Phillies' clubhouse. When the Shibe Park announcer came over to Stallings for the Braves' lineup, Stallings chased him away, hurling a few choice insults.

Now, the A's were no babies at this sort of stuff. They had been through several Series and they knew all the retorts. But this sort of insulting was different. It was contempt, rather than abuse, and it bothered them.

In the first game of the Series, in Philadelphia, the Braves exploded against Chief Bender in the second inning, scoring 2 runs. George Whitted walked, then Hank Gowdy, who had hit a lowly .243 during the season, started things off with a slashing double off the fence, driving in the Braves' first run. Maranville singled and Gowdy scored. In the fifth inning, Gowdy tripled, and another Maranville single gave the Braves a 3–1 lead. In the sixth inning the Braves really got to Bender, scoring 3 runs, then added to the Athletics' discomfort by working a double steal in the eighth inning for another run as Bender was driven from the mound. It was the first time in World Series history that an Athletics pitcher had been taken out of a game.

With that kind of hitting, Dick Rudolph had little difficulty against the A's as he struck out 8 and allowed the Athletics but 5 hits and a lone run. The Braves were off and running with their first win by a lopsided 7–1 margin.

In the second game, the Braves were more arrogant than ever, but they had a real dogfight and just won, 1–0. Bill James pitched one of his greatest games as he allowed the hard-hitting A's but 2 hits, striking out 8, while the Braves reached Eddie Plank for 7 hits and 1 run.

There was no holding back the Braves as they returned like conquering heroes to Boston and were met by a thunderous crowd of more than five thousand fans, who paraded around town with the players on their shoulders. Boston throbbed with excitement. The denouement to baseball's most wondrous fairy tale was at hand, and the city was in a frenzy.

When the Braves left Philadelphia after the 2 Series wins, Stallings ordered that all their traveling equipment, road uniforms, and trunks be sent back to Boston. He proclaimed, "We won't be coming back. It'll be all over after two more games in Boston."

In the third game of the Series, before a smashing crowd of more than thirty-five thousand fans, Stallings trotted out his third pitching ace, Lefty Tyler. Connie Mack used Bullet Joe Bush. It was the only game in the Series in which the A's led the Braves. Three times they were in front. Three times the "miracle men" caught up with them. The Braves were lucky once again. They played sloppy ball but they won.

The Athletics' first batter, Ed Murphy, a .317 hitter, led off with a ringing two-base hit. Rube

The 1914 World Champion "Miracle Team," the Boston Braves

Oldring sacrificed Murphy to third. Eddie Collins lined sharply to Joe Connolly, but Connolly let the ball go by him and Murphy scored, to give the A's a 1–0 lead.

The Braves came back in the second inning as Maranville walked, stole second, and scored when Gowdy doubled into the stands.

The A's took a 2–1 lead in the fourth. Stuffy McInnis doubled into the temporary bleachers in right field. Then Jimmy Walsh singled to score McInnis. But the Braves bounced right back as Butch Schmidt singled, took second on an infield groundout, and scored when Maranville bounced a single to center field. Now it was a 2–2 tie, and the game progressed into the tenth inning.

In the top of the tenth, Schang singled, Bush struck out, then Murphy beat out a bunt, and both runners advanced as Evers tossed out Rube Oldring. Eddie Collins walked to fill the bases. And then Johnny Evers made what he considered the dumbest play of his entire career. Frank Baker slashed a wicked ground ball to Evers, and Johnny fumbled the ball. Schang scored on the play, and as Evers picked up the ball and cussed it, Murphy kept on running and dashed safely across the plate as Evers stood frozen in the field with the ball in his hands. The score was 4–2 and the huge crowd started for the exits.

Then, in the bottom of the inning, Hank Gowdy, the Braves' leading hitter, stepped up to hit as Stallings yelled, "Hit it out of the park, Hank, and we'll win."

Gowdy nodded, stepped into the first pitch, and drove a fastball far into the center field bleachers for a home run. Josh Devore struck out. Then Bush walked Moran. Evers singled, sending Moran to third. A moment later he scored on Connolly's fly ball to center.

It was a 4–4 game as the teams went into the twelfth inning. It was growing dark, and Bill James, who had relieved Tyler in the eleventh inning, was able to get the side out without any further scoring.

Then the obstreperous Hank Gowdy delivered his third hit, a scorching two-bagger to the bleachers. Les Mann ran for Gowdy, a notoriously slow runner. Gilbert walked. Moran, attempting to bunt, hit the ball right to the pitcher, Bush, who scooped it up and threw wildly to third, and Les Mann dashed home with the winning run, which gave the Braves their third straight win, 5–4.

For the fourth game, Stallings selected Dick Rudolph, who had become a proud papa as the Series opened. He was opposed by Bob Shawkey, another of the Athletics' young stars, who had won 16 games in his second big-league season.

But the Braves would not be denied. They scored a run in the fourth inning, when John Evers walked, reached third as Collins fumbled Connolly's sharply hit grounder, and scored when Schmidt hit a soft pop fly over second base that fell in for a hit. The A's tied the score in the fifth inning, when Jack Barry singled over third base, went to second on Schang's grounder, and scored on Shawkey's single to center. Now it was 1–1.

The Braves countered with 2 big runs in their half of the fifth inning. With 2 out, Rudolph singled to center. Moran doubled to left, and with a 3 and 2 count, Evers singled to center scoring both men to wrap up the game, 3–1, and the Braves were world champions. It was a fitting climax to a miraculous season.

The Braves of 1914 occupy a unique spot, not merely in baseball but in American athletic tradition. They have become a symbol of the underdog, demonstrating by their gritty persistence that nothing is ever impossible.

It was truly a great chapter in the history of sports, a miraculous page in baseball, fashioned by the miracle man himself, George Tweedy Stallings, aided and abetted by as spirited a group of athletes as ever banded together in any sport.

And the conservative city of Boston went completely wild with joy. There were parties and parades that lasted for nearly a week.

For the players the long winter was too short for there were parties and banquets all winter long. They were the rich little poor boys.

Boston Red Sox Versus Philadelphia Athletics "How I Lost the 1915 World Series," by Grover Cleveland Alexander*

"The 1915 World Series was a disappointment to me. It was not so much the result, which went against my team, Philadelphia, but my own individual showing, which was so far from what I hoped it might be. Everyone knows that the Red Sox beat us four wins to our one, but I feel it might have been different if I had lived up to expectations.

"I have never yet given alibis and I am not going to begin now. But I would like to explain to all my fans and friends why I think I failed in the Series.

"Let me begin with a day during the final month of the pennant race. It was Labor Day. We opened a crucial series with Brooklyn. The Robins were right on our heels, and our manager, Pat Moran, and our boys felt, with good reason, that we must come out on the winning side of this encounter. I believe no one on our team even considered that we might not win a single game. And that is exactly what happened.

"I was picked to pitch the opener. Moran depended a great deal upon winning that game. If we won, we'd have that one on ice and we'd

be confident besides. It is my own feeling that Moran did not exaggerate the importance of winning that first game. I always feel that a visiting team should put its best foot forward. The home team has obvious advantages, and it is important for a visiting manager to balance those advantages as soon as he possibly can.

"Larry Cheney was the Dodger pitcher. He had just been acquired from the Cubs, and I detected an unusual determination on his part to justify the move that had brought him to Brooklyn.

"Brooklyn scored one run off me in the first inning. After that the game settled down into one of those contests where neither team will budge an inch and the pitchers must work their hearts out. Cheney, while wild, as was natural with spitball pitchers, was invincible. We could not get a single hit off him for six innings. In the seventh, he strained himself and had to leave

*Alexander's comments are from an interview with the author, in 1944, on the author's *Sports Show*, on New York radio station WINS.

the mound. It was then that our boys fell on the opposition and drove in three runs.

"We began the eighth with a two-run lead. Moran felt that the game was won. I hoped it was when Jake Daubert went out on my first pitch. But then something happened. I have never been able to understand it, but in some way I strained my shoulder and back muscles. I also had the misfortune of getting a blister on my middle finger and it bothered me considerably. Ballplayers don't pay much attention to such minor injuries, but try as he will a pitcher can hardly get results from his pitching hand when his fingers are sore.

"And now, I just couldn't control my pitches, and when I tried to ease up, and not throw my hardest, the Brooklyn hitters would hit me. And they hit the ball hard in the eighth.

"By the end of the inning they had scored five runs and won a game that we felt was safely in the bag.

"And to make matters even worse, our first-string catcher, Bill Killefer, got hurt, and now our prospects for the pennant were indeed gloomy as we lost all three games to Brooklyn.

"I didn't tell Moran that I had wrenched my shoulder in the Brooklyn series; he had enough worries without me. And I was lucky enough to pitch a one-hitter against the Boston Braves that clinched the pennant for us.

"It has never been my disposition to worry about things, but if there was one time in my entire life when I wanted to be in the best pitching form, it was for the World Series against the Red Sox. I would willingly give up my share of the receipts to have been able to pitch my team to the championship of the world. That is my answer to the oft-repeated suggestions that we ballplayers think only of the money involved in the game.

"The newspapers played up the Series on the front pages all over the country. And they said I was nervous in that first game. All right, I was. They hit me pretty hard, but that didn't worry me. There was a time when I used to throw my hardest on every single pitch, but a pitcher grows wiser as he gets older. The fact that Boston was hitting me didn't worry me as long as I was able to scatter the hits. What did worry me was the

Grover Cleveland Alexander led the Phillies to the pennant with 31 victories, then went on to win the opening game of the Series.

fact that our boys didn't seem to be able to hit Ernie Shore as much as the Red Sox were hitting me. At that the Sox only put their hits together in a single inning, the eighth, when they scored one run. However, I must admit that we got all the breaks as we only were able to get five hits off Shore, but scored three runs, and that was enough to beat them, three to one.

"As I look back upon the Series, I can forgive myself because at times I was too careful, too exact, too conscious of myself. When I am at my best, I can get the ball to break as I want it to, with little effort. And I can get my fastball to sweep across the plate just where I want it to go. A pitcher can always work best when he has to use the least thought and care. The more he has to supplement tired muscles by mental effort, the more he loses that fine edge. I tried to foresee every contingency, to guard against every accident, because I was not right. Had I been in my best form, I would have given these things scarcely a second thought. I would have pitched the best I could and trusted the ability of my fielders.

"Again, a pitcher in a World Series game has none of the assurance that he may have during the season. In the short Series he has to do whatever he is going to do then or never at all. If just one slip occurs it is too late to change it. He has one, or two, or perhaps three chances to deliver, and if he fails it is too late. During the regular season, if he loses a game or two, it doesn't matter much. He feels that he will have time later on to redeem himself. But in the World Series it is now, or perhaps never again.

"In my second game, and the game that was destined to be my last in the Series, I had hoped that I would feel in perfect shape. It was the third game of the Series. Boston had taken the second by a two to one margin.

"We got off to an early lead with one run in the third inning. But the Red Sox came right back at me and scored a run in the fourth inning. And from the fourth inning until the ninth, Dutch Leonard and I were knotted in a pitchers' duel. I think I was pitching better than I did in the first game, but as fate would have it, Leonard was even better.

"The crucial point for me came in the last of the ninth inning. With the potential winning run on base, I elected to pitch to Duffy Lewis. My critics contend that I should have walked Lewis, a two-ninety-one hitter during the season, and I should have pitched instead to Larry Gardner, who had hit about two-fifty during the season. That thought did occur to me, too, but I decided to pitch to Lewis for a number of reasons. In the first place, he had been hot in the Series, and I figured the percentages were bound to catch up with him. Besides, I had faced him in twelve games on a previous All-Star tour, and he had made only two hits off me. On one occasion I struck him out four straight times.

"All my reasonings were wrong. It was Lewis's hit that won the game by a two to one score.

"After my bitter loss in the third game, I knew our club was down and out. After all, I had won

thirty-one games during the regular season and they felt that I was practically unbeatable. Now with the loss they were depressed. We lost the fourth game, two to one. It was Ernie Shore who pitched and won for Boston. It was interesting to note that Shore allowed just seven hits in this game, which he won, compared to the five he allowed in the first one which he lost.

"Now we were behind in the Series, three games to one, and our hopes were all but shattered. A great deal has been written about that fifth game. I was slated to pitch, and, in fact, intended to pitch, until the last moment. I never wanted to pitch a game so much in my life. How I would have loved to beat Boston in that fifth game and put us right back into the Series!

"I knew when I started to warm up that I just didn't feel right. My arm was tight as a drum instead of feeling loose and easy. I had to choose between my own instinctive desire to pitch and my own knowledge that I was in no condition to properly pitch for my team. Finally, I decided to tell Moran how I felt. And I have to give him credit for taking this information without any great demonstration or disappointment.

Recognized as one of the greatest outfields in baseball, the Red Sox's stars (*left to right*) Harry Hooper in right field, Tris Speaker in center, and Duffy Lewis in left powered the Bosox to the Championship.

" 'Hell, Alex, if you're not right, the rest of us will have to carry on. Now, don't worry.'

"Moran expressed a fine sentiment, but unfortunately, it just didn't work out very well. Once again it was Mr. Duffy Lewis who was our nemesis. He belted a home run into the bleachers and Harry Hooper put the game on ice with his second homer of the game. Again, it was a game decided in the ninth inning, and Boston finally won by a score of five to four.

"I do not wish to disparage the work of our pitchers, Jim Mayer and Jephtha Rixey. They did a fine job. Had the fates been kinder in the ninth, they would have gained a victory. But be that as it may, as long as I live I will always wonder how I might have fared had I pitched the fatal fifth game of the 1915 World Series.

"No matter what anyone else may say, I know that the reason I lost the Series was that I was not in the proper physical condition to give my team the very best I could.

"I shall always think of this Series as a great personal disappointment. I was unable to live up to the expectations of my teammates and friends and I just wasn't able to perform."

Boston Red Sox Versus Brooklyn Dodgers

When Bill Carrigan graduated from Holy Cross College in 1907 and joined the Red Sox, his teammates hung on him a nom de diamond, which was apt and which stuck. One look at the lantern-jawed Irishman with the steely blue eyes and his tough and determined manner was enough to tag him for life as Rough Carrigan.

Carrigan came from Lewiston, Maine, where he had been a standout baseball and football star in high school. Bill had come to Holy Cross as an infielder, but the baseball coach, Tom McCarthy, noting his husky build and catlike quickness, made him a catcher. And it was as a catcher that the Boston Red Sox signed Rough Carrigan.

Six years after leaving college, in 1913, Carrigan was named manager of the Red Sox, succeeding Jake Stahl. It was not the most opportune time to assume that position. There were financial problems in the front office and trouble among the players.

The 1916 Sox had such stars as Duffy Lewis, Harry Hooper, Larry Gardner at third base, Everett Scott, a remarkable shortstop with a pair of incredible hands, Jack Barry at second base and Dick Hoblitzel on first. Bill Carrigan and Hick Cady handled the catching chores, while the "big four" of the pitching staff were Ernie Shore, Dutch Leonard, George Foster, and a new left-hander who had won 18 games in 1915, his first year as a starter, George Herman "Babe" Ruth.

At this stage of his career, Ruth was a slim, well-developed twenty-year-old, six feet two inches tall with a good pair of shoulders, sturdy arms, and powerful wrists, not yet weighing 200 pounds.

As a small boy, Babe had been sent to the St. Mary's School in Baltimore, an industrial school for boys who needed some direction and discipline. At St. Mary's they taught Ruth to be a tailor so that he might earn a respectable living. But they also put a bat in his hands, and taught him how to play baseball.

One of the teachers, Brother Gilbert, was soon convinced that Ruth had unusual baseball talent. He asked his friend, Jack Dunn, one of baseball's great managers, then skipper of the famed Baltimore Orioles, to visit St. Mary's to "take a look at one of our players." After several such letters, Dunn finally came out to the school to visit with Babe Ruth and to watch him play a few innings.

After an hour's workout, Dunn approached Brother Gilbert. "How much money do you want for him, brother? How much?" he asked.

"Jack, Ruth isn't mine to sell. All that I want for him is a good home, proper care, and the chance for him to make good in the world, no more, no less."

Jack Dunn and Brother Gilbert talked at length about Ruth's situation; then Dunn arranged to prepare formal papers, which would make him

The 1916 Series is noted principally for these remarkable Red Sox stars: (*left to right*) Carl Mays, Ernie Shore, George Herman "Babe" Ruth, and Dutch Leonard.

Ruth's guardian. Dunn further agreed to pay Ruth the sum of $600 to play ball with the Orioles during the 1914 season. The agreement stipulated that Ruth was to be Dunn's ward and responsibility first, and then a pitcher for the Orioles.

Ruth was overjoyed at the unbelievable prospect of getting paid to play ball and with the great Orioles. "Jeez!" he told his pals. "Imagine getting all that dough to play ball."

Ruth took Dunn's guardianship literally, and when the Orioles assembled for spring training at Fayetteville, North Carolina, a few days later, he trotted after Dunn onto the field like a puppy in more ways than one. He was just a 20-year-old kid, away from the home for the first time; he was awkward, shy, and above all he was terribly anxious to have everyone like him. He had to make good and stay with the team. He had nothing else.

It was on the first day of practice that Ruth was to get his nickname, which would stick with him for the rest of his life. Hal Steinman was a coach for the Orioles and Dunn's field assistant, and when Ruth arrived, trotting on Jack Dunn's heels, it was Steinman who said, "Here comes Jack Dunn with his newest babe."

It was Babe Ruth from that day on.

Even then, Babe Ruth was big. He was tall, lean, solidly muscled with the legs of a ballet dancer. His hair, ink-black, often fell over his forehead. He was outgoing, full of laughter, easy to meet, and had a vocabulary that would make a gambler blush, and at Fayetteville he fell for every prank the older players rigged up for him. To get him away from the older players and their pranks, Dunn had Ruth room with Roger Pippen, then a savvy sportswriter for the *Baltimore News Post*.

"In the first game I saw him play," said Pippen, "Ruth caught a pitch with the fat part of his big bat and drove the ball clear over the right field fence." It was Ruth's first home run in professional ball.

It was Ruth's pitching, rather than his hitting, that first made the headlines. In preseason games in North Carolina and at Baltimore against the world champion Athletics, the young, inexperienced Babe Ruth calmly breezed through such great hitters as Home Run Baker, Eddie Collins, Stuffy McInnis, and Wally Schang as though they were schoolboy batters at St. Mary's. He posted a string of early shutout innings and impressed all who saw him pitch. John McGraw was so impressed with Ruth that he contacted Jack Dunn and said, "Jack, that young left-hander you had out there today looked very good. Whenever you're ready to put Ruth on the market, I want to get first crack at him." McGraw always insisted that Jack had agreed, but Dunn was having too many financial worries then and he didn't pay much attention to McGraw's remarks.

In 1914 the Orioles' attendance fell off to a point where they were drawing fewer than fifty fans a day to the ballpark. Rather than go bankrupt, Dunn decided he had to sell his players. In perhaps the biggest deal, Babe Ruth, Ernie Shore, and catcher Ben Egan went to the Red Sox for a mere $20,000. It was estimated by baseball men, that of the $20,000 total, Ruth cost the Red Sox about $15,000.

Despite the loss of the incomparable Tris Speaker, who was sold to the Cleveland Indians for $50,000, manager Rough Carrigan guided the Red Sox to the 1916 pennant with a pitching staff that featured twenty-two-year-old Babe Ruth, who developed into the finest left-hander in the league with a 23-12 record.

Over in the National League, Wilbert Robinson's Robins took the pennant by 2½ games over the Phillies. As a matter of fact, all four of the eastern teams, Brooklyn, Philadelphia, Boston, and the Giants, charged down the home stretch in September in a furious finish that had the fans frantic with excitement.

Wilbert Robinson was the son of the village butcher in Hudson, Massachusetts. By the time he was twenty-two years old, Robbie was offered a contract to play for the Haverhill, Massachusetts, team in 1885. He was a fine catcher and gradually moved up in the ranks of the minor leagues and by 1892 became the regular catcher for the Baltimore Orioles.

When the Orioles won the pennant in 1894, Robbie and his pal John McGraw battled each other in an attempt to lead the team in batting. That year Robbie won out with a magnificent .353 average, while McGraw hit .340.

Jovial, genial, and an object of mirth, Robbie added some 35 pounds to his smallish, five-foot-eight-inch frame. He ballooned to 225 pounds when he became manager of the Brooklyn team in 1914. By that time he had become one of the most popular figures in the game. He was so beloved in Brooklyn that the team became known as the Robins. The great sportswriter Damon Runyon wrote about Robbie and his team almost on a daily basis and began to refer to him as "Your Uncle Wilbert" and then changed it to "the Round Robin." "Even when he bawled out

Fred Merkle appeared in three World Series with the Giants, then was traded to the Dodgers, for whom he played first base in the 1916 Series.

Brooklyn's Ebbets Field hosted its first Series in 1916.

a player," Grantland Rice wrote, "it sounded like the woof-woof of a friendly Newfoundland."

The team that Robbie assembled was a hodge-podge ball club, consisting mostly of trades and players dropped from the other clubs. Chief Meyers, Rube Marquard, and Fred Merkle were ex-Giants; pitcher Larry Cheney, an 18-game winner, had come from the Cubs; Mike Mowrey, at third base, was a Pirate castoff; Ivy Olson, at shortstop, was from the Indians; Jack Coombs, an ex-Athletic hurler, won 13 games. Other Dodgers included Casey Stengel, Zack Wheat, Jake Daubert, George Cutshaw, and hurlers Nap Rucker, Sherry Smith, and Jeff Pfeffer, the team's leading pitcher that season with 25 wins.

The Series opened in Boston on October 7 before some seventeen thousand screaming fans, who roared with every pitch, every play. Remembering that Rube Marquard had defeated

the Sox twice in 1912, Robbie started the former Giant star, but the Bosox had no trouble with Rube's slants and hit him hard throughout the first eight and a half innings as they led the Brooks by a 6–1 score.

Ernie Shore, pitching for Boston, had held the Dodgers throughout the game, and now in the Brooklyn half of the ninth inning, the fans began to leave the ballpark. Jake Daubert, Brooklyn's leading batter, opened the inning with a walk. Casey Stengel rapped a single to left field, but Shore scooped up Zack Wheat's attempted bunt and his throw just nipped Daubert at third. Cutshaw walked, filling the bases. Mowrey slugged the first pitch thrown to him on the ground, but Hal Janvrin, the Sox' second baseman, threw the ball away and Stengel and Wheat scored. Jim Johnson singled once more, filling the bases. Hy Myers fouled out, but pinch hitter

Merkle walked, forcing in Cutshaw. Carl Mays the great submarining hurler then came in for Shore and promptly shot a fastball in to Hy Myers, and Myers, up for the second time in the inning, beat out a ground ball to third base for a hit. On the play, Mowrey scored the fourth Brooklyn run of the inning. Now it was a 6–5 game with the Bosox holding on for dear life.

Jake Daubert, up to bat for the second time in the inning, slashed a sharp ground ball to deep short, but Everett Scott went deep into the hole, made an incredible stop of the ball and, as he was falling to the ground, tossed the ball to first and beat Daubert to the bag for the final out. And the Sox had won the game by a hairbreadth.

Bill Carrigan finally gave Babe Ruth his long deferred opportunity to pitch in a World Series in the second game at Boston, and Ruth pitched the greatest game of his career, as he held the hard-hitting Robins scoreless for thirteen innings. The Robins only scored off Ruth in the first inning as Hy Myers slashed a wicked liner to center field. The ball bounded over Tilly Walker's head in center and rolled to the distant fences as Myers sped around the bases, like a frightened rabbit, for a thrilling inside-the-park home run to give Brooklyn a 1–0 lead.

In the Red Sox half of the third inning, Everett Scott slashed a triple to left-center field. Ruth, the next batter, slugged a hard drive right at third baseman George Cutshaw, but in his anxiety to cut off the run, George took his eyes off the ball, fumbled it, and Scott came in with the tying run.

From the third inning to the fourteenth, the game developed into a brilliant pitching duel with both Ruth and Sherry Smith cutting down opposing hitters without another score.

In the fourteenth inning, Smith walked Hoblitzel to start the inning. Mike McNally went in to run for Hobby as Del Gainor pinch-hit for Gardner. Del took two called strikes, then drove the third pitch high into left field, but by that time it was so dark that it was difficult to follow the flight of the ball and it fell for a two-base hit, and the speedy McNally streaked across the plate with the winning run.

In the clubhouse after the victory, a beaming

Babe Ruth shouted to Carrigan, "I told you I could handle those National League sons of bitches."

Charlie Ebbets, the Brooklyn owner, had a minor revolution on his hands as the teams prepared for game three at Brooklyn on October 10. Ebbets had increased his ticket prices from three to five dollars per seat. But thousands of Brooklyn fans decided they would not pay for the more expensive seats and stayed home for the rest of the games.

Only about twenty-one thousand fans turned out for the fourth game and they missed one of the most exciting games of the entire Series, for Jack Coombs, the onetime ace of the Philadelphia Athletics, held the Red Sox scoreless for five innings, while the Robins pounded the formidable submarine pitcher, Carl Mays, for 4 runs and a 4–0 lead before George Foster, one of the heroes of the 1914 Series, relieved him.

However, the Sox came to life in the sixth inning, to score 2 runs off Coombs to make it 4–2, Brooklyn.

In the seventh inning, Larry Gardner's home run made it 4–3, Brooklyn, and that remained the score for the duration of the ball game.

The next afternoon the Brooklyn defense collapsed as they made 4 costly errors that paved the way for 4 runs and a 6–2 Boston triumph.

The fifth and final game of the Series was played in Boston on Columbus Day, and the Series vied with news of World War I on the front pages of the nation's newspapers as German submarines were pounding and sinking British and French merchant ships off the coast of Nantucket. Yet the final game set a new Series record for attendance and receipts, with 42,620 fans paying $83,873. The thousands of fans who did get in to see the game witnessed a "Roman holiday" as the Bosox won a convincing 4–1 victory.

This time pitcher Ernie Shore of the Red Sox was practically invincible, as he allowed the Dodgers just 3 base hits to clinch the championship for the Red Sox.

Brooklyn scored their lone run in the second inning. Cutshaw walked and went to third as Mowrey and Olson hit ground balls for two outs. Then one of Shore's fast pitches tore right through

The 1916 National League Champions, the Brooklyn Dodgers

The 1916 World Series champs, the Boston Red Sox

catcher Cady's glove for an error, and Cutshaw sprinted home for the Dodgers' run.

Brooklyn gave the Red Sox an unearned run in the bottom of the second inning when Lewis singled, but Zack Wheat allowed the ball to get away from him and Lewis tore into third base. Then Gardner sent a high fly ball to Wheat, who attempted to throw Lewis out after the catch. But Zack's throw was wide of the plate and Lewis easily scored.

In the third inning Cady bounced a single over Daubert's outstretched arms at first base. Hooper walked and then Janvrin slapped the ball to Olson at short stop. It looked like an easy double play, but Olson fumbled the grounder, then threw wildly to first as Cady scored and Hooper reached third. Chick Shorten drove in Hooper with a single to center and the Bosox were out in front to stay, 3 to 1.

Just to make certain of the decision, Hooper singled in the fifth inning and came all the way around on Janvrin's long two-base hit, which actually was a long fly ball that Hy Myers completely misplayed. Now it was 4 to 1 Boston and that's how the game ended.

Ernie Shore's sparkling 3-hit victory had won the Series for the Sox and his artistry throughout the Series made his name a household word. He returned home to his native town, Winston-Salem, North Carolina, where a fellow Tarheel greeted him with, "Hi ya, Ernie. Been away? Ain't seen you around for a couple of weeks."

For the champion Red Sox, Duffy Lewis and Harry Hooper were the offensive stars. Lewis hit for a .353 average, while Hooper was right behind him at .333. One thing that Brooklyn fans had to cheer about was the play of the twenty-seven-year-old right fielder who led all Brooklyn hitters with a rousing .364 average for the Series. His name, Casey Stengel.

By the time the season was over, Joe Lannin, the Red Sox owner, had become so tired of the constant bickering with Ban Johnson and other officials—in addition to his failing health—that he sold the team to New York theatrical producers Harry Frazee and Hugh Ward. The *Boston American* reported that the price paid for the team was more than one million dollars.

Chicago White Sox
Versus New York Giants

Charlie Comiskey was a man of set ideas, as he demonstrated time and again during his lifetime. It was one of Comiskey's theories that a big-league manager need not be a former player. If a manager had high-caliber players who could perform, it didn't matter who sat on the bench to run the team, and to prove it he signed Clarence "Pants" Rowland to manage the White Sox for the 1915 season.

Clarence Rowland had never played major league ball; he had never even progressed beyond the "Three Eye League" (a Class C league) when Comiskey gave him the White Sox post. He was called Pants simply because he preferred to dress in cream-colored trousers and a matching jacket during a period when most big leaguers dressed like truck drivers.

In Rowland's first season, 1915, the White Sox finished in third place. In September 1916, the White Sox suddenly caught fire and ripped off 16 straight victories, just failing to win the pennant. But in 1917, after a seesaw struggle with the Boston Red Sox, the teams battled neck and neck in a stretch run that had baseball fans agog with excitement. Suddenly, the White Sox put on a spirited drive, spurted away, and grabbed the pennant by 9 games over Boston.

There are sound baseball men today who consider the 1917 Chicago White Sox the greatest team ever assembled, or, at worst, just a shade below the 1927 Yankees.

Spark plug of the team was Arnold "Chick" Gandil, who two years later was to be the key man of the infamous "Black Sox" World Series scandal that rocked the nation. Obtained from the Cleveland Indians in 1916, Chick was a marvelous first baseman, who roamed all over the infield making one sensational play after another. A fine hitter, particularly in the clutch, Chick was a spirited, hustling player who hit .273 for the year. The White Sox infield also included Swede Risberg at shortstop, Buck Weaver at third, magnificent Eddie Collins at second. Oscar Felsch was a center fielder, who roamed the outfield like a deer. "Shoeless" Joe Jackson, in left field, was one of the finest natural hitters ever to play baseball, with an arm like a rifle. Shano Collins and Nemo Leibold alternated in right field and Ray Schalk was the catcher. The pitching staff was led by the master of the shine ball, Eddie Cicotte, who had won 28 games during the season; Reb Russell and Claude Williams won 15 and 17 games, respectively; spitball ace Red Faber posted a 16-13 record, while Davey Danforth won 11 games.

The New York Giants, under the leadership of John J. McGraw, still moving on the momentum of a remarkable 26-game winning streak during September 1916, galloped to an easy pennant as they romped over the second-place Phillies by 10 games.

McGraw had performed quite a facelift on his old championship team. Only Art Fletcher, George Burns, Jeff Tesreau, and Buck Herzog remained from the 1911, 1912, and 1913 winners. Heinie Zimmerman was the new third baseman. The new outfield included Benny Kauff, who had played for the Indianapolis team of the Federal League in 1914 and won the batting title with a smashing .370 average; in 1915 Kauff had hit for a .342 average with the Brooklyn club. Giant hurlers included Slim Sallee, Rube Benton, and Pol Perritt. Fred Anderson, a clever southpaw, who won 21 games, had been nursed along by McGraw since 1913 and by 1917 was one of his aces.

Many sportswriters looking back at the Series thought that McGraw and the Giants had underestimated the White Sox. Certainly, McGraw underestimated Pants Rowland and did not pass up an opportunity to taunt him with the term "busher." McGraw, who had matched strategy with the likes of Connie Mack, George Stallings, and Pat Moran, thought he had a soft touch in Rowland and treated him with contempt.

Rowland, on the other hand, respected and admired McGraw and went out of his way to be decent to him.

At the first game at Comiskey Park, on October 6, a packed crowd of some thirty-two thousand frenzied White Sox fans witnessed an old-fashioned pitching duel between Ed Cicotte, the slightly built curveball artist, and Harry "Slim" Sallee, a string-bean southpaw; and when the shades of night had fallen over Lake Michigan, Chicago fans were jubilantly toasting the names of their stars, Joe Jackson and Happy Felsch.

The Sox scored in the third inning, when Collins streaked home after Fred McMullin popped a short single in front of Ben Kauff, who misjudged the ball and let it fall in for a two-base hit.

In the fourth inning, Felsch started things off with a smashing drive that cleared the center field fence for a home run and it was 2–0, Chicago.

Urban "Red" Faber, ace hurler for the White Sox, won 3 games for the Pale Hose in the Series.

In the Giants' half of the fifth, Lew McCarty, the catcher, slammed a Cicotte fastball, a drive that carried out to the bleachers in center field for a triple. Slim Sallee then slapped a single to left scoring McCarthy.

From there, Cicotte took charge completely. Only two Giants reached base for the remainder of the ball game. With 1 out in the seventh, Joe Jackson made a sensational one-handed diving catch of McCarthy's line drive to prevent a certain Giant run. That was New York's last threat, and they went down in rapid order in the eighth and ninth innings to give Eddie Cicotte a marvelous 2–1 triumph.

For the second game, Rowland came right back with his great spitball pitcher, Red Faber, who toyed with the Giants, allowing them but

8 hits, while the Sox pounded four Giant hurlers for 14 blows, posting a 7–2 victory. Buck Weaver and Jackson each drove out 3 hits, while Eddie Collins banged out 2 base hits for the Pale Hose.

The teams moved back to New York on October 8, on the same train, and the rival ball-players glowered at each other as they passed on their way to the dining car. "You ain't getting too many hits, Benny," growled Weaver and Chick Gandil. Kauff had gone hitless in 8 trips to the plate in the two games in Chicago. "You won't be shooting your mouth off so much after we get through with you in New York," shot back Art Fletcher.

Fletcher was right. It rained on October 9 and the two-day respite was just what the Giants needed to regain their shattered equilibrium.

When play was resumed on October 10, McGraw and his legions came back smartly, behind a remarkable pitching effort by Rube Benton. The burly left-hander, winner of 15 games during the season, pitched his finest game of the season as he set the Sox down with but 5 base hits and came away with a brilliant 2–0 shutout over Cicotte. Benton also had the distinction of being the first left-handed pitcher to register a shutout in modern World Series play.

Davey Robertson continued his outstanding batting, knocking out a triple and 2 singles. His triple in the fourth inning, followed by Walt Holke's two-base hit, produced a run. Then Holke scored after Burns's infield hit and the Giants had 2 runs, all that were necessary to wrap up the third game.

Convinced by Benton's marvelous pitching that his theory of utilizing left-handers against the Sox was correct, McGraw started his fourth left-hander, Ferdie Schupp, in the fourth game. Ferdie, who had been driven out of the box early in the second game, went on to duplicate Benton's performance as he blanked the Sox, 5–0.

The fourth game also belonged to Benny Kauff, for it was one of the highlights of his career.

In the fourth inning, Kauff scored the Giants' first run of the game when he smashed a line drive over Happy Felsch's head in deep left-center field, and sped around the bases for an

Jim Thorpe, America's greatest athlete, appeared as a pinch hitter in the Giants lineup in the 1917 Series.

inside-the-park home run, as Giant fans whooped it up.

In the eighth inning, with Danforth pitching for the Sox, Kauff rifled one of Dave's fastballs into the upper reaches of the right field stands for his second homer of the game, to give the Giants its easy 5–0 victory, tying the Series at 2 games.

When the Series returned to Comiskey Park for the fifth game, Rowland decided to start Reb Russell, a left-hander with a sizzling fastball, instead of Cicotte, and Reb lasted long enough for just 3 batters to face him. He walked George Burns, the leadoff batter. Buck Herzog singled to center, sending Burns to third. Ben Kauff slugged a ringing double against the right field fence, scoring Burns. Cicotte relieved Russell and Zimmerman hit Cicotte's first pitch to Weaver. Hank scooped up the hard grounder, tossed the ball to catcher Ray Schalk, and Schalk tagged Herzog out at the plate. Art Fletcher, the next batter, hit sharply to McMullin at third base, and McMullin's throw to the plate just nabbed Kauff, attempting to score. However, Davey

Robertson singled, scoring Heinie Zimmerman, and the Giants were off to a rousing 2–0 lead.

For the fifth straight time, McGraw had called on a left-hander; this time it was Slim Sallee. Slim, pitching smoothly and effortlessly for the first six innings, seemed to have the game safely in hand. Chick Gandil doubled home a run for the Sox in the third inning, cutting the Giant lead to 2–1. However, the New Yorkers came back with a vengeance in the fourth inning, aided by 3 Sox errors, to score 2 runs and increase their lead to 4–1.

Sallee had a 5–2 advantage going into the seventh inning, when suddenly the White Sox batters started clubbing everything that Sallee offered. With 1 out, Jackson and Felsch singled in succession, and the ubiquitous Chick Gandil doubled to score both runners. An infield out put Gandil on third base with the potential tying run and the stands went into an uproar as Ray Schalk walked and then stole second. On the play, catcher Bill Rariden's throw hit the dirt in front of Herzog and Gandil came in with the tying run. It was now a 5–5 game.

In the eighth inning, Shano Collins singled and was sacrificed to second base. Ed Collins put the Sox ahead by singling to center, scoring Shano Collins. On a hit-and-run play, Jackson singled and Collins sped to third. On Robertson's throw to third base to get Collins, he threw the ball into center field and Collins scored. That was finis for Sallee. Perritt came in to pitch for the Giants and Felsch greeted him with a single to center, which scored Jackson. Now the White Sox led 8–5.

Red Faber pitched the final two innings for the Sox and received credit for the win, his second of the Series.

The sudden and dramatic surge of the White Sox brought many ugly repercussions. Chicago mobsters and big New York gamblers who had bet hundreds of thousands of dollars on the Giants pitched into McGraw for not relieving Slim Sallee earlier. They felt McGraw had kept Slim in much too long after the Sox had belted him about and that added to McGraw's anger. He turned his anger on his captain, Buck Herzog, and said the game was lost by balls hit through Herzog's position at second base. This

Babe Ruth won 2 Series games and extended his scoreless inning streak to 29 games in World Series play.

led to a McGraw-Herzog feud and shortly after the Series, Buck was traded from the ball club for the third time.

The sixth game was a nightmare for New York. The fourth inning, in particular, haunted McGraw to the end of his days.

For this historic game, Rowland started pitcher Red Faber and McGraw countered with his sixth left-hander, Rube Benton. Both pitchers were outstanding during the first three innings of a scoreless pitching duel.

Eddie Collins opened the fourth inning with a sharp ground ball to Zimmerman at third base. Heinie scooped up the ball, but threw it past his first baseman, Holke, and it went for a two-base error. Dave Robertson compounded the felony by dropping an easy fly ball by Jackson, and Collins sped to third. Felsch hit back to the pitcher, and Benton now had Collins trapped between third and home. However, Eddie jockeyed back and forth in order to give Jackson and Felsch an opportunity to advance as far as they could before he was tagged out. Then Benton threw to Zimmerman. At that moment, catcher Bill Rariden had moved up toward third base and Collins suddenly darted past the Giant catcher for the unprotected home plate. Zimmerman at third base took off after Collins, but Eddie was a step ahead of Zimm as the two players raced for home. Zimmerman, with his arm outstretched, ball in hand, tried to tag Collins all the way down the third base line, but Eddie crossed the plate for an easy score.

So famous has this play become that one of the legends connected with it is that Collins ran at half speed to lure Zimm into chasing him instead of throwing the ball. That simply was not true, for there was nobody covering the plate, and nobody for Zimm to throw to. McGraw always blamed Walt Holke for not coming in from first base to protect home plate.

Many years later, after he was out of baseball, Zimmerman still raged at the coals of fire which he believed had always been unjustly heaped upon his head for chasing Collins home. "Who the hell was I going to throw the ball to? Klem?" (Bill Klem was the umpire.)

After the furor caused by "the big chase" subsided, Chick Gandil slammed a long single to left scoring Jackson and Felsch, and the Sox had a 3–0 lead.

The Giants were now down, but not out. They came back in the fifth inning with 2 quick runs. Rariden and Wilhoit walked. Herzog then doubled, bringing in both runners. But that was all for the Giants and the Sox took the game 4–2, and with the game the Series.

The defeat left John McGraw sick at heart, as it was his fourth straight World Series setback. Added to that was Ban Johnson's publicly gloating over the victory. "McGraw and his Giants aren't so tough anymore. They just talk tough. They're our meat," said Johnson, making the loss even more bitter.

Eddie Collins and Red Faber emerged as the Series' heroes. Collins, the future Hall of Fame second baseman, hit for a stunning .409 average, while the three magnificent pitching victories for Red Faber placed him in the illustrious group of Bill Dinneen, Deacon Phillippe, Christy Mathewson, Babe Adams, Jack Coombs, Smokey Joe Wood, and, in later years Lew Burdette, Bob Gibson, and Mickey Lolich.

The 1917 World Series was only the second Series to take in as much as $400,000 at the gate. The final tally showed receipts amounting to $425,878. The winning White Sox players each received $3,669, while the losing Giant shares amounted to $2,442.

Boston Red Sox Versus Chicago Cubs

On April 6, 1918, with the United States fully involved in World War I, Secretary of War Newton Baker issued an order that the regular baseball season must end by September 1. But by that time there was not too much interest in baseball. The big show was happening elsewhere.

Newspapers were running front-page stories consisting of column after column with headlines that read MEN ENLISTED IN THE ARMY, along with the number of those needed to fill the quota. About twenty-five thousand draftees paraded along New York's Fifth Avenue, and were cheered by thousands of spectators. The army organized its first camouflage company, and appealed to the nation for volunteers to learn "the art of military concealment." Song sheets of "Slide, Kelly, Slide" and "Our National Game" took on a patriotic fervor. The Washington Senators became the "Statesmen." Sarah Bernhardt, the famous actress, appealed to ballplayers and other athletes to aid the war effort. Colonel Teddy Roosevelt became a military columnist for the *Kansas City Star* and appealed to the nation to "defeat the Hun and his allies." And by September 1, every major league baseball club had lost nearly half its players to the armed forces.

But the games continued.

The Boston Red Sox finished 4½ games in front of the Cleveland Indians in the American League, while the Cubs outdistanced the Giants by some 17½ games to capture the National League flag.

A group of Red Sox stars including manager Jack Barry had enlisted in the Navy; others were Duffy Lewis, Ernie Shore (who had pitched a perfect no-hit, no-runners game in 1917), Del Gainor, Mike McNally, Chick Shorten, Herb Pennock, Jim Walsh, Fred Thomas, and a number of substitutes. The Cubs lost their great star pitcher, Grover Cleveland Alexander, and a host of other first-rate players, but they were confident they could take their first World Series since their great victory in the 1908 Series.

Owner Harry Frazee appointed Ed Barrow the manager of the Bosox when Jack Barry left for the Navy. Barrow, with years of solid experience as a manager at Detroit, Toronto, and Montreal, as well as several years serving as president of the International League, knew baseball as well as any man in the game. He was a big, two-fisted, no-nonsense guy, who gave orders like a field marshal and expected his players to toe the line. Once, as manager of the Toronto team, he was arguing with an umpire, and decided to end the argument by punching the umpire in the jaw.

Most major league teams practiced short-order drills during spring training in 1918.
Here the Yankees go through their paces as World War I rages.

Several times during the 1918 season, Babe Ruth, feeling his oats, became troublesome and obnoxious. One day Barrow called Ruth into his office, locked the door, and said, "Now Babe, let's cut out the bull. We'll see who the better man is. Put up your dukes." When the door opened, a contrite Ruth was much more cooperative.

To bolster the Red Sox offense in 1918, Barrow decided on a daring move. With Duffy Lewis, his great outfielder, in the Navy, Barrow tried to find more use for Babe Ruth's long-distance hitting when the Babe wasn't on the mound. He experimented with playing Ruth in left field against right-handed pitchers, and the move was a revelation. In 95 games, Ruth hit .300 and drove out 95 base hits. However, what startled the baseball world was the big guy's high percentage of extra-base hits: 26 doubles, 11 triples, and 11 home runs. His 11 home runs tied Tilly Walker for the American League lead. In addition to his duties as an outfielder, Ruth still found the time to pitch and win 13 games.

Because of wartime travel restrictions, it was decided that the first three games of the World Series would be played in Chicago; then the Series would finish in Boston.

The first game was a marvelous pitching duel between Ruth and the Cubs' Jim Vaughn. Babe vindicated his manager's judgment by outpitching Vaughn to win a great 1–0 decision before a small opening-day Series crowd of some nineteen thousand excited fans.

The two pitchers who had been rivals in the third game of the 1914 Braves-Athletics Series— George Tyler, now with the Cubs, and Bullet Joe Bush—faced each other in game two, and once again Tyler was victorious, by a 3–1 margin. Bush had just one poor inning, the second, when the Cubs battered him for their 3 runs.

It was a warm, pleasant afternoon in Chicago on September 7, and the crowd grew to some twenty-seven thousand fans as the third game began. For three innings both Jim Vaughn, and his opponent, Carl Mays, were letter-perfect; neither pitcher had allowed a hit.

In the fourth inning, George Whiteman was hit by a pitch, and then, suddenly, the roof fell in on Vaughn, as McInnis, Schang, and Scott singled in succession and 2 runs were across the

First baseman Fred Merkle starred for the Cubs in the 1918 Series.

plate. After Scott's hit, only two other Red Sox batters reached base, but they had enough runs to win the game. The Cubs scored their only run when Charlie Pick doubled and came in on Fred Merkle's single.

In the Chicago half of the fourth inning, Whiteman made a sensational one-handed, running, diving catch of Dode Paskert's drive, which had home run written all over the ball. The play brought the crowd to its feet, and they roared in a stirring, five-minute tribute to Whiteman's catch. But that was the last Cub threat, as the submarine ace, Carl Mays, blanked the Cubs for the last five innings, and the Sox had their second Series win, 2–1.

For the fourth game in Boston, on September 9, manager Ed Barrow sent Babe Ruth to the mound, while George Tyler, who had won the second game for the Cubs, took the mound for Chicago; it was a pitching duel worthy of a World Series, for neither pitcher allowed a single base hit for the first three innings.

Ruth, however, was wild, but he explained that he was breaking in a new curveball and was having some difficulty in controlling it, while Tyler was pitching his usual sound, steady game for the Cubs.

Tyler found himself in a bit of a hole in the fourth inning as he walked the leadoff man, Dave Shean. Amos Strunk popped up. Shean then stole second, and Whiteman walked. Now Tyler, in trouble for the first time in the game, quickly bore down and got McInnis on a grounder to the pitcher. Tyler quickly scooped up the ball and snapped it to third base to get Shean. There were 2 outs and two men on base.

Then Babe Ruth came up to hit and Shean quickly snapped off two wicked curveballs that Ruth swung at and missed. Then Tyler made one of his few mistakes. He grooved a pitch and the Babe caught the ball on the fat part of his bat and slashed a long fly ball over the right fielder's head for a three-base hit that scored 2 runs, and the Red Sox suddenly were out in front, 2–0.

Ruth wasn't in the best condition to pitch this game for he had scuffled with a substitute player, Joe Kenney, on the train from Chicago and had injured the knuckles of his pitching hand against the steel frame of the train. Overnight the middle finger had swollen to twice its normal size. Despite the bad finger, Ruth had pitched a remarkable game for seven full innings. He had given up but 7 base hits and had held the Cubs scoreless until the eighth inning when his great pitching streak of 29⅔ ended as the Cubs scored twice to tie the game at 2–2. In the Red Sox half of the eighth inning, Wally Schang singled, went to second on a wild pitch, and scored when Phil Douglas, now pitching for the Cubs, threw a bunt attempt by Hooper into left field and the Sox were again out in front, 3–2.

Ruth was very tired by the time the ninth inning started and he walked Merkle and Rollie Keider, the first two Cub batters. Manager Barrow sent in Joe Bush to relieve Ruth and sent Ruth to left field. Then Bullet Joe went to work. A brilliant stop by Stuffy McInnis saved a run. Then Scott ended a potential Cub rally and the game with a sensational double play on Turner Barber's smash, and Ruth had his second World Series victory and a World Series record of 29⅔ consecutive scoreless innings.

Outfielder Greasy Neale is put out in an attempted steal of home in game two.

A crowd of about twenty-five thousand was on hand at Fenway Park for the fifth game and the fans entering the park were amazed to see no activity on the field. The players were in uniform in the dressing room and refused to come out. The admission price to the games had been reduced, and the players were angry when it became obvious that the winners' and losers' shares of the Series play would be meager. They demanded that the commissioner should agree to a flat $1,500 for the winners' share, and that losers ought to receive $1,000. The players would not lift a bat until those conditions were met.

Finally, after Boston's mayor, Honey Fitzgerald, the baseball commissioner, and managers of both teams appealed to the players telling them that the nation at large would be horrified at ballplayers asking for more money while the nation was at war, the players relented after a two-hour delay and both ball clubs took the field.

Jim Vaughn's fine pitching was finally rewarded in this game as he shut out the hard-hitting Bosox with just 5 base hits for a 3–0 victory.

The Red Sox came back the following day, behind the artistry of submariner Carl Mays, whose weird slants completely handcuffed the Cubs, and the Sox came away with a 2–1 win. The Cubs' pitcher, George Tyler, also pitched remarkable ball, allowing the Sox just 5 hits. However, the Sox bunched 2 hits plus 2 bases on balls to score their 2 runs in the third inning, enough runs to win the game, and the World Series.

Despite his marvelous play at bat and in the field, rookie George Whiteman, who became the darling of the Red Sox fans for his super play in the Series, was shipped back to the minor leagues when the Red Sox stars returned at war's end.

Each winning Boston player received $1,108 per share while the losing Cub shares amounted to $671 per player.

Ed Barrow, who later became general manager of the magnificent Yankee teams said, "We were a war team and we didn't hit very well. But we did hit enough to win. The one thing about that that has often been overlooked was the fact that we had an unbelievable defensive team. Our play, particularly on defense, was the greatest I've ever seen in a World Series. We made only one error in the six games that we played. That was the chief difference between our victory and the Cubs' defeat."

1919

Cincinnati Reds Versus Chicago White Sox

On the evening before the first game of the 1919 World Series, Eddie Roush, star center fielder of the Reds, was standing in front of the posh Sinton Hotel in Cincinnati, taking in the exciting evening scene, wondering what the morrow, the start of the all-important World Series, would bring.

A boisterous fan slipped up behind Eddie and grabbed his arm. "Hey, Ed, do you know what the hell is going on: It all looks and smells funny. It's in the bag. So put all your dough on the Reds. You'll get great odds. The Series is in the bag. The Sox are going to throw it."

Roush turned away angrily, walked into the hotel, and crossed the lobby. "Damned if you don't hear the strangest things at World Series time," he said aloud. "The Series fixed. You hear that every damn time. I wonder how in hell those rumors get started."

The excitement in Cincinnati on the eve of the Series can well be imagined. For the first time in National League history, the Reds had succeeded in winning the pennant. Now they were in the Series and the entire town was in a holiday mood and throngs milled around the streets discussing the coming Series with the unbeatable Chicago White Sox, champions of the American League.

Garry Herrmann, owner of the Reds, and proud as punch, had set up an elaborate press head-quarters at the hotel, which set a pattern for every World Series thereafter.

There was no question that the White Sox had a formidable ball club. They had defeated the New York Giants in the 1917 Series, 4 games to 2, and with practically the very same club. Many of the leading sportswriters called the Pale Hose team of 1919 the greatest team of all time.

The Sox had led the league in batting, the marvelous Joe Jackson leading the club with an extraordinary .351 average. The team was second in team fielding with a tight, scrappy infield that fought for and grabbed every ball hit. Pitcher Ed Cicotte had accumulated a 1.82 ERA, a record exceeded only by the Senators' remarkable Walter Johnson, and all season long, pitchers Dickie Kerr and Lefty Williams had allowed their opponents less than 3 earned runs per game.

By any logical analysis, the White Sox should have been heavy favorites to win the Series. But oddly enough, the gamblers had bet huge sums on the Reds. Strange characters had been appearing in the hotel lobbies, and on the streets. The famous sportswriter, John Lardner, a guest at the Metropolitan Hotel, recalled seeing New York and Chicago gamblers with fistfuls of hundred-dollar bills, stalking the lobby, placing huge bets on the Reds. And by game time, oddsmakers had made the Reds the favorites, 8–5.

The World Series opened on October 1, in Cincinnati, on a blistering 90-degree afternoon before a jam-packed crowd that filled every inch of space in the ballpark to see the two great teams face each other.

Because of the intense national postwar interest in this Series, the baseball officials decided to make the 1919 classic a best-of-nine Series.

The huge crowd was treated to a dazzling performance by the Reds' pitcher, Dutch Ruether, as he hurled a complete-game 6-hitter, and at the plate, the remarkable Ruether went 3 for 3 (2 of his hits were booming triples) and batted in 3 runs. Outfielder Greasy Neale, who would go on to lead the Reds in batting in this Series with a sparkling .357 average and later became an outstanding football coach, and first baseman Jake Daubert also collected 3 hits apiece.

An ashen-faced Kid Gleason, kicking dirt all the way to the mound, angrily yanked his pitcher Ed Cicotte from the mound in the fourth inning after the Reds had pounded him for 4 runs. Gleason kept shaking his head in disbelief as he walked back to the bench.

But the Reds continued to bombard relief pitchers Roy Wilkinson and Grover Lowdermilk for 2 additional runs to ring up a stunning 9–1 upset over the Sox as thousands of Red rooters poured out onto the diamond, after the final out had been made, to celebrate the great victory.

In the White Sox clubhouse after the game, manager Kid Gleason was livid. "Those miserable sons of bitches aren't playing the kind of ball I know they can. Something's rotten here, and I'm gonna do something about it."

Little Ray Schalk accosted his manager. "That dirty louse, Cicotte, shook off my curveball signs. He didn't want to throw a curveball. Now why in hell did he do that? Kept shaking me off."

The second game played in Cincinnati was another strange contest, but it brought another victory to the Reds. The two pitchers were both left-handers; Slim Sallee of the Reds and the crafty Claude Williams, a 23-game winner during the season. And although the Sox outhit the Reds 10–3, the Reds again won by a 4–2 score. Williams, who had had pinpoint control all year long, suddenly lost his poise and walked 3 Red batters. Roush inserted a single between 2 bases

on balls. Then Larry Kopf selected a pitch he liked, tripled, and the Reds picked up 3 more runs to win the game.

Thus far, despite the nasty rumors and suspicions heard all over the city, nothing appeared in the sports pages about the games being fixed. What was not known to the public was that Kid Gleason had talked with team owner Charles Comiskey in the middle of the night, after the second game, and complained that there were "a lot of funny things happening." Comiskey, in turn, discussed it with the commissioner of the National League, John A. Heydler. However, after hearing Comiskey explain manager Kid Gleason's suspicions and his thoughts on the matter, Heydler closed his eyes for a moment, looked at Comiskey, then snorted,

"Fix a World Series? Charlie, it's impossible. Nothing to it."

The erratic, almost bush league play that had marked the first two games provided more talk of something fishy going on. But it was all talk. Some sportswriters gave lengthy explanations of the White Sox stars, who they said were choking up. But that was laughed at in the more knowledgeable circles.

The third game brought the Series to Comiskey Park, Chicago, and a crowd of more than twenty-nine thousand wild-eyed Sox fans surged to the park to cheer for their favorites in an effort to spark them on to a win.

The Sox responded, beautifully, behind the masterful 3-hit pitching of little Dickie Kerr, who shut out the overconfident, cocky Reds and defeated them, 3–0. Kerr struck out 5 Red batters and did not allow an extra-base hit. Chick Gandil's single drove in 2 Sox runs in the second frame and Risberg's triple in the fourth inning led to another score, when he and Ray Schalk executed a perfectly timed squeeze play.

The long-delayed win restored much confidence in the badly shaken White Sox players, and brought out a crowd of some thirty-five thousand for the fourth game. However, pitcher Jimmy Ring of the Reds dashed their hopes by pitching a sensational game, allowing the Sox just 3 hits, winning the game, 2–0.

Eddie Cicotte was back on the mound once more for the White Sox and performed very well.

White Sox (Black Sox stars): (*left to right*) Nemo Liebold, Ed Murphy, Eddie Collins, Joe Jackson, and Happy Felsch

He allowed the Reds just 5 hits; however, 2 of those hits in combination with 2 errors by Cicotte in the fifth inning proved to be his undoing.

There was 1 out in the fifth when Duncan tapped a slow roller to pitcher Cicotte, but Eddie's toss to first was so wild that Duncan pulled up at second. Then Kopf hit a line drive to Jackson in left field; Joe fielded the ball and threw wildly toward the plate. The throw was deflected by Cicotte and then rolled all the way to the fence as Duncan scored and Kopf went to second. Neale doubled, scoring Kopf, and that was the ball game, with the Reds in front by a 2–0 margin.

The White Sox were now trailing 3 games to 1 and things looked bleaker than ever for them.

For the fifth game, manager Pat Moran of the Reds trotted out his great shine-ball star, Hod Eller. Eller was at his level best in this game and had the Sox hitters at his mercy. He allowed them just 3 base hits, struck out 9 White Sox

batters, and easily took the game by a 5–0 score. In the second and third innings, Eller fanned 6 Sox batters in a row, beginning with Gandil, then Risberg, Schalk, Williams, Leibold, and Ed Collins. In the fourth inning, Eller struck out Felsch and also threw out both Weaver and Joe Jackson—thus individually retiring the entire White Sox lineup from top to bottom. It was a pitching performance without parallel in World Series play.

The Reds were now out in front, 4 games to 1, as the Series moved to Cincinnati for the sixth game on October 7. And all of Cincinnati was trying to jam their way into a ballpark that could only seat some thirty-two thousand fans. As the crowd milled about the entrance and poured into the stadium, the police closed the gates.

Walter "Dutch" Ruether, winner of the first game, opposed little, five-foot-three-inch Dick Kerr of Chicago. For two and a half innings both pitchers were invincible. Then in the third inning, the Reds jumped all over Kerr's offerings for 2 runs. In the fourth frame, the Reds continued their attack driving across 2 more runs to jump out to a commanding 4–0 lead.

The Sox, who had not scored in 26 consecutive innings of play in the Series, now tied into Ruether's offerings with a vengeance. They scored a run in the fifth inning, and in the lucky seventh, the Sox hammered Ruether for 3 runs, tying the game at 4–4.

The score remained deadlocked at 4–4 going into the tenth inning, when Buck Weaver of the Sox slugged his second double of the game. Chick Gandil followed with a single scoring Weaver to give the White Sox a great come-from-behind 5–4 victory.

Ed Cicotte's third and final chance in the Series came in the seventh game, on October 8 in Cincinnati, before a sparse crowd of some fourteen thousand fans. This time, Cicotte's performance was marked with success, as he pitched his way to a 7-hit 4–1 victory over the Reds.

The Sox were ahead all the way in the seventh game as Joe Jackson led the Chicago nine, driving in a run in the first inning and another in the third. Felsch singled with the bases full in the fifth frame to score Ed Collins and Weaver, and it was a 4–0 game with the Sox out in front. In the sixth inning, Groh slammed a two-base hit with 1 out. Ed Roush, the next batter, hit the ball to Cicotte. It was a routine play for the pitcher, but instead of throwing to third to get Groh, Cicotte elected to throw out Roush at first. Then Duncan singled to give the Reds their lone run.

Hugh Fullerton, one of the nation's leading sportswriters, recalled a conversation he had heard in the men's lounge at Comiskey Park before the eighth and final game of the Series:

"It'll be all over in the very first inning," said a well-known Chicago gambler. "Watch for the Reds' big first inning."

"He could have been a rabid Reds rooter," said Fullerton later, "but it was more likely he knew something we didn't know."

Lefty Williams had lost 2 games to the Reds; in each of the games he lost, he allowed just 4 hits. Now Lefty was Kid Gleason's last hope to tie the Series, but this time he was driven from the mound before the fans were seated. He gave up 4 solid base hits in a third of an inning, as the Reds pounded him from pillar to post. Lefty got Rath on a hard ground ball for out number one, but Jake Daubert, Groh, Roush, and Duncan stung him for successive base hits.

Kid Gleason rushed in pitcher Bill James, then Roy Wilkinson, but the Chisox were now 4 runs behind before they had a turn at bat. The Reds continued to hit the White Sox pitchers, getting another run off James in the second inning.

Shoeless Joe Jackson provided a glimmer of hope for the Sox in the third inning as he drove a pitch far and wide over the left field fence for a long home run.

Still the Reds continued to peck and scratch out hits and runs through the next several innings.

In the eighth inning, the Sox rallied briefly for 4 runs off Eller, but by that time the Reds were just playing the string out. They had the ball game, and the championship, safely tucked away, by the score of 10–5.

The Reds were world champions, victors in 5 of 8 games against a team that had been regarded as the strongest ever assembled. And the sports world wondered how in hell something like that could have happened. And they wondered. And wondered.

The outstanding hero of the Series was Dickie Kerr, who had emerged with 2 wins, despite the strange happenings behind him on the diamond. Twenty years later, Dickie Kerr, manager of the Daytona Tigers, had one of his star pitchers play in the outfield. One day the star pitcher-outfielder caught a long fly ball, then fell heavily on his left shoulder after a marvelous catch. It was a serious injury and Kerr suggested that the player should switch positions permanently. Kerr offered the young ballplayer free room and board, for the player and his pregnant wife, until he could make the grade. The pitcher-turned-outfielder did finally make it to the major leagues, and played and became one of the great all-stars in baseball. He played with the Cardinals for twenty-two years and was recently named to baseball's Hall of Fame. His name was Stan Musial.

After the final game of the Series, White Sox owner Charles Comiskey, cognizant of all the rumors about the Series being fixed, offered a

More White Sox Stars: (*left to right*) Nellie Wolfgang, Dane Danforth, Red Faber, Joe Benz, Red Russell, Lefty Williams, and Ed Cicotte

$10,000 reward to any person who had hard evidence that the Series wasn't on the level. It wasn't until a year later, in the final weeks of the 1920 race for the pennant, when the Sox, the Yankees, and the Indians were in a three-way race for the pennant, that evidence of a fix was presented to a Chicago grand jury and eight members of the White Sox were named and indicted.

The evidence consisted mainly of the confessions of Ed Cicotte, Claude Williams, and Joe Jackson and evidence concerning notorious gamblers, former featherweight champion Abe Attell, and Arnold Rothstein, a big-time New York gambler and fixer. But the case of the state of Illinois was jeopardized when suddenly all the court papers in the district attorney's office, including the grand jury's findings and the signed confessions of Cicotte, Jackson, and Williams, were stolen.

It was necessary to build an entirely new case, which was done largely by Ban Johnson. However, on August 2, 1921, a Cook County jury acquitted the players of criminal conspiracy. Yet, if the accused players had any hopes that the acquittal would allow them to return to baseball,

Judge Kenesan Mountain Landis, who by that time had become the commissioner of baseball, quickly disillusioned them.

In a statement issued immediately after the acquittal, Landis said: "Regardless of this verdict of the jury, no player that throws a ball game, no player who entertains proposals or promises to throw a game, no player who sits in a conference with a group of crooked players and gamblers where the ways and means of throwing games are discussed, and does not promptly tell his club officials about it, will ever gain play major league baseball."

Attempts have been made from time to time to have a number of the players restored to good standing. An especially vigorous effort was made to restore Buck Weaver, and a petition with more than ten thousand signatures was taken to Landis. While Buck admitted he had sat in on two of the meetings, where the players talked about throwing the Series, he insisted he never took a dime and played every game to the best of his ability, submitting his World Series record as evidence. But the fiery old judge gave the pleas of Weaver and friends very little consideration.

1920

Cleveland Indians Versus Brooklyn Dodgers

Manager Tris Speaker's Cleveland Indians led the American League pennant race virtually every step of the way in 1920. While the Indians were taking a 3-game series from the St. Louis Browns, the White Sox were taking 3 straight from the Detroit Tigers, and the two contenders battled each other in Chicago on September 23, 1920, just as the first rumblings of the 1919 Black Sox scandal began to emerge from the Cook County Grand Jury in Chicago. It was an ominous day for all of baseball.

Although the crooked members of the White Sox must have known their careers were at stake, they went to work and trounced the Indians, 10–3, cutting the Cleveland lead on first place by just half a game.

The following day, while the grand jury was issuing subpoenas to those who were accused in the conspiracy, Duster Mails, a young former Dodger left-hander, took the mound for the Indians and won what may have been the most important ball game of his life.

Mails was superb, tossing a brilliant 3-hit shutout to defeat the White Sox, 2–0, and ensure the Indians' hold on first place through the series.

Two days later, on September 28, Ed Cicotte, the great pitching star of the White Sox, cracked under the relentless grilling of the district attorney in Chicago and told the complete story of his complicity in the conspiracy.

Once Cicotte's confession was reported, Charles Comiskey had no choice but to send the following wire to each of the White Sox players named: "You and each of you are hereby notified of your indefinite suspension as a member of the Chicago baseball club."

Despite the instantaneous uproar created by the suspension of the White Sox players, there could be no drowning out of a World Series in which the participants were the Cleveland Indians and the Brooklyn Dodgers. Then, and for more than thirty-five years thereafter, those two franchises stood alone in the major leagues for the sheer hysteria of their fans. In each of the cities, no matter who owned the team, the club belonged to the fans.

The Indians were the sentimental favorites across the nation. That was due to the incredible heartwarming drive they made following the death of their classy shortstop Ray Chapman, who was struck on the head by a fastball hurled by Yankee pitcher Carl Mays.

The first day of the World Series at Brooklyn, October 5, was a raw, cold, blustery day and Charlie Ebbets thoughtfully passed out half-pint bottles of rye to the sportswriters in the press box. One of the writers was so indiscreet as to discuss this in his story the next day, and before the game that day, a squad of federal agents swooped down on the park and ransacked Ebbets's offices for evidence of the liquor. However, Charlie had been tipped off that the feds were coming and removed the evidence.

For the first game, manager Wilbert Robinson utilized his experienced pitcher, Rube Marquard, a twelve-year star, while manager Tris Speaker countered with his curveball ace, Stan Coveleski, a 24-game winner. In the second inning, a bad play by shortstop Ivy Olson yielded a run for the Indians, and they hammered in another score as George Burns's fly ball fell just out of Ed Konetchy's reach in short right field, and when Koney tried to get Burns at second, Olson failed to cover the base and Koney's throw went into left field. Burns scored on the play. Joe Wood walked, Joey Sewell singled, and then Steve O'Neill slammed a two-base hit, scoring Wood. In the fourth inning, doubles by Wood and O'Neill resulted in the third run for the Indians.

The Dodgers fought back, and tried every trick that Robbie had in his repertoire, but they were held scoreless by the tricky slants of Coveleski until the seventh inning, when Zack Wheat finally was able to slam out a two-base hit. Two infield outs scored Wheat, and the Dodgers had their first and only run of the game. The first game of the Series ended with the Indians ahead, 3–0.

For the second game, both managers utilized their best pitchers. Burleigh Grimes had won 23 games during the season for the Dodgers. Grimes was opposed by Jim Bagby, who had won 31 games for the Indians. And both pitchers were brilliant, each allowed just 7 hits. However, Grimes was more effective in the pinches, and the Dodgers took game two with a 3–0 shutout.

In the third game, manager Speaker selected 20-game winner Ray Caldwell for his Indians. Caldwell, a crafty ten-year veteran, was opposed by southpaw Sherry Smith.

The Dodgers tore right into Caldwell in the very first inning: Ivy Olson walked, and Jim Johnson sacrificed him to second base; then shortstop Joey Sewell fumbled Tom Griffith's grounder, and with men on first and second, Zack Wheat laced a sharp single to left, scoring Olson. Hy Myers lifted a texas leaguer into right field, scoring Griffith, and Caldwell was taken out of the game and replaced by Duster Mails, who promptly shut out the Dodgers for the remainder of the game. But the two runs they had scored were all they needed to win the game, 2–1.

In Cleveland for the fourth game of the Series, Stan Coveleski won for the second time as he outpitched Leon Cadore in the 5–1 contest. The Indians feasted on the Brooklyn hurlers as they cracked out 12 base hits to easily win the game.

An incident that became a cause célèbre hit the front pages of newspapers across the nation

The 1920 National League flag bearers, the Brooklyn Dodgers

Player-manager Tris Speaker led his Cleveland Indians to their first-ever World Series triumph in 1920.

As if to bear out the old adage that anything is likely to happen when Brooklyn and/or Cleveland is involved, this game also saw the first home run to be hit by a pitcher in World Series history. Jim Bagby hit one out of the park with two men on base against Grimes.

The 2 home runs accounted for 7 of the runs the Indians racked up in winning the fifth game, 8–1.

In the fifth inning, with Pete Kilduff on second and Otto Miller on first base, Clarence Mitchell sliced a line drive toward right-center field. Wamby, playing close to the base, leaped high in the air, snared the ball, and came down right on second base, doubling Kilduff; then he turned toward first and seeing that Miller was on his way to second base, it was a simple matter for Wamby to run down the Brooklyn catcher and tag him for the third out and an unassisted triple play. It was also the first triple play in Series history.

Manager Tris Speaker now had a 3 games to 2 lead and decided to take a chance on his young pitcher, Duster Mails, and Mails responded with the finest game of his career as he outpitched Sherry Smith in an exciting 1–0 duel. Mails allowed the Dodgers just 3 hits.

In the seventh game, Burleigh Grimes took the mound once more in a vain effort to turn things around for the Dodgers, but there was little he could do as Stan Coveleski simply outpitched him to win his third game of the Series. Grimes was good in this game, allowing the Indians just 7 hits. But Covey, the big Pole from Shamokin, Pennsylvania, was almost perfect, allowing just 5 base hits, hurling a 3–0 shutout to win the championship for the Cleveland Indians. It was the first Series triumph for the Indians, who overcame the most traumatic year in their history. In the heat of the pennant race, twenty-nine-year-old Ray Chapman, the shortstop, and one of the most popular players on the club, was struck by a pitched ball, on August 16, in a game against the Yankees, and died the following day.

When Ed Konetchy forced Hy Myers at second base for the final out of the Series, Wambsganss, who had taken the throw, tossed the ball to manager Tris Speaker in center field. Speaker forced his way through the delirious mob of fans

as pitcher Rube Marquard, who had started the Series for the Dodgers was arrested in his hotel room and charged with scalping Series tickets. Specifically, he tried to sell eight box seat tickets for $400. When the story broke and the Rube was released from police custody after being fined $25 by Judge Harry Silbert, Ebbets declared, "That miserable person will never pitch for Brooklyn again." True to his word, Marquard was traded to the Reds after the Series.

The fifth game of the Series was one of the most bizarre in the history of the postseason event. It produced not only the ultimate in individual offensive plays—a home run with the bases filled, by Elmer Smith who hit it off Grimes in the first inning—but that rarest of all defensive plays, an unassisted triple play, made by second baseman Bill Wambsganss in the fifth inning.

The historic fifth game of the World Series was marked by an astounding un-assisted triple play: The Indians' second baseman, Bill Wambsgans (*far left*), caught the line drive off Clarence Mitchell (*center*) and immediately stepped on second base to double out Pete Kilduff (*left*). Then Wambsgans dashed over toward first to tag Otto Miller (*right*) and completed the triple play.

who had danced out onto the field and reached a box seat where his mother, who had come up from Texas, was sitting and gave her the game ball that brought the World Championship to the Cleveland Indians for the first time in the club's long history.

While far away in Brooklyn all was gloom.

Manager Wilbert Robinson, who had been so near, and yet so far, from a championship, went glumly home to Dover Hall in Brunswick, Georgia, to seek forgetfulness in hunting and fishing. But he felt much better several days later, when Charles Ebbets called to tell him he was sending him a new three-year contract at a nice increase in salary and asking him to please sign it and send it right back.

1921

New York Giants Versus New York Yankees

In the spring of 1919, at the Red Sox training camp in Tampa, manager Ed Barrow finally decided that the time had come for him to convert his phenomenal young pitcher Babe Ruth, into a full-time outfielder. In spite of the fact that Ruth was the finest left-handed pitcher in the American League, his great power at the plate could help the team even more. The move was a tremendous success. In his first year as a regular left fielder, Ruth, batting fourth in the Sox lineup, hit for a .322 average and belted out a record 29 home runs. No major league player had ever hit that many homers in the course of a single season.

Babe Ruth's name flashed across the country, and wherever the Red Sox played, the crowds swarmed to see Ruth. In New York, Colonel Jake Ruppert and Colonel Tillinghast Huston, the Yankee owners, looking on at Ruth's prowess and tremendous crowd appeal, wanted him. They were ambitious to make the Yankees the greatest team in baseball. Here, people were saying, was the greatest player, and certainly the most spectacular, the most awe-inspiring in baseball. He belonged, they felt, in a New York Yankee uniform.

Colonel Huston was a self-made man, an engineer who had grown up in Ohio and made a fortune in Cuba after the Spanish-American War in construction projects. He was a heavy-set man, a careless dresser, open and friendly, who considered the sportswriters and ballplayers as his particular pals. In contrast, partner Jake Ruppert was a New York aristocrat whose father had been a multimillionaire brewer. Ruppert dressed meticulously, had a valet, collected objets d'art, and moved easily in New York society. He always called Babe "Babe Root" and never called anyone by his or her first name. He could not remember first names.

The Red Sox owner, Harry Frazee, had always been a wealthy, colorful figure. He started work as a bill poster in his hometown, Peoria, Illinois. No pinchpenny promoter, Frazee made and lost several million dollars in various Broadway theatrical productions. With Babe Ruth making the turnstiles hum in 1919, and a couple of his shows losing money, Frazee was putting money in one pocket and taking it out of another. But not even Ruth could square the deficit, and Frazee was nearly broke again.

So, Harry went to New York and asked his friend Colonel Jake Ruppert for a $500,000 loan.

The colonel immediately countered with an offer to purchase Ruth, mentioning large sums of cash and players. Frazee dashed back to Boston to consult with manager Ed Barrow.

"You want cash, don't you?" Barrow asked.

"Yes," said Frazee.

"Well, get the money. The hell with the players. I don't want any players from that club. Get the dough." Frazee was back in New York the next day and made a deal for Babe Ruth. Ruth was to go to the Yankees for $100,000. And as a bonus, Frazee got a personal loan of $350,000 from Ruppert, who took Frazee's mortgage on Fenway Park as collateral.

The Red Sox fans almost went berserk when they heard about the sale of Babe Ruth, and threatened to boycott the Red Sox.

The Babe had no particular liking for New York. He had founded a cigar company in Boston and his picture was on each cigar package and the business was booming. He also had a farm near Sudbury, Massachusetts, and had little reason to want to go to New York.

"New York is so goddam expensive," he said. "Hell, a taxi ride costs a dollar, seventy-five cents and a show on Broadway is five bucks. Who in hell can pay those prices? Besides, everybody in Boston knows and likes me. Nobody knows me in New York. Too goddam big."

But whether he liked it or not, Ruth finally reported to the Yankees. There he was to give them a championship image, and to read one day, when the great new Yankee Stadium had been constructed, that it was "the House That Ruth Built."

Never before had the sale of one major league player created such a stir. Ruth had not only smashed all existing home run records in 1919, but he plainly was at the very beginning of a career as a batter who would revolutionize the game.

The innocent bystanders victimized by this incredible deal, the biggest so far in baseball history, were the great New York Giants. Up to that period, they had kept the edge in the torrid fight for patronage, but now they had no one to match the prowess, and color, of Babe Ruth, and it was quite certain that once the season opened, the Yankees would emerge as the leading team in New York.

With the Bambino leading the way in 1920, the Yankees moved into a three-way race for the pennant with the White Sox and the St. Louis Browns. However, the Browns dropped off the pace, but the Yanks and White Sox battled each other and their opponents until the very last two days of the season as the Sox went on to win the pennant by 1½ games from the surging Yankees.

There was, however, great rejoicing in New York. Although the Yanks finished in second place, they had won 95 games, more than any Yankee team in history. And Ruth's performance in 1920 was a baseball landmark. He hit 54 home runs, 9 triples, 36 doubles, and scored 158 runs. His slugging average was an amazing .847, still the major league record.

In 1921, the Yankees, with a new general manager in Ed Barrow, a new manager, Miller Huggins, and with Ruth blasting 59 home runs, swept to their first American League pennant by 6½ games over the Indians.

The Yankee pennant was made possible by deals that Colonels Ruppert and Huston made with the Boston Red Sox.

After purchasing Ruth in 1920, the Yankee dragnet snared Carl Mays and all Mays did was win 27 games during the season. But if the Mays deal was not enough, the Yankees also purchased pitchers Waite Hoyt, Ernie Shore, and Harry Harper; catcher Wally Schang; outfielder Duffy Lewis; and a crack third baseman, Mike McNally.

In the National League, John McGraw's Giants, smarting after World Series losses in 1911, 1912, 1913, and 1917, were determined to win their first championship. They staged one of their most magnificent pennant races in years to win. The Giants trailed Pittsburgh by 7½ games as the Pirates came into New York on August 24, for a vital 5-game series. They went out with blood in their eyes after a typical McGraw fight talk before the game, and defeated the Pirates 5 times in a row, and in late September, the Giants vaulted over Pittsburgh and captured the pennant by 4 games in one of the most spirited, thrilling finishes on record—a finish that had all of New York rooting for them.

Even as the Giants were smashing the opposition and snatching the National League flag, the Yankees continued to win the big-play coverage in the sports pages and fan support at the turnstiles. Most of the older fans were still faithful to the Giants, but now they were completely outnumbered by those newer fans whose imaginations had been fired by the heroics of Babe Ruth and who now swore allegiance to the Yankees. The changeover was reflected in the papers; most of the first-string writers had been

The 1921 American League Champions, the New York Yankees

assigned to the Yankees ever since Ruth came on board with his big bat.

It was understandable that the altered situation rankled the colorful, aggressive John McGraw. For the first time since his rise to greatness as a baseball figure, he was overshadowed, and right in his own backyard. It galled him to hear the crowds roar for Ruth where once they had cheered lustily for McGraw and his Giants.

The impending Series would be a bitter struggle, not between him and Miller Huggins, the Yankee manager, but between him and Ruth. The writers seized upon that and played it up with front-page stories and photographs every day. What would happen when the mastermind of the Giants had to match wits with Ruth in a pinch situation?

"Why in hell should Ruth worry me," asked McGraw. "Why all this excitement about him. We've been pitching all along to better hitters than Ruth ever will be."

Of all the shrewd managers he had to contend with, the Babe had the most to fear from McGraw, who had studied Ruth very closely in the spring of 1919, when the Giants and Yankees had engaged each other in several exhibition games. In those games, McGraw found that Ruth could be held somewhat in check by off-speed pitches, combined with a slow curveball on the inside.

The Giants' lineup for the 1921 Series included George Kelly at first base, Johnny Rawlings at second, Dave Bancroft at short stop, Frank Frisch at third, Irish Meusel in left field, George Burns in center field, and the brilliant Ross Youngs in right. Frank Snyder and Earl Smith shared catching duties, and the pitchers included Art Nehf, Phil Douglas, Jesse Barnes, and Fred Toney.

The Yankees had Wally Pipp on first base, Aaron Ward at second, Roger Peckinpaugh at short, Home Run Baker at third, Babe Ruth in left field, Elmer Miller in center, and Bob Meusel, younger brother of Irish, in right field. The big pitchers included Carl Mays, Waite Hoyt, Bob Shawkey, Jack Quinn, and Harry Harper. Wally Schang did most of the catching.

The 1921 Series was the last one to be a five-out-of-nine Series and the first played under the jurisdiction of the new baseball commissioner,

Judge Kenesaw Mountain Landis. All of the games were to be played at the Polo Grounds, with the teams alternating daily as the home team.

Miller Huggins decided to start the Series with his great left-handed submarine ace, Carl Mays, a 27-game winner. John McGraw opted to start Phil Douglas, his 15-game winner.

The Yankees immediately jumped on Douglas in the first inning, with Ruth stroking a long single to left field to score Elmer Miller, who had walked and had then gone to second and third on groundouts.

In the fifth inning, Yankee third baseman Mike McNally electrified the great crowd as he made a clean steal of home after he had doubled and advanced to third on a sacrifice fly, giving the Yanks a 2–0 advantage.

The Yankees scored another run in the sixth inning and then coasted easily to a 3–0 victory. Carl Mays taunted the big Giant hitters with his sneaky submarine pitches that just seemed to float in the air, then suddenly dived into the ground as the batters lunged wildly and missed. Mays allowed the Giants just 5 hits and the Giant third baseman Frankie Frisch was the only Giant hitter able to solve the mystery of Mays's pitching. Frisch had 4 of the 5 Giant hits.

The next day McGraw changed his pitchers but his luck was still bad. Bob Meusel stole home this time while Earl Smith, the Giants' catcher, watched and McGraw stewed. Smith had a clubhouse reputation as a talker, but he came out second best in a talk with McGraw after the game and also was relieved of $200 by Landis for an inflammatory speech he had made at home plate after Meusel had scored. The Giants, meanwhile, made only 2 hits off Waite Hoyt and for the second straight day lost by a score of 3–0.

The Yankees kept rolling along in the third game. They scored four times off Toney in the third inning before Toney got anybody out, and now the Giants were 2 games and 4 runs down and still hadn't scored a run of their own in the series. Besides, no team in the twenty year history of the World Series had spotted a rival 2 games and survived.

However, McGraw's club rallied with the help

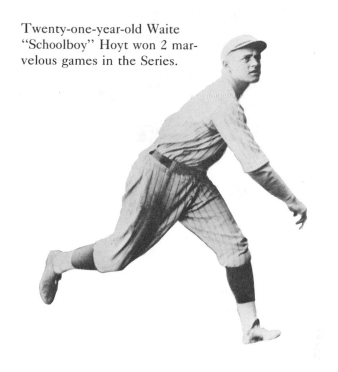

Twenty-one-year-old Waite "Schoolboy" Hoyt won 2 marvelous games in the Series.

of 3 bases on balls by Yankee pitcher Bob Shawkey, and the Giants made one of their remarkable comebacks. They scored 4 runs in the home half of the third inning, then 8 more in the seventh inning for a Series record as they stormed to a 13–5 win. John McGraw was elated as his Giants clubbed out a total of 20 base hits, 4 each by George Burns and Frank Snyder.

McGraw felt better now. And he felt even better when the Giants evened things by winning the fourth game, 4–2, despite a home run by Ruth in the sixth inning. It was Ruth's first World Series homer—the first of 45 during the next dozen years.

The next day the Yankees went back ahead in the Series with a 3–1 victory, and Ruth made even bigger news. He beat out a bunt. However, he also developed an abscess on his left elbow and, except for one appearance as a pinch hitter, he was finished in the Series. Without their great star, for all practical purposes, the Yankees were finished. Without their champion, they did not win another game as the Giants tied the Series by winning the next game, 8–5; went ahead with a 2–1 win in the seventh game; and then in the most exciting of all the games, the Giants' Art Nehf finally defeated his Yankee nemesis, Waite Hoyt, in a thrilling pitchers' battle, 1–0,

The magnificent defensive unit of the Giants provided the spark to the championship in this Series: (*left to right*) first base George Kelly, second base Johnny Rawlings, Davey Bancroft at short, and Frankie Frisch on third base.

to win the championship. Nehf allowed the Yankees just 4 hits and kept the big hitters back on their heels throughout the tense duel.

McGraw, who had lost in all four Series he had been in since 1905, was treated to one of those rare moments of unbelievable delight in the last inning of the last game. First, his big rival Babe Ruth pinch-hit for Wally Pipp and grounded out. Then Aaron Ward walked and Home Run Baker lined a pitch toward right field. But John Rawlings, the young second baseman, lunged for the ball, knocked it down on the rim of the outfield, and, still on his knees, threw out Baker at first base. Ward had rounded second and was en route to third, but Kelly, the first baseman, relayed Rawlings's throw across the infield to Frank Frisch, who ended the Series by tagging Ward at third base, while McGraw's cup ran over.

It ran far, far into the night, in a typically roaring celebration in the Giants' suite at the Waldorf. They had won the pennant at the final hour, had won the Series at the eleventh hour,

and were headed for four straight seasons of unmatched prosperity. But for John McGraw, there was only one victory worth crowing about.

"I signaled every pitch to Ruth," he said, savoring every boast from his first encounter with the big guy. "In fact, I gave the sign for practically every ball our pitchers threw. They wanted it that way. You could see Snyder or Smith turn and look at me on the bench before signaling the pitcher. We pitched only nine curves and three fastballs to Ruth during the entire Series. All the rest of the pitches were slowballs, and of the twelve of those, eleven set him on his back side."

The 1921 World Series catapulted baseball to the threshold of a new era, the million-dollar gate, which was to come with the opening of the new Yankee Stadium two years later. It was the beginning of baseball's upswing from the Black Sox scandal to start its greatest period of prosperity, which was to continue for a full decade. It was fitting that John J. McGraw and the 1921 Giants should be a part of it.

New York Giants Versus New York Yankees

Despite the thirty-nine-day suspension of Babe Ruth and Bob Meusel for taking part in an unauthorized barnstorming tour at the end of the 1921 season, the Yankees once again captured the American League pennant, but only after a season-long battle with the St. Louis Browns. The Browns, with seven of their regulars hitting above the .300 mark, fought to remain even with the Yankees until the very last days of the season before losing finally by 1½ games.

Meanwhile, the Giants easily captured the National League flag over the Cincinnati Reds by a margin of 7 games. But there was one potential scandal that for a few days threatened the good name of baseball as much as the Black Sox affair of 1919.

Pitcher Phil Douglas, a 15-game winner for the Giants, a nine-year veteran who had played with several major league teams, and a constant source of problems for McGraw since he had joined the team in 1919, had written a letter to outfielder Les Mann of the Cardinals. In the letter, Douglas offered that if the Cardinal players would make it worthwhile, "I will go fishing for the rest of the season and this way the Cards could win the pennant."

Mann turned the letter over to McGraw and the manager of the Giants called a press conference and announced that Douglas would immediately be placed on the ineligible list.

It was a shock to McGraw and the Giants, for the loss of Douglas, an outstanding pitcher who could win the big games, was enormous. But McGraw plugged the gap by purchasing Hugh McQuillan from the Boston Braves for $100,000 and acquiring Jack Scott from the Reds, and both pitchers helped the Giants' cause. McGraw also acquired Jim O'Connell, a .375 hitter, from San Francisco for a record price of $75,000 for a rookie. Two other vital acquisitions, which were to help the Giants for years to come, were Travis Jackson, an infielder from Arkansas, and Bill Terry, a budding star who would go on to succeed McGraw as the Giants' manager.

Then the big show was on, the Yankees versus the Giants.

The Yankees scored first in the fifth inning as Whitey Witt led off with a triple, then tried to score when Joe Dugan bounced a grounder to shortstop Dave Bancroft. But Banny threw the ball home and intercepted Witt, who was trapped between third and home, but who managed before he was tagged to hop back and forth long enough to allow Dugan to reach second base. Dugan then scored from second when Ruth followed with a long single to right field.

It was the second straight year that Ruth had got in the first lick against McGraw by driving across the first run. But for the second straight year, McGraw was destined to have the last

The indomitable Casey Stengel hit for a dazzling .400 average for the Giants in his first World Series.

laugh. It was the only run produced by Babe Ruth in the entire Series.

The Yanks scored again in the seventh, increasing their advantage to 2–0, with Bullet Joe Bush holding the Giants all the way. In the home half of the eighth, Bancroft singled, Groh singled, Frisch singled, and the bases were loaded with nobody out. Then Irish Meusel singled home Bancroft and Groh. Miller Huggins rushed in Waite Hoyt, but Youngs lifted a long fly to Witt and Frisch came in with the winning run and a 3–2 victory.

With the third game approaching, McGraw was ready for a big gamble.

"Jack Scott is going to be my pitcher," he told reporters.

They could scarcely believe him. Scott? The castoff?

Jack Scott had been a tobacco farmer in North Carolina. He was a big, raw-boned, right-handed thrower, and had played for the Braves for four years. In 1921, Jack was traded to the Reds. Then, in 1922, he was assailed by a number of injuries, and to increase his woes, the crops on

his farm were completely burned in a fire. The Reds released him and for several months he remained at home trying to salvage his farm. When things at home were once more in good order, he traveled to New York to plead with McGraw for a chance. He was broke and desperate. John McGraw looked at the big, earnest guy, pleading for his last chance of a comeback, and believed in him.

"Look, Scott," said McGraw, "we're going on the road. Stay here in New York, work out every day at the park. If your arm comes around, feels good enough to pitch by the time I get back, we'll work out something. But don't talk to anybody about this."

"I won't talk to anybody and I won't ever forget you, Mr. McGraw. This ol' arm ain't dead. I'll pay you back in the pitcher's box."

By the time the Giants returned to New York, Scott was pitching like his old self. His arm felt sound and strong.

On October 6, Jack Scott pitched the biggest game of his life. Throwing nothing but fastballs, keeping them high and tight, and an occasional off-speed pitch, Scott even handcuffed the great Babe Ruth, while the Giants pecked away at Waite Hoyt and Sam Jones for the 3 runs that gave them the game.

A steady downpour of rain fell during the fourth game but it did not prevent the Yankees from hitting the hell out of McGraw's $100,000 pitcher, Hugh McQuillan, in the first inning for 2 runs. Witt singled to open the game, and Jumping Joe Dugan singled. Ruth hit a 450-foot drive toward the stands in center field, but Billy Cunningham made a great running stop to rob him of an extra-base hit. Wally Pipp, however, singled and Witt scored. Meusel singled, scoring Dugan, and the Yankees had a 2–0 lead.

The great Carl Mays was just that, great, for four and a half scoreless innings. However, in the fifth inning, everything came up roses for the Giants. McQuillan hit a hard shot to Joe Dugan at third base, and it bounced off Joe's glove for a double. Bancroft smashed another hard drive right at Ward off second base, and at the last moment the ball bounded over his head for a single. Groh hit one back to the pitcher's mound, and Carl Mays knocked it down, but

Wally Pipp starred for the Yankees on first base in the 1921, 1922, and 1923 World Series.

In the first game of the World Series played at Yankee Stadium, the ex-Fordham star Frank Frisch rapped out 4 base hits for the Giants.

Groh was safe with a single. Then came a sacrifice, an infield out, and a single, and the Giants had 4 runs and the game by a 4–3 score.

The next day was Sunday, October 8, and 38,551 people packed the Polo Grounds—the largest crowd that had ever seen a World Series game in New York. They watched the Yankees build a 3–2 lead, then, when the Giants went to bat in the eighth inning, saw the furies break loose.

With 1 out, Groh singled and Frisch doubled. Meusel hit a ball to Everett Scott at shortstop, and Scott threw the ball home to cut down Groh at the plate. Huggins then resorted to some grand strategy and ordered Yankee pitcher Joe

Bush to walk the hard-hitting lefty, Ross Youngs. Bush did as he was told and pitched to George Kelly and Kelly lined the first pitch into center field for a two-run single that brought in the go-ahead run. Then Lee King singled, scoring Youngs, giving the Giants a 5–3 edge and the ball game—and the Series.

Now the huge crowd was dancing all over the field, screaming for McGraw and shouting his praises, and as he came out of the dressing room to doff his cap, the cheers for McGraw could be heard all the way across the Hudson to New Jersey.

A very old woman broke through the crowd to shake John McGraw's hand and she said, "I can go home now. I've shaken the hand of the greatest manager in baseball."

That night in the Giants' suite at the Waldorf-Astoria, McGraw and Horace Stoneham hosted the celebration that lasted throughout the night. There were hams and steaks and turkey for all the guests and rye and Scotch. There were such colorful guests as Lillian Russell; Diamond Jim Brady; Bet a Million Gates; the new heavyweight champion, Jack Dempsey, and his manager, Jack Kearns; boxer Mickey Walker; and every sportswriter in the area. It was one of the greatest nights of John McGraw's life.

New York Yankees
Versus New York Giants

With the start of the 1923 season, the rivalry between the Giants and the Yankees had reached its pinnacle. It was reflected not only in the boisterous arguments among the fans but in the relations between officials of the two clubs.

Horace Stoneham, a stock broker, had purchased controlling interest in the Giants from the Brush family, after John Brush passed away, for $1 million. Now with his manager John McGraw, Stoneham had come to hate the Yankees and the Yankee officials. The two sides hated each other and heaped insults on their adversaries at every opportunity.

McGraw and Stoneham had driven the Yankees from the Polo Grounds and compelled them to build their own ballpark, which was completed in the fall of 1922. And although they were to realize one day that it was a sorry mistake, the Giants were smugly content with having the Polo Grounds to themselves once again.

Across the Harlem River the magnificent Yankee Stadium opened in the spring of 1923 and a crowd of more than seventy thousand roaring fans welcomed Babe Ruth to the Yankees' new home in the Bronx.

In spite of the mounting popularity of Babe Ruth and the rest of the Yankees, it was a pleasant summer for John McGraw. Although challenged seriously for several weeks by the Brooklyn Dodgers and by his former bosom buddy, Wilbert Robinson, the Giants won another National League pennant by 6½ games over the Cincinnati Reds, as the Dodgers slumped badly and finished in sixth place.

The Yankees, meanwhile, ran roughshod over their American League rivals, the Detroit Tigers, by some 16 games, despite the great batting of Ty Cobb and of Harry Heilmann, who hit .403.

Once more, John McGraw had won three pennants in a row. Now an ever greater prize lay just in front of him. Three World Series in a row. No manager had ever achieved that.

In the first game of a World Series that broke existing attendance records with a crowd of 55,307 wildly excited fans, the Yankees were beaten by the Giants in a hard-fought, thrilling tussle.

Ironically, the player who proved the biggest obstacle in the Yankees' path to World Series supremacy was Casey Stengel, who more than a quarter of a century later would gain lasting fame as the most successful manager in Yankee history. A thirty-three-year-old outfielder for the Giants, Stengel was the hero of the first World Series game ever played at Yankee Stadium, and he also delivered the home run that won the third game of the Series.

There were two outs in the top of the ninth inning of the first game and the score was 4–4, when Casey lined a Joe Bush pitch into deep

99

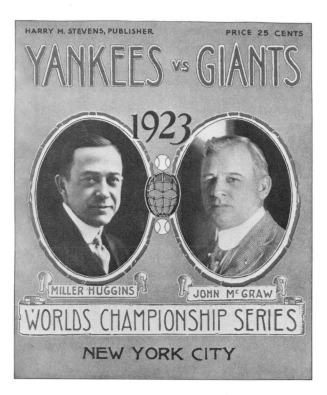

HARRY M. STEVENS, PUBLISHER   PRICE 25 CENTS

YANKEES vs GIANTS

1923

MILLER HUGGINS   JOHN McGRAW

WORLDS CHAMPIONSHIP SERIES

NEW YORK CITY

The cover of the 1923 World Series program

left-center field. The ball rolled to the wall, and Stengel, puffing and running as hard as his thirty-three-year-old bandy legs could carry him, with one shoe half off, fell across home plate. The inside-the-park home run gave the Giants a dramatic 5–4 victory.

In game two, Babe Ruth slugged 2 home runs and Aaron Ward smashed another, while the Yankees' ace, Herb Pennock, held the Giants to 2 runs; the Yankees took the game by a 4–2 margin. Irish Meusel of the Giants also homered.

The third game, played at Yankee Stadium, featured a dramatic pitching duel between the Yankees' Sam Jones and the Giants' Art Nehf, with both hurlers holding the opposition scoreless for six innings. Then once again, the pesky Stengel homered for the Giants in the seventh inning, giving the Giants a 1–0 lead, as Nehf held the Yankees scoreless to clinch the victory.

The Yankee sluggers finally came to life in the fourth game as they cranked up and teed off against the Giant pitchers for 13 hits and trounced them, 8–4.

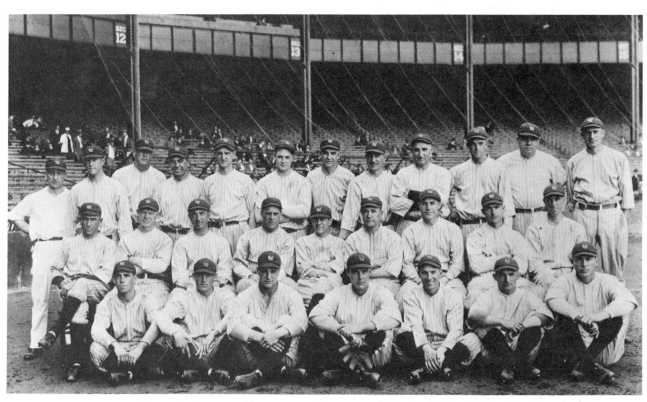

The 1923 World Champions, the New York Yankees

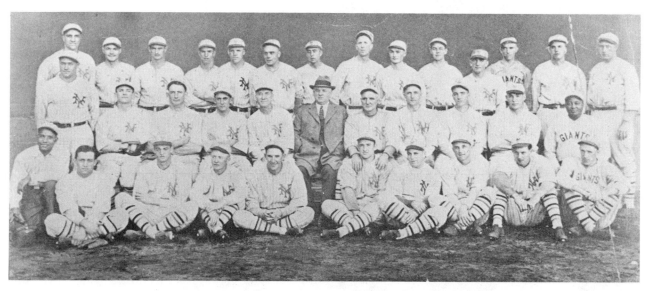

The 1923 Giants were one of John McGraw's greatest teams.

Jack Scott, hero of the 1922 Series, was bombed for 6 runs and knocked out of the box in the second inning. In an attempt to stem the Yankee tide, McGraw used five hurlers, but the Bronx Bombers continued their cannonade to win the game.

Back in the Bronx for game five, Joe Bush held the Giants to just 3 base hits as the Yankees continued their batting assault against four Giant pitchers, for 14 hits and an easy 8–1 win.

The Yankee sluggers finished off the Giants in game six to capture the vital game and the World Series.

Babe Ruth got the Yanks off and running with a long home run in the first inning. But the Giants hung in gamely and clubbed Herb Pennock for 10 hits, and led 4–1 going into the eighth inning. But the Yanks rallied, and came to life with a 5-run outburst in their half of the inning. The key hit was provided by Bob Meusel, a timely single that scored 2 runs, lifting the Yanks to a 5–4 lead. The Yankees scored another run before the inning was over, and Jones came on in the bottom of the eighth to relieve Pennock and hold the Giants in check, wrapping up the game and the Series.

The Series was Babe Ruth's first big postseason show. He smashed out 3 home runs, 2 in succession in the second game. He also had a long triple, which could have been an inside-the-park homer, but the Babe was tired and just made it to third base. Ruth also drove out a double and 2 singles and slugged the ball for a tremendous .368 average (he also walked 8 times), as the Yankees pounded their way to their very first World Championship.

There was another noteworthy event in 1923 that was to give the Yankees the greatest one-two batting punch in baseball as Columbia's Lou Gehrig made his first appearance at the stadium in a Yankee uniform.

The Yankees' chief scout, Paul Krichell had seen Lou play the outfield for Columbia University in a game against Rutgers and had been astonished by the raw hitting power he displayed.

"I think," he told general manager Ed Barrow that night, "I saw another Babe Ruth today. And I'm going to try and sign him."

Let us pause for a moment to look at the kid as he enters the Yankee clubhouse to put on a Yankee uniform for the first time. He is twenty years old, six feet two, and weighs about 190 pounds. His hair is cut closely and his face is lean. He is awed by his surroundings, for this is no ordinary ball club he is joining. The men scattered about the clubhouse getting into their uniforms are the Yankees, twice pennant winners and on their way to a third pennant and the championship of the world.

Giants shortstop Travis Jackson, a star in the 1923 and 1924 Series, was one of John McGraw's favorite players.

The big guy with the muffin face, the huge chest, skinny legs, and the booming voice is "Mr. Baseball," Babe Ruth. And that tall, lean, dour-looking fellow next to him is Bob Meusel. The slim, smiling guy is Herb Pennock. The boyish fellow is Waite Hoyt. And there are Wally Schang and Aaron Ward and Joe Dugan. That tall, quiet guy is first baseman Wally Pipp.

Paul Krichell walks Gehrig into the manager's office.

Miller Huggins is a little man. Spindly-legged, flat-footed, thin face. He is in uniform and is reading some scouting reports. He shakes hands with Krichell and nods at Lou.

"You're Gehrig." He spoke quietly. "Krich has told me about you. Glad to see you. Let's go out onto the field."

The Yankees were just beginning to start batting practice and Joe Dugan moved in to hit, when Huggins said, "Wait a minute, Joe. Let this boy hit a few balls."

Lou, nervous as a cat, picked up a bat—it happened to be one of Ruth's by some curious chance—and advanced to the plate. He looked big and menacing as he waited for the pitch. Obviously nervous, he missed the first three pitches, then bounced one weakly over second base, and the players laughed.

The Lou squared his shoulders and drove the next ball on a line over second base. It was a base hit in any league. Then another pitch, and this time Lou drove it high into the left field bleachers, where only Ruth could hit the ball. He hit another in the same place and another, and another. His swing was now a thing of beauty as he crashed one pitch after another into the stands.

"That's enough, Gehrig," Huggins yelled.

"His name's Lou Gehrig," Huggins said to no one in particular, "and he may be around for a long time if he hits like that."

Casey Stengel has just hit an inside-the-park home run in the new Yankee Stadium. He just makes it to home after his baseball shoe slipped off as he rounded third base.

1924

Washington Senators Versus New York Giants

Early on a rather cool morning in 1924, a twenty-seven-year-old ballplayer for the Washington Senators, on a golfing holiday in Tampa, Florida, where he had gone a month before reporting for spring training, received a special delivery letter from Clark Griffith, president of the Senators.

"Dear Bucky, I think you can do a very good job for us as manager of the ball club," Griffith wrote. "If you want the job, it is yours. But I must have your answer by Saturday. Call me long distance when you receive this letter. That is, if you'd like to manage the Senators."

The young ballplayer was nonplussed as he read and reread the letter; then, regaining his composure, he dashed to the nearest phone and reached Griffith in Washington.

"Hello, Mr. Griffith, I do want that job," he blurted.

But Bucky was talking into a very poor phone connection. "I can't hear you very well," said Griffith.

Harris was now screaming into the mouthpiece. Though he could hear Griffith, he couldn't make himself heard. Griff, impatient, cursed all the phone poles from Washington to Tampa and hung up. Bucky Harris panicked. A big-league job was his for the asking and he was helpless. Then he thought of a new approach and dashed to the nearest Western Union office and wired Griff: I'LL TAKE THE JOB AND WIN WASHINGTON'S FIRST AMERICAN LEAGUE PENNANT. He gave the Western Union clerk a twenty-dollar bill and said, "Send this wire right away and repeat it every hour for the next four hours."

Bucky Harris had every reason to be astonished at Griff's selection of him as manager. He was only twenty-seven years old, and had a scant three years of major league experience; he wasn't an outstanding player and actually had thought he was in the owner's doghouse at the time. A few weeks earlier Griff had caught him playing professional basketball in violation of his baseball contract and had actually threatened to fine Bucky. It was not a happy occasion, for after Harris had agreed to terms ($7,000) for the season, Griff told him, "We've got a chance to get the great Eddie Collins from the White Sox as our new manager. He'd play second base. Do you think you could move over to third?"

Bucky Harris wasn't born on a baseball diamond, but on Ball Street in Port Jervis, New York. His Welsh parents had gravitated to the coal fields of Pennsylvania where his grandfather was a fire boss, a job that required testing the safety of the mine.

Young Bucky had worked in the coal mines, first as a breaker boy sorting chunks of slate from coal, then graduating to the weighmaster's office, at $4.30 a week, in Pittston, Pennsylvania. When he wasn't working, he was playing baseball. He was living in a mining sector of a state that was rich in baseball tradition. Such stars as Christy

Mathewson, Ed Walsh, Hughie Jennings, Steve O'Neill, the two Coveleski brothers, all hailed from that area, and they all made the grade in the major leagues. Many returned to the small mining towns at the end of their careers and thrilled the local kids with stories of their halcyon days.

At the age of nineteen, Bucky Harris received a wire asking him to report to the training camp of the Detroit Tigers in Texas. Manager Hughie Jennings had seen Bucky playing for one of the mine teams and liked his play in the infield.

By 1924, Bucky Harris, the youngest player on the Senators, was named to be the manager of some of the finest major league players in baseball, Joe Judge, Walter Johnson, Sam Rice, Tom Zachary, the slugging Goose Goslin, George Mogridge, Muddy Ruel, and others.

For more years than anyone could remember, quiet, pleasant, placid Walter Johnson had expended his great right arm in a hopeless cause. A standard quip among comedians of the day went, "Washington, first in peace, first in war, and last in the American League."

This was Johnson's eighteenth year, and, as he had already won 374 games for the Senators it might reasonably be assumed that there weren't too many good games left in the great arm. His total victories for the Senators as the 1924 season began was 1 more than that of the great Christy Mathewson, Johnson's rival for the title of baseball's number one pitcher.

Now it seemed as if Johnson had reached back into the well of those great years of his youth, for his fastball zipped in to the batters as sharply as ever. During July and August, Walter won game after game and by the team's last western trip, he had won 13 consecutive games and the Washington Senators found themselves atop the American League in a tie with the Yankees.

In the pennant-hungry nation's capital, the Senators sweated out the final two days of the season, which would tell the pennant story.

On a bright, beautiful Monday afternoon, late in September, Fred Marberry and Tom Zachary teamed up to defeat the Red Sox, 5–3, as the entire city of Washington sat glued to their seats and listened to their radios; following the Senators' victory, the Yankees needed to defeat Philadelphia to tie the Senators for first place.

Teammates and roommates, Walter Johnson (*left*) and Clyde Milan (*right*) played with the Senators for seventeen years before they won their first pennant and played in the 1924 Series.

But the Athletics' marvelous knuckleball ace, Eddie Rommel, stifled the big Yankee bats and the Senators remained in first place—the new champions of the American League.

Even during the normally apathetic period when Calvin Coolidge was President, it was quite easy to get Washington residents excited about baseball, and when the Senators returned from Boston after clinching the pennant, there was as much hysteria in town as there had been six years earlier over the first armistice. Congressmen and senators, even Presidents, were merely transient visitors to Washington, but the Washington Senators' ball club was the town's very own.

For the eighth time in fourteen years, the National League's representative in the World Series was the New York Giants. This year, however, manager John McGraw's team, despite having a team batting average of .300, had had the battle of their lives and had just managed to win the pennant by 1½ games over the Brooklyn Dodgers.

McGraw had added several new faces to the team in 1924 following the trade of Casey Stengel and Davey Bancroft to the Boston Braves: Travis Jackson took over as the shortstop; two

Some of baseball's greatest stars posed for this photo prior to the start of the 1924 World Series: (*left to right*) Frank Lieb, chief scorer for the Series, Nick Altrock, Ty Cobb, Babe Ruth, John J. McGraw, Walter Johnson, George Sisler, and Christy Walsh, sportswriter and manager of Ruth.

rookies who would develop into superstars, Bill Terry and Hack Wilson, gave the Giants added power; and eighteen-year-old Fred Lindstrom performed like a ten-year veteran at third base.

Walter Johnson and Giant veteran Art Nehf were the opening-game pitchers, and both hurlers went the distance in what proved to be a thrilling, pulsating twelve-inning battle.

George Kelly and Bill Terry slugged home runs to give the Giants an early 2–0 lead, and Nehf held the Senators hitless until the sixth inning. Then, Earl McNeely doubled and took third on a groundout. He scored on Sam Rice's slow roller to third. Now it was a 2–1 game and the Senators' fans went crazy. In the ninth inning, Ossie Bluege of the Senators beat out an infield hit. Roger Peckinpaugh brought the crowd up on its feet as he slashed a drive into left field for a double, scoring Bluege. Now it was 2–2.

All through the tense tenth and eleventh innings, Johnson and Artie Nehf set their respec-tive opponents down in rapid order. Then, in the twelfth frame, Johnson suddenly lost his control and walked Hank Gowdy to open the inning. Nehf sent a high fly ball to McNeely in center field. But in his haste to grab the ball and make a play on Gowdy, Earl misjudged the ball and it rolled away from him for a hit and Gowdy went on to third and Nehf reached second base. McGraw now sent in pinch hitter Jack Bentley to hit for Lindstrom and he walked on four pitches, filling the bases. Frisch hit a hard ground ball to Harris at second base and Bucky's accu-rate throw to the plate nabbed Gowdy. Then Youngs singled to center, scoring Nehf, and the Giants were out in front, 3–2. Big George Kelly hit a towering fly ball that dropped in safely, and another run scored to make it 4–2, Giants.

In the Senators' half of the twelfth inning, Harris singled in Mule Shirly, who had opened the inning by cracking a double to center field. But that was all the scoring the Senators would do and the Giants finished on the winning end of a nerve-tingling 4–3 Series opener.

For the second game, Harris called on his left-handed star, Tom Zachary, while McGraw countered with another left-hander in Jack Bentley as a crowd of more than thirty-five thousand fans settled down for what they hoped would be another exciting matchup. Sam Rice started the Senators off with a first inning single. Then Goose Goslin brought the home crowd up and roaring as he drove a pitch into the stands for a 2-run homer.

There was no further scoring until the fifth inning, when the irrepressible Bucky Harris slashed a tremendous homer into left-center field and the Senators had a 3–0 lead.

In the seventh inning the Giants suddenly awakened from their lethargy. Kelly walked and legged it to third base on Meusel's single. Then Hack Wilson hit the ball to Harris, who stepped on second base for the double play. On the play, Kelly scored the Giants' first run of the game.

Tom Zachary, well on his way to an easy victory, had handcuffed the Giants until the ninth inning and had a 3–1 lead, but this was a season when nothing came easy for the Senators. Frankie Frisch walked to start the Giants' half of the inning. Then George Kelly slapped a sharp single to left field; Frisch, running at the crack of the bat, raced all the way home from first base. Wilson singled, and Kelly scored the tying run. There was a very close play at the plate as Kelly came down the third base line like a runaway train and barreled into catcher Muddy Ruel, sending Ruel sprawling about ten feet away. Bucky Harris then called on his relief star, Firpo Marberry and Firpo fanned Travis Jackson, the next batter, on three whizzing fastballs.

In their half of the ninth inning, the Senators quickly took over. Judge walked, and Bluege sacrificed him to second with a beautiful bunt. Then it was up to Peckinpaugh, and Peck once more equal to the task, slashed a fastball into left field that scored Judge with the winning run. This time the Senators were on the right side of a 4–3 score.

The Series then moved on to the Polo Grounds, and a huge crowd of some forty-eight thousand jammed every inch of Coogan's Bluff.

Bucky Harris selected Firpo Marberry for this vital game; it was Marberry who had saved the game for Washington the day before. John McGraw's choice was Hugh McQuillan.

Behind 3–0 in the fourth inning, the Senators pounded McQuillan for 3 hits and 2 runs before Rosy Ryan came in to relieve Hughie and stopped the Senators' surge. Ryan made history when he drove out a home run in the fourth inning. It was the first home run by a National League pitcher in a World Series.

The Giants were in front of the Senators by a 3–2 margin going into the ninth inning, when, with 1 out, Washington filled the bases. But reliever Johnny Watson retired the next two Senator batters and the Giants had their second win, 6–4.

In the fourth game of the Series, Goose Goslin, who had been a hitting fool since the first game, slugged his Senators to another victory as he pounded across 5 runs on 4 base hits. The Goose hit a homer with two men on base and was responsible for driving in 2 more runs. Goslin had two accomplices in this victory drive in Ossie Bluege and Earl McNeely. Both players smashed out 3 hits to help power the 7–4 Senators triumph that evened the Series at 2 games.

A crowd of more than forty-nine thousand fans sat stunned through the fifth game and only the most rabid Giant rooters had the heart to enjoy the game. There had been a feeling that Walter Johnson, the great Washington hurler, was under tremendous pressure in the first game, knowing the eyes of the nation were on him, and he would be a completely different pitcher in his next game.

But on this lovely afternoon, the great Johnson had even less stuff than in game one and he lost to the Giants, 6–2. The Giants pounded Johnson unmercifully for 13 base hits, including a 2-run homer by his pitching opponent Jack Bentley. Freddy Lindstrom, the Giant's eighteen-year-old phenom, battered the great Johnson for 4 solid base hits to lead the Giant attack.

Back in Washington for the sixth game of the Series, the Senators were still full of fight as Tom Zachary took the mound and demonstrated his mastery over the Giants. Zach hurled one of the finest games of his career as he outpitched Art Nehf and Ryan, allowing the Giants just 7 hits to eke out a 2–1 win for the fighting Senators, now back on even terms with the Giants, with 3 victories for each club.

The Series now had followed the pattern of 1909, with the National League winning all the odd-numbered games, and the Senators, the even-numbered contests. Would the rhythm continue into the seventh game?

The President and Mrs. Coolidge were on hand for the final game of the Series, and they were accompanied by some thirty-four thousand prayerful rooters as the Senators trotted onto the field for the historic game.

As the game began, the fans buzzed with interest and even anger when they noticed an obscure pitcher, Curly Ogden, who had barely won 9 games during the season, taking the mound for Washington.

Bucky Harris hadn't missed a trick throughout the Series. Now, when it came to the all-important seventh game, he completely surprised McGraw and the experts by starting Ogden. But Ogden was only the bait, and was quickly taken out of the game in favor of left-handed George Mogridge. McGraw didn't fall for the ruse immediately, and permitted left-handed Bill Terry to bat twice. But when Bill came up to bat for the third time, McGraw had Irish Meusel pinch-hit for Terry. Harris then inserted Marberry, and wound up with Johnson, and when the game went into extra, pulsating innings, Terry's big bat against the right-handed pitchers was sorely missed. Bill might have won the game, and Series, for the Giants.

"The Boy Wonder," Bucky Harris, led his Senators out of a scoreless tie in the fourth inning, when he drove a tremendous home run into the stands, and the Senators held on to that 1–0 advantage until the Giants came to bat in the sixth inning.

The first batter for the Giants, Ross Youngs, walked, and when George Kelly slashed a single to left field, Ross raced to third base. Meusel, hitting for Terry, lifted a fly ball to center field, scoring Youngs with the tying run after the catch. Wilson then singled, and two successive errors, by the usually reliable Joe Judge and Bluege, allowed Kelly and Wilson to score. The Giants now led, 3–1.

There was 1 out in the Senators' half of the eighth inning when Nemo Leibold, batting for

The headlines in this Minneapolis paper tell the story.

Tom Taylor, belted a long two-base drive to left-center field. Then Muddy Ruel delivered his first hit of the Series, a timely single to left, and Leibold went to third on the drive. Ben Tate, hitting for Marberry, walked to fill the bases. And now the Senators' fans were up on their feet, screaming for a base hit. The cheers of the crowd turned to a roar as Earl McNeely, who had hit the ball solidly throughout the Series, came up to the plate. But this time Earl hit a long fly ball to center field and now there were 2 outs.

Now the Senators were down to their last hitter, Bucky Harris, and Bucky took a terrific swipe at the first ball pitched, and missed. Another fastball, another swing for strike 2. Then, as the roaring of the Washington fans rose above the stadium, Harris set for the next pitch and

The Giants' captain, Frank Frisch (*left*), greets the captain of the Senators, Bucky Harris (*right*), prior to game one of the Series.

sent a hard ground ball sizzling down the third base line. Just as Giant third baseman Lindstrom reached for the ball, it hit a small pebble or clot of loose dirt, and bounced high over his head for a hit. Two runs scampered across the plate and it was now a 3–3 ball game as the cheers of the Senators' rooters threatened to shake the very foundation of the stadium.

John McGraw called on Art Nehf, his ace reliever, and Nehf ended the inning by retiring Sam Rice for the third out.

By now Harris was, as the saying went, "fresh out of pitchers," or so it seemed. But Bucky once again called on his "big guy," Walter Johnson, who had already lost 2 games in this Series.

There were literally millions of fans listening to the game on radio and the tenseness of the situation held them all, frozen to every word of the announcer, as George Kelly came up to hit. It was a paralyzing moment for all except Walter

Johnson who, in the shadow of a third loss, seemed to get new energy into his tired old arm. Walter simply blew Kelly down on three pitches. Ross Youngs walked, but was left on first base as Johnson retired the next two batters.

Now, with the tension near the bursting point, Johnson reached back for a new source of the youthful energy of old and in the tenth inning struck out Frisch. In the eleventh inning, Johnson momentarily faltered and walked Youngs. But he quickly regained his composure and reared back and fired three fastballs past Kelly to retire the Giants.

In the twelfth inning, after allowing Meusel to get a base hit, Johnson once again set the Giants down in one-two-three order.

In the Senators' half of the twelfth inning, Ruel, the first batter, hit a high pop fly between home and first. It should have been an easy out, but Hank Gowdy, circling under the ball, got his foot stuck in his own discarded mask, and just like a big bear caught in a bear trap, he tried to shake the mask loose, but failed and lost the ball, then lunged for it, and it dropped to the ground. While all of that was going on, Ruel never stopped running and he got to second base. Walter Johnson, the next batter, slapped a sharp ground ball to Travis Jackson at shortstop, who fumbled the ball, and everybody was safe. Earl McNeely hit a sharp ground ball toward third base, and, as Lindstrom bent forward to dig the ball out of the turf, it suddenly took a high hop over his head. Ruel thundered home from second base with the winning run, and the Washington Senators were world champions.

Washington went absolutely wild with jubilation, as though it had just received word of a great naval victory on some distant shores.

President Coolidge issued a presidential proclamation congratulating the new, unlikely world champions, the Washington Senators.

Senator heroes included pitcher Tom Zachary, who won 2 vital games; "the Big Train," Walter Johnson, for his skillful relief pitching in the final game; manager Bucky Harris for his leadership throughout the Series and his timely hitting throughout the year; Goose Goslin, who clubbed out a .344 Series average including 3 home runs; shortstop Roger Peckinpaugh, who had a .417 Series average; and Joe Judge, with a .385 average in the Series. Giant heroes included Bill Terry, with a .429 batting average; and Frank Frisch and Freddy Lindstrom, both of whom hit for a .333 average.

John McGraw was dazed by the loss of his second World Series in a row, and particularly by the loss of the twelve-inning seventh game, because of a pebble on the ground. Added to all this bitterness was his battle over salary differences with Bill Terry and other players, plus a scandal that had threatened to tear the fabric of the team apart in the middle of the pennant race. Suddenly the game wasn't much fun anymore.

A kind of pall settled over McGraw and the Giants as he gathered his team and pals for a final party before the players scattered. Somehow, even with all the delicious food and drink, it seemed as though the days of John McGraw and his glorious role in baseball were already beginning to slip into the past.

Pittsburgh Pirates Versus Washington Senators

Bucky Harris, who had signed a contract in 1924 for $7,000 before he knew he would be the team's manager, was handed a new contract for the 1925, 1926, and 1927 seasons. It called for a salary of $30,000 per season, making Bucky one of the highest-paid men in baseball.

Bucky was overjoyed with the result of the 1924 World Championship and his new three-year contract, but now had to face 1925 with a realization that he had won with an old team, which was now a year older.

The big problem, Harris and owner Clark Griffith decided, was the state of the club's aging pitching staff. Griff's solution—and it was one of his great triumphs—was to reach into the National League and pick up Dutch Ruether, onetime ace of the Brooklyn Robins. Then Griff worked out a deal with the Indians for Stan Coveleski, a 15-game winner in 1924. To bolster the infield, Griff obtained Yankee shortstop Everett Scott for the ailing Roger Peckinpaugh and, with his infield set and an outfield that consisted of Sam Rice, Earl McNeely, and one of the game's great sluggers, Goose Goslin, the Senators romped to their second straight pennant by some 8½ games over second-place Philadelphia.

In the National League, owner Barney Dreyfuss's Pirates finally snapped the Giants' string of titles as they easily captured the pennant from the second-place Giants by eight and a half

games. The Pirates were led by canny Bill McKechnie, who had never been more than a utility infielder for eleven years, but nevertheless was one of the brainiest baseball men in the league. The Pirates had a talented infield that consisted of Pie Traynor at third base, Glenn Wright at shortstop, Ed Moore at second base, and George Grantham at first. The outfield consisted of Max Carey, a .340 hitter; Kiki Cuyler, a slugger who hit .354 in his first season, and .357 the next. In left field was the surefooted, strong-armed Clyde Barnhart. The Pirate pitchers included Vic Aldridge, Emil Yde, Lee Meadows, and Babe Adams, the star of the 1909 World Series who was still winning games after eighteen major league seasons.

October 7 in Pittsburgh dawned cool and crisp. Forbes Field was festooned for the occasion and the jam-packed crowd, estimated at about forty-two thousand, could not wait for the opening pitch that would see the magnificent Walter Johnson match his cunning with the speed of the Pirates' Lee Meadows.

And Johnson did not disappoint the crowd. They gasped as the game began and Big Train just reared back and fired his fastball, which came in to the batters like a cannon shot. Moore and Carey, the first two hitters, quickly struck out, as if they were happy to get away from Johnson's blinding pitches. Then in the third inning, there was a shout of horror as a Johnson fastball pounded into Max Carey's body and Max fell as if shot. But only for a moment, and he was up and on first base. He was the only base runner for the Pirates until the fifth inning.

Meanwhile, Joe Harris, the Senators' right fielder, slugged a pitch by Meadows into the left field seats and the happy Senators had a 1–0 lead. In the fifth, they added 2 more runs as Harris and Bluege singled; then Sam Rice came through with another base hit and Harris and Bluege scampered home making the score 3–0, Washington. Meanwhile, Johnson had the Pirates at his mercy as he fanned 10, allowing the hit-hungry Pittsburgh batters just 5 hits and the Senators took the game 4–1.

However, joy in the Senator's clubhouse was tempered by the sudden and tragic news that the great Christy Mathewson, ill with the dreaded tuberculosis for many months, had died at his home in Saranac Lake, New York.

In the second game, Stan Coveleski, his bad back massaged and taped, was on the mound for the Senators, and Vic Aldridge was his opponent.

The early pattern of the game pointed to another Washington win, as the Senators took the lead in the second inning when Joe Judge slammed an Aldridge fastball into the stands for a home run. But the irrepressible Pie Traynor matched Judge's drive with a homer of his own, in the fourth inning, and the score was tied at 1.

Coveleski and Aldridge battled each other through four scoreless innings. Then, in the bottom of the eighth inning, Moore hit an easy roller to shortstop, but Peckinpaugh allowed the ball to roll right up his sleeve and Moore was safely on base. Then Cuyler slashed a home run over the center field fence and the Pirates quickly led by a 3–1 margin.

The Senators battled back in the ninth inning. Harris walked and McNeely was sent in to run for him. A single and a walk filled the bases; then Bobby Veach, pinch-hitting for Ruel, sent a high fly ball to center field, and McNeely scored after the catch to give Washington their second run. The Senators' rally died out after Ruether fanned Rice to give the Pirates an exciting 3–2 win.

The third game was played despite a windstorm that almost blew the pitchers off the mound, but Griff didn't mind the wind and his Senators won another nail-biting game from the Pirates, 4–3.

The Senators actually won the game in the seventh inning. Leibold walked and Harris then singled, and two men were on base as the Pittsburgh infield moved back on the grass as Goose Goslin came up to hit. Everybody was expecting the Goose to hit for the fences, and that belief was substantiated when Goose swung wildly at the first pitch and missed. Then on the next pitch, Goslin surprised the Pirates and every fan

Walter "Big Train" Johnson was magnificent as he won 2 games against the Pirates in the World Series by scores of 4–1 and 4–0.

The Senators' workhorse reliever Fred Marberry pitched 2 games against the Pirates, but lost both.

in the park by laying a perfect bunt down the third base line. Judge flied to center field and McNeely scored after the catch with the tying run. Then Joe Harris singled, to score Bucky Harris with the winning run.

From the moment Bucky Harris announced that Walter Johnson would pitch the next day, there wasn't much doubt about the outcome. His opponent on the mound for the Pirates was Emil Yde, and both Johnson and Yde pitched hitless ball until the fourth inning.

In the fourth inning, Sam Rice singled, Bucky Harris walked, and Goose Goslin strode up to the plate swinging three big bats. Swinging at the first pitch, the Goose caught it on the fat part of his big bat and sent the ball out into the distant center field bleachers for a 3-run homer and a 3–0 lead for the Senators. Joe Harris, the next batter, followed suit with another crashing drive into the bleachers and the score was 4–0. Those 4 runs were all the Senators got, but with Johnson hurling one of his finest games, they didn't need any more. Walter allowed the Bucs just 5 hits as he set the Pirates down in order in the eighth and ninth innings to give the Senators another win. The Senators, now with a Series

lead of 3 games to 1, seemed to have the championship in their hands.

The night before the fifth game, Bucky Harris wrestled with a momentous pitching decision for the next day. Should he use left-handed Dutch Ruether or Zachary, or perhaps Coveleski once again? Sensing victory, Harris gambled on Covey. It was a bad choice, for the Pirates, who had already beaten the ailing Covey, slugged him for 13 base hits and a 6–3 victory, to bring themselves within a game of a tie in the Series.

The Pittsburgh win threw Harris's pitching plans into a turmoil. For game six, he selected Alex Ferguson, and Bill McKechnie sent in Ray Kremer to oppose Fergy. But Bucky Harris had additional, more personal worries. For, in addition to his pitching problems, he was playing with a badly spiked hand that gave him a great deal of pain. It was taped and almost immobile and he was of little value to the team at the plate, but he did play well in the field.

The sixth game was a rarity, as both teams, knowing it was a decisive game, took no chances and played strictly defensive baseball. The Pirates, with Pie Traynor and Glenn Wright leading the way, were just a mite better. In the fifth inning, Moore slugged a long home run to give the Bucs the big run they needed to win by a 3–2 score. The Senators scored on Goslin's home run in the first inning. Judge singled and scored on Peckinpaugh's double for the Senators' other score. Both pitchers were outstanding, but Kremer deserved to win the contest, yielding 7 hits, while Ferguson gave up 6 hits in the seven innings he worked.

Now the World Series was knotted, 3 games to 3.

Few among the crowd assembled on October 5 thought the game would be played as a cold, torrential rain pounded the field. However, Judge Landis ordered that the game be played and the teams trudged onto the muddy field.

Once again, Harris called on his great star, Walter Johnson, who was opposed by Vic Aldridge. Each pitcher was making his third start of the Series.

Knowing that Johnson's injured leg would not allow him great mobility and that he would not be able to fully utilize his fastball, the Senators decided to go for an early lead in order to give Walter some breathing room. In the first inning, the Senators, aided by a couple of base hits, a walk, a balk, and a wild pitch, scored 4 runs, and it looked like a runaway for Washington.

But the Pirates gamely hung in and pecked away at the lead; in the third inning, they put together 3 straight singles and a two-base hit for 3 runs. Now it was a 4–3 game.

In the fifth inning, Rice and Goslin singled in succession. Joe Harris, a hitting fool throughout the Series, smashed a long double, scoring 2 runs. Now the Senators had a 6–3 lead.

But the Pirates put together doubles by Kiki Cuyler and Max Carey to add another run, making the score 6–4.

The Pirates tied the score in the fateful seventh inning as Moore reached first base on an error. Carey doubled, scoring Moore. Pie Traynor tripled to left-center field, scoring Carey, to make it a 6–6 game.

On the quagmire that once was a diamond, the Senators went ahead in the eighth inning. As if he had to atone for his several errors, Peckinpaugh blasted a long home run into the bleachers and it was now a 7–6 game with Washington in front.

In the Pittsburgh half of the eighth inning, Johnson, tiring, but holding on for dear life, pitched carefully to Wright and McInnis and got both men on fly balls. Johnson then whizzed two fastballs past Smith for strikes, but on the third pitch, Smith caught a fastball and blasted it into left field for a long double. Then Yde, running for Smith, scampered all the way home when Carson Bigbee, hitting for the pitcher, doubled. The Pirates now came on like gangbusters. Moore walked and Carey smashed a hard drive right at Peckinpaugh, but Roger's throw to second base was off the mark and all hands were safe. It was Peck's eighth error, a Series record. Now the bases were full as Cuyler came up to hit; he promptly came through with a line drive two-base hit scoring 2 runs and it was 9–7, Pittsburgh. The game, and Series, ended with Goslin vainly trying to get the big hit, but he struck out, and the final score remained 9–7, Pittsburgh.

After the final game, many Pittsburgh players and fans gathered at the Senators' dressing room searching for Walter Johnson. And always the message was the same: "We're glad we won, but sorry you had to be the loser, Walter."

"Well," said Johnson. "We'll get you next year." But two years later, after a series of accidents and a severe bout with the flu, Johnson retired and never pitched another game in the major leagues.

The 1925 American League champs, the Washington Senators

1926

St. Louis Cardinals
Versus
New York Yankees

From the first day the Cardinals reported at Terrell Hills, Texas, for their 1926 spring training, there was one man who never had any doubt where the Cardinals were headed. That was the fiery, aggressive Texan, manager Rogers Hornsby, who had been one of baseball's greatest hitters since he entered the league in 1915.

Hornsby began his major league career in 1915 with the Cardinals, and before he was traded to the Giants in 1927, managed to annex a batting average that astonished even the shrewdest experts. In 1915, Rogers hit for a .246 average. The next year he hit .313. Then followed the most incredible batting career in the history of baseball. In 1917 he hit .327, then in 1918 he hit .318, .370 in 1919, .397 in 1921, .401 in 1922, .384 in 1923, .424 in 1924, and .403 in 1925. No one in baseball, not Cobb, Speaker, Ruth, Wagner, Williams, DiMaggio, Mantle, or Mays, has ever had batting averages that could compare with those of "the Rajah." He is still considered the greatest right-handed batter in baseball history.

Rogers Hornsby was a strange man. He was sunny and happy one moment, moody and surly the next. A man who walked alone, he was called a mystery man, and thought of as one who played a dark, sinister role on the big-league stage, a thorn in the side of club owners.

According to his own account,* when he called his players together for the first squad meeting of the 1926 season, he told them: " 'I want you guys to listen to every word I say. We are going to win the pennant this year. Now, don't go around telling everyone we're going to win. But we are going to win just the same. If there's anybody here who doesn't believe we are going to win, why, there's a train leaving for the North tonight, and our secretary, Clarence Lloyd, will have a ticket for him. I'll trade anyone who doesn't think we are going to win. If there's one man here who thinks we're a second division ball club, well, I just don't want him around here.'

"We had a well-balanced pitching staff with Flint Rhem, Jesse Haines, Bill Sherdel, Herman Bell and when I heard that Joe McCarthy of the Cubs decided he didn't want Grover Alexander anymore and had asked for waivers, we got Alex for the waiver price of $4,000. That was one of the best bargains in the history of the St. Louis Cardinals.

"The National League race was a battle all

---

*The Hornsby quotations in this chapter are from Rogers Hornsby, *My Kind of Baseball*, and from interviews with the author, in 1946 and 1950–51, on his *Sports Show*, on New York radio station WINS.

through the summer. It was late in September, with only a couple of days of the season still to go, before we finally clinched the pennant by beating the Giants at the Polo Grounds, to make it impossible for the Reds, who had been crowding us down the final stretch, to overhaul us.

"Nobody figured the Cardinals had a chance against the powerhouse Yankees in the World Series. The Yanks were regarded as one of baseball's greatest teams with too much power for our young Cardinals. Miller Huggins had the two greatest sluggers in Babe Ruth and Lou Gehrig. With Babe in the outfield, the Yanks had Bob Meusel and Earle Combs. Gehrig's fellow infielder's were Tony Lazzeri, Mark Koenig and Joe Dugan. Hank Severeid, Pat Collins and Ben Bengough were the catchers.

"Huggins had great pitchers too, in Herb Pennock, Urban Shocker, and Waite Hoyt, Bob Shawkey, and Dutch Ruether."

By an odd shuffle of the baseball cards, Miller Huggins, manager of the Cardinals from 1913 to 1917, was now the manager of the Yankees, and with Babe Ruth leading the way with 47 home runs, had just managed to beat out the second-place Indians by 3 games in an exciting pennant race.

While many of the stars of Huggins's 1923 championship team—Ruth, Muesel, Dugan, Hoyt, Pennock, Shawkey, Jones, and Bengough were on the roster, Huggins had made a number of vital changes in his lineup. He replaced Wally Pipp with a kid first baseman, Lou Gehrig; and had a new keystone combination, shortstop Mark Koenig and second baseman Tony Lazzeri, who performed brilliantly. Earle Combs had pushed Whitey Witt from his center field job, and Urban Shocker and Dutch Ruether were added to the Yank pitching staff.

Hornsby's team included Les Bell at third base, Tommy Thevenow at short stop, Hornsby at second base, Jim Bottomley at first; Bob O'Farrell was the catcher, and Chick Hafey, Taylor Douthit, and Billy Southworth were in the outfield. Pitchers eligible for the Series included, Jesse Haines, Willie Sherdel, Flint Rhem, Bill Hallahan, Herman Bell, and Grover Cleveland Alexander.

"Sherdel was really the hard-luck pitcher in the Series," said Hornsby. "Bill, a little guy

with an old-fashioned slow ball was up against the crafty left hander, Herb Pennock, and we lost the first game, 2 to 1. Pennock allowed us just 3 base hits. But with a break here and there, we could have won this game."

In the second game, Grover Cleveland Alexander was opposed by Urban Shocker, a 19-game winner during the regular season.

The Yankees began the scoring in the second inning as Meusel, Lazzeri, and Dugan singled in succession. Attempting to break up a Yank double steal, Alex threw the ball into left field and 2 runs came home. In the third inning, Combs singled but was left stranded as Alexan-

In one of the most dramatic moments in Series history, thirty-nine-year-old Grover Cleveland Alexander came on in relief of Jesse Haines in the seventh inning of the seventh game of the 1926 Series and calmly proceeded to strike out dangerous Yankee Tony Lazzeri, with the bases full, to end the Yankee threat. Then he held the Yankees to win the game and Series for the Cardinals.

Babe Ruth was simply magnificent in this Series. All he accomplished for the Yankees was to hit 4 home runs and bat an even .300.

der got the side out. Throughout the remainder of the game, Alex was masterful as he set down 21 Yankee hitters in a row.

Meanwhile, the Cards tied the score in the third inning when Douthit bunted and beat out the throw. Southworth singled and then Hornsby advanced both runners with a sacrifice bunt. Then Bottomley slashed a single to left, scoring Douthit and Southworth. The game remained tied at 2–2 until the seventh inning, when Southworth rifled a fastball into the left field seats for a home run with O'Farrell on base to give the Cards a 4–2 edge.

In the ninth inning, Tommy Thevenow hit a high fly ball that rolled by Babe Ruth, and while Ruth searched for the ball, which had rolled into a gulley, Thevenow raced around the bases for an inside-the-park home run and the Cards romped to a 6–2 victory.

"We moved back to Sportsman's Park St. Louis for the third game of the Series," said Hornsby, "and we got a tremendous welcome from our fans. It was a welcome that became even happier when Jesse Haines pitched us to a 4 to 0 shutout over the Yankees and Dutch Ruether. Jesse helped us out with a 2 run homer and allowed the Yankees just 5 base hits."

The fourth game, at Sportsman's Park, on October 6, was a slugfest with both teams hitting the ball to all parts of the ballpark for 14 hits apiece. The outstanding performer was Babe Ruth. In the third game, won by St. Louis, Ruth had downgraded the shutout win pitched by Jesse Haines. "I'll kill that guy the next time I face him," glowered Ruth. "Tomorrow I'll hit two homers."

For once, Ruth's boast was an understatement, for he slugged 2 consecutive home runs off Flint Rhem and then another off Herm Bell, to pace the Yankees to a 10–5 romp.

Cardinal fans were quite sober the following day as the crafty Herb Pennock repeated his first-game win over Bill Sherdel, winning 3–2 this time, in ten thrilling innings.

The win gave the Yankees a big 3 games to 2 advantage as they returned to Yankee Stadium to wind up the Series.

Hornsby talked to his team in the locker room before the game: " 'If we can't do it today, there ain't any more Series. But, goddamn it, there is going to be more Series. We're going out there today and we've got to win and we've got to win tomorrow. So, get out there and fight your butts off; knock the ball down the pitcher's throat and don't concede one damn thing to those Yanks.' "

"Alex pitched for us in that sixth game," said Hornsby, "and we finally got around to giving him some decent support. Herm Bell was our big guy in this one as he drove out 5 runs with a homer, double and a single. We won by 10 to 2, and so we had the Series all squared away again."

Hornsby continued: "After the game, the second for Alex and his second win, I told him to take it easy that night.

" 'I may need you, Alex,' I told him. 'You're the best we've got and if we get into any trouble you're it. So get to bed as early as you can and get some rest. You've got a long winter ahead when you can do whatever you please.'

" 'I'll be ready, if you need me, Rog,' was all he said, and I didn't worry about him. I knew if he could walk from the bull pen to the mound he'd be all right if we got into a jam.

"We got into the jam, all right. We got out in front, scoring three runs after Ruth hit a homer in the third inning off Haines, but the Yankees made it 3 to 2 in the fifth inning, and in the seventh the Yanks filled the bases with two outs. Jesse Haines had a great knuckle ball, but he had been throwing it so much that a blister had developed on his gripping finger. And when he walked Gehrig, filling the bases, I knew we had to do something. Haines had mentioned that the blister was now beginning to bother his control. So with the bases filled and two outs, I figured Alexander was our best bet.

"People have asked me many times about what happened that day, in that seventh inning clutch, when I called Alex in from the bull pen to relieve Haines. They all wanted to know what I said and what Alex said, and whether he had a bottle out here in the bull pen, whether he had a tough night the night before.

"Well, I left my position at second base and walked out toward the bull pen to meet him as he came in. Naturally I wanted to get a close look at him, to see what kind of shape he was

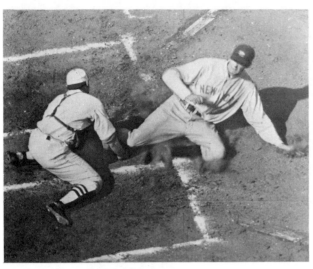

Outfielder Bob Meusel attempts to score from second base in game six, but a great throw by Bill Southworth to catcher Bob O'Farrell nabs him at the plate.

in. And I also wanted to tell him what the situation was, just in case he'd been dozing. He was a great guy to relax, and probably had got himself a little shut-eye in the bull pen. But he was wide awake when I met him. His eyes were clear as usual, and he knew we were in deep trouble.

" 'We're still ahead, three to two,' I told Alex. 'It's the seventh inning, two out, but the bases are filled and Tony Lazzeri's up.'

"Alex didn't say very much. 'Bases filled, eh?

" 'Well, don't worry about me. I'm all right. And I guess there's nothing much to do except give Tony a lot of hell.' "

Alex warmed up in that leisurely, methodical way of his. But the ball fairly sizzled as it came in to his catcher, Bob O'Farrell. He tossed half a dozen pitches and announced he was ready to pitch to Lazzeri, the great young star from the Pacific Coast League.

Alex was outwardly calm and as unconcerned as if it were a spring exhibition game. And

throughout the park there came a silence. The fans slid forward in their seats, tense and anxious.

What occurred in the next few minutes is recorded for posterity on the Grover Cleveland Alexander placque at the Baseball Hall of Fame in Cooperstown, New York.

Tony Lazzeri was an absolute terror in the pinches, ranking second only to Babe Ruth in runs batted in with 114. Now with the eyes of forty-five thousand fans watching him, Tony took the first pitch for a strike, then drove his bat viciously into the next one, sending a slashing drive down the left field line, foul by inches.

"A foot made the difference between being a hero and a bum," said Alex after the game.

Alexander wasn't wasting any pitches with Lazzeri. He shot in another fastball that cut across the outside corner of the plate, and Lazzeri, swinging with everything he had, from the heels, missed the ball for strike 3.

Even the partisan Yankee crowd roared approval for the marvelous pitching exhibition of Grover Cleveland Alexander.

"Two innings still had to be played," recounted Hornsby, "but Alex protected that squeaky 3 to 2 lead we had, and emerged as the popular hero of the Series, one of the most exciting that has ever been played. And being in it, we all felt that way about it.

"That was a great celebration on the way home. Alex drank enough black coffee to float a battleship as we tried to have him in condition for the great reception we knew was ahead of us back in St. Louis.

"St. Louis certainly did put on a show for us and that great Cardinal bunch that won the first pennant and world championship. The big reception, of course, was when we won the pennant. They say that no New York celebration, over a Lindbergh or a returning Army, ever was a greater celebration than the one they had for us in 1926 after we beat the Yankees."

New York Yankees Versus Pittsburgh Pirates

Prior to 1927, the Yankees had inspired no great dread as World Series competitors. Of the four World Series in which they had opposed the National League, they had been successful only in 1923. But in 1927 they began a golden era in which they paid back the National League for early humiliations. For the Yankees, it was a season of overpowering conquest and one-sided triumphs. To get close to the Bombers was to invite destruction.

Joe Judge, the great star of the Senators, said it best: "Those Yankees not only beat the tar out of you, they tear your heart out. I wish the season was over right now so we wouldn't have to play them anymore."

The pennant was clinched on Labor Day, and the Yankees went on to win 110 games to finish 29 games in front of the second-place Philadelphia Athletics.

The Pittsburgh Pirates, under former shortstop Donie Bush, had just managed to squeak by the Cardinals by 2½ games, while the Giants finished in third place, 2 games behind the Cards.

The Pirates were no match for the power-laden Yankees, but they had a well-balanced team with several outstanding hitters. Paul Waner, their great outfielder, led the league in batting with a super .380 average. His kid brother, Lloyd, was right behind with a stunning .355 average; third baseman Pie Traynor, one of the great hitters on that club, hit for a .342 average,

and George Grantham, Clyde Barnhart, and Kiki Cuyler all hit over .300. Pitchers included Lee Meadows, with 19 wins during the season; Carmen Hill, with 22; Ray Kremer, with 19; and Vic Aldridge, 15.

It was often said that the Yankees won the 1927 Series before it even started. It was to open in Pittsburgh, but just before the first game the Yankees put on a hitting demonstration during batting practice that awed the curious Pitt players who happened to be watching.

Ruth, Gehrig, Meusel, and Lazzeri ripped one ball after another over the center field fence. It was a display of hitting that no Pirate players had ever seen and it left them shaken.

The first game in Pittsburgh, on October 5, began under fair skies as Donie Bush selected Ray Kremer to hurl the first game, while Miller Huggins selected Waite Hoyt. Each club picked up a run in the first inning. In the Yankee half, there were 2 outs when Ruth singled on Kremer's first pitch. Then Lou Gehrig tripled to center and Ruth scored the Yankees' first run.

The Pirates quickly responded as Lloyd Waner singled and sped on to third base when brother Paul doubled. Glenn Wright flied to center field and Waner scored after the catch to make it a 1–1 game.

The Yankees picked up their attack in the third inning when Grantham fumbled Mark Koenig's ground ball; then Ruth slapped his second

May 23, 1927

My dear Mr. Barrow:

As requested in your telegram of even date, I am giving you be-low our office records, made from the New York player contracts, which were sent here for approval:

Bengough, Bernard O. - Contract 4/8/27 approved 4/13/27. $8000 for season of 1927.

Collins, Patrk. E. - Contract 2/15/27 approved 4/13/27. $7000 for season of 1927.

Combs, Earle B. - Contract 3/12/27. Approved 4/13/27. $10,500 for season of 1927.

Dugan, Joseph A. - Contract 4/8/27. Approved 4/13/27. $12,000 for season of 1927.

Gehrig, H. L. - Contract 4/8/27. Approved 4/13/27. $8000 for season 1927.

Hoyt, Waite C. - Contract 2/15/27. Approved 4/13/27. $11,000 for season of 1927. Club will pay player a bonus of $1,000 if he wins twenty (20) of the games he pitches for the Club during the championship season of 1927.

Koenig, Mark A. - Contract 4/8/27. Approved 4/13/27. $7000 for season 1927.

Lazzeri, Anthony - Contract 4/8/27. Approved 4/13/27. $8000 for season 1927. Club further agrees to pay travelling expenses, including Pullman accommodations and meals enroute of the player's wife from San Francisco to New York, at the beginning of the 1927 playing season, and to pay the like traveling ex-penses of the player and his wife from New York to San Francisco at the close of said season.

Meusel, Robt. W. - Contract approved 4/13/27. $13,000 for season of 1927, and an aggregate salary of $13,000 for his skilled services during the playing season of 1928, including the World's series or any other official series in which the Club may participate, and in any receipts of which the player may be entitled to share in each of said years.

Moore, Wilcey - Contract 2/21/27. Approved 4/13/27. $2500 for season of 1927. Club will pay an additional sum of $500, if player is retained in service of Club for entire championship season of 1927.

Pennock, Herb. J. - Contract approved 4/13/27. $17,500 for season of 1927, and an aggregate salary of $17,500 for his skilled ser-vices during each of the playing seasons of 1928 and 1929, including the World's series or any other official series in which the club may participate, and in any re-ceipts of which the player may be entitled to share in each of said years. If the player wins 25 twenty-five (25) of the ball games he pitches for the Club in any year covered by this contract, towit, 1927, 1928, and 1929, the club will in that event pay the player a bonus of $1000 at the close of the playing season of such year

Ruether, Walter H. - Contract 4/8/27. Approved 4/13/27. $11,000 for season 1927. Club will pay player bonus of $1000 if the player wins fifteen (15) of the games he pitches for the Club during the championship season of 1927.

Ruth, George H. - Contract 4/8/27. Approved 4/13/27. $70,000 for the season of 1927, and an aggregate salary of $70,000 each for the seasons of 1928 and 1929, including the World's Series or any other official series in which the player may participate, and in any receipts in which the play-er may be entitled to share in each of said years.

Shawkey, J. Robt. - Contract 4/8/27. Approved 4/13/27. $10,500 for season 1927.

Shocker, Urban J. - Contract approved 4/13/27. $13,500 for season of 1927.

A historical letter to Ed Barrow, the Yankees' general manager

single to left. Gehrig walked, filling the bases; Meusel walked, forcing in Koenig; and Lazzeri hit to short, forcing Meusel at second base, but the double play was avoided and Ruth scored on the play. Gehrig was caught between third base and home on an attempted double steal. But Smith, the Pirates' catcher, fumbled the throw and Gehrig scored for the third run of the inning.

Each team scored once in the fifth, the Yankees when Koenig stroked a two-base hit, Gehrig hit a fly ball to center, and then Koenig scored on Ruth's infield out. The Pirates, undaunted, came right back on a Waner double and Barnhart single that scored Waner. The score was now 5–3, New York.

Pirate fans raised quite a clamor in the eighth inning as Waite Hoyt, the Yankee ace, was knocked out of the box after Wright and Traynor singled in succession. But Miller Huggins relieved Hoyt with Wilcy Moore, and Moore held the Pirates in check for the first Yankee win, a 5–4 victory.

One of the most amazing players ever to wear the Yankee pinstripes, Wilcy Moore was brought up from the South Atlantic League in 1927. His pitching assets were limited, but quite adequate. It consisted of a sinker ball, a low fastball that broke sharply downward as it reached the plate, almost flawless control, and nerves of steel. He also had, or thought he had, a curveball, and he would beg Huggins to let him throw it once in a while. But Hug always shook him off. "Your curveball," said Huggins, "wouldn't go around a button on my vest."

Moore came up to the Yankees in 1927 and was utilized almost exclusively as a relief pitcher, yet he won 19 games. Those who played with Moore say he was the best relief pitcher in the history of baseball.

The Yankees laughed at Moore's attempts to hit the ball. And with good reason. He had a perfect stance at the plate and a near perfect swing. The trouble was that he always swung in the same spot, no matter where the ball was pitched. One year, Ruth bet Wilcy $300 that he wouldn't get 3 hits all season. He got 5 hits. After the season, when he got home he wrote Ruth: "The $300 came in very handy. I used it to buy two mules. I named one Babe and the other Ruth."

The Yankee shortstop Mark Koenig sparked the Yankees in the Series with a smashing .500 average as they swept the Pirates.

Huggins had a surprise for the second game. He started young George Pipgras, who in half a season in 1927 had compiled a 10-3 record. Pipgras outpitched three Pirate hurlers—Aldridge, Cvengros, and Dawson—allowing the hit-hungry Pirates just 7 hits, as he coasted to a 6–2 victory, for the Yankees' second straight win.

Huggins selected Herb Pennock for the first game in New York, defying those pundits who claimed that no left-handed hurler could beat the Pirates. And for seven innings, pitching against Lee Meadows, Pennock did not allow a single hit. The way he was pitching, it looked as if he would be the first pitcher to win a no-hit Series game. Ironically, he was stalled by his own teammates, for in the seventh inning the Yankees drove Meadows from the mound by scoring 6 runs. While sitting on the bench for nearly thirty minutes as his teammates pounded Pirate pitchers, Pennock's arm cooled off. In the eighth inning he got rid of Glenn Wright, the first batter, but Pie Traynor singled, Barnhart dou-

Pirates star Lloyd Waner beats out an infield hit in the fourth game of the Series as Lou Gehrig attempts to put him out.

bled, and Pie scored the first Pittsburgh run. In the ninth inning, Lloyd Waner singled for the final Pirate base hit.

Pennock had missed a no-hit game and a shutout as well. But his marvelous 3-hit performance, and 8–1 victory, still stands as one of the finest ever seen in any World Series game.

It is doubtful that there has been any finish with as much drama as the fourth game of the 1927 Series. Carmen Hill started for the Pirates, and he was opposed by Wilcy Moore, a surprise choice.

Besides not being able to handle Babe Ruth, Hill did a fine job of pitching. Ruth drove in Combs in the first inning with a base hit, and in the fifth inning he blasted a long home run with Combs again on base. It was the Babe's second homer of the Series, and now the Yankees were riding high and handsome with a 3–1 lead until the Pirates tied the game in the seventh inning.

John Miljus, a big, hard-throwing right-hander, relieved Hill in the seventh inning and battled Moore, pitch for pitch, until the fateful ninth. Combs walked to open the inning, and Mark Koenig caught the Pirates' infield by surprise as he laid down a perfect bunt and beat it out. Ruth was purposely walked. The bases were full, with nobody out, the score tied at 3–3, and the mighty Lou Gehrig, who had hit 47 home runs during the season, was the batter.

Speedy Earle Combs was edging off third base with each pitch, trying to upset Miljus. But John went about his business and struck out the mighty Gehrig, and then had the fans roaring as he fanned Meusel on three fastballs.

Now it was up to Tony Lazzeri.

Then it happened. Miljus threw a fastball, with something extra on the ball. It broke so sharply that catcher Johnny Gooch lost the pitch and Combs dashed home with the run that gave the Yankees the World Series.

It was a strange ending for the Yankees' greatest season, for here was a team that was power personified, a club that had set a season home run record and swept a World Series, achieving its greatest victory through the lowly medium of a single wild pitch.

Perhaps the strangest part of the 1927 World Series—and it is a tribute to the versatility of that Yankee team—was that they had won on their pitching, rather than their slugging ability; they had won because the Pirates did not have a single good inning against Yankee pitchers.

The Yankee winners' shares amounted to $5,592, while the individual Pittsburgh shares came to $3,728. It was quite an increase over the Pirates' previous World Series purse, when they had received the sum of $1,825 for winning the 1909 Series over the Detroit Tigers.

New York Yankees
Versus
St. Louis Cardinals

It happened one afternoon late in the 1928 season, as the Yankees, leading the American League, were heading into Chicago for a series with the White Sox. Not only were the Yankees leading the American League, but they were also having a great deal of fun off the field. Often, the players would come into the hotel after a night of carousing just as the sun was coming up the next morning. Of course, chief among the celebrants was Babe Ruth, who was leading the league in home runs, as well as leading the team in after-hours visits to every night spot in every town in which the Yankees played.

Manager Huggins decided this day to remonstrate with the Babe. "I don't like to do it," Huggins said to Mark Roth, the Yankees' traveling secretary, "but it's for his own good. I'll ball the hell out of him for his after-hours tours, but just before game time today."

But when he reached the clubhouse, Huggins decided to wait until after the game.

That afternoon, Ruth hit 2 home runs, one off Red Faber, the other off the ace of the Red Sox staff, Ted Lyons. That evening after dinner, Huggins and Roth were sitting in the hotel lobby when the Babe stepped jauntily off the elevator. He wore a pair of spotless white flannels, brown

sports jacket, a huge, fancy Panama hat with a brown sash around the crown, and brown and white sport shoes. "Judge," as the players called him, was really stepping out for another good time.

Roth, who knew that Huggins hadn't talked to the Babe at the ballpark, poked Huggins. "Go on, Hug. Talk to him now."

"Oh go shut up," said the manager.

"Go on," said Roth. "He's gonna stay up late again."

"So what," said Huggins. "He got three hits today and won the game with those two homers. Let's go to the movies."

The Yanks were still out in front of the field, late in August, by some 17 games, and then a flock of injuries threatened to derail the Bronx express.

Ruth sprained his ankle and was so crippled he could barely walk. Gehrig was taped from head to foot; Pennock's arm was sore; Lazzeri was injured; Combs, the flashy outfielder, had a bad wrist; and Joe Dugan's knee was so sore he could barely walk.

Leo Durocher, a brash, but good defensive shortstop, had been brought up by the Yankees in 1925, but had been sent back down to St. Paul. Now, in 1928, Leo was brilliant.

Shortstop Leo Durocher was the defensive magician for the Yankees in the 1928 Series.

On September 9, there was a memorable doubleheader against the Athletics, and a crowd of more than eighty thousand attended the game. The die was cast for this series. The Yankees knew that unless they won both games, they were finished. Rousing themselves from their lethargy, they defeated the A's in both games. George Pipgras pitched a brilliant shutout in the first game, and "Schoolboy" Waite Hoyt took the second game.

Now the Yankees were in first place to stay, and they clinched the pennant in Detroit on September 28. Babe Ruth had another incredible season, smashing out 54 home runs. Lou Gehrig led the club in batting with a resounding .374 average. Hoyt won 23 games and Pipgras won 24.

But the Yankees were just about held together by yards of adhesive tape as they moved into the Series against a tough St. Louis team, managed by the canny former Pittsburgh skipper, Bill McKechnie.

The Cards captured their second pennant by the slender margin of 2 games over their old rivals from New York, the Giants. There had been a number of vital changes in the team since 1926. The two most important included a new second base-shortstop combination in Frankie

Frisch and Rabbit Maranville. Jim Wilson became the regular catcher, while the pitchers included Grover Cleveland Alexander, Bill Sherdel, and Jesse Haines, who were expected to give the Yankees a most difficult Series.

It was interesting to note that more than half of the sportswriters covering the Series selected the Cardinals to win, in view of the injured state of the Yankee stars. But since 1927 it had been a poor policy to sell the Yankees short in a World Series. And experience should have taught that when Babe Ruth was seemingly handicapped with injuries, he was increasingly dangerous. As matters did turn out, an injured Babe Ruth gave perhaps the greatest of all World Series hitting exhibitions.

In the 1926 Series, manager Rogers Hornsby had given Ruth little opportunity to hit the ball, walking him 12 times in seven games. In this Series, Bill McKechnie decided he would pitch to Ruth: He was walked only once and was afforded every opportunity to hit the ball, and he took advantage of the chances. He finished the Series with the highest batting average ever of a regular player in the Series, .625, as he clubbed out 10 hits, including 3 homers and 3 two-base hits in 16 times at bat. He scored 9 times and batted in 4 more runs. Gehrig was right behind Ruth for honors. He slugged 4 home runs, a double, and a single for a stunning .545 average.

When the Series opened at Yankee Stadium, on October 4, Willie Sherdel was on the mound for the Pirates. He was opposed by his old rival, Waite Hoyt. And Sherdel wasn't any luckier than he had been in the 1926 Series, as the Yankees won the opener by a 4–1 margin.

Hoyt was in marvelous form; he allowed the Birds just 3 hits while the Yankees scored in the first, fourth, and eighth innings to wrap up the ball game.

Following the same pitching schedule employed by Hornsby in the 1926 World Series, McKechnie selected Grover Cleveland Alexander to pitch the second game for the Cardinals, while Miller Huggins's choice was his second-game winner in the 1927 Series, George Pipgras. But Alex was now forty-one years old, and the 1928 Yankees had a greater awareness of their

The flawless home-run swing of Babe Ruth as he pounded out a 3-run homer in this Series

might and power than the 1926 club had had; they drove the grand old star out of the box in the second inning with a 4-run barrage. His successor was a left-handed spitball pitcher, Clarence Mitchell, who could not hold the Yankee sluggers, and the Yankees easily romped to a 9–3 victory.

The teams traveled to St. Louis for the third contest, and a great crowd of more than thirty-nine thousand rabid Cardinal fans packed the ballpark and roared their support for their team.

On the mound for the Yankees was Tom Zachary, and Jesse Haines was his rival for this vital third game. The Cards got off to a flying start in the first inning by jumping on Zachary for 2 runs, but the Yanks came roaring back as Lou Gehrig slashed a tremendous home run over the center field fence in the second inning.

The Cards were leading 2–1 in the fourth inning, when Babe Ruth led off the inning with a base hit. Then Gehrig slugged his second homer to give the Yanks a 3–2 edge. In the fifth inning, the Cards scored a run to tie the game at 3–3.

In the sixth inning, the Yanks tore into Cardinal pitching for 3 runs and in the seventh the Yankees sewed up the game with another tally for a 7–3 victory.

The Yankees had now taken 3 straight World Series games from the Cards and were just 1 game short of another Series triumph.

Waite Hoyt started his second game of the Series, and once again he was opposed by Bill Sherdel for St. Louis. The Cards touched Hoyt for a run in the third inning, but Ruth tied the game in the fourth with a tremendous home run blast. When the Cardinals came up to hit in the fourth inning, they scored a go-ahead run to give them a 2–1 lead.

Then occurred one of the most bitter arguments in World Series history.

Mark Koenig grounded out, and Ruth came up to hit. Sherdel quickly shot 2 strikes over on the Babe, then caught him napping. With his foot still on the pitching rubber, Sherdel quickly whirled and shot another strike across the plate.

Then all hell broke loose.

"You can't do this," Ruth yelled.

"The hell I can't," said Sherdel. "I just did."

Huggins and the Yankees rushed from the dugout and swirled around umpire Pfirman, behind the plate. Wilson turned on Pfirman. Sherdel charged in to home plate with Frisch and Maranville at his side. The Yankees yelled that the pitch was illegal; the Cards screamed that Ruth had been struck out.

Pfirman pushed the players aside, and said, "Ruth isn't out. Sherdel will have to pitch all over to him."

"But it is legal," McKechnie and his players shouted at Pfirman. "It is a perfectly legal pitch according to the National League rules."

The other umpires—Cy Riegler, Brick Owens, and Bill McGowan—rushed to Pfirman and they all discussed the pitch and finally agreed it was legal. However, they neglected to inform the rival managers or the two pitchers. Finally, when all of the pushing, shoving, and shouting was over, it was agreed that Ruth would be allowed to hit once more.

The Babe promptly belted the first pitch into the right field seats, tying the score. And then Lou Gehrig hammered an even longer drive over the left field wall, and the Yankees were out in front. The Yanks continued to pound away at Sherdel, and 2 more runs scored, making it 6–3. In the eighth inning, with old Grover Cleveland Alexander on the mound, Cedric Durst clubbed a fastball for a home run. Koenig grounded out, and then Ruth hit his third home run of the game in his third successive time at bat.

The ninth inning was eventful, as it gave the colorful Pepper Martin his first chance to crack into a World Series box score. Pepper ran for Earl Smith, who had singled. He went to second, stole third base, and then scored on Wattie Holm's infield out. There were 2 outs when Ernie Orsatti and Andy High each singled to start a Cardinal rally. Frisch then hit a long foul fly ball that seemed headed for the seats, but the Babe, despite a shower of confetti and score cards tossed in his direction, hobbled over, leaned into the box seats, and made a great one-handed catch to end the game. As he caught the ball, Ruth proudly held it high in the air, and jogged into the clubhouse, and the crowd roared a tribute to the Bambino.

The 1928 World Champion New York Yankees

The Yankees had won the game, 7–3, and wrapped up their second straight 4-game sweep of the World Series.

No championship was ever celebrated as boisterously as this Yankee sweep. The sky was the limit, and the fun and high jinx started from the moment the Yankees' *Special* train pulled out of St. Louis for the ride back to New York. The wildest feature of the wild night was a midnight parade of the players right through the entire train, led by catcher Pat Collins, without pajamas, and followed by Babe Ruth, Lou Gehrig, Tony Lazzeri, and the fresh rookie Leo Durocher. Everyone on the train had to yield his shirt or his pajama top or it would be ripped off.

Huggins went through the train the next morning asking, "Did anyone see my teeth? I can't find them."

1929

Philadelphia Athletics Versus Chicago Cubs

Who was the smartest manager ever to lead a team in a World Series?

There have been many candidates: John J. McGraw, Miller Huggins, Joe McCarthy, Casey Stengel, Leo Durocher, Charlie Dressen, Billy Southworth, Walt Alston, Billy Martin, among others. But in our opinion, only one man in World Series history merits the adjective "Napoleonic." The smartest manager in World Series play was Connie Mack.

The smart managers mentioned above became famous largely for their successful application of what in baseball is known as "the percentage." The percentage says that a left-handed pinch hitter who pulls the ball should be utilized at a certain moment in a late-inning rally. The percentage also says that a pitcher who throws a type of pitch likely to induce a ground ball should be brought in to choke a rally. The percentage says to bunt in certain situations, to hit-and-run in others, to play for one run when you're ahead, to put in a defensive outfielder to protect a slim lead—and to do a hundred other things. If you play the percentage intelligently, and if, as Casey Stengel said, "you have the men who can execute," then you can win ball games, including World Series games. A good general, too, plays the percentage and if he has a big enough army, he wins the battles. But Napoleon became famous by winning even when

he had a small army, and he did it by going beyond the percentage and doing things that caught the German and Russian generals by surprise! Surprise is the name of the game.

Very few managers have ever intentionally surprised the opposition during a World Series. Nearly always, a manager in the Series relies on the very same players and strategy that had enabled him to win the pennant. The only striking exception to this rule is what Connie Mack did in the World Series against the Chicago Cubs in 1929.

Mack won eight pennants and five World Series for the Athletics, between 1903 and 1914. He also had some dreary stretches of disappointments. After the disastrous 1914 Series against the Miracle Braves, some of his players deserted to the short-lived Federal League, and he sold other stars. The A's then finished in last place for seven consecutive years. Among the hundreds of tributes paid to Mack in his later years was one from Sam Breadon, longtime Cardinal owner: "Connie Mack won pennants and world championships, but he kept the fans coming with a consistent tail-ender. If I finished last twice in succession in St. Louis, the fans would tar and feather me and run me out of town."

Baseball was a different game back in 1862, when Connie Mack was born in East Brookfield, Massachusetts, on December 22. His formal education was limited to a few years in grammar school, for he had to quit to work in a shoe factory to help support the very large McGillicuddy family.

Connie was a catcher, and a good one, and he was the only man on the team to wear any kind of glove. The distance from the pitcher's mound to home plate then was 40 feet, instead of 60 feet, 6 inches, today's mark. Catchers stood about 12 to 15 feet behind home plate and took the pitch on the first bounce. Pitchers threw underhand at that time. But they were fast, and the batters had the privilege of calling for the kind of pitch they wanted, either high or low balls.

Catching for Hartford in the New England League in 1885, Connie began the practice of moving up close behind the batter. A foul tip held by the catcher was an out. And by snapping his bare hand into his glove, Connie produced the same sound made by a foul tip. "You're out!" the umpire would shout, and the hitter would scream with rage. It was Connie's success with this ruse in the National League that led to a rule change. Now, of course, the batter is out only if the catcher can hold a foul tip.

Connie was not a good hitter when he first arrived in the major leagues with the Senators in 1886, but the Senators wanted a pitcher named Frank Gilmore, and Frank wouldn't go along unless Connie was in on the deal.

Connie played with the Senators for four years, then played for Buffalo in 1890, and then in 1894, he was named manager of the Pirates. In 1901 the new American League placed a team in Philadelphia, and Mack was selected to manage it. He was with the A's for the glory years of 1905, 1910, 1911, 1913, and 1914. Then followed a big blackout for the Athletics, seven dark, dismal years in last place.

In 1927, Connie acquired the incomparable Ty Cobb, one of the immortal stars of the game, and his Athletics began to challenge the Yankees for first place in the American League. Finally, in 1929 the Athletics once again were back on top.

Behind such great power-hitters as Jimmy Foxx, Al Simmons, Mickey Cochrane, Bing Miller, and Ty Cobb, the A's were almost unbeatable, and their defense was just as good, with Joe Boley

and Max Bishop, one of the slickest shortstop-second base combinations ever to play together. Above all, the marvelous pitching of Lefty Grove, Rube Walberg, George Earnshaw, Eddie Rommel, an almost impossible-to-hit, knuckleball star, and veteran reliever Jack Quinn made the A's tough to beat.

Among the little utilized pitchers on the staff was a veteran with fourteen solid years of major league experience who was now just barely hanging on with the Athletics. His name was Howard Ehmke. He was aging and had only pitched in 55 innings during the year, and in the final month of the pennant race he was not called on at all. About the only person on the ball club who remembered that Ehmke was still on the A's' roster was his manager Connie Mack.

The 1929 World Series was a most unusual one, since the adversaries were both well known far in advance. The Chicago Cubs, managed by Joe McCarthy, won their pennant in the National League almost as decisively as the Athletics did.

In 1929 the Cubs were awesome, with the great Rogers Hornsby hitting .380, Kiki Cuyler hitting .360, Hack Wilson hitting .345 and slugging 39 homers, and Riggs Stephenson hitting

Howard Ehmke, the A's' pitcher, had been relegated to the bench during the final weeks of the pennant drive. But in one of the great comeback stories in Series history, Ehmke fanned thirteen Cub hitters to win the opening game of the Series, 3–1.

.362. Their line drives and home runs rattled fences throughout the league, and they drove the enemy pitchers to all corners of the diamond.

The World Series that year looked as if it would be an evenly matched battle pitting Lefty Grove and George Earnshaw, the marvelous Athletic hurlers, against the thundering power of the Cub hitters. And since all the Cub hitters were right-handed, and Grove, the A's' biggest winner, was a left-hander, judicious sportswriters gave the edge to the Cubs.

Who would Connie Mack use as his starting pitcher for the first game?

"Earnshaw," opined one group of experts, because he was right-handed. "Lefty Grove," argued others, because of his blinding speed, which exceeded even that of his teammate, and because he would give the Cubs the swiftest pitches they had ever seen.

About a month before the pennant race ended, Howard Ehmke received a phone call requesting him to come to the front office. "Well, I guess this is the end for me. I guess I ought to pack my bags. Could be good-bye to all of this for me," he sighed.

"I guess this is the end of my days as a big leaguer," said Ehmke to himself as he entered the office and saw Mack waiting there.

"Mr. Mack, I know that I'm not as fast as I used to be, but I'm a lot smarter. I think I can pitch a couple of good ones for you. I'd like to try."

Surprisingly, Mack nodded in agreement. "I think you're right, Howard," he said. "And I'll tell you what we're going to do. I don't want you to do much pitching for the next month. Just keep throwing the ball, keep the arm nice and loose. But I'd also like for you to spend the next thirty days following the Cubs. I want you to spend time studying those big hitters. Find out what they like to hit, what's their weaknesses and see how we can stop them, then come back to me and we'll see. And Howard, let's not talk to anyone about this. It's between us."

When the World Series opened in Chicago on October 8, a crowd of more than fifty thousand rabid Cub rooters were on hand to cheer their favorites on to victory.

Right up to warm-up time, there still was speculation as to whether Mack would open with Grove or Earnshaw.

Then, Connie Mack dropped his bombshell. "Howard Ehmke will be my starting pitcher," said Mack.

The announcement shocked all the experts, the Cubs, the spectators, and even most of the Athletics.

Catcher Mickey Cochrane was flabbergasted. "How in hell can we win with Ehmke. He hasn't pitched at all." Mack crinkled his eyebrows. "Why, yes, it's Ehmke. If it's all right with you, Mickey."

Charlie Root, the Cubs' ace, had won 26 games in 1927, 14 in 1928, and 19 in 1929. He was a tough competitor in an important game, and this was an important game.

Through the first six innings, Ehmke was superb and had the big Cub hitters vainly waving at his slow curveball and striking out in every inning. In the seventh inning, Howard got Cuyler on 3 fastballs for another strikeout. Then he fanned Hornsby, and Hack Wilson, and now the crowd was on his side, howling with delight at every pitch.

But Root was also pitching a beautiful game, until the seventh inning, when Jimmy Foxx blasted a long home run into the bleachers to make it 1–0, Philadelphia.

The Cubs were snarling as they came up to hit in the seventh. Cuyler had struck out 3 times, but now he singled sharply up the middle. Riggs Stephenson singled, and now there were two men on base and nobody out. Charlie Grimm laid down a perfect sacrifice bunt, advancing both runners. Cliff Heathcote, the next batter, sent a short fly ball to center. Simmons raced in, caught the ball, and his perfect throw to the plate held Cuyler at third. Gabby Hartnett, pinch-hitting, struck out on three tantalizing curveballs, and Ehmke was out of a tough inning. He had now struck out 12 of the toughest batters in baseball and had set a World Series strikeout record.

In the ninth inning, the A's scored twice when Miller singled with the bases full, and they now led the Cubs 3–0.

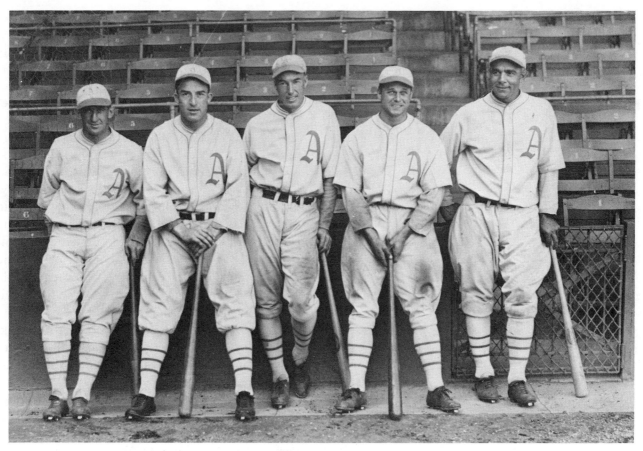

Philadelphia Athletics stars (*left to right*) Mickey Cochrane, Al Simmons, George Haas, Jimmy Foxx, and Bing Miller as they got ready to take the field for the first game.

In the Cubs' half of the ninth inning, Hack Wilson, the first Cub batter in the inning, drove a vicious line drive right back at Ehmke. The force of the blow knocked Howard off his feet. He quickly arose, fielded the ball, and tossed it to first base for the out, and then collapsed. Players, coaches, and even the umpires rushed to the mound. Howard was helped to his feet; he shook off Mack's efforts at relieving him, tossed a few warm-up pitches, and signaled his catcher that he was ready to pitch.

Cuyler then hit a slow curveball to third. Jimmy Dykes fielded the ball but threw wildly to first, and Cuyler raced on to second. Riggs Stephenson then slugged a single to center, scoring the Cubbies only run, and the fans were up and cheering. Then Charlie Grimm singled, sending Stephenson to second. Footsie Blair hit to Dykes at third, and Jimmy made a great stop of the ball and then tossed while off balance to second base to get Grimm. Now there were 2 outs and Chuck Tolson, pinch-hitting for Guy Bush was at bat. Ehmke got Tolson on 3 pitches for his thirteenth strikeout to end the game with a final score of 3–1, Athletics. Ehmke had allowed the Cubs just 3 hits to fashion one of the great pitching performances in World Series history.

Connie Mack's daring strategy left him in complete command of the Series. Now his two aces, Lefty Grove and George Earnshaw, were ready to be used for the second and third games.

By a strange twist of baseball statistics, in the second game the A's had a second 13-strikeout win, 9–3, as Grove and Earnshaw divided the honors, Grove fanning 6 Cubs and Earnshaw 7.

It was a game of threes, the A's scoring 3 runs

Slugger Jimmy Foxx sparked the A's' hitters as he drove out 3 home runs and hit for a Series average of .350.

in both the third and fourth innings, and the Cubs knocking out Earnshaw with a 3-run blast in the fifth. Jimmy Foxx hit a 3-run homer for the A's in the third inning to lead the Athletics to an easy victory.

Oddly enough, Connie Mack, again acting on a hunch, used the same strategy he'd used nineteen years before when he pitched Jack Coombs in both the second and third games, with only one day's rest. This time, Connie came back with Earnshaw for the third game. On the train to Chicago, he told the big pitcher from Swarthmore College, "George, I'm going to pitch you again in Philadelphia. You were working too fast yesterday when they knocked you out of the box. Now take more time between pitches tomorrow. Step off the mound, look around at your outfielders, rub the ball, pick up some dirt. Just slow down your rhythm and you'll beat those Cubs."

Earnshaw followed instructions and did very well; once again he pitched a magnificent game, allowing the Cubs just 6 hits, while striking out 10. But the A's simply could not bunch their hits to score. They clubbed Cub pitcher Guy Bush for 9 hits, but were able to score only 1 run. In the sixth inning, the Cubs put together a walk to Bush, an error enabling Hartnett to get on base, and a base hit by Hornsby that scored Bush. Then Cuyler singled to drive in 2 more runs, giving the Cubs a 3–1 win.

The fourth game, played on Saturday, Columbus Day, has no parallel in World Series history, producing perhaps the most spectacular rally in the entire history of World Series play. And none was ever staged under more dramatic circumstances, or with the stakes so high. It left the Philadelphia fans berserk with excitement, while National League fans simply slumped in their seats in pain.

The Cubs scored 2 runs in the fourth inning, 5 more in the sixth, another tally in the seventh to give them an 8–0 advantage, and to all intents and purposes the game was over.

Al Simmons opened the Athletics' seventh inning with a home run off Root. It was the first run for the A's, and Root, with an 8–0 lead, perhaps was easing up. At any rate, the roof suddenly fell in on him.

Jimmy Foxx, Miller, and Dykes followed with successive singles, and then Joe Boley singled and the A's had 2 more runs across the plate. Bishop singled, scoring Dykes, and now it was 8–4. Root was taken out and Art Nehf came in to relieve him. That was a bit of strategy that would be discussed by sportswriters for years to come. Then Mule Haas, a solid, free-swinging left-handed hitter, came up to bat. Mule had been jeered at and taunted by the Cub fans throughout the Series, and this time he struck back. He slugged Nehf's first pitch, a screaming line drive that Hack Wilson kicked around as Haas sped around the bases for an inside-the-park home run, and 3 more runs came in. The Cubs' once big lead had now been shaved to 1 run: It was an 8–7 game.

Now a shaken Nehf walked Mickey Cochrane and he was immediately relieved by Sheriff Blake. But the A's were on fire. Simmons and Foxx singled, another run came in, and the score was now 8–8—and the crowd went absolutely mad with excitement.

Pat Malone came in to pitch for the Cubs, and Bing Miller singled off Malone's first pitch; the bases were once again full. Then Jimmy Dykes rammed a shot to left field. Riggs Stephenson overran the ball and it bounded away for a double as Simmons and Foxx dashed across the plate to give the A's a 10–8 lead. Finally, Malone struck out Boley and Burns, and the Cubs' nightmare was over. But the Athletics had scored 10 runs, making World Series history by establishing a record for the most runs ever scored in an inning.

Lefty Grove came in for the Athletics in the eighth inning, and Lefty took good care of the Cub hitters for the remainder of the game to sew up the victory by a 10–8 margin.

Joe McCarthy's final defeat, on Monday, October 14, was almost as humiliating and painful as the rout on Saturday, as the Athletics once again came from behind, this time in final inning, to score 3 runs and win the game in spectacular fashion.

Connie Mack gave Howard Ehmke another chance to win in the Series finale. But after four solid innings, Howard had lost his magic touch and was knocked out of the box. With 2 outs in the fourth inning, Cuyler doubled, Stephenson walked, and successive singles by Grimm and Taylor scored 2 big runs for the Cubs. Rube Walberg relieved Ehmke and retired the side and then pitched marvelously, allowing the Cubs just 2 hits during the remainder of the contest.

Pat Malone, with a 2-run lead, was nearly perfect, giving up only 2 hits and pitching to only 26 batters, through the first eight innings.

In the ninth inning, Walt French, a former All-American halfback at Army, pinch-hitting for Walberg, struck out. Bishop singled, and then the Cub fans almost collapsed as Mule Haas blasted a home run to tie the score at 2–2.

The fans were in utter bedlam, yelling and stamping their feet. Then Simmons came up to the plate and drove a pitch up onto the scoreboard in center field for a double, and now everybody in the park was standing. Foxx walked, and then Bing Miller promptly walloped a smash off the wall for a double, scoring Simmons with the winning run for a 3–2 victory.

It was the first World Championship for Connie Mack and the Athletics since 1914, and it gave Mack the added distinction of being the

Jimmy Foxx crosses the plate after his home run in the ninth inning of the fifth game of the Series.

Magnificent was the word to describe the pitching of Lefty Grove as he won 2 games for the A's in the Series.

first manager to win four World Series.

After the game had ended, Connie Mack escaped from the frenzy of the clubhouse and took the elevator to his private office up in the Shibe Park tower. Three office girls burst in and fought for the privilege of kissing Mack, but Connie shyly dodged them with the excuse that three newspapermen were on their way to interview him. He dodged the newsmen too, saying, "Boys, you must excuse me just a little while. I'm afraid I overdid things a bit."

While the clubhouse revelry was going on and the entire city was caught up in a joyous celebration, Connie Mack lay down on a battered couch in his office and promptly fell sound asleep.

1930

Philadelphia Athletics Versus St. Louis Cardinals

For a good part of the 1930 season, Wilbert Robinson's Brooklyn Robins led the National League, but the unhappy Robins toppled from first to fourth place in the final ten days of the pennant race and the Giants and Cubs finished in front of them. But the Cardinals in the final days of the race spurted to a string of victories that enabled them to capture the pennant over the scrambling Cubs by a 2-game margin.

"For weeks it looked as if Brooklyn and the Athletics were going to be in the World Series," said Connie Mack to a reporter, "and I was really looking forward to battle the Robins. I always had a fondness for Robinson, and I believe he felt the same way about me." And then, with a shy smile, he added, "I think Brooklyn would have been less trouble for us than the Cardinals."

Mack anticipated a great deal of trouble from the Cards in the 1930 Series and he got it. "We're a very good club," he told his squad in the clubhouse before the first game, "but those red-hot Cardinals are an aggressive ball club."

Manager Gabby Street's Cardinals were truly red-hot, winning 39 of their final 49 games to finish in front of the Phillies, Giants, and the Dodgers in one of the most exciting pennant races in years.

The Series opened at Shibe Park, Philadelphia, on October 1, and a capacity crowd was in attendance as Lefty Grove and Burleigh Grimes warmed up on the sidelines and the crowd whooped it up for their hometown favorites.

The opening game demonstrated the Athletics' power as Grove was touched for 9 base hits, while the A's were only able to get 5 hits off Grimes, yet the A's took the game by a 5–2 margin. Although the A's were only able to get 5 hits, each of them went for extra bases. Mickey Cochrane and Al Simmons exploded for home runs; Jimmy Foxx and Mule Haas belted long triples and Jim Dykes hit a single. And each of the hits was good for a run, as the Athletics stranded just 2 runners.

The following day it was big George Earnshaw on the mound and he proved his mastery over the Cardinals. Connie Mack had an easy afternoon as the A's scored runs in pairs, in the first, third, and fourth innings. And with masterful pitching by Earnshaw, Connie just sat back and relaxed as the A's easily took the game, 6–1. Although the Cards managed to get 7 hits, their only run was scored when George Watkins homered in the second inning.

The train ride from Philadelphia to St. Louis enabled manager Street a chance to rally his

The 1930 World Champion Philadelphia Athletics

battered team. "Don't let those two beatings get to you. Remember how bad we looked in early August. Then we got going and we shellacked everybody in sight. So, pull up your socks and let's go get 'em."

The Cardinals listened to their manager, and promptly battled back, defeating the A's in the next 2 games to tie the Series.

In the third game, Rube Walberg pitched very well for the A's for four innings. Then Taylor Douthit blasted a home run into the bleachers to give the Cards a 1–0 edge. In the fifth inning, singles by Ray Blades, Jim Wilson, and Charlie Gelbert gave the Cards an additional run, and when Rube walked his mound rival, pitcher Bill Hallahan, Connie Mack quickly relieved him with Bill Shores, who halted the Cards in their tracks. However, in the seventh inning, Shores met his Waterloo, when he was hit hard for 2 runs. An additional run in the eighth inning gave the Cards a 5–0 win.

A wildly enthusiastic crowd of some forty thousand fans were on hand for the big Sunday game, as Jesse Haines, an eleven-year St. Louis favorite, opposed the ace of the A's staff, Lefty Grove. The two pitchers were at their best in a great duel, but Haines, the thirty-seven-year-old Card star, pitching in his third Series for the Redbirds, was the 3–1 winner.

The Cardinal players had it figured correctly. The fifth game was the turning point. Both Mack and Gabby Street also agreed that that was the one they had to win. For seven innings it was a magnificent pitchers' battle between Burleigh Grimes and George Earnshaw and both hurlers were in top form. They fought each other with every weapon in their pitching armory. As a result, it was a brilliantly fought battle, tense and tight for seven innings. Going into the eighth inning there was still no score, and each pitcher had allowed just 2 hits. But in the eighth inning, Grimes, who had been acquired from the Boston Braves in June, got into trouble when he loaded the bases with 1 out. But the great spitball pitcher forced Dykes and Max Bishop to hit into force-outs and the inning was over.

The Athletics came up in the ninth inning determined to score, as the crowd, now frantic with excitement, implored the Cards to hold them. Mickey Cochrane, the first batter, walked. Simmons popped up, and now it was up to slugger Jimmy Foxx, who had hit 37 home runs during the season. Foxx swung at Grimes's first pitch, caught the ball squarely on the fat part of his big bat, and hit one of the longest home runs ever seen. It was a dramatic and unexpected blow. Two runs were in and the Athletics had won the big game, 2–0.

The sixth game was anticlimactic. George Earnshaw pitched his third game of the Series, and it was a romp for the Athletics. Cochrane and Bing Miller drove out run-scoring doubles in the first inning and Al Simmons hit a home run in the third. Jimmy Dykes slugged reliever Sy Johnson for a 2-run homer in the fourth and it was all over as the A's had a 7–1 victory, and the Series.

The Cards' outfielder Pepper Martin ran wild in the Series. He stole bases, hit homers, and slugged out a .500 average.

Al Simmons crosses the plate after his home run in the seventh inning of game three as catcher Gus Mancuso of the Browns looks on.

The defensive play of the Athletics' infield was a chief factor in their Series victory: (*left to right*) Jimmy Dykes, John Boley, Dibrell Williams, Eric McNair, Max Bishop, Jimmy Foxx, and Phil Todt made sparkling plays throughout the Series.

St. Louis Cardinals Versus Philadelphia Athletics

Connie Mack won his third straight pennant and the ninth of his career in 1931. The victory put him only one under his great National League rival, John McGraw. Mack's Athletics won a record total of 107 games to easily romp over the second-place Yankees by 13½ games.

The terrible national Depression, which had begun with the stock market crash in the fall of 1929, was now eating deeper and deeper into the national income. Thousands of workers were unemployed and many of the Athletics' most faithful fans, once employed in the numerous factories and shipyards in the Philadelphia area, were out of work. Yet the Athletics' payroll had zoomed higher and higher. Al Simmons had signed a three-year contract which called for $100,000; Lefty Grove and Mickey Cochrane were in the $25,000-a-year class, with other stars not far behind, and Connie Mack and Tom Shibe were greatly concerned when they matched their payroll and compared it with the leaner gate receipts.

While the Great Depression cut across all America by 1931, most St. Louisans forgot their economic fears and turned to their pennant-winning Cardinals, who had dazzled the National League and romped past the Giants to win the flag by 13 games.

Manager Gabby Street said of his 1931 Cardinals, "I've seen a lot of great ball clubs in my time, but for pitching, hitting, spirit, and all around balance, I'm willing to back my '31 team against any of them."

The Cards' outstanding pitching staff included Bill Hallahan, Burleigh Grimes, and Flint Rhem, and the farm system had produced a jewel in the husky right-hander from Kentucky, Paul Derringer, a 24-game winner for Rochester in 1930.

Chick Hafey, the Cards' left fielder, captured the batting title with a smashing .3489 average in the closest batting race in history. Bill Terry of the Giants hit .3486, and Jim Bottomley of the Cards hit .3482.

Manager Street finally utilized John "Pepper" Martin, at the player's own insistence. Pepper had been shunted back and forth between the minor leagues and the Cards. Then one day he burst into Branch Rickey's office insisting, "I'm tired of riding the bench, I want to get into the game or I want you to trade me to some team that will play me." Rickey cleared the way for Pepper by trading center fielder Taylor Douthit to the Reds.

John Leonard Martin was a bundle of energy that couldn't sit still. As a youngster he starred in football at Oklahoma's Irving High School and left school to take two jobs. He delivered shoes for a shoe store and he also had a newspaper route, which led him to read the glowing stories about Babe Ruth and his success, and he made up his mind to be a ballplayer as famous as Ruth. He started in the minor leagues as a pitcher, like Ruth, at Ardmore, Oklahoma in 1923, and quickly moved up to Greenville as an outfielder, and then back to Ardmore, where he was signed by the Cardinals.

By 1930, Pepper was advanced to Rochester, where he hit .363 and developed into one of the most exciting, most colorful players in the International League. By 1931, Pepper was the Cardinals' center fielder.

Branch Rickey loved to tell sportswriters his favorite Pepper Martin story: "We purchased his contract in 1928 from Greenville and the next thing I'd heard he was in jail. It seems that he hitchhiked his way from Oklahoma by riding the rails. He looked like a bum and was arrested by the railroad police and locked up. He was dirty, oil-smeared, wore torn khaki pants and an old hunting jacket, and when we finally got him released, he reported to camp with a week's growth of beard, his face was smeared with tar and oil. He looked like hell," laughed Rickey. "But when we cleaned him up, suited him, he was pure magic on the field, pure magic."

High-spirited, full of fun, Pepper soon had developed a reputation for off-the-field pranks that made him a national celebrity. One afternoon he and Rip Collins disguised themselves as the hotel electricians. They barged into a Philadelphia hotel banquet and started a fake fight that threw the entire group into an uproar; the episode ended when the police, who had been called to the scene, recognized Pepper and Collins and joined in the hilarity.

In 1931, Martin had a fine rookie season, batting .300, and earned a reputation as a daring base runner who would slide headfirst into the bag, amidst a cloud of dirt. It was an exciting play and the fans roared his name every time Pepper got on base, and that was often.

At a clubhouse meeting before the first game of the Series, the top brass of the National League met for an informal conference. Martin

Cardinal star Jim Bottomley scores the first run of the fifth game in the 1931 Series.

was present at the meeting and remembered the addresses by John McGraw and Branch Rickey, in particular: "McGraw with his cussing and fire and brimstone speech and Rickey with his shrewd understanding of the players and wonderful command of the language; both men urged us to beat hell out of the Athletics," said Martin. "And when we left the locker room I was floating on air. No team could beat us. In my mind we were champions already."

In the first game of the Series, Cardinal pitcher Paul Derringer began the game in much the same fashion as a young Christy Mathewson, by striking out 4 of the first 6 batters to face him. In the third inning, however, it was another matter as Jim Dykes and Dib Williams both singled. Mule Haas doubled, scoring Dykes. Derringer walked Cochrane and then Jimmy Foxx slugged a drive that only good fielding held to a single as 2 more runs came in, giving the Athletics a 4–2 lead.

In the seventh inning, Derringer was rocked by a Cochrane single and a long home run by Al Simmons, and the Athletics took the first game, 6–2.

"You've got to get us even," manager Street pleaded with Bill Hallahan as he named the swift left-hander as his second-game pitcher. Hallahan knew that he had to be at the peak of his game to beat the formidable George Earnshaw, his opponent on the mound for the A's.

Pepper Martin practically stole the show for the Cardinals. In the second inning, Pepper singled to left, and Al Simmons lazily tossed the ball back to his pitcher only to discover that Martin had not stopped running after his single, but had turned the corner and torn down to second base safely. Then on the very next pitch, Martin flashed down to third base and slid head-first for a clean steal. He scored on Wilson's fly ball to center. In the seventh inning, Martin hurled himself around the bases again. He singled, stole second base, and sped to third on Wilson's bunt. By that time the ballpark was a bedlam. The crowd was going absolutely crazy as Martin edged off third for a moment, then streaked for home. The pitch was already on its way, and Gelbert squared away, bunted the ball beautifully down the first base line, and Martin scampered home, giving the Cards a 2–0 margin, which was the final score.

The third game's excitement centered again around the Series' darling, Pepper Martin. In the second inning, Martin singled, moving Bottomley, who had walked, to third base. Hack Wilson singled, scoring Bottomley, and Martin raced all the way to third base, arriving there after he dove headfirst practically into the base. A moment later, Pepper scored on a long fly ball to center field. In the fourth inning, Chick Hafey singled and Pepper slugged a long drive up against the center field wall for a two-base hit, and ultimately 2 more runs came across the plate as the Cards pasted Lefty Grove with another defeat, this time by a 5–2 count. Pepper Martin figured in the scoring of 4 of the 5 runs.

Big Moose Earnshaw duplicated Grimes's 2-hit game the following afternoon, October 6, as he shut out the Cards by a 3–0 margin. Once again, it was Pepper Martin who provided the only action for the Cardinals as he connected for the only 2 hits the Cards were able to manage off Earnshaw.

For the fifth game, manager Gabby Street moved Martin into the cleanup spot of the batting order, instead of his customary fifth place, and Pepper ran wild. In the first inning, with two men on base, Martin slashed a long fly ball to deep center field that enabled Frankie Frisch, who was on third base, to score the first run for the Cards. In the fourth inning, Pepper caught the A's completely napping as he laid down a beautiful bunt, and he reached first base. This time he did not advance, as the Cards were retired. In the sixth inning, Frisch doubled, then Martin drove one of Waite Hoyt's fastballs into the stands for a long home run. As he crossed the plate after scoring, the frenzied crowd burst into unrestrained cheering, and Martin was called out from the dugout to take an additional bow. It probably was the first time in Philadelphia history that the partisan Athletics crowd cheered for an opponent. In a Cardinal box seat, Mrs. Pepper Martin burst into tears as the crowd continued to applaud Pepper for a full five minutes.

In the eighth inning, with the score 3–1 and Watkins on second base, Martin came to bat and promptly lined a sharp single to left field, scoring Watkins. It was the fourth run driven in by Pepper; the final score was 5–1, Cardinals. By now, every baseball fan in the nation was singing the praises of the bright new World Series hero, who had already collected 10 hits. Overnight, Pepper Martin had become a national hero.

After a day off in order to travel to St. Louis, Grove and Derringer were ready to face each other once more. As in the first game, the A's rocked Derringer with a 4-run inning, and then jumped all over Jim Lindsey, who relieved Derringer, for 4 additional runs in the seventh inning, to romp to an 8–1 victory over the Cards.

Thus once again a World Series went thrillingly down to the seventh game finale.

In the final game, George Earnshaw faced the veteran Burleigh Grimes; they were two great pitchers, each of whom would give his all to win the decisive game. In the first inning, Earnshaw received several bad breaks, beginning with two texas leaguers that dropped in safely. Frankie Frisch then advanced both runners with a perfect bunt, and the crowd gave Pepper Martin a standing ovation as he came up to hit. The cheers did not stop until Pepper backed off the plate to doff his hat in a salute. Then he stepped in to hit.

Earnshaw wasn't the type of pitcher to worry about any batter, and he certainly wasn't worried now as he looked across the plate at the rookie who had become an overnight national hero. Perhaps Earnshaw became a bit too careful in pitching to Martin; at any rate his first pitch was way over the head of his catcher Mickey Cochrane, who leaped high in the air; but the ball shot by Mickey before he could deflect it, and 1 run was scored on the wild pitch. Earnshaw, unsettled now, walked Martin, and Pepper promptly stole second. Perhaps Cochrane also became rattled, for he missed the next pitch; it went through his glove, rolled to the backstop, and George Watkins scored the second run of the inning for the Cards.

In the third inning, Watkins came up to hit with a man on base, and slammed Earnshaw's first pitch into the left field seats for a 2-run homer. Then Earnshaw, bearing down, retired the next 15 men in a row before being relieved in the seventh inning with the score 4–0 in favor of the Cards.

Meanwhile, the A's found Grime's spitball almost impossible to hit and they went into the ninth inning on the short end of a 4–0 score. But Connie Mack rallied his troops and they responded with a single, 2 bases on balls, and another single; 2 runs were in, and it was a 4–2 game.

Manager Gabby Street then relieved Grimes with Wild Bill Hallahan, who faced Max Bishop, the first batter. Bishop hit Hallahan's first pitch to deep center field, and it looked as if the drive would be an extra base hit. But Martin, off with the crack of the bat, raced over to left-center field and grabbed the ball with a spectacular one-handed catch, and the game, and the World Series, were over.

It was a perfect ending. Pepper Martin had set a World Series record by slugging out 12 base hits, including 4 doubles and a home run, in 24 at bats, for a .500 average. He scored 5 runs, drove in 5 more, and stole 5 bases. Pepper had electrified the entire nation with his daring, gutsy head-first slides that turned him into one of the most colorful World Series heroes of all time.

Immediately after the Series ended, Judge Landis summoned the youthful Martin to his box for congratulations. "I wish I could trade places with you, young man," said Landis. "Give me your fifty thousand dollars, Judge, and take my five-thousand-dollar salary, and it's a deal," said Pepper.

In 1954, twenty-three years after his meteoric feats in the 1931 World Series, Martin was managing the Portsmouth team in the Class B Piedmont League. There was a very close ball game in an important series. A base hit was needed to win the game, and Pepper Martin, age fifty, inserted himself into the lineup, lined the first pitch to center field, sprinted to first base, rounded the bag, headed for second, and made it to second base with a headfirst slide that brought the crowd up screaming with delight.

1932

New York Yankees Versus Chicago Cubs

The 1932 Series was based on a grudge. Joe McCarthy, winning his first of a string of Yankee pennants, had suffered on the Chicago bench during the 1929 Series, when the Athletics scored 10 runs in one inning. He was fired as manager of the Cubs because, in the words of owner Bill Wrigley, "he could not bring me a world championship team." Now, three years later, Joe not only won the 1932 Series, but rubbed the Cubs' noses in the dirt by taking it from them in 4 straight games.

In 1932, McCarthy had a ball club that matched the 107 victories of the 1931 Athletics. Babe Ruth had hit for a .341 average with 41 home runs; Lou Gehrig walloped 34 home runs and had a .349 average; Earle Combs batted .321; Tony Lazzeri hit an even .300; Bill Dickey hit .310. McCarthy had such marvelous pitchers as Lefty Gomez, Red Ruffing, George Pipgras, Johnny Allen, and Herb Pennock.

Babe Ruth was now in his nineteenth season and had lost some of his zest and speed, with his weight up around 250 pounds. Pennock, too, after twenty great years, was now being used in relief. Bill Dickey had developed into one the the league's outstanding young catchers, and Joe Sewell, the kid shortstop of the 1920 Indians, was now the new third baseman. Charlie Grimm, the banjo-playing Cub first baseman, had relieved Rogers Hornsby as manager of the team on August 2 (Hornsby could not get along with the front office), and had driven the team to a pennant after a red-hot September race with the Pirates.

The Cubs still had Kiki Cuyler, Riggs Stephenson, Gabby Hartnett, and Joe Moore, players who had won for the Cubs in 1929. However, Grimm had added Billy Herman, a very talented infielder, who took over at Hornsby's post at second base. Bill Jurges was the shortstop, and Woody English was shifted to third base. Lon Warneke, the lanky Arkansas fastball pitcher, won 22 games for the Cubbies, while such standbys as Pat Malone, Guy Bush, Burleigh Grimes, and Charlie Root were able to pitch in with solid games when needed. Ex-Yankee Mark Koenig was picked up by the Cubs, and he filled in beautifully at shortstop when Jurges was injured.

But to win the pennant, McCarthy had to meet and overcome other problems. There were a number of players on the Yankees who disliked their manager. Many believed that Babe Ruth should have been chosen as the Yankee manager after illness forced Huggins to resign. Ruth was personally disappointed, but he did not let his feelings interfere with his game. There was, however, a marked coolness between the two men.

Joseph Vincent McCarthy had never played a game of baseball in the major leagues. Square-

Cub fans had hooted and jeered Babe Ruth every time he made a play during the Series. In the fifth inning of game three, the Babe had had enough. He had 2 strikes on him when he pointed majestically to the center field bleachers to indicate where he would hit the next pitch and that's exactly what he did. It was one of the most dramatic plays in Series history and one of the longest homers Cubs fans had ever seen.

In 1931, McCarthy was named manager of the Yankees and they finished in second place, behind the world champion Philadelphia Athletics. As the 1931 season finally ended, McCarthy had a talk with his boss, Colonel Jake Ruppert.

Ruppert told him, "I will stand for your finishing second this year, because you are new in this league. But I warn you, Joe, I don't like to finish second."

And McCarthy, looking straight back at Ruppert, said, "Neither do I, Colonel. We'll get it next year."

The 1932 World Series opened in New York on September 28, with Red Ruffing pitching for the Yankees and Guy Bush, a 19-game winner, taking the mound for the Cubs. The opener was an odd game, as the Cubs outhit the power-laden Yankees 10–8; but they left 11 men on base, and the Yanks cracked out a 12–6 win. The Yankees scored 3 runs in both the third and seventh innings, brought in 5 in the sixth, and scored again in the eighth. Lou Gehrig was the hitting star of the game, with a double and a home run, driving in 4 runs. Red Ruffing, although hit hard, struck out 10 Cub hitters to get the win for New York.

jawed, broad-shouldered, tough, and tenacious, he made the most of his limited abilities as a player by the thoroughness with which he studied the game and the zeal with which he played. In the minors he was a good fielder, a quick thinker, and a fair hitter, and he took each and every game to bed with him, playing and replaying strategic moves he should have made and would make the next day.

In 1921, Joe won a pennant for Louisville, and now baseball men around the country were talking about him. They were saying he was the best minor league manager. In 1925, McCarthy won another pennant for Louisville, and William Wrigley, the Chicago Cubs' owner, named him to replace Rabbit Maranville. The Cubs under McCarthy's leadership began to move up. They finished fourth in 1926 and third in 1928. In 1929 they won the pennant, then lost to the Athletics in the World Series, and in 1930 Joe was out as the Cubs' manager.

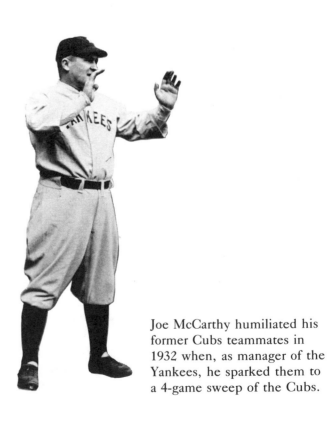

Joe McCarthy humiliated his former Cubs teammates in 1932 when, as manager of the Yankees, he sparked them to a 4-game sweep of the Cubs.

The second-game crowd was over fifty thousand as manager McCarthy selected Lefty Gomez to pitch, while Lon Warneke hurled for Chicago. Once again it was the muscular Lou Gehrig who dominated the game for the Yankees, with 3 hits. Lou scored 2 runs and drove in a third as the Yankees outplayed and outhit the Cubs for a 5–2 victory.

The third game, in Chicago on October 1, provided the most thrilling and dramatic contest of the Series. Another capacity crowd jammed every square inch of the Chicago ballpark on the day the Cubs were going to get revenge for the 2 straight losses. George Pipgras started for the Yankees, against Charlie Root, and it was anybody's ball game as it wound down to the very last inning.

The Bombers were off and running in the first inning. Combs singled, Sewell walked, and then Ruth stepped in to hit. The Babe was furious as he swung three heavy bats before stepping into the box. The day before, as the Yankees reached their Chicago hotel, Ruth and his teammates were pelted with sawdust, booed and hissed at, and some unruly fan tossed a bag of water at Ruth and his wife. Now the Babe, mad as hell, meant to get even. Ruth had been held to just 2 singles by the Cubs' pitchers, but now, with 2 on base, the Bambino swung from the heels and slugged a 3-run bomb over the left field wall, and it was 3–0 before many Cub fans were even seated.

The Cubs came back with a run when Billy Herman walked and came all the way around, scoring on Cuyler's double, to make it a 3–1 contest.

Lou Gehrig opened the third inning with a home run, but the Cubs, now fighting mad, picked up 2 runs to make the score 4–3. In the Cub's half of the third, Cuyler hit a home run. Then Stephenson singled and manager Charlie Grimm doubled, to score Stephenson. In the fourth inning, the Cubs tied the score when Jurges doubled and Lazzeri fumbled a grounder by English, allowing Jurges to score.

When the Yanks came up to bat for their epic fifth inning, Joe Sewell struck out, and then Babe Ruth stepped up to hit. He was greeted with a thunderous barrage of boos from the stands

Lou Gehrig was unstoppable in the Series. All Columbia Lou did was to slug 3 homers, a double, and a single and drive in 9 runs to post a .529 average.

and the Cubs' bench. He just stood defiantly and watched the first pitch, a fastball, zip by him. The Babe then pointed deep into the center field bleachers, and took a second strike, actually calling it on himself. Again, by pantomime, Ruth indicated that his target would be the center field bleachers. The Cubs rose, and jeered and booed and hissed him. Then Root came in with another fastball, right down the middle, and the Babe connected with a savage swing and hit the ball exactly where he had pointed, to the deepest part of the bleachers in center field, for a tremendous home run. Then Lou Gehrig followed Ruth and slugged another home run, into the right field bleachers. The great Yankee one-two punch knocked Root out of the box and brought in Pat Malone. To all intents and purposes, the World Series was over right then.

Ruth and Gehrig hit 2 home runs each. Ruth batted in 4 runs and scored twice himself. And the Yankees had their third straight Series victory, 7–5.

The saddest day of all for the Cubs was Sunday, October 2. Before a crowd of more than forty-nine thousand fans, the Yankees clubbed five Chicago hurlers for a total of 19 hits to romp over the hapless Cubs by a 13–6 margin.

Chicago hit hard and early with 4 runs in the first inning that featured Frank Demaree's homer with a man on base. But the respite was only a brief one as the Yankees kept up the pressure, scoring twice in the third inning and twice in the sixth. Then they came up with 4 runs in the seventh and 4 more in the ninth, to overwhelm the Cubs with a 13–6 victory.

Both Ruth and Gehrig were held to 1 hit apiece, but Tony Lazzeri smashed out 2 home runs and a single. Earle Combs homered and slammed out 2 singles, and Bill Dickey and Joe Sewell each had 3 base hits. Herb Pennock hurled the last three innings for the Yankees and allowed the Cubs just 2 hits and 1 run.

No lineup, except the Athletics of 1910, has ever finished a World Series with as many .300 hitters as the 1932 Yankees. Gehrig hit for a .529 average; Bill Dickey, .438; Combs, .375; Ruth, .333; Joe Sewell, .333.

The Series was Babe Ruth's tenth, and his last. In the 41 Series games in which he played, Ruth hit for a .326 average and slugged a record 15 home runs.

And the Yankees, once again world champions, had run their string of consecutive victories in World Series play to 12 games.

New York Giants Versus Washington Senators

The Washington Senators were making money in 1933 even though the nation was in a severe Depression. But they hadn't won a pennant in seven years, and Clark Griffith wasn't very happy with his manager, the great Walter Johnson. Johnson had been named to replace Bucky Harris in 1929, but Griffith felt that Johnson was too easygoing, and the contrast with Bucky Harris's tough, aggressive leadership of 1924 and 1925 was too great. So he fired Johnson at the end of the 1932 season.

There was no great outcry by the Washington fans. They still revered Johnson as a pitching idol, but they had not seen him bring any quality of inspiration or leadership to the team. Thus, Griffith was easily able to ease his conscience over the firing. He had given Johnson every opportunity, had also paid him the highest salary of any pitcher in the league from 1912 to 1927. At one period, Johnson's salary had reached $25,000.

Three names were suggested by Griffith aides for consideration as the new Washington manager. They were the veterans Sam Rice, Joe Judge, and the great Goose Goslin, but Griffith refused comment until late in October, when he called a press conference to introduce Joe Cronin, the new manager.

It was a shock to the sportswriters, to the fans, and to Griffith's inner circle of pals, for Cronin was only twenty-six years old, and had less than five years of major league experience.

Griffith had his reasons and told the press, "Cronin's a scrapper. He thinks nothing but baseball. I like these young guys who fight for everything. I made no mistake with Bucky Harris. I think I've got another Harris."

For the young Irishman Cronin, his elevation to the managership of a major league team at the age of twenty-six was a dream come true. But it wasn't his first stroke of high good luck. Back in San Francisco he had lived out a child's ultimate dream. His school, Mission High, burned down, and at fourteen he had been free to play baseball all day for the balance of the year.

Joe Devine, a scout for the Pirates, spotted Cronin and Wally Berger playing ball around San Francisco, and in 1924 offered Joe a contract with Pittsburgh. There were stops after that, at Johnstown, a Pirates farm team, then New Haven, and then Kansas City in 1927.

Joe Engel, Griffith's chief scout, saw Cronin play in 1928 and bought him for $7,500. By 1929, Cronin was the Senators' regular shortstop, a .281 hitter who was getting distance and could make all the plays necessary to shore up a weak Washington defense. By 1930, Joe Cronin was the best shortstop in the American League, with his batting average way up to .346.

Owing to Joe Cronin's inspired play and leadership, and the acquisition of three outstanding pitchers—Earl Whitehill, a curveball specialist

These outstanding Giants pitchers carried the hopes of the team in the Series: (*left to right*) Hal Schumacher, Carl Hubbell, and Freddy Fitzsimmons.

with ten years as a winner for the Tigers; Jack Russell, a big right-hander, from the Red Sox; and another curveball artist, Walt Stewart, from the Browns—the Senators began to win. Through most of the season, the Senators battled the Yankees and the Athletics for first place, but by July they were 9 games in front of the Bronx Bombers, and they clinched the pennant late in September.

In the National League, Bill Terry, a big, raw-boned first baseman who joined the Giants in 1923, was farmed out and then brought back to the Giants in 1924, and by 1925 had become one of the league's leading hitters, with a .319 average. What John McGraw did not like about Terry was his independence. Terry had a very good off-season position with the Standard Oil Company and had been offered an executive post with them any time he left baseball. So he took none of John McGraw's abuse. One year after he hit for an astounding .401 average, in 1930, he was ready to quit baseball if he couldn't get the salary increase he wanted. He and McGraw argued back and forth, until finally he got what he wanted. He was one of the few players McGraw tolerated after a bitter salary dispute. But even

John McGraw wasn't firing or trading a .400 hitter.

On June 3, 1933, the Giants were at the Polo Grounds. They had not played for two days because of rainy weather, and McGraw, who had not been well the past two years, suddenly felt that his entire world was coming apart. The team was floundering, going nowhere; players were getting to him; he was just sick of all the back-biting and arguing, and he called in Bill Terry.

"Bill," said McGraw. "How'd you like to be manager of the Giants?"

When his head stopped spinning, Terry asked, "Why? Are you quitting?"

McGraw said, "Yes, and I'd like to have you succeed me."

"I'd love to manage the Giants, Mr. Mc-Graw," said Terry. "But I would have to be the real manager, not just a front for you."

"That's the way it will be," said McGraw. "You'll be the boss. I'm just gonna sit on the sidelines this year. It's your team."

McGraw's decision to quit had been one of the most carefully guarded secrets in the history of baseball. All over town, all over the nation, the news became a front-page sensation.

The 1933 season was an exciting year for the Giants, for at last they were paying off on the promise they had made to McGraw to win in 1932. This was the team: Terry on first base; Hugh Critz at second; Blondy Ryan at shortstop; John Vergez at third; outfielders Lefty O'Doul, Joe Moore, and Curt Davis; and the incomparable pitching staff of "King" Carl Hubbell, Fred Fitzsimmons, Hal Schumacher, Roy Parmelee, and relievers Dolf Luque and Herm Bell, who were all tough, competitive, and winners.

By July the Giants were pressing ahead of the Pirates and the Cubs, and finally, in September, they clinched the pennant by 5 games over the Pirates.

It was the Washington Senators versus the New York Giants after a nine-year hiatus, and the brand-new managers were racing for the win.

Joe Cronin at age twenty-six was the youngest player-manager to guide his team to a World Series.

The Series had its premiere at the Polo Grounds on October 3, before a crowd of some forty-seven thousand, and, as expected, the brilliant Carl Hubbell, tossing his great screwball, won the opening game by a 4–2 margin. Hubbell's performance was a masterpiece of pitching as he allowed the hard-hitting Senators but 5 hits and struck out 10.

The second game saw a marvelous pitching battle between young Hal Schumacher and Al Crowder. Goose Goslin blasted a home run in the third inning to give the Senators a short-lived 1–0 lead, but in the sixth inning the roof fell in on Crowder, and the Giants batted around, scoring 6 runs and winning the game.

President Franklin Roosevelt was the honored guest at the third game, in Washington on October 5, and he brought good luck to the Senators. Earl Whitehill was manager Cronin's pitching selection, while Bill Terry chose Fred Fitzsimmons. Whitehill completely dominated Fitz and the Giants as he throttled their attack, shutting them out and allowing only 5 base hits.

The Senators scored in the first inning. Buddy Myer greeted Freddie Fitzsimmons with a single, and took third when Goslin doubled off the right field wall. Cronin's infield hit scored Myer, and then the Goose came home when Fred Schulte slugged a two-base hit off the left field fence, and it was 2–0 in favor of the Senators. In the third inning, successive two-base hits by Bluege and Myer resulted in another Washington run. The Senators added another run in the seventh, to give them a 4–0 lead as Whitehill held the Giants at bay for the win.

In the fourth game, manager Cronin selected Monte Weaver as his choice to duel with Carl Hubbell, and the pitching battle that ensued was the highlight of the entire Series. Weaver matched the Giants' ace pitch for pitch in the first three innings. Not a man reached base on either team until the fourth. Then Bill Terry slammed a tremendous home run deep into the seats in the left field section of the park, to give the Giants a 1–0 lead.

In the sixth inning, Myer singled, stole second, and went to third on a groundout. Then Heinie Manush smashed a ground ball toward third, and Hughie Critz scooped it up and tossed

The 1933 World Champion New York Giants

the ball to Hubbell, who was covering the bag for Terry, who was out of position. It was one of those quick-as-lightning plays, difficult to make a call on, and the umpire, Charlie Moran, after a momentary pause, called Manush out. The "out" call nullified the run that scored on the play since it was the third out. When Moran made the call, Manush and the entire Washington infield joined in a protest around him. After a few moments, Manush, losing the argument, brushed his hand across the umpire's back and Moran wheeled and thumbed Manush out of the game. Then there was another, louder argument and discussion on the play. Manush held up the game for fully ten minutes before he was finally able to be talked off the field.

On the mound once again, Weaver blanked the Giants in the seventh inning, and then the Senators tied the score. Joe Kuhel beat out a bunt, Bluege sacrificed him to second base, and

then Luke Sewell singled Kuhel home. Now the score was 1–1.

Weaver and Hubbell battled through the eighth, ninth, and tenth innings on even terms. Terry used some of his managerial strategy in the Giants' half of the eleventh inning. Knowing that the Arkansas kid had lost much of his speed, Terry flashed a bunt sign when he noted that Bluege was playing well back on the grass at third base. Jackson laid down a perfect bunt and raced to first as the ball slowly wended its way down the third base line. Then Gus Mancuso sacrificed Jackson to second, and the inspirational player of the 1933 season, Blondy Ryan, sent Travis home with the winning run as he sent a screeching single to left. The Giants won by a score of 2–1.

The fifth and final game of the Series was played in Washington. Hal Schumacher was manager Bill Terry's choice to wrap up the finale for the Giants, while Joe Cronin selected Al Crowder to hurl the Senators up from the ashes of defeat. And both pitchers gave it their best.

The Giants were off and running in the second inning with a 2–0 lead. In the sixth, the Giants bombarded Crowder, as Davis and Mancuso doubled to give the Giants another run. Jack Russell came in to relieve Crowder and checked the rally.

The Senators, now fighting with their backs to the wall and with 2 outs in the sixth inning, started to move. Manush and Cronin singled, and then Schulte had the Senators in a frenzy of joy as he caught a Schumacher fastball and slugged it out of the park for 3 runs, to tie the game, 3–3.

Both teams brought in relief pitchers to begin the tenth inning: Dolf Luque of the Giants and Jack Russell for the Senators. In the Giants' half of the tenth, 2 men were out when Mel Ott came up to hit. Ott had hit the ball hard all through the Series and was a threat to hit a long ball with his unique foot-in-the-air batting stance. This time, Mel caught one of Jack Russell's fastballs and drove the pitch on a line over Schulte's head in center field. Schulte made a dive for the ball, got his fingertips on it, deflecting the ball into the bleachers, and then toppled headfirst into the bleachers and was lost to view. Umpire Pfirman declared it a home run and the Giants were out in front by a 4–3 score.

In the Senators' half of the tenth, Dolf Luque bore down with everything he had and struck out Joe Kuhel to end the game and win the Series for the Giants.

President Franklin D. Roosevelt throws out the first pitch to open the Series.

John J. McGraw lived just long enough to see his painful 1924 defeat to the same Senators avenged. He died several months later.

St. Louis Cardinals
Versus Detroit Tigers

With all due respect to the championship New York Yankees of the Babe Ruth-Lou Gehrig era, the most colorful, picturesque club of modern baseball was the famous 1934 Gashouse Gang of St. Louis. In the sense that that name suggests a bunch of rowdies who played dirty, anything-goes baseball after the fashion of the old Baltimore Orioles or the Cleveland Spiders, it was really a misnomer. Manager Frank Frisch and his team always played hard-driving, heads-up baseball, but his tactics were clean.

The main cogs in the Gashouse Gang were frolicsome, exuberant spirits with boundless energy: Pepper Martin, Dizzy Dean, Rip Collins, Leo Durocher, Ernie Orsatti, Joe Medwick, Bill DeLancey. And they had the perfect manager for that kind of team in Frank Frisch, "the Fordham Flash."

The son of the prosperous linen importer, Frank Frisch was born in Queens, New York, on September 9, 1898, and began to play ball as soon as he entered grade school. At Fordham University, Frisch starred in basketball, football, and baseball. It was his baseball coach, Art Devlin, a former Giant third baseman, who put together some of college baseball's finest teams.

By 1921, Frisch had already played two short seasons with the Giants. Frankie had taken over third base, easily beating out three candidates for the regular job at the "hot corner." By 1922,

Frank Frisch was being called the Fordham Flash; he led all third basemen in the National League, hitting an astounding .341. And his manager, John McGraw, was saying, "Eddie Collins was the best third baseman I've ever seen. But Frankie Frisch can do everything that Collins could do."

Frisch was much like McGraw in personality, and many believed that as time went on Frank would eventually replace McGraw as the Giants' manager. But Frisch and the little Napoleon had a falling out in 1926, and that winter Frisch was sent to the Cardinals for Rogers Hornsby, in a trade that stunned the fans of both cities.

When Frisch reported to the Cardinals, he played his position flawlessly and hit .337. St. Louis fans took him to their hearts, and in 1933 Frisch was named manager, succeeding Gabby Street in mid-season.

"Early in May, Branch Rickey made the deal that helped us win the pennant," recounted Frisch.* "He announced at a press conference, 'I have obtained a suitable shortstop for our club. I've traded pitchers Paul Derringer and Al Stout and infielder Sparky Anderson for Leo Durocher.' A lot of eyebrows were raised over this expensive deal, but I think it was a great

*In an interview with the author, 1955, on author's *Sports Show*, New York radio station WINS

152

one for us. Then we acquired Jack Rothrock, who played for the Red Sox and White Sox, and he was a fine outfielder for us in 1934. By 1934, Joe Medwick had become one of the finest hitters in the league, and to plug the outfield we got Ernie Orsatti and Chick Fullis, and our outfield was set. Our infield was sound. We had Rip Collins at first base, Pepper Martin at third, I was still good enough at second base, and Durocher was the key to the entire infield. Our pitching was first-rate, for we had Tex Carleton, a sixteen-game winner, Bill Hallahan, and Bill Walker as our solid big three, and we had the Dean brothers, the greatest one-two pitching duo that I've ever seen.

"The most colorful, most exciting player was Dizzy Dean. Without Dizzy we'd never even be in the pennant race. He won thirty games for us, and his kid brother, Paul, won nineteen. That's forty-nine games, and we won the pennant by two and a half games. There has never, ever been a pitcher character like Dizzy Dean in the history of the game."

Dizzy Dean's father, Albert, could never afford to stay in one place long enough for his sons to get an education. But, inadvertently, he did introduce them to something that would one day enable them to earn more money than many college graduates and become national heroes. Al Dean taught his kids how to play baseball. In the early days of his marriage, before he had been burdened by children, Al was a very good third baseman and played several seasons for the club in Hartford, Connecticut.

"They let Dad keep that old Hartford uniform," said Diz. "He always carried it with him. I'll never forget how great it looked on him. It was blue and nearly wore out, but it looked great to all us kids. We were always beggin' him to wear it."*

The Dean family was baseball-crazy. They played every chance they got: in the falling dusk after a day's work in the fields; on Sundays; and sometimes, when traveling from job to job, they would stop the dust-covered old Ford and pile out in a nearby field to play catch.

"I read once how Bob Feller's dad taught him

*In 1954 interview with the author on WINS

how to pitch," said Diz. "Dad told us some rules of the game, but he sure didn't have to teach us how to throw the ball. It just came natural. I never know'd much about this playing ball for money until I was about fourteen, and I never saw a big-league game until I played in one."

Diz joined the army when he was sixteen years old, with the help of his stepbrothers, Claude and Herman, who thought it would do Diz a world of good. He was big and strong, and when he told the recruiting officer he was eighteen, nobody doubted him. Besides, the 12th Field Artillery needed a pitcher and Diz could throw hard.

He played ball in the army for three and a half years, and word got around that the 12th Field Artillery had a fine pitcher. That was the beginning of his famous career. By 1930, the most popular, most beloved ballplayer in the history of Texas baseball, Dizzy Dean, was brought up to the St. Louis Cardinals.

In his first major league game, against the tough Pittsburgh Pirates, Dizzy allowed the hard-hitting Pirate team to get 2 hits in the first inning, apologized to manager Gabby Street for his poor pitching, and then shut out the Pirates, allowing just 1 more hit for the rest of the game.

In 1932, Dean was the number one pitcher on the Cardinal team, winning 18 games and lead-

Pepper Martin, on a tear once again, slides into home as Detroit catcher Mickey Cochrane vainly awaits the ball. Action occurred in game two of the Series.

The Great One, Dizzy Dean, won 2 games for the Cards in the 1934 Series.

ing the Cardinal pitchers in strikeouts and innings pitched. In 1933, Dizzy won 20 games and led the entire league in strikeouts, with 199.

Meanwhile, Dizzy Dean had become the most talked about member of the Gashouse Gang, and he began to tell the Cardinals' general manager, Branch Rickey, and manager, Frank Frisch, about his kid brother, Paul, "who could throw even harder than me. Me and Paul can win a pennant for the Cards," said Dizzy.

Surprisingly, Branch Rickey sent for Paul Dean, who had been pitching successfully in Texas, and it turned out that Dizzy's boast wasn't far off base.

In 1934, Paul and Dizzy began to perform like no two brothers ever had, but the Cardinals still were seemingly out of the pennant race, as the 1933 world champion New York Giants had a 6-game lead after the Labor Day holiday in September. But suddenly, the Giants lost 6 of their last 7 games to the Braves, Phillies, and Dodgers

as the Cards thundered on. On the final Saturday of the season, the Cards slipped into first place, and on the final Sunday, they won the pennant. Dizzy had won 30 games and kid brother Paul had won 19.

While the Cardinals were snatching the pennant in a most dramatic finish, the Detroit Tigers, under the leadership of their great catcher, Mickey Cochrane, and with such stars as the fabulous pitcher Lynwood "Schoolboy" Rowe, who had a winning streak of 18 in a row, the Tigers shot from fifth place in 1933 to win their first pennant since 1909.

Detroit had a marvelous group of players, including the great slugging first baseman Hank Greenberg, who had hit for a .339 average and 26 home runs; Charlie Gehringer, perhaps one of the two or three greatest second basemen of all time; Bill Rogell at shortstop; and Marv Owen at third base. In the outfield the Tigers had Goose Goslin, Pete Fox, and Joe White. The pitchers included Rowe, Eldon Auker, Tom Bridges, Al Crowder, Fred Marberry, and Elon Hogsett, a full-blooded Indian curveball star.

Detroit had waited a quarter of a century for a World Series game, but the forty-two thousand-odd fans who were present on October 3 at Navin Field had little to cheer about, as Dizzy Dean and the Cardinals won in a romp by an 8–3 score.

Detroit tied the Series the next day, as Lyn Rowe, the big El Dorado, Arkansas, star, pitched one of the most classic Series games ever in bringing home the 3–2 win for Cochrane and the Tigers in twelve torrid innings. Despite Bill Hallahan's poor showing during the season, manager Frisch started him and he battled Rowe until the Tigers tied the score at 2–2, in the

ninth inning. Bill Walker, another left-hander, relieved him and lost the game in the twelfth, when the Tigers' "G Men" finally began to hit the ball. Bill Walker walked Gehringer and Hank Greenberg, and then Goose Goslin came through with a big single to drive in Gehringer with the winning run.

From the beginning of the third inning, when the Cardinals scored their second run, no Cardinal reached base until Pepper Martin doubled in the eleventh inning, but Martin got no farther as Rowe retired the side. Schoolboy Rowe retired 22 successive Cardinal hitters in notching the victory for the Tigers.

When the Series shifted to St. Louis on October 5, Dizzy's brother, Paul, the silent Dean, took up the burden and outpitched the marvel-

Shortstop Leo Durocher of the Cards slides home with the winning run in the sixth game of the Series.

ous curveball artist of the Tigers, Tommy Bridges, to take a 4–1 win for the Cards.

Mickey Cochrane was livid at Hank Greenberg's lack of hitting. Hank had struck out several times with the bases full. Thus, in the fourth game, Cochrane dropped Greenberg from the number 4 batting spot to number 6, and moved Goslin to the number 4 spot.

The Cardinals, led by Paul Dean and Pepper Martin, harangued big Hank Greenberg for his batting demotion, and they were to rue the day. For this got Big Hank fighting mad, and he finally busted loose. On October 6, in the fourth game, Hank slugged out 2 doubles and 2 singles (4 for 4) and drove in 3 runs, as the Tigers blasted the Cardinal pitchers from pillar to post for 13 hits and a 10–4 romp. Eldon Auker, the Tigers' submarine pitcher, had an easy time with the Cardinal batters as the Tigers slugged five St. Louis pitchers: Carleton, Vance, Walker, Haines, and Mooney.

In the fourth inning, Dizzy Dean was sent in to run for Virgil Davis, the Cardinals' slow-moving catcher, and as Billy Rogell, the Tigers' shortstop, tried for a double play, his throw hit Dean on the back of the head and Dizzy was knocked out. He was carried to the clubhouse, then rushed to the hospital. X rays indicated no serious damage. And one sports editor reported the story in this manner: "X rays on Dizzy Dean's head this morning showed NOTHING THERE."

The next day, October 7, reporters and the more than thirty-eight thousand fans were amazed to see Diz warming up just before the game began, and even more astounded to see Frisch starting Dizzy against the Tigers for the fifth game.

But the surprised Tigers in turn surprised everyone with an attack that outscored the Cardinals and won the game, 3–1. Tommy Bridges held the Cards to 7 hits and struck out 8 Cardinal batters. The Tigers too had only 7 hits, but their mechanical man, Gehringer, hit a long home run. Then Rogell singled and came home on Greenberg's long drive to Rothrock. The lone St. Louis run came in the seventh inning when Bill DeLancey hit a home run off Bridges.

Now leading in the Series 3 games to 2 as

they returned to Detroit, Cochrane and his Tigers felt confident. The biggest crowd of the Series, 44,551, was on hand at Navin Field on October 8, waiting to see Schoolboy Rowe win the World Series for the Tigers.

Paul Dean opposed the Schoolboy, and fortunately for Paul, this was the one game in which the "All-American Out," Leo Durocher, was a hitting fool. After going hitless in the first three games, Leo had a .110 Series average, and no one paid too much attention to him. But as the game progressed, Leo was positively the most dangerous hitter on the field.

It was soon evident that Rowe wasn't going to retire 22 hitters in a row: The game opened with Rothrock doubling and then scoring on Joe Medwick's single. But the Tigers came right back and tied the score in the third inning, when White walked, stole second, reached third on an error by Frisch, and raced home as Cochrane beat out an infield single. The score was 1–1 as the Cardinals started to belabor Rowe in the fifth inning. Durocher singled, then went to second on a groundout, and scored on Pepper Martin's single. Goslin tried to get Durocher out with a throw from deep left field, but that throw was wild and Martin tore around the bases and also scored. The Tigers roared right back again in

Ernie Orsatti, Cardinal outfielder, escapes Mickey Owen's tag at third base. Action occurred in the second inning of game two.

the next inning with 2 runs of their own, knotting the score at 3–3.

In the seventh inning, Durocher doubled, and scored when Paul Dean won his own game with a long single, giving St. Louis a 4–3 edge. Dean bore down in the seventh and eighth innings and retired the Tigers without further damage, clinching the victory that evened the World Series at 3 games each.

The seventh game saw Dizzy Dean primed for his third start in the Series, while Cochrane had to use Eldon Auker for the game that would mean the championship. And more than forty thousand hopeful Tiger fans trooped into Navin Field in Detroit on October 9 to witness the final battle.

It was just like the Gashouse Gang to wind up a most incredible season with a never-to-be-forgotten World Series game. The Gang broke through with a 7-run bombardment in the third inning. Dean started things for the Cards when he doubled with 1 out. After that, Tiger fans were almost blinded by the pyrotechnic display: a bunt by Martin; a walk to Rothrock; Frisch's

double to left, which knocked Auker out of the box. Then Collins singled, DeLancey doubled, and there followed singles by Leo Durocher and Dizzy, up for the second time, and a walk to Martin. And the Cards had 7 very big runs.

Mickey Cochrane paraded almost his entire pitching staff before the game was over: Hogsett, Bridges, Marberry, and Crowder. But the Cards were unstoppable, and peppered the Tiger pitchers for 17 base hits and an 11–0 shutout. Rip Collins got 4 hits, Dean got 2 hits, and Durocher slugged a triple and single, while Dean allowed the Tigers just 6 hits.

And so in the darkening dusk there was little glory for the Tigers, but the Cardinals were whooping it up in their dressing room with a hilarious festival of joy, led by Dizzy Dean and the rest of the Gashouse Gang.

Dizzy Dean was selected the Most Valuable Player of the Series. He was also selected Player of the Year by the New York Baseball Writers. Dizzy Dean accepted the award, all decked out in the first tuxedo he had ever worn.

1935

Detroit Tigers Versus Chicago Cubs

Two early World Series rivals of the first decade of the century—the Detroit Tigers and the Chicago Cubs—clashed again in 1935 after an interval of twenty-six years.

The Tigers, led by their great catcher and manager Mickey Cochrane, edged out the second-place Yankees by 3 games to win the American League flag. The Cubs, under manager Charlie Grimm, romped to their pennant after a sensational 21-game winning streak in September, which carried them to the final day of the season.

The Cubs, however, had been considerably changed since the 1932 Series. Gabby Hartnett, Charlie Root, Lon Warneke, Billy Herman, Bill Jurges, and Frank Demaree remained as valuable regulars, but Charlie Grimm strengthened his lineup with the acquisition of nineteen-year-old Phil Cavarretta at first base. Cavarretta was to develop into one of the great first basemen in the league, and to be a Cub mainstay for more than twenty-two years. The rest of the Cubs' lineup included Stan Hack, who had taken over at third base, Augie Galan, Fred Lindstrom, and the former Phillies slugger Chuck Klein. The new pitchers were Bill Lee, Larry French, Tex Carleton, Roy Henshaw, and Fabian Kowalik.

The first game opened in Detroit on October 2, and the Cubs, still red-hot from their winning streak, continued to play well and came on,

behind the 4-hit pitching of Lon Warneke, to shut out the Tigers by a 4–0 score.

The second game, played on a cold, windy afternoon before a crowd of more than forty-six thousand fans, saw the Tigers' first four batters all hit Cub pitcher Charlie Root for 4 base hits. Even before the crowd was properly seated, the Tigers had scored 4 big runs. White singled, then Cochrane doubled, scoring White. Charlie Gehringer then singled, scoring Cochrane, and Hank Greenberg blasted the ball completely out of the park for a home run. At that point Charlie Root, the most unlucky Cub pitcher (he never won a World Series game), was taken out of the game and replaced by Roy Henshaw, who finally got the Tigers out.

In the fourth inning, the Tigers continued their assault, pouncing on little Henshaw (he was five feet seven and weighed only 150 pounds) for 3 more runs. With 2 outs, Henshaw hit Marv Owen with a pitch, Tommy Bridges beat out an infield hit, White walked, and the bases were filled. A wild pitch scored Owen. Cochrane walked, and a Gehringer single scored Bridges and White, putting the Tigers well in front by a 7–0 margin. The final score was 8–3.

Grimm's third pitcher, Fabian Kowalik, a name that appeared but briefly in baseball lore, will always be remembered as the pitcher who hit Hank Greenberg with a fastball. The pitch smashed Greenberg's wrist. An X ray the next day showed that Greenberg's wrist was broken, and he was out of the Series and sidelined for most of the 1936 season.

Now the Tigers, although considerably weakened, grimly outlasted the Cubs in a torrid eleven-inning battle in Chicago, by a 6–5 margin. Both managers used a parade of hurlers. Auker, Rowe, and Hogsett for the winning Tigers, and Lee, Warneke, and French for the Cubs.

The Cubs scored quickly in the second inning, as Frank Demaree, who had hit the ball hard throughout the Series, slammed an Auker pitch over the fence. Hack then singled, stole second base, and scored on an infield out. The Cubs added a third run in the fifth inning, on Jurges's walk, Lee's sacrifice, and Augie Galan's single. Meanwhile, Bill Lee was pitching runless ball for the Cubs. The Tigers managed finally to break through in the sixth inning on Goslin's single and Pete Fox's long triple to left field. Then Lee picked Fox off third base and the resulting argument stalled the game for fifteen minutes.

The Chicago fans were just about ready to celebrate a hard-fought 3–1 victory, going into the eighth inning, when the Tigers snarled back and struck with a 4-run barrage that sent the Cubs reeling. Joe White walked, went to third base on Gehringer's two-base drive, and both men scored on Goslin's long single. Now it was a 3–3 game and the fans were up and screaming for the Cubs, as Warneke came in to pitch.

Fox and Rogell singled in succession, scoring Goslin, and then Rogell was trapped in a rundown play. While Rogell was being put out, Fox sneaked home for the fourth run of the inning, giving the Tigers a 5–3 advantage.

In the ninth inning, a desperate Chicago team, battling furiously with every pitch, tied the score. Chuck Klein and Ken O'Dea, two pinch hitters, came through with timely base hits and 2 big runs, to make it a 5–5 game.

The teams battled through a scoreless tenth, and then came the dramatic eleventh inning. Rogell bunted and was safe. Marv Owen then hit the ball hard but right at the Cubs' second baseman, Herman, and Rogell was out. Clifton was safe as Lindstrom misplayed his ground ball at third base. Then Joe White scored Owen with a single to left for the winning run, as Schoolboy Rowe ended the long game by striking out Chuck Klein and Wally Stephenson, and the Tigers went ahead in the Series, 2 games to 1.

Al Crowder had been trying to win a Series game, but in vain, ever since 1933. But now, in 1935, in the fourth game, in Chicago, Crowder pitched one of the finest games of his lengthy career. He allowed the Cubs just 5 base hits to eke out a 2–1 victory.

The Cubs kept the Series alive by winning the fifth game on October 6 by a 3–1 margin. A big Sunday crowd packed Wrigley Field in Chicago for the critical game, and they were thoroughly rewarded with a victory for the home team. Lon Warneke had to leave the mound after six innings. He had allowed the Tigers just 3 hits and no runs, but had injured his arm as he courageously pitched his heart out for his team. As Lon gave the ball to teammate Bill

Goose Goslin (4) and the Tiger mascot congratulate Hank Greenberg after Hank's 2-run homer in the second game of the 1935 Series.

Charlie Gehringer, one of baseball's greatest second basemen, led the Tigers to their first-ever Series victory with a sparkling .375 batting average.

Lee, who had been shelled off the mound two days before, he told Lee, "Bill, we've got to get this one. Or it's all over." And Lee responded with as brilliant a relief job as the World Series had ever seen. Lee held the Tigers scoreless in the seventh and eighth innings. They did score 1 run in the ninth but it was not enough. The Cubs had risen from the ashes and rallied, to take the Series lead, 3 games to 2.

The sixth game, at Detroit, was a tremendous one from the very first to the final inning. It was a game that saw the two pitchers, Tommy Bridges for the Tigers and Larry French for the Cubs, pitch brilliantly at times; while at other times both pitchers were hit hard. But when the chips were down and the championship was on the line, it was little Tommy Bridges who won the day hurling shutout ball for the last four innings to close down the ever-threatening Cubs.

The Tigers had an opportunity to nail down the game in the very first inning. With 1 out,

Cochrane and Gehringer singled in succession; Goslin popped out, but Fox slammed a two-bag hit over third, scoring Cochrane. Then Walker walked, filling the bases. With an opportunity to pile up a big lead, Bill Rogell slapped a weak roller back to the pitcher, French, whose throw nipped Gehringer at the plate.

The Cubs ripped back in the third inning on singles by Jurges, Galan, and Billy Herman. But once more the Tigers forged ahead as Walker singled. Rogell also singled. Marv Owen's bunt forced Rogell at second base, but Walker went to third and scored on the play at second base.

Now the seesaw battle continued as the Cubs went ahead. French singled, and then Billy Herman just about deflated the Tigers' hopes with a tremendous home run, giving the Cubs a 3–2 edge.

But the never-say-die Tigers roared right back in the sixth inning. Rogell doubled to left field. Then Owen, hitless so far in all 6 games, lined a single to left to score Rogell, and it was a 3–3 game.

The teams battled through the seventh and eighth innings without further scoring, and then Stan Hack exploded with a resounding triple to open the ninth. The crowd sat frozen in their seats, the stadium silent as a tomb, as the Cubs were 90 feet away from a big run. But stout-hearted Tommy Bridges, spitball and all, was equal to the task. Putting every ounce of energy behind every pitch, Tommy struck out Jurges, then got French on a tap to first base, holding Hack on third. Then he faced the hard-hitting Galan, and took care of him, forcing Augie to pop out as the grandstand became a bedlam. Yet even the noise that followed Galan's out was but a murmur compared to the roars of excitement that tore out of Navin Field during the next ten minutes.

The Tigers began the ninth inning with Clifton striking out and then hurling his bat into the stands in disgust with himself. But Mickey Cochrane started the action by ripping a single to left, and then tore into second base on a poor throw by Augie Galan. Now it was up to Goose Goslin, and he was equal to the job at hand. The Goose picked out a fastball, one of Larry French's best pitches of the game, and tore into it, ramming it solidly to right field, and a grinning, crazy-looking Cochrane, jumping up and down like a jack-in-the-box, scored the winning run. And then, there was pandemonium as players and fans tore onto the field to carry off Bridges and Goslin into the clubhouse.

The Detroit Tigers were world champions, and the Tigers' first modern championship set off the greatest celebration ever seen in baseball. Crowds screamed and yelled at the ballpark for forty-five minutes, then marched down to Cadillac Square and Grand Circus Park, snake dancing, shouting, waving banners until well past midnight, while all the bars and night spots stayed open until the sun rose the next morning. Detroit had a terrible hangover, but the championship was worth it.

New York Yankees
Versus New York Giants

Joe DiMaggio arrived at the Yankee spring training camp in 1936 after a series of delays over his signing. Once his contract was set, Joe made the trip from San Francisco to St. Petersburg in a car with Tony Lazzeri and Frank Crosetti. Tony didn't know Joe well, had never seen him play with the San Francisco Seals, where Joe had been the most sensational player in Pacific Coast League history, but Tony readily had adopted him because he was another Italian kid off the sandlots of San Francisco, just as he had adopted Crosetti for the same reason three years before.

It was Tony's idea that the three of them should share the driving chores on the coast-to-coast haul. Tony took the wheel and drove steadily for four hours and then moved over to make room for Crosetti in the driver's seat. When Frankie tired, after four long hours, Tony motioned to Joe.

"All right," he said. "Joe, it's your turn."

"I'm sorry," Joe said. "I don't drive."

Lazzeri and Crosetti looked at each other.

"Let's throw the bum out and leave him here," Tony said.

DiMaggio settled himself more comfortably in the backseat.

"Get going," he said with a laugh. "I got a date with the Yankees."

It isn't likely there was much conversation on the trip. None of the three players even remotely resembled a chatterbox. One day that summer, Jack Mahon, the *International News* sportswriter, reported a scene in his column featuring the three players in the lobby of the Chase Hotel, where the Yankees stayed in St. Louis (see below).

The first time DiMaggio appeared at Yankee Stadium and began to hit, he quickly convinced McCarthy, the players, and the sportswriters that

---

I came down in the elevator. And the three of them—DiMaggio, Crosetti, and Lazzeri—were sitting there, watching the guests coming and going. I bought a paper and sat down near them and after a while became aware of the fact that none of them had uttered a single word. Just for the hell of it, I timed them to see how long they would maintain their silence. Believe it or not, no one spoke a word for an hour and thirty minutes. At the end of the time, DiMaggio cleared his throat.

Crosetti looked at him and said: "What did you say, Joe?"

And Lazzeri said: "Shut up. He didn't say a thing."

the stories of his skill and power had not been exaggerated. He drove pitch after pitch into the stands with a display of power that caused all players to stop in their tracks and take another good, long look at the youngster. In the outfield, Joe pulled down everything hit in his general area, and his throws to the catcher were accurate. There was the unmistakable stamp of a major league player on him and an aura of greatness about him.

A painful foot injury kept Joe out of the lineup for about ten days, but when he was finally inserted again, the Yankees caught fire and quickly spurted into first place. Overnight they began to click.

Before the season opened, an angry, frus-

In the opening game of the 1936 Series, the Giants' curveball wizard, Carl Hubbell, allowed the Yanks just 6 hits to post a 6–1 victory.

trated, embittered Babe Ruth, denied in his efforts to win the job as the Yankee manager, asked for and secured his release from Colonel Ruppert. He would immediately be named a vice president and assistant manager of the Boston Braves. And thus a Yankee baseball legend was gone.

Now Lou Gehrig, always overshadowed by Ruth, would finally come into his own as the brightest star of the Yankees in his fifteenth year. In 1936, Lou would drive out 49 home runs, hit for a stellar .354 average. Others in the lineup included Ben Chapman in center field; George Selkirk in right; Frank Crosetti at shortstop; Red Rolfe at third base; Tony Lazzeri on second; and Bill Dickey, in his ninth season, had developed into the finest catcher in the major leagues. Pitchers included Lefty Gomez, Red Ruffing, Bump Hadley, Pat Malone, Monte Pearson, and relief pitcher, Johnny Murphy.

By August all the other clubs in the league had wilted under the tremendous rush of the Yankees' continuous assaults. On September 9, the Yanks clinched the pennant.

The New York Giants hustled their way to the National League flag by 5 games over the Cubs. The Giants lineup included manager Bill Terry at first base; Joe Moore in right field; Dick Bartell, shortstop; Burgess Whitehead on second; Travis Jackson, third base; Jim Ripple in center field; Mel Ott with 33 homers in right field; Gus Mancuso, catcher; Hank Lieber, in center field. Pitchers included Carl Hubbell, the MVP in 1936 with a 26–6 record; Fred Fitzsimmons; Hal Schumacher; Harry Gumbert; Clyde Castleman; and Dick Coffman.

"When I look back over the record of my first season with the Yankees, I'm still amazed that one team could show such power," said Joe DiMaggio.* "I had a three-twenty-three average for my first year and twenty-nine home runs. I tied with Red Rolfe for the league lead in triples with fifteen. Bill Dickey led the club with a three-sixty-two average, and Gehrig, who was right behind him with three-fifty-four, topped

*This account of the 1936 World Series was given by Joe DiMaggio during a series of interviews with the author in 1951 on New York radio station WINS.

The Yankees' murderers row of 1936: (*left to right*) Tony Lazzeri, Joe DiMaggio, Jake Powell, Lou Gehrig, Bill Dickey, George Selkirk and Red Rolfe were enough to strike terror into any pitcher in the 1936 Series.

the circuit with forty-nine home runs, and for the sixth time in his great career batted in more than one hundred fifty runs (one-fifty-two) and for the fifth time had more than four hundred total bases.

"Only two regulars hit less than three hundred, and one of them, Tony Lazzeri, hit seven home runs in a span of four consecutive games, two of them with the bases loaded. Crosetti, the only other regular to hit under three hundred, was at two-eighty-eight, with fifteen homers. Jake Powell hit three-oh-one and stole twenty-six bases. Our seven pitchers were among the first fifteen in the league in won and lost records. All told, the Yankees won one hundred two games and took the pennant from the Tigers by nineteen and a half games.

"The above statistics constitute a pretty good background for any club to bring into a World Series. We were the favorite over the Giants in the first Subway Series in thirteen years, but learned right off the reel that you can't be bringing your scrapbooks into the World Series.

"Despite a chill, penetrating rain, bad enough to call off any World Series game, the [first] game was tight. We came up in the eighth behind by two to one and Crosetti got to Hubbell for a double. Rolfe bunted in front of the plate to move Frankie over, but got a single when Hubbell slipped in the mud attempting to field the ball. I then hit a low liner toward right and Burgess Whitehead, playing second for the Giants, snagged it just before it hit the ground and then doubled Rolfe off first base.

"It wasn't much of an exhibition to cheer my mother and my brother Tom, who had come in from the West Coast for the game. Even though I did make a single, one of our seven hits off Hubb, I also was one of the eight strikeouts he hung up.

"The rain, which had started with the ball game, kept up all afternoon and all night, and after an inspection of the almost flooded Polo Grounds next morning, Judge Landis postponed the second game.

"It was in this game that I finally had the

thrill of playing before the President of the United States, a thrill which had been denied me when I missed the opening game [of the season] in Washington. Mr. Roosevelt was here for the game and he really saw something, because we went to town by an eighteen to four score. There were twelve records broken or equaled in this long one-sided game.

"Lazzeri hit a home run with the bases filled, the second in [World Series] history. We got seventeen hits and my contribution was a double and two singles.

"I tied one of the Series records by making three putouts in one inning, the ninth, and I made the last one under novel circumstances. Joe Moore opened the inning with an ordinary fly ball to me, and then Dick Bartell doubled. Terry hit a low liner to center and I came in to take the drive at my shoe tops. Then Big Hank Lieber really exploded one, a long, high fly that I had to chase almost to the edge of the clubhouse steps where I made the catch.

"All spectators had been asked to remain seated until the President left the grounds after the game. I was only a few yards from the steps to our dressing room and I was undecided whether to go on up or not, but I saw all our other players standing where they were and the Giants, too. So I remained at the foot of the stairs and Mr. Roosevelt's car passed within a few feet as it left the park. He gave a wave and a grin, but whether it was for me personally or for the wildly cheering fans in the bleachers, I can't say.

"When the Series moved to Yankee Stadium, we beat Fred Fitzsimmons by two to one in a real tough ball game. A single by Crosetti off Fitz's glove won the game for us. Fred, one of the best fielding pitchers in the game, couldn't pick up the ball, and neither could Whitehead, who came charging in from second. Fitz held us to four hits, one a long homer by Lou Gehrig. I made a double but it didn't figure in the scoring.

"My San Francisco cronies, Crosetti and Lazzeri, were the big noises. Frank with the game-winning single he smashed off Fitz's glove to score Powell, and Tony with a great catch of a line drive by Travis Jackson, which saved the day for Bump Hadley.

"I was horse-collared by Hubbell in the fourth game, but didn't care much as we beat him, five to two, before a record crowd—sixty-six thousand six hundred sixty-nine—and Lou Gehrig hit another home run. Monte Pearson breezed in for us and we all felt the Series would end without us having to return to the Polo Grounds. We didn't count on the pitching skill and courage of Hal Schumacher, who beat us five to four in ten innings the next day.

"Schumacher was in hot water all the way, but invariably he got a third strike by when he had to. We left nine on base as Hal fanned ten of us. He got me twice, once in the third with the bases full and no outs. He followed up his strikeout of me by fanning Gehrig, and then got Dickey on a fly ball. A hit by any one of us might have had him out of there.

"That exhibition by Schumacher cooled us off somewhat. We held a wobbly six to five lead

Yankee outfielder Jake Powell just reaches first base as Bill Terry of the Giants misses the tag.

Freshman Joe DiMaggio in his first World Series was a Yankee standout in 1936 with a .346 average.

move would be. I figured Terry would charge across the diamond at me and force me to make a break. When he threw to Mayo, who had moved in behind me, I took off for the plate as soon as Bill cocked his arm.

"Danning had the plate well guarded and I knew I couldn't make it by going in feet first with an orthodox slide. The only thing to do was dive over and around Harry, which I did, sweeping my hand across the plate.

"In the light of what happened after I scored, that run didn't mean much, but I got a great thrill out of it. We went on to score six more runs, for a total of seven in the inning, and walked away with the game, and with the Series, by a score of thirteen to five.

"That inning proved the truth of an old saying around the American League, an adage that was in good standing back in the days when I played on the Old Horse Lot in San Francisco: Give the Yankees an inch and they'll take a mile. One run on a very close play opened the gates for us and we had seven runs before the inning was over.

"My mother was almost hysterical with joy when we won the Series. She didn't know much about baseball, of course, but she could follow the general trend of the play from the shouts of the crowd.

"One of the biggest thrills she got was seeing the Statue of Liberty. She seemed surprised that it looked just the same as it did when she arrived in this country, some thirty-four years before, from Palermo.

"I took the train for San Francisco after the victory party. I was very happy with the Series and the season. And I'd take a lot of stories back home to the old gang at Columbus and Taylor Street."

after eight innings of the sixth game and knew that if the Giants won out, they'd have a well-rested Hubbell for the seventh game. I opened the ninth with a single and was chased to third for Gehrig's single.

"Art Fletcher, coaching at third, was whooping it up. 'Got to get this one in, Joe,' he yelled. 'Get this one in and we're home. On your toes now.'

"I broke for home when Dickey grounded toward first and seemed trapped when Terry came up with the ball. Bill, however, instead of throwing to Danning at the plate, threw behind the runner to Mayo, playing third for the Giants. When Terry came up with the ball, I stopped, halfway home, waiting to see what the next

New York Yankees
Versus New York Giants

When the 1937 season began, Joe DiMaggio was no longer the only DiMaggio in the major leagues. His older brother, Vince, was playing for the Boston Braves under Casey Stengel, and Vince led the team in home runs with 13. There were other stops later on for Vince, with the Reds, Pirates, and Giants. His best year was to be in 1941, with the Pirates, when he hit 21 home runs and drove in 100.

One afternoon, following a short practice session during the Yankees' spring training at Clearwater, Florida, the Yankees' court jester, Lefty Gomez, was holding forth.

With a wink and a sly smile at the bystanders in the locker room, Lefty said: "Sure is a hell of a nice guy, this DiMaggio of ours. His brother, Vince, gets him a tryout with the Seals in San Francisco, then what do you know? He beats his brother out of a job."

"I never did that," said DiMaggio with a scowl, annoyed.

"Sure you did," Gomez said. "You were together with the Seals in the spring of 1933, weren't you?"

"Yes," said Joe.

"Vince was a regular in the outfield, wasn't he? And after a while you were a regular?"

"That's right."

"And whose place did you take?"

"Well, but?"

"But what?" Gomez said, grinning.

"I don't know."

"Joe, you don't know what happened to Vince?"

"Hollywood bought his contract?"

"Hear that, guys, Hollywood bought him," Gomez said. "You mean the Seals sold him to Hollywood to make room for you! See, this DiMaggio is nothing but an ungrateful bum who beat his brother out of a job."

Joe smiled, enjoying the fun that Gomez was poking at him.

None of the other Yankees ever talked to Joe that way. Still somewhat shy, he would remain that way throughout his fifteen years with the team. He preferred his privacy. His shyness, he now believes, developed when his parents used to tease him about his mistakes in speaking Italian as a youngster in San Francisco. Still, in his shyness, he enjoyed Lefty Gomez; they had dinner together on trips, and they went out on the town together. They were baseball's odd couple—the introverted slugger and the extroverted pitcher. "Opposites attract," Joe explained once.

Except for demeanor, however, they weren't that opposite. Their roots were similar—both were from California, and, remarkably, both had played for the Seals before the Yankees purchased them.

There were many laughs for the Yankees in

1937 as they breezed to another pennant, by 13 games over the Tigers. The Tigers were never a threat after their great player-manager, Mickey Cochrane, was hit in the head by pitcher Bump Hadley of the Yankees. For days it seemed as if Cochrane would not leave the hospital alive. When he finally recovered, he was never to play again.

DiMaggio, instead of being bothered by the so-called sophomore jinx, was sensational in 1937. He hit for a .346 average, with 46 home runs. Lou Gehrig had another banner year, collecting a .351 average, with 37 home runs. Dickey hit .332, with 29 homers. Ruffing won 20 games, and Johnny Murphy was simply unbelievable as he relieved Yankee hurlers in game after game, winning 13 himself.

In 1937 a new face appeared in the Yankee lineup: hawk-nosed, boyish Tommy Henrich, who joined the team after he received a $25,000 bonus. Henrich was to enrich Yankee fans for the next eleven years, and earned the nickname Old Reliable for his remarkable ability to come through with the big hit when the Yankees needed one.

Another fine rookie joining the team in 1937 was the Georgia University former All-Southern halfback Spud Chandler, who was a sprint and hurdles star with the track team. A tough, solidly built right-hander with a bulletlike fastball, Chandler would go on to become a Yankee mainstay for eleven seasons, and twice during that period would win 20 games.

In the National League the winning Giants made a few changes in their lineup, though it was practically the same club that met the Yankees in the 1936 Series. Carl Hubbell, ace of the Giants' pitching staff, was the league's leading hurler, with a 22-8 record, and a young southpaw, Cliff Melton, won 20 games for the Giants during the season. Now it was felt that the Giants, who barely squeezed by the Cubs to win the pennant by 3 games, were in a much better position to challenge the Yankees with a one-two duo of pitching aces in Hubbell and Melton.

Lefty Gomez opposed Carl Hubbell in the first game, at Yankee Stadium, and it began as if it would turn out to be like one of those

Shortstop Dick Bartell of the Giants was the defensive star of his team in the 1937 Series.

marvelous Marquard-Plank pitching duels of bygone years as the teams battled each other on even, though scoreless, terms for four innings.

The Giants broke through in the fifth inning when Jim Ripple and McCarthy both singled. Gus Mancuso hit into a double play, but Ripple scored on the play. And just when Giant fans were beginning to believe that the 1 run would be enough to win, the Yankees dropped their atom bomb.

Hubbell started the seventh inning by walking Gomez. It was the first indication that Carl was beginning to lose his stuff. Crosetti then singled, followed by consecutive singles by Rolfe and DiMaggio. Gehrig walked and Bill Dickey singled home 2 runs. Then, following a single by Selkirk, Hubbell was removed. By that time it was a 5–1 game.

Dick Coffman came in to pitch to Lazzeri and Tony shot a hard grounder to Whitehead, who messed up the play, and 2 more runs were in and it was a 7-run inning. In the eighth inning, Lazzeri slammed a home run and it was 8–1, and that was the final score.

The second game resulted in the same score as the first, although the Yankees spread their scoring over three innings: the fifth, sixth, and seventh. Charlie Ruffing started the game for the Yankees; he was opposed by Cliff Melton, the rookie Giant hurler. Melton held the Yanks in check for five innings before the Bombers shelled him from the mound to easily win their second straight game.

In the third game, at the Polo Grounds, on October 8, Monte Pearson was opposed on the mound by Hal Schumacher. There were early signs that the Yankees would continue their bombardment of Giant pitching. They scored 1 run in the second inning, 2 more in the third, and 1 in each of the fourth and fifth innings off Schumacher to take a commanding 5–0 lead, as Monte Pearson forgot about all his arm problems and held the Giants to but 4 hits through the eight innings he pitched.

In the ninth inning, the Giants finally stirred. Ott singled and then Ripple and Lieber walked, and the bases were full. Manager McCarthy removed Pearson, brought in "the Fireman," Johnny Murphy, and John got Danning to hit a short fly to DiMaggio. Although the Giants scored 1 run, game three was soon history.

Even though the Giants were down by 3 games, interest perked up considerably as the pitchers were announced for the fourth game of the Series. Bill Terry of the Giants announced that Carl Hubbell would take the mound, while manager Joe McCarthy surprised everyone with his selection of Bump Hadley, an 11-game winner during the season.

The Yankees scored in the very first inning as Red Rolfe lined a triple to left field. DiMaggio singled to score Rolfe, and the Yanks had a 1–0 lead.

It was a short-lived lead, however, for the Giants came roaring back in the second inning. Lieber, McCarthy, and Danning singled in succession, and Lieber came in on Danning's hit. Burgess Whitehead's grounder hit Danning and Harry was automatically out. Hubbell slammed a grounder to Lazzeri, scoring McCarthy, as Tony's throw was wide of the plate. Moore then singled, scoring Whitehead, who had walked.

Ivy Andrews relieved Hadley at that point, and Bartell greeted him with a long single to left, scoring Hubbell. Ripple walked, again filling the bases. Lieber came up to hit for his

The Giants' catcher, Harry Danning, sparked the Giants' offense with 3 straight hits in the fourth game of the Series for the team's only win.

Tony Lazzeri led all Yankee batters with a rousing .400 average in the 1937 Series.

second time in the inning, and again singled, scoring Bartell and Moore, and it was 6–1, Giants.

The Yanks scored in the second inning, and again in the ninth on Gehrig's home run. (It was to be Lou's last home run in a World Series.) But the Giants were out in front to stay and won, 7–3.

Hubbell's victory was but a short respite for the Giants, as the Yankees took the final game of the Series on Sunday, October 10, by a 4 to 2 margin.

After a scoreless first inning, Myril Hoag, the Yankees' left fielder, led off the second inning with a smashing home run on Melton's first pitch, to give the Yanks an early 1–0 lead. In the third inning, DiMaggio drove another Melton pitch into the stands, to give the Yanks a 2–0 lead.

But the Giants came right back in their half of the second inning as Mel Ott blasted a home run into the seats with Bartell on base, to tie the score at 2–2. But it was the last Giant gasp; Lefty Gomez held the Giants in check for the remainder of the game.

In the fifth inning, the Yanks broke the deadlock when Lazzeri drove a long drive into left-center field that went for a triple; then Gomez singled, scoring Tony. Then it was up to Lou Gehrig, and Lou came through with a ringing double, scoring Gomez with the fourth and final run of the Series. Gehrig, with a triple and a double, knocked in 2 of the Yankees' 4 runs, and once again the Yankees were World Series champions.

In addition to Gehrig, Tony Lazzeri was also outstanding for the Yanks. He hit for a .400 average. Red Rolfe and Myril Hoag were the only other Yanks to hit .300. DiMaggio was held to .273. Top man for the Giants was Joe Moore, with a .391 average.

Each Yankee share amounted to $6,471. Each Giant share was a substantial $4,489.

New York Yankees
Versus Chicago Cubs

There were a number of important changes in the Yankee lineup for 1938, and despite the changes, the Yanks continued to hammer away and defeat all challengers, particularly the Red Sox, who folded in the final month of a torrid race. The Yankees thundered home to win the pennant by 9½ games.

Tony Lazzeri, a key player in the Yankee infield for some twelve years, was traded to the Chicago Cubs at the end of the 1937 season, and a newcomer who had starred for the Yankee farm team in Newark was given the opportunity to break into the lineup at second. His name, Joe Gordon.

Oscar Vitt, Gordon's manager at Newark, said of Gordon's ability: "Joe Gordon is going to be the greatest second baseman you ever saw. I've seen 'em all: Lajoie, Evers, Hornsby, Frisch, Gehringer. Right now this kid is on a par with them and he will be even better."

In spring training, McCarthy was delighted as he watched Gordon and Crosetti flipping the ball back and forth, weaving and floating around second base. Joe said he hadn't been too happy with the play of his second basemen and short-stops in the last few seasons, but this year, in the spring of 1938, he was delighted with the combination of Gordon and Crosetti.

Tom Henrich had recovered from several injuries and easily won an outfield position. But

there was some concern about the play and all-around movement of Lou Gehrig. He seemed to have lost his power at the plate, and his maneuverability at first base seemed limited, slow.

The Chicago Cubs, who had won pennants every third year since 1929, bounced back as the National League pennant winner under the inspired leadership of manager Gabby Hartnett, who had replaced Charlie Grimm halfway through the season.

The Cubs made headlines at the end of the 1937 season, when they acquired the onetime most valuable pitcher in the league, the colorful, incredible Dizzy Dean, from the Cardinals. The acquisition was reported to have cost the Cubs $250,000, as well as several players. With manager Hartnett carefully picking spots for Dizzy, Dean managed to win 7 big games for the Cubs at a period when every game spelled *pennant*. Other new Cubs included ex-Yankee Tony Lazzeri, Carl Reynolds, Jack Russell, and Rip Collins (another ex-Gashouse Gang member).

First-game pitchers were Bill Lee for Chicago and Red Ruffing for the Yankees as the Series opened at Wrigley Field in Chicago on October 5. Lee showed the effects of his team's furious September grind in a most difficult pennant race by giving up 12 base hits, while Ruffing, effective in the pinches, allowed the Cub batters 9 hits, to win the opening game, 3–1.

The second game featured stout-hearted Dizzy Dean in a masterful display against Yankee star Lefty Gomez. The game, played at Wrigley Field on October 6, was a sellout, and fans paid as much as $100 for a box seat. They came to see Dean beat the Yankees.

But Dizzy didn't have much speed on his fastball that afternoon, only a dinky curveball and a lot of soft stuff, instead of the fog and speed he threw back in 1934. But the Yanks were so eager to hit him, they were popping the ball into the air or into the dirt. They wouldn't have had a run going into the eighth inning if it hadn't been for some poor fielding behind Diz in the second inning. Even so, he was leading 3–2 when the Yankees came to bat in the eighth.

But he was dog-tired now. He had stood the Yankees off for seven innings with his head and great heart, and now they were crowding him. Selkirk opened with a ringing single to right. Joe Gordon forced Selkirk, and Hoag, hitting for Gomez, forced Gordon. With 2 outs, Crosetti came up to hit. Frank hit a slow ball, timed beautifully, far and high over the right-field fence, scoring Hoag ahead of him and putting the Yanks in the lead, 4–3.

Johnny Murphy, who had replaced Gomez on the mound for the Yanks, turned the Cubs back in their half of the eighth inning, and then the Yanks were up again. Tommy Henrich led off with a sharp single to right. Joe DiMaggio stepped in, took the first pitch for a strike, then flattened the next pitch with the fat part of his bat and the ball shot out of the park for a home run, and Dizzy was then taken out of the box.

Well, Dean had given the Yankees a tussle. But they defeated him after a mighty struggle, 6–3, and that really clinched the Series for them. The teams left for New York that night for the next two games.

The third game of the Series, played before a crowd of better than fifty-five thousand fans, saw a superlative pitching duel between Yankee star Monte Pearson and young Clay Bryant of the Cubs. The Cubbies broke the ice when Stan Hack opened the inning with a ringing double. Cavarretta was safe on an error, and then Hack scored as Joe Marty forced Cavarretta.

Joe Gordon evened the score when he homered in the fifth inning. It was the first Yankee hit off Bryant. Then Pearson came through with a base hit, Crosetti walked, and Red Rolfe golfed another single, which brought Pearson across the plate, and it was quickly a 2–1 game.

In the sixth inning, the Yanks erupted in a hurry, as DiMaggio and Lou Gehrig singled and Selkirk walked, filling the bases. Joe Gordon then slapped a hard single to center field, scoring DiMaggio and Selkirk. Russell came in to relieve Bryant and put out the Yankee fire for the moment. In the eighth inning, the Yanks scored once more when Dickey hammered a home run to give the Yankees their fifth and final run, and a 5–2 win.

For the fourth game, the Yankees started Red Ruffing and the Cubs started Bill Lee, who was effective in only the first inning. The second inning was a disaster for the Cubs and for Lee, as the Yanks pounded him for 3 big runs.

There were two Yanks on base when Frankie Crosetti drove a high, arching drive into left-center field that fell in for a triple, and 2 more runs were in. In the eighth inning, Crosetti once again faced Dizzy Dean, who was relieving Tex Carleton, with the bases full, and drove a long fly ball between right and center field that could

In his fourth World Series with the Yankees, in 1938, Bill Dickey led all his teammates with a nifty .400 batting average.

The 1938 World Champion New York Yankees

not be handled and fell in for a two-base hit. Two more Yankees scored, to give the Yankees an 8–1 margin.

The Cubs fought back in their half of the eighth and scored 2 runs, but then Ruffing handcuffed them in the ninth to wrap up a well-deserved 8–3 victory. And the Yankees were world champions for the third straight year.

After the game, Dizzy Dean pushed his way through the jam in the Yankees' dressing room to shake Joe McCarthy's hand.

"Congratulations, Joe," he said. "You got a great club."

"Thanks, Diz," Joe said. "I was sorry we had to beat you the other day. You pitched a great game."

"That's all right, Joe," Diz said. "I got beat by a great team."

They were both right.

1939

New York Yankees
Versus Cincinnati Reds

No one could figure out what was wrong with Lou Gehrig during the spring of 1939. He'd had, for him, rather a poor year in 1938. He had made a good start, but was gripped in a terrific slump soon after the halfway mark in the schedule. His average skidded. His home runs became fewer.

"I don't know what's wrong with him," McCarthy said, "but it isn't merely that he is slowing down as a player. There is something physically wrong with him, something that is robbing him of his power. He isn't popping up, striking out, or just getting a piece of the ball. He is hitting the ball squarely, but it isn't going anywhere."

Because of his fine start, Lou wound up with 29 home runs and a .295 average, but that was 56 points below his average in 1937. That was the first time since 1925 that he failed to hit .300 or better. In the World Series he got just 4 singles. There was no power there at all.

Now, in the spring of 1939, Lou couldn't hit or field. He was slow getting down for a ground ball, slow getting up, slow covering the bag. Nobody said a word to him. The baseball writers, out of admiration and sympathy for him, were guarded in their comments. Now and then one of them asked McCarthy a question about

Lou. But McCarthy would either evade a reply or just shake it off.

The season had opened and the team had played eight games, when on the night of April 30 the Yankees left for Detroit. When they reached Detroit on the morning of May 2, Lou talked to his manager.

"Joe, I'm benching myself."

McCarthy was silent for a moment. And then: "Why, Lou?"

"For the good of the team," Lou said. "I just can't seem to get going and nobody has to tell me how bad I've been and how much of a drawback I've been to the team. I've been thinking maybe the time has come for me to quit."

"Quit? You don't have to quit. Take a rest for a week or so. Maybe you'll feel better."

Lou shook his head. "No, Joe. I don't think so."

"All right, Lou," Joe said. "Take a rest for a few days. I'll put Dahlgren on first base today. But you remember, that's your position, and whenever you want it back, just walk out and take it."

For the first time since June 1, 1925, Lou Gehrig sat in the dugout as the Yankees took the field. His string of 2,130 consecutive games had been broken. The story flashed across the country, hit the headlines on every sports page, was shrilled through radio programs all over the nation:

"Gehrig benched! Dahlgren on first base for Yankees!"

On June 20 the nation was shocked. Gehrig had been to the Mayo Clinic in Rochester, Minnesota, for tests and observation, and the report from Mayo was: "Lou Gehrig is suffering from amyotrophic lateral sclerosis, a form of infantile paralysis." He could never play baseball again.

Back at Yankee Stadium, the team kidded Lou. They told him he would be okay. They made gentle fun with him, and letters and wires poured in from the fans all over the country.

Then, on July 4, at Yankee Stadium, New York paid to Lou Gehrig the finest tribute a ballplayer had ever received. It was Lou Gehrig Appreciation Day, and it was the big town's way of saying, or trying to say, with gifts and roaring cheers and laughs and tears, how much they thought of him.

Many of the old Yankees were there—the Yankees of 1927: the Babe, Bob Meusel, Herb Pennock, Waite Hoyt, Tony Lazzeri, Ben Bengough, Art Fletcher, Bob Shawkey, Earle Combs. Also present were celebrities from the theater, the mayor and the governor. And Lou made a speech that day that will never be forgotten. No one who heard it will ever forget not only the words but also the sound of his voice, the emotion, and the way he stood out there bravely. And when Babe Ruth walked over and hugged Lou, the well of emotion was almost too much to bear.

Without Gehrig in the lineup, the Yankees continued their fine play and rolled over their opponents, and by June 15 they were 20 games ahead of the Red Sox. At season's end, the Yankees had a 17-game advantage over Boston.

Batting sixth in the lineup, Joe DiMaggio was unbelievable as he pounded 30 homers and finished with an .381 average. Ruffing was the big winner among Yankee pitchers, with 21 wins. Steve Sundra won 11 in a row before losing his only game of the year.

The Cincinnati Reds had captured the National League flag for the first time since 1919.

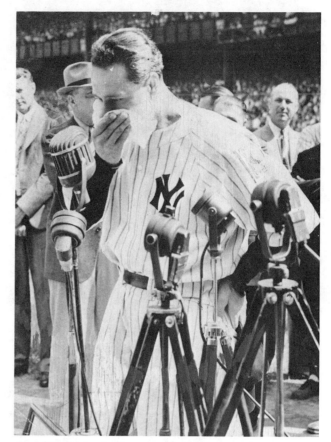

Lou Gehrig's famous farewell speech to his teammates, July 4, 1939

Manager Bill McKechnie was a hero, and so were Paul Derringer, Bucky Walters, and Ernie Lombardi. Bill McKechnie thought that the Reds actually could beat the Yankees.

"Let them come," said McKechnie. "We're ready."

The World Series opened at Yankee Stadium, with Red Ruffing against the Reds' ace, Paul Derringer, and the first game turned out to be the best of the Series.

The Reds scored first in the fourth inning, when Ivy Goodman walked, stole second, and then scored as McCormick rammed a single past Rolfe at third base. The Yanks tied the game in the fifth inning, when Joe Gordon singled, Babe Dahlgren smashed a double down the left field line, and Gordon came in on a close play at the plate. There was no further scoring until the ninth inning, when Charlie Keller drove a high liner toward the center field bleachers. Goodman leaped high into the air and almost caught the

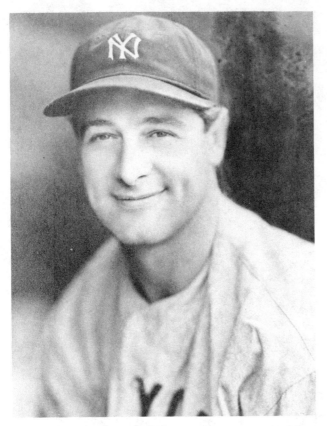

A Yankee immortal, Lou Gehrig played in 2,130 consecutive games from June 1, 1925, to April 30, 1939.

ball, but it rolled away from him and Keller raced to third. Then DiMaggio walked and Bill Dickey ended the game by punching a single to left and Keller danced home with the game-ending run, for a thrilling 2–1 victory.

Monte Pearson, who had won impressively in each of the last three World Series, made his greatest effort in the second game of the Series by allowing the Reds only 2 base hits, shutting them out for a 4–0 win. Pearson pitched no-hit ball for eight innings before Lombardi lined a single over second base. In the ninth inning, Bill Werber singled with 2 outs but Pearson then shut the Reds down.

When the Series moved to Cincinnati for the third game, on October 7, Red fans hoped for better days. Junior Thompson, a 13-game winner, was manager McKechnie's choice, while Lefty Gomez started for New York. But Lefty

injured his side and was replaced in the second inning by Hadley.

The Reds outhit the Yankees in this game, 10 to 5, but the 5 Yankee blows were good for 17 bases. Keller hit 2 home runs, and Dickey and DiMaggio each hit 1 homer. All 10 of the Reds' hits were of the one-base variety. The Yanks won handily, 7–3.

The fourth Series game saw Paul Derringer as the Reds' starting hurler, while manager McCarthy selected Oral Hildebrand.

For six innings, the game was one of those tense 0–0 battles with both pitchers hurling magnificently.

The the Bronx Bombers struck.

Charlie Keller drove out a home run to lead off the seventh inning. Then, almost before the Cincinnati fans could take another breath of air, Dickey slugged another homer and it was 2–0, New York.

The Reds surprised and thrilled their fans by coming back in their half of the seventh to score 3 times and take a 3–2 lead. Suddenly they seemed to be back in the Series.

In the eighth inning, Goodman led off the Reds' half of the inning with a double, and now the crowd was up and roaring for a hit. Big Ernie Lombardi responded by singling Goodman home, to give Cincinnati a 4–2 lead.

Bucky Walters came in to protect the Reds' 4–2 lead in the ninth inning, and the first batter for the Yanks was Charlie Keller, who had already battered the Reds' pitchers for 3 homers, a double and a single. Now, in the ninth, Walters pitched carefully to Keller, had 2 strikes on him, when suddenly Keller singled to left. DiMaggio also singled. Then Bill Dickey hit a perfect double-play ball to Lonny Frey. But Frey threw high to second base, and everybody was safe as Keller scored. That was the break the Bombers needed. Gordon hit a screaming drive to Werber at third, but Bill's throw was too late to head off DiMaggio, who scored, and the Yanks had tied the game with 2 big runs.

Crosetti walked to start the ninth inning, and Red Rolfe moved him to second on a sacrifice bunt. Then Myers fumbled Keller's grounder and Crosetti went to third base on the error.

Then came the big payoff play. DiMaggio

drove a pitch into left-center field. Goodman fumbled the ball, then made a long throw to the plate. But Crosetti had already scored, and then Keller dashed for the plate. Just as Lombardi grabbed Goodman's throw, Keller came charging in like a fullback, hit Lombardi as the ball arrived, and knocked him off his feet; both Keller and Lombardi were stunned. But Charlie recovered and touched home plate while Lombardi still lay there just a couple of feet from the ball. Then, as Lombardi made no motion to get to his feet, coach Art Fletcher waved DiMaggio home.

Lombardi appeared ludicrous, lying on the ground, still dazed, not knowing what was happening, while the Yankees literally ran away with the final game, 7–3, and the World Series.

Charlie Keller was, of course, the Series hero, with 7 hits and a .438 average for the Series in his first year with the Yankees. DiMaggio was the only other Yankee to hit above .300, at .313.

This was the last Series trip that the captain of the Yankees, Lou Gehrig, would ever make, and the celebration on the train back to New York was toned down by McCarthy out of respect for Lou.

Joe McCarthy became the first manager to win four World Championships in succession. It was the eighth title for the Yankees, and the seventh since 1927, of which five were sweeps.

The amazing Yankees had won 28 World Series games out of 31, for an incredible .901 percentage. They now owned practically every World Series record in the books.

Aboard the "Yankee Special" en route to Cincinnati for game three, the dinner menu for the ballplayers included sirloin steak and all the extras. Price: $2.25 for the dinner.

Cincinnati Reds Versus Detroit Tigers

The year 1940 was one of great travail and sorrow for the Cincinnati Reds. One of the most popular members of the team, catcher Willard Hershberger, committed suicide a day after the team had lost a crucial game to the Giants at the Polo Grounds, 5–4. The loss moved the Dodgers into first place, shoving the Reds into second.

After the game, a despondent Hershberger told McKechnie, "I lost the game. I called for the wrong pitch and Danning hit a home run. That call could cost us the pennant."

"Forget it," his teammates said. "We're just half a game off. We'll get it back tomorrow." But Hershy continued to brood.

When the game was over, McKechnie, who had encountered almost every vagary of human personality in his dealing with ballplayers through the years, took young Hershberger to dinner and talked to him.

The catcher suddenly told his manager he was contemplating suicide. McKechnie was startled, and seeing the youngster was deeply troubled, Bill talked with him far into the night and finally seemed to have restored his sense of balance.

The next day, with a doubleheader scheduled, Hershberger did not appear at the ballpark. And a search of his room disclosed that the young catcher had slit his throat.

The terrible tragedy threw a pall over the team. They returned home and played listlessly.

The Cincinnati fans seemed to understand and reacted quietly.

Then their great pitching star, Johnny Vander Meer, who had amazed the sports world by hurling successive no-hit games late in 1938, had slumped badly in 1939 and was sent to Indianapolis to recover his confidence. He was recalled in 1940, about the time of the Hershberger tragedy, and Vandy began to win. The team slowly straightened out its affairs, and in a must-win game against the Brooklyn Dodgers, the Reds behind Vander Meer won the game and went on to capture their second straight National League pennant.

The 1940 Detroit Tigers won the American League flag with a .584 percentage, just barely nosing out the Indians by 1 game.

The Tigers were not a great club, but like most Tiger champions before it, the 1940 edition packed plenty of power. They were led by Hank Greenberg, who hit 41 homers and slugged out a .340 average; Rudy York hit 33 home runs; Barney McCoskey hit for a .340 average; Charlie Gehringer hit .313. They got marvelous pitching from Bobo Newson, who won 21 games; Tommy Bridges, the great curveball star, won 12 games; and Schoolboy Rowe, in his eighth year with the Tigers, winning 16 games.

Manager Del Baker, a former Tiger catcher and coach for many years, had added such promising youngsters as Barney McCoskey; Bruce Campbell, who survived two attacks of meningitis; and Billy Sullivan, and three promising pitchers in Dizzy Trout, Fred Hutchinson, and John Gorsica. And they were ready and fired up with enthusiasm to play the Reds.

The World Series opened in Cincinnati on October 2, and it looked like another picnic for the American League. Paul Derringer was bombed out of the game in the second inning, and the Tigers coasted to a 7–2 victory behind the fine pitching of Bobo Newsom, who allowed the Reds just 8 base hits and practically laughed his way to victory.

In the second game the Reds' ace, Bucky Walters, made a shaky start against the Tiger star Schoolboy Rowe by allowing 2 runs in the very first inning.

But the Reds came fighting back in the second frame, driving out 4 successive base hits and scoring 2 runs to tie the game, 2–2.

In the Reds' half of the third inning, Goodman singled and then scored when Jim Ripple drove a ball out of the park for a 2-run home run. Successive two-base hits by Walters and Werber gave the Reds another run and a 5–2 lead. The Tigers came back to score a run in the sixth inning, but it wasn't quite enough, and the Tigers were held scoreless for the remainder of the game for an easy 5–3 Reds victory.

In the third game, played at Navin Field in Detroit on October 4, Tommy Bridges of the Tigers and the veteran hurler for the Reds, Jim Turner, faced each other in a remarkable pitching duel for six innings. Then, with the score tied, 1–1, both teams began to slug the ball. Bridges allowed 10 hits, but his Tiger teammates rapped Turner and two Cincinnati relievers for 13 base hits and a 5–1 lead. Rudy York and Pinky Higgins of the Tigers blasted 2-run homers to lead the Tigers' attack.

The Reds battled gamely as they scored a run in the seventh and 2 more in the eighth to make it a tight 5–4 game.

Joe Beggs came in to pitch for the Reds in the eighth inning and Greenberg greeted him with a lusty triple. Campbell singled to center, scoring Hank. Then Higgins drove in Campbell with a sharp double, and it was 7–4, Detroit.

With a 2–1 edge in games, manager Del Baker decided to start pitcher Dizzy Trout, who had a poor 3-7 record during the regular season. Paul Derringer, who had been knocked out in the opening game of the Series, came back to oppose Trout in the fourth contest and was in marvelous form as he allowed the Tigers just 5 hits and came away with a 5–2 victory.

With the Series deadlocked at 2 games each, Del Baker started Bobo Newsom, and Bobo pitched "a game for Dad" on Sunday, October 6. Newsom's dad had passed away three days before.

Manager McKechnie utilized pitcher Gene Thompson, who held the Tigers for two scoreless innings. In the third inning, Thompson allowed McCoskey and Gehringer to get on base,

Tiger ace Bobo Newsom won 2 games for the Tigers in the 1940 Series.

Catcher Ernie Lombardi hit for a .333 average against the Tigers in the Series.

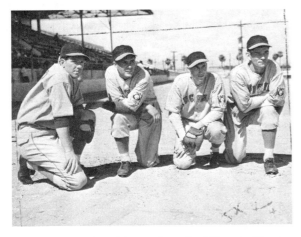

All set to turn the tide against the Tigers, Cincinnati's "big four" pitchers: (*left to right*) Paul Derringer, Johnny Vander Meer, Bucky Walters, and Lee Grissom

and then Greenberg hit Tommy's first pitch over the left field wall for a home run, and it was 3–0, Detroit. In the fourth inning, the Tigers wrapped up the game with 4 more runs, then got another in the eighth inning to romp to an 8–0 whitewash of the hapless Reds. Bobo Newsom was in flawless form, striking out 8 Reds and allowing just 3 base hits, all singles. It was one of the finest pitching performances in Newsom's twenty-year career.

Plucky Bucky Walters was the Reds' pitcher when the Series returned to Redland on October 7. He was opposed by the great Schoolboy Rowe, and once again Walters was invincible. He held the vaunted Tigers to just 5 hits, while the Reds pounded Rowe and Fred Hutchinson for 10 hits. His efforts delighted the thirty thousand Reds fans with a 4–0 shutout to tie the Series.

Manager Del Baker of the Tigers, faced with the herculean task of coming up with a pitcher to match Derringer in the seventh game, selected Bobo Newsom, who took up his pitching chores with only one day off.

The Tigers scored in the third inning. Bill Sullivan singled, went to second on Newsom's sacrifice, and then, when Charlie Gehringer smashed a grounder down the third base line, Werber scooped up the ball and made a marvelous stop, but his throw to first base was way off the mark and Sullivan scored the first run of the game.

The score remained 1–0 until the seventh inning, when Frank McCormick brought the Reds fans up on their feet as he slashed a two-base hit down the third base line. Then it was up to Jim Ripple, and he responded by slugging another long drive that was headed for the top of the fence. McCormick, on second base, didn't know if right fielder Bruce Campbell would catch the ball and so he hesitated between second and third. Campbell could not catch the fly ball, but did retrieve it off the wall and fired it right into Bartell at second base, who was standing with his back to the plate. McCormick scored while Bartell held the ball, and it became the most discussed play of the entire World Series. (Later, motion pictures of the play showed that a good throw by Bartell would have nipped McCormick.) But that was only the game-tying run,

The Tigers' great slugger Hank Greenberg has just hit a 3-run homer in game five of the Series.

and a still tougher run for the Tigers was to follow.

Jim Wilson, who was the shining star of this Series, sacrificed Ripple to third base. That left it all up to Bill Myers, a .130 hitter in this Series, and a Series goat in 1939. Myers chopped a single to left-center, and Ripple scored with that precious run, the run that gave the Reds a 2–1 lead.

In the ninth inning, Paul Derringer brought the house down as he got the Tigers, one-two-three, and the Reds were world champions.

1941

New York Yankees Versus Brooklyn Dodgers

The day before the 1937 World Series opened, a Series in which Brooklyn Dodger fans had no interest save a natural desire to see the New York Giants have their brains knocked out by the Yankees, Burleigh Grimes, the Dodgers' manager, completed a deal on which he had been quietly at work for the past several weeks. He sent Joe Stripp, Johnny Cooney, Jim Bucher, and Roy Henshaw to the St. Louis Cardinals for a fellow named Leo Durocher. Durocher was the finest fielding shortstop in baseball. As a matter of fact, he was one of the best baseball had ever known.

"He can't hit much," a scout had said of him when he was in the minor leagues, "but I never saw anybody who could handle a ball better."

He was referred to by fans as the All-American Out, but veteran critics compared him on defense to Dave Bancroft, Honus Wagner, Joe Tinker, and all the great shortstops of the past. He had come up to the Yankees in 1925 from Hartford, but had been sent out for further seasoning, first to Atlanta, then to St. Paul, and had been recalled to the Yanks in 1928.

Durocher walked into the clubhouse at St. Petersburg in 1928 as though he owned the place. And although he had two fine years in New York, by 1929 his stay with the Yankees was over.

Leo was known as a pop-off guy. He made wisecracks to the umpires, the opposing players, and his teammates, and he was mixed up in a dozen brawls on the field. Manager Miller Huggins and some of the players were getting tired of his antics. In September 1929, Huggins died, and in November, Bob Shawkey, who replaced Huggins as manager, asked for waivers on Leo. The seven other American League clubs wanted no part of him, and so he went to Cincinnati.

The swiftness with which he had been shunted out of the American League troubled Leo, yet he lost none of his liveliness on the field or in the dugout. He tried to keep out of trouble with manager Dan Howley and his teammates. Leo spent three full years with the Reds, and in 1933 was traded to the Cardinals for Paul Derringer.

Cardinal manager Frank Frisch had no great liking for Durocher, but he and Leo made a great shortstop-second base combination from the start. By 1934, when the Cards won the pennant and World Series, Leo was sensational.

After four years with the Cardinals, Durocher went to the Dodgers. It was one of the most important transactions the Dodgers ever made. In 1939 he was appointed manager.

In 1941 the Dodgers won the pennant by 2½ games over the St. Louis Cardinals, and now they were ready to face the challenge of the mighty New York Yankees. The Yankees had wrapped up the pennant by late August and were set for their ninth World Series and all of New York had baseball fever.

The Dodgers had a good ball club in 1941: Dolph Camilli, the MVP of the National League, on first base; Pete Reiser, the youngest batting champion in NL history, at twenty-two years of age, in center field; Dixie Walker, a former Yankee, in right field; Billy Herman at second base; Pee Wee Reese, at short; Cookie Lavagetto at third base; in left field, the old Gashouse Gang member, Joe Medwick; Mickey Owen was the catcher; and the pitchers included Whit Wyatt, Fred Fitzsimmons, Curt Davis, Larry French, Hugh Casey, Kirby Higbe, and Johnny Allen. Wyatt was the ace of the Dodger staff with a 22-10 record.

Manager Joe McCarthy had made a few changes in his latest Yankee model. Three young stars, graduates of the Kansas City farm team—Phil Rizzuto, first baseman John Sturm, and pitcher Ernie Bonham, a California giant—had played their way into the regular lineup.

This was also the year that Joe DiMaggio ran off his 56-game hitting streak and won the league's Most Valuable Player award.

The Brooklyn mob came across the bridges and through the tunnels to flock into Yankee Stadium for the opening game of the World Series on October 1. They outnumbered the Yankee fans, so that there was a louder roar from the stands as the Dodgers came out onto the field.

Durocher surprised everyone by starting Curt Davis, a big, hard-throwing right-hander, who was a 13-game winner during the season. His opponent on the mound for the Yankees was their ace, Red Ruffing, a 15-game winner.

In the Yankees' half of the second inning, Joe Gordon, who was to plague the Dodgers throughout the Series, homered into the left-field stands and the Yankees were out in front, 1–0. In the fourth inning, Keller walked and Bill Dickey drove out a long two-base hit that scored Keller for the Yankees' second run. Leo Durocher then removed David from the mound and brought in Hugh Casey, and the veteran Casey prevented further damage.

Leo Durocher is surrounded by his stars, Dolph Camilli (*left*) and Billy Herman (*right*), in 1941 after the Dodgers had won their first pennant in twenty-one years.

Pee Wee Reese opened the fifth inning with a single and raced home on Mickey Owen's drive that went for three bases. But the Dodger rally stalled right there.

The Yankees came back in the sixth inning, when Keller again walked and Dickey and Gordon singled to score Keller, for what proved to be the winning margin.

The Dodgers made an exciting game of it in the seventh inning, when Lavagetto hit to Rizzuto and was safe when Phil's throw pulled Sturm off first base. Reese singled to left, sending Lavagetto to third, and Cookie scored when pinch hitter Lew Riggs singled, to make the score 3–2, Yankees. But there was no further scoring, and the Yankees came away with a hard-fought, well-pitched game from both hurlers.

In the second game, Durocher selected Whit Wyatt as his pitcher, while Spud Chandler took over pitching chores for the Yankees.

The Yankees came into the fifth inning with a 2–0 lead, and the Dodgers came back fighting. Camilli walked and then Medwick slugged a two-base hit to left field. However, fast fielding held Camilli at third. Then Lavagetto walked,

Dixie Walker sprints to first base as Joe Gordon's throw pulls Yankee first baseman John Sturm off the bag in the second game of the Series.

Prior to the first game of the 1941 Series, manager Leo Durocher gives his Dodgers a pep talk before they go onto the field to battle the Yankees.

filling the bases. Reese, with an opportunity to break the game wide open, forced Lavagetto, but Camilli scored. Then Owen punched a single to center, and Medwick scored the tying run, making it a 2–2 ball game.

In the sixth inning, Walker hit a ground ball to Gordon but was safe on Joe's wild throw. Then Billy Herman slapped a single to left, sending Walker to third. Manager McCarthy took

out pitcher Spud Chandler and sent in his relief ace, Johnny Murphy, and Murph struck out Pete Reiser. Dolph Camilli drew a terrific roar from the Brooklyn fans as he tore into Murphy and singled to right, scoring Dixie Walker, and putting the Dodgers in front, 3–2. And that's the way the game ended, as neither team scored in the last two innings.

Newspapermen visiting the Dodgers' dressing room after the game walked into a scene that is usually reserved for a victory in the final game of a Series.

"We've got 'em now," the Dodgers yelled. "Wait till we get them in Brooklyn. We'll murder them bums."

A crowd of more than thirty-three thousand, including New York's Governor Herbert Lehman, were in Ebbets Field to see the third game.

After putting up a terrific tussle against Yankee southpaw Marius Russo and pitching seven scoreless innings, Fred Fitzsimmons left the game. There were 2 outs in the eighth inning, with Joe Gordon on second base, when Marius Russo slammed a hard line drive right back to Fitzsimmons. The ball struck Fred on his left thigh with such force that it bounded some thirty feet into the air, and Pee Wee Reese caught it near second base. Fitz went down as if shot. He was in no condition to continue; he was carried from the field, and Hugh Casey relieved him.

Casey pitched carefully to Red Rolfe. Rolfe singled to right. Then Tom Henrich beat out a grounder to Camilli, and the Yankees were threatening to score. Two men were on base and Joe DiMaggio came up to hit; he promptly lined a single to left, scoring Rolfe. Then Keller singled Henrich home, and it was a 2–0 ball game.

The Dodgers fought back gamely in their half of the eighth inning. Dixie Walker drove a sharp liner out toward Henrich in right field. Tommy dove for the ball, but it eluded him and Dixie had reached second base by the time Tommy came up with it. Then Russo struck out Augie Galan. But Pee Wee Reese came through with a timely single that scored Walker, and the roar of thunder that greeted Dixie as he crossed the plate shook the old stadium. Billy Herman should have been the next batter, but Billy, a tough

The most famous passed ball in history: Dodger catcher Mickey Owen misses the ball as Tom Henrich swings for the third strike that would have ended the fourth game of the Series. Henrich got to first. The Yankees had a new life and rallied to win the crucial game.

hitter in a pinch situation like this, had injured his side taking a few practice swings and could not bat. Pete Coscarart replaced Herman and struck out. Now it was a 2–1 game, and it remained that way as Russo took care of Reiser, Medwick, and Lavagetto in order to end the game with a Yankee win.

The next game was one of the darkest days in Brooklyn baseball history, for never had victory been torn so rudely from the grasp of the Dodgers.

It was a game of many pitching changes, with the Yankees utilizing Atley Donald, Marv Breuer, and Johnny Murphy, while Leo Durocher trotted out Kirby Higbe, Larry French, John Allen, and Hugh Casey.

The Yankees quickly jumped off to a 1-run lead in the first inning, when Red Rolfe singled, DiMaggio walked, and then the ever-dangerous Charlie Keller slapped a single just out of Camilli's reach off first base, scoring Rolfe. Two more runs in the fourth gave the Yankees a 3–0 lead.

In the Dodgers' half of the fourth inning, Owen and Coscarart walked, and then Jim Wasdell, hitting for French, punched a two-base hit to deep left field. Pete Reiser, who hadn't hit very well in the Series, became a hero in the next few minutes when he drove a fastball over the left field fence with Dixie Walker on base. The fans cheered Pete for fully five minutes.

As the Yankees came up to hit in the top of the ninth inning, the score was Brooklyn 4, New York 3. Hugh Casey, who had relieved Johnny Allen in the fifth inning, had pitched magnificently, retiring the Bronx Bombers as quickly as they came up to bat. And it looked like there would be a great Dodger win as Johnny Sturm, the Yankee first baseman, hit Casey's first pitch to Coscarart at second base and Pete easily threw him out. Then Casey got Rolfe on another easy groundout. Only 1 more out to go.

With a count of 2 strikes and 3 balls, Tommy Henrich took a terrific swing at a low curveball, missed it for strike 3, and the ball game should have been over. Then came disaster. The ball had slipped through Mickey Owen's glove and spun off to the right of the plate, rolling to the grandstand, and Henrich raced to first base and got there before Owen's frantic throw.

The crowd was stunned. Some fans had already raced onto the diamond, but were quickly chased behind the barriers. The ballpark was in pandemonium.

But the game wasn't over.

The Yanks had a man on first and Joe Di-Maggio was the hitter, and behind him, Keller, Dickey, and Gordon. And nobody, including Durocher, had the presence of mind to call a time-out, so that Casey and Owen might have a chance to recover from the blow that had fallen upon them.

Now Casey pitched quickly to DiMaggio and Joe belted a long single to left field. Casey, now floundering, got 2 strikes on Keller, and then Charlie slammed the ball against the right field wall for two bases, scoring both Henrich and DiMaggio and putting the Yankees out in front by a 5–4 margin.

Casey was completely beside himself with rage now, firing the ball, but he could not find the plate. Dickey walked and Gordon doubled to left, scoring Keller and Dickey, and it was now 7–4, Yankees. Rizzuto walked as Ebbets Field was exploding with rage. Finally Murphy hit a grounder to Reese, and the inning and agony was over for Brooklyn. So was the game, as the Dodgers went scoreless in the bottom of the ninth, the final tally remaining 7–4, Yankees.

The fifth game the next day was strictly an anticlimax. Even the thirty-four thousand never-say-die fans who entered the park with a dazed expression on their faces feared the worst.

Durocher roused himself for the game, fought with the umpires, baited the Yankees, cajoled and even threatened his players, but they were a beaten team.

Tiny Bonham, pitching for the Yankees, was in rare form and allowed the Dodgers only 4 base hits, to help the Yankees to a 3–1 victory.

The Yankees garnered another raft of records into the book. They now had won 5 World Championships in 6 years. During that stretch they had rolled up 20 wins against 4 losses. McCarthy passed Connie Mack and became the first manager to win the Series six times.

For the Dodgers, it was a year of bright achievement. They had brought a pennant to Brooklyn for the first time in twenty-one years, and had played to a record crowd of one million fans at home and more than one million on the road. And Leo Durocher had established himself as one of baseball's finest managers.

St. Louis Cardinals Versus New York Yankees

On January 16, 1942, roughly five weeks after Pearl Harbor, President Franklin D. Roosevelt wrote a letter to Judge Landis in reply to the commissioner's plea for guidance during the war years. Roosevelt's letter was a hearty endorsement of baseball. The war, he said, afforded a unique opportunity for young servicemen from all over the country to see their favorite teams play at home. Thousands of soldiers, sailors, marines, and coast guardsmen were admitted free to ball games around the country.

In the National League the talk was all about the remarkable drive of the young St. Louis Cardinals team, comparing it with the legendary climb of the 1914 Boston Braves from the cellar to the pennant.

The Cardinals of 1942 were 10 games behind by August 6. But they put on a furious late-season drive, winning 34 out of 40 of the final games to win the pennant.

Nobody outside St. Louis thought the Cards would win the Series. The team that Bill Southworth had put together consisted of fast, hustling youngsters, of small-town and farm boys, most of whom had never seen a major league team in action until they were the participants. Southworth placed great emphasis on the youth of his players and their refusal to become intimidated.

He had himself played on the 1926 World Series champion club.

The 1942 team had few veterans. Twenty-six-year-old Enos Slaughter was practically an old-timer, with four seasons of major league play. The fiery team captain, Terry Moore, a brilliant center fielder, was the oldest man on the team at thirty. The third outfielder was a young ex-pitcher who had injured his arm, switched to the outfield, and then fought his way into the lineup by hitting at a .315 clip. His name was Stan Musial. A tall, gangling kid named Marty Marion had earned the nickname Mr. Shortstop; a wild, reckless, daring Whitey Kurowski, with a withered left hand, played third base; Jim Brown was at second base; and Johnny Hopp was the first baseman; Walker Cooper, a right-handed batter, was the catcher; and the pitchers included Mort Cooper (Walker's brother), and hard-throwing kids like John Beazley, Ernie White, Max Lanier, Murry Dickson, and Howie Pollet.

The first game, at Sportsman's Park in St. Louis, on September 30, saw the Yankee ace Red Ruffing facing the Cardinals' star, Mort Cooper, a 22-game winner during the season. The game was scoreless until the fourth inning, when DiMaggio singled and Dickey walked; then Buddy Hassett picked out a fastball and

In his first World Series in 1942, twenty-one-year-old Stan Musial played an outstanding defensive game for the Cardinals.

The Yankees continued to hit Cooper freely, and by the eighth inning Cooper had given up 7 runs and 10 hits. At that point he was taken out and relieved by Harry Gumbert, who was later replaced by Max Lanier.

Meanwhile, Red Ruffing was putting in his bid for a Series no-hit game. He had pitched hitless ball for seven and two-thirds innings and had mowed down the Cardinals in order, until Terry Moore drove out a single with 2 outs in the eighth inning. It was a remarkable performance by the veteran right-hander.

The Cardinals had 2 outs in the ninth inning when Walker Cooper singled to left; it was only the second hit of the game for the Cards. Then Ruffing made a mistake by walking Sanders, and he was not able to get another man out. Marty Marion hammered Red's first pitch for a booming triple, and the Cards had 2 runs. Ken O'Dea singled and Marion scored. After another base hit, by Jim Brown, Spud Chandler came in to relieve Ruffing. But the Cardinals continued to hammer Chandler. Moore and Slaughter singled in succession, and the Cards had the tying run at the plate in the person of hard-hitting Stan Musial, up for the second time in the inning. But the best Stan could do was hit a sharp grounder to Hassett, and Buddy made the putout and the game was over, leaving three Cardinals on base.

Though beaten 7–4, that ninth inning rally with 2 outs practically amounted to a moral victory for the Cards.

In the second game, still spirited and red-hot from their ninth-inning rally the night before, the Cardinals couldn't be stopped, and even though they were outhit in the game 10 to 6, they thrilled their fans by halting the Yanks' big stopper, Tiny Bonham, and winning, 4–3.

Country Slaughter was the defensive star of this game as he came up with several outstanding plays. One was a magnificent stop of Buddy Hassett's drive to right field. As Tuck Stainback raced from first to third on Hassett's hit, Slaughter scooped up the ball and, in the same motion, threw it on a line right into Whitey Kurowski's hands at third base, and Whitey tagged Stainback as he slid into the bag. That was the end of a budding ninth-inning Yankee rally.

drove it to deep center field for a double, scoring DiMaggio with the first run of the game.

In the fifth inning, Red Rolfe singled to open the inning; then Roy Cullenbine slammed a drive down the third base line that was good for two bases and Rolfe scored to make it a 2–0 game.

The scene shifted to Yankee Stadium for the third game, on October 3, before a record crowd of 69,123, where the Cardinals won, 2–0, and went ahead in the Series, 2 games to 1. Ernie White, whose sore left arm had been useless earlier in the year, pitched a remarkable game and received even more remarkable support. The shutout was the first World Series white-wash performed against the Yankees since Jesse Haines had one in the third game of the 1926 Cardinal Series.

The fourth game, on Sunday, October 4, before a record crowd of 69,902 fans, was a free-for-all, yet it developed into another example of the remarkable resiliency of the Cardinal kids. It was a game that the Cards early on thought they had wrapped up, when they pounded Hank Borowy for 6 runs in the fourth inning; running the Yankees almost dizzy as they stole bases almost at will. At that point, the game should have been a cinch for the Cardinals, but suddenly pitcher Mort Cooper lost his poise and control, blew up, and the Yankees sailed into

Joe DiMaggio slides safely into third base during game one after Bill Dickey's single. Waiting for the ball is Whitey Kurowski, and umpire Cal Hubbard stands by to make the call.

him with their own barrage, including Charlie Keller's second homer of the Series, with two men on base, for a total of 5 big runs, to tie the score, 6–6.

Far from being upset at the unexpected turn of events, the Cards came fighting back. Atley Donald, the new Yankee pitcher, walked both Slaughter and Musial, and the Yankee infield was now jittery, because both of those Cardinal players had taken an extra base every time they got a base hit.

Walker Cooper came up to bunt, but Bill Dickey noticed that Slaughter had a big lead off second base. Attempting to catch Slaughter off base, Dickey threw the ball into center field. Enos went to third on the throw. Then Cooper singled to center, scoring Slaughter, and the Cards had a 7–6 lead. At that point, manager McCarthy signaled to his bullpen and Tiny Bonham came in to pitch for the Yankees. Bonham walked Kurowski, and the bases were full. Marion then sent a long fly ball to DiMaggio in center field, and easily beat Joe's throw to the plate. Now it was 8–6.

In the ninth inning, the Cards added an insurance run as Hopp singled, went to second on a sacrifice, then scored the final run as Max Lanier brought him home with a sharp single to center. And the Cardinals had come from behind to win by a 9–6 margin, their third straight win over the great Yankees.

Four straight wins in a World Series used to be a Yankee trademark. They had done it in 1927, 1928, 1932, and 1939, but now it looked as if the Cardinals were going to get a dose of it themselves.

It was dark and rainy when the ninth inning of the fifth and final game rolled around, with the score tied 2–2.

Catcher Walker Cooper, always dangerous, opened the inning by bashing out a single to left field. Then Johnny Hopp sacrificed Cooper to second. Up to the plate stepped Whitey Kurowski, a twenty-one-year-old youngster just a year out of a Cardinal farm team. What manager Southworth told Whitey just before he stepped up to hit nobody ever knew. Perhaps Whitey decided to take matters into his own sturdy hands. Whitey smashed into the first pitch by

In the 1942 Series, Joe DiMaggio banged out 7 hits, drove in 3 runs, and hit for a sparkling .333 average.

Beazley and hit the ball with the fat part of his big thirty-four-ounce bat. The ball streaked through the mist of a drizzly afternoon, and on the wings of that drive, which landed in the far center field bleachers, there came to an end one of the most remarkable World Series dynasties baseball has ever known. For with that one blow the Cardinals brought down Joe McCarthy's champion New York Yankees, 4–2, to win their fourth straight game. It captured the World Championship for Billy Southworth's National League champions, 4 games to 1, and completed the most amazing upset in Series history since 1914, when the Miracle Braves bowled over Connie Mack's heavily favored Athletics.

"The great thing I remember about the World Series," reflected Stan Musial,* "was that Whitey Kurowski hit that big home run in the ninth inning that won it for us. Kids with a handicap would do well to remember Whitey Kurowski, who played a remarkable game without a part of his right forearm [the ulna bone], as a result of boyhood osteomylitis. And to compensate for the diseased bone that was removed, Whitey developed powerful muscles. Because the right arm was short, he crowded the plate in a defiant stance that made him a target for high and tight pitches.

"In the clubhouse after we beat the Yankees, Whitey was the center of a shrieking clubhouse mob. We tore his shirt and pants right off him for souvenirs. The only thing he kept was the bat, with which he'd hit the homer.

"For me it was the greatest thrill, the greatest Series I've ever played in, since it was my first—and then the thrill of beating the great Yankees with DiMaggio, Keller, Dickey, Ruffing, Joe Gordon. All those incredible players and then we beat them four in a row. It has to be one of the great thrills of my entire life."

* In an interview with the author following the 1943 Series, on author's *Sports Show*, New York radio station WINS.

New York Yankees Versus St. Louis Cardinals

The war flames licked deeper into the baseball structure after the 1942 World Series. The Cardinals, made up largely of young fathers, had retained their manpower well up to that time, losing only rookies. But in the winter of 1942–43, team captain Terry Moore, Enos Slaughter, and John Beazley entered the armed services. During the 1943 season, Jimmy Brown and pitchers Howie Pollet and Murry Dickson were called into the army.

But once again the Cardinals' marvelous farm system proved adequate to take up this slack. Harry Walker, a brother of the Dodgers' Dixie, was outstanding in center field, and Lou Klein, up from Columbus, was sensational at second base. Harry Brecheen, George Munger, and Al Brazle were the pitchers, advanced to the Cards from their farm system, and Debs Garms and Frank Demaree were also added to the team.

Lukasz Musial was a stern, if kindly, father. A Polish immigrant, he had worked hard. He didn't want Stanley, elder of two boys and younger than his four sisters, to have to work in the steel mills at Donora, Pennsylvania. So when Andy French, manager of the Moncssen (Pennsylvania) team, called one night to talk about Stan and a baseball career, Lukasz Musial said no. Stanley was going to college. The boy was a star at basketball and several big universities had offered him a scholarship.

French, who had seen Stan pitch and strike out row after row of batters in a game for the Donora Zinc Company, tried to paint an alluring picture of a baseball career. But Pop was boss and it was no! That is until Stanley started to cry.

That did it. Mama Musial blew Stan's nose, wiped his eyes, and the Musials relented, and in 1939 Lukasz signed a baseball contract for his son.

Within two years, after pitching in West Virginia, Musial was sent to Daytona Beach in the Class D Florida League and under the tutelage of little Dickie Kerr, who pitched for the infamous 1919 White Sox, Musial won 15 and lost 5. When a shortage of outfielders posed a real problem for Daytona, Stan Musial, who could hit the ball for distance, was used in center field.

One day, while diving to catch a low line drive, Musial fell on his left (pitching) shoulder. That night a big knot formed on the shoulder and he could never throw hard again.

Now with a bad shoulder, he was finding it difficult to play ball at all. When he did play, the $100-per-month salary hardly paid the bills, particularly with a new baby coming.

Cardinal shortstop Marty Marion was the leading St. Louis batter with a .357 Series average.

Musial took his troubles to his manager Dickie Kerr, who in 1919 had actually won two World Series games from the Cincinnati Reds, when his teammates were throwing the Series.

Kerr had faced and conquered a great deal of adversity in his life, and knew what Musial was going through. He liked the youngster and just knew that Stan would develop into a major leaguer.

"You can't quit baseball and go back to the mills in Donora. You've got a great future here and someday you're gonna be a star. You've got a great future ahead as an outfielder."

Kerr did something more than preach about "the game." He rented a larger home, so there would be room for Stan and his new wife. He watched over Stan, worked with him on the field and despite all the pressure from the main office to release Stan, he did not do so, but worked even harder with him. And it began to pay off.

In 1940 at Springfield, Massachusetts, Musial, now an outfielder, was an absolute sensation. He hit for a .369 average, including 29 home runs. Stan Musial was on his way up.

The next season, Stan Musial was at Rochester. In his first game with Rochester, he hit a homer with the bases full, and he was hitting at a .327 clip when Billy Southworth sent for him to help the Cardinals battle the Dodgers for the 1941 pennant.

By 1942, Stan Musial was the most talked about rookie in the Grapefruit League; his batting during the regular season was one of the principal factors by which the Cards won the pennant. He sprayed home runs, triples, and doubles all over the field for a .315 average. One year later in 1943, Musial was the leading hitter in the National League with a sparkling .357 average, and he led the Cards to another pennant. Musial was now the dominant player as the Cardinals drove toward another Series win with some talented newcomers and the remainder of the 1942 club; Johnny Mize, John Hopp, Whitey Kurowski, Danny Litwhiler, Marty Marion, and Walker Cooper the Cards once again proceeded to spread-eagle the field, destroying the second-place Reds by 18 games. The Cards clinched the pennant on September 16, one of the earliest dates on record.

Sportswriters agreed that the New York Yankees would need a solid rebuilding job after their disastrous loss to the Cardinals in the 1942 Series. But Yankee president Ed Barrow, and manager Joe McCarthy disagreed and made only a few minor changes in the Yankee lineup.

As the season progressed, several players were called up for duty in the armed forces. Phil Rizzuto and George Selkirk went into the navy. Red Rolfe left for a coaching job at Yale. Lefty Gomez and Red Ruffing went to work in defense plants.

A leading candidate for an infield post was

rugged, old-fashioned, tobacco-chewing, head-first-sliding George Stirnweiss, who was rejected by the army because of stomach ulcers. A deal was made with Cleveland, and the Yanks received Roy Weatherly, an outfielder, and Oscar Grimes, an infielder. Nick Etten, a first baseman, was bought from Pittsburgh.

And then came the crushing but expected announcement from Joe DiMaggio that he had enlisted in the army.

The Series opened in New York on October 5 with Spud Chandler, for the Yankees, facing Max Lanier, a 15-game winner, for the Cardinals. A crowd of some sixty-nine thousand attended the game, including several thousand servicemen who were admitted free of charge.

In the second inning, Marty Marion slammed a ringing double to left field to score Walker Cooper, who had previously singled, for the first run of the Series.

But the Yanks came right back in the fourth inning after Lanier had handcuffed the Bombers for three innings. Frank Crosetti reached first base when Lanier muffed his grounder. He then stole second and went to third on Johnson's safe bunt. Then, when Keller hit into a double play, Crosetti scored. With the bases empty, Joe Gordon scorched a tremendous home run, a 450-foot drive, into the bleachers, and it was a 2–1 game.

Ray Sanders walked in the fifth inning, stole second, and reached third on a groundout. Then pitcher Lanier helped his own game by slapping a single to center, scoring Sanders, and tying the game, 2–2.

Crosetti beat out an infield hit to start the sixth inning and went to third on Billy Johnson's single. Lanier, trying to put some extra "stuff" on the ball, threw a wild pitch with disastrous results. Catcher Cooper couldn't see where the ball had rolled. As a result, Crosetti scored and Johnson reached third base, and scored a moment later when Dickey singled, to give the Yanks a 4–2 advantage. Spud Chandler held the Cardinals scoreless through the rest of the game for the Yankees.

In the early morning of October 6, the father of the Cardinals' Cooper brothers died at his home in Independence, Missouri. Bob Cooper

Manager Joe McCarthy won his seventh World Series in 1943.

was a great fan and a tutor for his two boys and had been following the Series on the radio. The brothers did not go home for the funeral, but elected to stay with the team in New York, saying, "Dad would have wanted it that way." Mort Cooper hurled a brilliant 6-hit game and defeated the Yankees, 4–3.

The third game proved to be the most exciting one of the Series, and was won by the Yankees, 6–2. Hank Borowy started for the Bombers against the lanky Oklahoma cotton picker, Al Brazle.

Stan Musial started the fourth inning with a single. Whitey Kurowski followed with a smashing double down the third base line. Sanders walked, and then Danny Litwhiler drove in Musial and Kurowski with a single up the middle, to give the Cards a 2–0 lead.

Brazle had allowed the world champions just 2 base hits in the first five innings, but in the sixth inning he ran into trouble. Hank Borowy led off with a two-base hit. Stainback fouled to Musial, and Borowy went to third after the catch. Johnson, the next Yankee hitter, slugged a sharp ground ball down to Kurowski at third, but Whitey fumbled it, allowing Borowy to score the Yanks' first run.

A transplanted pitcher, now an outfielder for the Yankees, Johnny Lindell, opened the eighth inning with a single and took an extra base when Walker fumbled the ball. Snuffy Stirnweiss, the former fleet-footed North Carolina gridiron star, batted for Borowy, and tapped the ball right at Sanders, who steadied himself and hurled the ball across the infield to Kurowski for a play on Lindell at third base. Umpire Beans Reardon waved Lindell out, but reversed himself when Whitey dropped the ball while putting it on the runner. Lindell, all six feet four inches of California brawn, hit Whitey like a Sherman tank rolling into a pillbox. Both players were bruised and shaken up, and there was a good deal of criticism of Lindell for the force of his slide. But McCarthy brushed off reporters with this quip after the game: "This ain't no pink tea party, and Lindell had the right of way."

The Yanks now had runners on third and first with no outs. On Stainback's fly ball to Litwhiler, Lindell held third, but Stirnweiss moved to second. Then Southworth took a gamble ordering Brazle to walk Crosetti, a weak hitter, but one who had been bothering Cardinal pitchers throughout the Series. That brought up Bill Johnson, a tough hitter in a clutch, and Johnson lashed a tremendous triple between Litwhiler and Walker that brought in 3 runs. Before the inning was over, Southworth rushed in first Howie Krist, then Harry Brecheen, as the Yankees piled up 5 big runs. When the dejected Brazle, head hanging on his chest, walked off the field, the record Yankee Stadium crowd stood up and cheered Alpha. But the Yanks had a commanding 6–2 lead, and Borowy and then Johnny Murphy held the Cards for the win.

The Series wasn't resumed until three days later in St. Louis, and the Cooper brothers took advantage of the big gap in the schedule to attend their father's funeral, after all.

The fourth game was played on a beautiful Sunday afternoon, October 10. Some of the faithful fans stood in line for twenty-four hours for the few unreserved seats, and there was much fight talk that an inspired Cardinal team would face and defeat the Yankees on the Cards' home grounds for the rest of the Series.

Manager Joe McCarthy took a daring gamble in the fourth game, pitching Marius Russo, his left-handed star, who had been bothered with a sore arm for over two seasons. Russo's 1943 record was a mediocre 5 wins and 10 losses. However, Russo was at his very best on this sunny afternoon in St. Louis, and won a tense, exciting game from Max Lanier by a 2–1 margin. Russo was both the batting and pitching star in this game, as he smacked out 2 doubles and scored the Yankees' winning run.

The Cardinals' lights were knocked out on October 11, in the fifth game, another painful one for the Redbirds. They managed to reach Yankee pitcher Spud Chandler for 10 solid base hits, but simply could not put the hits together and were held scoreless. Mort Cooper also pitched scoreless baseball for the first five innings, but in the sixth frame Keller singled and Bill Dickey slugged a home run off the pavilion wall to give the Yankees a 2–0 edge, which they maintained to win the game and the World Series.

Despite the Yankee win, the two clubs finished almost even in batting. The Yanks clubbed out 35 hits for a .220 team batting average, while the Cards had 37 hits for a .224 average.

The Yankee stars included catcher Bill Dickey, who hit a home run to clinch the finale, and Billy Johnson, the only Yank regular to hit .300. For the Cardinals, Walker Cooper and Ray Sanders hit for a .294 average, while Marty Marion was a surprise with a gaudy .357 batting average.

Radio broadcasts of the games were heard all over the world by the armed forces radio network, and the Army-Navy Relief Fund received $308,373 from the World Series fund. The Yankees' individual shares for winning amounted to $6,139, while the Cardinals' shares amounted to $4,321 per player.

St. Louis Cardinals
Versus St. Louis Browns

The third war season, 1944, saw something new in World Series competition. The Yankees and the Giants had fought subway battles in 1921, 1923, 1936, and 1937; Chicago had had its all-Windy City Series in 1906, and now St. Louis had a Mississippi River World Series of its own as the once lowly St. Louis Browns, aided and abetted by a formidable number of 4-F's and players released from the armed forces, managed to finish on top of the American League by nosing out the Detroit Tigers on the very last day of the season.

It was the first and only American League pennant the Browns would ever win, and they won with only one regular player, Mike Kreevich, hitting over .300.

One feature of the Browns during the year was the marvelous defensive play of the infield, consisting of George McQuinn on first base; ex-Gashouser Don Gutteridge at second; hard-hitting Junior Stephens at short; and Mark Christman, a St. Louis homebred, at third. The outfield consisted of Chet Laabs, Mike Kreevich, and Gene Moore. McQuinn, an ex-Yankee farmhand, tried in heroic fashion to win the Series for the Brownies single-handedly, and hit for a terrific .438 average, but he had little offensive support from his teammates. The Browns had a team batting average of .183. Laabs had won the final game of the pennant race against

the Yankees by slugging out 2 home runs, and was expected to lead the offense against the Cards, but he hit so poorly in the Series that he was benched in favor of Al Zarilla.

In the National League, it was a third straight Cardinal romp, as the Southworth men—led by Stan "the Man" Musial, who hit for a .347 average; Johnny Hopp, with a .336 average; and Walker Cooper, with a .317 average—demolished all opposition, winning the pennant over second-place Pittsburgh by 14½ games.

The 1944 World Series proved to be a pitchers' series. The pitchers of the two clubs struck out a record 92 batters, a record that still stands, with the Cardinal pitchers striking out 49, and the Brown's pitchers 43.

The first game, played on October 4, was a heartbreaker for the Cardinals' Mort Cooper. He yielded only 2 base hits to the Browns in a remarkable pitching duel against Denny Galehouse, who scattered 7 Cardinal hits. The Browns eked out a 2–1 win for their first Series victory.

The Cardinals tied the Series the next day, October 5, in an eleven-inning battle that thrilled the thirty-five thousand fans present. The game started with Max Lanier opposing Nellie Potter. The Cardinals gave Max a 2-run lead by scoring in the third and fourth innings as a result of spotty defensive play by the Browns' infield. But after Lanier held the Browns to a bunt single for

St. Louis Browns' jubilant players celebrate after winning first game of the Series: (*left to right*) George McQuinn, Denny Galehouse, and Gene Moore.

George McQuinn, the Browns' first baseman, hit a 2-run homer in the first game of the Series to win the game. Gene Moore (15) and Mark Christman (6) are shown scoring ahead of McQuinn. Walker Cooper, the Cards' catcher, looks on.

One-armed Pete Gray did not see action in the Series, although he was a sensational player during the 1944 season and an inspiration to the team.

six innings, the American League champs came to life in the seventh inning and tied the score. Moore's single, a long double by Ray Hayworth, and another single by Gus Mancuso made it a 2–2 game.

The score remained deadlocked at 2–2 as the teams prepared to play the eleventh inning. In the Cards' half of the eleventh, Sanders, a home-town boy, singled and took second on Kurowski's sacrifice; then Ken O'Dea became an instant hero when he whistled a smashing single to left field that scored Sanders with the winning run, making the score 3–2, Cardinals.

Brownie fans were delighted when their club shot to a 6–2 victory in the third game of the Series, on October 6, behind the steady pitching of Jack Kramer. Kramer allowed the Cards a run in the first inning, but the Browns came back with a concentrated attack in the third, when 5 successive base hits resulted in 3 runs that knocked Cards' pitcher, Ted Wilks, from the box and brought in Freddy Schmidt. The Browns scored another run off Schmidt and they had a 4–1 lead into the seventh inning.

The Browns picked up 2 more runs in the seventh on a walk to Stephens and base hits by Gutteridge and McQuinn, and chalked up a convincing 6 to 2 win. McQuinn was the key to the Browns' attack, with 3 hits and 3 runs.

Following the 1944 World Series, Stan Musial again discussed the games with the author on WINS: "We got back into the Series largely on the clutch pitching of Harry 'the Cat' Brecheen, for whom my admiration was to increase through the many years he was to pitch for us.

"On Sunday afternoon, before nearly thirty-seven thousand fans, we finally went ahead, but only after a great pitching duel between Mort Cooper and Denny Galehouse of the Browns.

Home runs by Ray Sanders and Dan Litwhiler gave us an exciting three to two win in a game in which the pitchers set a World Series record by striking out twenty-two men. Cooper fanned twelve for us.

"The Cardinals won the 1944 World Series with a three to one victory in the sixth game, in which Max Lanier and Wilks, who took over in the sixth inning, allowed only three base hits. Fact is, the Browns wound up with a one-eighty-three team batting average for the Series. Yet I salute them as an inferior team that just wouldn't quit. They didn't know the meaning of the word.

"I hit three-oh-four in that Series, but like many batting champions, including even greater ones like Ty Cobb, Rogers Hornsby, and Ted Williams, I never was a World Series standout. I'm just thankful I never was a Series bust, either.

"The World Series share in 1944 was skimpier: $4,626 for each winning share, and $2,743 for the losers' share. I was grateful for the share. Grateful for playing, for winning, and for the birth that December of our second child, daughter Geraldine.

"I had been able to play ball for two war years. In baseball I don't believe you'll find many who consider 1942 a war year, and I was really relieved to go into service when my Donora draft board finally called me in January 1945.

"I chose the navy and was sent to Bainbridge, Maryland, for basic training. A merciless barber at boot camp skinned my head like a grape. A photographer took my picture and the barber said, apologetically, 'Why didn't you tell me who you were? I wouldn't have cut your hair so short.' "

1945

Detroit Tigers Versus Chicago Cubs

In 1945 major league baseball came back in full strength as most of the star players who had been drafted or enlisted in the services returned to action once World War II had ended. The nation once again found diversion and surcease from the terrible tragedies of the long war in two spirited and exciting pennant races.

In 1944 the Tigers lost the American League pennant to the never-say-die St. Louis Browns on the very last day of the season. Manager Steve O'Neill, in his third season as Tiger skipper, guided his 1945 Tiger edition to the American League flag on the last day, when Hank Greenberg, discharged from the service just six weeks earlier, and still hampered by his three and a half years of baseball inactivity, slugged a dramatic ninth-inning bases-full home run as dusk was beginning to fog in the stadium, to give the Tigers a thrilling 6 to 3 victory over the Browns. The victory meant the pennant over the second-place Washington Senators and the first for the pennant-hungry Tiger fans since 1935.

They called the 1945 Tigers "the nine old men," for the club had such graybeards as forty-year-old Doc Cramer, thirty-four-year-old Hank Greenberg, thirty-five-year-old Eddie Mayo, and Jim Outlaw, Paul Richards, and Skeeter Webb (manager Steve O'Neill's son-in-law). However, the club's pennant victory was due largely to the magnificent work of the club's great left-hander,

Hal Newhouser, who won 25 games. Hal was backed by Paul "Dizzy" Trout who won 18 games. Other pitchers included Stubby Overmire, Al Benton, and George Caster, who saved a number of crucial games.

Charlie Grimm, the Cubs' manager in 1932 and 1935, returned to the Cubs after a period as manager in Milwaukee. He had an efficient ball club, including several players who had been with the Cubs in the 1938 Series. They were Stan Hack, a fine third baseman; Phil Cavarretta, an outstanding first baseman; Don Johnson; Peanuts Lowrey; Andy Pafko; and Bill Nicholson, solid baseball men with years of valuable experience in the major leagues.

In mid-season, a break in the schedule afforded manager Charlie Grimm and club general manager Jim Gallagher a day off. They went on a fishing trip and talked of acquiring another pitcher for the Cubs. Another first-line pitcher could possibly result in a meaningful run for the pennant.

It was very late when Gallagher returned to his home after the trip. He was told by his wife that New York had been calling all through the afternoon and evening. Tired and disgusted, Gallagher was about to retire and forget about fish, pitchers, and phone calls from New York. He still shudders whenever he recalls what might have happened if he had adhered to that plan.

199

Finally, he put the call through to New York and it was Larry MacPhail, the president of the Yankees, on the other end.

"What will you give in cash for Borowy?" MacPhail wanted to know. (Hank Borowy had been a first-line pitcher for the Yankees since 1942, and had won 15 games in his first year with the Bombers. He won 14 in 1943 and in 1944 was the Yanks' top pitcher with 17 wins.) Gallagher wasn't sure that he had heard Mac-Phail correctly. In his judgment, and others around the league, Borowy was the best pitcher on the Yankees. He asked MacPhail to repeat what he had said.

"How much for Borowy?" asked MacPhail. "How much cash?"

"How in hell can you ever get waivers on him?" Gallagher demanded. "Every team in the league would want him?"

"I've already got waivers on him," said Larry. "Do you want him, or don't you?"

There was a great deal more talk. And then finally, a price of $100,000 cash and a parcel of ballplayers was agreed on. The deal thrilled Cub fans when they heard about it. It assured the Cubs the pennant, as Borowy won 11 and lost 2 games. Borowy, in fact, was the pitcher of record on September 28, when the Cubs clinched the pennant by defeating the Pirates, 4–3.

Sportswriters from all over the nation had assembled in Detroit when the Cubs arrived for the first game of the 1945 World Series. An Associated Press writer made his rounds, asking each individual sportswriter which club he thought would win. When he approached the well-known sportswriter Irv Kupcinet, he expected to get the customary "Cubs" reply—"such is civic pride"— but he was startled to be told:

"I don't think either one of them can win it."

That came close to being the best forecast made.

The Series went the full seven games before the Tigers took the odd game and became world champions. However, long before that point was reached, even the players themselves had given up trying to figure out what might happen next. Fly balls were dropping beside fielders, who made no effort to catch them. Players were tumbling going around the bases. The baseball skill

(*left to right*) Pitcher Hal Newhouser, manager Steve O'Neil, and Hank Greenberg celebrate their win over the Cubs in game five.

shown was as far removed from previous major league standards as was possible without accusations being made that the players were imposters obtaining money under false pretenses. As a matter of fact, sportswriters dubbed it "the world's worst Series."

The Series started out most dismally for the Tigers. A shocked crowd of some fifty-five thousand Tiger fans, on a bleak October 3, watched in utter dismay as Hal Newhouser, the Tigers' ace, was hit hard from the very outset. He was knocked out of the box within three innings, as the Cubs routed the hapless Tigers by a 9–0 score.

It was the worst defeat suffered by a team in forty-two World Series openers, and, to make matters worse, it was the first time the National League had taken the first game since the all-New York Series of 1936.

But what added further salt to the wound was that the Cub shutout was administered by the former Yankee pitcher, Hank Borowy. Hank pitched with all of his skill and cunning, allowing the hard-hitting Tigers just 6 hits. When the Tigers did get men on base, and they did get 10 men on base, Borowy, with the help of three lightning-fast double plays and some outstanding clutch pitching, prevented any scoring.

Manager Steve O'Neill gambled it all in the second game, calling on pitcher Virgil Trucks.

The recently discharged sailor faced the Cubs' Hank Wyse, a 22-game winner, and for four innings, Wyse was as brilliant as Borowy had been the day before.

The Cubs practically stole their lone run in the fourth inning. With 1 out Phil Cavarretta hit an ordinary single to center, and before the startled Cramer knew what had happened, Phil had stretched the hit into a double. He then scored a moment later on Nicholson's single.

That run evidently made the Tigers angry and, after being held scoreless for thirteen successive innings, they broke loose with a rash of hits in the fifth. Skeeter Webb started things by slapping a single to left. Eddie Mayo walked, moving Webb to second. Cramer then atoned for his fielding lapse by lining a single to left that scored Webb. Then big Hank Greenberg dropped a bomb. With the count 1 and 1, Hank connected with a fastball and sent it soaring 375 feet into the bleachers. As Mayo and Cramer happily pranced home ahead of Greenberg, the crowd went absolutely wild with glee. They roared Greenberg's name for a full five minutes as Hank stepped out of the dugout to accept the cheers.

The final score of the second game was 4 to 1, Tigers.

In the third game, a crowd of almost fifty-six thousand sat in awed silence as Claude Passeau pitched one of the greatest games in the history of the fall classic, a magnificent 1-hit game, which he won by a score of 3–0. It was the first 1-hit game in a Series since an earlier Cub pitcher, Ed Reulbach, held the White Sox to a lone run in the second game of the all-Chicago Series in 1906. Passeau was so deadly effective that only 2 Tigers reached base. Rudy York spoiled the no-hitter when he singled in the second inning, and catcher Swift walked in the sixth.

As the Series shifted to Chicago for the fourth game, on October 4, the Cubs felt rather sure of themselves. Their pitchers had held the Tigers scoreless in every inning but one, and the Cubs had always been known as a strong home team.

"This time we're going to win. They can't stop us," said Charlie Grimm.

Manager Steve O'Neill had held Dizzy Trout

Just released from the navy, Virgil Trucks wasted little time as he allowed the Cubs just 7 hits and beat them in game two of the Series.

on the bench since the first game, as the big guy had a cold and a sore back. Steve asked him how he felt on the morning of the game in Chicago, and Dizzy replied, "I'm feeling good, boss. I'm ready to pitch the game of my life."

Ray Prim, a 13-game winner during the season, was Grimm's selection for the Cubs, and he delighted a Chicago crowd of forty-three thousand fans with his effectiveness. He set down the first ten men to face him, and then struck out Skeeter Webb to start the fourth inning. But that was the beginning of the end for Prim. Cramer fired a single to right, and then Greenberg came through with another single. Roy Cullenbine doubled, scoring Cramer. Right then, Prim was taken out and relieved by Paul Derringer, and Paul walked Rudy York. Jimmy Outlaw hit into a force play, scoring Greenberg, and then Richards's single sent Cullenbine home with the fourth run.

That was all the scoring for the Tigers, and more than they needed, for the Cubs would not have scored at all off Trout but for some of the fielding madness that characterized the Series.

Don Johnson led off the sixth inning with a smashing triple. Lowrey tapped a slow roller to Outlaw, but Johnson was trapped between third and home. Outlaw chose to let him run and made a play at first base for Lowrey. Instead of continuing on to score, Johnson reversed himself and broke back for third base, with Outlaw in hot pursuit. York saw Johnson scuttling back to third, and threw to third to try to get Johnson, but York's throw was wild, and Johnson reversed direction again and scored the Cubs lone run. The final tally was 4–1, Tigers.

With the Series tied at 2 games each, the opening-game pitchers, Hank Borowy for the Cubs and Hal Newhouser for the Tigers, were at each other's throats once more in game five.

There was no quick start against Newhouser this time, and Borowy needed several spectacular plays by Pafko and several long drives to keep the score at a 1–1 tie through the first five innings.

In the sixth inning, the Tigers suddenly found their batting eyes and began to savage Borowy. Cramer singled and went on to second when Pafko fumbled the ball. Greenberg slammed his second two-bagger and Cramer scored on the long hit. Cullenbine beat out a bunt along the third base line; then Rudy York singled, scoring Big Hank. Borowy was taken out and relieved by Hy Vandenberg. Outlaw's sacrifice fly, and successive walks to Richards and Newhouser, forced in Cullenbine, and York scored the fourth run on Webb's groundout, producing a final score of 8–4, Detroit.

The sixth game was perhaps the daffiest ever played. The struggle, and it was indeed one, for the players and fans alike, lasted three hours and twenty-eight minutes. And each team utilized nineteen players, to make the box-score compilation something that official scorers remember to this day. It was the longest World Series game ever played.

Claude Passeau, the 1-hit hero of game three, was pitted against Virgil Trucks, and the game probably never would have been close if Passeau hadn't injured the middle finger on his pitching hand by knocking down Outlaw's smash in the sixth inning. Claude came back for the seventh inning with a torn nail and bleeding finger, and he couldn't grip the ball properly. Until that point, Passeau had allowed only 2 hits, and the Cubs had a 5–1 lead. Neither Wyse nor Prim could check the Tigers, and with his lead slowly frittering away, Grimm called on Borowy to save the game.

Rudy York had started the scoring in the second inning by smashing out a two-base hit to score Cullenbine, who had walked. In the fifth inning, singles by Mickey Livingston, Hughes, Hack, and Cavarretta, a walk to Lowrey, and an error by catcher Richards gave the Cubs 4 big runs, and a 4–1 lead.

The Tigers finally began to come back with 2 runs in the seventh, to make it a 7–3 game. The most ludicrous play resulted when Chuck Hostetler, who had walked, advanced to third on a hit and tried to score on Doc Cramer's single. He slipped, fell flat on his face, and tried to crawl on the rain-soaked turf. He kept slipping, sliding, crawling, falling, and then fell facedown in the mud as he was tagged out, as the crowd howled and hooted.

The Tigers again came back to the attack in the eighth inning, to tie the game 7–7.

Neither team scored in the ninth, and the game went into extra innings. Frank Secory, hitting for Oscar Merullo, singled in the twelfth inning. Hack then hit a fly ball to left, and Greenberg tore in to make the play. But the ball hit a flat rock, bounded over Hank's head, and rolled all the way to the fence as Schuster, pinch-running for Secory, charged all the way home with the winning run.

A furor broke out over the play and the scorer's decision to charge Greenberg with an error. It seemed like the ball had hit a hard spot over a drainpipe, and several hours after the game ended, the official scorer reversed his decision and no error was charged on the play. However, that decision had no bearing on the final result, as the Cubs squeeked by with an 8–7 win to tie the Series at 3 games each.

Borowy was selected to pitch the final game, and once more he was opposed by Newhouser. But Hank simply had nothing left. He lasted long enough to pitch to three hitters, and all three men singled. The Tigers had 1 run before all the spectators had been seated. Paul Derringer replaced Borowy on the mound, but he was also ineffective, walking Cullenbine and York. Then Richards sent the crowd into despair as he slammed out a long double, clearing the bases, and the Tigers had 5 big runs.

The 5 runs were more than Newhouser needed, as the final score was 9–3. Manager Grimm had trotted out his entire pitching staff in a vain effort to halt the slugging Tigers. But the Tigers could not be halted. Newhouser allowed 10 hits, and fanned 10 batters. And the Tigers were world champions.

The World Series set new attendance and receipt records, with a total attendance of 333,457 for the games and total receipts of $1,592,454.

Each happy member of the Tigers received $6,443, while the losing Chicago Cubs were much more generous. They divided their shares with everybody on the squad and even the clubhouse boys shared in the bounty. Each Cub share amounted to $3,930.

The champion Tigers were feted at a big citywide dinner at the chic Book Cadillac Hotel on the night of October 11. Several players were speakers; Hal Newhouser was awarded *Sporting News*'s Major League Player of the Year Award and Hank Greenberg spoke for the entire club when he said, "We won this championship for manager Steve O'Neill. There was no man on the ball club who didn't want to win for Steve— a guy who never second-guessed a ballplayer and always understood our every problem."

1946

St. Louis Cardinals Versus Boston Red Sox

Recalling the 1946 World Series, Stan Musial said: *

"In 1946 the Cardinals and Dodgers went down the stretch neck and neck and ended the season in a dead heat on the final day. This necessitated a two-out-of-three playoff series. A season's high of more than thirty-four thousand fans at St. Louis watched the scoreboard as much as the action on the field. At Brooklyn, our former teammate Mort Cooper was pitching the Braves to a shutout over the Brooks that helped us tie the Dodgers. We got off in front against Chicago when I hit a third-inning homer off Johnny Schmitz, a troublesome left-hander. But just about the time the four to nothing final score at Brooklyn was posted, the Cubs knocked out George Munger in a five-run sixth inning.

"Chicago's eight to three win over us not only set up the historic first playoff, but enabled the Cubs to tie the Braves for third.

"Even though we backed into the playoffs, we were keyed up by the pressure of playing a best-of-three series. A World Series has all the glamour, but it doesn't pack the pressure of a playoff. After all, once you're in the Series, win or lose, you're in the money.

"We never felt we'd lose to Brooklyn. The

*In an interview with the author, 1947, on author's *Sports Show*, New York radio station WINS

Dodgers had indeed won three of the last four they'd played against us, but we had taken fourteen of twenty-two games during the regular season, and that margin had been necessary to reach a tie, ninety-six wins and fifty-eight defeats.

"Despite a bad back, Howie Pollet scored his twenty-first victory over the Dodgers in the first playoff game at St. Louis. I tripled in that game, but the real star was Joe Garagiola, who got three big hits, and we beat Ralph Branca and the Dodgers, four to two.

"Two days later at Brooklyn, we trounced the Dodgers once more with a thirteen-hit attack for an eight to four victory, and for the fourth time in my four seasons with the Cardinals we were pennant winners. It was a marvelous feeling.

"The Red Sox, who had breezed to the American League flag by some twelve games over the Tigers, were big favorites to beat us. Not only did the Red Sox have four three-hundred hitters to our three—Kurowski, Slaughter, and me—but they had much greater power in the heart of their batting order. Dom DiMaggio, after nearly four years in the service, had returned and had his finest year in the major leagues with a three-sixteen average, and once Dom got on base he was a cinch to steal another. Johnny Pesky hit for a three-thirty-five average, and he too was a threat on the bases, and Ted Williams, Rudy

York, and Bobby Doerr had the muscle that could terrorize any pitcher. Williams hit for a three-forty-two average and drove out thirty-eight home runs, for one of the best seasons in his magnificent career.

"The big individual duel all the sportswriters were writing about was between Williams and me. I had had a very good year, hitting for a three-sixty-five average to lead the National League for the second time, and I also hit fifty doubles, twenty triples, and sixteen home runs.

"The Red Sox pitching, with Boo Ferriss, Tex Hughson, Harris, and Dobson, was well established, and they had tradition going for them as well. They hadn't lost a World Series in five tries.

"We had tradition going for us too, and we lived up to part of it. For the eighth time in nine starts in World Series competition, we lost an opening game. And this one had to be the most disheartening of all. For eight innings, Howie Pollet, despite his sore back, had the Red Sox beaten as we held a two to one lead going into the ninth inning. But a freak hop on a ground ball by Pinky Higgins, the Sox' third baseman, enabled the Sox to score a run and tie the score. And in the tenth inning Rudy York walloped a home run to give the Sox a three to two win.

"One thing about baseball, the sun always rises the next day. Harry Brecheen was our pitcher for game number two, and Boston's left-hander, Mickey Harris, opposed him.

"I didn't feel very good myself in the third game, the first one at Fenway Park, where we had been humiliated in the All-Star Game that summer. I got one hit, walked, and stole second, and was picked off base. In the very first inning, Rudy York hit a three-run homer off Murry Dickson, and the Red Sox right-hander, Dave Ferriss, breezed to a four to zero win. My only hit was a ninth-inning triple that didn't help us.

"Eddie Dyer, our manager, had set up an unusual shift of our infielders and outfielders against Williams to encourage him to hit to left field. We left only Marion, our shortstop, on the left side of the infield, moving Kurowski, the third baseman, to the right side of second base. Schoendienst, the second baseman, was moved

deep into the hole toward first, and our outfield swung around toward right field. I'd have hit a ton against that kind of defense, but Ted Williams chose to challenge it.

"And by the third game, Ted had only two singles and was fit to be tied. But he insisted on challenging our defense, and, finally Ted bunted the ball in the third game and it went into left field for a hit. Next day a Boston paper had the headline, TED BUNTS!

"In the fourth game, manager Eddie Dyer decided to gamble with George Munger, and we made it easy for Big Red (who was six feet two and weighed two hundred twenty pounds) as we routed the Red Sox twelve to three. We really clobbered Hughson, Jim Bagby, Brown, Bill Zuber, and Mike Ryba for twenty hits. Every member of our club got at least one hit.

"The Red Sox came right back in the fifth game and moved to within one game of the championship when Joe Dobson pitched one of

Broadcaster Red Barber in a rare interview with Ted Williams before the first game of the 1946 Series

Catcher Joe Garagiola was one of the hitting stars in the 1946 Series. Joe hit for a .316 average for the Cards.

the best games of his career as he gave us just four hits and beat us six to three. Howie Pollet's back gave him all kinds of problems, and as a result his off-speed pitches and tantalizing curve-balls could not be controlled, and the Sox belted Howie, Brazle, and Beazley for eleven hits and an easy victory. As if that wasn't enough, Slaughter was hit on the right elbow by a pitch and was forced to leave the game, perhaps for the rest of the Series.

"On the train from Boston to St. Louis for the sixth game of the Series, our trainer, Doc Weaver, worked with hot and cold packs all through the night on Slaughter's shoulder, but Dr. Hyland, the team physician, suggested that Slaughter be kept out because a clot at the elbow might move and cause serious problems. But Slaughter would have none of that nonsense. And barely able to grasp a bat, he delivered the last of five hits by

which we knocked out Harris. And Harry Brecheen pitched a marvelous game, allowing the Red Sox just seven hits, and we won the sixth game, four to one, to even the Series.

"The seventh game was one of the most exciting in World Series history. Murry Dickson opposed Boo Ferriss, and we had a three to one lead going into the eighth inning. Then the Red Sox made its bench strength count. Pinch hitters Rip Russell and George Metkovich singled and doubled to put the tying runs on second and third with nobody out.

"Brecheen, who had but one day's rest, replaced Dickson. As Harry trotted in to rescue Dickson, his pal and roommate, Murry left the mound with tears in his eyes. He dressed quickly, left the clubhouse, and couldn't be found until the next day.

"It looked as though Brecheen might rescue the game for Dickson and his three to one lead. He struck out dangerous Wally Moses and got rid of pesky Johnny Pesky on a short fly ball to Enos Slaughter. Two outs now. But Dom DiMaggio crashed a screaming line drive that went for two bases, and two runs came in and it was now a three to three game. Boston had the game tied, but suddenly Dom DiMaggio was down on the turf. He had twisted his ankle, badly, rounding first base, and had to be carried off the field. Leon Culberson took his place. Then Ted Williams had a chance to win the game, but Brecheen pitched him carefully, and got Ted to pop up to Schoendienst.

"In the eighth inning, Slaughter singled to center. Then, with two outs, Enos broke for second base, so that when Walker lined the ball over shortstop Pesky's head into left-center field, Slaughter was nearing second at the time. Rounding the base, he made up his mind to go all the way home. He roared into third, and Mike Gonzalez, our third base coach, prepared to stop him, but Enos thundered past third, ignored Gonzalez's pleas to stop, and sped for the plate. Pesky had already caught the throw by Culberson. His back was to the plate, and when he suddenly realized that Slaughter was going for home, he cocked his arm and threw off-balance, so that the ball sagged as catcher Roy Partee went out to meet it; at the same time a savagely sliding Slaughter crossed the plate, safely.

"The drama didn't end with that first-to-home dash on a single, however. In the Boston ninth, singles by York and Bob Doerr put two men on base with no outs. We huddled around Brecheen on the mound, talking over our bunt defense. So when Higgins slapped the ball hard enough to third base to compel the third baseman to handle the ball, thereby eliminating the chance for a play at third, Kurowski reacted quickly. Instead of throwing to me at first base, Whitey pegged the ball to Marion at second for a force-out on Doerr.

"That unorthodox play not only kept the potential winning run out of scoring position, but it proved extremely important after Partee fouled to me. McBride, pinch-hitting, grounded to Schoendienst, who juggled the ball. Our hearts stood still as the ball rolled up Red's right arm. Red looked like a magician pulling a rabbit out of his sleeve when he finally flipped the ball to Marion, just in time for a Series-ending force play. If the runner had been on second base, not on first, Schoendienst wouldn't have been able to get the ball to me in time to retire McBride.

"The thrilling four to three win represented St. Louis's sixth championship. In this one, three-game winner Brecheen and Slaughter had been the Series heroes. I hadn't contributed very much, hitting just two-twenty-two, but in my head-to-head test against Ted Williams, I had the edge. My six hits included four doubles, a triple, and I'd driven in four runs. Ted got just five singles and hit for a two hundred average.

"We had voted to waive the one hundred seventy-five thousand Series broadcasting dollars, so that the players' pension fund could be started.

"And we of the 1946 St. Louis team have particular pride in the pension plan now existing, because it was the creation of our great shortstop, Marty Marion, and our trainer, Doc Weaver, devised one rainy day.

"As for me, it was a great and wonderful and exciting World Series, my fourth Series in my first four years."

1947

New York Yankees
Versus Brooklyn Dodgers

The vicissitudes of war and numerous other happenings had brought about some strange changes on the big-league chessboard. Larry MacPhail, the Dodger president in 1941, bobbed up as president and part owner of the Yankees, and Branch Rickey, who had built the world champion Cardinal teams in St. Louis, was the new honcho and a big stockholder of the Brooklyn Dodgers. Bucky Harris, who had won a sensational Series for Washington as the "boy manager" in 1924, and blown a 3–1 lead over the Pirates in 1925, became the field tactician of the Yanks.

The 1947 Series actually developed into something of a grudge fight between the two presidents, MacPhail and Rickey. As an aftermath of the feud between those two colorful figures, Leo Durocher, the Dodger manager, was suspended for the 1947 season by Baseball Commissioner Happy Chandler. Rickey then named Burt Shotton, his old pal from the Browns and Cardinals as Dodger manager, and the modest, unspectacular Shotton led the Dodgers to an unexpected thrilling victory over the Cardinals to win the pennant.

The Yankees, thanks to a mid-season winning streak of 19 consecutive victories, won one of those easy victories à la Joe McCarthy, and finished some 14 games ahead of the second-place Tigers.

But the biggest story of the year, and one of the biggest sports stories of all time, began back on October 26, 1945, when Jackie Robinson, a twenty-six-year-old black, former All-American baseball and football star at the University of Southern California, was signed by Branch Rickey to play ball for Montreal, the Dodgers' number one farm club. At the same time, Rickey emphasized that Robinson would be given every opportunity to advance in the Dodger organization.

In his crucial year at Montreal, Robinson played brilliantly and led the Montreal Royals to a world championship. By 1947, Jack had developed into the most exciting second baseman in the International League. The Dodgers needed a new second baseman, and they needed Jackie Robinson.

On April 9, 1947, a note was passed to the press box at Ebbets Field as the Montreal Royals prepared to take the field to play an exhibition game against the Dodgers. The note indicated that Robinson's contract "had been purchased" by the Dodgers. On the following day, Jackie Robinson wore the Dodger uniform for the first time.

In Jackie's first season, there were some dreadful incidents with the Phillies and their manager Ben Chapman, and with the Cardinals. Both clubs threatened to strike if Robinson took the field against them. And in both instances the new commissioner, Ford Frick, warned the teams. "I don't care if half of the National League strikes," he thundered. "Those who do so will be punished."

And there were no strikes.

The incidents, however, continued, and somehow the Cardinals and Dodgers were always involved. During one incident, Slaughter painfully spiked Jackie as he crossed first base. Another time, Joe Garagiola was a little rougher on Jackie than was necessary. Things were quite difficult for Jackie, but he had promised Branch Rickey that he would turn the other cheek when any ugly incidents occurred and he kept his promise.

Jackie played first base brilliantly, hit for a .297 average, and walked away with the Rookie of the Year Award.

Eddie Stanky and Pee Wee Reese also had fine years, and developed into a crack combination around second base.

The Dodgers, in the meantime, struggled on, blazing, fighting, shining one day, stumbling the next, blazing and shining again, giving their loyal followers cause to cheer, to despair, and then to cheer again. On the last day of the season, the Dodgers were idle. But the Cardinals lost to the Cubs and the Dodgers won the pennant.

On the final Saturday of the season, there was a Jackie Robinson Day at Ebbets Field. The master of ceremonies, Bill Robinson, the great black dancer, who idolized the Dodgers, addressed the crowd.

"This year," said Robinson, preparing to present Jackie with the keys to a spanking-new Chrysler, "I've seen something I never expected to see in this world. Ty Cobb in Technicolor." And the crowd of more than thirty-four thousand stood and cheered and cheered. The roar was heard all over Brooklyn and all over America.

The World Series opened at Yankee Stadium on September 30 before a record crowd of 73,365. Jackie Robinson talked about that opening of the Series on the author's radio program several years later:

"My greatest thrill in baseball," said Jackie, "didn't come from any ball I hit, from any base I stole, or from any play I made. It came when

Dodgers teammates hoist Cookie Lavagetto to their shoulders after Cookie's double won the fourth game of the Series.

I heard Robert Merrill and the orchestra play the national anthem just before the start of the first game. Goose bumps jumped up and down my spine and I was trembling. They lined up the Yankees along the first base line and us Dodgers lined up along the third base line. Then Merrill sang and the band played the national anthem and the flag went up out there in center field. I don't remember much else about this particular game except that we lost it. But what happened before the game gave me the greatest thrill in my life."

The pitchers for the opening game of the Series, played at Yankee Stadium, were Frank Shea for the Yankees and the former NYU star, Ralph Branca, for the Brooks.

Jackie Robinson walked after Stanky struck out, and on the next pitch Jackie stole second base. Then Dixie Walker, a former Yank, singled, scoring Robinson with the first run of the Series, and Brooklyn had a 1–0 lead.

But in the fifth inning, the Yankees struck back, like a bolt of lightning. Joe DiMaggio started the action with a slashing single to left field. Then George McQuinn walked on four straight pitches, and that seemed to visibly upset

Brooklynites all over town celebrated the Dodgers' win over the Yankees as they jammed the streets in parades and marches.

Branca. He then hit Billy Johnson with a pitch, and suddenly the bases were full. Johnny Lindell picked a blazing fastball and cracked out a double, scoring DiMaggio and McQuinn. Rizzuto and Bobby Brown walked, forcing in Johnson with another run. Tommy Henrich singled and 2 more runs came in, and the Yankees had a 5–1 advantage.

After a rocky first inning, Frank Shea pitched four and a half strong innings, and then was taken out, and Joe Page finished the game for the Yankees. Page, the Yankees' left-handed relief star, gave up single runs in the sixth and seventh innings, but bore down in the eighth and ninth to hold the Dodgers and preserve the Yankees' 5–3 margin.

The second game at Yankee Stadium saw the Dodger pitchers at their worst, as the Yanks clubbed four Dodger hurlers, Vic Lombardi, Hal Gregg, Rex Barney, and Hank Behrman, for 15 hits. The Yankees scored in every inning but the second and eighth to win, 10–3.

"Four straight games," the sportswriters said. "Four straight. That's all the Yanks need. They're going to sweep the Series!"

But the experts had reckoned without the switch of the Series from the almost somber atmosphere of Yankee Stadium to the raucous and, to the Dodgers, inspiring and cheering background of Ebbets Field.

It was reminiscent of 1941 as the Dodgers and Yankees moved into Brooklyn, and you would have thought that Durocher was back in the dugout, instead of in a box seat with Danny Kaye.

But just as it seemed as if the Yanks would ram through for four straight wins and another World Series victory, the Dodgers rallied with a one-two punch of their own, to take the third game, squeaking out a 9–8 thriller.

The following day, October 3, the Dodgers evened the Series by winning the fourth game at Ebbets Field in a contest that had more than thirty-three thousand fans stark, screaming mad. It was the kind of game that makes the World Series the event that it is and explains its hold on the American public.

Floyd Bevens, a towering six-foot-four, 220-pound giant with the Yankees since 1944, had won 16 games in 1946, but slumped badly in 1947 and only had 7 wins all season. But Bucky Harris thought a well-rested Bevens was ready, and if he could control his fastball, Bucky figured, "we could easily beat the Dodgers. They'll not be able to hit him." Bucky was almost right, for the big Yankee came within one pitch of immortality, of twirling the first no-hitter in World Series history. But when Cookie Lavagetto doubled with 2 outs in the ninth inning to produce the Dodgers' only hit, it not only shattered Bevens' no-hit game, and his heart, but also knocked him for a 3–2 loss.

The Yankees had a glorious chance to put the game on ice for Big Floyd in the very first inning, when Barney Shotton decided he would gamble with his pitcher. He selected Harry Taylor, a big right-hander with a great curveball. Taylor had suffered an arm injury late in the season, but had come on strong after recovering and won 10 games during the late-season pennant drive.

Taylor pitched to just 4 batters in the first inning. After singles by Stirnweiss and Henrich and an error by Reese on Yogi Berra's ground ball, the bases were loaded. Manager Shotton then brought in Hal Gregg, and Hal turned in a magnificent relief job. He forced McQuinn to hit a short pop fly to Reese, and then got the dangerous Billy Johnson to hit into a double play to end the Yankee threat. In the fourth inning, the Yankees made it a 2–0 game when Johnson tripled and scored on Johnny Lindell's ringing double.

After that rally, the Yanks had numerous scoring opportunities, but the 2-run lead was all that Bevens had to work with.

In the fifth inning, the Brooks finally broke through. Jorgensen and Gregg walked, and Eddie Stanky sacrificed both runners. Then an infield out by Pee Wee Reese scored Jorgensen and gave the Dodgers a run, without a base hit. But Bevens bore down and held the Dodgers until the ninth inning, with the Yanks out in front in a 2–1 ball game.

Dodger rooters then experienced every conceivable thrill that could possibly come to a fan in an incredible last inning. It looked as if the Yankees finally would give Bevens some breathing room in their half of the ninth, when Lindell and Stirnweiss singled. Bevens then tried a bunt and everybody was safe on catcher Edwards's poor throw to first base. Now the bases were full of Yankees. Manager Barney Shotton called a time-out and brought in his ace relief pitcher, Hugh Casey, and Casey got the Yanks out with one big pitch. He hurled a fastball, low and inside, to dangerous Tommy Henrich, and Tommy slammed the ball back to Casey. Hugh scooped up the ball, fired it to the plate to Edwards, his catcher, for one out, and Edwards's throw got Henrich at first. It was a lightning-fast

Jackie Robinson slides into second base and flips Phil Rizzuto in the air in the first inning of the sixth game of the Series. Snuffy Stirnweiss is at left.

World Series game called on account of autograph: The sixth game was halted when this five-year-old dashed onto the field for Joe DiMaggio's autograph.

play, and the Dodger fans reacted with a thunderous cheer.

It still was Bevens's game, and the only question was whether Floyd would be able to get his no-hitter.

In the Dodgers' last at bats, Bruce Edwards drove a pitch that went high into the air in left field, and Lindell backed right against the wall for the catch. One out now. Carl Furillo worked Bevens for his eighth walk, and then John Jorgensen fouled out to McQuinn for the second out.

Manager Shotton sent in Pete Reiser to hit for Casey, and Al Gionfriddo, a reserve outfielder, to run for Furillo, and Al promptly stole second on Berra's poor throw. It was a most opportune steal for the Dodgers.

Bevens was ordered to walk Reiser, and now Shotton attempted another piece of strategy. He called on Cookie Lavagetto to hit for Stanky. Cookie took a terrific cut and missed the first pitch, but then drove a screaming double off the right field wall. The ball caromed back past the startled Henrich, and both Gionfriddo and Eddie

Miksis (who ran for Reiser) scored, giving the Dodgers the ball game by a 3–2 score.

Maddened Dodger fans, completely overjoyed with the incredibly sudden victory after all was seemingly lost, leaped over the fences, knocked down the special police and ushers, attempting to hug the grinning Lavagetto, to slap his back, and to hug any Dodger player around. Cookie was almost mobbed by the happy throngs that surrounded him as he was carried back into the dugout by the sweep of the crowd.

And now the World Series was tied at 2 games each.

The following day, October 4, the Yankees, behind the 4-hit pitching of Young Frank Shea, went ahead of the Dodgers by winning an exciting pitchers' battle, 2–1. It was the lightest-hitting contest of the Series, as the winning Yanks managed to get just 5 hits off the combined efforts of Barney, Hatten, Behrman, and Casey.

Yet those amazing Dodgers snapped back on Sunday, October 5, to come from behind once more, taking an 8–6 thriller.

Allie Reynolds, the Yankees' Big Chief, started the game against the Dodgers' Vic Lombardi. But each pitcher was merely the first of a string of pitchers to follow, as both Bucky Harris and Barney Shotton tried desperately to win this vital game.

The Dodgers quickly jumped out in front, with 2 runs in the first inning and 2 more in the third. The Yanks came back furiously, however, knocking out Lombardi with 4 big runs in the third, and then went ahead 5–4 as Branca gave up singles to Robinson, Henrich, and Berra.

Then there was a surprise thrill for the fans, as the Dodgers came back with 4 runs in the sixth inning. Edwards singled, took second on Furillo's double, and scored on Lavagetto's fly ball to Berra in right field. A double by Bobby Bragan scored Furillo. Then Stanky and Reese singled in succession, accounting for 2 more runs, and the Dodgers now had an 8–5 lead.

Then came the most dramatic moment. Joe Hatten was on the mound for the Dodgers; he walked Stirnweiss, Berra singled, and then DiMaggio stepped up to the plate.

If DiMag could just hit the ball out of the

park. . . . Then it was all over!

Joe swung at Hatten's first pitch and drove the ball on an arc, high into the evening dusk. Everybody in the ballpark knew that it was heading for the left field stands. The ball was earmarked, home run!

With the crack of the bat, however, Al Gionfriddo, who was patrolling left field, raced back into the shadows of the deepest part of his territory. It seemed that Al was going to give it the old college try, and just as he reached the 415-foot mark, Al twisted around, reached up and out, and caught the ball as it was about to exit over the barrier and into the stands.

For just a precious moment, Dodger fans were stunned, and as they realized the impact of the catch, they broke out in a roar that could be heard all over Brooklyn.

The Yanks tried to come back in the ninth inning as Bill Johnson walked and McQuinn slapped a single to right field. But then Hugh Casey came in to pitch and, for the fifth time in the Series, got the Yankees out after 1 run had scored. But that was not enough and the Dodgers took an 8–6 squeaker. And the World Series was now tied at 3 games.

The seventh and final game of the Series seemed anticlimactic after the sensational sixth game as the Yankees, behind the marvelous relief pitching of Joe Page, won by a 5–2 margin. Page had the Dodgers at his mercy during the final five innings, facing just 16 Dodgers, and the Yankees once again came from behind to chalk up another World Series.

Bobby Brown, who is the current American League president, made history with his hitting during this Series. Bobby hit 2 doubles, a single, and walked in 4 times at bat as a pinch hitter, and batted 1000.

Each Yankee received $5,830 as the winner's share of the Series, while each Dodger received $4,081 for his efforts.

1948

Cleveland Indians Versus Boston Braves

"The photographers kept asking me to smile," said pitcher Johnny Sain.* "A whole crowd of them filled up the locker room. They posed me with Tommy Holmes, then Phil Masi, then Billy Southworth, and each time they repeated: How about a little smile, John? See how the guys are grinning? At least a little one, John? I just couldn't smile, I told the photographers; If a couple of breaks had gone the other way, you guys would be in the other locker room taking pictures of Bobby Feller. The game was too close to smile.

"It was just the greatest thrill of my life beating Bob Feller and the Cleveland Indians, one to nothing in the opening game of the 1948 World Series. But ballplayers can't get as excited as I was, they'd never be able to get their work done.

"For the fans, okay. But not the ballplayers. I was trying hard to take the whole thing in stride.

"It was a tremendous game, really close. We only got two hits off Feller, and I allowed the Indians four. That's how close it was.

"And it was important. Boston hadn't been in a World Series for thirty-four years, since 1914. And public interest made this a big game, the biggest game I'd ever pitched in my life.

*In an interview with the author, 1948, on author's *Sports Show*, New York radio station WINS

"Billy Southworth told me I was going to pitch the first game of the series about a week before. We were on the road then, the Red Sox were at home. They were in a three-team dogfight with the Yankees and Cleveland.

"I pitched five innings against the Giants at the Polo Grounds the day before the regular season ended. Then on the following Tuesday the Series began.

"The first game of the Series opened at Braves Field. It was slightly cloudy and a northeast wind was blowing towards the plate, the kind of weather good for pitchers. While I sat in the dugout before the game, I thought about the wind. Bill Salkeld, who was my catcher, came over and we discussed it.

"I said to Bill, 'The wind is blowing in. I'm going to keep the curveball high to their power hitters. I want to break it above their knees, not below.'

"He understood. Salkeld never said much, but he was very smart.

"So I threw curves, nothing but curves. The Indians must have expected them. It was my best pitch.

"I wasted my fastballs, then came in with my curveball. Every once in a while I used my slider, not too much, though.

"The strategy was working beautifully. In the first inning, all three Indian batters flied to the

214

outfield. I kept the curve high and the Indians were hitting up into the wind.

"Ken Keltner singled in the second inning, but he stayed there. Hegan reached first on an error, but I got the side out without further trouble.

"Meanwhile we weren't getting anywhere with Feller. He was strong, and fast when he had to be. We didn't get a hit off Bobby until the fifth inning, when Rickert singled, but he stayed there.

"Larry Doby singled in the sixth inning, but I didn't give up another hit. I felt good. My control was sharp. The eighth was our big inning.

"Salkeld walked and Masi ran for him. McCormick then sacrificed Masi to second. Feller then walked Eddie Stanky.

"It was a setup for their pickoff play. And no one was looking for it.

"The first guy I saw was Lou Boudreau sprinting towards second. Then Feller whirled, all of a sudden, and threw. It's a count play. The pitcher just watches the catcher, gets the sign, counts, then turns and throws to the base. The shortstop has to be there because the pitcher throws right over the base. Timing is everything.

"On the play, umpire Stewart called Masi safe. Boudreau put up a big holler, but the play was good.

The Indians' first baseman, Ed Robinson, stretches for the putout on Al Dark in the second game of the Series.

Player-manager Lou Boudreau led his Cleveland Indians to a Series triumph over the Red Sox in 1948.

"Holmes was the next hitter, and he banged a ball just inside the third base line, and Phil raced in with the only score of the game. And I had a one to nothing lead.

"In the ninth inning, I got Boudreau on a fly ball. Gordon fouled out, and I got Judnich on three straight curveballs, the best strikeout in my life. Then I was automatically walking back to our dugout.

"Players were all around me shaking hands, slapping me on the back. In the locker room, I heard all kinds of facts about the game. Someone yelled to me; 'You made ninety-five pitches, John. Feller made eighty-five. You know, that's the first one to nothing World Series game in twenty-five years. Since Casey Stengel's homer for the Giants, beating the Yankees one to nothing in 1923.'

"Later, talking to Salkeld, we learned just how much our strategy about throwing curveballs had paid off.

"Cleveland had hit fifteen flies to the outfield. Only two men went out on ground balls.

"Those are the things that make a pitcher feel wonderful."

The Cleveland Indians deadlocked the Series in Boston the next afternoon, behind the airtight pitching of Bob Lemon, 4–1. He was opposed by the Braves' ace southpaw, Warren Spahn, and although both pitchers allowed 8 hits, Lemon shut down the Braves just when it seemed they would break out and score a rash of runs.

A World War II hero, Gene Bearden was the Indians' star in the third game. During the war, Bearden was aboard the cruiser *Helen* in the South Pacific when the battlewagon was torpedoed. He floated unconscious for more than twenty-one hours in a life raft and almost bled to death from wounds in his head and knee. After two years of hospitalization with aluminum plates inserted in his head and knee, Bearden was playing ball once more, and in his first full season, 1948, with the Tribe, he won 20 games.

The Purple Heart hero shut out the Braves in the third game, allowing them but 5 hits, using tantalizing pitches, and had the Brave players popping up the ball for easy outs throughout the battle. Bearden helped himself and his team with 2 ringing doubles that scored 2 runs as the Indians chalked up a 2–0 victory.

Manager Southworth of the Braves selected Johnny Sain, his big star, winner of the first game, to pitch the fourth game of the Series, and Lou Boudreau of the Indians took what looked like a real gamble when he selected Steve Gromek as the Indians' hurler.

Larry Doby, the Indians' hard-hitting center fielder, provided the winning margin in the third inning as he slammed a long drive into the left field stands for a home run. Marv Rickert homered for the Braves' only run in the seventh inning. The final score was 2–1, Indians.

A record crowd of 86,288 fans jammed every inch of the huge Cleveland stadium on October

Bob Lemon, one of the ace Cleveland hurlers, won 2 games for the Indians in the Series.

Cleveland's great pitcher Bobby Feller waited for twelve years for the Indians to appear in a World Series.

10 for the fifth game of the Series. It was an unforgettable sight to see every seat filled and fans packed in like sardines in a can hoping to see their hero, Bobby Feller, who lost the opening game oppose Nelson Potter of the Braves.

But it didn't take long for fans to realize that Feller wasn't the Feller of three days ago, who had allowed the Braves 2 hits. Holmes opened with a single. Then Dark singled, and Bob Elliott, who had only 2 hits in the previous games, drove out a 3-run home run to give the Braves a 3–0 lead.

Dale Mitchell got 1 of those runs back in the Indians' half of the first inning by slugging a home run off Potter to make it a 3–1 game. But in the third inning, Elliott again belted a tremendous homer off Feller into the left field stands.

In the fourth inning, the Indians slugged back, scoring four times to give Feller a 5–4 advantage. Jim Hegan was the star of this Indian uprising as he belted a 3-run home run.

In the seventh inning, Salkeld homered off Feller, and then the Braves scored on 3 successive hits, and that was all for Feller, who walked dejectedly off the mound. By the time two Indian relief pitchers were in and out of the game, the Braves scored 5 runs and led by a score of 11–5, which Warren Spahn protected during the final two and a half innings. Spahn allowed the Indians just 1 hit from the time he relieved Potter in the fourth inning; he fanned 8 Indians, including 5 of the last 6 men he faced. The Indians looked inept as they tried vainly to hit Spahn's pitches.

However, it was succor for just a day for Billy

Television sets were expensive in 1948, so to promote sales, TV manufacturers placed the sets in parks, bars, and other areas to popularize them. The World Series was a giant promotion opportunity, as is shown here.

Southworth and his brave Braves, and they were beaten in Boston in the Series finale, 4–3.

It was a fine pitchers' battle for six innings, with the score 1–1, when Joe Gordon homered. The Indians scored again on a couple of singles, a force-out, and a sacrifice fly. In the eighth inning, the Indians scored their fourth and final run on successive singles by Ken Keltner, Joe Tucker, and Ed Robinson, making the score 4–1.

In the eighth inning, the Braves came back fighting mad. Tommy Holmes opened with a single, Earl Torgeson doubled, and Bob Elliott walked. Clint Conatser hit a fly ball to Tucker, and Holmes scored after the catch. Phil Masi doubled, scoring Torgeson. Masi's drive almost was a home run; it missed going over the fence by only a foot.

In the ninth, Spahn struck out 3 Indians in a row—Bearden, Kennedy, and Doby—and Brave fans began to yell for a rally. Eddie Stanky walked to start the ninth inning for Boston, but Sisti, the best bunter on the team, attempting to bunt, hit into a double play, and then Holmes ended the Braves' chances by popping the ball to Kennedy in left field, and the Cleveland Indians were world champions for the first time in twenty-eight years.

1949

New York Yankees
Versus Brooklyn Dodgers

Chances are that no one ever had more fun playing baseball than did the new manager of the New York Yankees, Casey Stengel, and while he had experienced all the woes with which managers are afflicted from time to time, he often looked back at the overall picture and said it had been a happy one.

Charles Dillon Stengel was born in Kansas City (hence the nickname KC, or Casey), July 30, 1890, and was fifty-eight years old when he was named manager of the Yankees.

As a player he was discovered in 1911 by Larry Sutton, the Dodgers' famous one-man scouting staff, and in view of his subsequent career, with its vagaries, and all the laughs, it was fitting that the discovery should have been accidental. Sutton, who roamed the country for the Dodgers looking for new talent, went to Aurora, Illinois, simply because he had never been there and wanted to see what the town looked like. Gravitating, naturally, to the ballpark, he saw Stengel hit the ball to all parts of the field. He liked the way Casey ran bases like a wild horse with his hair flying, then crashing into the base with a mad headlong slide that brought cheers from the crowds.

Casey had had but one season as a professional, playing with Kankakee and Maysville in the Blue Grass League, and on Sutton's recommendation the Brooklyn Dodgers decided to buy

this colorful clown. Casey reported to Montgomery in the Southern League in 1912, and before the season ended he was ordered to report to Brooklyn.

Dodger fans immediately took to the smiling, swaggering kid who had been a sandlot player, a cab driver, and a registered student for two years at the Western Dental College. When he learned that a left-handed dentist might find it difficult to build a successful practice, he promptly quit. (He was told that all dental tools were made for right-handed dentists.)

Casey played in Brooklyn for six years, and was traded to Pittsburgh after manager Wilbert Robinson discovered that Casey was the chief architect of a stunt that had the baseball world howling. It seems that Wilbert Robinson, the rotund manager of the Dodgers, had bet some of the Dodger players that he could catch a baseball dropped from the plane of a famous lady aviator at about 1,500 feet. The plane went up, and the aviatrix dropped not a baseball but a soft, squooshy half-rotten grapefruit. Robbie set himself for a catch, and the "ball" (grapefruit) came right on target. It hit Robinson in the face and he dropped to the ground as if he were shot. The fruit splashed all over him, and Robbie groaned in pain. He thought he was bleeding to death. As the players stood over him and howled with laughter, Robbie realized the

Yankee coach Bill Dickey greets baseball wives Mrs. Lou Gehrig (*left*) and Mrs. Babe Ruth (*right*) at the opening game of the 1949 Series.

stunt, got up, wiped his face, and noted that Stengel was among the chief plotters.

At season's end, Casey was shipped to Pittsburgh. In 1920, Casey was with the Phils and in the middle of the season was sent to the Giants.

In 1922, Casey helped the Giants beat the Yankees in the World Series, and in 1923, his 2 home runs helped the Giants win their only 2 Series games as the Yanks captured their first Series.

In 1923, Casey was traded to the Boston Braves. He then went on to a succession of teams: to Worcester as president of the club; Toledo as manager for six years; then back to Boston in 1938; then to Milwaukee; Kansas City; and Oakland for a couple of years. Then, to the surprise of almost all of the baseball world, he was named the new Yankee manager in 1949.

Casey spent several weeks consulting with general manager George Weiss, and then drew up extensive plans. For one thing, he wanted a second baseman to replace a fading George Stirnweiss. He tried to get Gerry Priddy of the Browns, but the Yankees had a youngster at St. Petersburg, Jerry Coleman, who played second base, shortstop, and even third base. And he was not yet twenty-five years of age.

On his arrival at spring training, Stengel, in conversation with several sportswriters, said, "I never had a ball club like this. Imagine having a fellow like Joe DiMaggio on your side!"

Late in August, the Yankees acquired John Mize from the Giants. John was to provide the Yankees with some immediate power in the final weeks of the pennant race.

On October 1 and 2, the Yankees defeated the Red Sox to take the American League flag by the margin of 1 game. In the National League, it looked as if the Cardinals had the flag all wrapped up, and the Cards' owner, Fred Saigh, had already printed World Series tickets. Suddenly, the Redbirds lost game after game and dropped to fourth place, enabling the Dodgers to just squeeze ahead by 1 game. However, the pennant remained in doubt until the tenth inning of Brooklyn's final game with the Phillies, which the Dodgers finally won in a 9–7 slugfest.

The Series opened at Yankee Stadium on October 5, and a crowd of some sixty-six thousand saw husky Allie Reynolds pitted against big Don Newcombe.

Newcombe was in superb form, and his blazing fastballs had the big Yankee hitters stopped cold. Don struck out 11 Yanks and allowed the Bombers just 5 hits. But the "Big Chief," Reynolds, was even better. Allie fashioned a brilliant 2-hit game. He fanned 9 Dodgers, and after eight and a half innings of the tightest pitching, the game blew up in the last half of the ninth.

Tommy Henrich slugged a home run into the right field stands, and the Yankees eked out a 1–0 win in game one.

The next day, seventy thousand fans, including more than a thousand standees, saw another remarkable pitching battle, between Preacher Roe, the Dodgers' fine left-hander, who won 15 games during the season, and the Yankee ace, Vic Raschi, a 21-game winner. The game was decided in the second inning by MVP Jackie Robinson. Jackie opened the inning with a slashing two-base hit, then sprinted to third when Jerry Coleman fell down after catching Gene Hermanski's foul fly. Jackie sped home when Gil Hodges rammed a single past Rizzuto at shortstop, and that lone run by the Dodgers evened the Series on a 1–0 shutout.

The third game, played at Ebbets Field before a capacity crowd, saw the Yankees emerge with

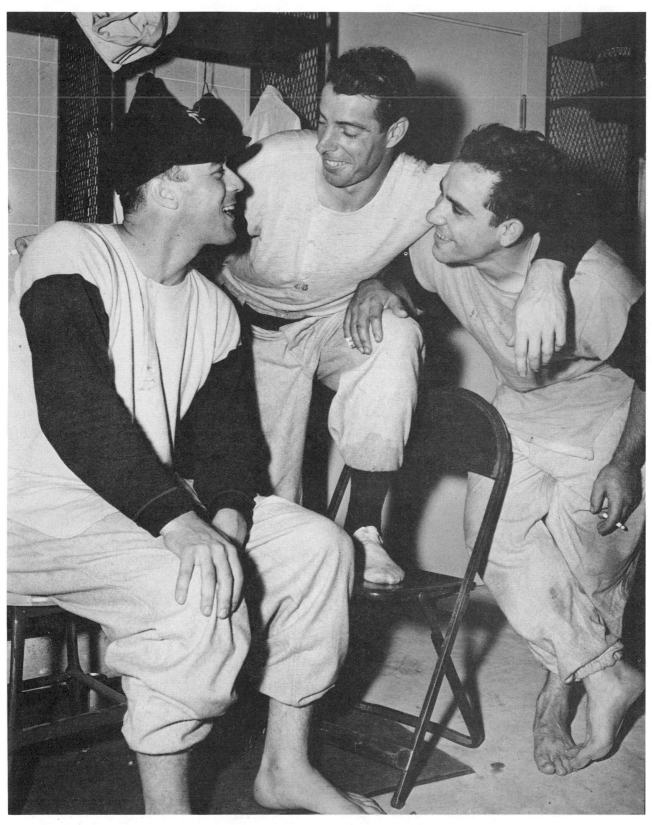

Yankee stars (*left to right*) Vic Raschi, Joe DiMaggio, and Yogi Berra relax in the clubhouse after the Yankee win in game five of the Series.

a 4–3 victory. It was an excellent game, which saw most of the action confined to one inning, the ninth.

Ralph Branca and Joe Page were practically invincible throughout the game. Suddenly, in the ninth inning, Branca walked Berra, Bobby Brown slugged a blazing fastball for a single, Gene Woodling walked, and then Mize, batting for Cliff Mapes, slammed a single to right field, scoring Berra and Brown. Then Coleman singled, scoring Woodling, and it was 4–1, Yankees.

In the bottom of the ninth inning, the Dodger bats, silent since the sixth inning, began to stir. Luis Olmo slammed a long home run into the left field stands, and Roy Campanella followed with another homer. But Joe Page had enough stuff left in reserve to strike out pinch hitter Bruce Edwards to end the game with the Yanks out in front by a 4–3 score.

Eddie Lopat, a 15-game winner, was Casey's selection for the fourth game, at Ebbets Field, and Don Newcombe was the Dodgers' selection. Newk, called back after his splendid win in the Series opener, just didn't have his usual stuff, and lasted until the fourth inning, when the Yankees pounded him for 3 runs. Hatten replaced Newk, and the Yankees jumped on Hatten for a second batch of 3 runs, highlighted by Bobby Brown's triple with the bases full of Yankees.

The 6-run lead made it look like a huge Yankee picnic. But suddenly, in the sixth inning, the Dodgers began to tee off on Lopat. The Brooks whacked out 7 hits for a total of 4 runs, and would have scored more if Snider hadn't hit into a double play following singles by Pee Wee Reese and Billy Cox. But Stengel called on Allie Reynolds in relief of Lopat, and the Big Chief promptly got the side out, then retired the next 7 Dodgers in a row to protect a 6–4 Yankee victory.

The fifth game saw Rex Barney on the mound for the Dodgers opposed by Vic Raschi for the Yankees. Barney, a big six-foot-three-inch, 215-pound giant, had a fastball that fairly sizzled as it reached a batter, that is, when Rex could locate the plate. He was splattered for 2 runs in the first inning and then driven to the showers in the third with a 3-run assault. Then, in succession, manager Shotton brought in a parade of Dodger pitchers in a vain but unsuccessful attempt to stop the Yankee onslaught as the Yanks piled up a 10–1 lead.

In the seventh inning, the Dodgers brought a ray of hope to their almost-lost cause, when Gil Hodges hit a bases-full home run off reliever Joe Page to make it a 10–6 game. But Page then bore down in the eighth and ninth innings and put an end to all the Dodger hopes as he ended further scoring to win the game and another championship for the Yankees.

While the World Series victory was the twelfth for the Yankees, it was the first one for Dan Topping and Del Webb since taking over complete control of the club from Larry MacPhail in 1947.

The experts said that Casey Stengel had brought in a World Series winner in his first year with the Yankees with "mirrors," and that his champions were not in the same class as some of Huggins's and McCarthy's teams. But despite the loss of the Yankee star Joe DiMaggio for the first 65 games, and more than seventy injuries to various players, and despite the fact that he took over a team that in the main resented him, Casey Stengel turned that resentment around and proved that he was a winner.

Yankee outfielders Gene Woodling (14) and Joe DiMaggio chase Pee Wee Reese's long double off the fence in the first inning of the fourth game of the 1949 Series.

New York Yankees Versus Philadelphia Phillies

If the 1949 Yankees looked impressive in defeating the Dodgers, the 1950 Bronx Bombers registered an even more emphatic win over the Philadelphia Phillies, the "Whiz Kids," so named by sportswriter Harry Grayson. The Yanks reverted to their earlier form by thrashing the "Kids" in 4 straight games to record their thirteenth World Championship. The sweep over the Phillies was their sixth in World Series competition.

The Whiz Kids were actually a spirited mix of youngsters and veteran players, the young consisting of twenty-two-year-old Granny Hamner at shortstop, twenty-four-year-old Mike Goliat at second base, twenty-four-year-old Willie Jones at third; in the outfield were Del Ennis at twenty-five, Richie Ashburn at twenty-three, and Dick Sisler at twenty-nine; twenty-nine-year-old Andy Seminick was the catcher; pitchers included twenty-three-year-old Robin Roberts, a 20-game winner, and twenty-one-year-old Curt Simmons, with a 17-8 record. Then there was the "old man," Jim Konstanty, who at thirty-three won 16 games and appeared in 74 games. And finally, Eddie Waitkus, a twenty-nine-year-old first baseman, who had been shot by a lovesick teenage girl, had recovered, and played first base as if he had been born there.

In 1985, Robert Redford produced and starred in the motion picture *The Natural*, a fictionalized version of the Waitkus shooting, which was one of the year's best pictures.

The surprising Phillies apparently seemed to have the pennant all locked up as the race dwindled down to the final week of the season. Then their sensational pitching staff suddenly came apart at the seams. Starters Bob Miller and Bubba Church received arm injuries and were sidelined. Curt Simmons, ace left-hander, was called up for active military duty, and by September 10, the Phils began a precarious slide, toward the waiting arms of the Dodgers.

The Whiz Kids charged into Ebbets Field with a 2-game lead, and 2 to play. In the first game on a sunny Saturday afternoon, the Dodgers whipped the Phils. One more Dodger victory the following day would mean a tie for first place, and a playoff.

The second game was a thriller, with both pitchers, Robin Roberts for the Phils, and Don Newcombe, pitching their hearts out as the game wound into the tenth inning, tied at 1–1.

In the top of the tenth, Dick Sisler, son of the immortal George Sisler, smashed a Newcombe fastball into the stands for a home run with two men on base, and the Phils were the National League champs by a score of 4–1. It was the Phillies' first pennant since 1915.

The Philadelphia "Whiz Kids" in 1950: (*left to right*) Richie Asburn, Dick Sisler, and Del Ennis sparked the Phils to their first pennant since 1915.

Meanwhile, there were few changes in the Yankee lineup. Casey Stengel was delighted that a healthy Joe DiMaggio was able to start the season, and there was a bright, fresh addition to the pitching staff, a towheaded, twenty-one-year-old left-hander out of Long Island City named Ed Ford, who for some reason was called Whitey. He was a product of the New York sandlots and a graduate of the Yankee farm system by way of Binghamton, Butler, Norfolk, and Kansas City.

The baby-faced Ford, sometimes mistaken by visitors to the dugout for the bat boy, won game after game as the Yankees slogged through the season.

As the season wore on, the Yanks once again proved victorious and took the pennant by 3½ games over the second-place Detroit Tigers.

Ford, incidentally, ran his string of wins to 9 in the closing days of the pennant race, but broke the string in a relief assignment in Philadelphia. That didn't matter to the brash rookie, for at the age of twenty-one and in his first year in the major leagues, he very definitely had played an integral role throughout the season.

The World Series between the Yankees and the Philadelphia Phillies, the Whiz Kids, pitted a bunch of boys against men, and, of course, the men had to win.

Eddie Sawyer, manager of the Phillies, surprised the experts by nominating his great relief ace, Jim Konstanty, to pitch the first game in Philadelphia, on October 4, against the Yankee ace, Vic Raschi. Konstanty, the league's MVP, hadn't started a game since joining the club in 1948, and Sawyer and Konstanty almost got away with the surprise. However, on that day, Raschi was razor-sharp and pitched near perfect ball, allowing the Phils just 2 base hits, and the Yankees took a squeaker by a 1–0 score.

The lone Yankee run came in the fourth inning. Bobby Brown crashed a long double past third base. Then two long sacrifice flies by Hank Bauer and Jerry Coleman brought Bobby home.

In the second game of the Series, on October 5 at Philadelphia, Robin Roberts, the Phils' young 20-game winner, matched his speed and control against the wily Allie Reynolds, and Robin lost this one, a heartbreaker, in the tenth inning, when he tried to slip a fastball by Joe DiMaggio, who had popped the ball up in six consecutive trips to the plate. This time, however, Joe guessed right, took a mighty swing, caught the pitch on the fat part of his bat, and the ball disappeared over the left field fence. It was Joe's first 1950 Series hit and won the game for the Yankees, 2–1.

The Whiz Kids had their chance to get back into the Series when the action shifted to New York for the third game, on October 6, and although they outhit the Yankees 10 to 7, the Phils were again losers in still another heartbreaker, by a 3–2 score.

In the Yankees' half of the ninth inning, with the score tied at 2 all, Gene Woodling and Phil Rizzuto singled in succession. Then Jerry Coleman hit a fly ball halfway between Sisler and Ashburn in the outfield. The ball dropped in as both players stood there, momentarily paralyzed, and Woodling raced across the plate with the winning run. Now the Yankees were just one game away from another championship.

Here is how Whitey Ford described the rest of the Series:*

* From an interview with the author, 1950, on his *Sports Show* on New York radio station WINS

"Stengel had named me to pitch the fourth game, and now I had a chance to make it the clincher. I held them scoreless throughout the first eight innings and we scored two in the first and three in the sixth and took a five to nothing lead into the ninth. I needed only three more outs.

"But the Phillies still had some fight left in them. Puddin' Head Jones led off with a single and I hit Del Ennis with a pitch. I got the next two hitters, and I thought the game, and the Series, was over when Andy Seminick hit a drive deep to left. But Woodling had trouble with the sun and dropped it for an error to score two runs and cut our lead to five to two.

"I thought I had a shutout, but I couldn't blame Woodling. Left field is tough to play, especially in October. A lot of outfielders had trouble with the sun out there at that time of year.

"I wanted to finish the game, but when Mike Goliat singled, the Phillies brought the tying run to the plate. And that brought Casey to the mound to make a pitching change. He took me out, and it was the worst booing I ever heard Casey take at the stadium. Half of the people booing him were my family and friends. But he was right.

"Casey brought in Allie Reynolds. The old man wasn't fooling around. He wanted to end it here and now. It was getting dark and the shadows were falling in Yankee Stadium. Usually, the first place the shadow falls is around home plate, which makes it even harder to pick up the ball because it's coming out of light into dark. Stan Lopata had no choice. Reynolds just pumped three fastballs past him and that was that. Lopata swung, but I'm not sure he ever saw the ball.

"It had been a great year, but a hectic one. I

Phil Rizzuto leaps high into the air to avoid Mike Goliat's slide as he drives into second base in game three.

was looking forward to doing nothing all winter except collect my World Series check, maybe buy some clothes, and just hang around and wait to report to spring training again.

"About two weeks after the Series, I was having a couple of beers with my friend Joe Gallagher in an Astoria bar called the Two-Way Inn. We were just up the street from the Con Ed building, which is also where the draft board was. I was eligible for the draft, and I was curious to know when I could expect my call up. I was wondering how much of the 1951 season I might have to miss.

"We walked up to the draft board and I asked the lady behind the desk if she could tell me when I could expect my call. She asked my name and address and I told her and she went away to look something up. A few minutes later, she came back smiling and said, 'You're leaving in two weeks.' "

1951

New York Yankees Versus New York Giants

"In 1951," recalled Leo Durocher,* "my Giants swapped training camps with the Yankees. They trained at our camp in Phoenix, and we trained at theirs in St. Petersburg. And we had the finest spring we ever had, and I felt that I was going back to New York with the very best team I'd ever managed. Before we broke camp, my wife, Laraine, and Fred Fitzsimmons's wife, Helen, dragged us down to an astrologist in the lobby of the hotel. Laraine took that kind of thing very seriously, and I'm so superstitious that I'll try anything. Not that I believe in anything like that. Oh no, just for the fun of hearing what they say.

"The astrologist, a nondescript middle-aged woman, told Fitz to change the number on his uniform from six to five. And she also told him to always wear something purple. Then she got to me. I was going to get off to the worst start I ever had, she said, and she was right. We won our opening game and then lost eleven straight. The first half of the season was going to be so bad, she said, that when I came up to my birthday we would be half a step from falling into last place. She was right. On July twenty-seventh, we were half a game out of the cellar. After my birthday, she said, things would change

*Leo Durocher discussed the 1951 World Series with the author on his *Sports Show*, New York radio station WINS.

and I would go on to have the greatest season of my life and end up winning everything.

"Freddy and I went up, laughing at the girls. How could we have that kind of miserable start with this good a team? Well, our eleven-game losing streak came to an end when Freddie changed his number and then started to wear purple undershorts. From there on, it was like we were following a Hollywood script. Superstitious as I am, I did everything to find that woman again. We wrote to the hotel, but they couldn't even tell us her name. Just an ordinary middle-aged woman."

The World Series began on October 4, one day after Bobby Thomson's dramatic game-winning home run in the ninth inning in a playoff game against the Dodgers, and the momentum that enabled the Giants to win 39 of their last 48 games carried them to victory in the first two games of the Series.

Leo Durocher selected Dave Koslo, a surprise starter, who had a mediocre 10–9 record during the season. But Koslo surprised everyone but his manager as he pitched magnificently, holding the slugging Yankees to just 7 hits, defeating them 5–1. Monte Irvin, the Giants' best batter, was the star of the contest, slashing out 4 hits, including a triple and 3 singles. Then to top off a big first inning, Monte stole home while Allie

Yankee stars celebrate after winning the first game of the Series: (*left to right*)
Bobby Brown, Vic Raschi, Gene Woodling, and Gerry Coleman.

Reynolds was winding up, and the Giants were off and running with a 2–0 lead.

The Yankees scored their lone run in the second inning, when Gil McDougald doubled and Jerry Coleman singled him home.

Al Dark clinched the game for the Giants in the sixth inning, when he homered with two men on base and the Giants had a 5–1 win.

In the second game, manager Stengel selected Ed Lopat, a 21-game winner, while Durocher nominated Larry Jansen, a 23-game winner to oppose the Yanks.

But Larry evidently suffered World Series jitters in the first inning, and the Yanks pushed over a run before a man was out. Mantle and Rizzuto both beat out drag bunts, and then Mickey raced in for the first score of the game when McDougald arched a texas leaguer past second base. In the second inning, Joe Collins, the Yankee first baseman, lifted a long fly ball into the right field bleachers for a home run, and it was a 2–0 game.

Jansen settled down and retired the next 13 Yankee batters in succession as he and Lopat matched pitch for pitch, until the seventh inning, when the Giants touched up Eddie for successive singles by Irvin and Lockman, and a sacrifice fly by Bill Rigney, for their lone run.

The Yanks picked up another run in the eighth inning, then held the Giants scoreless in the final inning for a 3–1 victory to even the Series.

The third game, at the Polo Grounds on October 6, saw the largest Series crowd thus far. More than fifty-two thousand fans jammed every inch of the historic home of the Giants to see two outstanding pitchers, the Giants' Jim Hearn and Yankee ace Vic Raschi. For five innings, it was one of the finest games played in the Series. The Giants had scored a run in the second inning and were leading 1–0 going into the fifth. Suddenly the Giants lashed out and exploded with 5 runs off Raschi. Whitey Lockman applied the crusher for the Giants with a long home run with two men on base, to give the Giants a 6–0 lead.

Second baseman Gerry Coleman leaps to avoid Monte Irvin's spikes, at the same time attempting to throw to first base for the double play on Bobby Thomson. Action occurred in the fourth game of the Series.

Eddie Lopat and Larry Jansen were the starting hurlers for their respective teams for the fifth game of the Series, at the Polo Grounds, and the Yankees bombarded Jansen and three other Giant pitchers for a total of 12 hits and a 13–1 shellacking, to take a 3 games to 2 Series lead.

Young Gil McDougald, the Yanks' rookie third baseman, blasted his way into the record books with a grand slam home run, the first by a rookie and only the third in World Series play to that time. DiMaggio once again hit the ball hard, with 3 base hits. Phil Rizzuto, the Yankees' MVP in 1950, exploded with a vengeance. Little Phil battered Giant hurlers with a home run, a single, 2 walks, and 3 runs, and was absolutely dazzling at shortstop.

Back at Yankee Stadium for the sixth game, on October 10, Vic Raschi of the Yankees and Dave Koslo of the Giants pitched their hearts out. It was a tense, exciting battle going into the sixth inning, with the score tied, 1–1.

Then Berra singled to start the Yankee half of the inning, and DiMaggio walked. Johnny Mize also walked, filling the bases. Then Hank Bauer, the burly ex-Marine, cleared the bases with a tremendous three-base hit to give the Yanks a 4–1 edge.

Big Jim Hearn, a former St. Louis Cardinal star, meanwhile had handcuffed the Yankee power hitters, allowing them just 4 hits, until a bad back forced him out. Shelly Jones came in to relieve Hearn and retired the Yankees after they scored single runs in the eighth and ninth innings. But the Giants' 6–2 lead was too much to overcome.

The Yankees tied the Series at 2 games each on October 8, when Joe DiMaggio suddenly came to life. Joe had been hitless in the first three games, but in the fourth, he hit a 2-run homer and then singled home an additional run to spark the Yankees to an easy 6–2 verdict. Allie Reynolds, aided by three snappy double plays, outpitched his rival, Giant ace Sal Maglie, who was banged for 12 hits by the Yankee sluggers. Al Dark of the Giants slugged out 3 consecutive two-base hits for the losers.

Bobby Thomson is out when Willie Mays hits into a game-ending double play: Rizzuto to Coleman to Joe Collins in the fourth game of the Series.

Outfielder Hank Thompson watches helplessly as Joe Collins's long drive shoots into the stands for a home run in the second game of the Series.

In the ninth inning, the Giants struck back. Eddie Stanky led off with a single. Al Dark followed with another single, and now the Giant fans were up and screaming for another hit. And Whitey Lockman slapped a single, filling the bases.

Casey Stengel then called in lefty Bob Kuzava to pitch against the Giants' two right-handed sluggers, Monte Irvin and Bobby Thomson. Irvin sent a fly ball deep but Woodling caught it on a dead run, and Stanky scored after the catch, making the score 4–2. And the Giants had slug-ger Bobby Thomson coming up to bat. Bobby slugged Kuzava's first pitch in the same general area of Irvin's fly, and again Woodling sprinted after the ball and caught it, and Dark scored after the catch. It was a 4–3 game, and the crowd was in a frenzy.

Durocher called on Sal Yvars, a powerful pinch hitter, to bat for Hank Thomson, and Yvars hit a sinking line drive that Hank Bauer chased and caught with a headlong drive, catching the ball just before it hit the ground. And the Yankees were once again world champions.

1952

New York Yankees Versus Brooklyn Dodgers

Leo Durocher once said of Eddie Stanky, his second baseman in Brooklyn from 1944 to 1947 and later with the Giants, "He can't hit, he can't run, he can't throw, but he's the best second baseman in baseball."

Casey Stengel might have said the same of his Yankee second baseman from 1950 to 1957. Not endowed with the remarkable defensive skills of a Rizzuto or the hitting of a Yogi Berra, Billy Martin was as important as either in winning the tough Series battles of the early 1950s.

Scrappy, talky, and cocky, a typical sandlot kid, Billy Martin, a Portuguese-Italian youngster from Berkeley, California, spent his boyhood on the streets. The situation at home was so bad that Billy lived with his grandmother and often swept out the local church in exchange for food for the family.

While still in high school, Billy played with the Oakland Oaks, a semipro team, and by 1946 he was good enough to win a berth in the Oakland farm setup. In 1947, Billy played for Phoenix in the Arizona-Texas League and was named the league's MVP; hit batting average was a brilliant .392.

"In 1948, I played for the Oakland team, under Casey Stengel," said Billy, "and we won the pennant. Then in 1949, Casey got the job with the Yankees and a year later I joined him."

Casey Stengel treated Martin as a son. Even before Billy had joined the team in 1950, Casey had been telling the Yankee players about "this kid of mine out in Oakland, who could be one of the best. He's got it here in his heart, where it counts," said Casey.

Martin didn't play too much during his first two years on the Yankees, in 1950 and 1951, because Jerry Coleman was so outstanding as the Yankees' second baseman, but by 1952, Billy became the regular second baseman, and although he only hit for a .267 average, his value, his inspirational play, and his will to win were contagious. The Yankees won and won and won.

The Yankees of 1952 represented Casey Stengel's top achievement as a Yankees manager. Despite the retirement of the great Joe DiMaggio, the loss of regulars Bobby Brown, Jerry Coleman, and Eddie Lopat for a good part of the year, Stengel was able to deliver his fourth pennant in a row. It was a feat achieved previously by only two other managers, Joe McCarthy, with the Yankees of 1936–39; and John J. McGraw, with the New York Giants of 1921–24.

In the National League, the Dodgers, who had been defeated two years running in photo finishes, came through for manager Chuck Dressen. The Dodgers feasted on the last three teams in the league, winning 17 games from the Reds, 18 from Boston, and 19 from the Pirates, and

Pee Wee Reese looks as active as an acrobat as he flips into the air to avoid Mickey Mantle's dive into second base in the 1952 Series. Larry Goetz is the umpire.

the innings sped by with neither team scoring. In the sixth inning, Pee Wee Reese opened with a single, and the Dodger crowd went into a paroxysm of joy as Duke Snider drove out a screaming line drive that cleared the right field scoreboard, and the Dodgers were out in front by a 3–1 margin.

In the eighth inning, Woodling tripled off the wall and scored on Hank Bauer's sacrifice fly,

breezed to the pennant by 6 games over the second-place Giants.

Joe Black, the twenty-eight-year-old right-handed fire-thrower, who was not even on the Dodgers' roster at the start of spring training, proved the Dodgers' lifesaver. Utilized strictly as a relief pitcher, Black led the Brooks with 15 wins against 4 losses and worked in 56 games. Manager Dressen rewarded Black by starting him in the first game of the Series. Stengel's choice was the ace of the Yankees' staff, Allie Reynolds.

The game began with a portent of things to come as Jackie Robinson, responding to the roars of the "faithful," slammed a home run in the second inning. But Gil McDougald evened the score with a drive into the left field seats in the third inning, to make it a 1–1 game.

Both Black and Reynolds had settled down and were now in a marvelous pitching duel as

Billy Martin dives for the ball and makes a breath-taking catch of a towering fly ball hit by Jackie Robinson with the bases full in the seventh game. This catch ended the Dodger threat.

Fans at Brooklyn's Ebbets Field cheer both teams in this great subway classic.

and the score was 3–2. But Pee Wee Reese drove a pitch into the lower left field stands, and the Dodgers happily toasted a 4–2 victory over their bitter New York rivals.

However, the next day, the Yankees, behind a masterful pitching performance by Vic Raschi, easily defeated the Dodgers, 7–1. Raschi was never in better form as he allowed the Dodgers but 3 base hits while striking out 9.

The third game of the Series, played at Yankee Stadium on October 3, was a pitching duel featuring two left-handed stars, Preacher Roe, the southpaw from Ashflat, Arkansas, and his southpaw opponent, Eddie Lopat. Roe allowed the Yanks but 6 hits, while his teammates pounded Lopat and reliever Tom Gorman for 11 blows, which enabled the Brooks to take a 5–3 verdict over the Bombers, and a 2 game to 1 edge in the Series.

In the fourth game, manager Stengel, unhappy with the play of first baseman Joe Collins, who had been unable to hit Dodger pitching in the first three games, started "Big John" Mize at first base. And Mize responded with a tremendous performance. He slugged a home run, a single, and a double, and in his fourth time at

bat, John walked to set up the second Yankee run, as the Yanks took a 2–0 squeaker.

In the fifth game, the Dodgers combined some solid hitting by Duke Snider and third baseman Billy Cox, plus airtight pitching by Carl Erskine. The Dodgers forged on to eke out a 6–5 victory in eleven innings at Yankee Stadium before a wildly screaming mob of seventy thousand fans.

It was a 5–5 game going into the eleventh inning, when Billy Cox bounced a single off McDougald's glove, then raced to third base on Reese's single to left, and scored the winning run for the Brooks on Snider's smashing two-base hit off the left field wall.

"I think we've got them Yanks now, especially winding up at home," Walter O'Malley, the Dodger owner, confided to intimates.

In the sixth game of the Series, at Ebbets Field, manager Dressen selected Billy Loes as his pitcher.

"You've got plenty of guts, and I'm going to let you finish those Yanks off," Chuck told his pitcher before the game. Billy had the guts, and pitched very well, but the Yanks prevailed to win an exciting 3–2 pitchers' battle.

There was no score in the game going into

the sixth inning, when Snider bombed a fastball over the right field wall to give the Dodgers a 1–0 lead. Yogi Berra responded in the seventh with a home run. Then Woodling singled, advanced to second on a balk by Loes, and scored the second Yankee run when Raschi bounced a hit off Billy Loes's knee, and the Yanks had a 2–1 lead.

Mickey Mantle led off the Yankee eighth inning with a solo home run, and the Yanks now had a 3 to 1 edge. In the Dodger's eighth inning, Duke Snider homered, to make it a 3–2 game. But Allie Reynolds held the Dodgers in check in the final inning, and the Yankees had tied the Series at 3 games.

In the seventh and final game of the Series, played at Ebbets Field on October 7, superb relief pitching by the Yankees was the deciding factor. Stengel started Ed Lopat, but Reynolds, Raschi, and Bob Kuzava were all in the game before it was over. The Dodgers' Carl Erskine, Roe, and Joe Black attempted to hold the Yankees.

Lopat started for the Yankees and Joe Black pitched for the Dodgers. After the Yankees scored a run in the fourth inning, the Dodgers came back in their half of the inning to fill the bases with nobody out. A single by Snider and safe bunts by Robinson and Campanella filled the bases, and Dodger rooters were up and in a

The Dodgers won the pennant by 6½ games over the Giants in 1952.

frenzy as their hopes mounted. But Stengel, in a masterful bit of strategy, removed Lopat and inserted Reynolds, and Allie retired the side at the expense of only 1 run.

In the fifth inning, Woodling drove out a home run, but Billy Cox got the run back for the Dodgers as he doubled and scored on Reese's single.

The high drama of the game came in the Dodgers' half of the seventh inning. By this time Allie Reynolds was arm-weary and had been replaced by Raschi, who walked the first batter, Furillo. Rocky Nelson popped out, Billy Cox singled, and Reese walked, to fill the bases. Now the thirty-two thousand faithful Dodger fans were in a constant uproar as the excitement mounted to a fever pitch.

Here, Stengel, once again realizing Raschi wasn't right, summoned lefty Bob Kuzava to face the always dangerous Duke Snider. The count went to 3 and 2, but on the next pitch Duke reached for a high fastball and popped the ball up.

Jackie Robinson had not been hitting the ball well throughout the Series, but now he came up to bat with a grim, determined look on his face. Again, the count went to 3 and 2. On the next pitch, the three Dodgers on base started to run as Jackie swung and lifted a high, high pop fly toward the rear of the pitching mound. First baseman Joe Collins took one look at the ball, and rushed over to make what looked like an easy catch. Then, suddenly, Joe stopped dead in his tracks. He had lost sight of the ball.

On the mound, Bob Kuzava just stood there looking up, as if he were transfixed, and two Dodgers had already crossed the plate. Billy Martin, the only infielder aware of the flight of the ball, made a wild last-minute, frantic dash from his post at second base. Tearing in at full speed, Billy speared the ball in the webbing of his glove just before it hit the ground.

Billy Martin's marvelous catch saved the game and the World Series for the Yankees, and snuffed

Dodgers outfielder Andy Pafko became an instant hero in the fifth game as he leapt high into the air to take a home run away from Yankee Gene Woodling in the 1952 Series.

out the Dodgers' 3-run rally. Bob Kuzava then breezed through the eighth and ninth innings without allowing another Dodger score, and the Yanks took the game, 4–2, chalking up their fifteenth success in nineteen World Series competitions.

1953

New York Yankees Versus Brooklyn Dodgers

The World Series of 1953 was the fiftieth played, and Commissioner Ford Frick celebrated the golden jubilee in fitting fashion. Survivors of the 1903 Pittsburgh-Boston teams had the distinction of throwing out the first ball in each of the six games. The honorable sextet was made up of Pirates manager-left fielder Fred Clarke, third baseman Tom Leach, and Otto Krueger, as well as Red Sox pitchers Cy Young and Bill Dinneen and shortstop Fred Parent.

The old interborough rivals, the Yankees and the Dodgers, were the participants in the 1953 Series. Both teams won their respective league titles in a romp.

The Dodgers breezed to their second straight pennant 13 games in front of the transplanted Boston Braves, who had moved to Milwaukee; and the Yankees finished 8 games ahead of the Cleveland Indians, winning an unprecedented fifth straight pennant. Nothing to equal that achievement had ever been accomplished in major league history. And then the incredible Casey Stengel went on to win an unheard-of fifth consecutive World Series. It was the fifteenth victory in sixteen Series since 1927.

In the opening game, at Yankee Stadium, the "Big Chief," Allie Reynolds, drew the opening assignment and took a 4–0 lead in the very first inning, when Carl Erskine, the Dodger pitcher, had trouble locating the plate.

Erskine walked the first three Yankees he faced, and they all scored when Bauer tripled. Then Billy Martin unloaded a tremendous three-base hit, to score Hank with the fourth run of the inning.

In the fifth inning, the Brooks came back with home runs by Junior Gilliam, Gil Hodges, and George Shuba to bring the Dodgers within striking distance, at 5–4. In the seventh inning, the Dodgers hit Johnny Sain hard, scoring a run on 3 base hits, and it was a 5–5 tie.

Joe Collins broke the tie with a solo home run off Clem Labine, and in the eighth inning the Yanks put the game away with 3 runs off Ben Wade, for a 9–5 victory.

Two southpaw pitchers, both featuring "junk" pitches, opposed each other in the second game, and, despite outhitting the Yankees 9 hits to 5, the Dodgers dropped a 4–2 decision to the Bombers. The Dodgers hit Lopat hard, but could not hit with men on base, and stranded 10 runners. Billy Martin and Mickey Mantle homered for the Yankees.

The desperate Dodgers, down two games, were now battling with their backs to the wall as the Series moved to Brooklyn for the third game. Manager Dressen had no alternative but to call on his hardworking ace, Carl Erskine. Carl responded with an awesome performance, allowing the slugging Yanks only 6 hits and

Pregame ceremonies at the opening game of the 1953 Series

Jackie Robinson slides home as Berra attempts to tag him. But Robbie is safe in this action photo in the sixth game of the Series. Umpire Bill Grieve and Gil Hodges (14) watch.

striking out 14, nailing Mickey Mantle and Joe Collins for 2 strikeouts each, to chalk up one of the great World Series wins for the Dodgers, a 3–2 squeaker.

In the eighth inning, with the score 2–2 and thirty-three thousand Dodger fans up and screaming for a hit, Roy Campanella responded by driving a terrific shot over the left field wall for a game-winning home run.

Duke Snider atoned for his ordinary performances in the three previous games, and took complete charge of the Yankees in the fourth game. The Duke of Brooklyn blasted a home run, and 2 doubles, driving in 4 runs to lead a 12-hit attack against four Yankee hurlers, and the Dodgers walked away with a 7–3 victory, tying the Series at 2 games each. Billy Loes held the Yankees to 2 runs and 8 hits until the eighth inning, when he tired, and Clem Labine shut down a budding Yank rebellion for the save.

The Yankees exploded with a vengeance in the fifth game to slug out an 11–7 victory that included a barrage of base hits off the Ebbets Field wall that rattled the old stadium. Yankees

Mickey Mantle, Billy Martin, Gene Woodling, and Gil McDougald unmercifully pounded five Dodger pitchers for home runs to sink Dodger hopes.

For the sixth game of the Series, manager Chuck Dressen decided to pitch Carl Erskine for the third time. It was a desperate decision, but the Dodgers had to win to stay in the Series, and Erskine was their ace. Whitey Ford was Stengel's choice, despite Whitey's having been knocked about by the Dodgers in the fourth game.

The game was a thriller from start to finish. The Yankees jumped out to a quick lead as Berra doubled, Mantle walked, and then Billy Martin drove a hard shot off Junior Gilliam's foot, scoring Berra. Rizzuto and Ford singled, and Mantle scored the second Yank run of the inning. In the third inning, Gene Woodling drove out a long fly ball, and Rizzuto scampered home for run number 3.

Both pitchers, Ford and Erskine, were in magnificent form until the sixth inning, as they set down batters in one-two-three order.

In the sixth, responding to the cries of the Dodger fans, Jackie Robinson doubled, and then, as Ford went into a sort of trance, Robinson stole third while Whitey was still holding the ball. Campanella swung, and topped the ball, which rolled to second base, and Jackie Robinson tore home with the first Dodger run, making it a 3–1 game.

Then Stengel, attempting to defuse the Dodgers, brought in Allie Reynolds in the eighth inning and Allie mowed down the Dodgers in order. But a Dodger storm was unleashed in the ninth.

There was 1 out when Allie walked Duke Snider. Furillo worked Reynolds to a full count; then, on the sixth pitch to him, Carl batted his way into the Dodgers' hall of fame as he slugged a tremendous home run, high over the right field stands, to tie the score at 3–3. And Dodger fans did a crazy war dance in the aisles beneath the vast portals of Yankee Stadium, and their cheers echoed throughout the Bronx.

But the Yankees, undaunted, put a damper on Dodger hopes in their half of the ninth. Clem

A happy group of Yankees celebrate after defeating the Dodgers in the opening game of the Series: (*left to right*) Hank Bauer, Yogi Berra, Billy Martin, and Joe Collins.

Now it's the Dodgers' time to celebrate after their second win over the Yanks: (*left to right*) Clem Labine, Junior Gilliam, Duke Snider, and Billy Loes.

Labine walked Hank Bauer; Mantle beat out an infield hit; and then scrappy Billy Martin broke every heart in Brooklyn with a slashing single to center field, and Bauer raced across the plate to win a thrilling, nerve-wracking 4–3 victory and the World Series. As the game ended, Martin was swept up and carried into the clubhouse by his uproarious teammates, and the victorious Yankees broke out the champagne.

Each World Series share was worth $8,280 for the Yankees, while the losing Dodgers received $6,178 each. The 1953 Series had grossed more money than any Series in history, just $20,000 short of a total gate of $3 million.

1954

New York Giants Versus Cleveland Indians

When National League ballplayers of the 1950s and 1960s discussed the other players in the league, they rarely had to say "Willie Mays." They merely said "Willie."

Willie got an early start in the game. His dad, a steelworker in Fairfield, Alabama (where Willie was born on May 6, 1931), was a fine semipro ballplayer. And Willie learned to throw and catch almost before he could walk. At Fairfield High, Willie was an outstanding three-sport star, and at age fourteen he was playing semipro baseball on Sundays, on the same team as his father. At age sixteen, Willie, in a tryout with the Birmingham Barons, made an outstanding impression, and the Barons took him on as a utility outfielder. A few weeks later, Willie had played his way onto the team as a regular. His light-hearted personality, his big smile, and his "Say hey" salutations were enough to start the locker room or bus rollicking with laughter.

Willie came to the attention of the New York Giants when a scout on the prowl for a first baseman spotted him one afternoon in Birmingham as he sparked one play after another in the field, and sprayed hits to all corners of the outfield in a superlative performance.

The scout forgot all about the first baseman he was supposed to get, signed Willie instead, and the following year Willie was sent to the Giants' farm team in Trenton, New Jersey, where

he hit .353. The next year, 1950, Willie was promoted to the Minneapolis Millers of the American Association and tore up the league with an incredible .477 average in the first 35 games of the season. Leo Durocher watched him carefully and decided that Mays was needed in the Giants' pennant fight.

The 1954 Indians had a remarkable team. They won 111 games, one more than had the 1927 Yanks, the former record holders. Their chief asset was probably the most powerful pitching staff ever assembled. Early Wynn and Bob Lemon each won 23 games; Mike Garcia won 19; Art Houtteman, 15; and the great Bobby Feller, used sparingly, won 13 big games. They had two brilliant young relief pitchers in Don Mossi and Ray Narleski, and plenty of offensive power at the plate. Bobby Avila was the league's leading hitter, with a .342 average, while Larry Doby slugged 32 homers, Al Rosen hit 24 home runs, and Vic Wertz, Jim Hegan, and Dave Philley supplied plenty of secondary power when needed.

The pitchers for the New York Giants could not match the massive power of the Indians' pitching staff. The backbone of the Giants was the veteran Sal Maglie, who had peaked in 1950 with 23 wins, but this season had won just 14 games. Young John Antonelli, in his first season with the Giants, won 21 games. They, together with Ruben Gomez, who had 17 victories, com-

Manager Leo Durocher in the lead car heads the ticker-tape parade up Broadway after the Giants' World Series win in 1954.

prised the first line of Giants hurlers. Jim Hearn, Don Liddle, and Hoyt Wilhelm were utilized in spots throughout the season. It was a good, solid staff for a short Series.

Durocher's stars included four outfielders: Willie Mays, Don Mueller, Monte Irvin, and James Lamar "Dusty" Rhodes. Willie Mays, back from nearly two years in the service, battled teammate Don Mueller for the batting crown throughout the season and just managed to nose out Don by hitting for a .345 average, while Mueller hit .342.

"In 1954, we not only won another pennant," said manager Leo Durocher,* "we swept the World Series in four straight. And once again I was a genius, and just in the nick of time too, because for two years I'd been just another bum. Just in case there are any skeptics, I can prove what a genius I was by the saga of Dusty Rhodes, the night rider, from Matthews, Alabama.

"At the start of the season I tried in every way I knew to trade Dusty Rhodes. Half of the time he was drunk and everybody else in the league had heard about his drinking problems, but no-

body would claim him. Thank the Lord nobody did.

"Every time we needed a pinch hit to win an important game, there was Dusty Rhodes to deliver it for us. Confident? The average fan may think a manager has to fight his men off when he's looking for a pinch hitter. Don't kid yourself. You look down on the bench and more often than not every eye is averted. But not Dusty Rhodes. Dusty would always be up on his feet, at the far end of the dugout, swinging a bat. 'Ah'm you're man,' he'd call down. 'What are you waiting for, Skipper?'

"He came through in the pinch all season long and I had to reward him with something extraordinary. Before the summer was over, I was leading him around to the best bars in the towns we played in and supplying him with whiskey. Training rules? They were forgotten where Dusty Rhodes was concerned."

In the opening game of the World Series, Sal Maglie opposed the Indian star, Bob Lemon. Maglie quickly fell behind as the Indians went ahead 2–0 in the opening innings.

The Giants tied the score in the third inning on singles by Lockman and Dark. Mays walked and Hank Thompson drove in 2 runs with a single to center.

In the eighth inning, Larry Doby walked, Al Rosen singled, and it looked as if the Indians were about to erupt for a couple of runs. Durocher took action and brought in Don Liddle to stem the Indian attack.

Vic Wertz, the first batter to face Liddle, slashed at Don's first pitch, a fastball, across the outside corner. As the ball shot off Wertz's bat, it did not appear to be a long drive, because its trajectory was low. That was deceptive, however, because the ball was hit so hard that it actually took off and began to rise as it reached the outfield. It seemed headed for the very top of the wall in center field.

Willie Mays, in center field, running at full speed with the crack of the bat, instinctively felt he had the ball tracked; he turned his back and kept on running as hard as he could toward the runway in deep center field, some 450 feet from home plate. Liddle was off the mound now, watching the flight of the ball, and Durocher

*Durocher discussed the 1954 Series in an interview with the author, on author's *Sports Show*, New York radio station WINS.

Willie Mays made perhaps one of the greatest defensive plays in Series history in the opening game of the 1954 Series. With the Giants and Indians tied at 2–2 and two Cleveland runners on base, Willie raced to deep center field and, with his back to the ball, made an over-the-shoulder catch of a 400-foot drive by Vic Wertz. Then Mays whirled and made a perfect throw to second base to hold Al Rosen from advancing to second on the catch.

and his players stood frozen in the dugout. The Indian runners were poised halfway between the bases, ready to dash home, and every eye was fixed on Mays, running for his life. At the very last moment, Willie put up his hands and caught the ball in the webbing of his outstretched glove, like a wide receiver. He stopped after the catch, pivoted, and got off a remarkably accurate throw on a line to Williams at second base. The throw was so accurate that Doby could only advance to third base, while Rosen remained at first.

"It was one of the greatest catches I've ever seen in all my years in baseball," said Durocher," and only Mays could have made it. And it meant the game for us."

In the Giants' half of the tenth inning, with the score still tied, 2–2, Willie Mays walked to start the inning. And on Lemon's first pitch to Thompson, Mays quickly stole second. Hank Thompson also walked. Then Durocher called a time-out and signaled to Dusty Rhodes to pinch-hit for Monte Irvin.

Dusty walked up to the plate swinging three big bats, tossed two of them to the side, strode into the batter's box, and slugged Lemon's first pitch high into center field. It finally settled into the left field stands for a home run. Three runs scored and the Giants had drawn first blood with a spine-tingling, tenth-inning 5–2 victory.

Leo Durocher remembered the rest of the

Series with equal excitement:

"The next day, Early Wynn was beating us one to nothing in the last of the fifth inning. We had two men on base and nobody was out and I again called on Dusty. This time he hit a short fly ball that dropped in center field, two men came in, and the score was tied. Before the inning was over, we scored another run and we were in front by two to one. Then, in the seventh inning, Dusty, up once more, hit a tremendous shot off Wynn. It must have been a fastball, because the ball carried more than three hundred fifty feet into the upper stands, and it's three to one. And we win another game.

"In the third game, I used Dusty even earlier. In the third inning, we were ahead by one to nothing over their big winner, Mike Garcia, and we loaded the bases. Dusty is up and hits a wicked line drive into the right field, and two more runs come in, and we won it six to two.

"Adding it all up, Dusty was now four for four and had driven in seven of the last nine we had scored. While he was at it, he had broken or tied four World Series records for pinch hits. And we had won three in a row, one more to go."

Indians manager Al Lopez now was in a pitch-ing quandary. He had expected to use Bob Feller in the fourth or fifth game, but he was in a spot where another defeat would end the Series. So he once again chose his ace, Bob Lemon. Durocher came back with Don Liddle.

In the second inning, Lemon walked Thompson, Monte Irvin doubled, and errors by Wertz and Wally Westlake gave the Giants 2 runs. They added another run in the third, and knocked Lemon out of the box in the fifth. Then the Giants hit Hal Newhouser and Narleski hard, to rack up 4 more runs, and give them a 7–0 lead.

The Indians rallied briefly in their half of the fifth inning to score four times when pinch hitter Hank Majeski homered with two men on base. They added another run in the seventh inning, but then Johnny Antonelli blanked the Indians in the eighth and ninth innings for a 7–4 win, and the Giants were world champions.

Although the Series ran only four games, the massive capacity at the Polo Grounds and Cleveland's Municipal Stadium made the 1954 Series one of the most lucrative on record. A record sum of $2,741,203 in receipts resulted from the four-game Series, with each winning player receiving a record $11,147 and the losing players receiving $6,000 each.

1955

Brooklyn Dodgers Versus New York Yankees

Baseball people have been wont to say that anything could happen in Brooklyn and usually did. Three men on third base at the same time, following a triple by the unforgettable Babe Herman; a sparrow flying from underneath Casey Stengel's hat; a fly ball hitting Babe Herman on the head; the longest game ever played (26 innings, against the Braves, which ended in a frustrating tie); and a game the Dodgers won when a ball rolled up and over the right field wall for a home run.

Everything had happened in Brooklyn baseball except one thing: a World Championship flag flying over the stadium.

All loyal Yankee fans agreed with the derisive stipulation that things were going to remain that way. The Dodgers could win pennants, if they wanted, but the World Championship was strictly for the Yankees.

In 1955 the Dodgers won another pennant, as manager Walt Alston guided his flock to an easy 13½-game margin over the second-place Milwaukee Braves, and all loyal Dodger fans eagerly looked forward to the World Series against the Yankees with the same combative confidence that had so dependably turned to groaning dismay in other years.

Through the seasons, there have been a number of Dodger heroes who won enduring affection in Brooklyn: Zack Wheat, Babe Herman,

Dazzy Vance, Pee Wee Reese, Jackie Robinson, Roy Campanella, Dixie Walker, Johnny Podres, Carl Erskine, Carl Furillo. But none of them made Ebbets Field his own private domain to quite the extent that the Duke did.

The Duke was a man who found home and happiness in Brooklyn. A native of California, Duke Snider had a navy dad who taught him to bat left-handed, on the theory that most major league ballparks give the left-handed hitter an extra step toward first base, surely an advantage. In high school, the Duke starred in football, basketball, and baseball. Once in a championship football game, the Duke tossed a forty-yard pass in the last few seconds of play to score the game-tying touchdown; then he calmly kicked the extra point to win the game 20–19. On the diamond, the Duke was the star hurler, and batted in the cleanup spot. One afternoon, after he had pitched a no-hit game against Beverly Hills High School, a Dodger scout signed Duke Snider and sealed it with a bonus of $750. The year was 1944. The Duke was just seventeen years old.

By 1952 the Duke was one of the stars of a great Dodger team. From 1952 to 1955, Snider hit 40 or more home runs in each season. His 42 homers in 1955 led an awesome Dodger team total of 201, and Brooklyn fans could hardly contain themselves as the team prepared to bat-

Mickey Mantle and Duke Snider check over their favorite bat before the first game of the 1955 Series.

tle their bitter rivals from across the East River, the champion New York Yankees.

The Yankees barely nosed out the aggressive Cleveland Indians by a slim margin of just 3 games in a hotly contested three-way pennant race, while the Chicago White Sox slumped in the final week to finish in third place, 5½ games off the pace.

Hobbled by injuries to Mickey Mantle and Hank Bauer, the Yankees limped into the first game of the Series at Yankee Stadium anxious to face the Dodgers' star pitcher, Don Newcombe, who had posted a record 27 wins during the regular season. Don was opposed by 18-game winner, Whitey Ford. But as the game pro-

The 1955 World Champion Brooklyn Dodgers

gressed, it was soon evident that both pitchers were off form and both were hit hard. The Yankees collected 9 base hits off Newcombe, while the Dodgers clobbered Ford for 10.

In the second inning, both teams exploded as Carl Furillo and Elston Howard slugged 2-run home runs. In the third inning, the Duke blasted a tremendous drive into the stands to give the Dodgers a 3–2 lead. But the Yankees charged back in their half of the inning to score a run and the score was now 3–3.

However, the Dodgers fell behind as Joe Collins, the Yankee first baseman, a .230 hitter during the season, smacked two successive home runs to give the Yankees a 6–3 margin as the teams went into the eighth inning. Dodger fans were already up and out of their seats and on the verge of leaving the ballpark as the Dodgers prepared to bat. Furillo led off the inning with a slashing single to left field, and then Jackie Robinson got the Flatbush faithful back to their seats as he smashed a hard ground ball that Gil McDougald fumbled. Furillo went to third and Robbie reached second on the error.

Don Zimmer (who would manage the Cubs in the late 1980s) scored Furillo with a long fly ball to deep center field and on the play Robinson sprinted to third. With the count 1 and 1 on pinch hitter Frank Kellert, Robinson, who had been taking daring leads off third base suddenly streaked for home as Whitey Ford hesitated for a long moment. Then regaining his poise, Whitey shot the ball to catcher Berra, but Jackie, racing for the plate like a whirling dervish, slid safely under Yogi's desperate tag. But that was all the scoring for the Dodgers and the Yankees took the game, 6–5.

In the second game, Dodger pitchers Billy Loes, Don Bessent, Karl Spooner, and Clem Labine all took turns attempting to contain the Yankee storm, which threatened to engulf the Dodgers. The Yankee pitcher, Tommy Byrne, was in great form as he held the struggling Dodgers to 5 hits and 2 runs and came away with the second straight Yankee victory, 4–2.

The Yankee fans began talking about a sweep of the Series.

"Why not?" they asked. "The Yankees have beaten the Dodgers in six out of seven. So, why not four?"

After hard-charging Bill Skowron bulls into catcher Roy Campanella, he knocks the ball from Roy's glove to score for the Yanks. Umpire Jim Honochick gives the safe sign.

With all the talk about a Yankee sweep of the Series, when the teams shifted to Brooklyn for the third game, more than thirty-four thousand fans roared a tremendous welcome to their defeated, but not yet conquered heroes.

While looking for a pitcher who might possibly stop the onrushing Yankees, manager Alston must have heard some of the Dodgers singing "Happy Birthday" in front of Johnny Podres's locker. It was John's twenty-third birthday and Alston must have selected Podres on a hunch, for there wasn't too much enthusiasm in the Brooklyn stands when Johnny walked out to the mound to warm up before the game. Sportswriter Jimmy Breslin wrote: "Johnny has been knocked out of the box so often, he's probably punch drunk."

Opposing him was the Yankee fireball star, Bob Turley, a wild but speedy right-hander. Turley managed to win 17 games during the year and was particularly tough in the stretch run for the pennant.

However, it looked as if the game might be over in the very first inning as Campanella smashed a towering home run with a man on base. But the Yanks came right back as Mickey Mantle slugged a 2-run home run over the left field fence to tie the score.

Then the Dodgers came on again; Robinson singled and Sandy Amoros was hit by a pitch

Sandy Amoros saves the Series for the Dodgers with this game-saving catch in the final game.

From the outset it was clear that the fourth game was being regarded as a grim piece of business for the Dodgers. Minutes after the game got under way, Gil McDougald smashed a home run into the center field stands. The Yanks tallied once again in the second inning, as Collins singled, advanced on a ground out, and scored on Rizzuto's single to center field.

Don Larsen, on the mound for the Yankees, held the Dodgers hitless until the third inning, when Amoros walked and stole second. Gillian then whacked a fastball inside third base and down the left field line. Amoros, off and running with the crack of the bat, didn't stop until he crossed the plate and it was a 2–1 game.

In the fourth inning, Erskine had to leave the game after his elbow began troubling him and Don Bessent replaced him on the mound. Yogi Berra singled and Collins walked; then Howard sliced a sharp ground ball to Bessent, and Don's throw was in time to force Berra at third base. On the next play, Collins reached third and scored when Billy Martin singled to right field. Now the Yankees had a 3–1 edge.

In the last of the fourth inning, Dodger bats began to erupt. Campanella blasted a long home run into the bleachers. It was Roy's second homer in two days. Furillo beat out an infield hit and then Gil Hodges followed with a smash over the right field fence, and the Dodgers were ahead, 4–3.

Gilliam led off the Dodgers' fifth inning with a walk, and Pee Wee Reese beat out a smash to the mound. Then Duke Snider brought the house down with a long drive over the left field wall; the crowd went wild. But the Yankees were not yet finished. They rallied for 2 runs in the sixth to make it a 7–5 game.

Campanella singled to start the seventh inning and Hodges promptly singled Campy to third. Reese singled, scoring Campanella, to give the Dodgers an 8–5 lead, which they maintained as Labine held the Yanks scoreless throughout the final three innings.

In the fifth game, manager Stengel decided to start rookie Bob Grim. He was opposed by another rookie, Roger Craig. But this day Grim had little luck against Duke Snider as the Duke rocked and socked Grim from pillar to post.

In the third inning, Snider slugged his third

and Podres safely bunted, filling the bases. Gilliam walked, and so did Reese, and 2 runs were in. The Dodgers had a 4–2 lead, and remained in front as Podres easily held the Yankees in the eighth and ninth innings for an 8–3 victory; and Brooklyn was back in the Series with both feet. After the game, Podres was surrounded by a horde of sportswriters in the clubhouse.

"What the heck," said the big, blond Podres, trying to answer as many of the questions as possible. "A good pitcher can beat any team on a given day, and today I had real good stuff. That's all there is to it, no mystery."

Answering a question about the kind of pitch he threw to Mantle, which Mickey hit over four hundred feet, Podres replied, "That one was a bad pitch. I wanted to throw the ball on the outside to Mickey, but I got it right over the plate and just above the knees and Mickey really hit the hell out of the ball."

homer of the Series, to give the Dodgers a 3–0 lead. In the fifth inning, Duke drove another Grim fastball over the scoreboard for another home run. That was all for Grim, as Stengel replaced him with the Yankees fastball ace, Bob Turley. But Snider had little respect for Yankee pitching this day, and rapped out a double off the fence. Duke hit the ball so hard that it rolled all the way back to second base. Clem Labine hurled the final three innings and held the Yankees to 2 hits and 1 run to gain credit for a 5–3 win. And now the Dodgers were up 3 games to 2.

Back at Yankee Stadium for the sixth game of the Series, Casey Stengel selected Whitey Ford as his starting pitcher, while Walt Alston's choice was a little-known rookie, Karl Spooner. But as early as the first inning, he was hit hard by every batter who faced him. Spooner pitched to six men; five reached base and scored. The big blow was a 3-run homer by Bill Skowron, giving Yankees a 5–0 lead.

Meanwhile, Whitey Ford was pitching one of his finest World Series games as he held the normally hard-hitting Dodgers to just 4 hits.

Whitey fanned 8 batters and the Yanks took the contest, 5–3.

With superior pitching, the Yanks were now odds-on favorites to win the seventh and final game. They had Tommy Byrne ready and well rested. Byrne had demonstrated that he could easily handle the Dodger hitters and was eager to get at them. The Dodgers, on the other hand, had a pitching problem. Newcombe was hurt, and as Walt Alston looked over his bruised and battered staff he found only man who had pitched a complete game, and that was young Johnny Podres.

For the first three innings, neither team scored. Then Roy Campanella started the action for the Dodgers with a searing two-base hit into left field. He moved to third on Furillo's ground out and when Hodges drilled a single to left, Campy danced home with the first score of the game.

In the sixth inning, Pee Wee Reese opened the inning with a single to left. Snider was safe on a beautiful bunt, and there were two men on base. Campy moved both runners along with a long sacrifice fly, and Casey ordered an intentional walk to Furillo that filled the bases. Grim

It may look like ballet, but Pee Wee Reese tries to beat out an infield hit and is called safe by umpire Bill Summers. Yank pitcher Johnny Kucks (53) was too late with his tag. First baseman Joe Collins (*left*) watches the play.

On his twenty-third birthday Johnny Podres celebrated by pitching the Dodgers to
an 8–3 win in game three of the 1955 Series.

relieved Byrne on the mound for the Yanks, and Gil Hodges sent a long fly ball to center field that scored Reese for the Dodgers' second run.

Billy Martin opened the Yankees' sixth inning by working Podres for a base on balls. McDougald surprised the Dodger infield, by dropping a perfectly executed bunt, and beat the throw to first base. Then the Yankees' most dangerous clutch hitter, Yogi Berra, came up to bat. Manager Alston had just installed Sandy Amoros in the left field post to bolster his defense, and the move paid off. Yogi, normally a sharp right field hitter, crossed everybody up by slicing a high fly ball down the left field line, about a foot inside the foul line. Sandy on a dead run had to come a long way to get near the ball, and it seemed as if the ball might just carry into the stands. But, suddenly, Sandy stuck up his glove, twisted his body, and extended his arm almost into the left field stands, coming away with the ball. It was an unbelievable catch, the finest defensive play of the Series. McDougald, running with the crack of the bat, was doubled off base; then Hank Bauer grounded

a slow roller to Reese for the final out and the Yankees' most serious threat was ended.

The Yankees were down but not yet out. In the eighth inning, with Rizzuto on third base and McDougald on second, Podres, pitching magnificently, got Yogi to pop up to left field and then fanned the dangerous Hank Bauer on three fast balls that shot by the bewildered Bauer and the last Yankee threat had been stymied.

The Dodgers had won their biggest game by a 2–0 margin and the World Championship came home to Brooklyn for the first time in their long history.

Both Podres and Amoros were the heroes of the Dodger victory, but the shining star was the Duke, who capped a magnificent season with four tremendous World Series home runs. It was the second time Snider had hit 4 homers in a Series. More important, this time the Duke's home runs were indispensable to Dodgers' victory.

Two years later, the Dodgers were no more the Brooklyn Dodgers. They left New York for Los Angeles and broke a couple of million hearts.

1956

New York Yankees Versus Brooklyn Dodgers

It was the beginning of the fifty-third World Series, on a cool, sunny day in Ebbets Field. Since the birth of the classic in 1903, hundreds of games had been played. None matched the color, the drama, the excitement, of this one.

President Dwight Eisenhower participated in the World Series opener to such an extent that he was a co-attraction, shaking hands, saluting ballplayers on both clubs, posing for the photographers, and generally comporting himself as any extraordinary fan would on a day such as this.

The Dodgers won the pennant after a bitter, season-long battle against the Milwaukee Braves and the Cincinnati Reds. Brooklyn actually tumbled into the pennant when the Braves slumped in the final week, lost several crucial games, and were out of the fight. The Dodgers finally won the pennant on the final day of the season, beating the harried Braves, 1–0.

The Yankees, meanwhile, had an easy time in the American League as they romped over the second-place Indians by 9 games as Mickey Mantle won the American League's triple crown with a smashing .353 average, 52 home runs, 130 RBI. Whitey Ford, Tom Sturdivant, and Johnny Kucks were expected to win their starting assignments in the Series against the Dodgers.

Manager Walt Alston selected one of his favorites, the veteran Sal Maglie, to pitch the Series opener. He was opposed by the Yankee ace, Whitey Ford.

And as the game progressed, it was evident that Maglie, the thirty-nine-year-old veteran of many wars, became the focus of all eyes. However, it appeared as if Sal might not last through the first inning as Slaughter singled on the first pitch, and Mickey Mantle drove a Maglie fastball high and far over the left field wall to give the Yankees a 2–0 advantage.

In the second inning, Jackie Robinson caught a pitch on the fat part of his bat, and drove it over the wall for a home run. The next batter, Gil Hodges, singled. Carl Furillo doubled, scoring Hodges, and it was a 2–2 game.

In the third inning, after Bauer and Slaughter singled in succession, Maglie settled down and showed the partisan crowd what he could do in a pinch as he fanned Mantle on three marvelous curveballs that everybody in the stands saw, but Mickey.

The Dodgers then jumped all over Ford and knocked him out of the box as Reese and Snider singled and then Hodges drilled a long home run into the stands.

Billy Martin homered in the fourth inning to

make it a 5–3 game. But the Dodgers came roaring back. Campanella doubled and then scored on Amoros's single. That was all the scoring in the game as Maglie held the Yankees in check for a 6–3 victory.

The second game produced one of the most amazing comebacks in Series history. The Dodgers fell behind 6–0 after one and a half innings. Amazingly, they smashed ahead and proceeded to win the game, 13–8. Don Newcombe gave up 1 run in the first inning and then was routed in the second during a 5-run outburst that featured Yogi Berra's grand slam homer. While the crowd of some thirty-six thousand watched with incredulity, the Dodgers rallied with 6 runs off Larsen, Kucks, and Byrne in their half of the second.

While Don Bessent, in a brilliant seventh-inning relief performance, held the Yanks to 6 hits and 2 runs, the Dodgers proceeded to hammer Tom Sturdivant, Tom Morgan, and Mickey McDermott for their remaining runs. Manager Stengel used seven pitchers in the three-hour,

twenty-six-minute game, the longest in Series history.

In the third game, the Dodgers were on their way to a third win, as they led the Yankees 2–1 going into the sixth inning, when Berra and Bauer singled and Enos Slaughter homered, to give the Yanks 3 big runs and a 4–2 lead. In the eighth inning, the Yanks scored an additional run to win, 5–3.

The Yankees got back on even terms with their rivals on October 7 at Yankee Stadium. This time, Tom Sturdivant, who was knocked around during the second-game slugfest, came back with a brilliant 6-hit performance for a 6–2 victory. After taking an early 3–1 lead against Dodger ace Carl Erskine, the Yanks clinched the verdict when Mickey Mantle hit a home run off Ed Roebuck. Bauer homered in the seventh off Don Drysdale. Now the Series was tied at 2 games, and the excitement, which had been brewing all over New York and Brooklyn, reached its peak as the teams prepared to face each other for the fifth game.

The Yankee pitching staff takes a workout before the opening game of the 1956 Series: (*left to right*) Bob Grim, Rip Coleman, Tom Sturdivant, Maury McDermott, John Kucks, Tom Morgan, Don Larsen, and Whitey Ford.

Don Larsen grew up in carefree southern California and began to play baseball as soon as he could walk. He was so obsessed with becoming a pitcher that he got his dad to spend hours at a time teaching and working with him. When the weather was cold, the father and son would practice pitching fundamentals in their basement.

Beginning in Aberdeen, there followed stops for Larsen at Springfield, South Dakota, and Wichita. He pitched for the army in 1951 and 1952, and in 1953 he was signed by the St. Louis Browns, just as the franchise shifted to Baltimore.

At Baltimore in 1954, Larsen posted the poorest won-lost record in the major leagues, 3-21. Then, in November 1954, in one of the biggest player deals ever made, the Yankees traded for Bob Turley and several other players, and only Casey Stengel could explain why one of them was Don Larsen.

In the second game of the Series, after the Yankees had given Don a 6-run lead, the Dodgers knocked him out of the box in the second inning, and there was little indication that Casey even considered using Larsen again. Pitching without a windup, Larsen had faced only twelve batters going into the fifth inning of the fifth game when Gil Hodges drove a fastball to deep left-center field. Mickey Mantle raced at top speed over to his right and managed to catch the ball. Amoros, the next batter, slugged a long drive that was foul by inches; then he quietly rolled out. The two plays drew a great cheer from the crowd as they were beginning to feel the pressure and excitement, when they realized that Larsen had set down fifteen batters in a row without a hit. Don was getting stronger as he breezed through the sixth inning, getting Furillo and Campanella, two dangerous Dodger batters, to pop out. Then he struck out Maglie on three whizzing fastballs.

In the last half of the sixth inning, the Yanks produced another run on a cluster of 3 singles, making the score 2–0.

Now the big question was, When would Larsen crack? The answer: Don wasn't about to.

After getting the Dodgers again in order, in the seventh inning, Don slipped into the runway

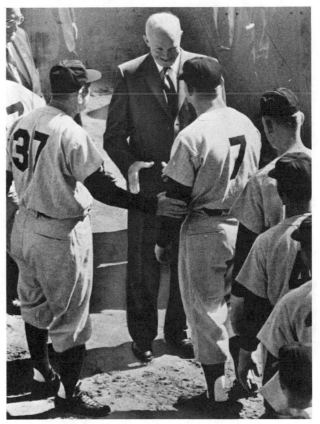

Casey Stengel (37) and Mickey Mantle (7) get a hand from President Eisenhower prior to the first game of the 1956 Series.

area of the dugout for a quick puff on a cigarette. He ran into Mantle.

"Do you think I'll make it, Mick?" He grinned at Mickey.

Mantle was shocked. Nobody is supposed to mention a possible no-hitter while the game is still on.

Now all eyes focused on Larsen as the innings sped by, and he cut each Dodger down without a hit. Tension mounted on the field and in the packed ballpark, and the crowd began to cheer Larsen's every pitch; the cheers mounted to a roar as the seventh and eighth innings went by with still no hits.

By the ninth inning, the noise was unbelievable and the tension incredible as Don faced hard-hitting Carl Furillo. And Furillo hammered two pitches, both long foul balls. Then Carl hit a short fly to Bauer. Two more batters to face.

The cartoon character on the wall seems to be laughing at Enos Slaughter's attempt to field Jackie Robinson's drive in the tenth inning of game six of the Series.

The scoreboard tells the story. Don Larsen winds up for the final pitch of his history-making game.

Campanella, up to hit, looked at a strike, then slashed at a sharp curveball and fouled it. He hit the third pitch on the ground to Martin. Billy scooped up the ball, and fired it to first base for the out.

The twenty-seventh batter, pinch hitter Dale Mitchell, former American League batting champion, was a dangerous left-handed line-drive hitter.

Now Larsen was talking to himself:

"Come on, slow down now. You've been ahead of these bastards all day." Strike one. "That's better. Now easy with this pitch."

On the next pitch, Mitchell swung at a curveball and missed, and the roar of the crowd was unimaginable. Everybody was standing, screaming.

Larsen came in once again with a fastball that slammed into Berra's glove with a report like a pistol shot.

"Strike three," cried umpire Babe Pinelli.

Led by Don Larsen's incredible perfect game, the Yankees had had three great pitching performances and turned the tables on the Dodgers. Now they were leading 3 games to 2 as the teams moved back to Ebbets Field for game six.

The Dodgers were worried now, not only about their lack of hitting; they couldn't seem to contain Yogi Berra and his big bat. It seemed that the stocky Yankee catcher was on base every time the Dodgers looked up; and whenever he came up to bat, he was a constant threat to hit the long ball.

The sixth game had two unforgettable surprises. First was the tremendous pitching of Clem Labine, a bull pen operator who proved to be just the man to deadlock this fierce competition between the Yanks and Dodgers. The second surprise highlighted the old truism that today's hero was tomorrow's bum. Unfortunately, it applied to Enos Slaughter, whose 3-run homer had won the first of the Yanks' three victories. The third of Slaughter's misadventures in left field cost Bullet Bob Turley the decision that sent the Series into its seventh game.

At the start of the tenth inning, the score was still 0–0. Junior Gilliam walked with 1 out in the tenth. Pee Wee Reese then laid down a perfect sacrifice bunt, sending Junior to second base and bringing up Duke Snider. Yankee strategy dictated an intentional pass for the Dodger slugger, and that brought up Jackie Robinson, who had left five runners stranded in three previous tries at bat. Jackie quickly lined Turley's second pitch into left field. Slaughter, battling the sun and shadows, charged. Too late, he saw his mistake as the ball soared past him, hitting the base of the left-center field wall and bringing in Gilliam with the game's only run to tie the Series at 3 games.

It was by this narrowest possible margin, the twelfth 1–0 game in World Series history, that Labine, whose eight previous Series appearances had been in relief roles, established himself as the newest star in this Series of stars.

October 10 was a sad, sad, day for the Dodgers.

With the Series deadlocked at 3 games each, manager Walt Alston called on his star, Don Newcombe, who had been pounded out of the box in game two when the Yankees bombarded him for 5 runs in the second inning. This day, however, Don was again hit hard from the outset as the Yankees scored 2 runs in the second inning, 2 more in the third, and by the fifth inning the game was a 5–0 Yankee rout.

While the big Yankee bats were mashing Dodger pitchers without mercy, Johnny Kucks pitched a marvelous game, allowing the Dodgers just 3 meager singles. The final score was 9–0, Yankees.

The big Yankee hero was, of course, Don Larsen, with his perfect game, but Berra, the gnomelike Yankee catcher, was right behind, with 9 hits, including 3 home runs. Mickey Mantle also enjoyed one of his great World Series, collecting 3 home runs. Both Duke Snider and Gil Hodges were standouts for Brooklyn, and by slugging his tenth World Series homer, the Duke tied Lou Gehrig for second place in the Series home run derby.

Each winning Yankee received $8,714, and each Dodger player pulled down a tidy $6,934 for his Series efforts. Total attendance zoomed to 345,903, and total receipts were $3,333,254.

Yogi Berra congratulates Don Larsen after Don's perfect game.

1957

Milwaukee Braves Versus New York Yankees

In spring training at Phoenix, Arizona, in 1951, young switch-hitting rookie Mickey Mantle had been driving the ball over the fences, batting left-handed and right-handed, and drawing raves and cheers from Yankee friend and foe alike. In batting practice, Mickey had hit every Yankee pitcher with some of the longest drives ever seen at a Yankee camp. In practice games he had hit every Yankee pitcher with ease; that is, every pitcher but rookie Lew Burdette.

Mickey was puzzled by his inability to get a single hit off Burdette. "Give me another pitch like the last one, Lew," Mickey said grimly. Burdette grinned at the husky Mantle.

"Take it easy, Mick. I'll throw you anything you want. That's what I'm here for."

Burdette, still grinning, hitched up his belt, tugged at his cap, and then came in with the pitch. Lew delivered the ball with a full motion, putting his entire body behind the pitch, and the ball just whizzed by as Mickey swung wildly.

"You're out," shouted umpire Ralph Houk.

Back in the clubhouse, Mickey sat beside Burdette. "Glad you're with us instead of against us. I'd hate like hell to hit against that spitball you throw."

"What spitball?" Lew grinned. "That's a little old dipsy doodle I came up with back in West Virginia."

"Well, whatever," said Mickey. "That's the same pitch you used last year when we played

at Kansas City. Keep on working that pitch and you'll have a spot here."

Lew pitched nineteen innings during spring training and allowed just 1 run, but, with so many outstanding pitchers on the roster, manager Casey Stengel decided to send Burdette out for more seasoning, and he went to San Francisco.

Then, one day in 1952, Casey Stengel decided he had to have Johnny Sain, one of Boston's top pitchers, in order to bolster his now shaky staff, and a deal was made for Sain that included sending Lew Burdette to the Boston Braves.

It is a recognized irony in baseball that a player, especially a pitcher, traded from one club to another, often comes back to haunt the team that traded him. And Burdette was no exception. He had always felt that the Yankees spurned him without good reason, and now he vowed to get even in 1957. Of course he had considerable help from Hank Aaron, Warren Spahn, and Eddie Mathews, but Burdette was the principal reason that Milwaukee, a team with a .269 batting average, won the 1957 World Series.

In the American League, the Yankees had traded away their fiery second baseman, Billy Martin. But they roared on to win another American League pennant by some 8 games over the White Sox, as Mickey Mantle won his second MVP title and hit a marvelous .365 during the season.

The Yankees, as usual, were the odds-on Series favorites, and they got off on the right foot at Yankee Stadium on October 2 before the more than sixty-nine thousand wildly cheering fans who turned out to see two great left-handers, Whitey Ford and Warren Spahn, the ace of the Milwaukee club, battle for honors.

After four scoreless innings, Spahn showed the first signs of weariness. Jerry Coleman led off the bottom of the fifth with a sharp single to center, then 2 infield groundouts sent Coleman to third, and he scored when Hank Bauer slashed a ringing two-base hit to left field. In the sixth inning, the Yanks continued to pound Spahn. Elston Howard singled, Berra walked, and when Andy Carey singled, Howard scored and Yogi sprinted to third. Manager Fred Haney took Spahn out of the game and inserted right-hander Ernie Johnson. Coleman then caught the entire Braves infield by surprise as he bunted safely, scoring Yogi Berra, and the Yankees had a 3–0 lead.

Meanwhile, Whitey Ford was superb, as he set down the spirited Milwaukee team in every inning but the seventh, when Covington doubled and scored the Braves lone run on Red Schoendienst's single up the middle. Ford allowed the Braves just 5 hits and struck out 6 Milwaukee hitters as the Yanks took game one by a 3–1 margin.

More than sixty-two thousand fans crowded into Yankee Stadium on October 3 for the second game of the Series; they were intrigued by the fact that they were going to see Lew Burdette, a former Yankee, attempt to stop the Bombers' rush for another Series victory. His opponent on the mound was another southpaw, Bobby Shantz, obtained during the season from the Athletics.

The Braves scored quickly in the second inning, as Mickey Mantle, playing with a badly bruised left knee, misjudged Aaron's line drive and it went for a triple. Joe Adcock brought in Aaron with a single, and the Braves led 1–0.

Slaughter walked to open the Yankees' half of the second inning. Tony Kubek singled, and then Coleman hit a soft dribbler to shortstop and beat the throw to first base, and the Yankees had the bases full. Then Bobby Shantz drove a low liner to left field, and Wes Covington made a difficult play with a fine one-handed running catch to save at least 2 runs and end a potential Yankee rally.

In the third inning, Logan homered for the Braves, and then Hank Bauer answered with a Yankee home run, and it was a 2–2 game. In the fourth inning, the Braves routed Shantz with 4 hits and 2 runs, to give Burdette a 4–2 lead. That was all that Lew needed as he bore down and pitched magnificent ball to shut out the Yankees with just 3 hits for the rest of the game. It was his finest effort of the year, and it gave the Braves their first World Series win.

The city of Milwaukee was a bedlam of World Series excitement. The town was alive with flags, bunting, and parades. Hotels were jammed, and many Milwaukee fans who had traveled for days to see the Braves and Yankees had to sleep on park benches or wherever they could safely stay, for this was the city's first-ever World Series.

But on this day of days for Wisconsin fans, it was twenty-one-year-old Tony Kubek, the Yankees' excellent shortstop, who provided the thrills. Tony, a Milwaukee resident, made a smashing debut in his hometown as he paced the Bombers to a 12–3 win. Kubek smashed 2 home runs to drive in 3 runs. Tony also scored 3 times as he led the Yankee attack on six Milwaukee pitchers to give the Yanks a 2 games to 1 Series advantage.

Milwaukee fans were in a frenzy during the fourth game, on October 6, when the Braves pulled out a tenth-inning thriller by a 7–5 score. The Braves had a 4–1 lead going into the ninth inning, and as the crowd began to move toward the exits, Berra and McDougald singled in succession, and then Elston Howard slammed a long home run over the left field wall, to give the Yanks 3 big runs and send the game into extra innings.

The ballpark was in pandemonium. Fans were now screaming wildly as the tenth inning began and the Yanks took a 5–4 lead.

But in the Braves' half of the tenth, Nippy Jones was hit by a pitch and went to first base. Felix Mantilla ran for Jones, and reached second on Red Schoendienst's sacrifice. Johnny Logan gave the Milwaukee partisans something to howl about as he slammed out a screaming two-base hit, scoring Mantilla and tying the game, 5–5. Then Eddie Mathews sent the Braves' delirious

Twenty-year-old Tony Kubek drives the first of his 2 homers for the Yankees in the Series.

Catcher Del Crandall points to first base and yells as Berra comes in to score on a squeeze bunt in the sixth inning of the opening game.

fans home in a frenzy of excitement as he slammed a home run to give the Braves a 7–5 victory, and tie the Series at 2 games each.

The following day, October 7, Lew Burdette gained additional revenge over his former Yankee teammates as he shut them down with just 7 hits and no runs, outpitching Whitey Ford to win his second Series game 1–0. Now the Braves had a 3 game to 2 margin over the champion Yankees.

On the return to New York for the sixth game on October 9, the Yanks, behind the fabulous 4-hit pitching of Bullet Bob Turley and home runs by Berra and Bauer, got back in the Series by winning a tense 3–2 battle. The game was tied 2–2 into the bottom of the seventh inning when Hank Bauer slammed a long home run into the upper stands at Yankee Stadium to win for the Bombers.

For the seventh and crucial game of the Series, manager Casey Stengel had hoped that Don Larsen might have some of the previous year's

magic in his arm, while manager Fred Haney had no alternative but to use Lew Burdette, despite the fact that Lew, winner of two Series games, had had but two days' rest.

But Larsen wasn't what Casey had hoped for, and after holding off the Braves and Burdette for two innings, the roof caved in on Big Don. The Braves put together 5 base hits for 4 runs before reliever Bobby Shantz was sent to the mound for the Yankees.

Del Crandall homered in the Braves' eighth to make the score 5–0. And that was the final score, giving the Milwaukee Braves their first World Championship.

"Lew Burdette surprised us Yankees," said Mickey Mantle,* "the same way that Johnny Podres and the Dodgers did two years ago. It

*After the Series that year, Mickey Mantle discussed it in an interview with the author on his *Sports Show*, New York radio station WINS.

wasn't a case of underrating these pitchers. We just didn't know they would prove to be as good as they were in the World Series.

"In the Series, Burdette was the big difference, mostly because of his amazing control. We had no idea that anybody could be so consistent in catching strikes on low pitches. The way we saw it before the Series, Burdette was a very smart pitcher, and we respected him for that, but we didn't know how really fast he could throw. We thought we could wait him out on his low stuff, and make him come up when he got behind on the count.

"His second-game performance had us gasping. He was even sharper than he was in the first game and didn't give us any time to think about forcing him to throw high.

"Although Burdette personally surprised us, he certainly proved two points I tried to make about World Series play. One is that pitching is not seventy or seventy-five percent of a World Series but ninety percent. The other is that the so-called book on hitters means very little in such a short series.

"Yogi Berra told our pitchers, 'Don't fool around, give me your best pitch.' Pitching depends on the pitcher, not on the book. Every pitcher has to come through with his most effective pitch in a jam, and the hitter knows what that pitch is. It boils down to who can do better, the pitcher or the hitter?"

The starting pitchers for game one: Milwaukee's Lew Burdette (*left*) and the Yankees' Don Larsen (*right*)

Hank Aaron was incredible in the 1957 Series with 3 long home runs.

1958

New York Yankees Versus Milwaukee Braves

Picking themselves off of the floor, the New York Yankees, perennial American League champions, made a remarkable comeback to defeat the Milwaukee Braves, 4 games to 3, gaining revenge in dramatic style for their 1957 loss.

The New York triumph was regarded by manager Casey Stengel as the "greatest in the remarkable history of the team," as the proud Yanks lost 3 of the first 4 World Series games and appeared to be doomed to another defeat at the hands of the spirited Braves. But their pride and indomitable spirit drove them on to their incredible comeback.

For Casey Stengel, the World Championship was his seventh, placing him in a tie with an earlier Yankee manager, Joe McCarthy. By defeating the Braves, the Yankees completed the cycle of defeating every National League club in at least one Series.

The major league season in 1958 was an unusual one in both leagues. The Braves repeated in the National League by 8 games over the surprising Pirates; Warren Spahn and Lew Burdette were the big winners for the Braves. Spahn won 22 games and Burdette won 20 during the season.

In the American League, the Yankees outdistanced the other clubs in the league and captured another pennant by 10 games over the second-place White Sox. Bob Turley was the best Yan-

kee pitcher, with 21 victories, and the remarkable Mickey Mantle pulverized American League pitching by slamming 42 home runs to lead the league.

The two Yankee heroes of the Series were Bob Turley and Hank Bauer. Bauer collected a total of 10 hits, 4 of them home runs, and drove in 8 runs. Led by hammering Hank, the Yankees clubbed a total of 10 home runs; the Braves drove in only 3.

In the opening game of the Series, in Milwaukee on October 1, the Braves started Warren Spahn, while manager Stengel selected Whitey Ford to hurl for the Yankees.

Bill Skowron opened the fourth inning by driving a home run into the left field stands. But the Braves came right back with 2 runs in their half of the inning on a walk to Hank Aaron, an error by Berra, and 3 consecutive singles by Del Crandall, Andy Pafko, and Spahn.

In the fifth inning, Ford walked, and then Bauer lashed the first of his 4 Series homers, to give the Yanks a 3–2 lead.

The Braves tied the score in the eighth inning. Eddie Mathews walked, Hank Aaron doubled, sending Mathews to third base, and then Wes Covington scored Mathews with a long fly ball to center field. It remained a 3–3 game at the end of nine innings.

In the tenth, Ryne Duren, the Yankee relief

Gil McDougald (*left*) is saluted by teammate Hank Bauer (*right*) after McDougald's tenth-inning homer, which clinched the opening game of the Series for the Yankees.

star, served up a fastball to Joe Adcock, and Joe whipped the pitch to left field for a single. Covington struck out, but Del Crandall slapped a single to left, and Billy Bruton, who had missed the entire 1957 Series with a badly injured knee, drove in the winning run with another sharp single, to give the Braves, a thrilling 4–3 victory in the opening game.

Lew Burdette was the Braves' hurler in the second game, in Milwaukee on October 2. He was opposed by Bullet Bob Turley, and Bob was lucky to get out of the first inning alive. The Braves' first batter, Billy Bruton, swung at a 3 and 2 pitch, and drove Turley's fastball out of the stadium. All told, the Braves pounded Turley and Duke Maas for 7 runs on 6 base hits, including a second home run in the inning, by Lew Burdette, with two men on base. Allowing only 7 hits in the battle royal, Burdette was tagged for 2 homers by Mickey Mantle and another by Hank Bauer. But the Braves had their hitting togs on that day, pounding Yankee pitchers for 15 hits, resulting in a 13–5 rout of the New Yorkers.

The third game, played, after a day's rest, at Yankee Stadium on October 4, provided a stage for Hank Bauer, as he put on a one-man hitting display to lead the Bronx Bombers to a 4–0 win.

The following day, October 5, the Yankees looked like anything but champions as they lost, 3–0, in front of a Sunday crowd of some seventy-two thousand patrons. Warren Spahn pitched his World Series masterpiece; a marvelous 2-hit shutout of the mighty Yankees. Mantle and Bill Skowron were the only Yanks to hit; Mickey was stranded after slugging a long triple, while Skowron ripped a single to account for the Yankees' entire attack.

The Yankees now were down 3 games to 1, and only the most rabid Yankee partisans gave them a chance to win. But Bob Turley brought a small ray of hope to the beleaguered cause when he pitched a 5-hit shutout on October 6 at the Yankee Stadium and won an easy 7–0 victory.

In the sixth inning, Elston Howard, in left field in place of Norm Siebern, made a catch that could be called the turning point of the Series. Bruton led off the inning with a single. Red Schoendienst followed with a low, slicing drive to left field. Howard came racing in, dove

The Braves' Warren Spahn was brilliant, winning 2 games in the Series.

The Braves' Red Schoendienst and Hank Aaron both arrive at third base as Jerry Lumpe (*upper left*) takes Berra's throw in an attempt to run down Schoendienst. Aaron (*upper right*) tries to stop at third base as he sees Schoendienst change his mind about going home. Red (*lower left*) runs past fallen Berra as the ball gets away from Yogi. But Don Larsen (*lower right*) scoops up the ball and tags Schoendienst for the out.

for the ball, and caught it just as it seemed to hit the ground. Bruton, already past second base, was an easy double-play victim.

In the sixth game, at Milwaukee on October 8, Warren Spahn, winner of the first game by a 4–3 score in ten innings, lost in ten innings by an identical score. Whitey Ford, making his third start for the Yankees, was bombed out of the game in less than two innings, but Art Ditmar, Ryne Duren, and Bob Turley all combined to pitch strongly in relief, and the Yankees took the tense thriller to even the Series at 3 games apiece. And now veterans in the press box were asking, "Can the Yankees do what Pittsburgh did in 1925?" Casey Stengel said they could.

In the seventh and climactic game, at Milwaukee, manager Fred Haney, grim-faced and dour over his team's slipping fortunes, said, "I'm pitching Lew Burdette, who won our deciding game for us a year ago, and I think he can do it again." In the other camp, Casey Stengel switched to Don Larsen as his starting pitcher, as an excited crowd of some forty-six thousand partisan Braves fans whooped it up for their home team.

The Braves had what looked like the beginning of a big first inning as they filled the bases, but they were held to only 1 run when Larsen struck out Del Crandall with three on base to end the inning. The Yankees struck back quickly, scoring twice on 2 bunts, 2 errors, and a couple of force-outs, to give them a 2–1 edge.

The third inning began with successive singles by Bill Bruton and Hank Aaron, and just when it looked as if the Braves might carve out a big inning, Casey Stengel called on his big fireball pitcher, Bob Turley, to relieve Larsen, and Tur-

ley put out the Braves rally without a run being scored. In the sixth inning, Del Crandall homered to tie the score at 2–2, but the Yankees were not to be denied this day.

In the eighth inning, Berra doubled with 2 outs, and Howard scored Yogi with a base hit to left. Andy Carey then singled, and big Moose Skowron delivered the coup de grace with a mighty 3-run blast into the bleachers to wrap up an incredible come-from-behind Series, and to win the championship by a comfortable 6–2 margin.

1959

Los Angeles Dodgers Versus Chicago White Sox

The California gold rush had its diamond version in the richest World Series in history, and one of the most dramatic from the standpoint of the clubs involved, when the Dodgers brought the World Championship to Los Angeles by defeating the Chicago White Sox.

Times were also changing in the baseball world, which had undergone its first relocation of a team in fifty years in 1953, with the transfer of the Boston Braves to Milwaukee. The St. Louis Browns moved to Baltimore in 1954; the Philadelphia Athletics, to Kansas City in 1955; and in 1958 the biggest transposition in baseball history occurred when the Giants moved to San Francisco and the Dodgers moved to Los Angeles.

The Brooklyn Dodgers tried for sixty-five years before they finally won the World Championship in 1955, but it took them only two years to accomplish the same feat in Los Angeles. They were the first team ever to rise from seventh place one year (in 1958) to the championship the next.

The Chicago White Sox won their first American League flag since 1919, when the infamous Black Sox played in the World Series and lost to the Reds. Behind the leadership of manager Al Lopez, the White Sox finished 5 games in front of the Cleveland Indians.

There were heroes galore for both teams. Ted Kluszewski and Nellie Fox were the hitting stars for the Sox, while the Dodgers had such heroes as Chuck Essegian, John Roseboro, Charlie Neal, and Carl Furillo. However, one player stood head and shoulders above all. An almost unknown twenty-four-year-old right-handed pitcher, Larry Sherry, was the relief pitcher is all four of the Dodger victories; of those games Larry won 2 games and saved 2 others.

A hundred years ago, a baby born with a clubfoot went through life handicapped, scorned, and humiliated at every turn. Today's medical science has changed all that, and now a clubfoot can be corrected. Of course, such a child can't be totally normal. He can't, for example, participate actively in sports; unless, that is, the child is really crazy about sports and can't be stopped.

Larry Sherry was born in Los Angeles on July 25, 1935, with a horrible clubfoot. But he loved to play baseball, and even when he couldn't run, he played ball. Larry had a strong arm and hated to lose. All the kids admired that never-say-die spirit. By the time he was in high school, Larry played all sports, with a limp, but he was outstanding. Of course, he got strong family support. His brother Norm, three years older, got a minor league contract as a catcher, and that brotherly rivalry helped inspire Larry. He swore he would make the grade in professional ball along with Norm.

Larry's father was a tailor, and his mother was a seamstress for the Hollywood Stars baseball club. Sometimes the players would let Larry work out with the team. Pretty soon the scouts began to notice the pleasant kid with the great arm, and they allowed him to pitch to some of the batters in practice. By 1959, Larry had won a contract with the Dodgers' farm team at St. Paul, where he continued to impress all the officials with his control and ability to save games for the regular pitchers. He had become an outstanding relief pitcher.

The World Series opened in Chicago on October 1, before some forty-eight thousand fans. The usually light-hitting White Sox, perhaps inspired by the great crowd, slugged five Dodger pitchers for 11 hits and 11 runs to rout the Dodgers by an 11–0 score.

The following day, the Sox again had their batting togs on; they jumped on the offerings of left-handed Johnny Podres for 2 runs, and led 2–0 going into the fifth inning. Then Charlie Neal of the Dodgers homered off White Sox hurler Bob Shaw, and it was 2–1 going into the seventh inning. With 2 outs in the seventh, Chuck Essegian, batting for Podres, belted a long home run to tie the score at 2–2. Jim Gilliam walked and then Charlie Neal drove out his second homer, to send the Dodgers out in front, 4–2. Young Larry Sherry was then sent to the mound for the Dodgers, and he protected the lead, burning back the Sox, in the eighth and ninth innings, allowing just 1 run on 2 hits and an error.

Two days later in Los Angeles, Don Drysdale, on the mound for the Dodgers, was opposed by Dick Donovan for the Sox. Drysdale was in trouble in the very first inning when Chicago filled the bases with 2 outs. But Drysdale got Sherm Lollar to foul out, and a promising Sox rally was cut short.

Donovan had won only 9 games during the season, but on this day Dick was working like a

The 1959 World Champion Los Angeles Dodgers

Gil Hodges smashes a tremendous home run in the fourth game of the 1959 Series.

charm, and allowed just 1 hit, a single, through the first six innings.

Suddenly, in the seventh inning, Donovan's control deserted him as he walked Norm Larker and Hodges to fill the bases. Gerry Staley then replaced Donovan, and Furillo hit Gerry's first pitch into center field for a single, scoring 2 runs and giving L.A. a 2–0 lead.

The grim White Sox rallied in the eighth inning on a single by Kluszewski, and when Wally Moon lost a high fly ball in the sun that fell in for another base hit, manager Alston removed Drysdale, and Larry Sherry went in to pitch for the Dodgers. Sherry hit Billy Goodman on the knee and the bases were full. Al Smith, a dangerous hitter, then came up, and Sherry fed him a waist-high screwball that broke viciously down and out. Smitty, who swung late at a pitch that was almost by him, slammed into a lightning-fast double play. Kluszewski scored on the play for the lone White Sox run.

In the ninth inning, Larry Sherry was magnificent as he struck out the three White Sox hitters, Norm Cash, Nellie Fox, and Jim Landis, and the Dodgers edged the Sox, 3–1.

In the fourth game, also played at the mammoth Los Angeles Coliseum, Early Wynn, the White Sox ace pitcher, was back, pitching against Roger Craig, his opponent in the first game of the Series.

The Dodgers broke the game open in the fourth inning, when four successive singles and an error enabled them to score 4 runs for a 4–0 lead. In the seventh inning, the Sox came to life with 3 successive base hits, capped by Sherm Lollar's home run to tie the game. Once more it became a dramatic battle of relief pitchers, Staley for the Sox and again Larry Sherry for the Dodgers.

In the last of the eighth innings, Gil Hodges put the Dodgers in front with a home run blast, and in the ninth inning, Larry Sherry handcuffed the White Sox hitters, Luis Aparicio, Nellie Fox, and Ted Kluszewski, in order, and the Dodgers had another squeaker, 4–3.

Now, on the verge of elimination, the White Sox fought back courageously to gain an exciting 1–0 victory in the best-played game of the Series, a game highlighted by the strategic maneuvering of managers Alston and Lopez. The lone run of the game was scored off Sandy Koufax in the fourth inning, when Fox singled, took third on a hit by Jim Landis, and ran home when Lollar hit into a fast double play.

The victory for the White Sox forced the clubs to return to Chicago for another game, and the Dodgers wasted no time in this one as they blasted their way to an easy 9–3 triumph.

The Dodgers picked up 2 runs in the third inning on Snider's home run and then ran up 6 more runs on 6 hits in the fourth inning to put the game beyond reach of the White Sox, who made a desperate effort to erase the 8–0 lead. The Sox rallied gamely in the fourth inning, when Ted Kluszewski slammed a 3-run homer to give the Sox their only runs of the game. But when the Sox continued to threaten, manager Alston took the ball from lefty Johnny Podres and inserted his relief pitcher par excellence, Larry Sherry. Sherry, pitching as if the game were close, shut out the White Sox with just 4 hits in the final four and a half innings to clinch the victory and the World Series for the Los Angeles Dodgers.

Twenty-four-year-old Larry Sherry, who had been a minor league pitcher for half the season, won 2 games for the Dodgers in the Series with a display of magnificent relief pitching.

Pittsburgh Pirates Versus New York Yankees

Every World Series takes its memorable place in the annals of the national pastime, but the 1960 meeting between the New York Yankees and the Pittsburgh Pirates is forever enshrined in the memories of baseball buffs as the weirdest and wackiest of all the blue-ribbon classics.

The Yankees, in a tussle with the Orioles for the pennant all season long, simply put together a 15-game winning streak toward the end of the season and walked away with their twenty-fifth pennant and the tenth in twelve years under Casey Stengel.

The Yanks set hitting records in the Series that made the slugging of the 1928, 1936, and other big Yankee years seem feeble. By the end of the sixth game of the Series, they had scored more runs and made more hits than any team in World Series history. And by the end of the seventh game they had scored 55 runs, almost 8 per game, and made an utterly incredible 91 hits, an average of 13 per game. Most impressive of all, they shattered the fifty-year-old batting-average record set by the Athletics of 1910, with a monstrous .338 team average. That fantastic figure was garnished with a dizzying, new total-bases record of 142, which averages to 20 total bases per game. Nothing remotely like it had been seen in any previous World Series. But the most incredible statistic hung up by the 1960 Yankees was that they lost the Series.

Reviewing the entire drama-packed story, one is tempted to conclude that the Yankees lost the 1960 World Series because of a disaster in a West Virginia mine some twenty years earlier. In that terrible tragedy one of the coal miners, among many others, suffered a terrible injury, an injury that ruined a lifelong dream of becoming a major league ballplayer. But Lew Mazeroski didn't let the bitterness destroy him. If he could never play the game he loved, he knew somebody who could, his young son, Bill. By the time Bill was fourteen, he was the regular shortstop for an outstanding organized sandlot team. By the time he was eighteen, Bill had turned down a number of college scholarships. Instead he signed with the Pittsburgh Pirates and received a handsome (for those days) $4,000 bonus.

Bill Mazeroski spent three years on the various Pirate farm clubs, and at the ripe age of twenty-one he won the regular second base job on the Pirates. In 1960, Bill won the prestigious *Sporting News*' Major League Player of the Year Award.

The 1960 Pirates consisted of a scrappy Don Hoak at third base; smart, steady Dick Groat at short; Mazeroski at second base; the wildly exciting home-run slugger Dick Stuart on first base; the great Roberto Clemente, Bill Virdon, and Bob Skinner in the outfield; and crafty Smokey Burgess as the catcher. The pitchers included Bob Friend, Vern Law, the great relief pitcher

Roy Face, and Harvey Haddix, who had pitched an unbelievable twelve-inning no-hitter during the season. The 1960 Pirates were not a sensational club; instead they played steady, solid baseball all season long to win the National League flag by 7 games over the second-place Milwaukee Braves.

From the very first game, played at Forbes Field in Pittsburgh, the pattern of play was as unexpected as Christmas in July. The Yankees shot off to an early lead in the first inning as Roger Maris blasted a Vern Law pitch into the bleachers for a 1–0 lead. But the Pirates stormed back with a barrage of line drives, aided by 2 Yankee blunders, for 3 runs.

In the last of the fourth, Jim Coates relieved Art Ditmar for the Yanks and walked Don Hoak. Mazeroski carefully looked over a couple of Coates's pitches; then, with a 2 and 0 count, Bill slugged a line-drive home run to give the Pirates a 5–2 lead.

The Yankees threatened in the seventh inning when they got two men on base. Danny Murtaugh, the Pirate manager, promptly put in his ace relief pitcher, Roy Face, and Face struck out Mantle, got Berra on a fly ball, and then struck out the dangerous Bill Skowron.

Howard hit a home run in the ninth inning, but Face then settled down and got Lopez to hit into a double play that ended the game with a 6–4 win for the Pirates.

The second game of the Series would have been a credit to the famed Yankees "Murderers' Row" of old, as the Bombers tore Forbes Field apart with a bombardment of 19 base hits, including 2 incredible tape-measure home runs by Mickey Mantle. One of the Mick's drives measured more than 475 feet.

Bob Friend, an 18-game winner, started for the Pirates. He was opposed by Yankee fireballer Bob Turley, but neither pitcher was around at the end of the game. Friend was taken out in

Bill Mazeroski's home run in the ninth inning wins the game and the Series for the Pirates.

Young Bobby Richardson drove in 6 RBIs in game three, including a bases-loaded home run.

These Yankee stars slugged a total of 9 home runs in the 1960 Series: (*left to right*) Mickey Mantle (2), Yogi Berra (1), Bill Skowron (2), Gil McDougald (1), Elston Howard (1), and Roger Maris (2).

the fourth inning after being battered for 3 runs. Clem Labine, the former Dodger hurler, relieved Friend, and the Yankees showed Clem no mercy as they pounded him for 5 runs. Before the onslaught had ended, the Yanks had battered four other Pirate pitchers in a record-setting 19-hit attack that netted the Bombers a 16–3 victory.

After an open date, the Series resumed on October 8 at Yankee Stadium where the Yankees' brilliant second baseman, Bobby Richardson, mounted a one-man offensive to set new Series records. Bobby slugged 2 singles and a bases-full home run to spoil Pirate manager Dan Murtaugh's forty-third birthday as the Yanks continued their all-out assault on Pirate pitching for a 10–0 rout. Richardson drove in 6 runs to set a new single-game RBI record.

The game Pittsburgh club, though, refused to stay buried and launched a brilliant comeback the following day behind the fine pitching of Vern Law and Roy Face, to eke out a 3–2 win and even the Series at 2 games each.

Manager Murtaugh started Harvey Haddix in the fifth game, while the Yanks called on Art Ditmar. Dick Stuart, the Pirates' first baseman, started things for the Pirates in the second inning with a single up the middle, but was forced by Gino Cimoli. Smokey Burgess slapped a two-base hit to center, but Cimoli stopped at third base. Then Don Hoak grounded to Kubek at third, and Cimoli scored on the out. Bill Mazeroski, hitting like a fiend, slammed a double to left, scoring Burgess and Hoak.

Maris homered in the second inning to give the Yanks their first run. They scored another in the third, and the score remained 4–2, Pirates, until the seventh inning.

Suddenly, as the seventh inning opened, Haddix walked a couple of batters and seemed to have lost his control. Without hesitation, Murtaugh inserted his ace reliever, Roy Face, and Roy held the Yankees hitless for the remainder of the game, to post a 5–2 win for the Pirates.

The Series once again shifted to Forbes Field on October 12, and the Yankees, with their backs to the wall, down 3 games to 2, brought in their great World Series winner, Whitey Ford, for the game they had to win. Whitey was in superb form as he shut out the Pirates with just 7 hits in an incredible 12–0 rout, and the Series was tied up once more, at 3 games. The Yankee attack was devastating, as they belabored five Pirate hurlers for 17 hits. John Blanchard, Maris, and Berra collected 3 hits each to lead the Yankee powerhouse.

The seventh and deciding game of the Series, played on October 13 at Pittsburgh, saw the

Mickey Mantle demonstrated his tremendous long-distance prowess as he hit 2 home runs in the Series. They were two of the longest ever hit in a World Series.

Pirates turn to Vern Law for the third time, while manager Stengel selected Bob Turley as his starting pitcher.

Bob Skinner, out with an injury since the first game, returned to left field, and Rocky Nelson took over first base, and the resulting changes paid off in the very first inning. Skinner, the first batter, walked. Rocky Nelson then smashed a long home run into the center field bleachers to give the Pirates 2 quick scores. In the second frame, Bill Virdon lined a base hit to center with two men on, for 2 additional runs, and the Pirates had a commanding 4–0 lead.

Vern Law held the Yanks scoreless until the fifth inning, when Bill Skowron powered a ball to the farthest reaches of Forbes Field for another long Yankee run. In the sixth inning, Richardson singled and Tony Kubek walked, and it looked as if the Yankees were about to launch an all-out attack as Law appeared tired. Manager Murtaugh, without hesitation, turned once more to Roy Face, for his fourth Series relief assignment, but Mantle slammed a long single to left, scoring Richardson, and then Yogi Berra drove a 3 and 2 pitch out of the park, to give the Yanks a 5–4 lead.

Face yielded 2 more runs in the eighth inning, and the Yankees appeared to be on their way to victory. It now became an almost impossible task for the Pirates to overcome the Yankee lead.

But the Pirates did it.

The Pirates opened the eighth inning as Cimoli, batting for Face, singled. Virdon rapped a ground ball to short, but the ball took a sharp bounce and hit Kubek in the throat for a base hit. Tony was hurt and was taken out of the game. Then Dick Groat singled, scoring Cimoli. That was enough for Stengel, and he brought in Jim Coates to pitch to Skinner, who sacrificed both runners along. Roberto Clemente beat out an infield hit that scored Virdon, and it was 7–6. Now it was up to a sub catcher, Hal Smith, and he delivered in sensational style with a home run that turned Forbes Field into an absolute madhouse as the Pirates now led 9–7.

That should have been the ball game, and the Series, for in came Bob Friend, determined to get the Yankees out.

Bobby Richardson opened the Yankees' half of the ninth inning with a sharp single. Dale

The Pirates' rubber-armed Roy Face relieved in 4 games for his team and saved 4 games in the Series.

Long, hitting for Joe DeMaestri, also singled. Now Harvey Haddix came in to replace Friend on the mound for the Pirates. Maris popped up and then Mickey Mantle slammed a single up the middle, scoring Richardson and moving Long to third base. The score was 9–8, Pittsburgh.

Next to bat was Berra, who took a terrific swing at Haddix's first pitch and hit a hard ground ball down the first base line. Nelson was right on the ball like a big cat; he gloved it, picked it up, and stepped on first base for the out. Then he straightened up, drew back his arm to throw to second base to complete the double play, and suddenly realized there was no reason to throw, for Mickey was standing just a few feet from him. At that moment, Mickey dived safely back to the base, eluding Nelson's frantic stab. All this while, McDougald scored the tying run, and the Pirates, unable to believe that such a thing could happen, were stunned. Had Nelson just reached over and tagged Mantle for the double play, the Series would have been over.

Was it a break or brilliant play? Both.

When Skowron ended the Yankee half of the ninth inning by grounding out, fate truly intervened. Bill Mazeroski, who had hit the ball all through the Series, came up to bat in Pittsburgh's half of the ninth inning.

As the crowd at Forbes Field screamed their heads off for a base hit, Mazeroski calmly looked at Ralph Terry's first pitch, a blazing fastball, then hit the next pitch over the left field fence, and the Pirates were champions.

There was pandemonium in Forbes Field then too, and it went on for more than an hour and a half. The fans spilled out over their seats and mobbed Mazeroski and the rest of the Pirates, and Bill actually had to fight his way to touch home plate. Then a man ran up to home plate with a shovel and dug it up.

New York Yankees Versus Cincinnati Reds

There were some severe reverberations after the Yankees lost the 1960 World Series. One was the termination of the twelve-year career of Casey Stengel as manager of the Yankees. There was criticism for his failure to start Whitey Ford in the opening game of the Series, which would have given Whitey three assignments, and for not getting more mileage out of the .338 team batting average, but actually it had been decided that since Casey was seventy years old, win or lose, he would be forced to retire after the World Series. However, few believed that Yankee owners Dan Topping and Del Webb would have risked public displeasure by firing Stengel had he won his eighth World Series.

Stengel's successor was coach Ralph Houk, former third-string catcher of the club and, during World War II, a hard-boiled, fighting major in the army. Ralph came out of the war with a Silver Star, a Bronze Star, and a Purple Heart. In between his Yankee catching and coaching chores, Ralph served three very successful years as manager of the Yankees triple A farm team in Denver. He was born to lead.

Even with the manager's portfolio passing from Stengel to Houk, there was no change in the end product of the Yankee production mill, the winning of the American League pennant. For most of the 1961 season, Houk's Yankees had to battle a surprisingly tough Tiger team, but in

late September the Tigers collapsed, and the Yankees captured still another American League flag by 8 games.

In the National League, the Cincinnati Reds, who were a sixth-place club in 1960, scrambled to the pennant under the inspired leadership of the former Tiger pitcher, Fred Hutchinson. The Reds won the pennant in the last week of play by 4 games over the Dodgers.

Manager Houk nominated Whitey Ford to hurl the first game for the Yankees, while Hutch selected another left-hander, Jim O'Toole, son of a Chicago police captain, as his pitching choice, and a capacity crowd jammed Yankee Stadium for the first game, on October 4. Whitey Ford was just about invincible as he pitched a magnificent 2-hit game to beat the Reds, 2–0. O'Toole also pitched well, allowing the Bombers 6 hits, 3 of them by Bobby Richardson. The Reds were beaten by a favorite Yankee weapon, the home run. One was hit by Ellie Howard in the fourth inning and the second by Moose Skowron in the sixth, to give the Yanks their winning margin.

Cincinnati's Joey Jay, a 21-game winner during the season, was manager Hutchinson's selection for game two, while Ralph Houk chose his 16-game winner, Ralph Terry. It was a tense, scoreless ball game for three innings, and then both clubs erupted to score 2 runs in the fourth inning. Gordy Coleman of the Reds connected for a home run with Robinson on base for the Cincinnati scores. The Yankee runs were provided by Yogi Berra, who slashed his twelfth Series homer with Roger Maris on base.

From the fifth inning on, the Reds had their own way. They picked up their third run on singles by Elio Chacon and Ed Kasko and a passed ball. Then, in the sixth inning, Wally Post doubled and scored on Edwards's single up the middle, and the Reds had a 4 to 2 lead. Cincinnati picked up 2 more runs in the eighth, to win the game, 6–2, as Joey Jay held the Bombers to just 4 hits.

The teams moved to Crosley Field, Cincinnati, for the third game, on October 7. It was

Whitey Ford started game four of the 1961 Series with twenty-nine consecutive scoreless World Series innings.

Manager Ralph Houk (*left*) is all smiles as he receives congratulations from Fred Hutchinson, the Reds' manager, after the Yankees won the Series.

Gordy Coleman follows through with his big swing after driving a long home run in the second game of the Series.

Second baseman Bobby Richardson was the Yankees' leading hitter with 9 base hits and a lusty .391 average in the 1961 Series.

the only game in which the Reds' fans had a real run for their money. With Bob Purkey of the Reds pitching brilliantly against a trio of Yankee pitchers, Bill Stafford, Bud Daley, and Luis Arroyo, the Reds outhit the Yanks 8 to 6, but after being held scoreless by Purkey for six innings, the Yanks scored a run in each of the final three innings to win by a 3–2 margin.

First-game pitchers Jim O'Toole and Whitey Ford were in top form for the fourth game, and it was 0–0 going into the fourth inning when Maris walked. Mantle came through with a single, his only hit of the Series, sending Maris to third base. Ellie Howard grounded into a double play, and Maris scored on the twin killing. Again, in the fifth inning, the Yanks scored. Ford walked, and, with singles by Richardson and Kubek, trotted in for another tally. The Yanks got 2

more runs off Jim Brosnan in the sixth inning to go ahead 4–0. In the seventh inning, the Yankees hammered Brosnan for 3 more runs. Maris and Berra walked, then Lopez singled, scoring Maris and Yogi. Skowron hit a grounder, scoring Lopez, and the Yankees had a commanding 7–0 victory. Whitey Ford left the game in the sixth inning, but not before he broke Babe Ruth's 1918 shutout record of 29⅔ innings. Whitey hurled 33⅓ consecutive shutout innings in the World Series from October 8, 1960, to October 4, 1962.

The Reds felt they had a good bet going for them in the fifth game with the marvelous Joey Jay. Jay would certainly assure the Reds a trip back to New York. But October 9 was a blue Monday for the Reds and all of Cincinnati. Before his cheering hometown fans had settled in their seats, Jay was rocked by a savage cannonading in the very first inning, as the Yankees drove in 5 runs. They scored 5 more runs in the fourth inning, and then romped home in a breeze with a 13–5 rout of the forlorn Reds.

As the Yankees blasted the Reds for 15 base hits, manager Fred Hutchinson attempted vainly to halt the Bombers by utilizing practically his entire pitching staff—Jay, Jim Maloney, Roadblock Jones, Bob Purkey, Jim Brosnan, and Ken Hunt—and they were all hit hard by the slugging New Yorkers.

Ralph Terry started for the Yankees, but ran into trouble in the third inning as the Reds creamed him for 3 runs. Wally Post led the Reds' attack with a home run in the inning, but just as it looked as if the Reds were about to mount another rally, Bud Daley came in to relieve Terry and did a satisfactory job, allowing 6 hits and 2 runs for the rest of the game to post the win that gave the Yanks another World Series. It was the nineteenth World Series win in twenty-six appearances for the champion Yankees.

1962

New York Yankees Versus San Francisco Giants

The Los Angeles Dodgers had a 1-game margin over the second-place Giants on the final day of the season. But 2 decisive home runs spelled their doom. The first was struck by Gene Oliver, a Cardinal catcher, and it gave the Cardinals a 1–0 win at Los Angeles. The second was smashed by Willie Mays at San Francisco, and it provided the Giants with a 2–1 triumph over Houston. The schedule had run its course; the Dodgers and Giants were tied for the league lead, and now they would face each other in a playoff, the fourth in league history. The Dodgers had been involved in every one.

The first of the games played at Candlestick Park saw the Giants, with Billy Pierce on the mound, shut out the Dodgers 8–0. Willie Mays powered 2 home runs to lead the Giants. The second game at Los Angeles featured a 7-run outburst by the Dodgers in the sixth inning, and they eventually nosed out the Giants by an 8–7 score. In the final game, the Giants and Dodgers went at it hammer and tongs before the Giants captured an exciting 6–4 victory and the National League pennant.

When the Giants flew back to San Francisco, a riotous mob of fifty thousand fans milled around the airport to greet the winners.

The Giants were dog-tired from the tremendous pressure-packed series with the Dodgers. Still, they were determined to win the Series that they had fought so hard to participate in. Bill O'Dell, a 19-game winner during the season, was up against the Series' greatest winner, Whitey Ford, and the game was a thriller. The Giants scored a run in the second inning, another in the third, and were shut down the rest of the game by the "mechanical marvel" that was Ford. He allowed the Giants 10 hits, but kept them well scattered, while his teammates knocked out 11 hits for a 6–2 win.

The Giants came back with their ace, Jack Sanford, for the second game at San Francisco, while the Yankees started Ralph Terry. The Giants scored in the first inning when Chuck Hiller drove Terry's first pitch to right field for a double. Matty Alou bunted Hiller to third, and Hiller scored when Alou grounded out.

The teams battled along without further scoring until the seventh inning, when Willie McCovey smashed a tremendous home run over the left field wall to give the Giants an added run.

Jack Sanford had the Yankees eating out of his hand, as he held them to 3 base hits in a masterful exhibition to give the San Francisco Giants their first World Series victory, by a 2–0 score.

The Series shifted to New York, and the Yankees, behind the 4-hit pitching of Bill Stafford, defeated the Giants, 3–2. Billy Pierce pitched well as he held the Yankees to 5 hits, but this game was a "must" for the Yanks, and they came through in fine style. Stafford pitched his best game of the year as he held the Giants to 4 hits.

Whitey Ford started the fourth game of the Series, and he was opposed by Juan Marichal, the Giant star, winner of 18 games during the season. The score was 2–2 in the seventh inning as Jim Coates went to the mound for the Yankees, and Coates promptly walked Jim Davenport. Tom Haller then struck out, and Matty Alou, pinch-hitting for Jose Pagan, doubled to

Juan Marichal held the Yankees scoreless for seven innings in game four of the 1962 Series, finally winning, 7–3.

left. But Davenport stopped at third base. Manager Alvin Dark then inserted pinch hitter Bob Nieman, and manager Ralph Houk, attempting to outmaneuver Dark, ordered Coates to walk Nieman. The next batter, Harvey Kuenn, a dangerous hitter, smashed a fly ball to short left field, but the runners all held their bases as the ball was caught. Chuck Hiller was the next batter. A twenty-seven-year-old whom the Giants had vainly tried to trade during the early season, Hiller had made only 2 base hits in the Series.

With the count 1 and 1 on him, Hiller drove a long, high fly over Roger Maris's head in right field. The ball kept on going going, and suddenly it was gone into the left field stands for a bases-full home run. It was only the eighth grand slam homer in World Series history. Even more unusual, it was the first ever hit by a National League player. Now, with a 4-run lead over the Yankees, Dark called on his stopper, Bill O'Dell, in the last of the seventh. Billy held the Yankees to 1 run in the ninth inning, and the Giants had a 7–3 win. The Series was now tied at 2 games.

In the summers during the 1940s, when Tom Tresh was growing up in Chicago, the other kids on the block would go on vacations with their fathers to the beaches or the mountains. But Mike Tresh, Tom's father, never got any time off during the hot, steamy summertime. His job held him from April until October, and Tommy never wanted a holiday that would keep him out of Chicago in July and August.

The other guys' fathers may have held more lucrative jobs. Some of them had bigger cars and owned better houses. But the rest of the gang never seemed exactly sure what their fathers did. They worked in offices or big auto plants, but they didn't seem important.

It was different with Mike Tresh. The cop on the beat seemed glad every time Mike walked by. Guys crossed the street to say hello. Storekeepers would neglect their customers when Mike came into the store. And sometimes the papers ran Mike's pictures. There was never any doubt in Tommy's mind that he would be a ballplayer just like his dad. Mike Tresh was a catcher for the White Sox for over ten years.

Tommy Tresh was a shortstop, but the old

Willie Mays, rounding third, scores on Willy McCovey's hit in the first game of the Series.

The Yankee half of the eighth inning began with singles by Kubek and Richardson; then from up in a grandstand seat, Mike Tresh watched his kid come up to hit. It had never been like this for Mike. His White Sox team had always been in the second division. The money was small, and every game was a struggle. Now Mike sat up and watched Tommy at bat. And he prayed for his kid.

The first pitch to Tommy was a ball. The second was a fastball over the plate. Afterward, Tommy Tresh said he was astonished by the perfection of it. Tom swung and the ball rose in a great arc, higher and higher, and then disappeared into the bleachers. And that was the ball game. And not a seat in the big stadium was occupied. Everybody was up and screaming. High up in the stands a middle-aged man jumped up and down, up and down. But he wasn't yelling. Mike Tresh couldn't. He was weeping. Summer in Chicago had never been like this October day in New York. His kid had won a World Series game.

The teams traveled to San Francisco, but torrential rains idled the ballplayers for three days before the classic was able to continue.

Giant pitcher Billy Pierce took the mound in the sixth game, while Whitey Ford was manager Ralph Houk's selection. Pierce, a 16-game winner during the season, pitched the finest game of his career as he held the mighty Yanks to just 3 hits for a 5–2 victory.

Roger Maris homered for the Yanks in the fifth inning, but the Giants came back with 2 runs, on singles by Kuenn, Hiller, Felipe Alou, and Orlando Cepeda. A two-base hit by Clete Boyer and a single by Kubek gave the Yankees a run in the eighth inning, but Pierce set the Yankees down in the ninth without a run and earned his first World Series win, deadlocking the World Series at 3 games.

The seventh game provided the pitching gem of the entire Series as Ralph Terry shut down the Giants, allowing just 4 base hits, to take a stirring 1–0 victory. The Yankees got their only run in the fifth inning. Skowron and Boyer singled, and Skowron went to third on Clete's hit. Then Kubek grounded into a lightning-fast double play. However, Skowron came home on the

man advised him that he should be able to play other positions. "You never know when you'll get a ball club that has someone like Luke Appling. Guys go bad sitting on the bench, waiting for a chance to play." But Tommy was a natural shortstop, and he played briefly at New Orleans and Binghamton in the Yankees' chain.

Tony Kubek was the Yankee shortstop, and other guys could never beat him out of the job. But after a couple of only average seasons, Tony was let go and Ralph Houk put Tresh at shortstop. Then he moved him to the outfield, and that's where he played in the World Series.

In the fifth game of the Series, the Giants took a quick lead in the third inning on a couple of base hits. The Yankees tied it in the fourth inning, when Jack Sanford made a wild pitch and Tresh dashed home from third. In the sixth inning, the score was again tied, 2–2.

Jubilant Yankee pitcher Ralph Terry is hoisted up on the shoulders of his teammates after his 1–0 shutout over the Giants wins the Series for the Yankees.

twin killing to give the Yanks their run. The Giants made a tremendous, dramatic bid for the victory in the last half of the ninth inning. Matty Alou pinch-hit for O'Dell and caught the Yankees asleep as he bunted safely down the third base line. Terry pitched to Willie Mays, and Willie doubled to right field. On the play, Maris came up with the ball and fired it on a line to Boyer at third base, forcing Alou to stop at third base.

With the winning runs on base and the slug-ging Willie McCovey up to bat, manager Houk walked to the mound to talk with Terry. He had to decide whether to allow Terry to pitch McCovey, to walk him, or to take Terry out. Ralph finally decided to allow Terry to continue, and to pitch to McCovey. Willie hit the first pitch Terry threw right at second baseman Bobby Richardson. Bobby jumped into the air, stuck his glove up even higher, and snared the ball for the final out, and another World Series victory for the Yankees.

1963

Los Angeles Dodgers Versus New York Yankees

After a separation of seven years and some three thousand miles, the Yankees and the Dodgers went at each other again in a battle that would decide the baseball championship in 1963.

Walter Alston's Dodgers, rebounding from a late-season collapse in 1962, fought off the challenge of the St. Louis Cardinals in 1963 and finished six games in front of the Cards to capture the pennant. The Dodgers' World Series opponent this time was an old Dodger nemesis, the New York Yankees. In seven previous Series between the Yanks and Dodgers the Bronx Bombers had won six times.

This year the Yankees had tremendous power, as usual, with four players, Ellie Howard, Roger Maris, Tom Tresh, and Joe Pepitone, hitting 20 or more home runs. They had good pitching, too, in Whitey Ford with a 24–7 record, Jim Bouton with 21 wins, Ralph Terry with 17, and Al Downing coming through with 13 victories. And incredibly they made it through a season with injuries to Mantle and Roger Maris—injuries that would have decimated most teams but didn't stop the Yanks from persevering and prospering.

On a cloudless October afternoon, some sixty-nine thousand enthusiastic fans descended upon the famous ballpark in the Bronx to watch the two old, and bitter, rivals in action. At least that was the acknowledged reason they were there. In truth, they wanted to know whether that wunderkind from Los Angeles, the kid from Brooklyn, Sandy Koufax, could really outpitch one of the Yankees' great stars, Whitey Ford.

Expectations in the first game were for one of the great pitching duels in Series history, for Koufax had pitched his team to the pennant with a number of spectacular victories during the season and had won 25 games as the Dodgers swept aside all opposition.

And in the opening game both pitchers, Ford and Koufax, were spectacular. Ford was the same old Whitey Ford as he struck out two Dodgers and got the third out on an easy groundout. It was hard to see how Sandy could improve on that. But he did, striking out the first three Yankee hitters, Tony Kubek, Bobby Richardson, and Tom Tresh. The great pitching battle had begun.

In the second inning it came to an abrupt end. Frank Howard, the gigantic six-feet-seven, 255-pound outfielder for the Dodgers, lined a 460-foot double to left center field and the former Yankee Bill "Moose" Skowron came up to hit. This had been a bad season for Skowron, who had played for the Yanks for nine seasons. When

280

the Dodgers traded for him, they felt sure he would add punch to the Dodger lineup. He did not. Moose hit .203 and knocked in only 19 runs for the Dodgers, and the crowds in Los Angeles began to boo him whenever he was announced as the pinch hitter.

But this time Moose came through with a sharp single up the middle bringing Howard home with the first run of the game. Next up was Dick Tracewski, the second most famous citizen of Eynon, Pennsylvania. The most famous citizen of Eynon was Joe Paparella, who happened to be the umpire behind the plate. Tracewski had hit only .266 that year and was used for defensive purposes in most games he played in. This was Tracewski's first-ever World Series and he felt sick to his stomach as he walked up to hit. Paparella said "Dick, aren't you gonna say hello to me?"

Tracewski looked straight at Ford and said, "Please, Joe, not now. Next time I will." Then he promptly laced a single to center for a clean base hit. John Roseboro, the Dodger catcher, followed with a smash over the left field wall and the Dodgers had a 4–0 lead.

With this nice lead Sandy Koufax was beyond perfection for almost five innings. In order, he struck out Tony Kubek, Bobby Richardson, Tom Tresh, Mickey Mantle, and Roger Maris. Elston Howard fouled out. After Koufax got Clete Boyer on a groundout, he struck out Kubek, Richardson, Tresh, and Mantle in order once more.

In the fifth inning, Sandy got into trouble and filled the bases with two outs, then with the huge Yankee crowd cheering for a hit, Sandy struck out Hector Lopez on three fastballs to end the budding rally.

The Yankees finally scored in the eighth inning when Tom Tresh slugged a 2-run homer. But that was all for the Yankees. With his last pitch of the game, Koufax struck out Harry Bright to break Carl Erskine's 1-game Series strikeout record of 14. Sandy had struck out every Yank regular except Boyer at least once for a total of 15 strikeouts.

The second game was probably the decisive game of the series. Johnny Podres didn't exactly match Koufax's great feat, but he held the Yankee batters through eight innings, giving up just 6 base hits and 1 run. Meanwhile the Dodgers got off swinging. Maury Wills singled in the first inning, stole second, and went to third as Junior Gilliam singled. Willie Davis drove a sharp liner to Roger Maris in right field, but Roger slipped and fell, attempting to field the drive, and 2 runs came across the plate. Two quick runs. The Dodgers and Podres made certain that would be enough.

Johnny Podres, the pitcher who beat the Yankees twice in the 1955 Series, including a 2–0 shutout in the seventh game to give the Dodgers their first world championship, was in complete control of the game until the ninth inning when the Yankees finally scored their lone run.

In the first inning Howard made a sensational catch of a long drive by Mantle that had "home run" written all over the ball; then Johnny fanned two batters in a row in the second inning to end the inning. This started Podres on a run of 13 consecutive outs. Even after Tresh singled in the sixth inning, Davis ran down Mickey Mantle's long drive to center. And when Skowron sliced a home run down the right field line, the Dodgers had a 3-run lead.

Willie Davis was the Dodgers' second batter in the eighth inning. On September 13, when Willie had been getting ready to play against the

Tom Tresh became an instant World Series hero when his homer, with two men on base, won game five for the Yankees.

Frank Howard connects with a Whitey Ford fastball and smashes it 450 feet for a home run in the fourth game as the Dodgers sweep the Yankees in the 1963 Series.

Sandy Koufax fanned fifteen Yankee hitters in the first game of the 1963 Series to beat Whitey Ford and the Yankees. Here Whitey (*left*) congratulates the winning pitcher.

Phillies in Philadelphia, he had received a phone call from Ken Meyers, the scout who signed him five years earlier for a paltry five-thousand dollars. "Willie," said Meyers, "you're hitting only .220 because you are standing up there at the plate like a stick. Bend over a little so you can see the pitch better. You're too good a hitter to be hitting .220." So Willie went out to the ballpark and copied and practiced the stance used by Stan Musial. Since that date, Davis hit for a .344 average and was deadly in the 1963 Series.

Willie doubled in that eighth inning and quickly scored on a tremendous triple by his roommate, Tommy Davis.

Podres held the Yankees in the seventh and eighth and got one man out in the ninth, then admitted he was dog-tired. Manager Walt Alston brought in Ron Perranoski, now a Dodger pitching coach, who promptly squelched a Yankee rally and kept the score, 4–1, Los Angeles.

In the dressing room after the game, Tommy Davis shook Willie Davis's hand. "What do you say, roomie?" he asked.

"I say good-bye New York. We won't be back. Make it in four."

Los Angeles was ready for the third game of the Series, all the way from Disneyland to Pasadena and back downtown to the Follies strip joint at Main and Third, where top billing went to a sexy brunette named Sandi Cofacks.

The Dodger fans did not really believe their team could win three in a row from the power-laden Yankees. That season the fans had been persuaded that Don Drysdale, with 19–17, was only a fair pitcher, because his record was not as outstanding as it had been in 1962, when big Don had won 25 and lost only 9.

When Drysdale arrived at Dodger Stadium for the third game and walked out to the mound, he was an almost odds-on bet to lose, but on that afternoon Drysdale was the best pitcher in baseball.

Two hours and five minutes after the game had begun, Don Drysdale had pitched the finest game of this superbly pitched Series. His teammates gave him one cheap, lucky, precious run and Don defended it as if his very life were at

Ron Fairly leaps into the air as he joins the happy mob surrounding winning
pitcher Sandy Koufax as the Dodgers win the game and the Series.

stake. The lone run of the game came in the first inning as the Yankees' great 21-game winner, Jim Bouton, walked Jim Gilliam to first and wild-pitched him to second, and then Gilliam scored on a freak single by Tommy Davis.

There was a short cessation of activities in the sixth inning after the Yankees moved Tommy Tresh to third base and Mantle was the next batter. Suddenly Frank Crosetti, the Yankee third base coach, called time and appealed to umpire Larry Napp to look at the ball that Drysdale was throwing.

"It's a spitter," howled Crosetti. "Look, it's all wet and discolored."

Napp told Don to wipe off his fingers after bringing them to his mouth. Drysdale said of course. Two pitches later Don threw a sizzling pitch to Mantle that dipped down sharply for a third strike. Mickey looked at it and shook his head. Roseboro, the Dodger catcher, said it was a fastball. He did not even smile when he said it.

In the ninth inning with the score 1–0, Joe Pepitone ended the game with a high drive to right field that looked like a home run. Ron Fairly, the Dodger right fielder, backed right to the very edge of the fence and jumped high into the air to catch the ball for the final out. The Dodgers had won, 1–0. Now they needed one more win to sweep the Series.

Early in the morning of the day of the fourth game of the Series, a young man stood at the corner of Wilshire Boulevard and Rodeo Drive in Beverly Hills. He had a glass of scotch and water in his right hand, and he wore a Dodger cap with bright white rabbit ears stretching skyward. As each car came up to the corner he raised his glass and offered one bit of advice: "Relax with Koufax."

Despite a brilliant 2-hit performance by Whitey Ford, hero of ten previous World Series victories, it turned out that the man on Rodeo Drive was right. But nobody at that fourth game relaxed until the final out.

In this fourth game Sandy's fastball may not have been quite as sharp as in the first, but his curveball was possibly better. He retired the first nine Yankees in order, four via the strikeout route. The first Yankee hit, in the fourth inning, was actually a high pop fly that three Dodger outfielders allowed to drop among them, and speedy Bobby Richardson, who had hit the ball, reached second base. But he died there as Tresh fouled out and Mantle bounced out to Maury Wills.

In the fifth inning Whitey Ford, who had held the Dodgers hitless, tossed a slow curveball to Frank Howard, and Frank promptly hit the ball 450 feet into the second deck in left field. Never before had anyone hit a ball into that section.

But the run did not hold up.

Mickey Mantle, who had suffered through a most frustrating Series with 1 hit in thirteen trips to the plate, slashed a high drive into the center field bleachers to tie the score. As he crossed the plate, the entire Yankee bench rose to greet him. For the first time in thirty-four innings, the Yankees had come from behind to tie the game. It was Mickey's fifteenth Series home run, tying Babe Ruth's total.

That tie lasted for only 2 more outs.

In the bottom of the seventh Jim Gilliam hit a hard, high bouncer toward third base. It seemed as though the ball would soar over Clete Boyer's head when the great Yankee third baseman stretched his body like a jumping jack and got the ball in his big glove. His throw to Pepitone was perfect, but Pepi lost the flight of the ball. It bounced off his chest and bounded to the fence. By the time Joe retrieved the ball, Gilliam was perched on third base and Willie Davis was at bat. Ford's first pitch to Willie was a high, hard fastball and Davis slugged it straight to Mantle in right center field. Despite Mickey's fine throw home on one bounce, Gilliam scored and the Dodgers were out in front, 2–1.

The Yankees, still battling, managed to get the tying run on base in the eighth inning when Phil Linz singled. But Koufax got Kubek to hit into a double play and another Yank rally was shut down. In the ninth inning Richardson singled. But Koufax bore down and struck out Tom Tresh and Mickey Mantle and then got Hector Lopez on a roller to the shortstop Maury Wills, and Maury whipped the ball to first and the Dodgers had swept the Yanks in four games.

Sandy Koufax for the second time in four days had beaten Whitey Ford. He did it on 6 hits, a wing and a prayer, and Joe Pepitone's error. Whitey Ford had pitched one of his great games, allowing the Dodgers but 2 hits. But the name of the game is runs. Koufax's reward and that of the Dodgers was the biggest that baseball can offer: a World Championship.

Mickey Mantle summed up the Series with this sentence: "We've seen good pitching before, but never this good for four games straight. You just don't see this good pitching in this league, or any blankety-blank league."

St Louis Cardinals Versus New York Yankees

In 1959 seventeen-year-old Tim McCarver signed on as a catcher for the St. Louis Cardinals, and by 1963 the hard-hitting twenty-one-year-old had fought his way into the varsity lineup of the Cardinals and had become one of the fine young catchers in major league baseball.

Young Bob Gibson, too light for football, nevertheless did make it big as a baseball and basketball star at Creighton University in Omaha. After leaving Creighton, Gibson signed with the world-famous Harlem Globetrotters. After a year, Gibson tired of the constant travel, and decided to concentrate on baseball. He was a pitcher and became so successful that the Cardinals signed him in 1959. By 1964, the combination of Gibson pitching and McCarver catching was one of the major reasons for the Cardinals' winning the National League flag by a single game on the very last day of the season over the favored Philadelphia Phillies.

In the American League, rookie manager Yogi Berra replaced Ralph Houk as the Yankee manager (Houk had been promoted to general manager), and promptly led the Yanks to the pennant, just 1 game in front of the White Sox and 2 games in front of the third-place Orioles.

The World Series opened at St. Louis with Whitey Ford opposing the Cardinal ace, Ray Sadecki, a 20-game winner in the 1964 season. But both pitchers, Ford and Sadecki, were hit hard and often and were not around at the finish of the game.

The Yanks looked like the Bombers of 1927 as they racked up 3 runs in the second inning on a homer by Tresh and singles by Howard, Boyer, Ford, and Richardson. St. Louis pecked out single runs in the first and second innings, and it was a 4–2 game with the Yanks in front as the sixth inning began.

Then, in the bottom of the sixth, the Cards struck. Ken Boyer singled and young Mike Shannon homered. Then Tim McCarver doubled and manager Berra took Whitey Ford out and Al Downing came in for the Yankees. That did not stop the Cards, as they continued their attack against Downing; Carl Warwick singled, and then Curt Flood unloaded a three-base smash to give the Cards a 6–4 lead. The Cards rolled up 3 more tallies in the eighth inning off pitchers Pete Mikkelsen and Rollie Sheldon, to take the first game, 9–5.

Bob Gibson started the second game for the Cardinals at St. Louis, with only two days' rest. For eight innings, Gibson did an outstanding job as he held the Yankees to just 4 runs.

The real hero of game two was twenty-two-year-old Yankee pitcher Mel Stottlemyre, who surrendered only 7 hits to the Cards, as the Yankees evened the Series with an 8–3 victory. Yankee shortstop Phil Linz had 3 hits, including a home run, to lead the attack for his team.

The third game of the Series, in New York, was an exciting pitching duel between the Cardinals' left-hander Curt Simmons and the Yankees' "Bulldog" Jim Bouton.

The score was 1–1 going into the dramatic ninth inning. Mickey Mantle opened the inning facing the Cards' great relief star, Barney Schultz, whose tantalizing knuckleball pitching had helped the Cards win the pennant. Schultz came in with his first pitch, a knuckleball, but Mickey promptly timed the "floater," and slugged it into the top tier of the right field stands for a tremendous home run, giving the Yanks a 2–1 win and a 2 games to 1 edge in the Series.

The following day at Yankee Stadium, Ken Boyer, the Cards' great third baseman, evened the Series with one powerful swing of his big bat. The Yankees had a 3–0 lead going into the sixth inning, when the Cards loaded the bases; then Boyer drove an Al Downing pitch into the seats for a grand slam homer, to give the Cardinals an exciting 4–3 victory to even the Series at 2 games.

On the basis of the first four games, it appeared that the Yankees had the edge; the Card pitchers appeared tired and largely ineffective, and the hitters appeared to be handcuffed by the Yankee pitchers. There were, however, some Cardinal hopes as Tim McCarver, the Cards' fine catcher, had a .417 batting average, and Bob Gibson, with three full days' rest, seemed ready for the first time since the Series began.

A well-rested Bob Gibson, his fastball crackling

Bob Gibson stretches for the catch. His 2 wins over the Yankees enabled the Cards to win their first World Series since 1946.

into catcher Tim McCarver's big glove, had the Yankee hitters at his mercy for eight and a half innings as the Cards jumped out in front, scoring 2 big runs in the fifth inning, to lead the Yankees 2–0 in a real thriller.

Now, the Yanks came to bat in the last of the ninth inning, and most of the New York fans were heading for the exits as Mickey Mantle came up to hit. No longer the fast-as-lightning Mantle of yesteryear, Mickey still could hit the ball; he took a last-second lunge at a fastball, just dribbled a grounder to short, but beat it out and was safely on first base. Howard struck out, and then it was up to Joe Pepitone. It was the most dramatic play of the entire Series.

Joe drilled a low fastball right back to the mound. Gibson, half-turned by his pitching follow-through, felt the ball smack on his right hip, a bruising blow; then it rolled toward the third base line. Gibson, with great reaction, was on the ball like a flash, scooped it up, and fired it as he was falling to first base to get Pepitone by an eyelash. It was one of those incredible bang-bang plays, and it precipitated an argument over the umpire's call.

While the Yankees argued the decision, Gibson tried to recover his poise on the mound. Then, taking a deep breath, he made his first pitch to Tommy Tresh, and Tommy promptly drove the ball into the left field stands. The crowd, now back in their seats, erupted in a roar that could be heard all over New York.

With the score tied, 2–2, the Yankees' relief pitcher Pete Mikkelsen began the dramatic tenth inning by walking Bill White. Ken Boyer bunted and was safe on the play. Now the Cards had two men on and nobody out. Dick Groat hit into a force play, and with men on first and third and 1 out, manager Johnny Keane almost was convinced that his next batter, Tim McCarver, should bunt. Finally, after talking the situation over with Tim, Keane gave McCarver the hit signal, and the count went to 3 and 2 as the crowd screamed. McCarver, thinking "fastball," got set for the pitch, swung, and drove the ball deep into right field. Not until he was rounding first did McCarver realize that the ball had landed in the right field stands. "I was absolutely dazed," McCarver said afterward. "By the time I got to

It was grit, determination, and skill that made Jim Bouton a winner in 1964.

third base, I was laughing out loud."

In the Yankees' half of the tenth inning, Gibson, with a 5–2 lead, simply poured in his fastball and overpowered the three Yankee hitters, and the Cardinals now had a lead of 3 games to 2 in the Series as the two teams flew back to St. Louis for game six.

Ten thousand excited fans welcomed the Cardinals as they returned to St. Louis and proclaimed them "our coming world champions."

Jim Bouton again took to the mound for the Yankees, and Curt Simmons was manager Johnny Keane's choice for the sixth game. Simmons pitched brilliantly for six and a half innings, and the Cardinals had a 1–0 lead, but then Simmons tired, and the Yankees pounded him for 3 runs, featuring home runs by the Yankees' two M men, Maris and Mantle. The 2 home runs, coming one after another, marked only the fourth time in World Series play that such a one-two punch was delivered. Ruth and Gehrig did it in 1928 against the Cards and again in 1932 against the Chicago Cubs. The 2 home runs by Maris

Tom Tresh hit 2 home runs, 2 doubles, and drove in 7 runs during the 1964 Series.

and Mantle enabled the Yanks to easily defeat the Cards, 8–3, and even the Series at 3 games.

Now everything was on the line for the big seventh game in St. Louis on October 15. Bob Gibson and Mel Stottlemyre opposed each other for the third time. In the fifth game, Gibson had pitched the entire ten innings; Stottlemyre had pitched seven innings.

In the bottom of the fourth inning, Ken Boyer broke the ice with a sharp single to center. Then Stott walked Dick Groat, and that brought Tim McCarver up to bat. McCarver hit a line smash down the first base line, and Pepitone made a magnificent stop of the difficult drive and fired

the ball to second for the force-out. But Linz's throw to first to get McCarver was wild, and Ken Boyer, who had never stopped running, scored the first run of the game. Mike Shannon then lined a single to left, and McCarver, running the bases like one of the old Gashouse Gang Cards, sped to third base. Suddenly Shannon, who was on first base, broke for second, and when Ellie Howard threw down to second base, McCarver tore for home. Richardson intercepted the throw to second base, but his throw to the plate was late and McCarver scored the second run. Dal Maxvill then singled sharply up the middle and Shannon scored.

In the fifth inning, manager Berra decided to change pitchers, and brought in Al Downing to relieve Stottlemyre. Lou Brock saluted Downing's first pitch with a tremendous clout into the left field seats. Now the Cardinals were on target, hitting everything. White singled, and Ken Boyer, up once again, stroked a long double to center field, and both runners scored on Groat's bounder to second and McCarver's sacrifice fly.

Down by a 6–0 margin, seemingly out of contention, the Yankees fought back fiercely, as Richardson opened the sixth inning with a base hit. Maris followed with a single, and then Mickey Mantle brought the crowd up screaming as he pole-axed a fastball, sent it whistling into the left field seats, and suddenly it was a 6–3 game and the Yankees were back in the battle.

In the seventh inning, the Yankees sent Steve Hamilton in to pitch. Steve got the first two Cardinal hitters, but Ken Boyer drove a fastball into the seats for his second home run of the Series. It was 7–3, St. Louis.

Gibson was simply superb in the eighth inning as he got Mickey Mantle on three fastballs that Mickey could not hit at all. One out! Howard fanned! 2 outs! Pepitone popped up!

Tommy Tresh fanned to begin the ninth inning.

But Clete Boyer, Ken's brother, and not a slugger in the same vein as his older brother, crossed up everyone by driving a ball into the stands for a home run, bringing the score to 7–4.

Johnny Blanchard, pinch-hitting for Hamilton, struck out.

One out to go.

Again the crowd was up on their feet, this time screaming and jumping up and down, for little Phil Linz stroked Gibson's first pitch into the stands for a home run, making it 7–5, Cards.

Bobby Richardson, who had earlier in the game broken a fifty-two-year-old record for total hits in a Series, with his thirteenth hit, stepped in to hit. Behind Bobby was Tommy Tresh, and possibly a pinch hitter.

Now Gibson went to work with a vengeance. He put everything into a fastball, and Richardson popped the ball up for an easy out. Tommy Tresh struck out on three great pitches, and Gibson simply poured the ball over to Johnny Blanchard, and Johnny struck out, ending the game and the Series. The Cards had won it in a thriller, 7–5.

There were parades in Omaha for Bob Gibson—and in Memphis for Tim McCarver. Light-hearted Tim McCarver, currently a play-by-play broadcaster for the Mets, who wound up with a glittering .478 batting average for the Series, grabbed an advertising slogan button and stuck it in his right eye as a monocle. It read: WE TRY HARDER.

There would be no more World Series for Mickey Mantle, Whitey Ford, or for Richardson, Kubek, or Boyer, among others, for the once-almighty Yankees would not be back in a Series for twelve long years, and by that time all of the great stars of the 1964 team had retired.

In a strange twist of fate, both World Series managers were dismissed after the Series. The Yankees, unhappy with the way Berra handled the club, fired Yogi. John Keane, Cardinal manager, quit the team and several weeks later was named manager of the Yankees. The fact that neither pennant-winning manager would be back with his old team was one of the most stunning episodes in baseball history.

1965

Los Angeles Dodgers Versus Minnesota Twins

For the first time since 1907–09 the National League won three World Series in a row, when the Dodgers with their remarkable pitching twins —Sandy Koufax, who won 26 games, and Don Drysdale, who had won 23—captured the pennant by 2½ games in an exciting last-month battle with the San Francisco Giants.

In the American League the amazing Minnesota Twins whose power hitting gave them a large advantage over the White Sox, the Orioles, and the Detroit Tigers, won their first pennant, by a margin of 7 games over the second-place Chicago White Sox.

In the opening game of the Series, Don Drysdale was Walt Alston's selection to halt the slugging Twins, while Jim "Mudcat" Grant, a 19-game winner for the Twins, was manager Sam Mele's pitching choice. Ron Fairly, the Dodgers' slugging right fielder, opened the second inning by driving Grant's first pitch into the left field seats for a 1–0 lead. But the Twins' Don Mincher duplicated the homer to tie the game.

Then, suddenly, the Twins exploded in the third inning with a roar that could be heard throughout the Twin Cities. Minnesota sluggers pounded Drysdale and three relievers for 6 big runs, more than enough for the eventual 8–2 victory. The big blow of the inning was a tremendous 3-run homer by Zoilo Versalles, the Twins' hard-hitting shortstop.

The next day the Twins shocked the baseball world by pounding the almost unbeatable Sandy Koufax for 6 base hits in six innings and a 2–0 lead. Koufax left the game in the sixth inning and gave way to Ron Perranoski, the Dodgers' fine relief pitcher. But the Twins continued their assault on Perranoski, collecting 3 hits and 3 runs in the one and a half innings he pitched. The Twins, noted principally for their hitting prowess, also featured one of the great defensive plays of the Series, a catch by Bob Allison that saved the game.

In the fifth inning, Ron Fairly singled and Jim Lefebvre stroked a curving line drive to left field. Allison, playing out of position, raced for the ball, and managed to get to it with a great dive just as the ball was nearing the ground. Allison slid about fifteen feet after the catch to save the day for the Twins, who came away with a 5–2 triumph.

The third game of the Series, at Los Angeles, featured superb pitching by the Dodgers' Claude Osteen, who allowed the slugging Twins just 5 base hits, to gain a 4–0 win over an assortment of three Twin pitchers. Four of Minnesota's 5 hits were singles; the fifth, by Versalles, was a double.

Everything that the Twins had heard about the Dodgers, the classy pitching, the swift and alert baserunning, was demonstrated in the fourth game.

Maury Wills, leading off in the first inning,

beat out an easy roller. Willie Davis hit to Mincher, and he too beat the throw as Wills, running like a frightened colt, came all the way in to score.

In the second inning, Johnny Roseboro, the Dodger catcher, hit a shot past the shortstop, Frank Quilici, with Wes Parker, on second base, coming in to score run number 2 on the hit.

The Dodgers scored another run, but Tony Oliva of the Twins homered with a man on base in the sixth inning to make it a 3–2 game. The Dodgers, however, came on again with a vengeance, scoring 3 runs in the sixth inning and another in the eighth to sew up the game. Don Drysdale, pitching as if it were the final game of the Series, fanned 11 Twin hitters to win the game, 7–2.

Behind the magnificent pitching of Sandy Koufax, the Dodgers romped over the Twins in game five by a 7–0 margin. Sandy was unhittable, allowing the Twins just 4 base hits while striking out 10. Maury Wills, with 4 hits, and Ron Fairly, with 3, starred on offense for the Dodgers as they completely outplayed the hapless Twins.

When the teams traveled back to Minneapolis for the sixth game, the pressure was on the Twins, who had no choice but to call on Jim Grant once more. Although he'd had but two days' rest, the husky right-hander was equal to the challenge, pitching a masterful 6-hitter to beat Claude Osteen and the Dodgers, 5–1.

Grant put the game on ice as he personally slashed a 3-run homer in the sixth inning to give the Twins and himself a 5–0 lead. Grant became the seventh pitcher in Series history to hit a homer.

Manager Walt Alston puzzled over his pitching selection for the seventh and final game of the Series, finally selecting Sandy Koufax. Koufax allowed the Twins just 3 base hits and struck out 10 Twins hitters to rack up a marvelous 2–0 shutout to give the Dodgers the championship.

Lou Johnson, the thirty-two-year-old sub outfielder who came right out of the minor leagues to fill in at the beginning of the season when Tommy Davis suffered a fractured leg, drove out a home run off Jim Kaat in the fourth inning to give Sandy the only run he needed for the

victory. However, the Dodgers got an insurance run in the same inning when Fairly doubled and scored on a long single by Wes Parker, to make it 2–0.

The Twins threatened in the ninth inning, when Harmon Killebrew singled with 1 out, but Sandy then threw caution to the wind. He just threw that fastball three times past Earl Battey, and then struck out the dangerous Bob Allison, to bring back the World Championship to the Los Angeles Dodgers.

Dodger third baseman Jim "Junior" Gilliam makes a great stop of Twins' Zoilo Versalles's ground ball, ending the Twins' rally. This was the key play of the final game of the 1965 Series.

Ron Fairly greets teammate Lou Johnson after his eighth-inning home run.

Sandy Koufax was in brilliant form in the seventh game as he allowed the Minnesota Twins just 3 hits for a 2–0 shutout.

1966

Baltimore Orioles Versus Los Angeles Dodgers

Surely it had to be one of the most astounding of all World Series as the 100 to 1 underdogs, the Baltimore Orioles, swept the Dodgers in four straight games. The Dodgers, who on the very last day of the regular season won the National League flag over the San Francisco Giants by a margin of 2 games, were admittedly not a power-hitting ball club, but manager Walt Alston made the most of his outstanding pitching staff, excellent defense, speed on the base paths, and sound strategy.

The Orioles, on the other hand, were a tremendous offensive team. They hit 175 home runs and were led by one of baseball's greatest players, Frank Robinson, who smashed out 49 circuit clouts to lead home-run hitters in both leagues.

It was a long, long time, seventy years to be exact, between major league championships in Baltimore, but Ned Hanlon's earlier Orioles were a team any modern Baltimore championship club could well emulate. The Birds of the 1890s, led by John McGraw, were a fighting, aggressive, brawling club, but also a team of thinkers, men of initiative and daring, who ate, drank, and slept baseball.

The Orioles of 1966, with such stars as Frank Robinson, Brooks Robinson, Luis Aparicio, Boog Powell, Paul Blair, and Curt Blefary were just as aggressive, fiery, and combative under Hank

Bauer's leadership as the old Orioles, and they came into the 1966 World Series with but one thought: to win!

In the opening game at Los Angeles, a National League castoff, Moe Drabowsky, who was picked up by the Orioles in the 1965 major league draft, set one record and tied another in a dazzling relief job. In six and two-thirds innings in relief of starting pitcher Dave McNally, the Polish-born Drabowsky held the Dodgers to 1 hit and got credit for the victory, a 5–2 win. Drabowsky struck out 11 Dodger hitters, a World Series record for a relief pitcher. In both the fourth and fifth innings, Moe struck out the side, tying the mark established by Hod Eller of Cincinnati in 1919 against the White Sox.

If Moe Drabowsky became a sudden and unexpected hero in the first game of the Series, Willie Davis of the Dodgers became an equally abject scapegoat in the second game, committing 3 errors as the Dodgers completely collapsed. The Dodgers made 6 errors, failed to hit, and did just about everything wrong.

The defeat of Don Drysdale in the first game was damaging, but all odds favored the Dodgers as Sandy Koufax, with his 27-9 record, took the mound for the second game, against the Orioles' Jim Palmer, a 15-game winner. Refusing to be awed by Koufax, Palmer completely subdued the Dodgers, hurling 4-hit ball and striking out

Paul Blair is safe at home in the second game.
Dodger catcher (8) is John Roseboro.

Dodger shortstop Maury Wills leaps high to avoid
slide of Andy Etchebarren as the Orioles' catcher
was forced at second base. Action occurred in the
sixth inning of the final game of the Series.

Ron Fairly (6) dives for the bag as Davey Johnson
(15) gets off his throw to first to complete a double
play in the second inning of the third game.

6 Dodgers as he defeated them, 6–0, to become the youngest pitcher to win a World Series shutout. The big right-hander was just nine days shy of his twenty-first birthday.

With one dramatic swing of his big bat, center fielder Paul Blair put himself in baseball's record book, placed the Orioles within range of a clean sweep, and at the same time, avenged an old personal score with the Dodgers as the teams played the third game in Baltimore on October 8. The Birds' center fielder smashed a fastball 430 feet into the left field bleachers in the fifth inning to give the Orioles a 1–0 victory and a 3-game lead in the Series as a huge partisan crowd of some fifty-three thousand fans roared their approval.

The 100 to 1 Birds needed one more win.

The three-year reign of the National League as the world champions of baseball came to a humiliating end on October 9, when the underdog Orioles shut out the Dodgers for the third straight time and defeated them 4 in a row to win the Series.

The finale was a 1–0 triumph that was virtually a carbon copy of the October 8 game, in which Wally Bunker supplied the pitching and Paul Blair contributed the winning home run.

Dave McNally came back to start the fourth game for the Orioles, and this time the lefty had superb control in matching 4-hitters with Don Drysdale. Once again the hero of the day for the Orioles was Frank Robinson, who supplied the knockout punch. In the fourth inning, with 1 out, Robinson hit a Drysdale fastball far up into the left field seats for a tremendous home run, some 410 feet away; and that was the only run the Birds needed.

Not only did the Orioles dethrone the Dodgers as world champions, but they wrote Los Angeles into the record books with an embarrassing succession of zeroes. The Dodgers played the final 33½ innings of the Series without scoring a single run, breaking a record that had existed for sixty-one years. In 1905 the Giants blanked the Athletics for 28 straight innings while en route to the title. Leon Ames, Christy Mathewson, and Joe McGinnity put that record together then. Moe Drabowsky, Jim Palmer, Wally Bunker, and Dave McNally were responsible for the new one.

Owner Walter O'Malley summed the Series up in this way: "The Dodgers are beyond explanation. We don't mind too much being beaten, but we hate like hell being embarrassed."

1967

St. Louis Cardinals Versus Boston Red Sox

On October 1, the Red Sox completed one of baseball's great rags-to-riches stories by defeating the Minnesota Twins 5–3, to win the tightest American League pennant race in history. They won it before a roaring crowd of some thirty-six thousand in the 162nd and final game of the season—just one year after they had finished ninth in the league and twenty-one years after they had won their last pennant.

As a result, the Red Sox, a second division team for nine years, were dog-tired, worn out by the exhausting pennant race, yet they were grimly determined to win over the Cardinals as they trotted onto the field for the sixty-fourth World Series, at Boston, and the hearts of all of America's downtrodden underdogs were at Fenway Park rooting for them.

Opening game pitching selections featured Bob Gibson against a virtual unknown, twenty-one-year-old Jose Santiago.

For Santiago, the opportunity to open a World Series was both a vindication and a great thrill. Just three years earlier, he had spent a season with Kansas City without winning a single game. The Athletics shipped Jose right back to the minor leagues and, whether by accident or design, neglected to protect their rights to him. The Red Sox bought him from Vancouver, but not until the second half of the 1967 season did Joe win some games. Then, when the Red Sox

were valiantly fighting off the White Sox, Tigers, and Twins, Jose won 7 straight games to help the Sox capture the coveted flag.

In the opening game of the Series, the Cards scored in the third inning. Lou Brock singled, Curt Flood doubled, and Brock scored on Roger Maris's groundout. But the Red Sox came right back on Santiago's home run to tie the score. The 1–1 tie lasted until the seventh inning, when Brock singled, stole second, advanced to third on Flood's single, and scored on Maris's hit to short.

Meanwhile, Bob Gibson was masterful as he allowed the Red Sox just 6 hits while striking out 10 Boston batters for an exciting 2–1 victory.

Pitcher Jim Lonborg and Carl Yastrzemski were the two Red Sox heroes of the second game. Yaz had 2 home runs and a single as well as 4 runs batted in. The Red Sox took game two by a 5–0 score to even the Series at 1 game each.

The teams journeyed to St. Louis for the third game of the Series, on October 7, with Nelson Briles opposing Gary Bell. Briles was a 14-game winner for the Cards, while Bell won 12 games during the season. Bell was a pickup from the Cleveland Indians in June, where he had a mediocre 1-5 record, but suddenly he regained his form and was 15-8 for the Red Sox during the remainder of the season. But Gary lasted just two innings as the Cardinals bashed him for 5 hits and 3 runs. Brock opened with a triple and came home when Flood singled for a quick Cardinal score. In the second inning, Tim McCarver singled and Mike Shannon drove a home run deep into the left field stands. Then, in the sixth inning, Brock beat out a bunt and raced to third base on a wild pickoff throw by reliever Lee Stange. Maris continued the barrage of hits with a single, scoring Brock. In the eighth inning, the Cards scored their fifth run on a Maris single and a two-base hit by Orlando Cepeda as they defeated the Sox, 5–2.

Bob Gibson took the mound for the Cards for the fourth game, and once again he was opposed by Jose Santiago. This time Gibson was even better than in the first game; he yielded just 5 hits in a 6–0 shutout victory. The Cards exploded in the first frame to knock out Santiago, driving him to cover with 6 hits and 4 runs in two thirds of an inning. Then, with a nifty 4-run lead safely tucked in his back pocket, Gibson pitched his heart out, striking out 7 and

holding the Red Sox to 5 base hits to gain his second Series win.

Needing a victory to prolong the Series, the Red Sox put their fortunes, hopes, and desires onto the big shoulders of the six-foot-five-inch right-hander, Jim Lonborg, who had pitched the Sox to their only Series win, a 1-hitter. This time, pitching with a slight cold and a paper horseshoe in his hip pocket, Big Jim came close to duplicating his previous spectacular work. This time Lonborg did not allow a batter to reach base until Del Maxvill singled with 1 out in the third inning. Then Maris singled in the fourth. Lonborg got 12 straight Cardinal batters out until Julian Javier got on base on an error in the eighth inning. And finally, Maris hit a home run over the right field fence in the ninth, to give the Birds their lone score. The Red Sox scored once in the third inning and twice more in the ninth, giving them a clutch 3–1 victory. And now they were back in the Series.

Manager Dick Williams selected rookie Gary Waslewski to pitch for the Sox in the sixth game,

Roger Maris is out on a close play at the plate in the second game. No. 19 is Elston Howard.

Bob Gibson won 3 games during the Series for the Cardinals.

Waslewski tired badly in the sixth inning. He walked Maris and McCarver and had a 1 and 0 count on Shannon when manager Williams called in his relief ace, John Wyatt, who managed to get through the inning without any damage. In the seventh inning, Wyatt walked pinch hitter Bob Tolan; then Lou Brock hit a home run to tie the game, 4–4.

But the Red Sox, now fighting mad to stay in the Series, came back with an explosion of their own. Jones singled and Joe Foy bashed a triple to left, scoring Jones. Mike Andrews singled, Yastrzemski singled, and then Scott and Smith singled in succession, resulting in 4 runs and a healthy 8–4 Red Sox lead.

The Cardinals hit the ball hard in the eighth and ninth innings, but outstanding defensive plays by the Red Sox outfield, two by George Thomas in right field, saved the game for the

In his only World Series appearance after twenty-two years with the Red Sox, Carl Yastrzemski smashed out 3 home runs and a .400 average against the St. Louis Cardinals.

while Dick Hughes, a 16-game winner, toiled for the Cardinals as the teams settled back at Fenway Park in Boston. Waslewski retired the Cards in order in the first two innings and had a 1-run lead, on Rico Petrocelli's drive over the "Green Monster," the wall in left field. But Waslewski weakened in the third inning, as Javier doubled and Brock singled to tie the score at 1–1. Then Curt Flood singled, scoring Brock, and there was a 2–1 St. Louis lead.

In the fourth inning, the Red Sox exploded. Yastrzemski, Smith, and Petrocelli all smashed round-trippers, giving the Sox a 4–2 lead. But

Red Sox, and when Cepeda finally grounded out, they had evened the Series at 3 games.

The matchup for the seventh and final game of the World Series had historic overtones. Only once before had a seventh game of a Series brought together starting pitchers who both had 2-0 won-lost records in that Series. It happened in 1925, when Walter Johnson, for Washington, pitched against Pittsburgh's Vic Aldridge.

On October 12 at Boston, Lonborg obviously lacked the sharpness that had characterized his first two games and most of his 22 wins during the regular season. He got by the first two innings on sheer guts, but Del Maxvill opened the third inning with a rousing triple off the center field wall. Then, with the Boston infield playing in, Gibson lined to Joe Foy at third base, and Brock popped out. But Flood singled, scoring Maxvill, and Maris ripped a single past first base, moving Flood to third. A wild pitch allowed Flood to score, making it 2–0, but Lonborg ended the inning by getting Cepeda out on a grounder. Lonborg got 4 more outs before falling hopelessly behind. Gibson homered. Then Brock singled, followed by 2 steals and a walk to Flood.

A fly ball by Maris made the scene 4–0, St. Louis. Lonborg was tiring now, as McCarver opened the sixth inning with a long double. Mike Shannon's hard shot to Foy at third base bounded away for an error, and now there were two men on base. Javier slashed at Lonborg's first pitch and drove the ball into the left field screen for a 3-run homer, and the score was now 7–1.

Yastrzemski opened the ninth for the Red Sox with a long two-base hit. Gibson bore down, forced Ken Harrelson to hit into a fast double play, and then Gibson struck out Scott to end the game. For Gibson it was his third World Series victory, and he preserved the St. Louis record of never losing the seventh game. Their 8-3 record in championship play represents the greatest success of any National League club.

It had been a fabulous year for Carl Yastrzemski. He captured the triple crown, batting .326, hitting 44 home runs, and driving in 121 runs. He also hit for a .400 average in the Series. Jim Lonborg walked away with the Cy Young Award to end a magnificent yet heartbreaking year for the Red Sox.

1968

Detroit Tigers Versus St. Louis Cardinals

According to Bob Gibson, it is possible for a man to stand on a pitching mound in the center of a stadium and not be totally aware of a crowd of fifty-five thousand people. Still perspiring freely, his Cardinals cap jauntily tilted to the right, the big pitcher charged into the clubhouse right after defeating the almost invincible Denny McLain to win the opening game of the 1968 World Series with a 4–0 drubbing of the Tigers, striking out 17 Tiger batters to break the World Series record. Gibson walked 1 batter, and gave up just 4 singles and 1 extra-base hit, a double. Gibson opened the game in the first inning by striking out Dick McAuliffe, then added Al Kaline. In the second inning, one-two-three, he fanned Norm Cash, Willie Horton, and Jim Northrup, then added Bill Freehan and McLain in the third inning. Thus, he struck out 7 of the first 9 Tigers to face him, including 5 batters in a row.

In the ninth inning, Mickey Stanley raised some faint Tiger hopes as he singled sharply to open the inning. Then Al Kaline, who had fanned twice in succession, missed a slider for strikeout number 15. Gibson seemed serenely unaware of the milestone he had reached; however, thousands in the crowd knew. When Bob struck out Cash, he received a tremendous standing ovation from the entire crowd at the huge Cardinal stadium. Finally he threw a curveball past Will Horton, for his seventeenth strikeout and final

out of the day—and received another tremendous standing ovation.

When Mickey Lolich was three years old, he rode his bicycle off a curb in Portland, Oregon, and collided with a motorcycle. It fell on him, injuring his left shoulder so badly that doctors later recommended constant throwing—for example, throwing baseballs—as therapy.

In time, Mickey threw baseballs so well left-handed that he became a pitcher. He still does everything else right-handed, but since 1963 has been a star for the Tigers—left-handed.

To get his kicks during the season Mickey put on a crash helmet, selected one of his fleet of motorcycles, drove it up a ramp from cellar to the street and roared to Tiger Stadium some thirty miles away.

On a clear, cool afternoon, October 3, in St. Louis, Mickey Lolich outpitched four of the Cardinals' top pitchers, Nelson Briles, Steve Carlton, Ron Willis, and Joe Hoerner, during the second game of the Series. He allowed the defending champions only 6 base hits (all singles), 2 walks, and struck out 9 batters.

Willie Horton slugged Briles's first pitch into the left field seats in the second inning for Detroit's first run of the Series. It was Willie's thirty-seventh home run of the year. In the third inning, Mickey Lolich, who had not hit a home run in his six big-league seasons, slugged a 2 and 2 pitch into the seats, giving Detroit a 2–0 lead. Mickey was so surprised, he forgot to touch first base and had to retrace his steps.

Norm Cash led off in the sixth inning by driving a 1 and 1 pitch into the left field seats, and the Tigers had a 3–0 lead. Horton then beat out a bunt, and Steve Carlton came in to pitch, relieving Briles. Jim Northrup greeted Carlton with a smashing single up the middle. Wert walked, filling the bases. Dick McAuliffe hit a low line drive to center field that Flood trapped in his glove, but the catch was a difficult one and Curt let the ball get away from him; 2 runs scored on the error. Now it was 5–0, Tigers.

Brock walked to open the Cards' half of the sixth inning; he promptly stole second base and scored the Cards' first run when Cepeda singled.

In the ninth inning, the Tigers scored 2 more runs on singles by Cash and Kaline, a walk to Freehan, and a walk to Wert, which forced in a run. Then Lolich walked and another run came in, and the Tigers took the game by an 8–1 score.

In the third game, on October 5 at Tiger Stadium, Earl Wilson of the Tigers opposed Ray Washburn, and both hurlers pitched scoreless ball for two innings. Then Dick McAuliffe singled and Kaline slugged a home run, to give the Tigers a short-lived 2–0 lead.

In the Cardinals' half of the fifth inning, Brock led off with a single, stole second, and scored on Flood's double. Maris walked, and then Wilson suddenly called a time-out, beckoned to his manager, and complained of an injury to his leg. He was relieved by Pat Dobson, who served a hanging curveball to Tim McCarver, and Tim promptly drove it out of the park for a 3-run homer, to give the Cards a 4–2 advantage.

In the Tigers' half of the fifth inning, McAuliffe drove a Washburn pitch into the stands; then, suddenly losing control, Ray walked both Cash and Horton. Manager Red Schoendienst brought in Joe Hoerner, and the left-hander took immediate control of the game. He yielded just 1 hit in the final three and a half innings. To nail down the game, Orlando Cepeda slammed a 3-run homer in the seventh inning, and the Cardinals won by a 7–3 score.

Bob Gibson returned to the mound for the fourth game, on October 6 at Tiger Stadium, which began after a rain delay of more than seventy-five minutes. He held the Tigers to 5 base hits, while his teammates pounded six Tiger hurlers for 13 base hits and a 10–1 rout of Denny McLain and four other Tiger pitchers.

With Mickey Lolich again on the mound for the Tigers, manager Red Schoendienst sent in Nelson Briles to pitch in the fifth game. The Cards greeted Mickey with a barrage of base hits in the first inning that included a double by Brock, a single by Flood, and a 3-run homer by Cepeda, to give them a 3–0 lead, which lasted until the fourth inning, when the Tigers scored 2 runs on 2 triples and a single by Northrup.

Tigers star Al Kaline had to wait sixteen years for his first opportunity to play in a World Series. He finally made it in 1968 and hit for a smashing .379 average.

Norm Cash, the great Tiger hitter, led his club's offense with a sparkling .385 average in the Series.

Lolich led off the seventh inning with a single, and that hit seemed to ignite the Tigers. Suddenly, McAuliffe singled, and Mickey Stanley walked, filling the bases. Al Kaline drove out a sharp single to center, scoring 2 Tigers; Cash then singled, and now the Tigers had a 5–3 lead, which they held on to for the rest of the game. It was a game the Tigers had to win in order to prolong the Series.

The evening after the sixth game, on October 9, a chunky man with gray hair stood in the middle of the St. Louis locker room as the Tigers celebrated their 13–1 lambasting over the St. Louis Cardinals. His name was Dr. Harry Wright.

Wright was the doctor who gave Denny McLain an injection on Tuesday, October 8, that won the sixth game of the Series for the Tigers. A muscle problem in his right shoulder had kept McLain from pitching at his best in his two previous appearances. After the second loss,

Colorful Tim McCarver, the Cards' fine catcher, slugged a 3-run homer in game three of the Series and hit for a .333 average.

Portly Mickey Lolich, the great Tiger pitcher, led his team to the championship by winning 3 marvelously pitched games in the 1968 Series.

McLain had talked as if he were through for the Series. He had been taking treatment from Dr. Wright for the last six weeks, and now the shoulder was getting worse.

"What Denny had is an inflamed shoulder," Wright said after the sixth game. "Up to now we've been manipulating the muscle, attempting to work the soreness out. But it wasn't enough anymore. We gave Denny one shot of cortisone and a mixture of Xylocaine, and as soon as the shot got into his bloodstream, he felt the soreness just vanish."

McLain then went out, pitched the entire game, and held the Cardinals scoreless until the ninth inning, when they tallied their lone run.

Meanwhile, the Tigers simply cannonaded seven Cardinal pitchers for a total of 12 base hits and 13 runs, including a bases-full home run by Jim Northrup in a record-breaking third inning, when the Tigers batted around and scored 10 runs.

In the seventh and final game, everything was at stake as Bob Gibson once more faced his rival, portly Mickey Lolich. For seven innings it was a tense, nerve-wracking pitching duel, with both teams helping their respective pitchers by turning in sparkling plays that brought cheers and gasps from the huge crowd.

There was still no score going into the seventh inning, when Tiger lightning struck. With 2 outs, Norm Cash singled and Willie Horton followed with another base hit, through the hole at second base. Jim Northrup smashed a three-bagger to deep center field; two runs came in and the Tigers had a 2–0 lead. Then catcher Bill Freehan, who had just 1 hit in 22 trips to the plate, slashed a double, scoring Northrup, and the Tigers were ahead 3–0.

In the ninth inning, the terrific Tigers continued to pester Gibson. Horton, Northrup, and Wert all singled, and Dick Tracewski, running for Horton, scored, to make it a 4–0 game.

The Cards put up a last-ditch effort, as Mike Shannon homered to give them their lone run. But then Lolich simply poured his fastball over to retire the Cardinals.

Mickey Lolich had allowed the Cards just 5 base hits, and as he got McCarver to pop up for the final out of the game, catcher Bill Freehan threw himself into the arms of the portly Tiger pitcher and lifted him into the air, the only man in town with five motorcycles in his basement and a World Series win over Bob Gibson.

"All of my life," Lolich said as the champagne flowed all around him, "somebody has been the big star and Mickey Lolich was the number two guy. I figured my day would come, and this was it."

The 1968 World Champion Detroit Tigers

1969

New York Mets Versus Baltimore Orioles

There were a number of unrelated events occurring off the playing field that made for a considerable change in the structure of the baseball world in 1969.

The transplanting of major league baseball teams went back to the 1940s, when plans were set to move the old St. Louis Browns team to Los Angeles. But those plans were scuttled when the Japanese struck Pearl Harbor and World War II broke out.

In 1953, a month into the baseball season, the Boston Braves, who had lost tons of money through the years, were suddenly shipped to Milwaukee, where they attracted more than 1.8 million fans, almost three times the number they had drawn in Boston. The Braves' move started an unstoppable trend. At the end of the 1953 season, the Browns moved to Baltimore. In 1954 the Philadelphia Athletics were purchased from Connie Mack and his family and moved to Kansas City.

But the move of the Athletics was nothing compared to the move of the beloved Brooklyn Dodgers to Los Angeles in 1958. Shortly thereafter, the Giants moved on to San Francisco. The Braves had left Milwaukee for Atlanta in 1966. The Kansas City team of 1955–67 moved to Oakland in 1968. And after a horrible year at the gate in 1969, the Seattle club moved to Milwaukee.

In 1961, the American League, finding eight clubs too limiting in the face of the constant demands for new franchises and even larger television dollars, expanded to ten teams. The National League followed suit in 1962.

The additions to the American League included the new California Angels, the Kansas City Royals, the Seattle Mariners, and the Minnesota Twins (who were really the transplanted Washington Senators). In the National League, new teams included the Houston Astros, the Montreal Expos, and the San Diego Padres.

Recognizing the mistake of leaving New York without a National League team, the league awarded a franchise to Mrs. Joan Payson, who named the team the Mets.

In 1969, each league split into Eastern and Western conferences, each consisting of six clubs. There would be a playoff between the two division leaders to decide the pennant winners.

The New York Mets, born to be laughed at, were now laughing back at the rest of the world on October 4, 1969. Symbols of five-star futility for most of their eight years in the National League, caricatured with ten thumbs and two left feet, they had suddenly, as if by divine right, been transformed into the National League champions.

In the championship series with the Braves, the Mets again were the underdogs, but they

304

ignored the odds and defeated the Braves in a 3-game sweep that sent baseball experts to their couches.

Their former manager, Casey Stengel, called them the "Amazin' Mets." And "amazin' " they were.

In 1968 the Mets had a new manager, Gil Hodges. Hodges was something of a living legend in New York. He had been the great first baseman for the old Brooklyn Dodgers from 1943 to 1957, and then moved west with the Dodgers when the franchise had been shifted to Los Angeles. Then, Gil had been one of the original Mets who played their games in 1962–63 at the Polo Grounds. He lived in Brooklyn with his wife, Joan, and their four children. Even when he was managing the Washington Senators, from 1963 to 1967, his home base was Brooklyn, where in the off-season he ran a bowling alley and an automobile dealership.

Hodges had proved that he had a unique ability to handle young ballplayers, and that was exactly what he had in the Mets of 1968 and 1969. Mindful of the club's conspicuous weaknesses, Hodges stressed basics day after day, hour after hour—pickoff plays, cutoffs, double plays—until the players had their assignments down pat, and working.

With pitchers like Tom Seaver winning 16 games; Jerry Koosman winning 19 games; and Nolan Ryan, Dick Selma, and Al Jackson developing into winners, the Mets won 73 games in 1968 and finished in ninth place in the league.

But 1969 was the year of the Mets. Seaver won 25 games; Jerry Koosman, 17; and Gary Gentry, 13. Cleon Jones was amazing as he hit for a .340 average, while his pal Tommie Agee hit 26 home runs. And the rest of the Mets, Art Shamsky, Bud Harrelson, Ron Swoboda, Eddie Kranepool, Wayne Garrett, Al Weis, Jerry Grote, played as if every game were a World Series game. At season's end the Mets won the Eastern Division title, then swept past the Atlanta Braves and were ready to face a star-studded Baltimore Orioles. The Orioles were a team that had devastated the American League, winning 109 games, with such great stars as Boog Powell, who hit 37 home runs; Frank Robinson, who hit 32 homers; Brooks Robinson, who collected 23 homers and

Koosman and his catcher Jerry Grote celebrate with champagne after Koosman's second win of the Series.

covered third base like a vacuum cleaner; Paul Blair, with 26 homers; Don Buford; Mark Belanger; all of them veteran players who had reached full maturity and stardom and were gunning for the fresh upstarts from the National loop.

In the opening game, on Saturday, October 11, at Memorial Stadium in Baltimore, the Orioles started their ace left-hander, Mike Cuellar, a 23-game winner, against the Mets' ace, Tom Seaver, and before the game was a minute old, the Orioles had scored.

Left fielder Don Buford took a ferocious swing at Seaver's second pitch and drove the ball into the right field seats for a home run. In the fourth inning, Elrod Hendricks singled, Davey Johnson walked, and Mark Belanger drove in Hendricks with a ringing base hit to give the Orioles a 2–0 lead. Then Cuellar singled, and Buford doubled, to increase the Orioles' advantage to 4–0.

The Mets scored their lone run in the seventh inning, when Al Weis stroked a long sacrifice fly, scoring Clendenon, who had singled, stole second, and then went to third on a groundout.

The Mets threatened in the ninth inning, but Cuellar got Art Shamsky out on a ground ball with two men on base, and that was the ball game, the Orioles on top, 4–1.

Michael Koosman could not comprehend the significance of his father's achievement. But, then, Mike was just two years old when his dad, Jerry, tossed a marvelous 2-hit game against the

The Mets' brilliant Jerry Koosman won 2 games for his team during this Series.

Tom Seaver hurled the Mets to a victory in game four of the Series.

Orioles in the second game of the World Series. To the Orioles and the Mets, Jerry Martin Koosman's performance before some fifty-one thousand fans at Memorial Stadium in Baltimore on October 12 was illustrious. The twenty-six-year-old lefty out of Minnesota flirted zealously with no-hit stardom through the first six innings. Only in the second inning, when he issued a 2-out walk to Davey Johnson, did Koosman face more than three batters.

But Paul Blair, leading off in the seventh inning, drilled a single through the hole into left field for a base hit.

"I was relieved that the pressure was off," Kooz said after the game, "but I sure as hell was disappointed that one of my boyhood goals was spoiled."

In the Mets' fourth inning, Donn Clendenon homered to give the Mets a 1–0 lead. But Paul Blair's score in the seventh tied the game at 1–1. In the ninth inning, Ed Charles singled; then Al Weis ripped a slider to left field, scoring Charles. In the Orioles' half of the inning, Koosman got the first two batters out, then walked Frank Robinson and Powell, and now Koosman was in dire trouble, with 2 men on base, 2 outs, and the Mets in front by a 2–1 margin.

Manager Hodges brought in Ron Taylor to pitch to the dangerous Brooks Robinson. After running the count to 3 and 1, Robbie fouled off a pitch, then sent a hard ground ball to third base. Ed Charles trapped the ball, saw it bounce off his chest, and, quick as a cat, grabbed the ball and fired it to first base, just nipping Robinson for the final out. And the Mets had won their first-ever World Series game.

The Series moved to New York on October 14, and there wasn't an empty seat in Shea Stadium. Governor Nelson Rockefeller, Jackie Onassis, Mayor John Lindsay, and every celebrity in town was at the ball game to watch the magnificent Mets in action.

Tommie Agee staged a one-man show that began in the first inning when he drove Jim Palmer's first pitch into the right field bleachers for a home run. In the fourth inning, with Orioles on first and second bases, Tommie raced to the 400-feet sign in left-center field to make a backhanded, off-the-shoe-tops catch of a hit by Elrod

The Mets' Donn Clendenon is shown slugging the first of his 3 home runs in the Series. Don hit for a .357 average.

Hendricks. In the seventh inning, with three Orioles on base, Tommie made an even more spectacular catch, of Paul Blair's smash. It was a drive that looked as if it would go through the alley in right-center field for at least a triple. But Tommie dived for the ball, his body fully extended, and caught it in the fingertips of his glove just as it was about to hit the ground. The incredible catch saved at least 2 Oriole runs and brought the huge crowd up on their feet.

The Mets, inspired by Agee's splendid plays, added 3 runs to their total, including a home run by Eddie Kranepool in the eighth inning, to humble the Orioles with a 5–0 shutout.

In the fourth game, the Mets' ace, Tom Seaver, faced the great Cuban-born left-hander, Mike Cuellar, and the two starting pitchers began the first inning by getting the first three batters on each team out in order. In the second inning, Donn Clendenon, a thorn in the side of the Orioles throughout the Series, slugged Cuellar's second pitch into the left field seats and the Mets had a 1–0 lead. In the ninth, Seaver appeared to tire and allowed Frank Robinson and Paul Blair to knock out singles. Then Ron Swoboda made one of the greatest plays in Series history with a diving, one-handed stab of Brooks Robinson's line drive that might have won the game for the Orioles. Swoboda's gem of a catch saved the day for the Mets. But the run that the Orioles scored on the play tied the game, 1–1,

and the Mets went to work again in the tenth inning.

Jerry Grote slammed a high drive off pitcher Dick Hall that fell in for two bases. Al Weis walked. Pete Richert replaced Hall. J. C. Martin bunted Richert's first pitch, and when Richert's throw hit Martin on the wrist, the ball rolled to the dugout, enabling Rod Gaspar to score, and the Mets had won another World Series game, 2–1. It was the Amazin' Mets' third straight win.

In the fifth game, it looked as if the Mets' magic had vanished, as the Orioles jumped on pitcher Jerry Koosman for 3 big runs in the third inning, including home runs by Dave McNally and Frank Robinson.

But slowly, the magic reappeared. And the shoe polish industry never had a better day. In the sixth inning, Cleon Jones, with only 2 Series hits to that point, skipped to get out of the way of a low curveball. The ball ricocheted into the Mets' dugout and umpire Lou DiMuro called it a ball. Jones insisted the ball hit his shoe. And when manager Gil Hodges showed DiMuro that the ball was marked with a black smudge of polish, DiMuro waved Jones to first base. Then, just as the crowd had barely settled back in their seats, Donn Clendenon whacked a 3 and 2 pitch off the scoreboard and the Mets were right back in the ball game, trailing 3–2.

Leading off in the seventh inning, little Al Weis, who had hit every Oriole pitcher as if he

Al Weiss singles to drive in the winning run in the second game of the Series. His homer in the final game helped the Mets win the final and the World Series, 5–3.

Ron Swoboda's great one-handed, diving, back-handed catch of Don Buford's line drive, with two men on base, stopped a Red Sox threat of a big inning to help the Mets win the final game and the World Series.

owned him, slugged a home run over the 370-feet mark to tie the game at 3–3.

Jones opened the eighth inning by slugging a double off reliever Ed Watt. Clendenon grounded out. Then Ron Swoboda lined a hard shot to left field for a double, scoring Jones, and the Mets had a 4–3 edge. Charles then flied out and Grote smashed a grounder to Powell at first base. When Watt mishandled the toss, Swoboda scored the Mets' fifth run.

In the ninth inning, Koosman walked Robinson, but then got the next three Oriole batters and the Mets had done the impossible—they had won the World Series.

There was pandemonium in the ballpark. In the city of New York, the town erupted as cabs stopped in the streets. People tore away from their jobs and ran out into the streets. Strangers toasted other strangers with potent drinks in the nearest taverns.

And down in staid, conservative Wall Street, brokers and their assistants tossed out hundreds of thousands of pieces of confetti and ran about in the streets, singing and dancing over the Amazin' Mets of 1969—World Series champions.

1970

Baltimore Orioles Versus Cincinnati Reds

The 1970 World Series was one in which the hitters, rather than the pitchers, distinguished themselves. The outstanding star of the Series was the thirty-three-year-old third baseman of the Orioles, Brooks Robinson. Robinson did everything but turn in a triple play as the Orioles won their second championship in five years. He was so unbelievable in the field that an official of the Hall of Fame in Cooperstown asked Brooks for the glove he wore during the Series. Not only did Robinson defy imagination with his sensational fielding, but he had 9 hits in 21 at bats, including 2 home runs and a double, and he drove in 6 runs. He compiled a .428 average for the five-game series.

In the first game, the hard-hitting Reds climbed all over Jim Palmer for 3 runs in the first three innings, led by Lee May's 2-run homer. In the fourth inning, big Boog Powell blasted a 2-run homer to make it a 3–2 game. Then Elrod Hendricks hammered a home run in the fifth inning, and Brooks Robinson hit a tremendous shot in the seventh, to give the Birds a 4–3 triumph.

The next day, the Reds again jumped out to a 3–0 lead in the second game of the Series, also at Cincinnati, but once again Boog Powell hit a home run in the fourth inning, and in the fifth inning, the Birds batted around, scoring 5 runs, to put them ahead 6–4. Then Dick Hall, a forty-

year-old relief pitcher whose style was reminiscent of a giraffe on roller skates, came on to strangle the last 7 Reds without a hit, and the Orioles had a 2 games to none lead in the Series.

In the third game, the first played in Baltimore, it was Brooks Robinson's day at bat and in the field. Pete Rose and Bob Tolan hit successive singles to begin the game, and just when it looked like the Reds were set for a big inning, Robinson made a sensational grab of Tony Perez's wicked grounder, stepped on third, and then fired the ball to first for the double play to end the inning as the huge crowd of some fifty-two thousand stood and roared his name. Then, to add insult to injury, Robinson doubled with Frank Robinson and Don Buford on base, and both men scored. In the second inning, Robbie was marvelous as he raced in for Helms's slow ground ball and whipped the ball to first for the out. In the sixth inning, Robbie flung himself into the air to grab Johnny Bench's line drive. Also in the sixth, pitcher Dave McNally, showing how grateful he was to his teammates for their fine work, slugged a home run with the bases full. The final score was 9–3, Baltimore.

In the fourth game of the Series, with the Reds behind 5–3, Lee May jolted a 3-run homer in the eighth inning to give Cincinnati a 6–5 squeaker for their first victory.

At the start of the fifth game, it appeared that

the Orioles' pitcher, Mike Cuellar, would be in for a very rough afternoon. Rose led off with a double, Bench singled, and then May and Hal McRae also doubled, to give the Reds a 3–0 bulge. But those 3 runs were all the Reds were to get, as Cuellar shut them down with just 2 hits while the Birds pulled away for an easy 9–3 victory, and the World Series.

Paul Blair of the Orioles hit for a lusty .474 mark, and Brooks Robinson, ablaze in the field, hit for a .429 average and led his team in RBI.

Third baseman Brooks Robinson was the offensive star of the Orioles with 2 homers and a .429 average.

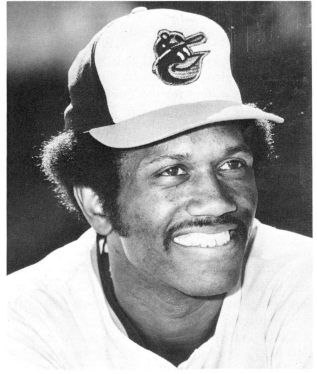

Paul Blair of the Orioles was the offensive star for the Orioles in the 1970 Series, hitting for a stunning .474 average.

Orioles first baseman Boog Powell slides home in the fifth inning of the final game of the 1970 Series as catcher Johnny Bench tries to block the plate. Umpire Dick Williams called Boog safe. Brooks Robinson (5) watches the play.

Orioles catcher Elrod Hendricks, in attempting to tag Bernie Carbo (25) of the Reds, smashes into umpire Ken Burkhart, who signals out. Replay showed later that Hendricks tagged Carbo without the ball, but there was no argument from the Reds and the play stood.

1971

Pittsburgh Pirates Versus Baltimore Orioles

It was early in the morning of the first game of the 1971 World Series. In his office off the locker room in Memorial Stadium in Baltimore, Orioles' manager Earl Weaver sat behind a desk, talking.

"I've got the best damn ball club in the universe," he told reporters. "Won over a hundred games three years in a row. Great spirit. Great ability. Great everything. We'll beat these Pirates. Not easy, but we'll beat 'em. I've got too good a club. They keep winning. I've heard it said anyone can manage this team. That's fine with me as long as I get the check each week.

"Now, I've got four twenty-game pitchers . . . all winners ready for the Series. McNally goes today; then Mike Cuellar; Jim Palmer will pitch Monday; Pat Dobson on Wednesday; then I'll come back with McNally with four days' rest or Cuellar on Thursday to wrap it up."

Weaver's analysis was almost correct, for in the first game of the Series McNally started against the Pittsburgh Pirates. But as the game got under way, Dave McNally's pinpoint control suddenly deserted him and he was roughed up for 3 runs in the second inning. But from the third inning on, he was sharp and pitched a remarkable game, retiring the next 19 Pirate hitters in order.

Frank Robinson and Merv Rettenmund led the Oriole attack with home runs. Then Don Buford hit one out of the park in the fifth inning,

to give the Birds a 5–3 win, as McNally sparkled, allowing the Pirates just 3 hits.

In 1971 nothing excited baseball fans in Baltimore like this simple announcement: "Batting sixth, and playing third base, number five, Brooks Robinson." It was a signal for a thunderous ovation for the thirty-four-year-old veteran of some sixteen major league seasons, an All-Star who has been referred to as "the Stan Musial of Baltimore" in tribute to his gentle nature and incredible talent.

The more than fifty-three thousand fans at the second World Series game, on October 11, including Mrs. Richard Nixon, daughter Julie, and son-in-law David Eisenhower, had plenty to cheer about. Robinson drove out 3 singles, drew 2 walks, and executed one of his patented miracle defensive plays in leading the Orioles to their second straight triumph over the Pirates, 11–3.

At Pittsburgh for the third game of the Series, on a cool, crisp October 12, Steve Blass brought the Pirates back from the brink of extinction when he defeated the Orioles, 5–1, before a crowd of fifty thousand screaming Pirate fans. Mixing a fastball, a curve, and a slider, the tall, slender Blass kept the Birds at bay until the fifth inning, when Brooks Robinson looped a single to left. Frank Robinson's homer in the seventh inning made it a 2–1 game. But then the Pirate first baseman, Bob Robertson, slugged a 3-run homer to give the Pirates a 5–1 victory.

The fourth game, on Wednesday, October 13, was the first night game in World Series history. It began as an Oriole parade—and ended in disaster.

The Birds jumped all over the Pirates' starting hurler, Luke Walker, for 3 runs, and twenty-one-year old Bruce Kison came in to pitch. Although Kison set a new one-game record by hitting 3 batters, he allowed the frantic Birds just 1 hit in six innings, while the Pirates kept pecking away at pitcher Dobson. The Pirates went ahead in the seventh after Dobson was taken out for a pinch hitter. Right-hander Ed Watt pitched the seventh inning for Baltimore and lost the game when Milt May singled home the go-ahead run for a 4–3 Pirate win.

The fifth game, played at Pittsburgh on a Thursday afternoon, was practically no contest. The Pirates' manager, Danny Murtaugh, gave the starting assignment to Nelson Briles, a veteran of two previous World Series with the Cardinals, and the right-hander pitched a magnificent ball game, allowing the Orioles just 2 hits.

Against such opposition, Baltimore's Dave McNally was no match for Briles. Bob Robertson opened the second inning by driving a McNally pitch 410 feet over the center field fence for a home run. Manny Sanguillen followed with a single, then pitcher Briles singled to center, scoring Sanguillen.

The Pirates scored a run in the third inning and then drove McNally to the showers with a barrage in the fifth. Gene Clines opened the inning with a triple over Blair's head in center field. Then Roberto Clemente, who had hit safely in 12 previous World Series games, singled up the middle, scoring Clines for the Pirates' fourth run. Then Briles set the Orioles down in the sixth, seventh, eighth, and ninth innings for a brilliant 2-hit 4–0 victory, which gave the Pirates a 3 games to 2 edge in the Series.

Frank Robinson and Brooks Robinson, baseball executioners, joined forces with one of their specialties, producing runs, in the tenth inning of game six, on October 16, and, as a result, the back-to-the-wall Orioles defeated the Pirates, 3–2, to even the Series at 3 victories each.

The Pirates got off to a 2-run lead in the first

Frank Robinson, the Orioles' great first baseman, slugged 2 home runs in the 1971 Series.

The Orioles' third-base magician, Brooks Robinson, made all those "impossible" stops in the 1971 Series. Here is just one example of his great play at third.

In his second World Series, Roberto Clemente drove out 12 base hits, including 2 home runs. Roberto scored 3 runs, drove in 4 more, and hit for a .414 average.

Pirates manager Danny Murtaugh (*left*) and his star pitcher, Nelly Briles (*right*), give each other a champagne bath after the Pirates defeated the Orioles in the 1971 Series.

three innings, the second run on an opposite-field home run by Roberto Clemente, who had tripled his first time up.

In the Orioles' half of the sixth inning, Don Buford led off with a home run; and in the seventh inning, Davey Johnson scored Mark Belanger with the tying run.

Now the pressure cooker was steaming:

Jim Palmer, taken out in the ninth inning for a pinch hitter, was replaced by Pat Dobson, who started the tenth with the score knotted at 2–2. Dave Cash singled with 1 out. Richie Hebner struck out, and on the third strike, Cash stole second. Clemente was purposely passed. McNally now came in to relieve Dobson. (It was the first time that a World Series game ever saw two 20-game winners relieve a third within two innings.) McNally walked Willie Stargell, filling the bases. But the threat was ended when Al Oliver flied out.

Then the Orioles made their big move:

Frank Robinson walked with 1 out, and then, running as if his life depended on it, Robbie rounded second and dived headfirst into third base on Rettenmund's long single to left. Gimpy leg and all, Robbie then scored the winning run on Brooks Robinson's short fly to Vic Davalillo.

The forty-four thousand fans didn't stop their shouting until a half hour after the game was over, for now the Series was tied at 3 games each.

Pirate manager Danny Murtaugh gave the ball to his pitching star, Steve Blass, for the World Series finale. Blass's only misadventure on a cool and cloudy Sunday, October 17, at Baltimore, occurred in the eighth inning. Until that time, the Orioles had managed just 2 hits.

Roberto Clemente, one of the great hitting stars of the Series, gave the Bucs a 1–0 lead in the fourth inning with his second Series homer. Stargell singled, and Pagan hit a double in the eighth inning, scoring Stargell, and the Pirates had a 2–0 lead.

The Birds could get only one of the runs back, on an infield out in their half of the eighth inning, and when Blass got Powell, Frank Robinson, and Rettenmund out in order in the ninth inning, that was the ball game and the Pirates were the world champions.

Thus, the Pirates had won their fourth seven-game World Series in as many tries.

Oakland Athletics Versus Cincinnati Reds

Years ago, growing up in Russelton, Pennsylvania, young Fury Tenace was a devout Yankee fan. The allegiance may have been from the rich Italian heritage of Yankee players: Tony Lazzeri, Frank Crosetti, Joe DiMaggio, Yogi Berra, Phil Rizzuto. Or maybe it was because the Yanks operated a farm club at nearby Butler, Pennsylvania. Whatever the reason, the teenage loyalty exploded one day and vanished when a Yankee scout, sizing up Gene Tenace's prospects as a future major leaguer, reported, "Not a chance."

Subsequently, the youngster was signed as a shortstop by Dan Carnevale, a scout for the Kansas City A's. The bonus was less than $10,000.

On October 14, 1972, the Yankees would have welcomed the onetime reject with open arms. Fury Gene Tenace had become one of the most promising catchers in the major leagues, and by 1972 had slowly edged his way into the regular lineup with a steady performance behind the plate.

When Oakland star Reggie Jackson injured his left leg sliding home against Detroit in the play-off series, he was scratched from the Series lineup. If the A's were to make a respectable showing, somebody would have to take up the hitting slack. Who but Tenace? In his first two at bats, Tenace slugged 2 home runs off pitcher Gary Nolan in the first game of the World Series to give the scrappy Athletics all the runs they needed

for a 3–2 victory. The 2 home runs were the first such accomplishment in a World Series since Rico Petrocelli of the Red Sox had done it in the sixth game of the 1967 Series against the Cardinals. But no one had ever homered twice in his first two World Series at bats.

Tenace unloaded his first blast in the second inning. With 2 outs, George Hendrick walked and scored when Tenace drove the ball out of the park, and the A's had a 2–0 lead.

The Reds retrieved 1 run in their half of the second inning, when Bench and Perez singled. Cesar Geronimo popped out, and Dave Concepcion smashed a hard grounder that scored Bench. But owing to Tenace's magnificent effort, the A's walked away with a 3–2 win.

In the second game, at Cincinnati, the A's, behind outstanding pitching by Jim "Catfish" Hunter, who won 21 games during the regular season, again stopped the Reds, 2–1.

Hunter had mastered the art of control as a youngster by throwing corn cobs through a hole in a barn fence at Hertford, North Carolina. On October 15, he had the Reds at his mercy, mixing his curveball, sliders, and an occasional fastball, allowing the Reds just 1 run on 6 base hits, to win game two for the Athletics.

In the cozy little family of the Cincinnati Reds, Jack Billingham responds to the nickname Rip. That does not mean that Jack is a ripsnort-

Pete Rose slides headlong into third base as Sal Bando makes a late tag. Action occurred in the seventh inning of game six of the 1972 Series.

ing, tearing-up kind of guy. His teammates merely concluded that any player who requires twelve to fourteen hours of sleep daily must be a lineal descendant of the fabled Rip Van Winkle.

However, there was nothing somnolent about the six-foot-four, 200-pound right-hander on the evening of October 18, 1972. Jack was invincible in the third game, allowing the hard-hitting Athletics just 3 base hits and striking out 8 as he pitched his ball club back into the World Series with a magnificent 1–0 victory.

The following night, the Reds almost had the Series tied, but then a furious last-minute rally by the Athletics gave the game to the A's. The Reds had a 2–1 lead going into the bottom of the ninth inning and, with 1 out, reliever Clay Carroll seemed to have the game under control. Suddenly, successive singles by pinch hitter Gonzalo Marquez, Tenace, Don Mincher, and Angel Mangual gave the A's 2 big runs and a 3–2 win, and a 3 games to 1 advantage in the Series.

Joe Morgan's contributions to the Cincinnati cause in the first four games of the World Series were hardly noticed. In 13 official trips to the plate, he did not get a hit. In the fifth game, Morgan continued on his hitless way. But the Reds would have lost the game were it not for Joe's 2 runs and some of the greatest defensive plays ever seen in a Series.

The Reds were trailing in the fifth inning by a 4–2 score with 2 outs when Morgan walked and stole second on Catfish Hunter's first pitch. Bobby Tolan singled and Morgan, running as if his life depended on it, scored all the way from second, making it a 4–3 game.

Three innings later, after Rollie Fingers had retired 7 consecutive batters, Morgan again walked and stole second. Then, in a repeat performance, Tolan singled and Morgan sprinted home with the tying run.

In the last of the ninth, the Reds were trying to protect a precarious 5–4 lead. John Odom was running for Tenace, who had walked; Odom was at third and Dave Duncan was on first. Bert Campaneris popped a high foul ball behind first base. Morgan waved everybody away, made the catch, then stumbled as Odom streaked for home plate. Then Joe fired the ball right on target to catcher Johnny Bench, and Odom was out, and the Reds had won a game that was an absolute must if they wanted to prolong the Series. They had defeated the Athletics in a thriller that had the more than forty-nine thousand spectators limp with exhaustion.

On Saturday, October 21, the Series resumed in Cincinnati and the Reds pounded the Athletics' starting pitcher, Vida Blue, and three relievers for 10 base hits, including doubles by Joe Morgan and Hal McRae, a triple by Concepcion, and a home run by Johnny Bench, to gain an easy 8–1 victory that tied the Series at 3 games each.

Freak plays make world champions, and the seventh game of the 1972 World Series had a number of weird happenings. Jack Billingham opened the game by retiring Campaneris on a routine fly ball to right field. Then Mangual drove a liner to center field that Bobby Tolan misjudged, and Mangual raced to third. Joe Rudi popped out, but Tenace chopped a grounder toward third base, and as Dennis Menke charged in for the ball, it hit a seam in the Astroturf,

Led by this menacing group of Oakland stars, the A's were favored to defeat the Reds in the 1972 Series: (*left to right*) Bob Locker, Mike Epstein, Reggie Jackson, Darrell Knowles, and Rollie Fingers.

leaped over Menke's head, and Mangual scored, giving the A's a 1–0 lead.

After facing only 13 batters in the first four innings, Odom tired, and when Perez singled and Geronimo walked in the fifth inning, Catfish Hunter came in to pitch to Hal McRae. On the first pitch, McRae drove a fastball to deep center field, but Mangual caught the ball at the wall. Perez scored after the catch and it was a 1–1 game.

Campaneris singled to open the sixth inning, and when Tenace stroked a two-base hit to left field, Campy scored the go-ahead run. Sal Bando, who led the Athletics in game-winning hits during the regular season, slashed a terrific drive to center field. Tolan streaked for the ball, but suddenly he was down on the turf; his left leg had crumpled. He gamely got up, played the ball to the infield, and collapsed once more as Campa-

neris scored, giving the Athletics a 1-run lead.

The Reds made a futile attempt to get back in the ball game in the eighth inning. Pete Rose singled and Joe Morgan slammed a double off the wall that sent Rose to third. The partisan Reds crowd was up on their feet yelling, pounding each other, for it looked as if the Reds had a big inning on the way. But pinch hitter Joe Hague popped out. Bench was intentionally walked, filling the bases. Perez sent a fly ball to center field and Rose scored after the catch, but Menke flied out to end the inning; and it was a 3–2 game with the Athletics in front.

The Reds again threatened in the ninth inning as they got Dick Chaney on base when he was hit by one of Rollie Finger's fastballs. But Pete Rose flied out to end the game that was a thriller from start to finish, and the Athletics were world champions.

1973

Oakland Athletics Versus New York Mets

The Oakland Athletics became the first team since the Yankees to win two successive World Series when they defeated the surprising New York Mets.

The Athletics had three 20-game winners in Ken Holtzman, Vida Blue, and Jim Hunter, and won the American League West over Kansas City by 8 games. Then they defeated the Baltimore Orioles, the Eastern Division winners, in 5 games.

The amazing New York Mets, at one time 12 games off the pace as late as August 5, won 20 of their final 28 games to capture their division title. They then went on to defeat the Western Division winners, the Cincinnati Reds, in a riotous five-day series.

Two fine left-handers opposed each other in the opening game of the World Series at the Oakland-Alameda Stadium, Ken Holtzman for the A's and Jon Matlack, a 14-game winner during the season, for the Mets.

Offensively, the Mets couldn't hope to cope with the power of the Oakland sluggers. Reggie Jackson had hit 32 homers; Sal Band, 29: Gene Tenace, 24; Deron Johnson, 19.

Although lacking in power, the Mets had the pitching craftiness and experience of Tom Seaver, who was approaching his greatest years, Jerry Koosman, Jon Matlack, and Tug McGraw.

Matlack was in marvelous form on opening

day, and the Athletics had difficulty hitting Jon's sweeping curveballs. As a result, they were able to get only 3 base hits. Unfortunately for the Mets' pitcher, all 3 hits came in the third inning and, combined with an unfortunate error, proved to be Matlack's downfall.

There were 2 outs and no one on base when Holtzman sliced a double down the third base line. Campaneris then grounded to Millan at second base, but Felix allowed the ball to go through him and Holtzman came all the way home to score. Campaneris then stole second and scored on Rudi's single. The 2 runs were all the A's needed to win game one by a 2–1 margin.

Tug McGraw, a free spirit who helped carry the Mets from sixth place to a National League pennant, with his team-rallying battle cries of "You gotta believe," found new converts in the camp of the Athletics on the afternoon of October 14, 1973.

McGraw entered the second game in the sixth inning when the score was 3–2, A's. He never let his teammates forget his proven battle cry, and at the finish, after the Mets had come from behind, time and time again, then won the game in twelve innings, 10–7, to tie the Series, Tug enjoyed perhaps the biggest moment of his career.

In a game that overflowed with rallies and counterrallies, outstanding and then shabby de-

318

fensive play, disputed plays throughout, and a parade of eleven pitchers, the Mets prevailed on the strength of a 4-run outburst in the third extra inning. After Bud Harrelson doubled to center, his third hit of the game, McGraw attempted to sacrifice the runner and slapped a bunt single, and both runners were safe when the pitcher kicked the bunted ball. Willie Mays, who had replaced Rusty Staub in the outfield, slashed a single over second base. Cleon Jones singled, and when Mike Andrews, the second baseman, made three successive errors, the Mets scored 3 big runs.

The A's rallied to tie the score. Bando walked; then Reggie Jackson and Tenace singled. Two runs scored and now it was a 6–6 game.

The action reached a climax as Harrelson led off the twelfth inning with a ringing double, his third hit of the game. Jones singled and Mays was walked, filling the bases. Grote then came through with a single, and the fourth Mets run of the inning crossed the plate, and now they had what looked like a safe 10–6 lead as the A's came up for their turn at bat in the twelfth.

The A's scored a run and filled the bases, and George Stone came in to relieve Tug McGraw. Stone finally induced the dangerous Campy Campaneris to hit the ball on the ground for an easy out. And the Mets had won a crucial game to tie the Series at 1 game each.

The Series shifted to New York for the third game, and the opposing pitchers, Tom Seaver for the Mets and Jim Hunter for the A's, were the aces of their respective clubs. A great pitching duel was anticipated by the fifty-five thousand goggle-eyed Met fans.

The Mets scored in the first inning as Wayne Garrett timed one of Jim Hunter's curveballs perfectly and slugged the ball into the stands for a home run. Felix Millan followed with a sharp single up the middle, and sprinted to third base when Rusty Staub singled. Millan then came in for the second Met run on a wild pitch.

Tom Seaver had mowed down the first three A's batters in order in each of the first five innings. But just as suddenly he tired, and Joe Rudi, leading off the sixth inning, timed a Seaver fastball, and slammed it to the far reaches of the ballpark before Don Hahn leaned into the stands to catch the drive. Then Sal Bando slugged a two-base hit. Tenace followed with another two-bagger, and the A's had their first run of the game.

The A's tied the score in the eighth inning. Campaneris opened the inning with a single to center field. He stole second on Tom's first pitch and scored as Joe Rudi singled.

As the eleventh inning began, Harry Parker, who had finally relieved Seaver, walked Ted Kubiak. Angel Mangual, the next batter, reached first base on a third strike that catcher Grote missed, and it rolled to the fence. Mangual saw Grote fumbling for the ball and continued on to second base. It was a costly error, as Campaneris then singled and Kubiak scored, and the A's had a 3–2 lead.

Rollie Fingers came in to pitch for the A's, and shut down the Mets without a tally in the eleventh inning, and that was the game.

The fourth game, at Shea Stadium, was highlighted by Rusty Staub Night, and the Mets' redheaded star had one of his greatest games.

Pitching star Tom Seaver of the Mets warms up before the start of game three of the 1973 World Series as his pitching coach, Rube Walker, looks on.

Reggie Jackson has just driven a pitch by Jon Matlack of the Mets over the left field wall for a 2-run homer in the 1973 Series. Jackson's homer occurred in the seventh game.

Rusty drove out 4 hits, including a home run and a walk in 5 visits to the plate, driving in 5 of his team's 6 runs as the Mets evened the Series with a resounding 6–1 victory.

In the fifth game, the upstart Mets then went out behind the airtight pitching of Jerry Koosman (six and a half innings) and Tug McGraw, who allowed the slugging A's just 3 base hits in a 2–0 thriller. Cleon Jones and Don Hahn were the hitting stars for the Mets. Jones doubled in the second and scored on John Milner's single, while Hahn tripled home a run in the sixth inning.

The action shifted to Oakland on October 20 for the sixth game of the World Series. Slugger Reggie Jackson's achievements thus far were hardly those of a leading candidate for the MVP Award. In the first five games, the Athletics'

outfielder, with 5 hits in 21 at bats, had compiled a .238 batting average. To make matters worse, Reggie had left 17 teammates stranded on the bases. But on the afternoon of October 20, before a jam-packed crowd of some fifty-thousand fans, the twenty-seven-year-old slugger responded crisply and emphatically with 3 hits in 4 at bats to lead his team to 3–1 victory, and tie the Series at 3 games each.

In the first inning of the game, with Rudi on first base, Reggie sliced a drive into left field and Rudi came all the way around to score. In the third inning, with 2 men out and Bando on first base, Jackson doubled off Tom Seaver, scoring Bando, to give the A's a 2–0 lead. In the eighth inning, Reggie led off with a single against Tug McGraw. But when center fielder Don Hahn

Celebrating their great win over the A's in the fifth game of the 1973 Series are (*left to right*) Tug McGraw, manager Yogi Berra, and Jerry Koosman.

let the ball skip by him, Jackson sped all the way to third base. Jesus Alou then lifted a high fly to left field that sent Reggie home.

The seventh and final game of the Series promised to be a pitchers' duel between the Mets' Jon Matlack and Kenny Holtzman. But the A's exploded in the third with a vengeance. There was 1 out when pitcher Holtzman sliced a double down the left field line. The next batter, Campaneris, outstanding on both offense and defense throughout the Series, drove a pitch out of the ballpark for a 2-run homer. Joe Rudi followed with a single, and then Reggie Jackson blasted a tremendous drive into the right field stands, and it was a 4–0 game.

Harry Parker came in to relieve Matlack, but the die was cast. The A's never relinquished their lead. In the sixth inning, successive two-base hits by Millan and Staub gave the Mets

their first run. But when Rollie Fingers came in from the bull pen to relieve Holtzman, the two runners were stranded as Rollie put down any further thoughts of a Mets rally.

The Mets made their final bid in the ninth inning when Milner led off with a walk. Hahn singled, and then Buddy Harrelson bunted, but the throw to first just got him and the Mets were down to their final out. Pinch hitter Ed Kranepool reached first base when Tenace bobbled his grounder, and Milner scored on the play.

The Mets now had the tying run at the plate as third baseman Wayne Garrett stepped up to bat. Rollie Fingers came in from the bull pen to pitch to Garrett, and got Wayne to pop the ball up—and the Oakland Athletics had defeated the Mets, 5–2, and had won their second straight World Championship.

1974

Oakland Athletics Versus Los Angeles Dodgers

They certainly were not Peace Corps candidates. Were they the modern-day counterparts of the brawling Gashouse Gang of fifty years ago? Well, they certainly might be if they continued to work at it.

On the afternoon of October 11, the Oakland Athletics, three-time champions of the American League, were awaiting the start of a team meeting in the visitors' clubhouse at Dodger Stadium in Los Angeles. Suddenly, and before most of the players were aware of what was going on, pitcher Rollie Fingers took out after Blue Moon Odom, a fellow pitcher, and the two men were punching and wrestling each other to the floor. Earlier in the season, there were scuffles between Reggie Jackson and Billy North, and when Ray Fosse, the peacemaker, tried to settle the fight, he suffered a crippling injury.

The Athletics did not leave their fighting spirit in the dressing room. They brought it right out onto the field at Dodger Stadium, and on the afternoon of October 12, before a record crowd of 55,974 howling baseball fans, the Athletics defeated the Dodgers 3–2 in classic A's style. The 1-run decision had become an Oakland hallmark. In the first game of the 1974 Series, the Dodgers squandered numerous scoring opportunities in nearly every inning and stranded 12 men on base.

Leading off in the second inning, Jackson slammed a pitch by Andy Messersmith for a home run, to give the A's a 1–0 lead. In the fifth inning, with no outs, pitcher Ken Holtzman pulled a double inside the third base line. Kenny advanced to third on a wild pitch, and then raced for the plate and scored as Campaneris dropped a perfectly executed suicide-squeeze bunt along the first base line, and it was 2–0, Athletics. The play caught the Dodgers completely by surprise and Holtzman scored easily.

In the fifth inning, the Dodgers shook off the lethargy that had marked their play and scored a run on a base hit, combined with errors by Tenace and Campaneris, and were back in the ball game, 2–1.

In the eighth inning, Sal Bando hit a chopper down to Ron Cey at third base. Ron scooped up the ball, but threw wildly to first, allowing Campaneris, who was on second base, to score.

With 2 outs in the ninth inning, Jim Wynn slugged a home run to bring the Dodgers to within 1 run of the A's. But Catfish Hunter protected the lead and the A's won by a 3–2 margin.

Vida Blue was manager Al Dark's selection in the second game of the Series. He was opposed by the Dodgers' most effective pitcher during the last half of the season, right-hander Don

Sutton. The Dodgers broke into the lead, scoring a run in the second inning, then adding 2 more in the sixth when Joe Ferguson homered with Steve Garvey on base. Meanwhile, Don Sutton had allowed the Dodgers just 4 hits, had struck out 10, and was in complete control of the situation as the Athletics came up to bat in the ninth inning.

Suddenly, the entire game changed. Bando, the first batter, was hit by a pitch. Jackson doubled to left, and that was all for Sutton, as manager Walt Alston brought in reliever Mike Marshall, who took the ball and promptly picked pinch runner Herb Washington off first base. Then, without even wasting a single motion, Marshall whipped over three curveballs to Angel Mangual. Mangual swung and missed each pitch and the game was over. The Dodgers had tied the Series with a sizzling 3–2 victory.

There was a day off, and the Series resumed at Oakland with a Tuesday night game that featured a surprise pitching choice for the Dodgers. Manager Walt Alston decided to pitch Al Downing, who had been ineffective most of the season. His opponent was Catfish Hunter.

Hunter, one of eleven children who grew up in a North Carolina farm family on the edge of a bear swamp, was a man with a high degree of native intelligence. But he would be the first to tell you that most of his life had revolved around three-, four-, and five-letter words, like *eat, sleep, work*. Hunter joined the Kansas City A's as a young nineteen-year-old with great potential. He won 8 games in his first year, and by 1974 had become a 25-game winner and one of the top pitchers in the league.

Undisturbed by the big crowd and his personal battles with owner Charles Finley concerning a long-overdue bonus, Catfish toyed with the Dodgers for seven and a third innings, allowing just 5 hits and 1 run, as he gained credit for a stunning 3–2 victory. It was the third such score in this Series in as many games, and the American League champions had gained a 2 games to 1 edge.

Andy Messersmith and Ken Holtzman, starting pitchers in the opening game of the Series, again opposed each other in the fourth game, at Oakland, before some forty-nine thousand fans. And once again Holtzman made a mockery of

Oakland's Sal Bando crashes into Dodger catcher Steve Yeager in the eighth inning of game one of the 1974 Series. Yeager held on to the ball and Bando was out on the play.

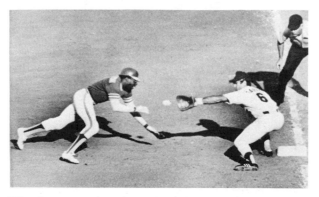

The former sprint champion Herb Washington of the A's was trapped off first base and put out in the ninth inning of the second game of the 1974 Series.

the American League's designated-hitter rule, first used in 1973, by starting the Oakland scoring, this time with a tremendous home run over the left field fence in the third inning. The Dodgers came right back in the fourth inning, when Bill Russell lined a 2-out triple to center, scoring Steve Garvey and Joe Ferguson, who had walked. They were to be the only scores for the Dodgers in the fourth game.

The A's wrapped up the game with a 4-run outburst in the sixth inning. North walked to open the inning. And when Messersmith attempted to pick him off first, he threw the ball away, and Billy sped to second. Bando then singled to center, and North scored. Jackson was purposely walked. Joe Rudi moved the runners along with a sacrifice fly, and when Claudell Washington walked, the bases were full. Jim Holt singled, scoring North and Bando. Then

Dick Green bounced into a force-out, scoring Reggie Jackson, and it was a 5–2 game, the A's in front; and that was the final score.

In the fifth game, the Dodgers and the A's were locked in a classic pitchers' battle between Vida Blue, making his fifth World Series start, and Don Sutton. The score was 2–2 going into the bottom of the sixth inning, with both pitchers allowing just 4 base hits. Mike Marshall took over for the Dodgers in the sixth, and retired the A's in order. He was preparing to pitch the first ball to the leadoff hitter, Joe Rudi, in the seventh, when suddenly there was a shower of missiles from the bleachers, and the umpires called a time-out. There was a fifteen-minute delay while the field was being cleared, and Rudi began to wonder about Marshall.

Unlike other pitchers, Marshall had his own ideas about the care and feeding of a pitcher's arm. He did not wear a protective sweater or jacket to keep his arm loose, during the interruption, nor did he take any warmup pitches when the action resumed.

When Rudi stepped into the box, Marshall had not made a pitch for at least fifteen minutes.

"Believe it or not," said Rudi, "but I sort of expected an inside fastball, and that's just what I got."

It was all Joe needed. He smashed into the pitch and drove it into the bleachers for a home run that gave the A's all they needed to win another World Championship, with a 3–2 decision.

Thus, the Athletics gained the distinction of being the only club other than the Yankees to win three successive World Championships.

Cincinnati Reds Versus Boston Red Sox

Two dreams nourished Luis Tiant through the eleven years he played major league baseball away from his native Cuba. One was to see his father again; the other was to pitch his Red Sox to a World Series championship.

But to pitch in a World Series game, to win it, to win it by a shutout over a team known to be one of the great clubs, and to do it with his beloved father sitting in the stands, was even beyond the wildest dreams of Tiant, the brilliant Red Sox right-hander.

Once again, Tiant was the dominant force in a ballpark normally dominated by big hitters. This time he stopped Cincinnati with just 5 hits to gain a surprising 5–0 shutout over the favored Reds in the first World Series game at Fenway Park. Tiant was cheered on almost every pitch by the Red Sox fanatics as he pitched perfect ball with his incredible spinning delivery until the fourth inning, when Joe Morgan singled to center field.

Tiant, himself, who had batted only once all year, because of the American League's designated-hitter rule, started the winning rally in the seventh inning with a single. It proved to be one of the biggest hits of the year for the Sox, when Dwight Evans followed with a bunt and beat out a poor throw for a base hit, and the Red Sox suddenly were threatening. Denny Doyle singled and the bases were full, and up came Carl Yastrzemski, the thirty-six-year-old hero of Boston since he joined the Sox in 1961. Carl singled to right field, and Tiant came home to score the first run of the game as Fenway Park vibrated with the cheers of the fans. Clay Carroll came in to pitch for the Reds and promptly walked Carlton Fisk, forcing in run number 2. Fred Lynn struck out, but Rico Petrocelli singled, and 2 more runs were home, for a 4–0 lead. Rick Burleson singled, driving in run number 5, and then Cecil Cooper gave the Sox fans a thrill as he powered the ball to the stands in right field, missing a homer by inches. Run number 6 came home after the catch.

And that was it: 6 runs for Boston, and the biggest inning in a World Series since the Tigers had scored 10 against the Cardinals in 1968.

The second game, played with rain falling through most of the contest, saw the Red Sox out in front by a 2–1 margin in an exciting battle until the top of the ninth inning. Then Johnny Bench, the first batter up, doubled to right, and Dick Drago was sent in to relieve Bill Lee. Drago got out the next two Red hitters, but Dave Concepcion hit a savage grounder up the middle that scored Bench. Concepcion then stole second base and scored the winning run on Ken Griffey's double as the Reds took a hard-fought thriller, 3–2. Cincinnati's speed on the bases was to be a constant threat throughout the Series.

Red Sox catcher Carlton Fisk homered in the twelfth inning to give the Bosox a 7–6 thriller in the sixth game of the Series.

The third game was made memorable by 6 home runs flying out of Riverfront Stadium in Cincinnati, by Bernie Carbo's pinch-hit home run, by record-tying back-to-back home runs, by a record-tying 2 errors by a catcher. But October 14, 1975, may be best remembered for a sacrifice bunt that traveled perhaps fifteen feet, but which unleashed streams of controversy and led to the Reds' victory in a ten-inning 6–5 cliff-hanger, giving them a 2 games to 1 edge in the World Series.

The hotly disputed play occurred in the tenth inning with Geronimo on first base. Jim Willoughby was pitching for Boston with nobody out, the score was tied at 5, and the more than fifty-five thousand fans in attendance were up on their feet, screaming for a Reds hit.

Eddie Armbrister, batting for pitcher Rawley Eastwick, dropped a bunt in front of the plate. Catcher Carlton Fisk, trying to reach the ball, collided with Armbrister, who seemed to hesitate before starting toward first base. After the brief collision, Fisk pounced on the ball, then threw wildly past second base as both runners advanced, Geronimo to third and Armbrister to second.

Then a full-scale argument ensued as the players and managers of both teams streamed out onto the field to argue with umpires Dick Stello and Larry Barnett. The Red Sox complained that Fisk was interfered with; the Reds, that Fisk reached for the ball and bumped Armbrister. When the furor subsided, the decision stood in favor of the Reds: There was no interference!

When play was resumed, Pete Rose walked, and then Joe Morgan slashed a sharp single to center, and Cincinnati had won another thriller, 6–5.

In the fourth game, on October 15, before 56,667 fans, the second largest crowd ever to watch the Reds at Riverfront Stadium, the Reds jumped out to a 2–0 lead in the first inning. But after a 5-run Red Sox rally in the fourth, Luis Tiant held the Reds in check for the remainder of the game. Although Tiant was sitting on the proverbial powder keg, it somehow never exploded. Fighting against faulty control and an unfamiliar pitching mound that gave him trouble, Tiant just managed to sidestep danger zones as he hurled the Red Sox to his second World Series victory, 5–4, deadlocking the Series at 2 victories apiece.

In the fifth game, Cincinnati's fine first baseman, Tony Perez, came out of his 0 for 15 slump with 2 long home runs to power the Reds to a 6–2 triumph over the Red Sox. But the slugging Perez had to share game honors with the Reds' star left-hander, Don Gullett, who pitched a magnificent game. Gullett, who worked eight and two-thirds innings, had allowed the Red Sox just 2 hits going into the ninth, and at one point had retired 16 consecutive Red Sox batters. He was taken out in the ninth inning after singles by Yastrzemski and Fisk and a double by Lynn gave the Sox 1 run. Then Rawley Eastwick came in to relieve a very tired Gullett, and Eastwick promptly fanned Petrocelli to end the game as the Reds took the fifth game.

The sixth game of the Series was postponed for four days by torrential rainstorms that swept through New England. The delay gave Luis Tiant four days of rest, and manager Darrell

Johnson, figuring that Tiant had the Reds' number, put him on the mound, opposed by the Reds' Gary Nolan.

In the first inning, with two Red Sox on base, Freddy Lynn slammed a 3-run homer into the right field stands to give the Sox a comfortable 3–0 lead. Tiant, trying for his third Series victory, sailed through the first four innings, but tired in the fifth frame and allowed the Reds to crash through for 3 runs to tie the game. Then the Reds surged ahead in the seventh inning, when they put together singles by Ken Griffey and Joe Morgan and then a double by George Foster to take a 5–3 lead.

Geronimo's homer in the eighth inning widened the Reds' lead to 6–3, and it appeared that they were almost certain winners as the Red Sox came up to hit in their half of the eighth. The Cincinnati Reds were just 4 outs away from the World Championship as Bernie Carbo, the hard-hitting Red Sox outfielder, came up to hit. Carbo took two pitches, both strikes, as the huge crowd implored Bernie, "Hit one out." And that's just what Carbo did on the next pitch, slugging the ball into the right field stands for a 3-run homer that tied the score.

Then, in the dramatic ninth inning, Denny Doyle opened the frame for Boston with a sharp single. And when Yastrzemski slashed a single to left, Doyle kept on running and dived into third base. And now the Red Sox fans were standing and screaming. Freddy Lynn then hit a short fly ball to left field, and Doyle, against instructions from the third base coach, tried to score after the catch, but was thrown out at the plate, and the crowd groaned. There was no further scoring as the heart-stopping thriller went into the tenth and then the eleventh innings.

Then, in the twelfth inning, Carlton Fisk enshrined his name in the Red Sox hall of fame as he slammed a long drive that caromed off the left field foul pole, fair by a few inches, to give the Red Sox one of the most exciting victories in World Series history, by a 7–6 score.

In the deciding seventh game, two left-handers, Don Gullett of the Reds and Bill Lee of Boston, defied the odds in the graveyard of southpaw pitchers, Fenway Park, by facing each other. For five innings, Lee held the Big Red Machine in complete control, spacing just 5 hits

Johnny Bench's home run in the third game aided the Reds in winning over the Bosox by a 6–5 margin.

and no runs as his teammates scored 3 runs in the third inning to give him a 3–0 cushion.

In the sixth inning, however, Lee became a victim of his teammates' blunders. Rose singled, and then Johnny Bench grounded to Rick Burleson for what should have been a double play. But Doyle, after taking the toss for a force-out on Rose, threw the ball into the Boston dugout and Bench went to second base. Then Tony Perez put the Reds right back into the ball game with a long home run.

Suddenly the Reds were alive and it was a 3–2 game. Their speed on the bases enabled them to tie the score in the seventh inning, when Griffey walked, stole second, and came all the way home on Rose's single. In the ninth inning, the Reds took the lead. Griffey walked, was sacrificed to second base, took third on an infield out, and then Joe Morgan singled him home with the run that gave the Reds a 4–3 win—and the World Series.

1976

Cincinnati Reds Versus New York Yankees

The New York Yankees won the pennant by defeating the Kansas City Royals in an intra-league battle royal that went to five games and was not decided until the very last man came to bat. The Yankees, appearing in their thirtieth World Series, but their first since 1964, bore no resemblance to the great Yankee teams of the past. They did, however, have a new manager, a sort of secret weapon, in Billy Martin, who had won with his teams in Oakland, Texas, Minneapolis, and Detroit. He was a proven winner and his teams displayed the same kind of arrogance and fight that their manager had always been proud of.

The Reds, sparked by several .300 hitters—Pete Rose, Joe Morgan, Ken Griffey, George Foster, and Cesar Geronimo—won the National League's Western Division title over the Dodgers, and then swept the Philadelphia Phillies, the Eastern Division champs, in 3 straight games.

Life as a baseball field-hand had not been all sunshine and roses for Tony Perez, veteran Reds first baseman. There were reports that management had grown dissatisfied with his production and his advancing years. And when he went 0 for 15 in the 1975 World Series, rumors of a trade were an almost daily occurrence.

But on October 16, 1976, Tony Perez put all his frustrations behind him in the first game of the World Series, driving out 3 hits and 1 run, and displaying bygone defensive moves as he led his team to a 5–1 victory over the slightly favored Yankees.

The Yankees surprised the Reds and everyone else by nominating Doyle Alexander as their starting pitcher, while the Reds' ace, Don Gullett, was primed for the opening afternoon game.

Joe Morgan, the Reds' great second baseman, started the Red Ball Express moving in the first inning by driving an Alexander fastball over the right field fence. The Yankees came right back on the attack in the second inning. Lou Piniella doubled and moved to third on a groundout, and scored the Yankees first run when Graig Nettles flied out.

The Reds scored again in the third inning on a triple by Concepcion, who ran home after Rose sent along fly to center field. In the sixth inning, Cincinnati added to their total on a walk to Pete Rose, a force-out by Griffey, and a single by Tony Perez, to make it a 3–1 game.

The Reds continued to hit Yankee pitching in the seventh inning, as Foster opened with a single and came in with the Reds' fourth run of the game when Bench slugged a triple off the right field wall. Sparky Lyle relieved Doyle Alexander, and his first pitch went over the head of his catcher, allowing Bench to score for the fifth and final run of the game.

The second game of the Series was played on a cold Sunday night, and both Catfish Hunter and Fred Norman were affected by the wind. Hunter, in particular, kept blowing on his pitching hand, but any relief from the cold, biting wind was temporary. In the second inning, the Reds jumped on the Catfish's offerings for 4 solid base hits and 3 big runs, and it looked as if this would be a very tough night for Hunter and the Yankees. In the fourth inning, however, the Bombers began to fight back, as Thurman Munson, Chris Chambliss, and Graig Nettles singled in succession for 1 run. In the seventh inning, another Yankee attack, headed by Willie Randolph, who singled, plus a two-base hit by Roy White, produced another score. A force-out that allowed White to score finally brought the Yankees to a 3–3 tie.

It appeared that the game would be forced into extra innings as Catfish retired the first 2 Reds in order in the ninth inning. But a throwing error by Yankee shortstop Fred Stanley enabled Ken Griffey to reach second base on an easy grounder. Joe Morgan was purposely passed, and then Tony Perez, the spoiler in this game, promptly belted Hunter's first pitch into left field for a single, scoring Griffey with the winning run, and the Reds had their second victory in two days, 4–3.

As a small boy in Waco, Texas, Pat Zachry dreamed big dreams of his future as a major league ballplayer. In his fantasies, he wore a white pinstripe uniform with "NY" emblazoned on his chest and cap. *If you're gonna dream,* thought the youngster, *you might as well go for the whole bundle.*

A portion of that childhood reverie came true the night of October 19, when Zachry, now twenty-four years old, walked onto the pitching mound at Yankee Stadium, wearing the double-knit grays of the Cincinnati Reds. And boyhood aspirations notwithstanding, Zachry pitched with poise and polish in pushing the Yankees one step closer to World Series extinction with a 6-hit, 6-strikeout performance and a 6–2 victory over the New Yorkers in game three.

A day of rain held off the fourth game of the Series, and when play was resumed on October 21, Gary Nolan was selected by manager Sparky

Anderson to clinch the Series for the Reds, while manager Billy Martin's choice was Ed Figueroa, a 19-game winner during the regular season.

Playing in 50-degree weather after an all-day rain, the Yankees jumped on Nolan in the first inning. Munson singled, and Chris Chambliss continued his effective play by driving in Thurman with a long two-base hit, and the Yanks were on the scoreboard with 1 run.

The Reds kept pecking away at Figueroa throughout the first three innings, but could not hit with men on base. That is, until the fourth inning, and then they hit Figgy with a vengeance. Joe Morgan walked to lead off the inning and promptly stole second. He scored when George Foster drilled a single to left. Then Johnny Bench slugged the first of his 2 home runs high up into the left field stands, making it 3–1, Reds.

The Yankees displayed a flash of their old aggressiveness when Mickey Rivers led off in

Chris Chambliss, Yankee first baseman, has just connected for a ninth-inning homer to win the play-offs for the Yankees.

In game four of the Series, Johnny Bench was a one-man wrecking crew as he blasted a 2-run and a 3-run homer to single-handedly demolish the Yankees. Bench hit for an amazing .533 average in the Series.

the fifth inning with a single and promptly stole second base. Thurman Munson then came through with another single, and Mickey scored to make it a 3–2 game.

That was the signal for Sparky Anderson to bring in his ace relief pitcher, Will McEnaney. McEnaney promptly shot a slow-breaking curveball to Chambliss, who swung hard but topped the ball, and it was an easy out and an end to the Yankee threat.

The Reds nailed the Yankee coffin shut in the ninth inning with a 4-run splurge that featured Bench's 3-run homer into the center field bleachers, giving the Reds a 7–2 lead.

The Yankees went down swinging in their half of the ninth inning, and the Cincinnati Reds were the world champions. Thus the Reds became the first team to win 7 straight postseason games, a pennant and a World Series sweep, since the beginning of the playoffs in 1969.

In his first full year as manager, Billy Martin brings his Yankees to the World Series.

1977

New York Yankees Versus Los Angeles Dodgers

The Los Angeles Dodgers began the year with rookie manager, Tommy Lasorda, who succeeded twenty-two-year veteran Walt Alston. Under Lasorda, the Dodgers won 22 of their first 26 games, racing into a lead in the National League. They began to tire late in the summer and slacked off a bit, but finally fought off several challenges by Cincinnati's Big Red Machine. The Dodgers took the Western Division title, then, after losing the opening game of the playoffs, won three straight from the Phillies to capture their sixteenth pennant since the turn of the century.

The Yankees, meanwhile, were reaching heights of soap opera drama as they struggled to take their second straight Eastern Division title in the American League. Their expensive free agents were riddled with injuries; manager Billy Martin fought constantly with owner George Steinbrenner and the team's new star, Reggie Jackson; the players quarreled in public with one another; and Martin was fired but reprieved while Jackson was benched for an important playoff game, but was later inserted back into the lineup. Notwithstanding, the Yankees won the division and American League flags.

In the opening game of the World Series, at Yankee Stadium, Billy Martin astounded the experts by starting Don Gullett, his high-priced free agent. The twenty-six-year-old fireballing left-hander, who had an outstanding 14-4 record during the season, had to be removed from the first playoff game because of a shoulder problem. Billy had figured Gullett was through for the season, but Gullett insisted he was all right.

Gullett had a shaky first inning, in which the Dodgers scored 2 quick runs that began with a walk to Davey Lopes, the leadoff batter, then a 400-foot triple by Bill Russell, a walk to Reggie Smith, and a long sacrifice fly by Ron Cey. Then it was Don Sutton's turn on the mound, and the thirty-two-year-old right-hander confessed that for him this was a night to remember: "I had been dreaming about pitching in Yankee Stadium all of my life. I've been pitching a lot of mental shutouts against the Yankees."

This time his fantasy was blurred before Sutton got the Yankees out in the first inning. He got Mickey Rivers and Willie Randolph out, but Munson singled and then Reggie Jackson looped a single to center. Chambliss scored Thurman with another single to center, and it was a 2–1 game.

The Yankees tied the score in the sixth inning on Randolph's home run. In the eighth inning, Munson ripped a hard drive down the left field line that was good for a double, scoring Randolph, who had walked, and the Yankees were out in front, 3–2. Then Elias Sosa, a righthander from the Dominican Republic, came in to strike out Piniella and Bucky Dent to end any further Yankee scoring in the inning.

Dusty Baker led off the Dodgers' ninth inning with a sharp single to left. Steve Yeager walked, and suddenly the Dodgers had a real threat going. With the game on the line, manager Billy Martin called a time-out and signaled for his ace reliever, Sparky Lyle. But Lee Lacy put the Dodgers right back into the game with a hard single to right, scoring Baker, to tie the game, 3–3.

The Yankees threatened in the tenth and eleventh, but failed to capitalize on their several opportunities. Then, in the twelfth inning, Willie Randolph shot a double to right field off reliever Rick Rhoden. Rhoden then walked

In the second game of the Series, Burt Hooten allowed the Yankees just 6 hits, to win, 6–1.

Munson, and Paul Blair, whose specific task was to sacrifice the runner along, fouled off two attempts. Then he slapped a hard single to left, and Willie Randolph scored with the winning run.

Yankee coaches questioned Martin's wisdom in starting Catfish Hunter in game two, for the Cat had not pitched for an entire month. In addition, he had experienced both arm trouble and a urinary infection. Nevertheless, Hunter started the game and was in immediate trouble.

With 2 outs in the first frame, Reggie Smith punched a double to center and Ron Cey poled a home run into the Dodger bull pen. The carnage continued in the second inning, when Steve Yeager hit a home run. And in the third inning Smith slugged a round-tripper with a man on base, and the Dodgers had a comfortable 5–0 advantage.

Meanwhile, Burt Hooton, humiliated and driven from the mound just five days earlier during the playoffs by the jeering and hooting of Philadelphia fans, came back beautifully in this game. He had the Yankees at his mercy, striking out 6 in three innings and allowing just 5 hits as he coasted to an easy 6–1 victory.

Tommy John was a thirty-four-year-old medical marvel whose left elbow had been operated on and completely rebuilt just three seasons earlier. The operation was so successful that John became a 20-game winner in 1977. Mike Torrez and lefty Tommy John were the pitching selections for the third game. It was the Yankees' first appearance in Los Angeles since 1963, and they quickly jumped on John. Mickey Rivers led off with a double; Willie Randolph was out on a ground ball to first, and Rivers dashed to third on the play. A moment later Mickey scored when Munson doubled past first base. Reggie Jackson followed with a single to left, scoring Thurman, and it was 2–0, New York. Lou Piniella kept up the attack on John with another single, and Jackson, running with the pitch, came all the way in to score the Yankees' third run off John.

There was 1 out in the Dodgers' half of the third inning when Reggie Smith singled to right. Garvey followed with another single, and then Dusty Baker, one of the four Dodgers to hit 30

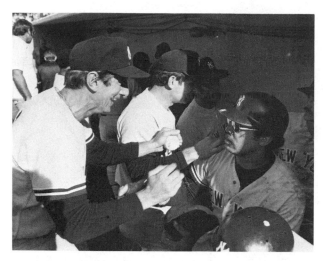

Billy Martin congratulates Reggie Jackson for his homer and double in the fourth game of the Series as the Yankees won, 4–2.

Loyal Dodger wives cheer for their husbands as the 1977 Series opens at Yankee Stadium: (*left to right*) Cindy Garvey, Gunnar Hooten, and Pattie Sutton.

Dodger fans greet their heroes at the L.A. airport, despite their loss to the Yankees in the 1977 Series.

Yankee outfielder Paul Blair is just about to be tagged at home by Dodger catcher
Steve Yeager in the first inning of game four.

homers during the season, drove a towering shot high into the Dodger bull pen for a home run, making it a 3–3 game.

Graig Nettles and Bucky Dent singled in succession to begin the fourth inning, and both runners advanced on a bunt by Mike Torrez. Rivers grounded out and Nettles scored on the play, to give the Yankees a 4–3 edge. The Yanks added a run in the fifth inning, giving them a 5–3 margin, as Mike Torrez held the Dodgers in check for another Yankee victory.

The next day, at Dodger Stadium, it was Tommy Lasorda's time to gamble on his pitching selection. He selected Doug Rau, a 14-game winner, to oppose Yankee Ron Guidry. Rau had come up with a sore arm and was of little use during the latter part of the season. But Lasorda had a hunch and played it. However, it was a poor one. The Yankees welcomed Rau with open arms, and knocked him from the box in the second inning.

Jackson doubled off Rau, and Piniella scored Reggie with an opposite-field single. Then Chambliss slammed a two-base hit and Reggie scored. Lasorda quickly brought in his fine relief pitcher Rick Rhoden. An infield out scored Piniella, and then Bucky Dent slapped an opposite-field single that scored Chris Chambliss. Three runs had been scored on 4 opposite-field base hits.

That was all the skinny, mustachioed Louisianian, Ron Guidry, needed. Guidry was at his very best as he allowed the Dodgers just 4 hits while striking out 9, to give the Yankees a 4–2 win and a decided 3 games to 1 edge in Series.

After batting practice before the fifth game, Lasorda called a crucial team meeting. Usually he was an evangelist in these meetings, but that day he was Father Flanagan, the famed founder of Boys' Town. "I told them how proud I was of them," Lasorda later said. "In my opinion, I told them, they were the best in baseball. I also told them that if they win today, they're gonna win 'em all."

And the Dodgers came out swinging their big bats. In the fourth inning, Davey Lopes led off with a sizzling drive over Rivers's head, and by the time the ball was retrieved, Lopes was on third base. Lopes scored on a Russell single up the middle. Ron Cey then smashed a long fly to Lou Piniella for an out. But Garvey doubled to left, scoring Russell. Then Dusty Baker scored Garvey with a hard single to left. Lee Lacy then smashed the ball to Graig Nettles at third base, but Nettles kicked the ball around and Lacy was safe at first. Billy Martin called time-out, and walked out to talk to Gullett. He reassuringly patted him on the back, then walked back to the dugout. Gullett stood on the rubber, kicked, and then fired his forkball into Steve Yeager. But the ball did not dip as sharply as it usually did, and Yeager drove the pitch out of the ball-park, making the score 5–0, Los Angeles. The Dodger crowd went wild with excitement.

Don Sutton eased up as the Dodgers picked up 5 additional runs; he gave up home runs to Munson and Jackson for 4 runs. But the Dodger lead was insurmountable, and Sutton coasted to an easy 10–4 win.

Mike Torrez was Billy Martin's pitching choice for the sixth game, hoping to wrap up the Series for the Yankees, while Tommy Lasorda came up with Burt Hooton. Lasorda's pitching selection seemed to be sound as Hooton got the Yanks out in one-two-three order in the first inning.

Torrez got the first two Dodger batters in the first inning, then Smith slammed a grounder to shortstop Dent and Bucky allowed the ball to go through for a hit. Smith then went to second as a pitch got away from catcher Munson. Ron Cey walked, and then Steve Garvey hammered a fastball for a long triple that scored Smith and Cey.

In the second inning, the Yankees tied the score when Jackson walked and Chambliss pounded a 400-foot home run into the bleachers. Reggie Smith again homered for the Dodgers,

Graig Nettles, the Yankees' great third baseman, makes an "impossible" catch in the third inning of the fourth game, on a hit by Dodger Davey Lopes.

in the third inning, to give the Dodgers a 3–2 lead. In the fourth, Munson singled and Reggie Jackson blasted a fastball into the bleachers, and the Yankees were back in front, 4–3. Hooton was replaced in the fourth inning by Sosa, and Sosa was in immediate trouble when Chambliss drove a towering fly ball to center that dropped between two Dodgers. Chris was safely on second base when the ball was retrieved, took third on a groundout, and scored on a sacrifice fly by Lou Piniella, and the Yankees had a 5–3 lead.

Rivers opened the fifth inning with a single, and then Reggie Jackson drove out his second home run to extend the Yanks' lead to 7–3. In the eighth inning, Reggie Jackson wrote his name in the record books with another, tremendous 450-foot blow for his third consecutive home run. And his fifth of the World Series.

The Dodgers got a meaningless run in the ninth inning to make the final score 8–4, New York.

And so the Yankees regained the World Championship they had last held in 1962.

1978

New York Yankees Versus Los Angeles Dodgers

"The Yankees had an abundance of talent in 1978," said Lou Piniella, in an interview with the author, "and we stayed eight to ten games over five hundred most of the first half of the year. The Red Sox, in the first place, were having a spectacular season. They were twenty games over five hundred at one point, and it looked like they would blow the league apart and march right into the World Series.

"And at Yankee Stadium, every day brought another fuss, another crisis. Mostly it had to do with Reggie Jackson and Billy Martin, and Thurman Munson and Steinbrenner.

"But we had those great stars. Ron Guidry, with a great fastball. And when Sparky Lyle taught him how to throw a nasty, vicious slider, he became one of the best pitchers in all of baseball. He was great late in 1977, but by 1978 he had a twenty-five and three record."

Billy Martin discussed his players in an interview with the author: "Graig Nettles at third base was one of the best, and Willie Randolph at second base was the league's finest. Bucky Dent was steady and reliable and made all the plays, while Thurman Munson was the absolute catcher, a great one. Speedy Mickey Rivers was one of a kind, and Roy White and Chris Chambliss were top-notch players. Our pitching staff

included Ed Figueroa, Ken Clay, Jim Hunter, Dick Tidrow, Jim Beattie, Ron Guidry, and the finest relief pitcher of them all, the fastball artist, Goose Gossage."

By July 19, the Yankees were fully 14 games behind the Red Sox, and seemingly out of the race. Then, after a series of bitter battles with Reggie Jackson and George Steinbrenner, Billy Martin, under great stress, resigned on July 24, and was replaced with Bob Lemon.

Lemon, a great pitcher for Cleveland for fifteen years, had managed at Kansas City and Chicago and knew he could handle the Yankees in this stressful period. Under Lemon, the Yankees began to move. They won 35 of their last 47 games and sprinted in front of the slumping Red Sox on September 11.

At season's end, the Yanks and the Red Sox were tied. In a three-game playoff, the Yankees beat the Red Sox on Bucky Dent's dramatic 3-run homer in the third game. They then defeated Kansas City in the American League playoffs and thus were well prepared for their thirty-second World Series, against their bitter West Coast rivals, the Dodgers.

The Dodgers fought their way past the Giants and the Reds to win their division title, then defeated the Phillies in the tenth inning of a thrilling finale to capture the National League flag.

The first game of the Series, in Los Angeles, featured a surprising barrage of base hits by the Dodgers, who had their batting togs on for the opening game and pounded four Yankees hurlers for 3 home runs, a total of 15 hits, and an 11–5 victory.

Lasorda's choice to pitch Tommy John was outstanding, for the clever curveball artist with a nasty slider had the Yankees at his mercy as they hit the ball up into the air, or drove it into the turf for easy outs. John held the Yankees scoreless until the seventh inning, when with a 7–0 lead he eased off, and Reggie Jackson drove out a home run. It was Reggie's eighth World Series home run. But Davey Lopes's 2 home runs, combined with 3 hits by Dusty Baker, gave the Dodgers an easy 11–5 win.

The second game was a spectacular battle that the Yankees, down by 1 game, were determined to win. They got off to a rousing start as Jackson smashed a double to left in the third inning, scoring Roy White and Munson.

In the fourth inning, Reggie Smith singled, and Ron Cey singled to bring in Smith. In the sixth, Cey homered with two on base for a 4–2 Dodger lead.

Roy White singled to start the seventh inning, and Terry Forster replaced the Dodgers' starting pitcher Burt Hooton. Paul Blair, the first Yankee to face Forster, greeted him with a double to left. Jackson grounded out and White scored on the play, to make it a 4–3 game with the Dodgers in front.

The Dodgers were leading by 1 run as the pressure-packed ninth inning began. The Yankees got their first two hitters on base with 1 out, and one of their most dangerous hitters, Thurman Munson, came to bat.

At that moment Tommy Lasorda had a hunch that his twenty-one-year-old fireballing ace, Bob Welch, could handle the situation. Welch, a year out of Eastern Michigan University, was a big winner in college circles and in the minor leagues, but now he was in a nail-biting crucial World Series game, against the mighty New York Yankees.

The Yanks had Bucky Dent on second base,

Paul Blair on first, and as Welch looked the situation over, he nodded to Lasorda and came in with his first pitch to Munson. A blazing fastball, which Thurman promptly hit to left field for an out.

Now it was all up to Reggie Jackson. Welch just stared at Reggie, hitched up his pants, and zinged his fastball past Jackson for a strike. Then a ball. Then strike 2. And then a whopping fastball that tore past Reggie, who swung and missed for strike 3.

The Yankee threat was ended and the twenty-one-year-old kid had knocked down the big Yankee hitters to win the Dodgers' second straight World Series encounter by a score of 4–3.

Some years prior to the 1978 World Series, a young second baseman, Graig Nettles, playing in the Twins' farm system, was asked to switch to third base because the club had several young and talented second basemen and they needed a third baseman at the time.

Dodger second baseman Davey Lopes leaps high into the air to avoid a rolling slide by Chris Chambliss, who attempts to break up a double play in the second inning of the third game.

Lee Lacy, Dodger pinch hitter, slides under Yankee second baseman Fred Stanley, attempting to break up a double play. Action occurred in the second inning of game one of the Series.

"I had considered myself as a hard-hitting second baseman," said Nettles, "but I had also seen Rod Carew play in the spring training games and I realized that my chances for making the majors were much better as a third baseman."

How well Graig Nettles succeeded was made clear on the night of October 13 in the third game of the World Series. While a crowd of more than fifty-six thousand at Yankee Stadium, and millions more on TV, watched in utter disbelief Nettles made perhaps half a dozen of the greatest plays ever seen at third base.

Roy White got the Yankees rolling in the first inning with a home run off Dodger starter Don Sutton. Then Nettles singled in the second inning, stole second, and scored on a groundout, to give the Yanks a 2–0 lead. The Dodgers got a run back in the third inning, when North walked, stole second, moved to third on a groundout, and scored on a single by Bill Russell.

Ron Guidry, who started for the Yankees, walked 7 batters and was in trouble on a number of occasions. But several double plays, plus a number of miracle plays by Nettles, saved the game for Guidry and the Yankees, who took a 5–1 decision from the Dodger Express, temporarily derailed by the combination of Guidry and Nettles.

Tommy John started for the Dodgers and Ed Figueroa was Bob Lemon's pitching choice for the fourth game of the Series at Yankee Stadium, and for four innings both pitchers held their respective opponents scoreless.

In the Dodgers' fifth inning, Yeager doubled, Lopes walked, and then Reggie Smith blasted a home run into the stands to give the Dodgers a 3–0 lead.

With 1 out in the sixth, Roy White singled and Munson walked as Tommy John seemed to tire. Jackson then singled, scoring Roy White, and Munson took second. Piniella smashed a line drive that hit off the heel of Bill Russell's glove, but the shortstop picked up the ball and stepped on second, forcing Jackson. Then Russell fired the ball toward first base in an attempt for the double play. The ball hit Jackson on the hip, bounced away from first baseman Garvey, and while that was going on, Munson scored.

The Dodgers, led by manager Lasorda, claimed that Jackson interfered with the throw. They said Reggie had leaned into the throw, and it hit him and was deflected. The Yankees, of course, argued that the throw hit Reggie. Finally umpire Frank Pulli ruled it was not interference and the play stood.

After the forty-five-minute argument, Dick Tidrow came in to relieve Figgy and held the Dodgers to just 3 hits and no runs in the three innings he pitched. Goose Gossage mopped up for the Yankees in the ninth and tenth innings, holding the Dodgers hitless. The Yanks scored 2 runs in the sixth inning and another in the eighth, to tie the score, 3–3.

In the tenth inning, Lou Piniella, hitless in four trips to the plate, came up to bat with runners on first and second and slammed Bob Welch's first fastball to right-center field for a clean hit, to give Yankees the run that meant victory.

Game five was a combination of timely Yankee hitting, poor Dodger fielding, and sensational pitching by a twenty-four-year-old Yankee rookie, Jim Beattie, who pitched his first complete game of the year that day, in defeating the Dodgers, 12–2.

Beattie, a six-foot-six-inch right-hander who was a fourth-round draft choice out of Dartmouth College just three years earlier, almost quit baseball during the 1978 season because he was so frustrated at his inability to win more than 6 games.

Jim scattered 9 hits in going the distance for the first time in the major leagues, and struck out 10 Dodgers, to give his team a 3 games to 2 advantage in the series.

The Dodgers, determined to tie the Series, started off the sixth game with a bang as Lopes greeted Catfish Hunter with a smashing drive that carried over the right field stands for a home run.

In the Yankees' half of the second inning, Graig Nettles led off with a single. Jim Spencer walked and Brian Doyle, subbing for an injured Willie Randolph, surprised Dusty Baker by slamming a pitch over Baker's head for a long double, tying the game. Bucky Dent singled, 2 runs came in, and the Yanks were in front 3–1.

In the Dodgers' third inning, Ferguson doubled and went to third on a sacrifice fly ball by Davalillo. Lopes singled, scoring Ferguson, and it was a 3–2 game.

In the sixth inning, Piniella singled and went to second on a wild throw. Then the double Ds went to work. Brian Doyle lined a sharp single up the middle and Piniella scored. Bucky Dent then smacked a single into left field, scoring Doyle. In the seventh inning, Jackson blasted a home run to deep right field with White on base, increasing the Yankee lead to 7–2. Hunter then calmly went about his business, retiring 10 Dodgers in a row. In the eighth inning, Goose Gossage took over and held the Dodgers in check, to give the Yankees their second straight World Series over the Dodgers.

Pittsburgh Pirates Versus Baltimore Orioles

Led by their seemingly indestructible thirty-eight-year-old captain, outfielder Willie "Call Me Pops" Stargell, the Pittsburgh Pirates came back after trailing the Baltimore Orioles 3 games to 1, to win 3 straight, and became only the fourth team in baseball history to win a World Series in such a manner.

Willie contributed a .281 batting average to his team during the regular season, plus a team record of 32 home runs, and provided the heart and soul of a great come-from-behind Pirate team as they whipped the Montreal Expos in the Eastern Division playoffs and then defeated the Cincinnati Reds in 3 straight games for the National League pennant.

The Baltimore Orioles had it easy in the Eastern Division of the American League, coasting to an 8-game lead over the Milwaukee Brewers. Piloted by their crusty manager, Earl Weaver, they defeated the California Angels to gain the American League pennant.

It rained so fiercely in Baltimore on the night of the first game of the World Series that Commissioner Bowie Kuhn postponed the game. It was the first time in Series history that a first game had ever been postponed.

The following night, Al Bumbry led off for the Orioles with a single. Mark Belanger walked and Ken Singleton bounced a double-play ball at Bruce Kison, who messed up the play, and

only Singleton was out. Eddie Murray walked, and then John Lowenstein hit another sure double-play ball to Phil Garner, who threw the ball away and both Bumbry and Belanger scored. Kison then tossed a wild pitch and Murray came home for the third run of the inning. Then Doug DeCinces unloaded a 2-run homer to make it 5–0 in the first inning, and that was all for Kison. Jim Rooker, the Pirates' capable relief pitcher, held the Orioles scoreless for the remainder of the game.

Meanwhile, Pittsburgh pecked away for a run in the fourth inning, 2 more in the sixth, and Willie Stargell homered in the eighth to put the Pirates within striking distance. But they couldn't get another run, and the final tally remained 5–4.

Eddie Murray, one of the game's leading batters, drove in 99 runs during the 1979 season. The fans anticipated a big hit each time "Edd-dee" came up to the plate.

In the second game, the Pirates moved out to a 2-run lead in the second inning on singles by Willie Stargell, Johnny Milner, and Bill Madlock, plus a sacrifice fly by Ed Ott. But then Murray walloped a long home run into the bleachers for the Orioles' first run, and it was a 2–1 game.

In the sixth inning, Murray scored Ken Singleton with a long two-base drive to tie the game at 2–2. Murray then went to third on an out and attempted to score on Lowenstein's fly to Dave Parker in center field. But Parker's throw was a thing of beauty. It came in on a clothesline to catcher Ed Ott, and Ott tagged Murray, and the Oriole threat was stopped cold.

The tie score was broken in the ninth inning as Ott, who had singled, went to second when Garner walked. Then Manny Sanguillen looped a long single to right field. Singleton scooped up the ball and fired it to the plate, but Murray intercepted the throw and wheeled and fired a perfect strike to the plate, attempting to get Ott, who was streaking for home. Ott just managed to get there and safely slid around catcher Rick Dempsey, who vainly tried to tag him. As Ott

scored the winning run, the crowd shrieked its appreciation of the beautiful precision of the play, and the Pirates chalked up a 3–2 decision.

When the Series shifted to Pittsburgh for game three, manager Earl Weaver selected Scott McGregor as the Orioles' pitcher, while manager Chuck Tanner selected John Candelaria to hurl for the Pirates. But Candelaria was raked for 8 hits and 6 runs in the three innings he pitched, and was relieved by Enrique Romo. Romo was also belted hard by the Oriole batters, and he in turn gave way to Kent Tekulve, the submarine pitcher.

Scott McGregor's balk in the first inning led to 1 run for the Pirates. He gave up 2 more in the second, as Garner drilled a double to left

Orioles pitcher Mike Flanagan, a 23-game winner during the year, outpitched four Pirate hurlers to win game one of the Series.

Appearing in his first World Series after eighteen years of play, Willie Stargell climaxed his great career, driving out 3 home runs in the Series.

The 1979 World Champion Pittsburgh Pirates

that scored Willie Stargell, who had singled, and Steve Nicosia, who had walked.

In the fourth inning, the Orioles filled the bases, and an obscure .247 batter for the team during the season, Kiko Garcia, smashed a triple, scoring 3 runs. In the seventh inning, Kiko singled in his fourth run of the game. Before the game was over, Kiko, whose only previous distinction was that his birthplace, Martinez, California, is the same as Joe DiMaggio's, had collected 4 straight hits to give him a Series average of .800.

Two long rain delays tormented both pitchers during the day, but McGregor seemed to get stronger after the game was resumed in the fifth inning, allowing the Pirates just 1 run as the Orioles coasted to an 8–4 triumph.

In the fourth game, at Pittsburgh, the Pirates jumped off to a 4–0 lead in the second inning, paced by Willie Stargell's tremendous home run. In the fifth inning, the Pirates added another run, and in the sixth, boosted their lead over the Orioles to 6–3. But the Birds started to hit in the eighth inning.

With the bases full, John Lowenstein slammed a double off Kent Tekulve that scored 2 runs. A few minutes later, as the Orioles again filled the bases, pinch hitter Terry Crowley doubled, and 2 more runs crossed the plate for the Birds. Tim Stoddard followed with a single, and the fifth run came across the plate. Finally, Al Bumbry grounded out, but the sixth run scored on the out and the Orioles took a 9–6 win.

For four innings, the fifth game of the Series at Pittsburgh was a brisk, efficient pitching duel between the red-haired Jim Rooker and Mike Flanagan, the Orioles' tough lefty. The Orioles finally broke through in the fifth to take a 1–0 lead. But the Pirates got a pair of runs in the sixth inning on 2 hits, and added 2 more runs in the seventh and 3 in the eighth, and they romped to a 7–1 victory.

John Candelaria, "the Candy Man," who was knocked out of the box in the fourth inning of the third game, made a great comeback in the sixth must-win game by hurling six strong innings, allowing the Birds just 6 hits, all singles. Kent Tekulve took over in the seventh inning and gave up just 1 base hit and struck out 4 to enable the Pirates to tie the Series at 3 games each, with a 4–0 shutout.

"Wonderful Willie" did it for the Pirates in the seventh and final game of the Series. That's Wonderful Willie Stargell. The "patriarch of the Pirate family" put his big bat where his stars were, over his heart, and delivered the big punch as the Pirates came from behind and defeated the Orioles.

Down 1–0 in the sixth inning, Willie Stargell exploded a 2-run homer off Scott McGregor to turn the game around for the Pirates. Pops Stargell also singled twice and slammed a double, giving him 25 total bases for the Series, tying Reggie Jackson's record set in 1977. Willie also set a Series record with 7 extra-base hits—4 doubles, and 3 home runs—and was voted the World Series MVP.

In the sixth inning, the Bucs took the lead on Stargell's home run with a man on base, and they were never caught. Going into the ninth inning the Pirates faced five different pitchers and scored 2 runs, to win the game, 4–1, and the World Series.

Although the outstanding star of the Series was Willie Stargell, who batted an even .400, Phil Garner, the Pirate second baseman, had the top batting average, an even .500. Kent Tekulve's 3 relief saves were one of the features of a championship team effort by Pittsburgh.

Philadelphia Phillies Versus Kansas City Royals

Of the sixteen teams playing major league baseball in 1903, two teams had not won a Series championship by the time 1980 rolled around, the St. Louis Browns and the Phillies.

The St. Louis Browns participated in their only World Series in 1944, but lost to the Cardinals. So when the franchise shuttled off to Baltimore in 1954, the Browns still had never won a Series.

The Kansas City Royals, defeated in the playoffs in 1976, 1977, and 1978, finally exacted revenge against their chief rivals, the Yankees, and swept three straight from the Bombers in the 1980 playoffs to finally win the American League flag. They were ready and more than able to challenge the only other team never to win the World Championship, the Philadelphia Phillies.

Long-suffering Phillies fans couldn't wait for the October 14 opening game, as a crowd of some sixty-six thousand jammed every inch of the huge Veterans Stadium. And for the first time in twenty-eight years, a rookie pitcher started and won the opening game, as the Phils rallied to defeat the Royals in an exciting 7–6 battle.

Bob Walk, a twenty-two-year-old Californian, was selected by the Phils for a very simple reason: The Phillies were exhausted by five tremendous playoff games against the Astros, did not have anybody else. And although Walk was burned by 2 home runs hit by Willie Aikens, and another by Amos Otis, he pitched with his head and heart into the eighth inning and more than fulfilled his role.

Manager Dallas Green once more watched his club start slowly before rallying, as they had throughout the season and playoffs. The KC Royals pounded Walk in the second inning as Amos Otis cracked a 2-run homer his first time at bat to give KC a 2–0 lead. In the third frame, Willie Aikens drove out a homer with a man on base to boost the KC lead to 4–0.

The Phils, however, revived in the third inning, blasting the KC pitcher, Dennis Leonard, for 5 runs. They added runs in the fourth and fifth innings, to give them a 7–4 advantage.

But just when they thought they had the game well in hand, Willie Aikens, celebrating his twenty-sixth birthday, slugged a tremendous home run, his second of the game with a man on base, to give the Phillies the "Willies" as they hung on to survive by a slim 7–6 margin.

In game two, at Philadelphia, the Phils staged a come-from-behind charge and delivered a rabbit punch to the Royals, defeating them, 6–4, in one of the most exciting games ever seen in Philly.

Behind 4–2 going into the eighth inning, the Phils blasted Dan Quisenberry, the submarine hurler, for 4 hits and 4 big runs to clinch the game.

Now it was a 2 game to 0 deficit for the Kansas City Royals, but that was only part of the bad news for KC. George Brett, KC's great star, who had tried desperately to hit .400 during the regular season but wound up with a .390 average, had to leave the second game after going 2 for 2 at the plate. It was disclosed that Brett was in considerable pain, suffering from hemorrhoids.

Then a medical miracle occurred. Brett entered the hospital, had minor surgery, and within twenty-four hours was in uniform, swinging a bat. And that was just about the worst news for the Phillies.

Just hours after leaving the hospital, Brett drove out a home run in the first inning of the third game off pitcher Dick Ruthven, and was on base once more in the tenth inning when Willie Aikens lashed a single to left. Streaking around the bases as if his life depended on it,

Brett came all the way home on the hit. The winning run by Brett brought the Royals their first World Series win ever played in Kansas City.

For the Phillies it was a night of squandering opportunities and that old matter of baseball being a game of inches. They tied a Series record by stranding 15 base runners.

Larry Christenson started on the mound for the Phils in the fourth game. He never knew what hit him after Willie Wilson, the first KC batter, shot a sharp single to left. A wild throw let Wilson sprint all the way to third base. Brett shot a triple to left-center, scoring Willie, and then Aikens slashed a long home run into the stands. Hal McRae doubled to left, and then Otis slugged another double. Four runs were in, and Christenson staggered out of the pitching box. Dick Noles, who relieved him, gave up the second consecutive home run by Aikens, and it was 5–1, KC.

The Phils threatened in the seventh and eighth innings, scoring in each, but Quisenberry shut down the Phils in the ninth inning and KC took

The Royals doused everyone in sight with champagne after winning the American League flag, beating the Yankees in 3 straight games.

Lefty Steve Carlton won game two of the Series, then followed four days later with a magnificent 7-hit win to give the Phillies their first-ever championship.

the game, 5–3, and the Series was even at 2 games each.

Manager Jim Frey selected twenty-two-year-old Marty Bystrom to pitch the fifth game of the Series. He was opposed by 18-game winner Larry Gura, and for three innings both pitchers shut down the opposition. But in the fourth inning, Bystrom, pitching too carefully to hard-hitting Mike Schmidt, tried to sneak a fastball by, and Mike slugged the ball out of the park for a 2-run homer and a 2–0 Phils lead.

The Royals came back in the fifth inning to score their first run. An inning later, Amos Otis, the first batter up, tied the game with a long homer. Clint Hurdle, the next batter, singled. So did Darrell Porter, and when U. L. Washington drove a fly ball to center, Clint scampered home with a go-ahead run, and the Royals had a 3–2 edge.

Quisenberry, the KC relief ace, came in to relieve Larry Gura in the seventh inning, the Royals still clinging to that 3–2 lead. Dan did a fine job holding the Phils scoreless until the top of the ninth, when Mike Schmidt got the Phils moving with a single off Brett's glove at third base. Del Unser, in a pinch-hitting role, slugged a long double to left-center, and Schmidt sprinted home with the run that tied the score, 3–3. Keith Moreland moved Unser to third base on a sacrifice, and then Manny Trillo chopped a single to center field and Unser galloped home, to put the Phils on top, 4–3.

Tug McGraw was sent in to pitch the ninth inning against KC, and sent quakes of fear rippling all the way to Philadelphia when he walked three batters. Then, with 2 outs, the huge crowd standing and screaming, McGraw hitched up his pants and struck out Jose Cardenal on three steaming fastballs, and the Phillies had a nerve-wracking but happy 4–3 victory.

For the sixth and what would prove to be the final game of the Series, manager Dallas Green called on his ace, Steve Carlton, who had pitched eight excellent innings in game two, while manager Jim Frey's choice was Richie Gale.

In the top of the third inning, Bob Boone walked and stole second base. Lonnie Smith beat out a grounder, and Pete Rose bunted, to fill the bases. Then Mike Schmidt popped a single to left field, 2 runs came in, and the Phils had a 2–0 lead.

The Phils pecked away, picking up 2 more runs by the end of the sixth inning. But the Royals managed to get two men on base in the eighth inning; Carlton was taken out and Tug McGraw, who had already appeared in three games, came in to hold back the tide. KC managed to get 1 run off Tug. In the ninth inning, the Royals filled the bases with 2 outs, and the crowd was up and screaming. They were in a frenzy, shouting for McGraw to hold the Royals.

McGraw looked at manager Green, standing near the dugout, hitched up his pants, and then came in with three of the swiftest pitches Willie Wilson had faced all season, and Wilson went down swinging. And the Phillies were world champions for the first time in their history.

1981

Los Angeles Dodgers Versus New York Yankees

"You gotta have heart . . . miles and miles and miles of heart," according to the hit song from the musical comedy *Damn Yankees*. And the 1981 edition of the Los Angeles Dodgers had enough heart to extend through a dozen zip codes. It was a team with a porous over-the-hill infield, a team constantly flirting with disaster, and, in the end, a team with remarkable courage.

In addition to courage, the 1981 Dodgers had added charisma in the person of Fernando Valenzuela, a roly-poly, twenty-year-old pitcher who in the course of a single season had become an instant folk hero. He arrived in Los Angeles in the fall of 1980 fresh out of the Texas League with two things going for him: a flamboyant personality, and a controlled screwball that danced a cha-cha as it broke over the plate. In 1981 "the Cha-cha Kid" won 13 big ball games for the Dodgers, games that meant the West Division title. The Dodgers, with outstanding pitching by Jerry Reuss, Burt Hooton, Valenzuela, and Bob Welch, snatched the division title from the Astros and the pennant from the Montreal Expos in a series of thrilling games, and were more than ready to do battle with the 1981 Yankees.

The Yankees had been idle for four days waiting for the National League pennant to be decided after they defeated the Milwaukee Brewers

to win the Eastern Division, and then, hardly working up a sweat, swept the Oakland A's in 3 straight games to win the pennant.

For manager Tommy Lasorda and his Dodgers, it was almost a case of déjà vu, starting the Series with leadoff man Davey Lopes in the first game at Yankee Stadium. Lopes slammed a ball to the left side of the infield. Graig Nettles, at third base, made a miraculous stop, then gunned him down with a great throw to first.

In the Yankees' half of the inning, Jerry Mumphrey singled, Lou Piniella doubled, and then Bob Watson drove a pitch over the left field wall to give Ron Guidry a 3–0 lead.

In the third inning, the Yankees scored another run off a tiring Reuss, after which Reuss was relieved by Bobby Castillo, who promptly walked four Yanks in a row. Now the Bombers were ahead 5–0.

Steve Yeager's solo home run in the fifth inning gave the Dodgers their first run of the game, and when Ron Guidry tired and left the game in the seventh inning, Ron Davis relieved him, walked two batters, and then the Yankees' ace reliever, Goose Gossage, took over. Pinch hitter Jay Johnstone, the first batter to face the Goose, singled home a run for the Dodgers, and then Dusty Baker's long fly ball brought in another

348

run. Steve Garvey caught hold of one of Gossage's fastballs and banged a murderous drive toward third base. But Nettles once again made one of his amazing saves. He flung himself, fully extended, off the ground to his right, and speared the ball in his glove tip. That catch halted a Dodger rally and saved the game for the Yankees, who took a 5–3 win.

"I get sick to my stomach watching Nettles make those plays," said Lasorda. "He must go to bed hoping and praying he can kill us with his glove."

In the second game, the Dodgers faced a former teammate, Tommy John, on the mound for the Yankees. The pitcher with the "bionic" arm, who was traded to the Yanks by the Dodgers in 1979 and was a 22-game winner in 1980, was at his very best as he allowed the Dodgers just 3 base hits in the seven innings he was on the mound. Gossage relieved John in the eighth inning and got the Dodgers out in order in the last two frames for a marvelous 3–0 shutout, and the Yankees' second straight win.

Once again the Dodgers had their backs to the wall. And when a mild earthquake hit southern California on the morning of the third game, Los Angeles fans took it as an omen of a disaster for the team. Even Ron Cey's 3-run homer in the first inning didn't seem to be enough as the

Yankees came back with a vengeance, roughing up Valenzuela on Bob Watson's homer, Rick Cerone's two-base hit, and a single by Larry Milbourne, which accounted for 2 runs. Then the Yanks pounded Fernando for another pair of runs in the third on Piniella's single and Cerone's home run, to take a 4–3 lead.

Suddenly, Valenzuela seemed to come apart; he could not get his screwball over the plate, and when he eased up on his fastball, the Yankees clobbered his pitches. The experts were now second-guessing Lasorda: Why was he staying with Valenzuela when the rookie didn't seem to have it?

Lasorda was thinking the same thing along about the fifth inning, with the score now 4–4, and the Dodgers had the bases full. Mike Scioscia slammed into a rapid-fire double play that gave the Dodgers a 1-run lead, but cut off a most promising Dodger rally.

Horrible baserunning by the Yankees and an incredible catch by Ron Cey in the eighth inning with two men on base gave the Dodgers a breather, and Fernando finished the game with a flourish, to give the Dodgers their first Series victory by a narrow 5–4 margin.

The Dodgers continued their come-from-behind battle in the fourth game at Los Angeles, and once again fate seemed to be riding with

Dodger third baseman Ron Cey has just smashed a line drive down the third-base line, but Graig Nettles dives for the ball, makes the catch, and flips it to second base for the double play in the second game of the Series.

Rival managers in the 1981 World Series, Billy Martin and Tommy Lasorda

the Dodgers as Yankee ineptness turned the tide. Bob Welch started for the Dodgers, but he was bombarded for 3 hits and 2 runs before he got a man out, and was relieved by Dave Goltz, who was not much better. By the end of three innings, the Yanks had a 4–2 lead, and by the bottom of the sixth inning they had extended the lead to 6–3.

However, a walk to Scioscia, followed by Jay Johnstone's pinch-hit homer off reliever Ron Davis, gave the Dodgers 2 runs to bring the score to 6–5, Yankees. Then Lopes hit a high fly ball to Reggie Jackson, who staggered around and then lost the ball in the sun, allowing Davey to reach second base. Bill Russell singled Davey home, and it was a 6–6 game. In the seventh

inning, another Yankee misplay gave the Dodgers 2 more runs as Bobby Brown misjudged Rick Monday's routine fly ball, resulting in 8–6 Dodger advantage.

Reggie Jackson homered in the seventh inning to bring the Yanks to within a run of the Dodgers, 8–7, but there was no further scoring and the Dodgers had come back to tie the Series.

The Dodgers, as defined by Jerry Reuss, are fighters who "don't know when they've had enough." They seem to be at their best when the lights are about to go out.

Ron Guidry was staked to the only run he seemed to need in the second inning of the fifth game when Reggie Jackson led off with a whistling double down the left field line. He went to third as Lopes kicked around Watson's grounder, and scored when Piniella singled. Thereafter, the Lightning Kid from Louisiana settled into a frightening groove. He struck out the side in the fourth inning, and when he got Dusty Baker in the seventh inning he had 9 strikeouts. Suddenly, in the seventh inning, Manny Mota, a Dodger coach, called to his next two batters, Pedro Guerrero and Steve Yeager, and whispered some instructions to them just before they went up to bat.

"Now, both you guys," he said, "stand a little back in the batter's box and don't swing as hard as you usually do. This will give you a better and longer look at Guidry's pitches."

Well, something worked, for both Guerrero and Yeager lined home runs into the stands and the Dodgers had a 2–1 edge.

Jerry Reuss retired the next 12 of the final 13 Yankee batters, firing in his fastball at speeds clocked at more than ninety miles per hour, limiting the Yankees to just 3 hits in the final two innings, and the Dodgers took a thrilling 2–1 squeaker from the Yankees.

The sixth game was anticlimactic, as the Dodgers invaded Yankee Stadium so intent on beating the Yanks in their own ballpark, they felt that nothing could hold them back.

But it wasn't that easy. The Yankees jumped off to a 1–0 lead in the first inning.

And the Dodgers came back fighting in the fifth. They got two men on base when Ron Cey pounded the Yankee pitcher, George Frazier, for a triple that brought in 2 runs. In the sixth inning, with Rick Reuschel on the mound for the Yankees, Cey drove in 2 more runs with a long single that gave the Dodgers a commanding 8–2 lead. pedro Guerrero's home run in the eighth inning made the final score 9–2, and the Dodgers had come from behind to win the World Series of 1981.

To call the Dodgers' comeback incredible

Twenty-one-year-old Fernando Valenzuela was invincible in the pinches and defeated the Yankees in game three of the Series.

would be an understatement. They had been down 2 games to 0 in the Series, and had done the unbelievable taken 4 straight games, exactly as the Yankees had steamrolled them in 1978.

After the game and the celebrations, Tommy Lasorda said, "This is the greatest thing that ever happened to me in nearly twenty-five years in baseball. These guys have given me a lifetime of thrills in a single season. I've always wished that if the good Lord ever let us win the World Series, it would be against these Yankees who beat us twice."

St. Louis Cardinals Versus Milwaukee Brewers

"It was the kind of beating that could affect a team's collective psyche. Just how good were those Milwaukee Brewers? This first game of the 1982 World Series was a disaster for us," said MVP Darrell Porter in an interview with sportswriter Dick Young.

"It started right in the very first inning at St. Louis, when Ben Oglivie drove in a run. Then, Gorman Thomas drove in another run, giving the Brewers a two to nothing lead.

"The Brewers then proceeded to trounce us by a score of ten to nothing, cuffing our pitchers for seventeen hits. Third baseman Paul Molitor became the first player in a World Series to get five hits in six trips to the plate. His teammate Robin Yount got four hits.

"Our starting pitcher, Bob Forsch, was taken out of the game in the sixth inning with the score four to nothing against us. Forsch was replaced by forty-three-year-old Jim Kaat. Kaat was the second oldest man ever to appear in a Series and was our only effective pitcher.

"Their pitcher, Mike Caldwell, was dazzling. He threw only fifty-two pitches in the first five innings, and by the time the game was over, a hundred and one, with sixty-four of these strikes. After I doubled in the second inning, he retired twelve of us in a row."

The next day, October 13, the Cardinals tied the World Series at 1 game apiece at St. Louis, when they defeated the Milwaukee Brewers, 5–4 on a highly unglamorous but fateful play, a walk with the bases full in the eighth inning.

In game three, just five months after he was promoted from the minor leagues, twenty-three-year-old Willie McGee stood in the glare of the World Series limelight and said, "I must be dreaming. I don't believe this." The young outfielder from San Francisco was the hero of the third game and was celebrated all over town for his 2 tremendous home runs and 4 runs batted in to spearhead the 6–2 win by the Cardinals.

Manager Whitey Herzog's joy with McGee was mixed with anxiety over Joaquin Andujar, his starting pitcher. Andujar had a 2-hit shutout going into the seventh inning when he was struck by a drive off the bat of Ted Simmons. The right-hander was carried off the field by teammates and taken to Mount Sinai Medical Center, where he was treated by the team's physician, Dr. Stan London.

In the fourth game, pitcher Dave LaPoint dropped a throw from Keith Hernandez on Ben Oglivie's ground ball in the seventh inning with the Cards out in front, 5–1. "It didn't seem very important at the time," said Oglivie.

But that dropped throw gave the Brewers a new life and they quickly made the most of it. Don Money followed with a line single, and the huge crowd of more than fifty-six thousand came alive. Then, with 2 outs, second baseman Jim Gantner lined LaPoint's first pitch to left-center for a double, scoring Oglivie, and before the inning was over the Brewers had cashed in 6 runs and had a 7–5 lead that they held on to for dear life. Now the Series was tied at 2 games each.

In game five at Milwaukee, Robin Yount and the Brewers were both expecting. The shortstop, who singled twice, doubled, and then finished his day with a long home run to help the Brewers to a 6–4 win, was happy that the game was over and his team had won. But he was also eagerly anticipating news from the hospital where his wife was awaiting the birth of their third child. She waited until the Series concluded before delivering their baby.

As delighted as they were about Yount's incredible play and the expected new member of the Yount family, the good citizens of Milwaukee were awaiting their city's first World Championship in twenty-five years, and the entire state of Wisconsin was agog with the excitement. Each time Yount came up to hit, the crowd shouted, "MVP, MVP, MVP," and with each at bat he tried to prove them right. In the very first inning, Robin singled and scored the game's first run. In the third, his two-base hit set up the Brewers' second run. In the seventh inning, his solo home run gave his team a 4–2 lead. Two more runs in the eighth inning wrapped up the game for the Brewers.

The Series moved back to St. Louis for the sixth game, and the Cardinals bounced back with a savage 13–1 trouncing of a hapless Milwaukee Brewers team. Rookie John Stuper, who had to wait out two rain delays, totaling a two-and-a-half-hour wait, was magnificent as he allowed the Brewers' heavy hitters just 4 hits while pitching the complete game and tying the Series at 3 games each. First baseman Keith Hernandez and catcher Darrell Porter were the batting stars for the Cards, as both players drove out 2-run homers. Hernandez drove in 4 runs and scored twice. Designated hitters Dane Iorg banged out 2 dou-

bles and a triple as the Cards exploded for 12 hits to deflate the Brewers under an avalanche of 13 runs.

The seventh and deciding game of the World Series, played in St. Louis, was won by Joaquin Andujar, who allowed the Brewers just 7 hits in seven innings, and just five days after a brief hospitalization to care for his injured right knee.

In the fourth inning of a scoreless tie in which both pitchers were working with great deliberation, Willie McGee and Tom Herr of the Cards singled in succession, then Lonnie Smith singled, scoring McGee. However, in the top of the fifth inning, Ben Oglivie hammered Andujar's first pitch high into the balcony, and it was a 1–1 ball game.

Then, in the sixth inning, both teams fired their best shots, and the Cards prevailed. In the top of the inning, Jim Gantner doubled, and then Paul Molitor laid a bunt down along the

Cardinals star Willie McGee sparkled in the field with three defensive gems, then slugged 2 home runs to win game three of the Series.

third base line. Andujar pounced on the ball and threw it wildly past first, and Gantner raced home and Molitor went to second. Yount singled and Molitor went to third, and then scored on a sacrifice fly by Cecil Cooper. Now the Brewers had a 3–1 advantage.

In the bottom of the sixth, Ozzie Smith singled and Lonnie Smith doubled. Manager Harvey Kuenn yanked Pete Vuckovich and replaced him with Bob McClure, a ninth-inning hero in a pervious game. But that didn't work at all. Gene Tenace walked and the Cards had the bases full. Keith Hernandez, batting at this dramatic moment, and on his twenty-ninth birthday, gave himself and his team a big present by smashing a single to center, scoring 2 runs and tying the game at 3–3. George Hendrick, up to hit with first and third occupied, pushed an opposite-field single to right that scored the third run of the Cards' rally, and they now led 4–3.

In the bottom of the eighth inning, the Cards wrapped up the game and the Series with 2 more runs. The St. Louis Cardinals had won their ninth World Championship.

"This is the most fun I've had playing baseball in my entire career," said catcher Darrell Porter. "I can't believe this."

To the surprise of many baseball people, Darrell Porter was voted the World Series MVP.

Milwaukee catcher Darrell Porter won game six for the Brewers with a 2-run homer to tie the Series.

1983

Baltimore Orioles Versus Philadelphia Phillies

The National League champion Phillies and the American League champion Orioles were as different as cheese steaks and crab cakes, but they did have a couple of things in common. One was a firm belief in two-platoon baseball. The other was outstanding pitching.

The Orioles were clearly the Series favorites even though they couldn't utilize Ken Singleton in his favorite spot as the club's designated batter. That could hurt the Birds, for Singleton was one of the club's top hitters and a home run threat.

It was a rainy, cold night on October 5 when some fifty-two thousand fans, many dressed in yellow or orange slickers and looking like thousands of autumn leaves, started screaming, "Eddie! Eddie! Eddie!" for their favorite Oriole home run slugger, Eddie Murray. Then the cheers burst into a full-throated roar of, "Reagan! Reagan! Reagan!" as President Ronald Reagan and a large entourage of Washington politicos entered the stadium.

Jim Dwyer started the excitement as he selected a 3 and 2 fastball hurled by the Phillies pitcher, John Denny, and crashed his big bat into the pitch, connecting solidly for a home run into the bleachers. The big bad Birds were off and running with a 1-run lead.

Scott McGregor faced only 16 batters through five innings, one more than the minimum. But

then, with 2 outs in the sixth inning, Joe Morgan jumped on a curveball and drove it into the seats for a homer, and the game was tied at 1–1. The next batter facing McGregor was Garry Maddox, and Garry slugged a pitch into the seats, putting the Phils in front, 2–1.

John Denny left the game in the eighth inning, after Al Bumbry doubled. Al Holland, who threw nothing but fastballs, got the side out in the eighth and ninth innings, and the Phillies had done the improbable—beaten the Orioles in Baltimore in game one by a 2–1 margin.

Mike Boddicker, just out of Norway, Iowa (population 633), pitched his way into the hearts of Oriole fans in game two with a dazzling 3-hitter. Mike had the Phils' big bats completely baffled as he fanned 7 batters, issued no walks, and no earned runs, and tamed the Phils, 4–1. Boddicker's performance was the finest by a rookie pitcher since little Dickie Kerr spun a 3-hitter in the infamous 1919 World Series for the Black Sox against Cincinnati.

When the teams shuttled via Amtrak to Philadelphia on October 14 for the third game, the Phils were all hopped up by a tremendous homecoming crowd of more than sixty-five thousand fans who welcomed the "Gee Whiz Kids as if they had already won the Series.

But the Birds eked out a tense, exciting pitching battle between two marvelous, combative

The Orioles' star Jim Palmer allowed the Phils just 8 hits in game three and won the game, 3–2.

There were three pitchers with a combined total of eight Cy Young Awards featured in the game: Mike Flanagan (one award), who started for the Birds but left the game in the fourth inning, trailing 2–0; Steve Carlton (four awards), who started for the Phils and lost the lead and the game; and Jim Palmer (three awards), who pitched two innings in relief for the Birds and was the winning pitcher.

Not many hours after the Birds had taken the 3–2 thriller, the two teams faced each other in game four at Philadelphia on a sunny autumn afternoon, October 15.

The starting pitchers for the fourth game, Storm Davis and John Denny, pitched three splendid scoreless innings before the Orioles got moving. The Birds filled the bases in the fourth

Catcher Rick Dempsey was the offensive star in the Series as he slugged out 4 doubles, a triple, and a home run for a .385 average.

pitchers, Mike Flanagan for the Orioles and lefty Steve Carlton, the first 300-game winner to ever pitch in a World Series, by the score of 3–2, merely because Benny Ayala sliced a base hit in the seventh inning, scoring Rick Dempsey, who had just doubled.

There was a curious and embarrassing change that manager Paul Owens made with his lineup in this game; he benched forty-two-year-old Pete Rose, one of the team's great stars. It began to look as if Owens was beginning to panic.

inning on consecutive singles by Jim Dwyer, Cal Ripken, and Eddie Murray. Then Denny fanned the dangerous John Lowenstein. But Rich Dauer slammed a long single to left and 2 runs crossed the plate.

The Phils came right back in their half of the inning when Pete Rose singled to center for the Phils' first hit. Mike Schmidt, hitless in 13 trips to the plate, hammered a single to left and Rose dived into third base on the play. Then Joe Lefebvre lined a two-base hit to left-center, scoring Rose, making the score 2–1. In the fifth inning, the Phils tied the game. Bo Diaz doubled, and then Denny hit a liner that Lowenstein misjudged and it fell for a single, scoring Diaz with the tying run. Then Pete Rose brought the huge crowd up on its feet with a long drive that went for a double, scoring Denny, and the Phils had a 3–2 edge.

But not for long. Manager Joe Altobelli sent up six pinch hitters in the unbelievable sixth inning, and the Orioles managed to squeeze out 2 runs to take a 4–3 lead. In the seventh, the Birds added another run, to make it 5–3.

The Phillies fought back in the last of the ninth and scored 1 run. But it was their last gasp as they lost the heartbreaker, 5–4.

For the fifth game of the Series, manager Altobelli called on his young star, Scott McGregor, while manager Owens's selection was second-game pitcher Charlie Hudson.

McGregor was dazzling. He allowed the Phillies just 5 base hits, allowing no more than 1 hit in any inning. Eddie Murray finally fulfilled the fans' continual cheers with 2 tremendous home runs to lead the Baltimore Orioles to a 5–0 romp over the Phillies, and wrap up another World Series for the Orioles, their first championship since 1970.

The day after the Series ended, the city of Baltimore virtually shut down. Hundreds of thousands of people lined the downtown streets hours before the scheduled noon victory parade. "This is the greatest parade in the history of American sports," said Orioles owner Edward Bennett Williams as he addressed the mob from the steps of City Hall. And when Rick Dempsey, the MVP of the Series, was introduced, the crowd's roar shook the building's foundations.

1984

Detroit Tigers Versus San Diego Padres

The Detroit Tigers bolted to a 35-5 start in the first month and a half of the 1984 pennant race, and then romped to the division title as they won 104 games, and 15½ games ahead of Toronto, their nearest rival. In the playoffs, they never trailed, even for half an inning, during their 3-game sweep of their bewildered rivals, the Kansas City Royals.

The San Diego Padres did the seemingly impossible in the playoffs against the Chicago Cubs, coming back from a 3–0 deficit in the fifth game of the National League championship series to beat the Cubbies and one of baseball's best pitchers, Rick Sutcliffe, 6–3. It was the first time that the sixteen-year-old Padres had even been in a playoff. San Diego had not had a major champion in any sport since the Chargers won the American Football League title in 1963.

The Tigers' Lou Whitaker started the fireworks in the first inning. He was the first batter and promptly smacked one of Mark Thurmond's fastballs for a solid two-base hit. Alan Trammell followed with a single, and Whitaker scampered home with the first run of the Series.

But the dead-game Padres came right back as Steve Garvey and Graig Nettles banged back-to-back singles, and when Terry Kennedy lashed a double to left-center, both Garvey and Nettles scored. The noisy Padres fans were beside themselves with excitement.

Neither team scored again until the Tigers' half of the fifth inning, when Lance Parrish doubled and then Larry Herndon slugged Thurmond's fastball into the right field seats and the Tigers had a 3–2 lead. Jack Morris held the Padres in check for the rest of the game, striking out 9 Padre batters for the victory.

The Tigers were leading 3–2 in the second game and seemed headed for win number 2, when the stumbler, Kurt Bevacqua, the Padres' thirty-seven-year-old utility outfielder, in and out of the major leagues since 1971 with half a dozen clubs, became an instant and unforgettable San Diego hero. Bevacqua came up to hit with Nettles and Kennedy on base and drove Dan Petry's second pitch, a slider that just seemed to hang in air, into the left field seats for only his second home run of the season, and the Padres were out in front, 5–3. Pitchers Andy Hawkins and Craig Lefferts held the Tigers for the rest of the game and the Padres had their first-ever World Series victory.

A World Series record was set in the third game, at Detroit on October 12, for the most men left on base. Together, both teams left 24 on base. Another World Series mark was for the most bases on balls surrendered by San Diego pitchers: 11.

The Tigers got 1 run in the second inning when Herndon walked with the bases full. Then,

Second baseman Lou Whitaker was the defensive star for the Tigers as they defeated the Padres in the 1984 Series.

Shortstop Alan Trammell drove out 2 home runs and led the Tigers' offense with a brilliant .450 average as they captured the Worlds Series over the Padres in 1984.

with his wife, Julie, looking on, cheering along with the fifty-one thousand other Tiger fans, Marty Castillo slugged a home run off Tim Lollar with a man on base. Then another run scored when Kirk Gibson was hit by a pitch in the third inning, also with the bases full.

The Padres, however, did threaten Tiger pitcher Milt Wilcox in the seventh inning, when they scored on a single by Tony Gwynn, a double by Steve Garvey, and a sacrifice fly by Nettles. But that was all the scoring for the Padres as they went down to their second Series loss, 5–2.

The fourth game, at Tiger Stadium on October 13, followed the pattern so evident in the Tigers' postseason play. Detroit jumped off to a quick lead in the first inning, when Whitaker

reached first on an error and then Eric Show, the Padres' hurler, fed Alan Trammell a 2 and 0 fastball and Trammell punched out a home run. In the third inning, Whitaker singled and once again Trammell slammed a home run, into the upper deck this time, and the Tigers were out in front, 4–1.

Tiger pitcher Jack Morris, who went the full nine innings in the opening victory, allowed the Padres just 5 hits and 2 runs. The Padres simply couldn't hit Morris's split-fingered fastball, which did a dipsy-doodle fadeaway as it reached the hitters.

Said Morris after the game, "Deep down I wonder if Babe Ruth could have hit the split-finger. I've seen Ty Cobb hit on film, and I know he couldn't hit a forkball."

Jack Morris, ace of the Tigers' staff, beat the Padres in game one, then four days later won his second game of the Series, allowing the Padres just 5 hits.

The former Michigan State grid star Kirk Gibson drove in 7 runs and hit for a .333 average in the 1984 Series for the Tigers.

The fifth and what proved to be the final game of the Series began with the familiar quality of the first four games. Lou Whitaker hit Mark Thurmond's first fastball for a solid single to open the game. Alan Trammell was out on a fielder's choice; then Kirk Gibson slugged one of the longest home runs ever seen in Tiger Stadium, landing the ball high in the upper deck in the right-center field. Then Thurmond fell apart and allowed singles by Lance Parrish, Herndon, and Chet Lemon, and the Tigers had a 3–0 lead. Thurmond was taken out and relieved by Andy Hawkins.

The Padres, however, not to be denied, began to peck away, scoring a run in the third and 2 more in the fourth, until it was a 3–3 game into the fifth inning.

Andy Hawkins had been holding the Tigers since their first-inning revolt, but got into trouble in the fifth. Gibson singled, Herndon walked, and Hawkins was relieved by Craig Lefferts. Rusty Kuntz hit a high pop fly to right field, but Gwynn lost the ball. Alan Wiggins, at second base, made the catch, but he was out of position to make any kind of a strong throw to the plate, and Gibson easily scored. That run proved to be the game-winner.

In the seventh inning, Goose Gossage relieved Lefferts as Lance Parrish came up to bat. Parrish fouled off Goose's first fastball, then drove the next pitch into the seats for a home run and the Tigers led 5–3.

In the eighth inning, Bevacqua moved the Padres closer, by smashing a home run into the left-center field seats, and making it 5–4. In the Tigers' half of the eighth, Kirk Gibson came up to bat with two men on base and slugged one of Gossage's pitches into the seats. The Tigers had an 8–4 lead that they held into the final inning to take the World Championship.

The World Series win made Sparky Anderson the first manager to win championships in both the National and American leagues. Anderson managed the champion Cincinnati Reds in 1975 and 1976 and the 1984 Tigers.

Kansas City Royals Versus St. Louis Cardinals

The 1985 World Series was the first all-Missouri Series since 1944 when the Cardinals and the St. Louis Browns clashed for the Championship. Now in 1985 the Cards had returned to the Royals' stadium to battle the Royals.

Kansas City, with an offense built around the spectacular hitting of George Brett, and the home run power of the rotund Steve Balboni, who hit 36 homers during the season, were a solid, steady, if not spectacular team. They had preciously won six divisional titles and two American League pennants, but were still striving to win their first World Series.

The St. Louis Cardinals, on the other hand, had been regular visitors to the Series. They were old, experienced hands who had appeared in thirteen previous championship Series during the past sixty years and had won nine World Series.

For the first game at Kansas City, manager Dick Howser selected twenty-three-year-old Danny Jackson, his 14-game winner during the season. Jackson was opposed by the Cardinal ace, Johnny Tudor, who had finished the 1985 pennant race in a blaze of glory, winning 20 of his last 21 games.

KC jumped out ahead, 1–0, in the second inning, when Jim Sundberg walked and moved to second base on Darryl Motley's single. Then big Steve Balboni punched out a long single to left, scoring Sundberg with the first run of the game.

The Cardinals bounced back in the third inning. After Terry Pendleton walked, catcher Dyrrell Porter bounded a single up the middle. Tudor flied out to center field, and Willie McGee grounded out, Pendleton scoring on the play. In the fourth inning, Tito Landrum doubled and scored on Cesar Cedeno's two-base drive, and the Cards had a 2—1 advantage, which they held on to going into the ninth inning. The Cards delivered the kayo punch when Tommy Herr singled and Jack Clark scored Herr with a smashing line drive to left-center field, giving the Cards a 3–1 win.

In the second game, it was Charlie Leibrandt who proved that he could be invincible in a big game. Charlie's off-speed pitches had the Cards off balance most of the game as he allowed them just 2 base hits, struck out 6 hitters, and was leading 2–0 going into the ninth inning.

In the ninth inning, Willie McGee opened with a smash off George Brett's glove that was good for a double. Then Leibrandt settled down and retired Ozzie Smith on a groundout and got Tommy Herr on a long fly ball, and it was up

Cardinals first baseman Jack Clark drove out 6 hits in the Series in a vain effort to defeat KC. It wasn't enough.

The sportswriters were calling shortstop Ozzie Smith of the Cardinals the Magician for his astonishing defensive play in the Series.

to the Card slugger, Jack Clark. With a 3 and 0 count on him, Jack slammed the ball past Brett at third base, scoring McGee, and suddenly it was a 2–1 game. Hard-hitting Tito Landrum then slapped a two-base texas leaguer, but the slow-moving Clark held up at third base. Cedeno was purposely walked, and Pendleton, with a 2 and 1 count on him, just managed to make contact with the ball. It fell in for a two-base hit and 3 runs scored, giving the Cards a 4–2 victory. The Cardinals became the first Series team since the 1939 Yankees to enter a game in the ninth inning 2 runs behind and then go on to win.

Game three belonged to the twenty-one-year-old right-handed star of the Royals, Bret Saberhagen, a second-year major leaguer, who in 1985 had developed into one of the finest pitchers in the major leagues, posting a 20-6 record. Pitching with the knowledge that he might become a

father, for the first time, while the game was in progress, Saberhagen later said he had had the jitters in the first couple of innings.

Saberhagen had but one momentary lapse; it came in the sixth inning, when successive singles by Lonnie Smith, Herr, and Jack Clark trimmed the KC lead to 4–1. But the Royals struck again and scored 2 more runs to seal a decisive 6–1 win over the Cardinals.

John Tudor started game four for the Cards. Dick Howser's choice was Bud Black. But it was Tudor who dominated this game as he allowed KC just 5 base hits and struck out 8 batters to post an outstanding 3–0 victory for the Cardinals. He was in trouble in just one inning as he recorded his sixteenth straight victory in Busch Stadium and his twenty-third win in twenty-five starts since starting the 1985 season. Now the Cardinals had a command-

Dick Howser, manager of the KC Royals

Twenty-one-year-old Bret Saberhagen won 2 games in the Series, including a 5-hit game in the last one that finalized Kansas City's first championship.

ing 3 game to 1 margin in the Series.

The Johnny Tudor story is one of the strangest in the long history of baseball. The young pitcher had come to the Cards from the Pirates in 1984, and had struggled all through the first ten weeks of the season. He had compiled a disastrous 1-7 record by late May and got the feeling that he was about to be sent down to the minor leagues.

One day he received a phone call from a Dave Bettencourt, who had been his catcher in high school. It seems that Bettencourt, while watching Tudor pitch on TV in a Cardinal game, had noticed a serious flaw in the pitching motion of his former battery mate. On the phone that day, he explained his thoughts to Tudor, and then Tudor adjusted the flaw in practice. The change in his pitching motion and the results were incredible. He began an amazing comeback, won 20 games during the rest of the 1985 season and

his success was one of the principal factors that sparked the Cards to the division championship.

In the fifth game, twenty-three-year-old Danny Jackson spun a dazzling 5-hit game to chalk up a 6–1 victory for the Royals' second win of the Series.

The exciting sixth game was filled with nail-biting tension as the two opposing pitchers from game two, Charlie Leibrandt and Danny Cox pitched shutout ball for seven grueling innings. Both pitchers were relieved in the seventh with the score still 0–0.

In the eighth inning, Terry Pendleton singled and went to second base on an error. He then scrambled all the way home when Brian Harper, batting for the pitcher, singled and it was 1–0, in favor of St. Louis. Jorge Orta beat out a ground ball and was safe at first. Then Balboni singled, sending Orta to second base. Hal McRae

KC's George Brett was the offensive star of his team, driving out 9 hits and compiling a .375 average as the Royals won their first championship.

walked and then Dane Iorg singled, scoring 2 runs, and the Royals had snatched a 2–1 squeaker to tie the Series at 3 games.

The two pitchers for the final game of the Series, John Tudor and Bret Saberhagen, did not last very long. Tudor simply couldn't get his curveball into the strike zone and had to rely on his fastball. When he switched to his fastball, he was hammered.

In the second inning, with the score 0–0, Balboni walked. Then Darryl Motley smashed a long home run to put Kansas City ahead 2–0. In the third inning, Tudor crumbled. Lonnie Smith walked, Brett singled for his fourth hit, and then Tudor walked Frank White and Jim Sundberg to force in run number 3.

Tudor was taken out of the box, and Bill Campbell came in to relieve him for the Cards. The first batter to face Campbell was Balboni and Steve promptly singled, scoring 2 more runs, making it a 5–0 game. In the fifth inning, the Royals pounded four Cardinal pitchers for 6 base hits and 5 more runs, turning the game into an 11–0 runaway, as Saberhagen swept the Cards down in order with only 5 base hits, all singles, and the Kansas City Royals were the world champions for the first time in the club's history.

1986

New York Mets Versus Boston Red Sox

It was only fitting that in the sixteenth and final inning of the longest and most dramatic game in postseason history of the National League, after the Mets had spurted ahead in the fourteenth inning and Bill Hatcher of the Astros tied the game with a dramatic home run, Ray Knight should deliver the tie-breaking run for a momentous 7–6 Mets victory. Knight's blow was a smashing line single to right field that followed Darryl Strawberry's double. It was a hit that won the pennant for the New York Mets.

Ray Knight, who knocked in clutch runs for the Mets in the ninth and sixteenth innings, said later, "This is my sixteenth year in professional baseball, and I've never been involved in anything as emotional or been under such pressure."

It was the third pennant won by the Mets since they had joined the league just twenty-five years earlier as comical underdogs. It was a performance filled with heroes, quirks, and even scuff marks on baseballs. The Mets hit only .189 as a team, but still defeated the Astros. Jesse Orosco came out of the bull pen four times and heroically won 3 games, including the finale.

And in Boston, with the ghosts of seventh games past lurking in every corner of Fenway Park, the Bosox buried their own cursed history and added another painful chapter to the history of Gene Mauch by defeating the Los Angeles Angels, 8–1 for the American League flag and a

berth against the Mets in the World Series.

Now the Red Sox were in New York, a town that hated them, to tangle with the Mets at Shea Stadium in a World Series that seemed anticlimactic for both clubs.

October 10 was the great Oktoberfest at Shea Stadium, and a jammed crowd bundled in winter gear waited for the cry "Play ball."

To open the first game, manager Davey Johnson selected Ron Darling, a 15-game winner during the season, while John McNamara, the Red Sox skipper, selected his 13-game winner, Bruce Hurst.

Both teams reached the World Series with solid offensive power, but in this first game it was strictly the pitchers who ruled the game. And for seven tense, exciting innings neither team was able to mount any sort of an attack.

There was still no score when Darling began the inning by walking Jim Rice. Then Ron wild-pitched and Rice moved on to second base.

Then came the first break of the game, costly for the Mets. Rich Gedman hit a grounder to Tim Teufel at second base that just sliced along the ground and suddenly scooted beneath Teufel's glove for an error. Rice scored as he beat Strawberry's throw to the plate, giving Boston a 1–0 advantage; and that was the final score.

In game two, Davey Johnson selected his young fastball ace, Dwight Gooden, while McNamara

The Mets' opening-game pitcher, Ron Darling, gets Wade Boggs out on this dazzling strike across the plate in the first inning at Shea Stadium.

Dwight Gooden pitches to the Red Sox's leadoff batter, Wade Boggs, in the first inning of the second game of the Series.

Lenny Dykstra slides home safely to score in the seventh inning of the third game of the Series at Boston.

Mets catcher Gary Carter waits for a late throw from the outfield as Bosox runner Dave Henderson drives in to score Boston's lone run of the game in the third inning of the third game.

went with his Cy Young star, Roger Clemens, who had chalked up 24 wins during the season. There was no score until the third inning, when the Red Sox quickly touched Gooden for 4 hits and 3 runs.

In the Mets' half of the third inning, they managed to get back 2 runs, making it a 3–2 game. Then in the fifth inning, Dwight Evans homered with a man on base. The 2 runs plus a run in the fourth inning put the Red Sox ahead by a 6–3 margin, and seemingly they were out in front to stay as they had hit Gooden freely and quite often.

But suddenly the Mets began to reach Clemens in the fifth inning. They put together a hit, a walk and a stolen base to score their third run and McNamara, realizing that Clemens was not up to par, removed his young pitcher and brought in Steve Crawford. Then, in the sixth inning, reliever Bob Stanley came in to pitch and held the Mets to 2 hits, while the Sox had a field day scoring 3 more runs to post an easy 9–3 victory.

The teams moved to Fenway Park in Boston with the Red Sox 2 games up in the Series. The situation now looked rosy for the Sox as the

teams squared off for game three. Left-hander Bob Ojeda, acquired from Boston in an eight-player trade that sent Cal Schiraldi, among others, from the Mets to Boston, was the Mets' pitching choice. He was opposed by Oil Can Boyd, a 16-game winner during the season. But Boyd was hit hard and often during the seven innings he worked.

Lenny Dykstra, the Mets' center fielder, led off the first inning with a long home run, and the Mets collected 3 more scores, 2 via Dan Heep's single with the bases full, before the inning was over. The Mets had a 4–0 lead. In the seventh inning, both Santana and Dykstra singled, Hernandez walked, filling the bases. Gary Carter lined a hard single to left-center field, scoring Santana and Dykstra and making it a 6–1 game. They added another run in the eighth inning on 2 base hits, and it was 7–1. McDowell, who had relieved Ojeda in the eighth inning, set the Bosox down in order in the final two innings, and the Mets tasted their first Series victory.

It was Gary Carter night in the fourth game, for Carter, who had driven in 3 runs in game three, drove in 3 more runs, as the Mets won a bitterly fought 6–2 verdict to even the Series at 2 games apiece. Carter slugged 2 tremendous home runs and Lenny Dykstra also contributed another homer with a man on base to give the Mets the game.

In winning the opening game of the Series Bruce Hurst, the Red Sox left-hander, had been magnificent, allowing the Mets just 4 base hits. Now, in game five, Hurst was hit freely; the Mets collected 10 solid blows, but each time it seemed as if the Mets were about to explode, Hurst called on his reserve strength, fired in the ball and got the team out. Hurst became so tough to hit with men on base that the Mets did not score their first run until Tim Teufel hit a home run in the eighth inning. They added another tally in the ninth, but that was all they could manage, and the Red Sox took the game by a 4–2 margin. Now the die was cast, for the Sox had a 3–2 advantage in the Series.

Dwight Gooden, the Mets' twenty-one-year-old speedster, was hit freely through the four innings he lasted, and was touched up for 9 hits and all 4 runs. Sid Fernandez came into relieve

Dwight in the fifth inning and held the Bosox scoreless.

In New York once again, the Mets clawed and scratched their way through the sixth game with the profuse assistance of horrible Red Sox fielding. Glaring errors on two eighth-inning bunts enabled the Mets to tie the game, 3–3, and then a wild pitch followed by another error brought in the tying and winning runs in the tenth inning. It was one of the most exciting games ever seen at Shea Stadium. Ray Knight, whose error led to Boston's third run in the seventh inning, singled home the first run in the tenth-inning rally. Then he took second on Bob Stanley's wild pitch while Kevin Mitchell tore home from third base with the tying run. The wild pitch came on Stanley's seventh pitch to Mookie Wilson. After the ninth pitch and with a 3 and 2 count Mookie hit a routine ground ball to first base and as Bill Buckner, a sure-handed first baseman, scampered over to field the ball it simply dribbled in between his legs while Ray Knight tore home with the game-winning run.

On a cold, gloomy, misty October 27 night, at Shea Stadium, the Mets defeated the Red Sox 8–5 in a dramatic come-from-behind effort that produced 8 runs in the final four innings as

No, it's not ballet, it's the Mets' third baseman Ray Knight (22) and shortstop Rafael Santana (3) as they both leap high for a pop fly in the sixth inning of the fifth game of the Series.

Tim Teufel, the Mets' second baseman, homers in the ninth inning of the fifth game as Bosox catcher Rich Gedman and umpire Ed Montague follow the play. Teufel was the Mets' leading hitter in the Series with a spectacular .444 average.

the New Yorkers captured their second World Championship in the twenty-five year history of the team.

The Red Sox quickly jumped on the offerings of Ron Darling for 3 runs in the second inning, which featured back-to-back home runs by Dwight Evans and Rich Gedman, and the Bosox were off to a 3–0 lead.

The Mets rallied late in the sixth inning when Lee Mazzilli singled, Mookie Wilson singled, and Tim Teufel walked to fill the bases. Now the fans began their famous chant: "Let's go, Mets. Let's go, Mets. Let's go, Mets." Then Keith Hernandez singled, driving in 2 runs. Carter drove out a long fly ball and Teufel scampered home, making it a 3–3 game.

And it was bedlam in New York's Shea Stadium.

In the seventh inning, manager McNamara brought in relief pitcher Cal Schiraldi to replace Hurst. It was a move that brought stunning results, in a hurry.

The first hitter to face Schiraldi, Ray Knight, waited on four pitches, then blasted a drive over the left field wall and the Mets were out in front, 4–3. Lenny Dykstra followed with a base hit, went to second on a wild pitch, and trotted home when Santana singled. Santana stole second, went to third on a groundout, and scored on Hernandez's sacrifice fly. Now it was a 6–3, Mets.

But the Red Sox were not out of the game by any means and fought back tenaciously. Buckner and Jim Rice singled in succession and both runners sprinted home on Evans's two-base drive. Now it was a 6–5 contest and the Mets' fans were biting their nails and screaming for the Mets to just hold 'em.

Darryl Strawberry became an instant sweetheart of the Mets when he homered in the eighth inning and Jesse Orosco punched out a long base hit to score Mazzilli, who had singled earlier.

Now it was 8–5 and Mets fans were breathing easier.

In the ninth inning, Orosco retired the Red Sox in order, and the Mets were world champions.

Minnesota Twins Versus St. Louis Cardinals

He was supposed to be the best man at his brother's wedding on October 17, 1987. Frank Viola thought the baseball season would be over, and he would fly to New York and stand beside his brother, John, when he and his bride took their wedding vows at St. Raphael Church in East Meadow, Long Island. Instead, the former St. John's University pitching ace was pitching and winning the first game of the World Series.

As much as he wanted to be best man for his brother, Frank had waited for this moment all of his life. He had pitched for St. John's, posting a 26-2 record there, and went to the College World Series. Then came the long trail to the major leagues and finally his appearance on the mound against the St. Louis Cardinals on October 17, 1987.

"When I was a little kid," said Viola, "I always wanted to pitch for the Mets. But you don't always get what you want in this game of baseball. The biggest thing for me was to get to the major leagues as early as I could. I knew the Twins needed pitchers, and if I made good in the minors they would rush me up into the big leagues, quicker than any other major league team."

In the first World Series ever played at Minnesota's Metrodome, Viola was superb as he allowed the hard-hitting Cardinals just 5 base hits, 1 run, and fanned 5 hitters while the Twins pounded three St. Louis pitchers for 11 hits and 10 runs to romp to a 10–1 victory.

The Twins' left fielder, Dan Gladden, capped a 7-run drive in the fourth inning with a home run with the bases full to give the Twins a 7–1 lead. After sending 11 batters to the plate in the fourth inning, the Twins pounded out 2 more runs in the fifth.

Dan Cox, the big Cardinal hurler, started the second game. An imposing sight, the twenty-eight year old right-hander looked more like a tight end at six feet four inches and 235 pounds. Yet, despite his size and swift delivery, Danny lasted just three and two thirds of an inning as the Twins leveled him with a barrage of 6 hits and 7 runs, continuing their devastating slugging to win game two, 8–4.

Bert Blyleven pitched for the Twins and did a fine job as he allowed the Cards just 6 hits and 2 runs to post the win.

The Cards were supposed to have won the third game of the Series played at St. Louis when the pitching assignments were first announced a week before the game. There was nothing to talk about. It was John Tudor, ace of the Cardinal pitching staff, against the unknown Les Straker, the first ballplayer from Venezuela ever to pitch in a World Series.

"I win this game," Straker said to the writer, "I am the biggest hero in my country. They gonna be so proud of me. I never have to work again, they take care of me."

As the game progressed, Straker proceeded to set the Cards down in order. Through six innings, the kid from Venezuela had outpitched the great John Tudor. He allowed the Cards just 4 base hits, struck out 4, and had the Twins out in front by a 1–0 margin. And back in Caracas via armed forces radio, the citizens of that great city were going crazy with joy.

In the seventh inning, Straker was hit hard as the Cards finally solved the mystery of his pitching. They scored 3 runs to clinch a hard-fought victory, 3–1.

In the fourth game, at St. Louis, Frank Viola, trying for his second Series win, did a creditable job for three and a half innings. Then, with the score tied at 1–1, Tom Lawless, the Cards' fine third baseman, who had hit but 1 home run in the 215 games he had played as a major leaguer, slugged a 3-run homer off Viola in an attack that left the ex-St. John's left-hander staggering under a 6-run assault. It gave the Cards a 7–1 lead that they never relinquished. They swept to their second straight win at home, 7–2.

Now the Series was tied at 2 games each.

The fifth game featured a head-to-head pitching duel that had the more than fifty-five thousand fans in Busch Stadium, standing and cheering the efforts of both pitchers as Bert Blyleven and Dan Cox pitched their hearts out in a scoreless six-inning battle.

In the Cardinals' half of the seventh, Vinny Coleman singled and Lon Smith beat out a bunt. Then Coleman and Smith pulled off a dazzling double steal, and Ford singled to score 2 runs. On the next play, shortstop Greg Gagne booted Jose Oquendo's grounder, and Dan Driessen scored, making it 3–0. The Cards added a run in the next frame.

The Twins scored twice, but that was all they were able to come up with and the Cards had their third straight victory, 4–2. All they needed was one more victory for the championship.

"We have no more games to play here in St. Louis," said Twins manager Tom Kelly. "It's no good here for us. It will be good to be back home on our own grounds. We can beat 'em there."

Frank Viola, former St. Johns pitching ace, won 2 games for the Twins, including a stunning 5-hit opening-game 10–1 victory over the Tigers.

October 24 was the ultimate day of irony for the St. Louis Cardinals. For once in the tortuous season, for once in seven horrible months of injuries and disasters, they finally had the best of all worlds. They needed to win one more game in Minneapolis to capture still another World Series. They had a 5–2 lead over the Twins in the Metrodome in Minneapolis in the fifth inning, and they had their great money pitcher, John Tudor, out on the mound to preserve their lead.

But it just didn't work out that way.

Tudor was raked for 11 base hits, the most he allowed all year. Ken Dayley, who was brought in from the bull pen to get just 1 out, threw 1 pitch and Kent Hrbek hit it over the center field fence for a grand slam homer. And the best of all worlds for the Cardinals collapsed with that one pitch. The Cards collapsed, sustaining an 11–5 beating that enabled the Twins to even the Series.

And now it all came down to the seventh game.

The Cards and the Twins played this game the way the seventh game of a World Series

Twins first baseman Kent Hrbek greets Steve Lombardozzi after Lombo's 3-run homer in the first game of the Series.

should be played. There was everything: masterful pitching; great clutch hitting; unbelievable defensive play; runners thrown out at home on split second and controversial plays that were hotly disputed. And the crowd going crazy with joy one minute, and downcast and disbelieving the next.

After a scoreless first inning, the Cards were off and running as they plastered Viola for 4 consecutive singles to score 2 runs in the second inning.

The Twins scratched out a run on a single by Steve Lombardozzi that brought in Tim Laudner in the second inning, making the score 2–1, St. Louis. Kirby Puckett slugged a two-base hit off the wall to drive in Gagne in the fifth inning to make it a 2–2 tie.

Catcher Tim Laudner of the Twins connects for a homer off pitcher Danny Cox in the first game of the Series.

Cardinals star Willie McGee slammed out 10 hits for a sparkling .370 average for the Series.

Twins manager Tom Kelly directs all the action from the dugout.

It was still tied at 2–2 in the sixth inning, when Danny Cox, who had relieved Joe Magrane, walked two successive hitters. Then Todd Worrell came in for the Cards, and promptly walked the next two batters to fill the bases. Gagne promptly drove the first pitch to Lawless at third base, who made a fine stop of the hard-hit ball, but his throw to first base was too late and Tommy Brunansky scored to give the Twins a 3–2 margin.

In the eighth inning, Laudner singled and sped all the way home on Dan Gladden's scorching two-base drive, and the Twins were now breathing a bit easier with at 4–2 lead.

Manager Tom Kelly now wisely decided to relieve Viola, who was laboring, and brought in his ace relief pitcher, Jeff Reardon, and Jeff held on to the lead.

He simply reared back and fired in his ferocious fast ball at the Card hitters in the eighth and ninth innings, got the Cards out in order, and the Twins had won their first World Series in the team's history.

There was pandemonium up in the stands and delirium on the field as the players pounded and jumped on each other in sheer ecstasy. It was the first major professional championship for a Minnesota team since the great George Mikan had led the Lakers basketball team to the NBA title in 1954.

When the baseball season had begun in April, Las Vegas bookmakers had determined that the odds were 125–1 that the Twins would not win the World Series. There were, however, no indications that any bettor had taken the odds on the Twins.

1988

Los Angeles Dodgers
Versus Oakland Athletics

How in the world did it ever happen?

How did a ball club with a half-crippled, patched-up minor league lineup resembling that of the Carolina Clippers wallop a team that was reminiscent of the all-time slugging stars, the 1927 Yankees?

All of the evidence points to the fact that Kirk Gibson's incredibly heroic home run in the ninth inning of game one was the most dramatic home runs in World Series history, and was the turning point in the Series.

Traditionalists will mention Babe Ruth's called homer at Wrigley Field in Chicago. Others will mention Carlton Fisk's monster drive in game six of the 1975 Series at Fenway Park. Others will say nothing ever could or would equal Bill Mazeroski's climactic drive in game seven at Forbes Field in 1960.

But none of those epochal drives had the theatrical elements of the drive by the half-crippled Gibson, who was not even sitting on the bench during the tense nail-biter that saw Oakland's Jose Canseco slam a bases-full home run in the second inning to give the A's what looked like an comfortable 4–2 lead after the Dodgers' Mickey Hatcher had driven a 2-run shot into the bleachers in the first inning.

Gibson could hardly move around the clubhouse without the aid of the Dodgers' trainer.

He had re-strained his left hamstring muscle in the fifth game of the National League playoff series and had not been able to swing a bat since he injured his right knee in the seventh game of that series. Kirk hadn't even been introduced with the rest of the team as is customary before game time.

Twenty minutes before the game began, Gibson still had not suited up with the rest of the team. He was sitting in the trainer's room underneath Dodger Stadium watching the progress of the game when he heard Vin Scully inform his national TV audience that Gibson, the heart and spark of the Dodger offense, would not play. When Kirk heard Scully's comments, he got up grabbed a bat. Despite strained and aching muscles that tore at his insides with every move, Gibson walked to the batting tee and began to hit some balls. He then put an icebag on his knee, tried to sit somehow in the whirlpool and then sent word to Tommy Lasorda that if he was needed in a desperate spot, he would be ready to pinch-hit.

The A's carried a 4–3 margin as the teams got ready for the fateful ninth inning, when Dennis Eckersley walked pinch hitter Mike Davis with 2 outs. When ball 4 sent Davis to first, the crowd of some fifty-six thousand Dodger fans erupted with the realization that this was one of the marvelous Hollywood moments. Like Roy Hobbs (the hero of *The Natural*), Gibson hit the ball out of the park.

And like Roy Hobbs, Kirk Gibson hobbled to the plate to pinch-hit. Before anyone realized it, the count on Gibson was 2 and 2, the next pitch was a wicked slider, but Gibson swung into the ball with every ounce of his 225 pounds, and drove it ten rows up into the bleachers, and the Dodgers had won an incredible 5–4 triumph. It was a game that broke the morale of the cocky Athletics and sent the Dodgers and their fans into a frenzied dance of victory.

In an encore performance the next evening, the Dodgers rested Kirk Gibson and turned the stage over to pitcher Orel Hershiser. In another incredible performance, Hershiser was just about invincible, allowing the hard-hitting A's just 3 measly singles, all by Dave Parker, as Tommy Lasorda's fighting Dodgers, his "team of destiny," routed the A's to take a 2 games to 0 lead in the eighty-fifth World Series.

It was a tense game until Hershiser lined a single to center field in the third inning that ignited a 5-run outburst. Mike Marshall provided the key hit of the game with a slashing 3-run homer off Storm Davis. The Dodgers scored another run in the fourth inning to make it a 6–0 game as Hershiser made it look easy as pie as he set the A's down for the remainder of the game without a single offensive threat.

"The shutout was a very satisfying thing, but the hitting was a great thrill," said Hershiser after the game. "After all, this is the World Series and I want to hit the ball as well as the other players. Hershiser's 3 hits in the game were the first time that a pitcher had got that many hits in sixty-four years. (Art Nehf of the Giants got 3 hits in the 1924 Series against Washington.)

Just as Gibson had given the Dodgers an emotional lift in the opening game of the Series, Mark McGwire gave the A's a tremendous lift in game three with a dramatic ninth-inning

Battered, bruised, barely able to swing a bat, Dodger star Kirk Gibson came off the bench to drive out one of the most dramatic home runs in Series history to win the opening game of the Series for the Dodgers.

Orel Hershiser pitched a shutout against the A's in game two of the Series. Three days later he allowed the A's just 4 hits to win his second Series game.

The Dodgers pour out onto the field to greet Gibson after his home run in the first game of the Series.

homer that won the game for the Athletics, 2–1. McGwire's homer came off a former teammate, Jay Howell, who had stirred controversy in the playoffs against the Mets when he was ejected for pitching with a smear of pine tar on his glove.

The Dodgers were completely thwarted this time by the outstanding pitching of Greg Caderet, Gene Nelson, and Rick Honeycutt, who produced four innings of shutout pitching. John Tudor, who started for the Dodgers, left the game in the second inning with a sore elbow and was replaced by right-hander Tim Leary.

The A's opened the scoring in the third inning. Glenn Hubbard singled, stole second, and then went on to third as Mike Scioscia, the catcher, threw the ball into left field. Then Ron Hassey singled Hubbard home for the A's first run in eighteen innings.

Bob Welch struck out the side in the first inning and had compiled 8 strikeouts by the time Jeff Hamilton singled to center for the Dodgers in the fifth inning. Alfredo Griffin laid down a sacrifice bunt, moving Hamilton to second. Then Franklin Stubbs doubled to left, scoring Hamilton and tying the game at 1–1. That was all the scoring there was until McGwire's dramatic game-ending homer in the ninth inning.

Game four was lost in the first three innings by the A's when a couple of mistakes—a walk, a passed ball, an error by Hubbard, and another error by Walt Weiss—allowed the Dodgers to run up a 3–1 lead, sparked by Mickey Hatcher's hit-and-run tactics, just as in the first two games.

The decisive run for the Dodgers came in the seventh inning after pitcher Dave Stewart walked Griffin with 1 out. Steve Sax singled to center, sending Griffin to third. Tracy Woodson then hit a hopper to short in a play that should have been an easy double play, but Sax had taken off as soon as Woodson made contact with the ball and the A's could only get 1 out. Griffin, however, scored on the play and it was now 4–2, Dodgers.

Walt Weiss singled to start the seventh inning and came all the way home when Dave Henderson smacked a double, and the score was now 4–3. The A's failed to score in the final two innings.

Now the Dodgers were 1 game away from the championship.

The fifth game, at Oakland, belonged to the Dodgers. They completed their dramatic run to the championship by doing to the A's what they did throughout the Series. They reversed the way the teams were supposed to hit. The Dodgers, who weren't supposed to hit, did; the A's, who had all the powerhouse sluggers, failed to hit. It was that simple.

When the final pitch of the season sailed through the strike zone and Tony Phillips, the A's last batter, swung and missed, with the Dodgers ahead by a 5–2 margin, it meant the World Championship belonged to the Dodgers.

The irregular army of crippled Dodgers that limped and then conquered, who were led by a unique hero of a pitcher, who sat on the bench between innings with eyes closed, singing church hymns to himself, were the new world champions. Hershiser was magnificent in pitching his crippled street fighters to victory as he allowed

Hershiser can hit as well as pitch. Here he lays down a perfect bunt in the second game of the Series.

Mickey Hatcher proved to be a combination of Pepper Martin and Mickey Mantle, both idols of his, as he hit like a fiend and ran the bases like a wild deer.

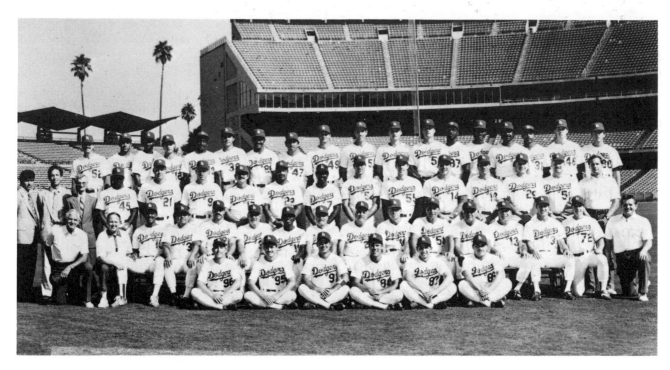

The 1988 World Champion Los Angeles Dodgers

the feeble-hitting Athletics just 4 base hits, while striking out 9 batters. Another pair of street fighters, Mickey Hatcher and Mike Davis, also delivered telling home runs when they were needed.

In a final address to his troops, manager Tommy Lasorda called the Dodgers, "my team of destiny," and urged the downtrodden of the nation to look to his team for inspiration. "They have to be an influence on everybody in the nation," said Tommy. "What they did here in this Series, when they didn't have the talent and they were all battered and crippled, is one of the greatest accomplishments I've ever seen anywhere. People who doubt that they can make a success in life should look to this great ball club as a role model. We did the impossible and it could happen to you."

1989

Oakland Athletics Versus San Francisco Giants

A. Bartlett Giamatti once wrote an essay about baseball beginning with this statement: "The game is designed to break your heart."

All Bart Giamatti ever wanted to be, he said, was president of the American League. Instead, he wound up holding baseball's two other ranking positions—president of the National League and commissioner of baseball.

But Giamatti served as commissioner for only five months of what was to have been a five-year term. That was denied him when he died of a sudden massive heart attack on September 1, 1989, shortly after arriving at his summer cottage on Martha's Vineyard in Massachusetts, and just nine days after he had suspended Pete Rose of the Cincinnati Reds for life. The suddenness of Giamatti's death stunned and shocked the world of baseball and the nation as well, for Giamatti, in his all-too-brief tenure, left an indelible mark on the game.

The day after Giamatti's death, baseball's executive council named Fay Vincent, a close friend and the deputy commissioner of baseball, as acting commissioner. Shortly thereafter, Vincent was named commissioner of baseball for a five-year term.

There were two rapid playoffs in the American and National Leagues that took five games apiece to decide who won the pennants. In the National loop, the Giants defeated the Chicago Cubs, while the A's easily won the crown in the American League by defeating Toronto, to clear the way for the first "subway Series" in thirty-three years; the second straight Series in southern California, and the first World Series ever played entirely in the San Francisco Bay Area.

It was the third World Series between California teams and the Athletics had figured in all three. In 1974 they defeated the Los Angeles Dodgers in five games in the first Series between West Coast teams. In 1988, the Dodgers turned on their California rivals and defeated the A's in five games.

The eighty-sixth World Series opened in Oakland on Saturday evening, October 14, before a roaring, festive crowd of nearly sixty thousand fans as pitcher Dave Stewart, the ace of the Athletics' staff, took to the mound for the home team. Giant manager Roger Craig selected his great young star, Scott Garrelts, to oppose Stewart.

Garrelts, with an incredible 14-3 record during the regular season, was supposed to be able to handle the big Oakland sluggers, but after getting by in the first inning, Scott was bashed for 3 hits and 3 runs in the second inning; a home run by Dave Parker in the third; and another homer by Walt Weiss in the fourth inning, to give the A's an insurmountable 5–0 lead.

Meanwhile, Stewart, the mainstay of the A's pitching staff during the past three seasons, was

379

Oakland's great pitcher Dave Stewart fires his first pitch against the Giants in game one of the Series.

Terry Steinbach is safe at home, sliding into the plate as the Giants' catcher Terry Kennedy loses the ball in the second inning of game one.

in remarkable form. He flashed an incredible forkball, that dipped, danced, and slammed into his catcher's big glove, striking out 6 hitters and allowing the Giants just 3 base hits to preserve the 5–0 victory.

In the second game of the Series, manager Roger Craig selected his portly, forty-year-old, six-foot-three pitcher, Rick Reuschel, while manager Tony LaRussa nominated the speedy Mike Moore. Moore, a veteran of seven years with the Seattle mariners, became a free agent in 1988 and signed with the A's for a record $3.95 million contract. He promptly won 19 games which clinched the pennant.

The A's jumped out to a 1-run lead in the first inning. In the third frame, Moore's character was tested for the first time when Terry Kennedy, the Giant catcher, singled to open the inning. Jose Uribe slammed a come-backer to Moore, who scooped up the ball, whirled, and threw to Weiss at second base to nab Kennedy. Brett Butler then singled to left, sending Uribe to third base. Robby Thompson lined a fly ball to Dave Henderson in center field and Uribe scored after the catch to tie the game at 1–1. Now with Butler in scoring position and Clark and Mitchell waiting to hit, Moore calmly whipped in 3 incredible split-finger pitches to strike out the most dangerous Will Clark. It was the last time the Giants were able to mount any kind of threat.

In the fourth inning, Canseco walked and Parker slugged the ball to the fence for a double, scoring Canseco. Dave Henderson walked and then Terry Steinbach connected for a home run, scoring Parker and Henderson to give the Athletics an easy 5–1 victory and a 2 games to 0 advantage in the Series.

It was a beautiful late afternoon scene in the Bay Area. Soft breezes, a setting sun, and a cloudless sky played on the senses of the ballplayers of both clubs as they prepared to take the field for the third game of the Series. Tailgating parties had begun earlier in the lot at Candlestick Park, site of the game, and fans were still streaming into the nearly jam-packed ballpark. It was a joyous, festive occasion, even if the home-team Giants were trailing the A's by 2 games to 0.

Oakland's Dave Parker slides headfirst into second base as shortstop Jose Uribe attempts a tag in the fourth inning of game two. Umpire Rennert (*left*) calls Parker safe.

Then without warning, this great playground was sent reeling and swaying as an earthquake that measured 7.2 on the Richter scale rolled through northern California, destroying buildings, roadways, bridges, disrupting power and all communications, and causing an estimated two hundred deaths and leaving thousands homeless.

Candlestick Park shook and swayed, and chunks of cement were jarred loose. Many fans and the ballplayers on the field dashed to their loved ones and left the field.

About forty-five minutes after the quake, game three was postponed by Baseball Commissioner Fay Vincent as the crowd, dazed and horrified, slowly filed out of the huge ballpark.

Some twenty-four hours later, Commissioner Vincent rescheduled the third game for October 27. The fourth game would be played on the twenty-eighth, and the fifth game, if necessary, on the twenty-ninth.

When the World Series resumed on October 27, it was a moving and somber evening. A crowd of more than sixty-two thousand fans observed a minute of silence for the earthquake victims, then joined in singing, "San Francisco," the tune from the old film that dramatized San Francisco's revival after the terrible quake of 1906.

Then baseball's battle of the Bay Area was restarted after the longest intermission in baseball history. And the A's, fresh from several days of training in Arizona, unfurled their full power to batter the Giants, 13–7, for a third consecutive win in a Series they had owned since the first pitch on October 14.

The A's opened their battery of artillery in the fourth inning when Dave Henderson and Tony Phillips drove out long home runs off pitcher Scott Garrelts. They roared again in the fifth inning when Canseco and Rickey Henderson homered off Kelly Downs, and they exploded once again when Carney Lansford homered in the sixth inning to pad the A's lead to 9–3.

Like a big cat, Rickey Henderson edges off first base, watching the Giants' pitcher's every move, just before stealing second base in game two of the Series.

Jose Canseco slams a 3-run homer in the fifth inning of game three of the World Series.

In the eighth inning, the A's continued to hammer the Giants pitchers. Singles by Walt Weiss, Tod Blankenship, Carney Lansford, and Jose Canseco gave the Giants 2 more runs and they added 2 additional scores to make it a 13–3 battering.

The Giants came to life in the ninth inning as Bill Bathe, pinch-hitting for pitcher Lefferts drove out a home run with two men on base to cut the A's lead to 13–6. Donnell Nixon singled and then Gregg Litton doubled, scoring Nixon for the Giants' seventh and final run of the game, making the final score 13–7, Oakland.

As the Giants took the field on October 29, three games down with no room for error, they knew that sixteen teams in the eighty-six-year history of the Series had lost the first three games and none had recovered. In fact, thirteen of the sixteen teams never did win a single game, and the three others won only one before being beaten.

As the teams prepared to take the field for the fourth game at Candlestick Park, the Giant manager Roger Craig said, "They've got a really great team. And at this moment they're a better ball club than we are. After the long break, they looked much sharper. We were rusty. But, we still think they can be beaten. It'd be a miracle if we did it, but there's still that possibility."

But when the game began, it was apparent that the Giants' pitcher, Don Robinson, a thirty-two-year-old Kentuckian, who hadn't started a game in more than a month because of a stretched ligament in his right knee, didn't have the stuff to stop the onrushing Oakland express.

The first batter for the A's was Rickey Henderson, who had tormented the Giant pitchers throughout the first three games with his frenetic base running and solid base hits. Robinson's first two pitches to Rickey were balls. The third pitch by Robby was a fastball right down the middle and Henderson slugged the ball over the left field fence for his seventh Series hit, and the A's had a 1–0 lead. In the second inning, Dave Henderson opened the inning with a ringing double. Steinbach flied out sending Henderson to third base. Tony Phillips grounded out. But Walt Weiss was purposely walked so Robinson could pitch to the A's pitcher Mike Moore, who had never had a hit in the major leagues.

Robby got two quick strikes on Moore; then Mike slugged the third pitch over Brett Butler's

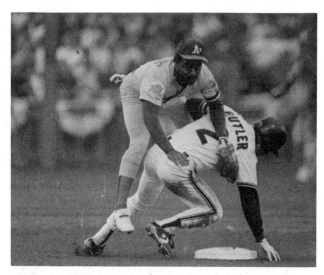

Brett Butler (*right*) breaks up a double play as he slides into second base and upends the A's' second baseman Tony Phillips. Butler was out, but teammate Ken Oberkfell was safe on first during action in the first inning of the fourth and final game of the Series.

head in deep center field for a double, and two more runners crossed the plate to make it 3–0 for the A's. Rickey Henderson continued his amazing hitting, slashing out a single to left field for his eighth hit and Moore scored to make it 4–0. In the fifth inning, the A's continued their bombardment by slugging pitcher Mike LaCoss for 3 hits including a booming triple by Steinbach and a double by Phillips that produced 3 more runs and a 7–0 lead. In the sixth inning, it was more of the same as Rickey Henderson tripled to left-center field and then scored on Carney Lansford's single. With the score now 8–0, it was no longer a contest.

In the sixth inning, the Giants rallied briefly for 2 runs when Will Clark singled and then

Kevin Mitchell walloped a long home run to give the Giants their first runs of the game.

In the seventh frame, after a tongue lashing by manager Craig, the Giants came to life with a bang. Kennedy walked and then Bob Litton smashed a home run to cut the A's lead to 8–4. Candy Maldonado tripled to left and Butler continued the assault by slashing a double to right field that scored Candy. Thompson singled to left scoring Butler. Now it was an 8–6 game and Giant fans were up for the first time and roaring for more. But the rally was stopped dead in their tracks when Clark and Mitchell both flied out to end the Giant hopes.

In the eighth inning, the relentless A's scored an additional run, increasing their lead to 9–6 and then Denny Eckersley ended any hopes for a Giant victory, as he mowed down the San Francisco hitters in order in the ninth inning to wrap up an easy victory and the World Series for the Athletics.

It was the first championship for the Athletics since 1974 when they captured the last of their three consecutive World Series with a bevy of glittering stars, who soon after that third title, left the team in the free agent revolution that swept the baseball world. And it was the fourth championship in five world Series since the A's had moved to Oakland from Kansas City, some twenty-one years before.

The A's World Series victory was also the first Series sweep since 1976, when the Cincinnati Reds had humiliated the Yankees in four games.

At the modest clubhouse celebration, sans the usual wild celebration, pitcher Dave Stewart was voted the MVP by the sportswriters. After he received the award, Stewart called over to Rickey Henderson, "This award is for you and me, Rick. But Mike Moore, Dave Henderson, Terry Steinbach, and Carney Lansford had MVP Series, too."

Appendix

WORLD SERIES STATISTICS

Individual Batting, Baserunning (in One game)

Most Runs

4 Babe Ruth, New York Yankees, October 6, 1926
Earle Combs, New York Yankees, October 2, 1932
Frankie Crosetti, New York Yankees, October 2, 1936
Enos Slaughter, St. Louis Cardinals, October 10, 1946
Reggie Jackson, New York Yankees, October 18, 1977

Most Runs Batted In

6 Bobby Richardson, New York Yankees, October 8, 1960

Most Hits

5 Paul Molitor, Milwaukee Brewers, October 12, 1982

Most Two-Base Hits

4 Frank Isbell, Chicago White Sox, October 13, 1906

Most Three-Base Hits

2 Thomas Leach, Pittsburgh Pirates, October 1, 1903
Pat Dougherty, Boston A.L., October 7, 1903
Walter Ruether, Cincinnati Reds, October 1, 1919
Bob Richardson, New York Yankees, October 12, 1960
Tommy Davis, Los Angeles Dodgers, October 3, 1963

Most Home Runs

3 Babe Ruth, New York Yankees, October 6, 1926, and
October 9, 1928
Reggie Jackson, New York Yankees, October 18, 1977

Most Home Runs with Bases Filled

1 Elmer Smith, Cleveland Indians, October 10, 1920
Tony Lazzeri, New York Yankees, October 2, 1936
Gil McDougald, New York Yankees, October 9, 1951
Mickey Mantle, New York Yankees, October 4, 1953
Yogi Berra, New York Yankees, October 5, 1956
Moose Skowron, New York Yankees, October 10, 1956
Bobby Richardson, New York Yankees, October 8, 1960
Chuck Hiller, San Francisco Giants, October 8, 1962
Ken Boyer, St. Louis Cardinals, October 11, 1964
Joe Pepitone, New York Yankees, October 14, 1964
Jim Northrup, Detroit Tigers, October 9, 1968
Dave McNally, Baltimore Orioles, October 13, 1970

Most Stolen Bases

3 John Wagner, Pittsburgh Pirates, October 11, 1909
Willie Davis, Los Angeles Dodgers, October 11, 1965
Lou Brock, St. Louis Cardinals, October 12, 1967, and
October 5, 1968

Most Times Stealing Home

1 Bill Dahlen, New York Giants, October 12, 1905
George Davis, Chicago White Sox, October 13, 1906
James Slagle, Chicago Cubs, October 11, 1907
Ty Cobb, Detroit Tigers, October 9, 1909
Charles Herzog, New York Giants, October 14, 1912
Charles Schmidt, Boston Braves, October 9, 1914
Michael McNally, New York Yankees, October 5, 1921
Bob Meusel, New York Yankees, October 6, 1921, and
October 7, 1928
Monte Irvin, New York Giants, October 4, 1951
Jackie Robinson, Brooklyn Dodgers, September 28,
1955
Tim McCarver, St. Louis Cardinals, October 15, 1964

Individual Batting, Baserunning (for World Series)

Most Series Played

14 Yogi Berra, New York Yankees, 1947, 1949, 1950,
1951, 1952, 1953, 1955, 1956, 1957, 1958, 1960, 1961,
1962, 1963

Highest Batting Average

4-game Series: .625—Babe Ruth, New York Yankees, 1928
5-game Series: .500—John Mclean, New York Giants, 1913
                Joe Gordon, New York Yankees, 1941
6-game Series: .500—Davis Robertson, New York Giants,
                1917
                Billy Martin, New York Yankees, 1953
7-game Series: .500—Pepper Martin, St. Louis Cardinals,
                1931
                John Lindell, New York Yankees,
                1947
                Phil Garner, Pittsburgh Pirates, 1979
8-game Series: .400—Charles Herzog, New York Giants,
                1912

Most Home Runs (in One Series)

5 Reggie Jackson, New York Yankees, 1977
4 Duke Snider, Brooklyn Dodgers, 1952 and 1955
  Hank Bauer, New York Yankees, 1958
  Gene Tenace, Oakland Athletics, 1972
  Willie Aikens, Kansas City Royals, 1980
3 Goose Goslin, Washington Senators, 1924 and 1925
  Joe Harris, Washington Senators, 1925
  Babe Ruth, New York Yankees, 1923, 1926, and 1928
  Lou Gehrig, New York Yankees, 1928 and 1932
  Charlie Keller, New York Yankees, 1939
  Johnny Mize, New York Yankees, 1952
  Mickey Mantle, New York Yankees, 1956, 1960, and 1964
  Yogi Berra, New York Yankees, 1956
  Henry Aaron, Milwaukee Braves, 1957
  Ted Kluszewski, Chicago White Sox, 1959
  Carl Yastrzemski, Boston Red Sox, 1967
  Don Clendenon, New York Yankees, 1969
  Tony Perez, Cincinnati Reds, 1975
  Reggie Smith, Los Angeles Dodgers, 1977
  Davey Lopes, Los Angeles Dodgers, 1978
  Willie Stargell, Pittsburgh Pirates, 1979

.500 Hitters

.625—Babe Ruth, New York Yankees, 1928, 10 for 16 (4 games, 9 runs)
.545—Hank Gowdy, Boston Braves, 1914, 6 for 11 (4 games, 3 runs)
  Lou Gehrig, New York Yankees, 1928, 6 for 11 (4 games, 5 runs)
.533—Johnny Bench, Cincinnati Reds, 1976, 8 for 15 (4 games, 4 runs)
.529—Lou Gehrig, New York Yankees, 1932, 9 for 17 (4 games, 9 runs)
  Thurman Munson, New York Yankees, 1976, 9 for 17 (4 games, 2 runs)
.500—Larry McLean, New York Giants, 1913, 6 for 12 (5 games, 0 runs)
  Dave Robertson, New York Giants, 1917, 11 for 22 (6 games, 3 runs)
  Mark Koenig, New York Yankees, 1927, 9 for 18 (4 games, 5 runs)
  Pepper Martin, St. Louis Cardinals, 1931, 12 for 24 (7 games, 5 runs)
  Joe Gordon, New York Yankees, 1941, 7 for 14 (5 games, 2 runs)
  Billy Martin, New York Yankees, 1953, 12 for 24 (6 games, 5 runs)
  Vic Wertz, Cleveland Indians, 1954, 8 for 16 (4 games, 2 runs)
  Phil Garner, Pittsburgh Pirates, 1979, 12 for 24 (7 games, 4 runs)

Individual Pitching Records

Most Series Played

11 Whitey Ford, New York Yankees, 1950, 1953, 1955, 1956, 1957, 1958, 1960, 1961, 1962, 1963, 1964

Most Games Won, Series

4-game Series: 2—Richard Rudolph, Boston Red Sox, 1914
  William James, Boston Red Sox, 1928
  Red Ruffing, New York Yankees, 1938
  Sandy Koufax, Los Angeles Dodgers, 1963
5-game Series: 3—Christy Mathewson, New York Giants, 1905
  John Coombs, Philadelphia Athletics, 1910
6-game Series: 3—Urban Faber, Chicago White Sox, 1917
7-game Series: 3—Charles Adams, Pittsburgh Pirates, 1909
  Stan Coveleski, Cleveland Indians, 1920
  Harry Brecheen, St. Louis Cardinals, 1946
  Lew Burdette, Milwaukee Braves, 1957
  Bob Gibson, St. Louis Cardinals, 1967
  Mickey Lolich, Detroit Tigers, 1968
8-game Series: 3—Bill Dinneen, Boston A.L., 1903
  Deacon Phillippe, Pittsburgh Pirates, 1903
  Joe Wood, Boston Red Sox, 1912

Most Saves, Total Series, Since 1969

6 Rollie Fingers, Oakland A's, 1972 (2), 1973 (2), 1974 (2)

Most Saves Series

4-game Series: 2—Bill McEnaney, Cincinnati Reds, 1976
5-game Series: 2—Rollie Fingers, Oakland A's, 1974
  Tippy Martinez, Baltimore Orioles, 1983
5-game Series: 2—Willie Hernandez, Detroit Tigers, 1984
6-game Series: 2—Tug McGraw, Philadelphia Phillies, 1980
  Rich Gossage, New York Yankees, 1981
7-game Series: 3—Kent Tekulve, Pittsburgh Pirates, 1979

Fewest Hits Allowed, Game, Nine Innings

0 Don Larsen, New York Yankees, October 8, 1956 (perfect game)

One- and Two-Hit Games, Nine Innings

1 Ed Reulbach, Chicago Cubs, October 10, 1906
  Claude Passeau, Chicago Cubs, October 5, 1945
  Floyd Bevens, New York Yankees, October 3, 1947
  Jim Lonborg, Boston Red Sox, October 5, 1967

2 Ed Walsh, Chicago White Sox, October 11, 1906
   Mordecai Brown, Chicago Cubs, October 12, 1906
   Ed Plank, Philadelphia Athletics, October 11, 1913
   Bill James, Boston Braves, October 10, 1914
   Waite Hoyt, New York Yankees, October 6, 1921
   Burleigh Grimes, St. Louis Cardinals, October 5, 1931
   George Earnshaw, Philadelphia Athletics, October 6, 1931
   Monte Pearson, New York Yankees, October 5, 1939
   Mort Cooper, St. Louis Cardinals, October 4, 1944
   Bob Feller, Cleveland Indians, October 6, 1948
   Allie Reynolds, New York Yankees, October 5, 1949
   Vic Raschi, New York Yankees, October 4, 1950
   Warren Spahn, Milwaukee Braves, October 5, 1958
   Whitey Ford, Edward C., New York Yankees, October 4, 1961
   Nelson Briles, Pittsburgh Pirates, October 14, 1971

Most Strikeouts, Series

4-game Series: 23—Sandy Koufax, Los Angeles Dodgers, 1963
5-game Series: 18—Christy Mathewson, New York Giants, 1905
6-game Series: 20—Chief Bender, Philadelphia Athletics, 1911
7-game Series: 35—Bob Gibson, St. Louis Cardinals, 1968
8-game Series: 28—Bill Dinneen, Boston Red Sox, 1903

Most Strikeouts, Inning

4 Orval Overall, Chicago Cubs, October 14, 1908

Most Strikeouts, Game

17 Bob Gibson, St. Louis Cardinals, October 2, 1968

Lowest Earned-Run Average, Series, 14 or More Innings

0.00—Christy Mathewson, New York Giants, 1905
      Waite Hoyt, New York Yankees, 1921
      Carl Hubbell, New York Giants, 1933
      Whitey Ford, New York Yankees, 1960 and 1961
      Joe McGinnity, New York Giants, 1905
      Walter Mails, Cleveland Indians, 1920
      John Benton, New York Giants, 1917

Miscellaneous Individual Records

Players on Championship Teams in Both Leagues

Terry Crowley, Cincinnati Reds, 1975; Baltimore Orioles, 1970

Mike Cuellar, St. Louis Cardinals, 1964; Baltimore Orioles, 1970
Murry Dickson, St. Louis Cardinals, 1942; New York Yankees, 1958
Lonnie Frey, Cincinnati Reds, 1940; New York Yankees, 1947
Billy Gardner, New York Giants, 1954; New York Yankees, 1961
Don Gullett, Cincinnati Reds, 1975–76; New York Yankees, 1977
Johnny Hoop, St. Louis Cardinals, 1942, 1944; New York Yankees, 1950–51
Jay Johnstone, Los Angeles Dodgers, 1981; New York Yankees, 1978
Roger Maris, St. Louis Cardinals, 1967; New York Yankees, 1961–62
Eddie Mathews, Milwaukee Braves, 1957; Detroit Tigers, 1968
Dal Maxvill, St. Louis Cardinals, 1964, 1967; Oakland Athletics, 1972, 1974
Don McMahon, Milwaukee Braves, 1957; Detroit Tigers, 1968
Merv Rettenmund, Cincinnati Reds, 1975; Baltimore Orioles, 1970
Paul Richards, New York Giants, 1933; Detroit Tigers, 1945
Pete Richart, Los Angeles Dodgers, 1963; Baltimore Orioles, 1970
Dutch Ruether, Cincinnati Reds, 1919; New York Yankees, 1927
Rosy Ryan, New York Giants, 1921–22; New York Yankees, 1928
Johnny Sain, Boston Braves, 1948; New York Yankees, 1951–553
Bill Skowron, Los Angeles Dodgers, 1963; New York Yankees, 1956, 1958, 1961–62
Enos Slaughter, St. Louis Cardinals, 1942, 1944, 1946; New York Yankees, 1956, 1958
Dick Tracewski, Los Angeles Dodgers, 1963, 1965; Detroit Tigers, 1968
Jim Turner, Cincinnati Reds, 1940; New York Yankees, 1943

Players Who Homered in Both Leagues

Enos Slaughter, St. Louis Cardinals, 1946; New York Yankees, 1956
Bill Skowron, Los Angeles Dodgers, 1963; New York Yankees, 1955, 1957, 1961
Roger Maris, St. Louis Cardinals, 1967; New York Yankees, 1960–62, 1964
Frank Robinson, Cincinnati Reds, 1961; Baltimore Orioles, 1966, 1969–71
Reggie Smith, Los Angeles Dodgers, 1978; Boston Red Sox, 1967

Players Who Homered in First World Series At Bat

Joe Harris, Washington Senators
George Watkins, St. Louis Cardinals
Mel Ott, New York Giants
George Selkirk, New York Yankees
Dusty Rhodes, New York Giants
Elston Howard, New York Yankees
Roger Maris, New York Yankees
Don Mincher, Minnesota Twins
Brooks Robinson, Baltimore Orioles
Jose Santiago, Boston Red Sox
Mickey Lolich, Detroit Tigers
Don Buford, Baltimore Orioles
Gene Tenace, Oakland Athletics
Jim Mason, New York Yankees
Doug DeCinces, Baltimore Orioles
Amos Otis, Kansas City Royals
Bob Watson, New York Yankees
Jim Dwyer, Baltimore Orioles

Players Who Have Stolen Home in a World Series Game

Bill Dahlen, New York Giants
George Davis, Chicago White Sox
Jim Slagle, Chicago Cubs
Ty Cobb, Detroit Tigers
Charlie Herzog, New York Giants
Charles Schmidt, Boston Braves
Mike McNally, New York Yankees
Bob Meusel (2), New York Yankees
Monte Irvin, New York Giants
Jackie Robinson, Brooklyn Dodgers
Tim McCarver, St. Louis Cardinals

Youngest Player to Appear in a World Series Game

Freddie Lindstrom, New York Giants, 1924—18 years, 10 months, 13 days

Oldest Player to Appear in a World Series Game

Jack Quinn, Philadelphia Athletics, 1929—45 years

Pitchers on Championship Teams in Both Leagues

Jack Coombs, Brooklyn Dodgers, 1916; Philadelphia Athletics, 1910–11
Hank Borowy, Chicago Cubs, 1945; New York Yankees, 1943
Johnny Sain, Boston Braves, 1948; New York Yankees, 1951

Don Larsen, San Francisco Giants, 1962; New York Yankees, 1956
Tommy John, Los Angeles Dodgers, 1978; New York Yankees, 1981

Managers Who Won a World Series in Both Leagues

Yogi Berra, New York Mets, 1973; New York Yankees, 1964
Alvin Dark, San Francisco Giants, 1962; Oakland Athletics, 1974
Joe McCarthy, Chicago Cubs, 1929; New York Yankees, 1932–33, 1937–39, 1941–43

General Records
First World Series Night Game

October 13, 1971, at Pittsburgh, Pittsburgh Pirates vs. Baltimore Orioles

Largest Attendance, Game

92,706, October 6, 1959, at Los Angeles, Chicago White Sox vs. Los Angeles Dodgers

Largest Attendance, Series

4-game Series: 251,507—New York Giants vs. Cleveland Indians, 1954.
5-game Series: 304,139—Baltimore Orioles vs. Philadelphia Phillies, 1983.
6-game Series: 420,784—Los Angeles Dodgers vs. Chicago White Sox, 1959.
7-game Series: 394,712—Milwaukee Braves vs. New York Yankees, 1957.
8-game Series: 269,976—New York Giants vs. New York Yankees, 1921.

Winning Series After Winning First Game

Accomplished 47 times

Club Records
Most Runs, Game, One Club

18 New York Yankees vs. New York Giants, October 2, 1936 (Won 18–4)

Largest Score, Shutout Game

New York Yankees, 12, Pittsburgh Pirates, 0, October 12, 1960.

Most Hits, Game, One Club

20 New York Giants vs. New York Yankees, October 7, 1921; St. Louis Cardinals vs. Boston Red Sox, October 10, 1946

Most Hits, Game, Both Clubs

32 New York Yankees, 19, Pittsburgh Pirates, 13, October 6, 1960

Most Home Runs, Game, One Club

5 New York Yankees vs. St. Louis Cardinals, October 19, 1928

Most Home Runs, Game, Both Clubs

6 New York Yankees, 4, Chicago Cubs, 2, October 1, 1932
New York Yankees, 4, Brooklyn Dodgers, 2, October 4, 1953
Cincinnati Reds, 3, Boston Red Sox, 3, October 14, 1975 (ten innings)

Most Series Played

33 New York Yankees, 1921, 1922, 1923, 1926, 1927, 1928, 1932, 1936, 1937, 1938, 1939, 1941, 1942, 1943, 1947, 1949, 1950, 1951, 1952, 1953, 1955, 1956, 1957, 1958, 1960, 1961, 1962, 1963, 1964, 1976, 1977, 1978, 1981.
17 Brooklyn/Los Angeles Dodgers, 1916, 1920, 1941, 1947, 1949, 1952, 1953, 1955, 1956, 1959, 1963, 1965, 1966, 1974, 1977, 1978, 1981.

Most Series Won

22 New York Yankees, 1923, 1927, 1928, 1932, 1936, 1937, 1938, 1939, 1941, 1943, 1947, 1949, 1950, 1951, 1952, 1953, 1956, 1958, 1961, 1962, 1977, 1978.

Most Consecutive Years Winning Series

5 New York Yankees, 1949, 1950, 1951, 1952, 1953.

Most Series Lost

12 Brooklyn/Los Angeles Dodgers, 1916, 1920, 1941, 1947, 1949, 1952, 1953, 1956, 1966, 1974, 1977, 1978
11 New York Yankees, 1921, 1922, 1926, 1942, 1955, 1957, 1960, 1963, 1964, 1976, 1981.

Most Consecutive Series Won, League

7 American League, 1947, 1948, 1949, 1950, 1951, 1952, 1953.

Most Home Runs, Inning, One Club

3 Boston Red Sox vs. St. Louis Cardinals, October 11, 1967

Most Series, Manager

10 Casey Stengel, New York Yankees, 1949, 1950, 1951, 1952, 1953, 1955, 1956, 1957, 1958, 1960.

Most World Series Winners Managed

7 Joe McCarthy, New York Yankees, 1932, 1936, 1937, 1938, 1939, 1941, 1943
Casey Stengel, New York Yankees, 1949, 1950, 1951, 1952, 1953, 1956, 1958.

Managers Representing Both Leagues

Joe McCarthy, Chicago Cubs, 1929; New York Yankees, 1932, 1936, 1937, 1938, 1939, 1941, 1942, 1943.
Yogi Berra, New York Yankees, 1964; New York Mets, 1973
Alvin Dark, San Francisco Giants, 1962; Oakland A's, 1974.
Sparky Anderson, Cincinnati Reds, 1970, 1972, 1975, 1976; Detroit Tigers, 1984.
Dick Williams, Boston Red Sox, 1967; Oakland A's, 1972, 1973; San Diego Padres, 1984.

TOP TWENTY WORLD SERIES PERFORMERS

Series

Yogi Berra	14
Mickey Mantle	12
Joe DiMaggio	10
Elston Howard	10
Babe Ruth	10
Hank Bauer	9
Phil Rizzuto	9
Bill Dickey	8
Frankie Frisch	8
Gil McDougald	8
Bill Skowron	8
Many tied with	7

Games

Yogi Berra	75
Mickey Mantle	65
Elston Howard	54
Hank Bauer	53
Gil McDougald	53
Phil Rizzuto	52
Joe DiMaggio	51
Frankie Frisch	50
Pee Wee Reese	44
Roger Maris	41
Babe Ruth	41
Carl Furillo	40
Jim Gilliam	39
Gil Hodges	39
Bill Skowron	39
Bill Dickey	38
Jackie Robinson	38
Tony Kubek	37
Three tied with	36

Batting Average (75+AB)

	AB.	PCT.
Lou Brock	87	.391
Home Run Baker	91	.363
Lou Gehrig	119	.361
Reggie Jackson	98	.357
Billy Martin	99	.333
Eddie Collins	128	.328
Babe Ruth	129	.326
Charlie Gehringer	81	.321
Steve Garvey	113	.319
Hank Greenberg	85	.318
Gene Woodling	85	.318
Johnny Evers	76	.316
Frank Schulte	81	.309
Bobby Richardson	131	.305
Frankie Frisch	197	.294
Harry Hooper	92	.293
Bil Skowron	133	.293
Willie McGee	79	.291
Enos Slaughter	79	.291
Two tied with	94 or 129	.287

Slugging Average (75+AB)

	AB.	SLG.
Reggie Jackson	98	.755
Babe Ruth	129	.744
Lou Gehrig	119	.731
Lou Brock	87	.655
Hank Greenberg	85	.624
Duke Snider	133	.594
Billy Martin	99	.566
Frank Robinson	92	.554
Home Run Baker	91	.538
Mickey Mantle	230	.535
Gene Woodling	85	.529
Johnny Bench	86	.523
Bill Skowron	133	.519
Goose Goslin	129	.488
Enos Slaughter	79	.468
Emil Meusel	87	.460
Willie McGee	79	.456
Yogi Berra	259	.452
Tommy Henrich	84	.452
Two tied with	85 or 92	.435

At Bats

Yogi Berra	259
Mickey Mantle	230
Joe DiMaggio	199
Frankie Frisch	197
Gil McDougald	190
Hank Bauer	188
Phil Rizzuto	183
Elston Howard	171
Pee Wee Reese	169
Roger Maris	152
Jim Gilliam	147
Tony Kubek	146
Bill Dickey	145
Jackie Robinson	137
Bill Skowron	133
Duke Snider	133
Gil Hodges	131
Bobby Richardson	131
Pete Rose	130
Three tied with	129

Runs

Mickey Mantle	42
Yogi Berra	41
Babe Ruth	37
Lou Gehrig	30
Joe DiMaggio	27
Roger Maris	26
Elston Howard	25
Gil McDougald	23
Jackie Robinson	22
Hank Bauer	21
Reggie Jackson	21
Phil Rizzuto	21
Duke Snider	21
Gene Woodling	21
Eddie Collins	20
Pee Wee Reese	20
Bill Dickey	19
Frank Robinson	19
Bill Skowron	19
Two tied with	18

Hits

Yogi Berra	71
Mickey Mantle	59
Frankie Frisch	58
Joe DiMaggio	54
Hank Bauer	46
Pee Wee Reese	46
Gil McDougald	45
Phil Rizzuto	45
Lou Gehrig	43
Eddie Collins	42
Elston Howard	42
Babe Ruth	42
Bobby Richardson	40
Bill Skowron	39
Duke Snider	38
Bill Dickey	37
Goose Goslin	37
Steve Garvey	36
Four tied with	35

Total Bases

Mickey Mantle	123
Yogi Berra	117
Babe Ruth	96
Lou Gehrig	87
Joe DiMaggio	84
Duke Snider	79
Hank Bauer	75
Frankie Frisch	74
Reggie Jackson	74
Gil McDougald	72
Bill Skowron	69
Elston Howard	66
Goose Goslin	63
Pee Wee Reese	59
Lou Brock	57
Roger Maris	56
Billy Martin	56
Bill Dickey	55
Gil Hodges	54
Phil Rizzuto	54

Doubles

Yogi Berra 10
Frankie Frisch.......... 10
Jack Barry 9
Pete Fox 9
Carl Furillo 9
Lou Gehrig 8
Lonnie Smith 8
Duke Snider 8
Home Run Baker 7
Lou Brock 7
Eddie Collins 7
Hank Greenberg....... 7
Chick Hafey 7
Elston Howard 7
Reggie Jackson 7
Marty Marion 7
Pepper Martin......... 7
Danny Murphy 7
Stan Musial 7
Jackie Robinson 7

Triples

Bill Johnson............ 4
Tommy Leach 4
Tris Speaker 4
Hank Bauer........... 3
Bobby Brown 3
Dave Concepcion 3
Buck Freeman 3
Frankie Frisch.......... 3
Lou Gehrig 3
Billy Martin........... 3
Tim McCarver 3
Bob Meusel........... 3
Fred Parent........... 3
Chick Stahl 3
Many tied with 2

Home Runs

Mickey Mantle 18
Babe Ruth 15
Yogi Berra 12
Duke Snider 11
Lou Gehrig 10
Reggie Jackson 10
Joe DiMaggio 8
Frank Robinson 8
Bill Skowron 8
Hank Bauer........... 7
Goose Goslin.......... 7
Gil McDougald 7
Roger Maris 6
Al Simmons 6
Reggie Smith 6
Many tied with 5

Runs Batted In

Mickey Mantle 40
Yogi Berra 39
Lou Gehrig 35
Babe Ruth 33
Joe DiMaggio 30
Bill Skowron 29
Duke Snider 26
Hank Bauer........... 24
Bill Dickey 24
Reggie Jackson 24
Gil McDougald 24
Hank Greenberg........ 22
Gil Hodges 21
Goose Goslin.......... 19
Elston Howard 19
Tony Lazzeri........... 19
Billy Martin........... 19
Home Run Baker 18
Charlie Keller 18
Roger Maris........... 18

Game-Winning RBI (1980–Present)

Mike Schmidt.......... 2
Steve Yeager 2
Many tied with 1

Bases on Balls

Mickey Mantle 43
Babe Ruth 33
Yogi Berra 32
Phil Rizzuto.......... 30
Lou Gehrig 26
Mickey Cochrane 25
Jim Gilliam 23
Jackie Robinson 21
Gil McDougald 20
Joe DiMaggio 19
Gene Woodling........ 19
Roger Maris 18
Pee Wee Reese........ 18
Gil Hodges 17
Gene Tenace 17
Ross Youngs 17
Pete Rose 16
Five tied with 15

Strikeouts

Mickey Mantle 54
Elston Howard 37
Duke Snider 33
Babe Ruth 30
Gil McDougald 29
Bill Skowron 26
Hank Bauer........... 25
Reggie Jackson 24
Bob Meusel........... 24
Joe DiMaggio 23
George Kelly 23
Tony Kubek 23
Frank Robinson 23
Jim Bottomley......... 22
Joe Collins........... 22
Gil Hodges 22
Steve Garvey.......... 21
Roger Maris........... 21
Tony Perez 21
Three tied with 20

Stolen Bases

Lou Brock 14
Eddie Collins 14
Frank Chance 10
Dave Lopes........... 10
Phil Rizzuto.......... 10
Frankie Frisch......... 9
Honus Wagner 9
Johnny Evers.......... 8
Pepper Martin......... 7
Joe Morgan 7
Vince Coleman 6
Jackie Robinson 6
Jimmy Slagle 6
Joe Tinker 6
Bob Tolan 6
Maury Wills........... 6
Dave Concepcion 5
Bob Meusel........... 5
Pee Wee Reese........ 5
Willie Wilson......... 5

ANNUAL BATTING AND PITCHING RECORDS

1903

COMPOSITE BATTING AVERAGES

Boston Red Sox

Player-Position	G	AB	R	H	2B	3B	HR	RBI	BA
Stahl, cf	8	33	6	10	1	3	0	3	.303
Ferris, 2b	8	31	3	9	0	1	0	6	.290
Freeman, rf	8	32	6	9	0	3	0	4	.281
Parent, ss	8	32	8	9	0	3	0	4	.281
Collins, 3b	8	36	5	9	1	2	0	1	.250
Dinneen, p	4	12	1	3	0	0	0	0	.250
Dougherty, lf	8	34	3	8	0	2	2	5	.235
Criger, c	8	26	1	6	0	0	0	4	.231
LaChance, 1b	8	27	5	6	2	1	0	4	.222
Young, p	4	15	1	2	0	1	0	3	.133
Farrell, ph	2	2	0	0	0	0	0	1	.000
O'Brien, ph	2	2	0	0	0	0	0	0	.000
Hughes, p	1	0	0	0	0	0	0	0	.000
Totals	8	282	39	71	4	16	2	35	.252

Pittsburgh Pirates

Player-Position	G	AB	R	H	2B	3B	HR	RBI	BA
Kennedy, p	1	2	0	1	1	0	0	0	.500
Sebring, rf	8	30	3	11	0	1	1	5	.367
Leach, 3b	8	33	3	9	0	4	0	8	.273
Beaumont, cf	8	34	6	9	0	1	0	2	.265
Clarke, lf	8	34	3	9	2	1	0	0	.265
Phelps, ph-c	8	26	1	6	2	0	0	1	.231
Wagner, ss	8	27	2	6	1	0	0	3	.222
Phillippe, p	5	18	1	4	0	0	0	1	.222
Bransfield, 1b	8	29	3	6	0	2	0	1	.207
Ritchey, 2b	8	27	2	3	1	0	0	2	.111
Leever, p	2	4	0	0	0	0	0	0	.000
Smith, c	1	3	0	0	0	0	0	0	.000
Thompson, p	1	1	0	0	0	0	0	0	.000
Veil, p	1	2	0	0	0	0	0	0	.000
Totals	8	270	24	64	7	9	1	23	.237

COMPOSITE PITCHING AVERAGES

Boston Red Sox

Pitcher	G	IP	H	R	ER	BB	SO	W	L	ERA
Young	4	34	31	13	6	4	17	2	1	1.59
Dinneen	4	35	29	8	8	8	28	3	1	2.06
Hughes	1	2	4	3	2	2	0	0	1	9.00
Totals	8	71	64	24	16	14	45	5	3	2.03

Pittsburgh Pirates

Pitcher	G	IP	H	R	ER	BB	SO	W	L	ERA
Veil	1	7	6	1	1	4	1	0	0	1.29
Phillippe	5	44	38	19	16	3	20	3	2	3.27
Thompson	1	2	3	1	1	0	1	0	0	4.50
Kennedy	1	7	11	10	4	3	3	0	1	5.14
Leever	2	10	13	8	7	3	2	0	2	6.30
Totals	8	70	71	39	29	13	27	3	5	3.73

1905

COMPOSITE BATTING AVERAGES

New York Giants

Player-Position	G	AB	R	H	2B	3B	HR	RBI	BA
Donlin, cf	5	19	4	6	1	0	0	1	.316
Bresnahan, c	5	16	3	5	2	0	0	1	.313
Devlin, 3b	5	16	0	4	1	0	0	1	.250
Mathewson, p	3	8	1	2	0	0	0	0	.250
McGann, 1b	5	17	1	4	2	0	0	4	.235
Gilbert, 2b	5	17	1	4	0	0	0	1	.235
Browne, rf	5	22	2	4	0	0	0	1	.182
Mertes, lf	5	17	2	3	1	0	0	3	.176
Dahlen, ss	5	15	1	0	0	0	0	1	.000
McGinnity, p	2	5	0	0	0	0	0	0	.000
Strang, ph	1	1	0	0	0	0	0	0	.000
Ames, p	1	0	0	0	0	0	0	0	.000
Totals	5	153	15	32	7	0	0	13	.209

Philadelphia Athletics

Player-Position	G	AB	R	H	2B	3B	HR	RBI	BA
Hartsel, lf	5	17	1	5	1	0	0	0	.294
Schreckengost, c	3	9	2	2	1	0	0	0	.222
Davis, 1b	5	20	0	4	1	0	0	0	.200
Murphy, 2b	5	16	0	3	1	0	0	0	.188
M. Cross, ss	5	17	0	3	0	0	0	0	.176
Plank, p	2	6	0	1	0	0	0	0	.167
Powers, c	3	7	0	1	1	0	0	0	.143
Seybold, rf	5	16	0	2	0	0	0	0	.125
L. Cross, 3b	5	19	0	2	0	0	0	0	.105
Lord, cf	5	20	0	2	0	0	0	2	.100
Bender, p	2	5	0	0	0	0	0	0	.000
Coakley, p	1	2	0	0	0	0	0	0	.000
Hoffman, ph	1	1	0	0	0	0	0	0	.000
Totals	5	155	3	25	5	0	0	2	.161

COMPOSITE PITCHING AVERAGES

New York Giants

Pitcher	G	IP	H	R	ER	BB	SO	W	L	ERA
Mathewson	3	27	14	0	0	1	18	3	0	0.00
McGinnity	2	17	10	3	0	3	6	1	1	0.00
Ames	1	1	1	0	0	1	1	0	0	0.00
Totals	5	45	25	3	0	5	25	4	1	0.00

Philadelphia Athletics

Pitcher	G	IP	H	R	ER	BB	SO	W	L	ERA
Coakley	1	9	9	9	0	5	2	0	1	0.00
Plank	2	17	14	4	2	4	11	0	2	1.06
Bender	2	17	9	2	2	6	13	1	1	1.06
Totals	5	43	32	15	4	15	26	1	4	0.84

1906

COMPOSITE BATTING AVERAGES

Chicago White Sox

Player-Position	G	AB	R	H	2B	3B	HR	RBI	BA
Rohe, 3b	6	21	2	7	1	2	0	4	.333
Donahue, 1b	6	18	0	6	2	1	0	4	.333
Isbell, 2b	6	26	4	8	4	0	0	4	.308
Davis, ss	3	13	4	4	3	0	0	6	.308
Hahn, rf	6	22	4	6	0	0	0	0	.273
Altrock, p	2	4	0	1	0	0	0	0	.250
Tannehill, ss	3	9	1	1	0	0	0	0	.111
Dougherty, lf	6	20	1	2	0	0	0	1	.100
Jones, cf	6	21	4	2	0	0	0	0	.095
Sullivan, c	6	21	0	0	0	0	0	0	.000
White, p	3	3	0	0	0	0	0	0	.000
Walsh, p	2	4	1	0	0	0	0	0	.000
Towne, ph	1	1	0	0	0	0	0	0	.000
Owen, p	1	2	0	0	0	0	0	0	.000
O'Neill, rf	1	1	1	0	0	0	0	0	.000
McFarland, ph	1	1	0	0	0	0	0	0	.000
Totals	6	187	22	37	10	3	0	19	.196

Chicago Cubs

Player-Position	G	AB	R	H	2B	3B	HR	RBI	BA
Brown, p	3	6	0	2	0	0	0	0	.333
Hofman, cf	6	23	3	7	1	0	0	2	.304
Schulte, rf	6	26	1	7	3	0	0	3	.269
Overall, p	2	4	1	1	1	0	0	0	.250
Steinfeldt, 3b	6	20	2	5	1	0	0	2	.250
Chance, 1b	6	21	3	5	1	0	0	0	.238
Kling, c	6	17	2	3	1	0	0	0	.176
Tinker, ss	6	18	4	3	0	0	0	1	.167
Evers, 2b	6	20	2	3	1	0	0	1	.150
Sheckard, lf	6	21	0	0	0	0	0	1	.000
Moran, ph	2	2	0	0	0	0	0	0	.000
Reulbach, p	2	3	0	0	0	0	0	1	.000
Pfiester, p	2	2	0	0	0	0	0	0	.000
Gessler, ph	2	1	0	0	0	0	0	0	.000
Totals	6	184	18	36	9	0	0	11	.196

COMPOSITE PITCHING AVERAGES

Chicago White Sox

Pitcher	G	IP	H	R	ER	BB	SO	W	L	ERA
Altrock	2	18	11	2	2	2	5	1	1	1.00
Walsh	2	15	7	6	3	6	17	2	0	1.80
White	3	15	12	7	3	7	3	1	1	1.80
Owen	1	6	6	3	2	3	2	0	0	3.00
Totals	8	54	36	18	10	18	27	4	2	1.67

Chicago Cubs

Pitcher	G	IP	H	R	ER	BB	SO	W	L	ERA
Overall	2	12	10	2	2	3	8	0	1	1.50
Reulbach	2	11	6	4	3	8	4	1	0	2.45
Brown	3	19⅔	14	9	7	4	12	1	2	3.20
Pfiester	2	10⅓	7	7	7	3	11	0	2	6.10
Totals	6	53	37	22	19	18	35	2	4	3.23

1907

COMPOSITE BATTING AVERAGES

Chicago Cubs

Player-Position	G	AB	R	H	2B	3B	HR	RBI	BA
Steinfeldt, 3b	5	17	2	8	1	1	0	2	.471
Evers, 2b-ss	5	20	2	7	2	0	0	1	.350
Slagle, cf	5	22	3	6	0	0	0	4	.273
Schulte, rf	5	20	3	5	0	0	0	2	.250
Sheckard, lf	5	21	0	5	2	0	0	2	.238
Chance, 1b	4	14	3	3	1	0	0	0	.214
Kling, c	5	19	2	4	0	0	0	1	.211
Howard, ph-1b	2	5	0	1	0	0	0	0	.200
Overall, p	2	5	0	1	0	0	0	2	.200
Reulbach, p	2	5	0	1	0	0	0	1	.200
Tinker, ss	5	13	4	2	0	0	0	1	.154
Zimmerman, 2b	1	1	0	0	0	0	0	0	.000
Moran, ph	1	0	0	0	0	0	0	0	.000
Pfiester, p	2	2	0	0	0	0	0	0	.000
Brown, p	1	3	0	0	0	0	0	0	.000
Totals	5	167	19	43	6	1	0	16	.257

1908

COMPOSITE BATTING AVERAGES

Chicago Cubs

Player-Position	G	AB	R	H	2B	3B	HR	RBI	BA
Chance, 1b	5	19	4	8	0	0	0	3	.421
Schulte, rf	5	18	4	7	0	1	0	2	.389
Evers, 2b	5	20	5	7	1	0	0	2	.350
Overall, p	3	6	0	2	0	0	0	0	.333
Hofman, cf	5	19	2	6	0	1	0	4	.316
Powers, c	5	19	2	5	0	0	1	5	.263
Tinker, ss	5	19	2	5	0	0	1	5	.263
Steinfeldt, 3b	5	16	3	4	0	0	0	3	.250
Kling, c	5	16	2	4	1	0	0	1	.250
Sheckard, lf	5	21	2	5	2	0	0	1	.238
Reulbach, p	2	3	0	0	0	0	0	0	.000
Brown, p	2	4	0	0	0	0	0	0	.000
Pfiester, p	1	2	0	0	0	0	0	0	.000
Howard, ph	1	1	0	0	0	0	0	0	.000
Totals	5	164	24	48	4	2	1	21	.293

1909

COMPOSITE BATTING AVERAGES

Pittsburgh Pirates

Player-Position	G	AB	R	H	2B	3B	HR	RBI	BA
Wagner, ss	7	24	4	8	2	1	0	7	.333
Leach, cf-3b	7	25	8	8	4	0	0	2	.320
Byrne, 3b	7	24	5	6	1	0	0	0	.250
Miller, 2b	7	28	2	7	1	0	0	4	.250
Gibson, c	7	25	2	6	2	0	0	2	.240
Abstein, 1b	7	26	3	6	2	0	0	2	.231
Clarke, lf	7	19	7	4	0	0	2	7	.211
Wilson, rf	7	26	2	4	1	0	0	1	.154
Adams, p	3	9	0	0	0	0	0	0	.000
Camnitz, p	2	1	0	0	0	0	0	0	.000
Willis, p	2	4	0	0	0	0	0	0	.000
Maddox, p	1	4	0	0	0	0	0	0	.000
Leifield, p	1	1	0	0	0	0	0	0	.000
O'Connor, ph	1	1	0	0	0	0	0	0	.000
Phillippe, p	2	1	0	0	0	0	0	0	.000
Hyatt, ph-cf	2	4	1	0	0	0	0	1	.000
Abbaticchio, ph	1	1	0	0	0	0	0	0	.000
Totals	7	223	34	49	13	1	2	26	.220

1907

COMPOSITE BATTING AVERAGES

Detroit Tigers

Player-Position	G	AB	R	H	2B	3B	HR	RBI	BA
Killian, p	1	2	1	1	0	0	0	0	.500
Rossman, 1b	5	20	1	8	0	1	0	2	.400
Jones, lf	5	17	1	6	0	0	0	0	.353
Coughlin, 3b	5	20	0	5	0	0	0	0	.250
Payne, c-pr	2	4	0	1	0	0	0	1	.250
Crawford, cf	5	21	1	5	1	0	0	3	.238
Cobb, rf	5	20	1	4	0	1	0	0	.200
Schmidt, c-ph	4	12	0	2	0	0	0	0	.167
Schaefer, 2b	5	17	0	1	0	0	0	0	.050
Donovan, p	2	8	0	0	0	0	0	0	.000
Mullin, p	2	6	0	0	0	0	0	0	.000
Siever, p	1	1	0	0	0	0	0	0	.000
Archer, c	1	3	0	0	0	0	0	0	.000
Totals	5	172	6	36	1	2	0	6	.209

COMPOSITE PITCHING AVERAGES

Chicago Cubs

Pitcher	G	IP	H	R	ER	BB	SO	W	L	ERA
Brown	1	9	7	0	0	1	4	1	0	0.00
Reulbach	2	12	6	1	1	3	4	1	0	0.75
Overall	2	18	14	4	2	4	11	1	0	1.00
Pfiester	1	9	9	1	1	1	3	1	0	1.00
Totals	5	48	36	6	4	9	22	4	0	0.75

Detroit Tigers

Pitcher	G	IP	H	R	ER	BB	SO	W	L	ERA
Donovan	2	21	17	9	4	5	16	0	1	1.71
Mullin	2	17	16	5	4	6	7	0	2	2.11
Killian	1	4	3	1	1	1	1	0	0	2.25
Siever	1	4	7	4	2	0	1	0	1	4.50
Totals	5	46	43	19	11	12	25	0	4	2.15

1908

COMPOSITE BATTING AVERAGES

Detroit Tigers

Player-Position	G	AB	R	H	2B	3B	HR	RBI	BA
Thomas, ph-c	2	4	0	2	1	0	0	1	.500
Cobb, rf	5	19	3	7	1	0	0	4	.368
Mullin, p	1	3	1	1	0	0	0	1	.333
Crawford, cf	5	21	2	5	1	0	0	1	.238
McIntyre, lf	5	18	2	4	1	0	0	0	.222
Rossman, 1b	5	19	3	4	0	0	0	3	.211
Summers, p	2	5	0	1	0	0	0	1	.200
Downs, 2b	2	6	1	1	1	0	0	1	.167
O'Leary, ss	5	19	2	3	0	0	0	0	.158
Schaefer, 3b-2b	5	16	0	2	0	0	0	0	.125
Coughlin, 3b	3	8	0	1	0	0	0	1	.125
Schmidt, c	4	14	0	1	0	0	0	1	.071
Killian, p	1	0	0	0	0	0	0	0	.000
Jones, ph	3	2	1	0	0	0	0	0	.000
Donovan, p	2	4	0	0	0	0	0	0	.000
Winter, pr-p	2	0	0	0	0	0	0	0	.000
Totals	5	158	15	32	5	0	0	14	.203

COMPOSITE PITCHING AVERAGES

Chicago Cubs

Pitcher	G	IP	H	R	ER	BB	SO	W	L	ERA
Brown	2	11	6	1	0	1	5	2	0	0.00
Overall	3	18⅓	7	2	2	7	15	2	0	0.98
Reulbach	2	7⅔	9	4	4	1	5	0	0	4.70
Pfiester	1	8	10	8	7	3	1	0	1	7.88
Totals	5	45	32	15	13	12	26	4	1	2.00

Detroit Tigers

Pitcher	G	IP	H	R	ER	BB	SO	W	L	ERA
Mullin	1	9	7	3	0	1	8	1	0	0.00
Winter	1	1	1	1	0	1	0	0	0	0.00
Donovan	2	17	17	8	8	4	10	0	2	4.24
Summers	2	14⅔	18	8	7	4	7	0	2	4.30
Killian	1	2⅓	5	4	3	3	1	0	0	11.57
Totals	5	44	48	24	18	13	26	1	4	3.08

1909

COMPOSITE BATTING AVERAGES

Detroit Tigers

Player-Position	G	AB	R	H	2B	3B	HR	RBI	BA
Delahanty, 2b	7	26	2	9	4	0	0	4	.346
Moriarty, 3b	7	22	4	6	1	0	0	1	.273
Bush, ss	7	23	5	6	1	0	0	3	.261
Crawford, cf-1b	7	28	4	7	3	0	1	3	.250
T. Jones, 1b	7	24	3	6	1	0	0	1	.250
D. Jones, lf-cf	7	30	6	7	0	0	1	1	.233
Cobb, rf	7	26	3	6	3	0	0	6	.231
Schmidt, c	6	18	0	4	2	0	0	4	.222
Stanage, c	2	5	0	1	0	0	0	2	.200
Mullin, p-ph	6	16	1	3	1	0	0	0	.188
McIntyre, ph-lf	4	3	0	0	0	0	0	0	.000
Donovan, p	2	4	0	0	0	0	0	0	.000
Summers, p	2	3	0	0	0	0	0	0	.000
Willett, p	2	2	0	0	0	0	0	0	.000
Works, p	1	0	0	0	0	0	0	0	.000
O'Leary, 3b	1	3	0	0	0	0	0	0	.000
Totals	7	233	28	55	16	0	2	25	.236

COMPOSITE PITCHING AVERAGES

Pittsburgh Pirates

Pitcher	G	IP	H	R	ER	BB	SO	W	L	ERA
Phillippe	2	6	2	0	0	1	2	0	0	0.00
Maddox	1	9	10	6	0	2	4	1	0	0.00
Adams	3	27	18	5	4	6	11	3	0	1.33
Willis	2	11⅔	10	6	4	8	3	0	1	3.08
Leifield	1	4	7	5	5	1	0	0	1	11.25
Camnitz	2	3⅓	8	6	5	2	2	0	1	13.50
Totals	7	61	55	23	18	20	22	4	3	2.66

Detroit Tigers

Pitcher	G	IP	H	R	ER	BB	SO	W	L	ERA
Willett	2	7⅔	3	1	0	0	1	0	0	0.00
Mullin	4	32	22	14	8	8	20	2	1	2.25
Donovan	2	12	7	4	4	8	7	1	1	3.00
Summers	2	7⅓	13	13	7	4	4	0	2	8.59
Works	1	2	4	2	2	0	2	0	0	9.00
Totals	7	61	49	34	21	20	34	3	4	3.10

1910

Composite Batting Averages

Philadelphia Athletics

Player-Position	G	AB	R	H	2B	3B	HR	RBI	BA
Collins, 2b	5	21	5	9	4	0	0	3	.429
Baker, 3b	5	22	6	9	3	0	0	4	.409
Coombs, p	3	13	0	5	1	0	0	3	.385
Davis, 1b	5	17	5	6	3	0	0	2	.353
Murphy, rf	5	20	6	7	3	0	1	8	.350
Bender, p	2	6	1	2	0	0	0	1	.333
Strunk, cf	4	18	2	5	1	1	0	2	.278
Thomas, c	4	12	2	3	0	0	0	1	.250
Lapp, c	1	4	0	1	0	0	0	1	.250
Barry, ss	5	17	3	4	2	0	0	3	.235
Hartsel, lf	1	5	2	1	0	0	0	0	.200
Lord, lf-cf	5	22	3	4	2	0	0	1	.182
Totals	5	177	35	56	19	1	1	29	.316

Chicago Cubs

Player-Position	G	AB	R	H	2B	3B	HR	RBI	BA
Chance, 1b	5	17	1	6	1	1	0	4	.353
Schulte, rf	5	17	3	6	3	0	0	2	.353
Tinker, ss	5	18	2	6	2	0	0	0	.333
Sheckard, lf	5	14	5	4	2	0	0	1	.286
Hofman, cf	5	15	2	4	0	0	0	2	.267
Zimmerman, 2b	5	17	0	4	1	0	0	2	.235
Archer, 1b-c	3	11	1	2	1	0	0	0	.182
Steinfeldt, 3b	5	20	0	2	1	0	0	1	.100
Kling, c-ph	5	13	0	1	0	0	0	1	.077
Overall, p	1	1	0	0	0	0	0	0	.000
McIntire, p	2	1	0	0	0	0	0	0	.000
Brown, p	3	7	0	0	0	0	0	0	.000
Richie, p	1	0	0	0	0	0	0	0	.000
Reulbach, p	1	0	0	0	0	0	0	0	.000
Pfiester, p	1	2	0	0	0	0	0	0	.000
Needham, ph	1	1	0	0	0	0	0	0	.000
Cole, p	1	2	0	0	0	0	0	0	.000
Kane, pr	1	0	0	0	0	0	0	0	.000
Beaumont, ph	3	2	1	0	0	0	0	0	.000
Totals	5	158	15	35	11	1	0	13	.222

Composite Pitching Averages

Philadelphia Athletics

Pitcher	G	IP	H	R	ER	BB	SO	W	L	ERA
Bender	2	18⅔	12	5	4	4	14	1	1	1.93
Coombs	3	27	23	10	10	14	17	3	0	3.33
Totals	5	45⅔	35	15	14	18	31	4	1	2.76

Chicago Cubs

Pitcher	G	IP	H	R	ER	BB	SO	W	L	ERA
Richie	1	1	1	0	0	0	0	0	0	0.00
Pfiester	1	6⅔	9	5	0	1	1	0	0	0.00
Cole	1	8	10	3	3	3	5	0	0	3.38
Brown	3	18	23	16	11	7	14	1	2	5.50
McIntire	2	5⅓	4	5	4	3	2	0	1	6.80
Overall	1	3	6	3	3	1	1	0	1	9.00
Reulbach	1	2	3	3	2	2	0	0	0	9.00
Totals	5	44	56	35	23	17	23	1	4	4.70

1911

Composite Batting Averages

Philadelphia Athletics

Player-Position	G	AB	R	H	2B	3B	HR	RBI	BA
Baker, 3b	6	24	7	9	2	0	2	5	.375
Barry, ss	6	19	2	7	4	0	0	2	.368
Murphy, rf	6	23	4	7	3	0	0	3	.304
Collins, 2b	6	21	4	6	1	0	0	1	.286
Lapp, c	2	8	1	2	0	0	0	0	.250
Coombs, p	2	8	1	2	0	0	0	0	.250
Davis, 1b	6	24	3	5	1	0	0	5	.208
Oldring, cf	6	25	2	5	2	0	1	3	.200
Lord, lf	6	27	2	5	2	0	0	1	.185
Bender, p	3	11	0	1	0	0	0	0	.091
Thomas, c	4	12	1	1	0	0	0	1	.083
Plank, p	2	3	0	0	0	0	0	0	.000
Strunk, ph	1	0	0	0	0	0	0	0	.000
McInnis, 1b	1	0	0	0	0	0	0	0	.000
Totals	6	205	27	50	15	0	3	21	.244

New York Giants

Player-Position	G	AB	R	H	2B	3B	HR	RBI	BA
Ames, p	2	2	0	1	0	0	0	0	.500
Crandall, p-ph	3	2	1	1	1	0	0	1	.500
Doyle, 2b	6	23	3	7	3	1	0	1	.304
Meyers, c	6	20	2	6	2	0	0	2	.300
Mathewson, p	3	7	0	2	0	0	0	0	.286
Herzog, 3b	6	21	3	4	2	0	0	0	.190
Devore, lf	6	24	1	4	1	0	0	3	.167
Merkle, 1b	6	20	1	3	1	0	0	1	.150
Fletcher, ss	6	23	1	3	1	0	0	1	.130
Snodgrass, cf	6	19	1	2	0	0	0	1	.105
Murray, rf	6	21	0	0	0	0	0	0	.000
Marquard, p	3	2	0	0	0	0	0	0	.000
Becker, ph	3	3	0	0	0	0	0	0	.000
Wiltse, p	2	1	0	0	0	0	0	0	.000
Wilson, p	1	1	0	0	0	0	0	0	.000
Totals	6	189	13	33	11	1	0	10	.175

Composite Pitching Averages

Philadelphia Athletics

Pitcher	G	IP	H	R	ER	BB	SO	W	L	ERA
Bender	3	26	16	6	3	8	20	2	1	1.04
Coombs	2	20	11	5	3	6	16	1	0	1.35
Plank	2	9⅔	6	2	2	0	8	1	1	1.96
Totals	6	55⅔	33	13	8	14	44	4	2	1.29

New York Giants

Pitcher	G	IP	H	R	ER	BB	SO	W	L	ERA
Crandall	2	4	2	0	0	0	2	1	0	0.00
Marquard	3	11⅔	9	6	2	1	8	0	1	1.54
Mathewson	3	27	25	8	6	2	13	1	2	2.00
Ames	2	8	6	5	2	1	6	0	1	2.25
Wiltse	2	3⅓	8	8	7	0	2	0	0	18.90
Totals	6	54	50	27	17	4	31	2	4	2.83

1912

Composite Batting Averages

Boston Red Sox

Player-Position	G	AB	R	H	2B	3B	HR	RBI	BA
Henriksen, pr-ph	2	1	0	1	1	0	0	1	1.000
Hall, p	2	4	0	3	1	0	0	0	.750
Engle, ph	3	3	1	1	1	0	0	2	.333
Speaker, cf	8	30	4	9	1	2	0	2	.300
Hooper, rf	8	31	3	9	2	1	0	2	.290
Wood, p	4	7	1	2	0	0	0	1	.286
Stahl, 1b	8	32	3	9	2	0	0	2	.281
Yerkes, 2b	8	32	3	8	0	2	0	4	.250
Gardner, 3b	8	28	4	5	2	1	1	4	.179
Wagner, ss	8	30	1	5	1	0	0	0	.167
Lewis, lf	8	32	4	5	3	0	0	2	.156
Cady, c	7	22	1	3	0	0	0	1	.136
Carrigan, c	2	7	0	0	0	0	0	0	.000
Collins, p	2	5	0	0	0	0	0	0	.000
Bedient, p	4	6	0	0	0	0	0	0	.000
O'Brien, p	2	2	0	0	0	0	0	0	.000
Ball, ph	1	1	0	0	0	0	0	0	.000
Totals	8	273	25	60	14	6	1	21	.220

New York Giants

Player-Position	G	AB	R	H	2B	3B	HR	RBI	BA
Wilson, c	2	1	0	1	0	0	0	0	1.000
Herzog, 3b	8	30	6	12	4	1	0	4	.400
Tesreau, p	3	8	0	3	0	0	0	2	.375
Meyers, c	8	28	2	10	0	1	0	3	.357
Murray, rf-lf	8	31	5	10	4	1	0	5	.323
Merkle, 1b	8	33	5	9	2	1	0	3	.273
McCormick, ph	5	4	0	1	0	0	0	1	.250
Devore, lf-rf	7	24	4	6	0	0	0	0	.250
Doyle, 2b	8	23	5	8	1	0	1	2	.242
Snod'ss, cf-lf-rf	8	23	2	7	2	0	0	2	.212
Fletcher, ss	8	28	1	5	1	0	0	3	.179
Mathewson, p	3	12	0	2	0	0	0	0	.167
Becker, pr-cf	2	4	1	0	0	0	0	0	.000
Crandall, p	1	1	0	0	0	0	0	0	.000
Shafer, pr-ss	3	0	0	0	0	0	0	0	.000
Marquard, p	2	4	0	0	0	0	0	0	.000
Ames, p	1	0	0	0	0	0	0	0	.000
Totals	8	274	31	74	14	4	1	25	.270

Composite Pitching Averages

Boston Red Sox

Pitcher	G	IP	H	R	ER	BB	SO	W	L	ERA
Bedient	4	18	10	2	1	7	7	1	0	0.50
Collins	2	14⅓	14	5	3	0	6	0	0	1.88
Hall	2	10⅔	11	6	4	9	1	0	0	3.38
Wood	4	22	27	11	9	3	21	3	1	3.68
O'Brien	2	9	12	7	5	3	4	0	2	5.00
Totals	8	74	74	31	22	22	39	4	3	2.68

New York Giants

Pitcher	G	IP	H	R	ER	BB	SO	W	L	ERA
Crandall	1	2	1	0	0	0	2	0	0	0.00
Marquard	2	18	14	3	1	2	9	2	0	0.50
Mathewson	3	28⅔	23	11	5	5	10	0	2	1.57
Tesreau	3	23	19	10	8	11	15	1	2	3.13
Ames	1	2	3	1	1	1	0	0	0	4.50
Totals	8	73⅔	60	25	15	19	36	3	4	1.83

1913

COMPOSITE BATTING AVERAGES

Philadelphia Athletics

Player-Position	G	AB	R	H	2B	3B	HR	RBI	BA
Baker, 3b	5	20	2	9	0	0	1	7	.450
Collins, 2b	5	19	5	8	0	2	0	3	.421
Schang, c	4	14	2	5	0	1	1	6	.357
Barry, ss	5	20	3	6	3	0	0	2	.300
Oldring, lf	5	22	5	6	0	1	0	1	.273
Lapp, c	1	4	0	1	0	0	0	0	.250
Bush, p	1	4	0	1	0	0	0	0	.250
E. Murphy, rf	5	22	2	5	0	0	0	0	.227
Plank, p	2	7	0	1	0	0	0	0	.143
McInnis, 1b	5	17	1	2	1	0	0	2	.118
Strunk, cf	5	17	3	2	0	0	0	1	.118
Bender, p	2	8	0	0	0	0	0	1	.000
Totals	5	174	23	46	4	4	2	23	.264

New York Giants

Player-Position	G	AB	R	H	2B	3B	HR	RBI	BA
Mathewson, p	2	5	1	3	0	0	0	1	.600
McCormick, ph	2	2	1	1	0	0	0	0	.500
McLean, ph-c	5	12	0	6	0	0	0	2	.500
Snodgrass, 1b-cf	2	3	0	1	0	0	0	0	.333
Fletcher, ss	5	18	1	5	0	0	0	4	.278
Murray, rf	5	16	2	4	0	0	0	1	.250
Merkle, 1b	4	13	3	3	0	0	1	3	.231
Shafer, cf-3b	5	19	2	3	1	1	0	1	.158
Burns, lf	5	19	2	3	2	0	0	1	.158
Doyle, 2b	5	20	1	3	0	0	0	2	.150
Herzog, 3b	5	19	1	1	0	0	0	0	.053
Meyers, c	1	4	0	0	0	0	0	0	.000
Marquard, p	2	1	0	0	0	0	0	0	.000
Crandall, p-ph	4	4	0	0	0	0	0	0	.000
Tesreau, p	2	2	0	0	0	0	0	0	.000
Grant, pr-ph	2	1	1	0	0	0	0	0	.000
Wilson, c	3	3	0	0	0	0	0	0	.000
Wiltse, pr-1b	2	2	0	0	0	0	0	0	.000
Cooper, pr	2	0	0	0	0	0	0	0	.000
Demaree, p	1	1	0	0	0	0	0	0	.000
Totals	5	164	15	33	3	1	1	15	.201

COMPOSITE PITCHING AVERAGES

Philadelphia Athletics

Pitcher	G	IP	H	R	ER	BB	SO	W	L	ERA
Plank	2	19	9	4	2	3	7	1	1	0.95
Bush	1	9	5	2	1	4	3	1	0	1.00
Bender	2	18	19	9	8	1	9	2	0	4.00
Totals	5	46	33	15	11	8	19	4	1	2.15

New York Giants

Pitcher	G	IP	H	R	ER	BB	SO	W	L	ERA
Mathewson	2	19	14	3	2	2	7	1	1	0.95
Crandall	2	4⅔	4	2	2	0	2	0	0	3.86
Demaree	1	4	7	4	2	1	0	0	1	4.50
Tesreau	2	8⅓	11	7	6	1	4	0	1	6.48
Marquard	2	9	10	7	7	3	3	0	1	7.00
Totals	5	45	46	23	19	7	16	1	4	3.80

1914

COMPOSITE BATTING AVERAGES

Boston Braves

Player-Position	G	AB	R	H	2B	3B	HR	RBI	BA
Gowdy, c	4	11	2	6	3	1	1	3	.545
Evers, 2b	4	16	2	7	0	0	0	2	.438
Rudolph, p	2	6	1	2	0	0	0	0	.333
Maranville, ss	4	13	1	4	0	0	0	3	.308
Schmidt, 1b	4	17	2	5	0	0	0	2	.294
Mann, rf-pr-ph	3	7	1	2	0	0	0	1	.286
Whitted, cf	4	14	2	3	0	1	0	2	.214
Deal, 3b	4	16	2	2	2	0	0	0	.125
Connolly, lf	3	9	1	1	0	0	0	1	.111
Moran, rf	3	13	2	1	1	0	0	0	.077
Cather, lf	1	5	0	0	0	0	0	0	.000
James, p	2	4	0	0	0	0	0	0	.000
Tyler, p	1	3	0	0	0	0	0	0	.000
Devore, ph	1	1	0	0	0	0	0	0	.000
Gilbert, ph	1	0	0	0	0	0	0	0	.000
Totals	4	135	16	33	6	2	1	14	.244

Philadelphia Athletics

Player-Position	G	AB	R	H	2B	3B	HR	RBI	BA
Wyckoff, p	1	1	0	1	0	0	0	0	1.000
Shawkey, p	1	2	0	1	1	0	0	0	.500
Walsh, ph-cf	3	6	0	2	1	0	0	1	.333
Strunk, cf	2	7	0	2	0	0	0	0	.286
Baker, 3b	4	16	0	4	2	0	0	2	.250
Collins, 2b	4	14	0	3	0	0	0	0	.214
Murphy, rf	4	16	2	3	2	0	0	0	.188
Schang, c	4	12	1	2	1	0	0	0	.167
McInnis, 1b	4	14	2	2	1	0	0	0	.143
Barry, ss	4	14	1	1	0	0	0	0	.071
Oldring, lf	4	15	0	1	0	0	0	0	.067
Lapp, c	1	1	0	0	0	0	0	0	.000
Bender, p	1	2	0	0	0	0	0	0	.000
Plank, p	1	2	0	0	0	0	0	0	.000
Pennock, p	1	1	0	0	0	0	0	0	.000
Bush, p	1	5	0	0	0	0	0	0	.000
Totals	4	128	6	22	9	0	0	5	.172

COMPOSITE PITCHING AVERAGES

Boston Braves

Pitcher	G	IP	H	R	ER	BB	SO	W	L	ERA
James	2	11	2	0	0	6	9	2	0	0.00
Rudolph	2	18	12	2	1	4	15	2	0	0.50
Tyler	1	10	8	4	4	3	4	0	0	3.60
Totals	4	39	22	6	5	13	28	4	0	1.15

Philadelphia Athletics

Pitcher	G	IP	H	R	ER	BB	SO	W	L	ERA
Pennock	1	3	2	0	0	2	3	0	0	0.00
Plank	1	9	7	1	1	4	6	0	1	1.00
Wyckoff	1	3⅔	3	1	1	1	2	0	0	2.45
Bush	1	11	9	5	4	4	4	0	1	3.27
Shawkey	1	5	4	3	3	2	3	0	1	5.40
Bender	1	5⅓	8	6	6	2	3	0	1	10.13
Totals	4	37	33	16	15	15	18	0	4	3.65

1915

COMPOSITE BATTING AVERAGES

Boston Red Sox

Player-Position	G	AB	R	H	2B	3B	HR	RBI	BA
Foster, p	2	8	0	4	1	0	0	1	.500
Lewis, lf	5	18	1	8	1	0	1	5	.444
Hooper, rf	5	20	4	7	0	0	2	3	.350
Cady, c	4	6	0	2	0	0	0	0	.333
Gainor, 1b	1	3	1	1	0	0	0	0	.333
Hoblitzell, 1b	5	16	1	5	0	0	0	1	.313
Speaker, cf	5	17	2	5	0	1	0	0	.294
Gardner, 3b	5	17	2	4	0	1	0	0	.235
Shore, p	2	5	0	1	0	0	0	0	.200
Thomas, c	2	5	0	1	0	0	0	0	.200
Barry, 2b	5	17	1	3	0	0	0	1	.176
Scott, ss	5	18	0	1	0	0	0	0	.056
Janvrin, ss	1	1	0	0	0	0	0	0	.000
Carrigan, c	1	2	0	0	0	0	0	0	.000
Henriksen, ph	2	2	0	0	0	0	0	0	.000
Ruth, ph	1	1	0	0	0	0	0	0	.000
Leonard, p	1	3	0	0	0	0	0	0	.000
Totals	5	159	12	42	2	2	3	11	.264

Philadelphia Phillies

Player-Position	G	AB	R	H	2B	3B	HR	RBI	BA
Rixey, p	1	2	0	1	0	0	0	0	.500
Luderus, 1b	5	16	1	7	2	0	1	6	.438
Chalmers, p	1	3	0	1	0	0	0	0	.333
Bancroft, ss	5	17	2	5	0	0	0	1	.294
Alexander, p	2	5	0	1	0	0	0	0	.200
Burns, c	5	16	1	3	0	0	0	0	.188
Paskert, cf	5	19	2	3	0	0	0	0	.158
Cravath, rf	5	16	2	2	1	1	0	1	.125
Stock, 3b	5	17	1	2	1	0	0	0	.118
Whitted, lf-1b	5	15	0	1	0	0	0	1	.067
Niehoff, 2b	5	16	1	1	0	0	0	0	.063
Mayer, p	2	4	0	0	0	0	0	0	.000
Dugey, pr	2	0	0	0	0	0	0	0	.000
Becker, lf	2	0	0	0	0	0	0	0	.000
Byrne, ph	1	1	0	0	0	0	0	0	.000
Killefer, ph	1	1	0	0	0	0	0	0	.000
Totals	5	148	10	27	4	1	1	9	.182

COMPOSITE PITCHING AVERAGES

Boston Red Sox

Pitcher	G	IP	H	R	ER	BB	SO	W	L	ERA
Leonard	1	9	3	1	1	0	6	1	0	1.00
Foster	2	18	12	5	4	2	13	2	0	2.00
Shore	2	17	12	4	4	8	6	1	1	2.12
Totals	5	44	27	10	9	10	25	4	1	1.84

Philadelphia Phillies

Pitcher	G	IP	H	R	ER	BB	SO	W	L	ERA
Alexander	2	17⅔	14	3	3	4	10	1	1	1.53
Chalmers	1	8	8	2	2	3	6	0	1	2.25
Mayer	2	11⅓	16	4	3	2	7	0	1	2.38
Rixey	1	6⅔	4	3	2	2	2	0	1	2.70
Totals	5	43⅔	42	12	10	11	25	1	4	2.06

1916

COMPOSITE BATTING AVERAGES

Boston Red Sox

Player-Position	G	AB	R	H	2B	3B	HR	RBI	BA
Gainor, ph	1	1	0	1	0	0	0	1	1.000
Carrigan, c	1	3	0	2	0	0	0	1	.667
Shorten, cf	2	7	0	4	0	0	0	2	.571
Lewis, lf	5	17	3	6	2	1	0	1	.353
Hooper, rf	5	21	6	7	1	1	0	1	.333
Walker, cf	3	11	1	3	0	1	0	1	.273
Cady, c	2	4	1	1	0	0	0	0	.250
Hoblitzell, 1b	5	17	3	4	1	1	0	2	.235
Janvrin, 2b	5	23	2	5	3	0	0	1	.217
Gardner, 3b	5	17	2	3	0	0	2	6	.176
Thomas, c	3	7	0	1	0	1	0	0	.143
Scott, ss	5	16	1	2	0	1	0	1	.125
Shore, p	2	7	0	0	0	0	0	0	.000
Mays, p	2	1	0	0	0	0	0	0	.000
Walsh, cf	1	3	0	0	0	0	0	0	.000
McNally, pr	1	0	1	0	0	0	0	0	.000
Ruth, p	1	5	0	0	0	0	0	1	.000
Henriksen, ph	1	0	1	0	0	0	0	0	.000
Foster, p	1	1	0	0	0	0	0	0	.000
Leonard, p	1	3	0	0	0	0	0	0	.000
Totals	5	164	21	39	7	6	2	18	.238

Brooklyn Dodgers

Player-Position	G	AB	R	H	2B	3B	HR	RBI	BA
Stengel, rf-ph	4	11	2	4	0	0	0	0	.364
Coombs, p	1	3	0	1	0	0	0	1	.333
Johnston, ph-rf	3	10	1	3	0	1	0	0	.300
Olson, ss	5	16	1	4	0	1	0	2	.250
Pfeffer, p-ph	4	4	0	1	0	0	0	0	.250
Merkle, ph-1b	3	4	0	1	0	0	0	1	.250
Wheat, lf	5	19	2	4	0	1	0	1	.211
Meyers, c	3	10	0	2	0	1	0	0	.200
Smith, p	1	5	0	1	1	0	0	0	.200
Myers, cf	5	22	2	4	0	0	1	3	.182
Daubert, 1b	4	17	1	3	0	1	0	0	.176
Mowrey, 3b	5	17	2	3	0	0	0	1	.176
Miller, c	2	8	0	1	0	0	0	0	.125
Cutshaw, 2b	5	19	2	2	1	0	0	2	.105
Marquard, p	2	3	0	0	0	0	0	0	.000
O'Mara, ph	1	1	0	0	0	0	0	0	.000
Rucker, p	1	0	0	0	0	0	0	0	.000
Getz, ph	1	1	0	0	0	0	0	0	.000
Cheney, p	1	0	0	0	0	0	0	0	.000
Dell, p	1	0	0	0	0	0	0	0	.000
Totals	5	170	13	34	2	5	1	11	.200

COMPOSITE PITCHING AVERAGES

Boston Red Sox

Pitcher	G	IP	H	R	ER	BB	SO	W	L	ERA
Foster	1	3	3	0	0	1	0	0	0	0.00
Ruth	1	14	6	1	1	3	4	1	0	0.64
Leonard	1	9	5	2	1	4	3	1	0	1.00
Shore	2	17⅔	12	6	3	4	9	2	0	1.53
Mays	2	5⅓	8	4	3	2	0	1	5.06
Totals	5	49	34	13	8	14	19	4	1	1.47

Brooklyn Dodgers

Pitcher	G	IP	H	R	ER	BB	SO	W	L	ERA
Rucker	1	2	1	0	0	0	3	0	0	0.00
Dell	1	1	1	0	0	0	0	0	0	0.00
Smith	1	13⅓	7	2	2	6	2	0	1	1.35
Pfeffer	3	10⅔	7	5	2	4	5	0	1	1.69
Cheney	1	3	4	2	1	1	5	0	0	3.00
Coombs	1	6⅓	7	3	3	1	1	1	0	4.26
Marquard	2	11	12	9	8	6	9	0	2	6.55
Totals	4	47⅓	39	21	16	18	25	1	4	3.04

1917

COMPOSITE BATTING AVERAGES

Chicago White Sox

Player-Position	G	AB	R	H	2B	3B	HR	RBI	BA
Risberg, ph	2	2	0	1	0	0	0	1	.500
E. Collins, 2b	6	22	4	9	1	0	0	2	.409
Leibold, ph-rf	2	5	1	2	0	0	0	2	.400
Weaver, ss	6	21	3	7	1	0	0	1	.333
Jackson, lf	6	23	4	7	0	0	0	2	.304
J. Collins, rf	6	21	2	6	1	0	0	0	.286
Felsch, cf	6	22	4	6	1	0	1	3	.273
Schalk, c	6	19	1	5	0	0	0	0	.263
Gandil, 1b	6	23	1	6	1	0	0	5	.261
Cicotte, p	3	7	0	1	0	0	0	0	.143
Faber, p	4	7	0	1	0	0	0	0	.143
McMullin, 3b	6	24	1	3	1	0	0	2	.125
Danforth, p	1	0	0	0	0	0	0	0	.000
Russell, p	1	0	0	0	0	0	0	0	.000
Williams, p	1	0	0	0	0	0	0	0	.000
Lynn, ph	1	1	0	0	0	0	0	0	.000
Totals	6	197	21	54	6	0	1	18	.274

New York Giants

Player-Position	G	AB	R	H	2B	3B	HR	RBI	BA
Perritt, p	3	2	0	2	0	0	0	0	1.000
Robertson, rf	6	22	3	11	1	1	0	1	.500
McCarty, c-ph	3	5	1	2	0	1	0	1	.400
Rariden, c	5	13	2	5	0	0	0	2	.385
Holke, 1b	6	21	2	6	2	0	0	1	.286
Herzog, 2b	6	24	1	6	0	1	0	2	.250
Schupp, p	2	4	0	1	0	0	0	1	.250
Burns, lf	6	22	3	5	0	0	0	2	.227
Fletcher, ss	6	25	2	5	1	0	0	0	.200
Sallee, p	2	6	0	1	0	0	0	1	.167
Kauff, cf	6	25	2	4	1	0	2	5	.160
Zimmerman, 3b	6	25	1	3	0	1	0	0	.120
Anderson, p	1	0	0	0	0	0	0	0	.000
Wilhoit, ph	2	1	0	0	0	0	0	0	.000
Tesreau, p	1	0	0	0	0	0	0	0	.000
Benton, p	2	4	0	0	0	0	0	0	.000
Thorpe, rf	1	0	0	0	0	0	0	0	.000
Totals	6	190	17	51	5	4	2	16	.256

COMPOSITE PITCHING AVERAGES

Chicago White Sox

Pitcher	G	IP	H	R	ER	BB	SO	W	L	ERA
Cicotte	3	23	23	6	5	2	13	1	1	1.96
Faber	4	27	21	7	7	3	9	3	1	2.33
Williams	1	1	2	1	1	0	3	0	0	9.00
Danforth	1	1	3	2	2	0	2	0	0	18.00
Russell	1	0	2	1	1	1	0	0	0	—
Totals	6	52	51	17	16	6	27	4	2	2.77

New York Giants

Pitcher	G	IP	H	R	ER	BB	SO	W	L	ERA
Benton	2	14	9	3	0	1	8	1	1	0.00
Tesreau	1	1	0	0	0	1	0	0	0	0.00
Schupp	2	10⅓	11	2	2	2	9	1	0	1.74
Perritt	3	8⅓	9	2	2	3	3	0	0	2.16
Sallee	2	15⅓	20	10	9	4	4	0	2	5.28
Anderson	1	2	5	4	4	0	3	0	1	18.00
Totals	6	51	54	21	17	11	28	2	4	3.00

1918

COMPOSITE BATTING AVERAGES

Boston Red Sox

Player-Position	G	AB	R	H	2B	3B	HR	RBI	BA
Schang, ph-c	5	9	1	4	0	0	0	1	.444
Whiteman, lf	6	20	2	5	0	1	0	1	.250
McInnis, 1b	6	20	2	5	0	0	0	1	.250
Shean, 2b	6	19	2	4	1	0	0	0	.211
Hooper, rf	6	20	0	4	0	0	0	0	.200
Ruth, p-lf	3	5	0	1	0	1	0	2	.200
Mays, p	2	5	1	1	0	0	0	0	.200
Strunk, cf	6	23	1	4	1	1	0	0	.174
Thomas, 3b	6	16	0	2	0	0	0	0	.125
Scott, ss	6	21	0	2	0	0	0	1	.095
Agnew, c	4	9	0	0	0	0	0	0	.000
Dubuc, ph	1	1	0	0	0	0	0	0	.000
Bush, p	2	2	0	0	0	0	0	0	.000
Jones, p	1	1	0	0	0	0	0	0	.000
Miller, ph	1	1	0	0	0	0	0	0	.000
Totals	6	172	9	32	3	0	6	.186

Chicago Cubs

Player-Position	G	AB	R	H	2B	3B	HR	RBI	BA
Hendrix, ph	2	1	0	1	0	0	0	0	1.000
Pick, 2b	6	18	2	7	1	0	0	0	.389
Merkle, 1b	6	18	1	5	0	0	0	1	.278
Flack, rf	6	19	2	5	0	0	0	0	.263
Mann, lf	6	22	0	5	2	0	0	2	.227
Tyler, p	3	5	0	1	0	0	0	2	.200
Hollocher, ss	6	21	2	4	0	1	0	1	.190
Paskert, cf	6	21	0	4	1	0	0	2	.190
Deal, 3b	6	17	0	3	0	0	0	0	.176
Killefer, c	6	17	2	2	1	0	0	2	.118
Zeider, ph-3b	2	0	0	0	0	0	0	0	.000
Wortman, 2b	1	1	0	0	0	0	0	0	.000
O'Farrell, ph-c	3	3	0	0	0	0	0	0	.000
McCabe, pr-ph	3	1	1	0	0	0	0	0	.000
Barber, ph	2	2	0	0	0	0	0	0	.000
Vaughn, p	3	10	0	0	0	0	0	0	.000
Douglas, p	1	0	0	0	0	0	0	0	.000
Totals	6	176	10	37	5	1	0	10	.210

COMPOSITE PITCHING AVERAGES

Boston Red Sox

Pitcher	G	IP	H	R	ER	BB	SO	W	L	ERA
Mays	2	18	10	2	2	3	5	2	0	1.00
Ruth	2	17	13	2	2	7	4	2	0	1.06
Jones	1	9	7	3	3	5	5	0	1	3.00
Bush	2	9	7	3	3	0	4	0	1	3.00
Totals	6	53	37	10	10	18	14	4	2	1.70

Chicago Cubs

Pitcher	G	IP	H	R	ER	BB	SO	W	L	ERA
Douglas	1	1	1	1	0	0	0	0	1	0.00
Hendrix	1	1	0	0	0	0	0	0	0	0.00
Vaughn	3	27	17	3	3	5	17	1	2	1.00
Tyler	3	23	14	5	3	11	4	1	1	1.17
Totals	6	52	32	9	6	16	21	2	4	1.04

1919

COMPOSITE BATTING AVERAGES

Cincinnati Reds

Player-Position	G	AB	R	H	2B	3B	HR	RBI	BA
Ruether, p-ph......	3	6	2	4	1	2	0	4	.667
Wingo, c	3	7	1	4	0	0	0	1	.571
Fisher, p	2	2	0	1	0	0	0	0	.500
Magee, ph........	2	2	0	1	0	0	0	0	.500
Neale, rf	8	28	3	10	1	1	0	4	.357
Eller, p	2	7	2	2	1	0	0	0	.286
Duncan, lf........	8	26	3	7	2	0	0	8	.269
Daubert, 1b	8	29	4	7	0	1	0	1	.241
Rath, 2b	8	31	5	7	1	0	0	2	.226
Kopf, ss..........	8	27	3	6	0	2	0	3	.222
Roush, cf.........	8	28	6	6	2	1	0	7	.214
Rariden, c	5	19	0	4	0	0	0	2	.211
Groh, 3b	8	29	6	5	2	0	0	2	.172
Smith, pr.........	1	0	0	0	0	0	0	0	.000
Sallee, p	2	4	0	0	0	0	0	0	.000
Luque, p	2	1	0	0	0	0	0	0	.000
Ring, p	2	5	0	0	0	0	0	0	.000
Totals	8	251	35	64	10	7	0	34	.255

Chicago White Sox

Player-Position	G	AB	R	H	2B	3B	HR	RBI	BA
McMullin, ph	2	2	0	1	0	0	0	0	.500
Jackson, lf........	8	32	5	12	3	0	1	6	.375
Weaver, 3b	8	34	4	11	4	1	0	0	.324
Schalk, c	8	23	1	7	0	0	0	2	.304
J. Collins, rf-cf .	4	16	2	4	1	0	0	0	.250
Gandil, 1b	8	30	1	7	0	1	0	5	.233
E. Collins, 2b.....	8	31	2	7	1	0	0	1	.226
Williams, p	3	5	0	1	0	0	0	0	.200
Felsch, cf-rf	8	26	2	5	1	0	0	3	.192
Kerr, p...........	2	6	0	1	0	0	0	0	.167
Risberg, ss	8	25	3	2	0	1	0	0	.080
Leibold, rf-ph.....	5	18	0	1	0	0	0	0	.056
Cicotte, p	3	8	0	0	0	0	0	0	.000
Wilkinson, p......	2	2	0	0	0	0	0	0	.000
Lynn, c	1	1	0	0	0	0	0	0	.000
Murphy, ph	3	2	0	0	0	0	0	0	.000
Lowdermilk, p.....	1	0	0	0	0	0	0	0	.0000
Mayer, p	1	0	0	0	0	0	0	0	.000
James, p	1	2	0	0	0	0	0	0	.000
Totals	8	263	20	50	10	3	1	17	.224

COMPOSITE PITCHING AVERAGES

Cincinnati Reds

Pitcher	G	IP	H	R	ER	BB	SO	W	L	ERA
Luque	2	5	1	0	0	6	0	0	0	0.00
Ring	2	14	7	1	1	6	4	1	1	0.64
Sallee	2	13½	19	6	2	1	2	1	1	1.35
Eller.............	2	18	13	5	4	2	15	2	0	2.00
Fisher	2	7⅔	7	3	2	2	2	0	1	2.35
Ruether	2	14	12	5	4	4	1	1	0	2.57
Totals	8	72	50	20	13	15	30	5	3	1.63

Chicago White Sox

Pitcher	G	IP	H	R	ER	BB	SO	W	L	ERA
Mayer	1	1	0	1	0	1	0	0	0	0.00
Kerr	2	19	14	4	3	3	6	2	0	1.42
Wilkinson	2	7⅓	4	2	4	3	0	0	2.45
Cicotte	3	21⅔	19	9	7	5	7	1	2	2.91
James	1	4⅔	8	4	3	3	2	0	0	5.79
Williams	3	16⅓	12	12	12	8	4	0	3	6.61
Lowdermilk	1	1	2	1	1	1	0	0	0	9.00
Totals	8	71	64	35	28	25	22	3	5	3.55

1920

COMPOSITE BATTING AVERAGES

Cleveland Indians

Player-Position	G	AB	R	H	2B	3B	HR	RBI	BA
Nunamaker, ph-c ...	2	2	0	1	0	0	0	0	.500
O'Neill, c	7	21	1	7	3	0	0	2	.333
Bagby, p	2	6	1	2	0	0	1	3	.333
Jamieson, ph-lf....	6	15	2	5	1	0	0	1	.333
Speaker, cf	7	25	6	8	2	1	0	1	.320
E. Smith, ph-rf ...	5	13	1	4	0	1	1	5	.308
Evans, lf-ph	4	13	0	4	0	0	0	0	.308
Burns, 1b-ph	5	10	1	3	1	0	0	3	.300
W. Johnston, ph-1b.	5	11	1	3	0	0	0	0	.273
Gardner, 3b	7	24	1	5	1	0	0	2	.208
Wood, rf-ph	4	10	2	2	1	0	0	0	.200
Sewell, ss	7	23	0	4	0	0	0	0	.174
Wambsganss, 2b....	7	26	3	4	0	0	0	1	.154
Coveleski, p	3	10	2	1	0	0	0	0	.100
Lunte, 2b	1	0	0	0	0	0	0	0	.000
Graney, ph-rf-lf ..	3	3	0	0	0	0	0	0	.000
Uhle, p	2	0	0	0	0	0	0	0	.000
Caldwell, p	1	0	0	0	0	0	0	0	.000
Mails, p...........	2	5	0	0	0	0	0	0	.000
Thomas, c	1	0	0	0	0	0	0	0	.000
Totals	7	217	21	53	9	2	2	18	.244

Brooklyn Dodgers

Player-Position	G	AB	R	H	2B	3B	HR	RBI	BA
Mitchell, ph-p	2	3	0	1	0	0	0	0	.333
Grimes, p	3	6	1	2	0	0	0	0	.333
Wheat, lf	7	27	2	9	2	0	0	2	.333
Olson, ss	7	25	2	8	1	0	0	0	.320
Myers, cf	7	26	0	6	0	0	0	1	.231
J. Johnston, 3b....	4	14	2	3	0	0	0	0	.214
Griffith, rf	7	21	1	4	2	0	0	3	.190
Sheehan, 3b	3	11	0	2	0	0	0	0	.182
Konetchy, 1b	7	23	0	4	0	1	0	2	.174
Krueger, c-ph	4	6	0	1	0	0	0	0	.167
Miller, c	6	14	0	2	0	0	0	0	.143
Kilduff, 2b	7	21	0	2	0	0	0	0	.095
Lamar, ph	3	3	0	0	0	0	0	0	.000
Neis, pr-rf	4	5	0	0	0	0	0	0	.000
Marquard, p	2	1	0	0	0	0	0	0	.000
Mamaux, p	3	1	0	0	0	0	0	0	.000
Cadore, p	2	0	0	0	0	0	0	0	.000
S. Smith, p	2	6	0	0	0	0	0	0	.000
Pfeffer, p.........	1	1	0	0	0	0	0	0	.000
McCabe, pr........	1	0	0	0	0	0	0	0	.000
Schmandt, ph	1	1	0	0	0	0	0	0	.000
Totals	7	215	8	44	5	1	0	8	.205

COMPOSITE PITCHING AVERAGES

Cleveland Indians

Pitcher	G	IP	H	R	ER	BB	SO	W	L	ERA
Mails	2	15⅔	6	0	0	6	6	1	0	0.00
Uhle	2	3	1	0	0	3	0	0	0.00
Coveleski	3	27	15	2	2	2	8	3	0	0.67
Bagby............	2	15	20	4	3	1	3	1	1	1.80
Caldwell	1	⅓	2	2	1	1	0	0	1	27.00
Totals	7	61	44	8	6	10	20	5	2	0.89

Brooklyn Dodgers

Pitcher	G	IP	H	R	ER	BB	SO	W	L	ERA
Mitchell..........	1	4⅔	3	1	0	3	1	0	0	0.00
S. Smith	2	17	10	2	1	3	3	1	1	0.53
Marquard	2	9	7	3	1	3	6	0	1	1.00
Pfeffer	1	3	4	1	1	2	1	0	0	3.00
Grimes............	3	19⅓	23	10	9	9	4	1	2	4.19
Mamaux	3	4	2	2	2	0	5	0	0	4.50
Cadore	2	2	4	2	2	1	1	0	1	9.00
Totals	7	59	53	21	16	21	21	2	5	2.44

1921

COMPOSITE BATTING AVERAGES

New York Giants

Player-Position	G	AB	R	H	2B	3B	HR	RBI	BA
Barnes, p..........	3	9	3	4	0	0	0	0	.444
Snyder, c-ph	7	22	4	8	1	0	1	3	.364
E. Meusel, lf	8	29	4	10	2	1	1	7	.345
Rawlings, 2b	8	30	2	10	3	0	0	4	.333
Burns, cf	8	33	2	11	4	1	0	2	.333
Frisch, 3b	8	30	5	9	0	1	0	1	.300
Youngs, rf	8	25	3	7	1	1	0	4	.280
Kelly, 1b	8	30	3	7	1	0	0	4	.233
Bancroft, ss	8	33	3	5	1	0	0	3	.152
Douglas, p	3	7	0	0	0	0	0	0	.000
Smith, ph-c	3	7	0	0	0	0	0	0	.000
Nehf, p	3	9	0	0	0	0	0	0	.000
Toney, p...........	2	0	0	0	0	0	0	0	.000
Totals	8	264	29	71	13	4	2	28	.269

New York Yankees

Player-Position	G	AB	R	H	2B	3B	HR	RBI	BA
Shawkey, p.........	2	4	2	2	0	0	0	0	.500
Ruth, lf-ph	6	16	3	5	0	0	1	4	.313
Schang, c	8	21	1	6	1	1	0	1	.286
Baker, ph-3b.......	4	8	0	2	0	0	0	0	.250
Ward, 2b	8	26	1	6	0	0	0	4	.231
Hoyt, p	3	9	0	2	0	0	0	1	.222
McNally, 3b	7	20	3	4	1	0	0	1	.200
Fewster, pr-lf	4	10	3	2	0	0	1	2	.200
R. Meusel, rf	8	30	3	6	2	0	0	3	.200
Peckinpaugh, ss ...	8	28	2	5	1	0	0	0	.179
Miller, cf	8	31	3	5	1	0	0	2	.161
Pipp, 1b	8	26	1	4	1	0	0	2	.154
Mays, p	3	9	0	1	0	0	0	0	.111
DeVormer, c-pr	2	1	0	0	0	0	0	0	.000
Quinn, p	1	2	0	0	0	0	0	0	.000
Collins, p	1	0	0	0	0	0	0	0	.000
Rogers, p..........	1	0	0	0	0	0	0	0	.000
Harper, p	1	0	0	0	0	0	0	0	.000
Piercy, p	1	0	0	0	0	0	0	0	.000
Totals	8	241	22	50	7	1	2	20	.207

COMPOSITE PITCHING AVERAGES

New York Giants

Pitcher	G	IP	H	R	ER	BB	SO	W	L	ERA
Nehf	3	26	13	6	4	13	8	1	2	1.36
Barnes	3	16⅓	10	3	3	6	18	2	0	1.65
Douglas	3	26	20	6	6	7	17	2	1	2.08
Toney	2	2⅔	7	7	7	3	1	0	0	23.63
Totals	8	71	50	22	20	27	44	5	3	2.53

New York Yankees

Pitcher	G	IP	H	R	ER	BB	SO	W	L	ERA
Hoyt	3	27	18	2	0	11	18	2	1	0.00
Piercy............	1	1	2	0	0	0	2	0	0	0.00
Mays	3	26	20	6	5	0	9	1	2	1.73
Shawkey	2	9	13	9	7	6	5	0	1	7.00
Rogers	1	1⅓	3	1	1	6	1	0	0	6.75
Quinn	1	3⅔	8	4	4	2	2	0	1	9.82
Harper	1	1⅓	3	3	3	2	1	0	0	20.25
Collins	1	⅔	4	4	4	1	0	0	0	54.00
Totals	8	70	71	20	24	22	36	3	5	3.00

1922

COMPOSITE BATTING AVERAGES

New York Giants

Player-Position	G	AB	R	H	2B	3B	HR	RBI	BA
King, cf	2	1	0	1	0	0	0	1	1.000
Groh, 3b	5	19	4	9	0	1	0	0	.474
Frisch, 2b	5	17	3	8	1	0	0	2	.471
Stengel, cf	2	5	0	2	0	0	0	0	.400
Youngs, rf	5	16	2	6	0	0	0	2	.375
Snyder, c	4	15	0	5	0	0	0	0	.333
Kelly, 1b	5	18	0	5	0	0	0	2	.278
J. Scott, p	1	4	0	1	0	0	0	0	.250
McQuillan, p	1	4	1	1	1	0	0	0	.250
E. Meusel, lf	5	20	3	5	0	0	1	7	.250
Cunn'ham, pr-cf	4	10	0	2	0	0	0	2	.200
Bancroft, ss	5	19	4	4	0	0	0	2	.211
E. Smith, ph-c	4	7	0	1	0	0	0	0	.143
Nehf, p	2	3	1	0	0	0	0	0	.000
Ryan, p	1	0	0	0	0	0	0	0	.000
J. Barnes, p	1	4	0	0	0	0	0	0	.000
Totals	5	162	18	50	2	1	1	18	.309

New York Yankees

Player-Position	G	AB	R	H	2B	3B	HR	RBI	BA
Hoyt, p	2	2	0	1	0	0	0	0	.500
R. Meusel, lf	5	20	2	6	1	0	0	2	.300
Pipp, 1b	5	21	0	6	1	0	0	3	.286
Dugan, 3b	5	20	4	5	1	0	0	0	.250
Witt, cf	5	18	1	4	1	1	0	0	.222
Schang, c	5	16	0	3	1	0	0	0	.188
Bush, p	2	6	0	1	0	0	0	1	.167
Ward, 2b	5	13	3	2	0	0	2	3	.154
E. Scott, ss	5	14	0	2	0	0	0	1	.143
Ruth, rf	5	17	1	2	1	0	0	1	.118
Shawkey, p	1	4	0	0	0	0	0	0	.000
El. Smith, ph	2	2	0	0	0	0	0	0	.000
McNally, 2b	1	0	0	0	0	0	0	0	.000
Baker, ph	1	1	0	0	0	0	0	0	.000
Jones, p	2	0	0	0	0	0	0	0	.000
Mays, p	1	2	0	0	0	0	0	0	.000
McMillan, ph-cf	1	2	0	0	0	0	0	0	.000
Totals	5	158	11	32	6	1	2	11	.203

COMPOSITE PITCHING AVERAGES

New York Giants

Pitcher	G	IP	H	R	ER	BB	SO	W	L	ERA
J. Scott	1	9	4	0	0	1	2	1	0	0.00
Ryan	1	2	1	0	0	0	2	1	0	0.00
J. Barnes	1	10	8	3	2	2	6	0	0	1.80
McQuillan	1	9	8	3	2	2	4	1	0	2.00
Nehf	2	16	11	5	4	3	6	1	0	2.25
Totals	5	46	32	11	8	8	20	4	0	1.57

New York Yankees

Pitcher	G	IP	H	R	ER	BB	SO	W	L	ERA
Jones	2	2	1	0	0	0	2	0	0	0.00
Hoyt	2	8	11	3	1	2	4	0	1	1.13
Shawkey	1	10	8	3	3	2	4	0	0	2.70
Mays	1	8	9	4	4	2	1	0	1	4.50
Bush	2	15	21	8	8	5	6	0	2	4.80
Totals	5	48	50	18	16	12	15	0	4	3.35

1923

COMPOSITE BATTING AVERAGES

New York Yankees

Player-Position	G	AB	R	H	2B	3B	HR	RBI	BA
Bush, p-ph	4	7	2	3	1	0	0	1	.429
Ward, 2b	6	24	4	10	0	0	1	2	.417
Ruth, rf-1b	6	19	8	7	1	1	3	3	.368
Shawkey, p	1	3	0	1	0	0	0	1	.333
Schang, c	6	22	3	7	1	0	0	0	.318
E. Scott, ss	6	22	2	7	0	0	0	3	.318
Dugan, 3b	6	25	5	7	2	1	1	5	.280
R. Meusel, lf	6	26	1	7	1	2	0	8	.269
Pipp, 1b	6	20	2	5	0	0	0	2	.250
Witt, cf	6	25	1	6	2	0	0	4	.240
Johnson, ss-pr	2	0	1	0	0	0	0	0	.000
Pennock, p	3	6	0	0	0	0	0	0	.000
Jones, p	2	2	0	0	0	0	0	0	.000
Haines, rf-cf-pr	2	1	1	0	0	0	0	0	.000
Hofmann, ph	2	1	0	0	0	0	0	0	.000
Hoyt, p	1	1	0	0	0	0	0	0	.000
Hendrick, ph	1	1	0	0	0	0	0	0	.000
Totals	6	205	30	60	8	4	5	29	.293

New York Giants

Player-Position	G	AB	R	H	2B	3B	HR	RBI	BA
Bentley, ph-p	5	5	0	3	1	0	0	0	.600
Stengel, cf-ph	6	12	3	5	0	0	2	4	.417
Frisch, 2b	6	25	2	10	0	1	0	1	.400
Youngs, rf	6	23	2	8	0	0	1	3	.348
E. Meusel, lf	6	25	3	7	1	1	1	2	.280
Groh, 3b	6	22	3	4	0	1	0	2	.182
Kelly, 1b	6	22	1	4	0	0	0	0	.182
Nehf, p	2	6	0	1	0	0	0	0	.167
Cunn'ham, cf-ph	4	7	0	1	0	0	0	0	.143
Snyder, c	5	17	1	2	0	0	1	2	.118
Bancroft, ss	6	24	1	2	0	0	0	1	.083
Ryan, p	3	2	0	0	0	0	0	0	.000
Gowdy, c-ph	3	4	0	0	0	0	0	0	.000
Maguire, pr	2	0	1	0	0	0	0	0	.000
McQuillan, p	2	3	0	0	0	0	0	0	.000
J. Scott, p	2	1	0	0	0	0	0	0	.000
Jonnard, p	2	0	0	0	0	0	0	0	.000
O'Connell, ph	2	1	0	0	0	0	0	0	.000
Barnes, p	2	1	0	0	0	0	0	0	.000
Watson, p	1	0	0	0	0	0	0	0	.000
Gearin, pr	1	0	0	0	0	0	0	0	.000
Jackson, ph	1	1	0	0	0	0	0	0	.000
Totals	6	201	17	47	2	3	5	17	.234

COMPOSITE PITCHING AVERAGES

New York Yankees

Pitcher	G	IP	H	R	ER	BB	SO	W	L	ERA
Jones	2	10	5	1	1	2	3	0	1	0.90
Bush	3	16⅔	7	2	2	4	5	1	1	1.08
Shawkey	1	7⅔	12	3	3	4	2	1	0	3.52
Pennock	3	17⅓	19	7	7	1	8	2	0	3.63
Hoyt	1	2⅓	4	4	4	1	0	0	0	15.43
Totals	6	54	47	17	17	12	18	4	2	2.83

New York Giants

Pitcher	G	IP	H	R	ER	BB	SO	W	L	ERA
Barnes	2	4⅔	4	0	0	4	0	0	0	0.00
Jonnard	2	2	1	0	0	1	1	0	0	0.00
Ryan	3	9⅓	11	4	1	3	3	1	0	0.96
Nehf	2	16⅓	10	5	5	6	7	1	1	2.76
McQuillan	2	9	11	5	5	4	3	0	1	5.00
Bentley	2	6⅔	10	8	7	4	1	0	1	9.45
J. Scott	2	3	9	5	4	1	2	0	1	12.00
Watson	1	2	4	3	3	1	1	0	0	13.50
Totals	6	53	60	30	25	20	22	2	4	4.25

1924

COMPOSITE BATTING AVERAGES

Washington Senators

Player-Position	G	AB	R	H	2B	3B	HR	RBI	BA
Shirley, ph-pr	3	2	1	1	0	0	0	1	.500
Peckinpaugh, ss	4	12	1	5	2	0	0	2	.417
Judge, 1b	7	26	4	10	1	0	0	0	.385
Goslin, lf	7	32	4	11	1	0	3	7	.344
Harris, 2b	7	33	5	11	0	0	2	7	.333
McNeely, cf-ph	7	27	4	6	3	0	0	1	.222
Rice, rf	7	29	2	6	0	0	0	1	.207
Bluege, 3b-ss	7	26	2	5	0	0	0	2	.192
Miller, 3b	4	11	0	2	0	0	0	2	.182
Leibold, cf-ph	3	6	1	1	1	0	0	0	.167
Johnson, p	3	9	0	1	0	0	0	0	.111
Ruel, c	7	21	2	2	1	0	0	0	.095
Marberry, p	4	2	0	0	0	0	0	0	.000
Taylor, pr-3b	3	2	0	0	0	0	0	0	.000
Tate, ph	3	0	0	0	0	0	0	0	.000
Zachary, p	2	5	0	0	0	0	0	0	.000
Mogridge, p	2	5	0	0	0	0	0	0	.000
Russell, p	1	0	0	0	0	0	0	0	.000
Martina, p	1	0	0	0	0	0	0	0	.000
Speece, p	1	0	0	0	0	0	0	0	.000
Ogden, p	1	0	0	0	0	0	0	0	.000
Totals	7	248	26	61	9	0	5	23	.246

New York Giants

Player-Position	G	AB	R	H	2B	3B	HR	RBI	BA
Groh, ph	1	1	0	1	0	0	0	0	1.000
McQuillan, p	3	1	1	1	0	0	0	1	1.000
Ryan, p	2	2	1	1	0	0	1	1	.500
Terry, 1b-ph	5	14	3	6	1	1	1	1	.429
Nehf, p	3	7	1	3	0	0	0	0	.429
Frisch, 2b-3b	7	30	1	10	4	1	0	0	.333
Lindstrom, 3b	7	30	1	10	2	0	0	4	.333
Kelly, cf-2b-1b	7	31	7	9	1	0	1	4	.290
Bentley, ph-p	5	7	1	2	0	0	1	2	.286
Gowdy, c	7	27	3	7	0	0	0	2	.259
Wilson, lf-cf	7	30	1	7	1	0	0	3	.233
Youngs, rf-lf	7	27	3	5	1	0	0	2	.185
Meusel, lf-rf	4	13	0	2	0	0	0	1	.154
Jackson, ss	7	27	3	2	0	0	0	1	.074
So'wo'h, pr-cf-ph	5	1	1	0	0	0	0	0	.000
Barnes, p	2	4	0	0	0	0	0	0	.000
Jonnard, p	1	0	0	0	0	0	0	0	.000
Watson, p	1	0	0	0	0	0	0	0	.000
Baldwin, p	1	0	0	0	0	0	0	0	.000
Dean, p	1	0	0	0	0	0	0	0	.000
Snyder, ph	1	1	0	0	0	0	0	0	.000
Totals	7	253	27	66	9	2	4	22	.261

COMPOSITE PITCHING AVERAGES

Washington Senators

Pitcher	G	IP	H	R	ER	BB	SO	W	L	ERA
Martina	1	1	0	0	0	1	0	0	0	0.00
Ogden	1	⅓	0	0	0	1	0	0	0	0.00
Marberry	4	8	9	6	1	4	10	0	1	1.13
Zachary	2	17⅔	13	4	4	3	3	2	0	2.04
Johnson	3	24	30	10	6	11	20	1	2	2.25
Mogridge	2	12	7	4	3	6	5	1	0	2.25
Russell	1	3	4	2	0	0	0	0	0	3.00
Speece	1	1	3	1	1	0	0	0	0	9.00
Totals	7	67	66	27	16	25	40	4	3	2.15

New York Giants

Pitcher	G	IP	H	R	ER	BB	SO	W	L	ERA
Baldwin	1	2	1	0	0	0	1	0	0	0.00
Dean	1	2	3	2	0	0	2	0	0	0.00
Jonnard	1	0	0	0	0	1	0	0	0	0.00
Watson	1	⅔	0	0	0	0	0	0	0	0.00
Nehf	3	19⅔	15	5	4	9	7	1	1	1.83
McQuillan	3	7	2	2	2	6	2	1	0	2.57
Ryan	2	5⅔	7	2	2	4	3	0	0	3.18
Bentley	3	17⅔	18	7	7	8	10	1	2	3.57
Barnes	2	12⅔	15	8	8	1	9	0	1	5.68
Totals	7	67⅓	51	26	23	29	34	3	4	3.07

1925

COMPOSITE BATTING AVERAGES

Pittsburgh Pirates

Player-Position	G	AB	R	H	2B	3B	HR	RBI	BA
Morrison, p	3	2	1	1	0	0	0	0	.500
Carey, cf	7	24	6	11	4	0	0	2	.458
Smith, c	6	20	0	7	1	0 *	0	0	.350
Traynor, 3b	7	26	2	9	0	2	1	4	.346
Bigbee, pr-ph-lf	4	3	1	1	1	0	0	1	.333
McInnis, ph-1b	4	14	0	4	0	0	0	1	.286
Cuyler, rf	7	26	3	7	3	0	1	6	.269
Barnhart, lf	7	28	1	7	1	0	0	5	.250
Moore, 2b	7	26	7	6	1	0	1	2	.231
Wright, ss	7	27	3	5	1	0	1	3	.185
Kremer, p	3	7	0	1	0	0	0	1	.143
Grantham, 1b-ph	5	15	0	2	0	0	0	0	.133
Aldridge, p	3	7	0	0	0	0	0	0	.000
Gooch, c	3	3	0	0	0	0	0	0	.000
Yde, p-pr	2	1	1	0	0	0	0	0	.000
Meadows, p	1	1	0	0	0	0	0	0	.000
C. Adams, p	1	0	0	0	0	0	0	0	.000
Oldham, p	1	0	0	0	0	0	0	0	.000
Totals	7	230	25	61	12	2	4	25	.265

Washington Senators

Player-Position	G	AB	R	H	2B	3B	HR	RBI	BA
Leibold, ph	3	2	1	1	1	0	0	0	.500
J. Harris, rf	7	25	5	11	2	0	3	6	.440
Rice, cf-rf	7	33	5	12	0	0	0	3	.364
Severeid, c	3	3	0	1	0	0	0	0	.333
Ruel, c	7	19	0	6	1	0	0	1	.316
Goslin, lf	7	26	6	8	1	0	3	6	.308
Bluege, 3b	5	18	2	5	1	0	0	2	.278
Peckinpaugh, ss	7	24	1	6	1	0	1	3	.250
Myer, 3b	3	8	0	2	0	0	0	0	.250
Judge, 1b	7	23	2	4	1	0	1	3	.174
Johnson, p	3	11	0	1	0	0	0	0	.091
S. Harris, 2b	7	23	2	2	0	0	0	0	.087
McNeely, cf-pr	4	0	2	0	0	0	0	0	.000
Ferguson, p	2	4	0	0	0	0	0	0	.000
Veach, ph	2	1	0	0	0	0	0	1	.000
Coveleski, p	2	3	0	0	0	0	0	0	.000
Marberry, p	2	0	0	0	0	0	0	0	.000
Ballou, p	2	0	0	0	0	0	0	0	.000
S. Adams, ph-2b	2	1	0	0	0	0	0	0	.000
Ruether, ph	1	1	0	0	0	0	0	0	.000
Zachary, p	1	0	0	0	0	0	0	0	.000
Totals	7	225	26	59	8	0	8	25	.262

COMPOSITE PITCHING AVERAGES

Pittsburgh Pirates

Pitcher	G	IP	H	R	ER	BB	SO	W	L	ERA
C. Adams	1	1	2	0	0	0	0	0	0	0.00
Oldham	1	1	0	0	0	0	2	0	0	0.00
Morrison	3	9⅓	11	3	3	1	5	0	0	2.89
Kremer	3	21	17	7	7	4	9	2	1	3.00
Meadows	1	8	6	3	3	0	4	0	1	3.38
Aldridge	3	18⅓	18	9	9	9	9	2	0	4.42
Yde	1	2⅓	5	4	3	3	1	0	1	11.70
Totals	7	61	59	26	25	17	30	4	3	3.69

Washington Senators

Pitcher	G	IP	H	R	ER	BB	SO	W	L	ERA
Marberry	2	2⅓	3	0	0	0	2	0	0	0.00
Ballou	2	1⅔	0	0	0	1	1	0	0	0.00
Johnson	3	26	26	10	6	4	15	2	1	2.08
Ferguson	2	14	13	6	5	6	11	1	1	3.21
Coveleski	2	14⅓	16	7	6	5	3	0	2	3.77
Zachary	1	1⅔	3	2	2	1	0	0	0	10.80
Totals	7	60	61	25	19	17	32	3	4	2.85

1926

COMPOSITE BATTING AVERAGES

St. Louis Cardinals

Player-Position	G	AB	R	H	2B	3B	HR	RBI	BA
Haines, p	3	5	1	3	0	0	1	2	.600
Thevenow, ss	7	24	5	10	1	0	1	4	.417
Bottomley, 1b	7	29	4	10	3	0	0	5	.345
Southworth, rf	7	29	6	10	1	1	1	4	.345
O'Farrell, c	7	23	2	7	1	0	0	2	.304
Douthit, cf	4	15	3	4	2	0	0	1	.267
L. Bell, 3b	7	27	4	7	1	0	1	6	.259
Hornsby, 2b	7	28	2	7	1	0	0	4	.250
Hafey, lf	7	27	2	5	2	0	0	0	.185
Holm, rf-ph-cf	5	16	1	2	0	0	0	1	.125
Alexander, p	3	7	1	0	0	0	0	0	.000
Flowers, ph	3	3	0	0	0	0	0	0	.000
Sherdel, p	2	5	0	0	0	0	0	0	.000
Rhem, p	1	1	0	0	0	0	0	0	.000
Toporcer, ph	1	0	0	0	0	0	0	1	.000
Reinhart, p	1	0	0	0	0	0	0	0	.000
H. Bell, p	1	0	0	0	0	0	0	0	.000
Hallahan, p	1	0	0	0	0	0	0	0	.000
Keen, p	1	0	0	0	0	0	0	0	.000
Totals	7	239	31	65	12	1	4	30	.272

New York Yankees

Player-Position	G	AB	R	H	2B	3B	HR	RBI	BA
Combs, cf	7	28	3	10	2	0	0	2	.357
Gehrig, 1b	7	23	1	8	2	0	0	3	.348
Dugan, 3b	7	24	2	8	1	0	0	2	.333
Ruth, rf	7	20	6	6	0	0	4	5	.300
Severeid, c	7	22	1	6	1	0	0	1	.273
Paschal, cf	5	4	0	1	0	0	0	1	.250
Meusel, lf	7	21	3	5	1	1	0	0	.238
Lazzeri, 2b	7	26	2	5	1	0	0	3	.192
Pennock, p	3	7	1	1	0	0	0	0	.143
Koenig, ss	7	32	2	4	1	0	0	2	.125
Ruether, ph-p	3	4	0	0	0	0	0	0	.000
Collins, c	3	2	0	0	0	0	0	0	.000
Shawkey, p	3	2	0	0	0	0	0	0	.000
Hoyt, p	2	6	0	0	0	0	0	0	.000
Shocker, p	2	2	0	0	0	0	0	0	.000
Thomas, p	2	0	0	0	0	0	0	0	.000
Adams, pr	2	0	0	0	0	0	0	0	.000
Gazella, 3b	1	0	0	0	0	0	0	0	.000
Jones, p	1	0	0	0	0	0	0	0	.000
Totals	7	223	21	54	10	1	4	19	.242

COMPOSITE PITCHING AVERAGES

St. Louis Cardinals

Pitcher	G	IP	H	R	ER	BB	SO	W	L	ERA
Keen	1	1	0	0	0	0	0	0	0	0.00
Haines	3	16⅔	13	2	2	9	5	2	0	1.08
Alexander	3	20⅓	12	4	3	4	17	2	0	1.33
Sherdel	2	17	15	5	4	8	3	0	2	2.12
Hallahan	1	2	2	1	1	3	1	0	0	4.50
Rhem	1	4	7	3	3	2	4	0	0	6.75
H. Bell	1	2	4	2	2	1	1	0	0	9.00
Reinhart	1	0	1	4	4	4	0	0	1	—
Totals	7	63	54	21	.19	31	31	4	3	2.71

New York Yankees

Pitcher	G	IP	H	R	ER	BB	SO	W	L	ERA
Hoyt	2	15	19	8	2	1	8	1	1	1.20
Pennock	3	22	13	3	3	4	8	2	0	1.23
Thomas	2	3	3	1	1	0	0	0	0	3.00
Ruether	1	4⅓	7	4	2	2	1	0	1	4.15
Shawkey	3	10	8	7	6	5	3	0	1	5.40
Shocker	2	7⅔	13	7	7	0	3	0	1	8.22
Jones	1	1	2	1	1	2	1	0	0	9.00
Totals	7	63	65	31	23	11	28	3	4	3.14

1927

COMPOSITE BATTING AVERAGES

New York Yankees

Player-Position	G	AB	R	H	2B	3B	HR	RBI	BA
Collins, c	2	5	0	3	1	0	0	0	.600
Koenig, ss	4	18	5	9	2	0	0	2	.500
Ruth, rf	4	15	4	6	0	0	2	7	.400
Pipgras, p	1	3	0	1	0	0	0	0	.333
Combs, cf	4	16	6	5	0	0	0	2	.313
Gehrig, 1b	4	13	2	4	2	2	0	4	.308
Lazzeri, 2b	4	15	1	4	1	0	0	2	.267
Dugan, 3b	4	15	2	3	0	0	0	0	.200
Moore, p	2	5	0	1	0	0	0	0	.200
Meusel, lf	4	17	1	2	0	0	0	1	.118
Bengough, c	2	4	1	0	0	0	0	0	.000
Pennock, p	1	4	1	0	0	0	0	1	.000
Hoyt, p	1	3	0	0	0	0	0	0	.000
Grabowski, c	1	2	0	0	0	0	0	0	.000
Durst, ph	1	1	0	0	0	0	0	0	.000
Totals	4	136	23	38	6	2	2	19	.279

Pittsburgh Pirates

Player-Position	G	AB	R	H	2B	3B	HR	RBI	BA
Kremer, p	1	2	1	1	0	0	0	0	.500
L. Waner, cf	4	15	5	6	1	1	0	0	.400
Grantham, 2b	3	11	0	4	1	0	0	0	.364
P. Waner, rf	4	15	0	5	1	0	0	3	.333
Barnhart, lf	4	16	0	5	1	0	0	4	.313
Traynor, 3b	4	15	1	3	1	0	0	0	.200
Harris, 1b	4	15	0	3	0	0	0	1	.200
Wright, ss	4	13	1	2	0	0	0	2	.154
Smith, c-ph	3	8	0	0	0	0	0	0	.000
Miljus, p	2	2	0	0	0	0	0	0	.000
Brickell, ph	2	2	1	0	0	0	0	0	.000
Gooch, c	3	5	0	0	0	0	0	0	.000
Aldridge, p	2	3	0	0	0	0	0	0	.000
Cvengros, p	2	2	0	0	0	0	0	0	.000
Dawson, p	1	1	0	0	0	0	0	0	.000
Rhyne, 2b	1	4	0	0	0	0	0	0	.000
Spencer, c	1	1	0	0	0	0	0	0	.000
Meadows, p	1	2	0	0	0	0	0	0	.000
Groh, ph	1	1	0	0	0	0	0	0	.000
Yde, pr	1	0	1	0	0	0	0	0	.000
Hill, p	1	1	0	0	0	0	0	0	.000
Totals	4	130	10	29	6	1	0	10	.223

COMPOSITE PITCHING AVERAGES

New York Yankees

Pitcher	G	IP	H	R	ER	BB	SO	W	L	ERA
Moore	2	10⅔	11	3	1	2	2	1	0	0.84
Pennock	1	9	3	1	1	0	1	1	0	1.00
Pipgras	1	9	7	2	2	1	2	1	0	2.00
Hoyt	1	7⅓	8	4	4	1	2	1	0	4.91
Totals	4	36	29	10	8	4	7	4	0	2.00

Pittsburgh Pirates

Pitcher	G	IP	H	R	ER	BB	SO	W	L	ERA
Dawson	1	1	0	0	0	0	0	0	0	0.00
Miljus	2	6⅔	4	1	1	4	6	0	1	1.35
Kremer	1	5	5	5	2	3	1	0	1	3.60
Cvengros	2	2⅓	3	1	1	0	2	0	0	3.86
Hill	1	6	9	3	3	1	6	0	0	4.50
Aldridge	1	7⅓	10	6	6	4	4	0	1	7.36
Meadows	1	6⅓	7	7	7	1	6	0	1	9.95
Totals	4	34⅔	38	23	20	13	25	0	4	5.19

1928

COMPOSITE BATTING AVERAGES

New York Yankees

Player-Position	G	AB	R	H	2B	3B	HR	RBI	BA
Collins, c	1	1	0	1	1	0	0	0	1.000
Ruth, rf-lf	4	16	9	10	3	0	3	4	.625
Gehrig, 1b	4	11	5	6	1	0	4	9	.545
Durst, cf	4	8	3	3	0	0	1	2	.375
Lazzeri, 2b	4	12	2	3	1	0	0	0	.250
Bengough, c	4	13	1	3	0	0	0	1	.231
Paschal, cf-ph	3	10	0	2	0	0	0	1	.200
Meusel, lf-rf	4	15	5	3	1	0	1	3	.200
Dugan, 3b-ph	3	6	0	1	0	0	0	1	.167
Koenig, ss	4	19	1	3	0	0	0	0	.158
Hoyt, p	2	7	0	1	0	0	0	0	.143
Robertson, 3b-ph	3	8	1	1	0	0	0	2	.125
Durocher, 2b	4	2	0	0	0	0	0	0	.000
Zachary, p	1	4	0	0	0	0	0	0	.000
Pipgras, p	1	2	0	0	0	0	0	0	.000
Combs, ph	1	0	0	0	0	0	0	1	.000
Totals	4	134	27	37	7	0	9	25	.276

St. Louis Cardinals

Player-Position	G	AB	R	H	2B	3B	HR	RBI	BA
Smith, c	1	4	0	3	0	0	0	0	.750
Maranville, ss	4	13	2	4	1	0	0	0	.308
High, 3b	4	17	1	5	2	0	0	1	.294
Orsatti, ph-cf	4	7	1	2	1	0	0	0	.286
Frisch, 2b	4	13	1	3	0	0	0	1	.231
Bottomley, 1b	4	14	1	3	0	1	1	3	.214
Hafey, lf	4	15	0	3	0	0	0	0	.200
Holm, ph-rf	3	6	0	1	0	0	0	1	.167
Harper, rf	3	9	1	1	0	0	0	0	.111
Douthit, cf	3	11	1	1	0	0	0	1	.091
Wilson, c	3	11	1	1	1	0	0	0	.091
Thevenow, ss	1	0	0	0	0	0	0	0	.000
Sherdel, p	2	5	0	0	0	0	0	0	.000
Johnson, p	2	0	0	0	0	0	0	0	.000
Alexander, p	2	1	0	0	0	0	0	1	.000
Mitchell, p	1	2	0	0	0	0	0	0	.000
Haines, p	1	2	0	0	0	0	0	0	.000
Blades, ph	1	1	0	0	0	0	0	0	.000
Rhem, p	1	0	0	0	0	0	0	0	.000
Martin, ph	1	0	1	0	0	0	0	0	.000
Totals	4	131	10	27	5	1	1	9	.206

COMPOSITE PITCHING AVERAGES

New York Yankees

Pitcher	G	IP	H	R	ER	BB	SO	W	L	ERA
Hoyt	2	18	14	4	3	6	14	2	0	1.50
Pipgras	1	9	4	3	3	4	8	1	0	3.00
Zachary	1	9	9	3	3	1	7	1	0	3.00
Totals	4	36	27	10	9	11	29	4	0	2.25

St. Louis Cardinals

Pitcher	G	IP	H	R	ER	BB	SO	W	L	ERA
Rhem	1	2	0	0	0	0	1	0	0	0.00
Mitchell	1	5⅔	2	1	1	2	2	0	0	1.50
Johnson	2	2	4	2	1	1	1	0	0	4.50
Haines	1	6	6	6	3	3	3	0	1	4.50
Sherdel	2	13⅓	15	7	7	3	3	0	2	4.73
Alexander	2	5	10	11	11	4	2	0	1	19.80
Totals	4	34	37	27	23	13	12	0	4	6.00

1929

COMPOSITE BATTING AVERAGES

Philadelphia Athletics

Player-Position	G	AB	R	H	2B	3B	HR	RBI	BA
Dykes, 3b	5	19	2	8	1	0	0	4	.421
Cochrane, c	5	15	5	6	1	0	0	0	.400
Miller, rf	5	19	1	7	1	0	0	4	.368
Foxx, 1b	5	20	5	7	1	0	2	5	.350
Simmons, lf	5	20	6	6	1	0	2	5	.300
Haas, cf	5	21	3	5	0	0	2	6	.238
Boley, ss	5	17	1	4	0	0	0	1	.235
Ehmke, p	2	5	0	1	0	0	0	0	.200
Bishop, 2b	5	21	2	4	0	0	0	1	.190
Earnshaw, p	2	5	1	0	0	0	0	0	.000
Grove, p	2	2	0	0	0	0	0	0	.000
Summa, ph	1	1	0	0	0	0	0	0	.000
Quinn, p	1	2	0	0	0	0	0	0	.000
Walberg, p	2	1	0	0	0	0	0	0	.000
Rommel, p	1	0	0	0	0	0	0	0	.000
Burns, ph	1	2	0	0	0	0	0	0	.000
French, ph	1	1	0	0	0	0	0	0	.000
Totals	5	171	26	48	5	0	6	26	.281

Chicago Cubs

Player-Position	G	AB	R	H	2B	3B	HR	RBI	BA
Blake, p	2	1	0	1	0	0	0	0	1.000
Wilson, cf	5	17	2	8	0	1	0	0	.471
Grimm, 1b	5	18	2	7	0	0	1	4	.389
Stephenson, lf	5	19	3	6	1	0	0	3	.316
Cuyler, rf	5	20	4	6	1	0	0	4	.300
Hornsby, 2b	5	21	4	5	1	1	0	1	.238
English, ss	5	21	1	4	2	0	0	0	.190
Taylor, c	5	17	0	3	0	0	0	3	.176
McMillan, 3b	5	20	0	2	0	0	0	0	.100
Heathcote, ph	1	1	0	0	0	0	0	0	.000
Gonzalez, c-ph	2	1	0	0	0	0	0	0	.000
Blair, ph	1	0	0	0	0	0	0	0	.000
Root, p	2	5	0	0	0	0	0	0	.000
Hartnett, ph	3	3	0	0	0	0	0	0	.000
Bush, p	2	3	1	0	0	0	0	0	.000
Tolson, ph	1	1	0	0	0	0	0	0	.000
Carlson, p	2	0	0	0	0	0	0	0	.000
Nehf, p	2	0	0	0	0	0	0	0	.000
Totals	5	173	17	43	6	2	1	15	.249

COMPOSITE PITCHING AVERAGES

Philadelphia Athletics

Pitcher	G	IP	H	R	ER	BB	SO	W	L	ERA
Grove	2	6⅓	3	0	0	1	10	0	0	0.00
Walberg	2	6⅓	3	1	0	0	8	1	0	0.00
Ehmke	2	12⅔	14	3	2	3	13	1	0	1.42
Earnshaw	2	13⅔	14	6	4	6	17	1	1	2.63
Quinn	1	5	7	6	5	2	2	0	0	9.00
Rommel	1	1	2	1	1	1	0	1	0	9.00
Totals	5	45	43	17	12	13	50	4	1	2.40

Chicago Cubs

Pitcher	G	IP	H	R	ER	BB	SO	W	L	ERA
Bush	2	11	12	3	1	2	4	1	0	0.82
Malone	3	13	12	9	6	7	11	0	2	4.15
Root	2	13⅓	12	7	7	2	8	0	1	4.73
Carlson	2	4	7	3	3	1	3	0	0	6.75
Blake	2	1⅓	4	2	2	0	1	0	1	13.50
Nehf	2	1	1	2	2	1	0	0	0	18.00
Totals	5	43⅔	48	26	21	13	27	1	4	4.33

1930

COMPOSITE BATTING AVERAGES

Philadelphia Athletics

Player-Position	G	AB	R	H	2B	3B	HR	RBI	BA
Simmons, lf-cf	6	22	4	8	2	0	2	4	.364
Foxx, 1b	6	21	3	7	2	1	1	3	.333
Moore, ph-lf	3	3	0	1	0	0	0	0	.333
Bishop, 2b	6	18	5	4	0	0	0	0	.222
Dykes, 3b	6	18	2	4	3	0	1	5	.222
Cochrane, c	6	18	5	4	1	0	2	4	.222
Miller, rf	6	21	0	3	2	0	0	3	.143
Haas, cf	6	18	1	2	0	1	0	1	.111
Boley, ss	6	21	1	2	0	0	0	1	.095
Grove, p	3	6	0	0	0	0	0	0	.000
Earnshaw, p	3	9	0	0	0	0	0	0	.000
Walberg, p	1	2	0	0	0	0	0	0	.000
Shores, p	1	0	0	0	0	0	0	0	.000
Quinn, p	1	0	0	0	0	0	0	0	.000
McNair, ph	1	1	0	0	0	0	0	0	.000
Totals	6	178	21	35	10	2	6	21	.197

St. Louis Cardinals

Player-Position	G	AB	R	H	2B	3B	HR	RBI	BA
Lindsey, p	2	1	0	1	0	0	0	0	1.000
Haines, p	1	2	1	1	0	0	0	1	.500
High, ph-3b	1	2	1	1	0	0	0	0	.500
Fisher, ph	2	2	0	1	1	0	0	0	.500
Grimes, p	2	5	0	2	0	0	0	0	.400
Gelbert, ss	6	17	2	6	0	1	0	2	.353
Mancuso, c	2	7	1	2	0	0	0	0	.286
Hafey, lf	6	22	1	6	5	0	0	2	.273
Wilson, c	4	15	0	4	1	0	0	2	.267
Frisch, 2b	6	24	0	5	2	0	0	0	.208
Watkins, rf	4	12	2	2	0	0	1	1	.167
Adams, 3b	6	21	0	3	0	0	0	1	.143
Blades, rf-ph	5	9	2	1	0	0	0	0	.111
Douthit, cf	6	24	1	2	0	0	1	2	.083
Bottomley, 1b	6	22	1	1	1	0	0	0	.045
Johnson, p	2	0	0	0	0	0	0	0	.000
Hallahan, p	2	2	0	0	0	0	0	0	.000
Puccinelli, ph	1	1	0	0	0	0	0	0	.000
Rhem, p	1	1	0	0	0	0	0	0	.000
Orsatti, ph	1	1	0	0	0	0	0	0	.000
Bell, p	1	0	0	0	0	0	0	0	.000
Totals	6	190	12	38	10	1	2	11	.200

COMPOSITE PITCHING AVERAGES

Philadelphia Athletics

Pitcher	G	IP	H	R	ER	BB	SO	W	L	ERA
Earnshaw	3	25	13	2	2	7	19	2	0	0.72
Grove	3	19	15	5	3	3	10	2	1	1.42
Walberg	1	4⅔	4	2	2	1	3	0	1	3.86
Quinn	1	2	3	1	1	0	1	0	0	4.50
Shores	1	1⅓	3	2	2	0	0	0	0	13.50
Totals	6	52	38	12	10	11	33	4	2	1.73

St. Louis Cardinals

Pitcher	G	IP	H	R	ER	BB	SO	W	L	ERA
Bell	1	1	0	0	0	0	0	0	0	0.00
Haines	1	9	4	1	1	4	2	1	0	1.00
Hallahan	2	11	9	2	2	8	8	1	1	1.63
Lindsey	2	4⅔	1	1	1	1	2	0	0	1.93
Grimes	2	17	10	7	7	6	13	0	2	3.71
Johnson	2	5	4	4	4	3	4	0	0	7.20
Rhem	1	3⅓	7	6	4	2	3	0	1	10.80
Totals	6	51	35	21	19	24	32	2	4	3.35

1931

COMPOSITE BATTING AVERAGES

St. Louis Cardinals

Player-Position	G	AB	R	H	2B	3B	HR	RBI	BA
Martin, cf	7	24	5	12	4	0	1	5	.500
Watkins, rf-pr	5	14	4	4	1	0	1	2	.286
Grimes, p	2	7	0	2	0	0	0	2	.286
Roettger, rf	3	14	1	4	1	0	0	0	.286
High, 3b-pr	4	15	3	4	0	0	0	0	.267
Gelbert, ss	7	23	0	6	1	0	0	3	.261
Frisch, 2b	7	27	2	7	2	0	0	1	.259
Adams, 3b	2	4	0	1	0	0	0	0	.250
Wilson, c	7	23	0	5	0	0	0	2	.217
Hafey, lf	6	24	1	4	0	0	0	0	.167
Bottomley, 1b	7	25	2	4	1	0	0	2	.160
Flowers, ph-3b	5	11	1	1	1	0	0	0	.091
Mancuso, ph-c	2	1	0	0	0	0	0	0	.000
Derringer, p	3	2	0	0	0	0	0	0	.000
Johnson, p	3	2	0	0	0	0	0	0	.000
Blades, ph	2	2	0	0	0	0	0	0	.000
Hallahan, p	3	6	0	0	0	0	0	0	.000
Lindsey, p	2	0	0	0	0	0	0	0	.000
Collins, ph	2	2	0	0	0	0	0	0	.000
Rhem, p	1	0	0	0	0	0	0	0	.000
Orsatti, lf	1	3	0	0	0	0	0	0	.000
Totals	7	229	19	54	11	0	2	17	.236

Philadelphia Athletics

Player-Position	G	AB	R	H	2B	3B	HR	RBI	BA
Cramer, ph	2	2	0	1	0	0	0	2	.500
Foxx, 1b	7	23	3	8	0	0	1	3	.348
Simmons, lf-cf	7	27	4	9	2	0	2	8	.333
Moore, ph-lf	2	3	0	1	0	0	0	0	.333
Williams, ss	7	25	2	8	1	0	0	1	.320
Miller, rf	7	26	3	7	1	0	0	1	.269
Dykes, 3b	7	22	2	5	0	0	0	2	.227
Cochrane, c	7	25	2	4	0	0	0	1	.160
Bishop, 2b	7	27	4	4	0	0	0	0	.148
Haas, cf	7	23	1	3	1	0	0	2	.130
Grove, p	3	10	0	0	0	0	0	0	.000
Earnshaw, p	3	8	0	0	0	0	0	0	.000
McNair, pr-ph-2b	2	2	1	0	0	0	0	0	.000
Walberg, p	2	0	0	0	0	0	0	0	.000
Mahaffey, p	1	0	0	0	0	0	0	0	.000
Hoyt, p	1	2	0	0	0	0	0	0	.000
Heving, ph	1	1	0	0	0	0	0	0	.000
Rommel, p	1	0	0	0	0	0	0	0	.000
Boley, ph	1	1	0	0	0	0	0	0	.000
Todt, ph	1	0	0	0	0	0	0	0	.000
Totals	7	227	22	50	5	0	3	20	.220

COMPOSITE PITCHING AVERAGES

St. Louis Cardinals

Pitcher	G	IP	H	R	ER	BB	SO	W	L	ERA
Rhem	1	1	1	0	0	0	1	0	0	0.00
Hallahan	3	18⅓	12	1	1	8	12	2	0	0.40
Grimes	2	17⅔	9	4	4	9	11	2	0	2.04
Johnson	3	9	10	3	3	1	6	0	1	3.00
Derringer	3	12⅔	14	10	6	7	14	0	2	4.26
Lindsey	2	3⅓	4	4	2	3	2	0	0	5.40
Totals	7	62	50	22	16	28	46	4	3	2.32

Philadelphia Athletics

Pitcher	G	IP	H	R	ER	BB	SO	W	L	ERA
Earnshaw	3	24	12	6	5	4	20	1	2	1.86
Grove	3	26	28	7	7	2	16	2	1	2.42
Walberg	2	3	3	1	1	2	4	0	0	3.00
Hoyt	1	6	7	3	3	0	1	0	1	4.90
Mahaffey	1	1	1	1	1	1	0	0	0	9.00
Rommel	1	1	3	1	1	0	0	0	0	9.00
Totals	7	61	54	19	18	9	41	3	4	2.06

1932

COMPOSITE BATTING AVERAGES

New York Yankees

Player-Position	G	AB	R	H	2B	3B	HR	RBI	BA
Gehrig, 1b	4	17	9	9	1	0	3	8	.529
Dickey, c	4	16	2	7	0	0	0	4	.438
Combs, cf	4	16	8	6	1	0	1	4	.375
Sewell, 3b	4	15	4	5	1	0	0	3	.333
Ruth, rf-lf	4	15	6	5	0	0	2	6	.333
Moore, p	1	3	0	1	0	0	0	0	.333
Lazzeri, 2b	4	17	4	5	0	0	2	5	.294
Chapman, lf-rf	4	17	1	5	2	0	0	6	.294
Crosetti, ss	4	15	2	2	1	0	0	1	.133
Ruffing, p-ph	2	4	0	0	0	0	0	0	.000
Gomez, p	1	3	0	0	0	0	0	0	.000
Pipgras, p	1	5	0	0	0	0	0	0	.000
Pennock, p	2	1	0	0	0	0	0	0	.000
Byrd, p	1	0	0	0	0	0	0	0	.000
Allen, p	1	0	0	0	0	0	0	0	.000
Hoag, pr	1	0	1	0	0	0	0	0	.000
Totals	4	144	37	45	6	0	8	36	.313

Chicago Cubs

Player-Position	G	AB	R	H	2B	3B	HR	RBI	BA
Stephenson, lf	4	18	2	8	1	0	0	4	.444
Jurges, ss	3	11	1	4	1	0	0	1	.364
Grimm, 1b	4	15	2	5	2	0	0	1	.333
Hartnett, c	4	16	2	5	2	0	1	1	.313
Demaree, cf	2	7	1	2	0	0	1	4	.286
Cuyler, rf	4	18	2	5	1	1	1	2	.278
Koenig, ss-ph	2	4	1	1	0	1	0	1	.250
Herman, 2b	4	18	5	4	1	0	0	1	.222
English, 3b	4	17	2	3	0	0	0	1	.176
Moore, cf	2	7	1	0	0	0	0	0	.000
Bush, p	2	1	0	0	0	0	0	0	.000
Grimes, p	2	1	0	0	0	0	0	0	.000
Gudat, ph	2	2	0	0	0	0	0	0	.000
Smith, p	1	0	0	0	0	0	0	0	.000
Warneke, p	2	4	0	0	0	0	0	0	.000
Hemsley, ph-c	3	3	0	0	0	0	0	0	.000
Root, p	1	2	0	0	0	0	0	0	.000
Malone, p	1	0	0	0	0	0	0	0	.000
May, p	2	2	0	0	0	0	0	0	.000
Tinning, p	2	0	0	0	0	0	0	0	.000
Hack, pr	1	0	0	0	0	0	0	0	.000
Totals	4	146	19	37	8	2	3	16	.253

COMPOSITE PITCHING AVERAGES

New York Yankees

Pitcher	G	IP	H	R	ER	BB	SO	W	L	ERA
W. Moore	1	5⅓	2	1	0	0	1	1	0	0.00
Gomez	1	9	9	2	1	1	8	1	0	1.00
Pennock	2	4	2	1	1	1	4	0	0	2.25
Ruffing	1	9	10	6	4	6	10	1	0	4.00
Pipgras	1	8	9	5	4	3	1	1	0	4.50
Allen	1	⅔	5	4	3	0	0	0	0	40.50
Totals	4	36	37	19	13	11	24	4	0	3.25

Chicago Cubs

Pitcher	G	IP	H	R	ER	BB	SO	W	L	ERA
Malone	1	2⅔	1	0	0	4	4	0	0	0.00
Tinning	2	2⅓	0	0	0	3	0	0	0	0.00
Warneke	2	10⅔	15	7	7	5	8	0	1	5.91
Smith	1	1	2	1	1	0	1	0	0	9.00
Root	1	4⅓	6	6	5	3	4	0	1	10.38
May	2	4⅔	9	7	6	3	4	0	1	11.57
Bush	2	5⅓	5	9	9	6	2	0	1	14.29
Grimes	2	2⅔	7	7	7	2	0	0	0	23.63
Totals	4	34	45	37	35	23	26	0	4	9.26

1933

COMPOSITE BATTING AVERAGES

New York Giants

Player-Position	G	AB	R	H	2B	3B	HR	RBI	BA
O'Doul, ph	1	1	1	1	0	0	0	2	1.000
Luque, p	1	1	0	1	0	0	0	0	1.000
Fitzsimmons, p	1	2	0	1	0	0	0	0	.500
Peel, cf-ph	2	2	0	1	0	0	0	0	.500
Ott, rf	5	18	3	7	0	0	2	4	.389
Davis, cf	5	19	1	7	1	0	0	0	.368
Hubbell, p	2	7	0	2	0	0	0	0	.286
Schumacher, p	2	7	0	2	0	0	0	3	.286
Ryan, ss	5	18	0	5	0	0	0	1	.278
Terry, 1b	5	22	3	6	1	0	1	1	.273
Moore, lf	5	22	1	5	1	0	0	1	.227
Jackson, 3b	5	18	3	4	1	0	0	2	.222
Critz, 2b	5	22	2	3	0	0	0	0	.136
Mancuso, c	5	17	2	2	1	0	0	2	.118
Bell, p	1	0	0	0	0	0	0	0	.000
Totals	5	176	16	47	5	0	3	16	.287

Washington Senators

Player-Position	G	AB	R	H	2B	3B	HR	RBI	BA
Rice, ph	1	1	0	1	0	0	0	0	1.000
Schulte, cf	5	21	1	7	1	0	1	4	.333
Cronin, ss	5	22	1	7	0	0	0	2	.318
Myer, 2b	5	20	2	6	1	0	0	2	.300
Crowder, p	2	4	0	1	0	0	0	0	.250
Goslin, rf	5	20	2	5	1	0	1	1	.250
Sewell, c	5	17	1	3	0	0	0	1	.176
Kuhel, 1b	5	20	1	3	0	0	1	1	.150
Bluege, 3b	5	16	1	2	1	0	0	0	.125
Manush, lf	5	18	2	2	0	0	0	0	.111
Stewart, p	1	1	0	0	0	0	0	0	.000
Russell, p	3	2	0	0	0	0	0	0	.000
Harris, ph-rf	3	2	0	0	0	0	0	0	.000
Thomas, p	2	0	0	0	0	0	0	0	.000
Bolton, ph	2	2	0	0	0	0	0	0	.000
McColl, p	1	0	0	0	0	0	0	0	.000
Whitehill, p	1	3	0	0	0	0	0	0	.000
Weaver, p	1	4	0	0	0	0	0	0	.000
Kerr, pr	1	0	0	0	0	0	0	0	.000
Totals	5	173	11	37	4	0	2	11	.214

COMPOSITE PITCHING AVERAGES

New York Giants

Pitcher	G	IP	H	R	ER	BB	SO	W	L	ERA
Hubbell	2	20	13	3	0	6	15	2	0	0.00
Luque	1	4⅓	2	0	0	2	5	1	0	0.00
Bell	1	1	0	0	0	0	0	0	0	0.00
Schumacher	2	14⅔	13	4	4	5	3	1	0	2.45
Fitzsimmons	1	7	9	4	4	0	2	0	1	5.14
Totals	5	47	37	11	8	13	25	4	1	1.53

Washington Senators

Pitcher	G	IP	H	R	ER	BB	SO	W	L	ERA
Whitehill	1	9	5	0	0	2	2	1	0	0.00
McColl	1	2	0	0	0	0	0	0	0	0.00
Thomas	2	1⅓	1	0	0	2	0	0	0	0.00
Russell	3	10⅓	8	1	1	0	7	0	1	0.87
Weaver	1	10⅓	11	2	2	4	3	0	1	1.74
Crowder	2	11	16	9	9	5	7	0	1	7.36
Stewart	1	2	6	4	2	0	0	0	1	9.00
Totals	5	46	47	16	14	11	21	1	4	2.74

1934

COMPOSITE BATTING AVERAGES

St. Louis Cardinals

Player-Position	G	AB	R	H	2B	3B	HR	RBI	BA
V. Davis, ph	2	2	0	2	0	0	0	1	1.000
Fullis, cf	3	5	0	2	0	0	0	0	.400
Medwick, lf	7	29	4	11	0	1	1	5	.379
Collins, 1b	7	30	4	11	1	0	0	4	.367
Martin, 3b	7	31	8	11	3	1	0	3	.355
Orsatti, cf	7	22	3	7	0	1	0	2	.318
Durocher, ss	7	27	4	7	1	1	0	0	.259
J. Dean, p-pr	4	12	3	3	2	0	0	1	.250
Rothrock, rf	7	30	3	7	3	1	0	6	.233
Frisch, 2b	7	31	2	6	1	0	0	4	.194
DeLancey, c	7	29	3	5	3	0	1	4	.172
P. Dean, p	2	6	0	1	0	0	0	2	.167
Hallahan, p	1	3	0	0	0	0	0	0	.000
W. Walker, p	2	2	0	0	0	0	0	0	.000
Carleton, p	2	1	0	0	0	0	0	0	.000
Vance, p	1	0	0	0	0	0	0	0	.000
Whitehead, pr-ss	1	0	0	0	0	0	0	0	.000
Haines, p	1	0	0	0	0	0	0	0	.000
Crawford, ph	2	2	0	0	0	0	0	0	.000
Mooney, p	1	0	0	0	0	0	0	0	.000
Totals	7	262	34	73	14	5	2	32	.279

Detroit Tigers

Player-Position	G	AB	R	H	2B	3B	HR	RBI	BA
Gehringer, 2b	7	29	5	11	1	0	1	2	.379
G. Walker, ph	3	3	0	1	0	0	0	1	.333
Greenberg, 1b	7	28	4	9	2	1	1	7	.321
Fox, rf	7	28	1	8	6	0	0	2	.286
Rogell, ss	7	29	3	8	1	0	0	4	.276
Goslin, lf	7	29	2	7	1	0	0	2	.241
Cochrane, c	7	28	2	6	1	0	0	1	.214
Bridges, p	3	7	0	1	0	0	0	0	.143
White, cf	7	23	6	3	0	0	0	0	.130
Owen, 3b	7	29	0	2	0	0	0	1	.069
Auker, p	2	4	0	0	0	0	0	0	.000
Doljack, ph-cf	2	2	0	0	0	0	0	0	.000
Crowder, p	2	1	0	0	0	0	0	0	.000
Marberry, p	2	0	0	0	0	0	0	0	.000
Rowe, p	3	7	0	0	0	0	0	0	.000
Hogsett, p	3	3	0	0	0	0	0	0	.000
Hayworth, c	1	0	0	0	0	0	0	0	.000
Totals	7	250	23	56	12	1	2	20	.224

COMPOSITE PITCHING AVERAGES

St. Louis Cardinals

Pitcher	G	IP	H	R	ER	BB	SO	W	L	ERA
Haines	1	2/3	1	0	0	2	0	0	0	0.00
Mooney	1	1	1	0	0	0	0	0	0	0.00
Vance	1	1⅓	2	1	0	1	3	0	0	0.00
P. Dean	2	18	15	4	2	7	11	2	0	1.00
J. Dean	3	26	20	6	5	5	17	2	1	1.73
Hallahan	1	8⅓	6	2	2	4	6	0	0	2.16
W. Walker	2	6⅓	6	7	5	6	2	0	2	7.11
Carleton	2	3⅔	5	3	3	2	2	0	0	7.36
Totals	7	65⅓	56	23	17	25	43	4	3	2.34

Detroit Tigers

Pitcher	G	IP	H	R	ER	BB	SO	W	L	ERA
Hogsett	3	7⅓	6	1	1	3	3	0	0	1.23
Crowder	2	6	6	4	1	1	2	0	1	1.50
Rowe	3	21⅓	19	8	7	0	12	1	1	2.95
Bridges	3	17⅓	21	9	7	11	12	1	1	3.63
Auker	2	11⅓	16	8	7	5	2	1	1	5.56
Marberry	2	1⅔	5	4	4	1	0	0	0	21.60
Totals	7	65	73	34	27	11	31	3	4	3.74

1935

COMPOSITE BATTING AVERAGES

Detroit Tigers

Player-Position	G	AB	R	H	2B	3B	HR	RBI	BA
Fox, rf	6	26	1	10	3	1	0	4	.385
Gehringer, 2b	6	24	4	9	3	0	0	4	.375
Crowder, p	1	3	1	1	0	0	0	0	.333
Cochrane, c	6	24	3	7	1	0	0	1	.292
Rogell, ss	6	24	1	7	2	0	0	1	.292
Goslin, lf	6	22	2	6	1	0	0	3	.273
White, cf	5	19	3	5	0	0	0	1	.263
Rowe, p	3	8	0	2	1	0	0	0	.250
Walker, ph-cf	3	4	1	1	0	0	0	0	.250
Greenberg, 1b	2	6	1	1	0	0	1	2	.167
Bridges, p	2	8	1	1	0	0	0	1	.125
Owen, 3b-1b	6	20	2	1	0	0	0	1	.050
Clifton, 3b	4	16	1	0	0	0	0	0	.000
Auker, p	1	2	0	0	0	0	0	0	.000
Hogsett, p	1	0	0	0	0	0	0	0	.000
Totals	6	206	21	51	11	1	1	18	.248

Chicago Cubs

Player-Position	G	AB	R	H	2B	3B	HR	RBI	BA
O'Dea, ph	1	1	0	1	0	0	0	1	1.000
Kowalik, p	1	2	1	1	0	0	0	0	.500
Herman, 2b	6	24	3	8	2	1	1	6	.333
Klein, ph-rf	5	12	2	4	0	0	1	2	.333
Hartnett, c	6	24	1	7	0	0	1	2	.292
Demaree, rf-cf	6	24	2	6	1	0	2	2	.250
French, p	2	4	1	1	0	0	0	0	.250
Jurges, ss	6	16	3	4	0	0	0	1	.250
Hack, 3b-ss	6	22	2	5	1	1	0	0	.227
Lindstrom, cf-3b	4	15	0	3	1	0	0	0	.200
Warneke, p	3	5	0	1	0	0	0	0	.200
Galan, lf	6	25	2	4	1	0	0	2	.160
Cavarretta, 1b	6	24	1	3	0	0	0	0	.125
Root, p	2	0	0	0	0	0	0	0	.000
Henshaw, p	1	1	0	0	0	0	0	0	.000
Lee, p	2	1	0	0	0	0	0	1	.000
Stephenson, ph	1	1	0	0	0	0	0	0	.000
Carleton, p	1	1	0	0	0	0	0	0	.000
Totals	6	202	18	48	6	2	5	17	.238

COMPOSITE PITCHING AVERAGES

Detroit Tigers

Pitcher	G	IP	H	R	ER	BB	SO	W	L	ERA
Hogsett	1	1	0	0	0	1	0	0	0	0.00
Crowder	1	9	5	1	1	3	5	1	0	1.00
Bridges	2	18	18	6	5	4	9	2	0	2.50
Rowe	3	21	19	8	6	1	14	1	2	2.57
Auker	1	6	6	3	2	4	1	0	0	3.00
Totals	6	55	48	18	14	11	29	4	2	2.29

Chicago Cubs

Pitcher	G	IP	H	R	ER	BB	SO	W	L	ERA
Warneke	3	16⅔	9	1	1	4	5	2	0	0.54
Carleton	1	7	6	2	1	7	4	0	1	1.29
Kowalik	1	4⅓	3	1	1	1	1	0	0	2.08
French	2	10⅔	15	5	4	2	8	0	2	3.38
Lee	2	10⅓	11	5	4	5	5	0	0	3.48
Henshaw	1	3⅔	2	3	3	5	2	0	0	7.36
Root	2	2	5	4	4	1	2	0	1	18.00
Totals	6	54⅔	51	21	18	25	27	2	4	2.96

1936

COMPOSITE BATTING AVERAGES

New York Yankees

Player-Position	G	AB	R	H	2B	3B	HR	RBI	BA
Malone, p	2	1	0	1	0	0	0	0	1.000
Pearson, p	1	4	0	2	1	0	0	0	.500
Murphy, p	1	2	1	1	0	0	0	1	.500
Powell, lf	6	22	8	10	1	0	1	5	.455
Rolfe, 3b	6	25	5	10	0	0	0	4	.400
DiMaggio, cf	6	26	3	9	3	0	0	3	.346
Selkirk, rf	6	24	6	8	0	1	2	3	.333
Gehrig, 1b	6	24	5	7	1	0	2	7	.292
Crosetti, ss	6	26	5	7	2	0	0	3	.269
Lazzeri, 2b	6	20	4	5	0	0	1	7	.250
Gomez, p	2	8	1	2	0	0	0	3	.250
Dickey, c	6	25	5	3	0	0	1	5	.120
Ruffing, p-ph	3	5	0	0	0	0	0	0	.000
Johnson, pr-ph	2	1	0	0	0	0	0	0	.000
Hadley, p	1	2	0	0	0	0	0	0	.000
Seeds, pr	1	0	0	0	0	0	0	0	.000
Totals	6	215	43	65	8	1	7	41	.302

New York Giants

Player-Position	G	AB	R	H	2B	3B	HR	RBI	BA
Leslie, ph	3	3	0	2	0	0	0	0	.667
Castleman, p	1	2	0	1	0	0	0	0	.500
Fitzsimmons, p	2	4	0	2	0	0	0	0	.500
Davis, ph-pr	4	2	2	1	0	0	0	0	.500
Bartell, ss	6	21	5	8	3	0	1	3	.381
Hubbell, p	2	6	0	2	0	0	0	1	.333
Koenig, ph-2b	3	3	0	1	0	0	0	0	.333
Ripple, cf-ph	5	12	2	4	0	0	1	3	.333
Ott, rf	6	23	4	7	2	0	1	3	.304
Mancuso, c	6	19	3	5	2	0	0	1	.263
Terry, 1b	6	25	1	6	0	0	0	5	.240
Moore, lf	6	28	4	6	2	0	1	1	.214
Jackson, 3b	6	21	1	4	0	0	1	1	.190
Whitehead, 2b	6	21	1	1	0	0	0	2	.048
Leiber, cf	2	6	0	0	0	0	0	0	.000
Schumacher, p	2	4	0	0	0	0	0	0	.000
Smith, p	1	0	0	0	0	0	0	0	.000
Coffman, p	2	0	0	0	0	0	0	0	.000
Gabler, p	2	0	0	0	0	0	0	0	.000
Danning, ph-c	2	2	0	0	0	0	0	0	.000
Gumbert, p	2	0	0	0	0	0	0	0	.000
Mayo, 3b	1	1	0	0	0	0	0	0	.000
Totals	6	203	23	50	9	0	4	20	.246

COMPOSITE PITCHING AVERAGES

New York Yankees

Pitcher	G	IP	H	R	ER	BB	SO	W	L	ERA
Hadley	1	8	10	1	1	1	2	1	0	1.12
Malone	2	5	2	1	1	1	2	0	1	1.80
Pearson	1	9	7	2	2	2	7	1	0	2.00
Murphy	1	2⅔	1	1	1	1	1	0	0	3.38
Ruffing	2	14	16	10	7	5	12	0	1	4.50
Gomez	2	15⅓	14	8	8	11	9	2	0	4.70
Totals	6	54	50	23	20	21	33	4	2	3.33

New York Giants

Pitcher	G	IP	H	R	ER	BB	SO	W	L	ERA
Castleman	1	4⅓	3	1	1	2	5	0	0	2.08
Hubbell	2	16	15	5	4	2	10	1	1	2.25
Schumacher	2	12	13	9	7	10	11	1	1	5.25
Fitzsimmons	2	11⅔	13	7	7	2	6	0	2	5.40
Gabler	2	5	7	4	4	4	0	0	0	7.20
Coffman	2	1⅔	5	6	6	1	1	0	0	32.40
Gumbert	2	2	7	8	8	4	2	0	0	36.00
Smith	1	⅓	2	3	3	1	0	0	0	81.00
Totals	6	53	65	43	40	26	35	2	4	6.79

1937

Composite Batting Averages

New York Yankees

Player-Position	G	AB	R	H	2B	3B	HR	RBI	BA
Ruffing, p	1	4	0	2	1	0	0	3	.500
Lazzeri, 2b	5	15	3	6	0	1	1	2	.400
Hoag, lf	5	20	4	6	1	0	1	2	.300
Rolfe, 3b	5	20	3	6	2	1	0	1	.300
Gehrig, 1b	5	17	4	5	1	1	1	3	.294
DiMaggio, cf	5	22	2	6	0	0	1	4	.273
Selkirk, rf	5	19	5	5	1	0	0	6	.263
Dickey, c	5	19	3	4	0	1	0	3	.211
Gomez, p	2	6	2	1	0	0	0	0	.167
Crosetti, ss	5	21	2	1	0	0	0	0	.048
Pearson, p	1	3	0	0	0	0	0	0	.000
Murphy, p	1	0	0	0	0	0	0	0	.000
Hadley, p	1	0	0	0	0	0	0	0	.000
Andrews, p	1	2	0	0	0	0	0	0	.000
Powell, ph	1	1	0	0	0	0	0	0	.000
Wicker, p	1	0	0	0	0	0	0	0	.000
Totals	5	169	28	42	6	4	4	25	.249

New York Giants

Player-Position	G	AB	R	H	2B	3B	HR	RBI	BA
Moore, lf	5	23	1	9	1	0	0	1	.391
Leiber, cf	3	11	2	4	0	0	0	2	.364
Ripple, rf	5	17	2	5	0	0	0	0	.294
Chiozza, cf	2	7	0	2	0	0	0	0	.286
Whitehead, 2b	5	16	1	4	2	0	0	0	.250
Danning, c	3	12	0	3	1	0	0	2	.250
Bartell, ss	5	21	3	5	1	0	0	1	.238
McCarthy, 1b	5	19	1	4	1	0	0	1	.211
Ott, 3b	5	20	1	4	0	0	1	3	.200
Mancuso, c-ph	3	8	0	0	0	0	0	1	.000
Hubbell, p	2	6	1	0	0	0	0	1	.000
Gumbert, p	2	0	0	0	0	0	0	0	.000
Coffman, p	2	1	0	0	0	0	0	0	.000
Berger, ph	3	3	0	0	0	0	0	0	.000
Smith, p	2	0	0	0	0	0	0	0	.000
Melton, p	3	2	0	0	0	0	0	0	.000
Leslie, ph	2	1	0	0	0	0	0	0	.000
Schumacher, p	1	1	0	0	0	0	0	0	.000
Brennan, p	2	0	0	0	0	0	0	0	.000
Ryan, ph	1	1	0	0	0	0	0	0	.000
Totals	5	169	12	40	6	0	1	12	.237

Composite Pitching Averages

New York Yankees

Pitcher	G	IP	H	R	ER	BB	SO	W	L	ERA
Murphy	1	1/3	0	0	0	0	0	0	0	0.00
Wicker	1	1	0	0	0	0	0	0	0	0.00
Ruffing	1	9	7	1	1	3	8	1	0	1.00
Pearson	1	8 2/3	5	1	1	2	4	1	0	1.04
Gomez	2	18	16	3	3	2	8	2	0	1.50
Andrews	1	5 2/3	6	2	2	4	1	0	0	3.18
Hadley	1	1 1/3	6	5	5	0	0	0	1	33.75
Totals	5	44	40	12	12	11	21	4	1	2.45

New York Giants

Pitcher	G	IP	H	R	ER	BB	SO	W	L	ERA
Brennan	2	3	1	0	0	1	1	0	0	0.00
Smith	2	3	2	1	1	0	1	0	0	3.00
Hubbell	2	14 1/3	12	10	6	4	7	1	1	3.77
Coffman	2	4 1/3	2	2	2	5	1	0	0	4.15
Melton	3	11	12	6	6	6	7	0	2	4.91
Schumacher	1	6	9	5	4	3	0	1	0	6.00
Gumbert	2	1 1/3	4	4	4	1	1	0	0	27.00
Totals	5	43	42	28	23	21	21	1	4	4.81

1938

Composite Batting Averages

New York Yankees

Player-Position	G	AB	R	H	2B	3B	HR	RBI	BA
Dickey, c	4	15	2	6	2	0	1	6	.400
Gordon, 2b	4	15	3	6	2	0	1	6	.400
Hoag, ph-lf	2	5	3	2	1	0	0	1	.400
Pearson, p	1	3	1	1	0	0	0	0	.333
Gehrig, 1b	4	14	4	4	0	0	0	0	.286
DiMaggio, cf	4	15	4	4	0	0	1	2	.267
Crosetti, ss	4	16	1	4	2	1	1	6	.250
Henrich, rf	4	16	3	4	1	0	1	1	.250
Selkirk, lf	3	10	0	2	0	0	0	1	.200
Rolfe, 3b	4	18	0	3	0	0	0	1	.167
Ruffing, p	2	6	1	1	0	0	0	1	.167
Powell, lf	1	0	0	0	0	0	0	0	.000
Gomez, p	1	2	0	0	0	0	0	0	.000
Murphy, p	1	0	0	0	0	0	0	0	.000
Totals	4	135	22	37	6	1	5	21	.274

Chicago Cubs

Player-Position	G	AB	R	H	2B	3B	HR	RBI	BA
Dean, p	2	3	0	2	0	0	0	0	.666
Marty, cf	3	12	1	6	1	0	1	5	.500
Hack, 3b	4	17	3	8	1	0	0	1	.471
Cavarretta, rf-ph	4	13	1	6	1	0	0	0	.462
Jurges, ss	4	13	0	3	1	0	0	0	.231
O'Dea, ph-c	3	5	1	1	0	0	1	2	.200
Herman, 2b	4	16	1	3	0	0	0	0	.188
Collins, 1b	4	15	1	2	0	0	0	0	.133
Demaree, lf	3	10	1	1	0	0	0	0	.100
Hartnett, c	3	11	0	1	0	1	0	0	.091
Reynolds, cf-lf-ph	4	12	0	0	0	0	0	0	.000
Lee, p	2	3	0	0	0	0	0	0	.000
Russell, p	2	0	0	0	0	0	0	0	.000
French, p	3	0	0	0	0	0	0	0	.000
Lazzeri, ph	2	2	0	0	0	0	0	0	.000
Bryant, p	1	2	0	0	0	0	0	0	.000
Galan, ph	2	2	0	0	0	0	0	0	.000
Root, p	1	0	0	0	0	0	0	0	.000
Page, p	1	0	0	0	0	0	0	0	.000
Carleton, p	1	0	0	0	0	0	0	0	.000
Totals	4	136	9	33	4	1	2	8	.243

Composite Pitching Averages

New York Yankees

Pitcher	G	IP	H	R	ER	BB	SO	W	L	ERA
Murphy	1	2	2	0	0	1	1	0	0	0.00
Pearson	1	9	5	2	1	2	9	1	0	1.00
Ruffing	2	18	17	4	3	2	11	2	0	1.50
Gomez	1	7	9	3	3	1	5	1	0	3.86
Totals	4	36	33	9	7	6	26	4	0	1.75

Chicago Cubs

Pitcher	G	IP	H	R	ER	BB	SO	W	L	ERA
Russell	2	1 2/3	1	0	0	1	0	0	0	0.00
Lee	2	11	15	6	3	1	8	0	2	2.45
French	3	3 1/3	1	1	1	1	2	0	0	2.70
Root	1	3	3	1	1	0	1	0	0	3.00
Dean	2	8 1/3	8	6	6	1	2	0	1	6.48
Bryant	1	5 1/3	6	4	4	5	3	0	1	6.75
Page	1	1 1/3	2	2	2	0	0	0	0	13.50
Carleton	1	0	1	2	2	2	0	0	0	—
Totals	4	34	37	22	19	11	16	0	4	5.03

1939

Composite Batting Averages

New York Yankees

Player-Position	G	AB	R	H	2B	3B	HR	RBI	BA
Keller, rf	4	16	8	7	1	1	3	6	.438
Ruffing, p	1	3	0	1	0	0	0	0	.333
DiMaggio, cf	4	16	3	5	0	0	1	3	.313
Dickey, c	4	15	2	4	0	0	2	5	.267
Dahlgren, 1b	4	14	2	3	2	0	1	2	.214
Selkirk, lf	4	12	0	2	1	0	0	0	.167
Gordon, 2b	4	14	1	2	0	0	0	1	.143
Rolfe, 3b	4	16	2	2	0	0	0	0	.125
Crosetti, ss	4	16	2	1	0	0	0	1	.063
Pearson, p	1	2	0	0	0	0	0	0	.000
Gomez, p	1	1	0	0	0	0	0	0	.000
Hadley, p	1	3	0	0	0	0	0	0	.000
Hildebrand, p	1	1	0	0	0	0	0	0	.000
Sundra, p	1	0	0	0	0	0	0	0	.000
Murphy, p	1	2	0	0	0	0	0	0	.000
Totals	4	131	20	27	4	1	7	18	.206

Cincinnati Reds

Player-Position	G	AB	R	H	2B	3B	HR	RBI	BA
Thompson, p	1	1	0	1	0	0	0	0	1.000
Hershberger, c-ph	3	2	0	1	0	0	0	1	.500
McCormick, 1b	4	15	1	6	1	0	0	1	.400
Goodman, rf	4	15	3	5	1	0	0	1	.333
Myers, ss	4	12	2	4	0	1	0	0	.333
Werber, 3b	4	16	1	4	0	0	0	2	.250
Simmons, lf	1	4	1	1	1	0	0	0	.250
Lombardi, c	4	14	0	3	0	0	0	2	.214
Derringer, p	2	5	0	1	0	0	0	0	.200
Craft, cf	4	11	0	1	0	0	0	0	.091
Frey, 2b	4	17	0	0	0	0	0	0	.000
Berger, lf-cf	4	15	0	0	0	0	0	1	.000
Bordagaray, pr	2	0	0	0	0	0	0	0	.000
Walters, p	2	3	0	0	0	0	0	0	.000
Gamble, ph	1	1	0	0	0	0	0	0	.000
Grissom, p	1	0	0	0	0	0	0	0	.000
Bongiovanni, ph	1	1	0	0	0	0	0	0	.000
Moore, p	1	1	0	0	0	0	0	0	.000
Totals	4	133	8	27	3	1	0	8	.203

Composite Pitching Averages

New York Yankees

Pitcher	G	IP	H	R	ER	BB	SO	W	L	ERA
Pearson	1	9	2	0	0	1	8	1	0	0.00
Hildebrand	1	4	2	0	0	0	3	0	0	0.00
Sundra	1	2 2/3	4	3	0	1	2	0	0	0.00
Ruffing	1	9	4	1	1	1	4	1	0	1.00
Hadley	1	8	7	2	2	3	2	1	0	2.25
Murphy	1	3 1/3	5	1	1	0	2	1	0	2.70
Gomez	1	1	3	1	1	0	1	0	0	9.00
Totals	4	37	27	8	5	6	22	4	0	1.22

Cincinnati Reds

Pitcher	G	IP	H	R	ER	BB	SO	W	L	ERA
Moore	1	3	0	0	0	0	2	0	0	0.00
Grissom	1	1 1/3	0	0	0	0	0	0	0	0.00
Derringer	2	15 1/3	9	4	4	3	9	0	1	2.35
Walters	2	11	13	9	6	1	6	0	2	4.91
Thompson	1	4 2/3	5	7	7	4	3	0	1	13.50
Totals	4	35 1/3	27	20	17	9	20	0	4	4.33

1940

COMPOSITE BATTING AVERAGES

Cincinnati Reds

Player-Position	G	AB	R	H	2B	3B	HR	RBI	BA
Werber, 3b	7	27	5	10	4	0	0	2	.370
Wilson, c	6	17	2	6	0	0	0	0	.353
Ripple, lf	7	21	3	7	2	0	1	6	.333
Lombardi, c-ph	2	3	0	1	1	0	0	0	.333
M. McCormick, cf	7	29	1	9	3	0	0	2	.310
Walters, p	2	7	2	2	1	0	1	2	.286
Goodman, rf	7	29	5	8	2	0	0	5	.276
Baker, c	3	4	1	1	0	0	0	0	.250
F. McCormick, 1b	7	28	2	6	1	0	0	0	.214
Joost, 2b	7	25	0	5	0	0	0	2	.200
Myers, ss	7	23	0	3	0	0	0	2	.130
Aronvich, ph-lf	1	1	0	0	0	0	0	0	.000
Riggs, p	3	3	1	0	0	0	0	0	.000
Derringer, p	3	7	0	0	0	0	0	0	.000
Moore, p	3	2	0	0	0	0	0	0	.000
Riddle, p	1	0	0	0	0	0	0	0	.000
Turner, p	1	2	0	0	0	0	0	0	.000
Beggs, p	1	0	0	0	0	0	0	0	.000
Thompson, p	1	1	0	0	0	0	0	0	.000
Vander Meer, p	1	0	0	0	0	0	0	0	.000
Hutchings, p	1	0	0	0	0	0	0	0	.000
Frey, ph-pr-2b	3	2	0	0	0	0	0	0	.000
Craft, ph	1	1	0	0	0	0	0	0	.000
Totals	7	232	22	58	14	0	2	21	.250

Detroit Tigers

Player-Position	G	AB	R	H	2B	3B	HR	RBI	BA
Campbell, rf	7	25	4	9	1	0	1	5	.360
Greenberg, lf	7	28	5	10	2	1	1	6	.357
Higgins, 3b	7	24	2	8	3	1	1	6	.333
McCosky, cf	7	23	5	7	1	0	0	1	.304
Bartell, ss	7	26	2	7	2	0	0	3	.269
York, 1b	7	26	3	6	0	1	1	2	.231
Gehringer, 2b	7	28	3	6	0	0	0	1	.214
Sullivan, c-ph	5	13	3	2	0	0	0	0	.154
Newsom, p	3	10	1	1	0	0	0	0	.100
Croucher, ss	1	0	0	0	0	0	0	0	.000
Tebbetts, c-ph	4	11	0	0	0	0	0	0	.000
Rowe, p	2	1	0	0	0	0	0	0	.000
Gorsica, p	2	4	0	0	0	0	0	0	.000
Bridges, p	1	3	0	0	0	0	0	0	.000
Trout, p	1	1	0	0	0	0	0	0	.000
Smith, p	1	1	0	0	0	0	0	0	.000
McKain, p	1	0	0	0	0	0	0	0	.000
Hutchinson, p	1	0	0	0	0	0	0	0	.000
Averill, ph	3	3	0	0	0	0	0	0	.000
Fox, p	1	1	0	0	0	0	0	0	.000
Totals	7	228	28	56	9	3	4	24	.246

COMPOSITE PITCHING AVERAGES

Cincinnati Reds

Pitcher	G	IP	H	R	ER	BB	SO	W	L	ERA
Vander Meer	1	3	2	0	0	3	2	0	0	0.00
Riddle	1	1	0	0	0	0	2	0	0	0.00
Walters	2	18	8	3	3	6	6	2	0	1.50
Derringer	3	19⅓	17	8	6	10	6	2	1	2.79
Moore	3	8⅓	8	3	3	6	7	0	0	3.24
Turner	1	6	8	5	5	0	4	0	1	7.50
Hutchings	1	1	2	1	1	1	0	0	0	9.00
Beggs	1	1	3	2	1	0	1	0	0	9.00
Thompson	1	3⅓	8	6	6	4	2	0	1	16.20
Totals	7	61	56	28	25	30	30	4	3	3.00

Detroit Tigers

Pitcher	G	IP	H	R	ER	BB	SO	W	L	ERA
Gorsica	2	11⅓	6	1	1	4	4	0	0	0.79
Newsom	3	26	18	4	4	4	17	2	1	1.36
Smith	1	4	1	1	1	3	1	0	0	2.25
McKain	1	3	4	1	1	0	0	0	0	3.00
Bridges	1	9	10	4	3	1	5	1	0	3.00
Hutchinson	1	1	1	1	1	1	1	0	0	9.00
Trout	1	2	6	3	2	1	1	0	1	9.00
Rowe	2	3⅔	12	7	7	1	1	0	2	17.18
Totals	7	60	58	22	20	15	30	3	4	3.00

1941

COMPOSITE BATTING AVERAGES

New York Yankees

Player-Position	G	AB	R	H	2B	3B	HR	RBI	BA
Gordon, 2b	5	14	2	7	1	1	1	5	.500
Chandler, p	1	2	0	1	0	0	0	1	.500
Selkirk, ph	2	2	0	1	0	0	0	0	.500
Keller, lf	5	18	5	7	2	0	0	5	.389
Rolfe, 3b	5	20	2	6	0	0	0	0	.300
Sturm, 1b	5	21	0	6	0	0	0	0	.286
DiMaggio, cf	5	19	1	5	0	0	0	1	.263
Henrich, rf	5	18	4	3	1	0	1	1	.167
Dickey, c	5	18	3	3	1	0	0	1	.167
Rizzuto, ss	5	18	0	2	0	0	0	0	.111
Rosar, c	1	0	0	0	0	0	0	0	.000
Ruffing, p	1	3	0	0	0	0	0	0	.000
Murphy, p	2	2	0	0	0	0	0	0	.000
Russo, p	1	4	0	0	0	0	0	0	.000
Donald, p	1	2	0	0	0	0	0	0	.000
Breuer, p	1	1	0	0	0	0	0	0	.000
Bonham, p	1	4	0	0	0	0	0	0	.000
Bordagaray, pr	1	0	0	0	0	0	0	0	.000
Totals	5	166	17	41	5	1	2	16	.247

Brooklyn Dodgers

Player-Position	G	AB	R	H	2B	3B	HR	RBI	BA
Higbe, p	1	1	0	1	0	0	0	0	1.000
Casey, p	3	2	0	1	0	0	0	0	.500
Riggs, ph-3b	3	8	0	2	0	0	0	1	.250
Medwick, lf	5	17	1	4	1	0	0	0	.235
Walker, rf	5	18	3	4	2	0	0	0	.222
Reiser, cf	5	20	1	4	1	1	1	3	.200
Reese, ss	5	20	1	4	0	0	0	2	.200
Wasdell, ph-lf	3	5	0	1	1	0	0	2	.200
Camilli, 1b	5	18	3	3	1	0	0	1	.167
Owen, c	5	12	1	2	0	1	0	2	.167
Wyatt, p	2	6	1	1	1	0	0	0	.167
Herman, 2b	4	8	1	1	0	0	0	0	.125
Lavagetto, 3b	3	10	1	1	0	0	0	0	.100
Coscarart, 2b	3	7	1	0	0	0	0	0	.000
Franks, c	1	1	0	0	0	0	0	0	.000
Davis, p	1	2	0	0	0	0	0	0	.000
Allen	3	0	0	0	0	0	0	0	.000
Fitzsimmons, p	1	2	0	0	0	0	0	0	.000
French, p	2	0	0	0	0	0	0	0	.000
Galan, ph	2	2	0	0	0	0	0	0	.000
Totals	5	159	11	29	7	2	1	11	.182

COMPOSITE PITCHING AVERAGES

New York Yankees

Pitcher	G	IP	H	R	ER	BB	SO	W	L	ERA
Murphy	2	6	2	0	0	1	3	1	0	0.00
Breuer	1	3	3	0	0	1	2	0	0	0.00
Ruffing	1	9	6	2	1	3	5	1	0	1.00
Bonham	1	9	4	1	1	2	2	1	0	1.00
Russo	1	9	4	1	1	2	5	1	0	1.00
Chandler	1	5	4	3	2	2	2	0	1	3.60
Donald	1	4	6	4	4	3	2	0	0	9.00
Totals	5	45	29	11	9	14	21	4	1	1.80

Brooklyn Dodgers

Pitcher	G	IP	H	R	ER	BB	SO	W	L	ERA
Fitzsimmons	1	7	4	0	0	3	1	0	0	0.00
Allen	3	3⅔	1	0	0	3	0	0	0	0.00
French	2	1	0	0	0	0	0	0	0	0.00
Wyatt	2	18	15	5	5	10	14	1	1	2.50
Casey	3	5⅓	9	6	2	2	1	0	2	3.36
Davis	1	5⅓	6	3	3	3	1	0	1	5.06
Higbe	1	3⅔	6	3	3	2	1	0	0	7.36
Totals	5	44	41	17	13	23	18	1	4	2.06

1942

COMPOSITE BATTING AVERAGES

St. Louis Cardinals

Player-Position	G	AB	R	H	2B	3B	HR	RBI	BA
Lanier, p	2	1	0	1	0	0	0	1	1.000
O'Dea, ph	1	1	0	1	0	0	0	1	1.000
Brown, 2b	5	20	2	6	0	0	0	1	.300
T. Moore, cf	5	17	2	5	1	0	0	2	.294
W. Cooper, c	5	21	3	6	1	0	0	4	.286
Kurowski, 3b	5	15	3	4	0	1	1	5	.267
Slaughter, rf	5	19	3	5	1	0	1	2	.263
Musial, lf	5	18	2	4	1	0	0	2	.222
M. Cooper, p	2	5	1	1	0	0	0	2	.200
Hopp, 1b	5	17	3	3	0	0	0	0	.176
Beazley, p	2	7	0	1	0	0	0	0	.143
Marion, ss	5	18	2	2	0	1	0	3	.111
Gumbert, p	2	0	0	0	0	0	0	0	.000
White, p	1	2	0	0	0	0	0	0	.000
Pollet, p	1	0	0	0	0	0	0	0	.000
Crespi, pr	1	0	1	0	0	0	0	0	.000
Sanders, ph	2	1	1	0	0	0	0	0	.000
Walker, ph	1	1	0	0	0	0	0	0	.000
Totals	5	163	23	39	4	2	2	23	.239

New York Yankees

Player-Position	G	AB	R	H	2B	3B	HR	RBI	BA
Rosar, ph	1	1	0	1	0	0	0	0	1.000
Rizzuto, ss	5	21	2	8	0	0	1	1	.381
Rolfe, 3b	4	17	5	6	2	0	0	0	.353
DiMaggio, cf	5	21	3	7	0	0	0	3	.333
Hassett, 1b	3	9	1	3	1	0	0	2	.333
Cullenbine, rf	5	19	3	5	1	0	0	2	.263
Dickey, c	5	19	1	5	0	0	0	0	.263
Ruffing, p-ph	4	9	0	2	0	0	0	0	.222
Keller, lf	5	20	2	4	0	0	2	5	.200
Priddy, 3b-1b	3	10	0	1	0	0	0	1	.100
Gordon, 2b	5	21	1	2	1	0	0	0	.095
Crosetti, 3b	1	3	0	0	0	0	0	0	.000
Chandler, p	2	2	0	0	0	0	0	0	.000
Bonham, p	2	2	0	0	0	0	0	0	.000
Breuer, p	1	0	0	0	0	0	0	0	.000
Turner, p	1	0	0	0	0	0	0	0	.000
Borowy, p	1	1	0	0	0	0	0	0	.000
Donald, p	1	2	0	0	0	0	0	0	.000
Selkirk, ph	1	1	0	0	0	0	0	0	.000
Stainback, pr	2	0	0	0	0	0	0	0	.000
Totals	5	178	18	44	6	0	3	14	.247

COMPOSITE PITCHING AVERAGES

St. Louis Cardinals

Pitcher	G	IP	H	R	ER	BB	SO	W	L	ERA
White	1	9	6	0	0	0	6	1	0	0.00
Lanier	2	4	3	2	0	1	1	1	0	0.00
Gumbert	2	⅔	1	1	0	0	0	0	0	0.00
Pollet	1	⅓	0	0	0	0	0	0	0	0.00
Beazley	2	18	17	5	5	3	6	2	0	2.50
M. Cooper	2	13	17	10	8	4	9	0	1	5.54
Totals	5	45	44	18	13	8	22	4	1	2.00

New York Yankees

Pitcher	G	IP	H	R	ER	BB	SO	W	L	ERA
Turner	1	1	0	0	0	1	0	0	0	0.00
Breuer	1	0	2	1	0	0	0	0	0	0.00
Chandler	2	8⅓	5	1	1	1	3	0	1	1.08
Ruffing	2	17⅔	14	8	8	7	11	1	1	4.06
Bonham	2	11	9	5	5	3	4	0	1	4.00
Donald	1	3	3	2	2	2	1	0	1	6.00
Borowy	1	3	6	6	6	3	1	0	0	18.00
Totals	5	44	30	23	22	17	19	1	4	4.50

1943

Composite Batting Averages

New York Yankees

Player-Position	G	AB	R	H	2B	3B	HR	RBI	BA
Russo, p	1	3	1	2	2	0	0	0	.667
Borowy, p	1	2	1	1	1	0	0	0	.500
Johnson, 3b	5	20	3	6	1	1	0	3	.300
Dickey, c	5	18	1	5	0	0	1	4	.278
Crosetti, ss	5	18	4	5	0	0	0	1	.278
Gordon, 2b	5	17	2	4	1	0	1	2	.235
Keller, lf	5	18	3	4	0	1	0	2	.222
Stainback, rf	5	17	0	3	0	0	0	0	.176
Chandler, p	2	6	0	1	0	0	0	0	.167
Metheny, rf	2	8	0	1	0	0	0	0	.125
Lindell, cf	4	9	1	1	0	0	0	0	.111
Etten, 1b	5	19	0	2	0	0	0	2	.105
Bonham, p	1	2	0	0	0	0	0	0	.000
Murphy, p	2	0	0	0	0	0	0	0	.000
Stirnweiss, ph	1	1	1	0	0	0	0	0	.000
Weatherly, ph	1	1	0	0	0	0	0	0	.000
Totals	5	150	17	35	5	2	2	14	.220

St. Louis Cardinals

Player-Position	G	AB	R	H	2B	3B	HR	RBI	BA
O'Dea, ph-c	2	3	0	2	0	0	0	0	.667
Marion, ss	5	14	1	5	2	0	1	2	.357
W. Cooper, c	5	17	1	5	0	0	0	0	.294
Sanders, 1b	5	17	3	5	0	0	1	2	.294
Musial, rf	5	18	2	5	0	0	0	0	.278
Litwhiler, lf-ph	5	15	0	4	1	0	0	2	.267
Lanier, p	3	4	0	1	0	0	0	1	.250
Kurowski, 3b	5	18	2	4	1	0	0	1	.222
Walker, cf-ph	5	18	0	3	1	0	0	0	.167
Klein, 2b	5	22	0	3	0	0	0	0	.136
Garms, ph-lf	2	5	0	0	0	0	0	0	.000
Hopp, cf	1	4	0	0	0	0	0	0	.000
Brecheen, p	3	0	0	0	0	0	0	0	.000
M. Cooper, p	2	5	0	0	0	0	0	0	.000
Brazle, p	1	3	0	0	0	0	0	0	.000
Krist, p	1	0	0	0	0	0	0	0	.000
Dickson, p	1	0	0	0	0	0	0	0	.000
Demaree, ph	1	1	0	0	0	0	0	0	.000
Narron, ph	1	1	0	0	0	0	0	0	.000
White, pr	1	0	0	0	0	0	0	0	.000
Totals	5	165	9	37	5	0	2	8	.224

Composite Pitching Averages

New York Yankees

Pitcher	G	IP	H	R	ER	BB	SO	W	L	ERA
Russo	1	9	7	1	0	1	2	1	0	0.00
Murphy	2	2	1	0	0	1	1	0	0	0.00
Chandler	2	18	17	2	1	3	10	2	0	0.50
Borowy	1	8	6	2	2	3	4	1	0	2.25
Bonham	1	8	6	4	4	3	9	0	1	4.50
Totals	5	45	37	9	7	11	26	4	1	1.40

St. Louis Cardinals

Pitcher	G	IP	H	R	ER	BB	SO	W	L	ERA
Krist	1	0	1	0	0	0	0	0	0	0.00
Dickson	1	⅔	0	0	0	1	0	0	0	0.00
Lanier	3	15⅓	13	5	3	3	13	0	1	1.76
Brecheen	3	3⅔	5	1	1	3	3	0	1	2.45
M. Cooper	2	16	11	5	5	3	10	1	1	2.81
Brazle	1	7⅓	5	6	3	2	4	0	1	3.68
Totals	5	43	35	17	12	12	30	1	4	2.51

1944

Composite Batting Averages

St. Louis Cardinals

Player-Position	G	AB	R	H	2B	3B	HR	RBI	BA
Lanier, p	2	4	0	2	0	0	0	1	.500
Verban, 2b	6	17	1	7	0	0	0	2	.412
O'Dea, ph	3	3	0	1	0	0	0	2	.333
W. Cooper, c	6	22	1	7	2	1	0	2	.318
Musial, rf	6	23	2	7	2	0	1	2	.304
Sanders, 1b	6	21	5	6	0	0	1	1	.286
Marion, ss	6	22	1	5	3	0	0	2	.227
Kurowski, 3b	6	23	2	5	1	0	0	1	.217
Litwhiler, lf	5	20	2	4	1	0	1	1	.200
Hopp, cf	6	27	2	5	0	0	0	0	.185
Fallon, 2b	2	2	0	0	0	0	0	0	.000
Bergamo, ph-lf	3	6	0	0	0	0	0	1	.000
M. Cooper, p	2	4	0	0	0	0	0	0	.000
Donnelly, p	2	1	0	0	0	0	0	0	.000
Wilks, p	2	2	0	0	0	0	0	0	.000
Schmidt, p	1	1	0	0	0	0	0	0	.000
Jurisich, p	1	0	0	0	0	0	0	0	.000
Byerly, p	1	0	0	0	0	0	0	0	.000
Brecheen, p	1	4	0	0	0	0	0	0	.000
Garms, ph	2	2	0	0	0	0	0	0	.000
Totals	6	204	16	49	9	1	3	15	.240

St. Louis Browns

Player-Position	G	AB	R	H	2B	3B	HR	RBI	BA
Mancuso, ph-c	2	3	0	2	0	0	0	1	.667
McQuinn, 1b	6	16	2	7	2	0	1	5	.438
Kreevich, cf	6	26	0	6	3	0	0	0	.231
Stephens, ss	6	22	2	5	1	0	0	0	.227
Laabs, lf-ph	5	15	1	3	1	1	0	0	.200
Galehouse, p	2	5	0	1	0	0	0	0	.200
Moore, rf	6	22	4	4	0	0	0	0	.182
Gutteridge, 2b	6	21	1	3	1	0	0	0	.143
Hayworth, c	6	17	1	2	1	0	0	1	.118
Zarilla, ph-lf	4	10	1	1	0	0	0	1	.100
Christman, 3b	6	22	0	2	0	0	0	1	.091
Baker, ph-2b	2	2	0	0	0	0	0	0	.000
Potter, p	2	4	0	0	0	0	0	0	.000
Muncrief, p	2	1	0	0	0	0	0	0	.000
Kramer, p	2	4	0	0	0	0	0	0	.000
Jakucki, p	1	0	0	0	0	0	0	0	.000
Clary, ph	1	1	0	0	0	0	0	0	.000
Hollingsworth, p	1	1	0	0	0	0	0	0	.000
Shirley, pr-p	2	0	0	0	0	0	0	0	.000
Byrnes, ph	3	2	0	0	0	0	0	0	.000
Turner, ph	1	1	0	0	0	0	0	0	.000
Chartak, ph	2	2	0	0	0	0	0	0	.000
Totals	6	197	12	36	9	1	1	9	.183

Composite Pitching Averages

St. Louis Cardinals

Pitcher	G	IP	H	R	ER	BB	SO	W	L	ERA
Donnelly	2	6	2	0	0	1	9	1	0	0.00
Schmidt	1	3⅓	1	0	0	1	1	0	0	0.00
Byerly	1	1⅓	0	0	1	0	1	0	0	0.00
Brecheen	1	9	9	1	1	4	4	1	0	1.00
M. Cooper	2	16	9	2	2	5	16	1	1	1.13
Lanier	2	12⅓	8	3	3	8	11	1	0	2.19
Wilks	2	6⅓	5	4	4	3	7	0	1	5.68
Jurisich	1	⅔	2	2	2	1	0	0	0	27.00
Totals	6	55	36	12	12	23	49	4	2	1.96

St. Louis Browns

Pitcher	G	IP	H	R	ER	BB	SO	W	L	ERA
Kramer	2	11	9	2	0	4	12	1	0	0.00
Shirley	1	2	2	0	0	1	1	0	0	0.00
Potter	2	9⅔	10	5	1	3	6	0	1	0.93
Muncrief	2	6⅔	5	1	1	4	4	0	1	1.35
Galehouse	2	18	13	3	3	5	15	1	1	1.50
Hollingsworth	1	4	5	1	1	2	1	0	0	2.25
Jakucki	1	3	5	4	3	0	4	0	1	9.00
Totals	6	54⅓	49	16	9	19	43	2	4	1.49

1945

Composite Batting Averages

Detroit Tigers

Player-Position	G	AB	R	H	2B	3B	HR	RBI	BA
Maier, ph	1	1	0	1	0	0	0	0	1.000
Walker, ph	2	2	1	1	1	0	0	0	.500
Cramer, cf	7	29	7	11	0	0	0	4	.379
Hoover, ss	1	3	1	1	0	0	0	1	.333
Greenberg, lf	7	23	7	7	3	0	2	7	.304
Mayo, 2b	7	28	4	7	1	0	0	2	.250
Swift, c	3	4	1	1	0	0	0	0	.250
Cullenbine, rf	7	22	5	5	2	0	0	4	.227
Richards, c	7	19	0	4	2	0	0	6	.211
Webb, ss	7	27	4	5	0	0	0	1	.185
York, 1b	7	28	1	5	1	0	0	3	.179
Outlaw, 3b	7	28	1	5	0	0	0	3	.179
Trout, p	2	6	0	1	0	0	0	0	.167
Mierkowicz, lf	1	0	0	0	0	0	0	0	.000
Newhouser, p	3	8	0	0	0	0	0	1	.000
Benton, p	3	0	0	0	0	0	0	0	.000
Tobin, p	1	1	0	0	0	0	0	0	.000
Mueller, p	1	0	0	0	0	0	0	0	.000
Trucks, p	2	4	0	0	0	0	0	0	.000
Overmire, p	1	1	0	0	0	0	0	0	.000
Caster, p	1	0	0	0	0	0	0	0	.000
Bridges, p	1	0	0	0	0	0	0	0	.000
McHale, ph	3	3	0	0	0	0	0	0	.000
Borom, ph-pr	2	1	0	0	0	0	0	0	.000
Eaton, ph	1	1	0	0	0	0	0	0	.000
Hostetler, ph	3	3	0	0	0	0	0	0	.000
Totals	7	242	32	54	10	0	2	32	.223

Chicago Cubs

Player-Position	G	AB	R	H	2B	3B	HR	RBI	BA
Becker, ph	3	2	0	1	0	0	0	0	.500
Cavarretta, 1b	7	26	7	11	2	0	1	5	.423
Secory, ph	5	5	0	2	0	0	0	0	.400
Hack, 3b	7	30	1	11	3	0	0	4	.367
Livingston, c	6	22	3	8	3	0	0	4	.364
Lowrey, lf	7	29	4	9	1	0	0	0	.310
Hughes, ss	6	17	1	5	1	0	0	3	.294
Pafko, cf	7	28	5	6	2	1	0	2	.214
Nicholson, rf	7	28	1	6	1	1	0	8	.214
Johnson, 2b	7	29	4	5	2	1	0	0	.172
Borowy, p	4	6	1	1	1	0	0	0	.167
Gillespie, c-ph	3	6	0	0	0	0	0	0	.000
Merullo, pr-ss	3	2	0	0	0	0	0	0	.000
Schuster, ss-pr	2	1	1	0	0	0	0	0	.000
Williams, ph-c	2	2	0	0	0	0	0	0	.000
Wyse, p	3	3	0	0	0	0	0	0	.000
Erickson, p	4	0	0	0	0	0	0	0	.000
Passeau, p	3	7	1	0	0	0	0	1	.000
Prim, p	2	0	0	0	0	0	0	0	.000
Vandenberg, p	3	1	0	0	0	0	0	0	.000
Chipman, p	1	0	0	0	0	0	0	0	.000
Derringer, p	2	0	0	0	0	0	0	0	.000
Block, pr	1	0	0	0	0	0	0	0	.000
McCullough, ph	1	1	0	0	0	0	0	0	.000
Sauer, ph	2	2	0	0	0	0	0	0	.000
Totals	7	247	29	65	16	3	1	27	.263

Composite Pitching Averages

Detroit Tigers

Pitcher	G	IP	H	R	ER	BB	SO	W	L	ERA
Mueller	1	2	0	0	0	1	1	0	0	0.00
Caster	1	⅔	0	0	0	0	1	0	0	0.00
Trout	2	13⅓	9	2	1	3	9	1	1	0.66
Benton	3	4⅔	6	1	1	0	5	0	0	1.93
Overmire	1	6	4	2	2	2	2	0	1	3.00
Trucks	2	13⅓	14	5	5	5	7	1	0	3.38
Tobin	1	3	4	2	2	1	0	0	0	6.00
Newhouser	3	20⅔	25	14	14	4	22	2	1	6.10
Bridges	1	1⅔	3	3	3	3	1	0	0	16.20
Totals	7	65⅔	65	29	28	19	48	4	3	3.84

Chicago Cubs

Pitcher	G	IP	H	R	ER	BB	SO	W	L	ERA
Vandenberg	3	6	1	0	0	3	3	0	0	0.00
Chipman	1	⅓	6	0	0	1	0	0	0	0.00
Passeau	3	16⅔	7	5	5	8	3	1	0	2.70
Erickson	4	7	8	3	3	3	5	0	0	3.86
Borowy	4	18	21	8	8	6	8	2	2	4.00
Derringer	3	5⅓	5	4	4	7	1	0	0	6.75
Wyse	3	7⅔	8	7	6	4	1	0	1	7.04
Prim	2	4	4	5	4	1	1	0	1	9.00
Totals	7	65	54	32	30	33	22	3	4	4.15

1946

Composite Batting Averages

St. Louis Cardinals

Player-Position	G	AB	R	H	2B	3B	HR	RBI	BA
Rice, c	3	6	2	3	1	0	0	0	.500
Walker, lf-rf-ph	7	17	3	7	2	0	0	6	.412
Dickson, p	2	5	1	2	2	0	0	1	.400
Slaughter, rf	7	25	5	8	1	1	1	2	.320
Garagiola, c	5	19	2	6	2	0	0	4	.316
Kurowski, 3b	7	27	5	8	3	0	0	2	.296
Dusak, ph-lf	4	4	0	1	1	0	0	0	.250
Marion, ss	7	24	1	6	2	0	0	4	.250
Munger, p	1	4	0	1	0	0	0	0	.250
Schoendienst, 2b	7	30	3	7	1	0	0	1	.233
Musial, 1b	7	27	3	6	4	1	0	4	.222
Moore, cf	7	27	1	4	0	0	0	2	.148
Brecheen, p	3	8	2	1	0	0	0	1	.125
Pollet, p	2	4	0	0	0	0	0	0	.000
Wilks, p	1	0	0	0	0	0	0	0	.000
Brazle, p	1	2	0	0	0	0	0	0	.000
Beazley, p	1	0	0	0	0	0	0	0	.000
Jones, ph	1	1	0	0	0	0	0	0	.000
Sisler, ph	2	2	0	0	0	0	0	0	.000
Totals	7	232	28	60	19	2	1	27	.259

Boston Red Sox

Player-Position	G	AB	R	H	2B	3B	HR	RBI	BA
Russell, ph-3b	2	2	1	2	0	0	0	0	1.000
Metkovich, ph	2	2	1	1	1	0	0	0	.500
Moses, rf	4	12	1	5	0	0	0	0	.417
Doerr, 2b	6	22	1	9	1	0	1	3	.409
Gutteridge, pr-2b	3	5	1	2	0	0	0	1	.400
Harris, p	3	3	0	1	0	0	0	0	.333
Hughson, p	3	3	0	1	0	0	0	0	.333
York, 1b	7	23	6	6	1	1	2	5	.261
DiMaggio, cf	7	27	2	7	3	0	0	3	.259
Pesky, ss	7	30	2	7	0	0	0	0	.233
C'son, ph-rf-cf-pr	5	9	1	2	0	0	1	1	.222
Higgins, 3b	7	24	1	5	1	0	0	2	.208
Williams, lf	7	25	2	5	0	0	0	1	.200
McBride, rf-ph	5	12	0	2	0	0	0	1	.167
Partee, ph-c	5	10	1	1	0	0	0	1	.100
H. Wagner, c	5	13	0	0	0	0	0	0	.000
Johnson, p	3	1	0	0	0	0	0	0	.000
Dobson, p	3	3	0	0	0	0	0	0	.000
Ferriss, p	2	6	0	0	0	0	0	0	.000
Bagby, p	1	1	0	0	0	0	0	0	.000
Zuber, p	1	0	0	0	0	0	0	0	.000
Brown, p	1	0	0	0	0	0	0	0	.000
Ryba, p	1	0	0	0	0	0	0	0	.000
Dreisewerd, p	1	0	0	0	0	0	0	0	.000
Klinger, p	1	0	0	0	0	0	0	0	.000
Campbell, pr	1	0	0	0	0	0	0	0	.000
Totals	7	233	20	56	7	1	4	18	.240

Composite Pitching Averages

St. Louis Cardinals

Pitcher	G	IP	H	R	ER	BB	SO	W	L	ERA
Wilks	1	1	2	1	0	0	0	0	0	0.00
Beazley	1	1	1	0	0	0	1	0	0	0.00
Brecheen	3	20	14	1	1	5	11	3	0	0.45
Munger	1	9	9	3	1	3	2	1	0	1.00
Pollet	2	10⅓	12	4	4	4	3	0	1	3.48
Dickson	2	14	11	6	6	4	7	0	1	3.86
Brazle	1	6⅔	7	5	4	6	4	0	1	5.40
Totals	7	62	56	20	16	22	28	4	3	2.32

Boston Red Sox

Pitcher	G	IP	H	R	ER	BB	SO	W	L	ERA
Dobson	3	12⅔	4	3	0	3	10	1	0	0.00
Ryba	1	⅔	2	1	0	1	0	0	0	0.00
Dreisewerd	1	⅓	0	0	0	0	0	0	0	0.00
Ferriss	2	13⅓	13	3	3	2	4	1	0	2.03
Johnson	3	3⅓	1	1	1	2	1	1	0	2.75
Bagby	1	3	6	1	1	1	1	0	0	3.00
Hughson	3	14⅓	14	8	5	3	8	0	1	3.14
Zuber	1	2	3	1	1	1	1	0	0	4.50
Harris	2	9⅔	11	6	5	4	5	0	2	4.66
Klinger	1	⅔	2	1	1	1	0	0	1	13.50
Brown	1	1	4	3	3	1	0	0	0	27.00
Totals	7	61	60	28	20	19	30	3	4	2.95

1947

Composite Batting Averages

New York Yankees

Player-Position	G	AB	R	H	2B	3B	HR	RBI	BA
Brown, ph	4	3	2	3	2	0	0	3	1.000
Houk, ph	1	1	0	1	0	0	0	0	1.000
Lollar, c	2	4	3	3	2	0	0	1	.750
Reynolds, p	2	4	2	2	0	0	0	1	.500
Lindell, lf	6	18	3	9	3	1	0	7	.500
Clark, ph-rf	3	2	1	1	0	0	0	1	.500
Shea, p	3	5	0	2	1	0	0	1	.400
Henrich, rf-lf	7	31	2	10	2	0	1	5	.323
Rizzuto, ss	7	26	3	8	1	0	0	2	.308
Johnson, 3b	7	26	8	7	0	3	0	2	.269
Stirnweiss, 2b	7	27	3	7	0	1	0	3	.259
DiMaggio, cf	7	26	4	6	0	0	2	5	.231
A. Robinson, c	3	10	2	2	0	0	0	1	.200
Berra, c-ph-rf	6	19	2	3	0	0	1	2	.158
McQuinn, 1b	7	23	3	3	0	0	0	1	.130
Page, p	4	4	0	0	0	0	0	0	.000
Newsom, p	2	0	0	0	0	0	0	0	.000
Raschi, p	2	0	0	0	0	0	0	0	.000
Drews, p	2	2	0	0	0	0	0	0	.000
Phillips, ph-1b	2	2	0	0	0	0	0	0	.000
Chandler, p	1	0	0	0	0	0	0	0	.000
Bevens, p	2	4	0	0	0	0	0	0	.000
Wensloff, p	1	0	0	0	0	0	0	0	.000
Frey, ph	1	1	0	0	0	0	0	1	.000
Totals	7	238	38	67	11	5	4	36	.282

Brooklyn Dodgers

Player-Position	G	AB	R	H	2B	3B	HR	RBI	BA
Bragan, ph	1	1	0	1	1	0	0	1	1.000
Vaughan, ph	3	2	0	1	1	0	0	0	.500
Furillo, ph-cf	6	17	2	6	2	0	0	3	.353
Hatten, p	4	3	1	1	0	0	0	0	.333
Reese, ss	7	23	5	7	1	0	0	4	.304
Robinson, 1b	7	27	3	7	2	0	0	3	.259
Miksis, ph-2b-lf	5	4	1	1	0	0	0	0	.255
Reiser, cf-lf-ph	5	8	1	2	0	0	0	0	.250
Stanky, 2b	7	25	4	6	1	0	0	2	.240
Walker, rf	7	27	1	6	1	0	1	4	.222
Edwards, c	7	27	3	6	1	0	0	2	.222
Jorgensen, 3b	7	20	1	4	2	0	0	3	.200
Hermanski, lf	7	19	4	3	0	1	0	1	.158
Lavagetto, ph-3b	5	7	0	1	1	0	0	3	.143
G'friddo, ph-pr-lf	4	3	2	0	0	0	0	0	.000
Branca, p	3	4	0	0	0	0	0	0	.000
Casey, p	6	1	0	0	0	0	0	0	.000
Gregg, p	3	3	0	0	0	0	0	0	.000
Barney, p	3	1	0	0	0	0	0	0	.000
Taylor, p	1	0	0	0	0	0	0	0	.000
Lombardi, p-pr	3	3	0	0	0	0	0	0	.000
Bankhead, pr	1	0	1	0	0	0	0	0	.000
Hodges, ph	1	1	0	0	0	0	0	0	.000
Totals	7	226	29	52	13	1	1	26	.230

Composite Pitching Averages

New York Yankees

Pitcher	G	IP	H	R	ER	BB	SO	W	L	ERA
Wensloff	1	2	0	0	0	0	0	0	0	0.00
Shea	3	15⅓	10	4	4	8	10	2	0	2.35
Bevens	2	11⅓	3	3	3	11	7	0	1	2.38
Drews	2	3	2	1	1	1	0	0	0	3.00
Page	4	13	12	6	6	2	7	1	1	4.15
Reynolds	2	11⅓	15	7	6	3	6	1	0	4.76
Raschi	2	1⅓	2	1	1	0	1	0	0	6.75
Chandler	1	2	2	2	2	3	1	0	0	9.00
Newsom	2	2⅓	6	5	5	2	0	0	1	19.29
Totals	7	61⅔	52	29	28	30	32	4	3	4.00

Brooklyn Dodgers

Pitcher	G	IP	H	R	ER	BB	SO	W	L	ERA
Taylor	1	0	2	1	0	1	0	0	0	0.00
Casey	6	10⅓	5	1	1	1	3	2	0	0.87
Barney	3	6⅔	4	2	2	10	3	0	1	2.70
Gregg	3	12⅔	9	5	5	8	10	0	1	3.55
Hatten	4	9	12	7	7	7	5	0	0	7.00
Behrman	5	6½	9	5	5	9	3	0	0	7.11
Branca	3	8⅓	12	8	8	5	8	1	1	8.64
Lombardi	3	6⅔	14	9	9	1	5	0	1	12.15
Totals	7	60	67	30	37	38	37	3	4	5.55

1948

Composite Batting Averages

Cleveland Indians

Player-Position	G	AB	R	H	2B	3B	HR	RBI	BA
Bearden, p	2	4	1	2	1	0	0	0	.500
Kennedy, rf	3	2	0	1	0	0	0	1	.500
Tucker, cf	1	3	1	1	0	0	0	0	.333
Doby, cf	6	22	1	7	1	0	1	2	.318
Robinson, 1b	6	20	0	6	0	0	0	1	.300
Boudreau, ss	6	22	1	6	4	0	0	3	.273
Hegan, c	6	19	2	4	0	0	1	5	.211
Gordon, 2b	6	22	3	4	0	0	1	2	.182
Mitchell, lf	6	23	4	4	1	0	1	1	.174
Keltner, 3b	6	21	3	2	0	0	0	0	.095
Judnich, rf	4	13	1	1	0	0	0	1	.077
Clark, rf	1	3	0	0	0	0	0	0	.000
Peck, rf	1	0	0	0	0	0	0	0	.000
Feller, p	2	4	0	0	0	0	0	0	.000
Lemon, p	2	7	0	0	0	0	0	0	.000
Gromek, p	1	3	0	0	0	0	0	0	.000
Boone, ph	1	1	0	0	0	0	0	0	.000
Klieman, p	1	0	0	0	0	0	0	0	.000
Christopher, p	1	0	0	0	0	0	0	0	.000
Paige, p	1	0	0	0	0	0	0	0	.000
Muncrief, p	1	0	0	0	0	0	0	0	.000
Tipton, ph	1	1	0	0	0	0	0	0	.000
Rosen, ph	1	1	0	0	0	0	0	0	.000
Totals	6	191	17	38	7	0	4	16	.199

Boston Braves

Player-Position	G	AB	R	H	2B	3B	HR	RBI	BA
Potter, p	2	2	0	1	0	0	0	0	.500
Torgeson, 1b	5	18	2	7	3	0	0	1	.389
Elliott, 3b	6	21	4	7	0	0	2	5	.333
Stanky, 2b	6	14	0	4	1	0	0	1	.286
M. McCor'k, cf-lf	6	23	1	6	0	0	0	2	.261
Salkeld, c-ph	5	9	2	2	0	0	1	1	.222
Rickert, lf	5	19	2	4	0	0	1	2	.211
F. McCo'k, ph-1b	3	5	0	1	0	0	0	0	.200
Sain, p	2	5	0	1	0	0	0	0	.200
Holmes, rf	6	26	3	5	0	0	0	1	.192
Dark, ss	6	24	2	4	1	0	0	0	.167
Masi, pr-c	5	8	1	1	1	0	0	1	.125
Conatser, cf-ph	2	4	0	0	0	0	0	1	.000
Sisti, pr-2b	2	1	0	0	0	0	0	0	.000
Spahn, p	3	4	0	0	0	0	0	1	.000
Barrett, p	2	0	0	0	0	0	0	0	.000
Bickford, p	1	0	0	0	0	0	0	0	.000
Voiselle, p	2	2	0	0	0	0	0	0	.000
Ryan, ph-pr	2	1	0	0	0	0	0	0	.000
Sanders, ph	1	1	0	0	0	0	0	0	.000
Totals	6	187	17	43	6	0	4	16	.230

Composite Pitching Averages

Cleveland Indians

Pitcher	G	IP	H	R	ER	BB	SO	W	L	ERA
Bearden	2	10⅔	6	0	0	1	4	1	0	0.00
Muncrief	1	2	1	0	0	0	0	0	0	0.00
Paige	1	⅔	0	0	0	0	0	0	0	0.00
Gromek	1	9	7	1	1	1	2	1	0	1.00
Lemon	2	16⅓	16	4	3	7	6	2	0	1.65
Feller	2	14⅓	10	8	8	5	7	0	2	5.02
Klieman	1	0	1	3	3	2	0	0	0	—
Christopher	1	0	2	1	1	0	0	0	0	—
Totals	6	53	43	17	16	16	19	4	2	2.72

Boston Braves

Pitcher	G	IP	H	R	ER	BB	SO	W	L	ERA
Barrett	2	3⅔	1	0	0	0	1	0	0	0.00
Sain	2	17	9	2	2	0	9	1	1	1.06
Voiselle	2	10⅔	8	3	3	2	2	0	1	2.53
Bickford	1	3⅓	4	2	1	5	1	0	1	2.70
Spahn	3	12	10	4	4	3	12	1	1	3.00
Potter	2	5⅓	6	6	5	2	1	0	0	8.44
Totals	6	52	38	17	15	12	26	2	4	2.60

1949

COMPOSITE BATTING AVERAGES

New York Yankees

Player-Position	G	AB	R	H	2B	3B	HR	RBI	BA
Byrne, p	1	1	0	1	0	0	0	0	1.000
Mize, ph	2	2	0	2	0	0	0	2	1.000
R. Brown, ph-3b	4	12	4	6	1	2	0	5	.500
Reynolds, p	2	4	0	2	1	0	0	0	.500
Woodling, lf	3	10	4	4	3	0	0	0	.400
Lopat, p	1	3	0	1	1	0	0	1	.333
Henrich, 1b	5	19	4	5	0	0	1	1	.263
Coleman, 2b	5	20	0	5	3	0	0	4	.250
Raschi, p	2	5	0	1	0	0	0	1	.200
Rizzuto, ss	5	18	2	3	0	0	0	1	.167
Bauer, rf-pr-ph	3	6	0	1	0	0	0	0	.167
Lindell, lf	2	7	0	1	0	0	0	0	.143
Johnson, 3b	2	7	0	1	0	0	0	0	.143
DiMaggio, cf	5	18	2	2	0	0	1	2	.111
Mapes, rf	4	10	3	1	1	0	0	2	.100
Berra, c	4	16	2	1	0	0	1	1	.063
Niarhos, c	1	0	0	0	0	0	0	0	.000
Silvera, c	1	2	0	0	0	0	0	0	.000
Page, p	3	4	0	0	0	0	0	0	.000
Stirnweiss, pr	1	0	0	0	0	0	0	0	.000
Totals	5	164	21	37	10	2	2	20	.226

Brooklyn Dodgers

Player-Position	G	AB	R	H	2B	3B	HR	RBI	BA
Edwards, ph	2	2	0	1	0	0	0	0	.500
Cox, ph-3b	2	3	0	1	0	0	0	0	.333
Reese, ss	5	19	2	6	1	0	1	2	.316
Hermanski, lf-rf	4	13	1	4	0	1	0	2	.308
Miksis, 3b-ph	3	7	0	2	1	0	0	0	.286
Olmo, lf	4	11	2	3	0	0	1	3	.273
Campanella, c	5	15	2	4	1	0	1	2	.267
Hodges, 1b	5	17	2	4	0	0	1	4	.235
Robinson, 2b	5	16	2	3	1	0	0	2	.188
Jorgensen, 3b-ph	4	11	1	2	2	0	0	0	.182
Snider, cf	5	21	3	3	1	0	0	0	.143
Furillo, rf-ph	3	8	0	1	0	0	0	0	.125
Newcombe, p	2	4	0	0	0	0	0	0	.000
McCormick, rf	1	0	0	0	0	0	0	0	.000
Rackley, lf	2	5	0	0	0	0	0	0	.000
Roe, p	1	3	0	0	0	0	0	0	.000
Branca, p	1	3	0	0	0	0	0	0	.000
Banta, p	3	1	0	0	0	0	0	0	.000
Hatten, p	2	0	0	0	0	0	0	0	.000
Erskine, p	2	0	0	0	0	0	0	0	.000
Barney, p	1	0	0	0	0	0	0	0	.000
Palica, p	1	0	0	0	0	0	0	0	.000
Minner, p	1	0	0	0	0	0	0	0	.000
Whitman, ph	1	1	0	0	0	0	0	0	.000
T. Brown, ph	2	2	0	0	0	0	0	0	.000
Totals	5	162	14	34	7	1	4	14	.210

COMPOSITE PITCHING AVERAGES

New York Yankees

Pitcher	G	IP	H	R	ER	BB	SO	W	L	ERA
Reynolds	2	12⅓	2	0	0	4	14	1	0	0.00
Page	3	9	6	2	2	3	8	1	0	2.00
Byrne	1	3⅓	2	1	1	2	1	0	0	2.70
Raschi	2	14⅔	15	7	7	5	11	1	1	4.30
Lopat	1	5⅔	9	4	4	1	4	1	0	6.35
Totals	5	45	34	14	14	15	36	4	1	2.80

Brooklyn Dodgers

Pitcher	G	IP	H	R	ER	BB	SO	W	L	ERA
Roe	1	9	6	0	0	3	1	0	0	0.00
Palica	1	2	1	0	0	1	1	0	0	0.00
Minner	1	1	1	0	0	0	0	0	0	0.00
Newcombe	2	11⅔	10	4	4	3	11	0	2	3.09
Banta	3	5⅔	5	2	2	1	4	0	0	3.18
Branca	1	8⅔	4	4	4	6	0	1	4.15
Hatten	2	1⅔	4	3	3	2	0	0	0	16.20
Erskine	2	1⅔	3	3	3	1	0	0	0	16.20
Barney	1	2⅔	3	5	5	6	2	0	1	16.88
Totals	5	44	37	21	21	18	27	1	4	4.29

1950

COMPOSITE BATTING AVERAGES

New York Yankees

Player-Position	G	AB	R	H	2B	3B	HR	RBI	BA
Lopat, p	1	2	0	1	0	0	0	0	.500
Woodling, lf-ph	4	14	2	6	0	0	0	1	.429
Brown, 3b-ph	4	12	2	4	1	1	0	1	.333
Raschi, p	1	3	0	1	0	0	0	0	.333
Reynolds, p	2	3	0	1	0	0	0	0	.333
DiMaggio, cf	4	13	2	4	1	0	1	2	.308
Coleman, 2b	4	14	2	4	1	0	0	3	.286
Berra, c	4	15	2	3	0	0	1	2	.200
Rizzuto, ss	4	14	1	2	0	0	0	0	.143
Mize, 1b	4	15	0	2	0	0	0	0	.133
Bauer, rf-lf	4	15	0	2	0	0	0	1	.133
Collins, 1b	1	0	0	0	0	0	0	0	.000
Mapes, rf	1	4	0	0	0	0	0	0	.000
Hopp, 1b-pr	3	2	0	0	0	0	0	0	.000
W. Johnson, 3b	4	6	0	0	0	0	0	0	.000
Ferrick, p	1	0	0	0	0	0	0	0	.000
Ford, p	1	3	0	0	0	0	0	0	.000
Jensen, pr	1	0	0	0	0	0	0	0	.000
Totals	4	135	11	30	3	1	2	10	.222

Philadelphia Phillies

Player-Position	G	AB	R	H	2B	3B	HR	RBI	BA
Hamner, ss	4	14	1	6	2	1	0	0	.429
Jones, 3b	4	14	1	4	1	0	0	0	.286
Waitkus, 1b	4	15	0	4	1	0	0	0	.267
Konstanty, p	3	4	0	1	0	0	0	0	.250
Goliat, 2b	4	14	1	3	0	0	0	1	.214
Seminick, c	4	11	0	2	0	0	0	0	.182
Ashburn, cf	4	17	0	3	1	0	0	1	.176
Ennis, rf	4	14	1	2	1	0	0	0	.143
Sisler, lf	4	17	0	1	0	0	0	1	.059
Silvestri, c	1	0	0	0	0	0	0	0	.000
Lopata, c-ph	2	1	0	0	0	0	0	0	.000
Bloodworth, 2b	1	0	0	0	0	0	0	0	.000
Mayo, ph-lf-pr	3	0	0	0	0	0	0	0	.000
Meyer, p	2	0	0	0	0	0	0	0	.000
Roberts, p	2	2	0	0	0	0	0	0	.000
Heintzelman, p	1	2	0	0	0	0	0	0	.000
Miller, p	1	0	0	0	0	0	0	0	.000
Whitman, p	3	2	0	0	0	0	0	0	.000
K. Johnson, pr	1	0	1	0	0	0	0	0	.000
Caballero, pr-ph	3	1	0	0	0	0	0	0	.000
Totals	4	128	5	26	6	1	0	3	.203

COMPOSITE PITCHING AVERAGES

New York Yankees

Pitcher	G	IP	H	R	ER	BB	SO	W	L	ERA
Raschi	1	9	2	0	0	1	5	1	0	0.00
Ford	1	8⅔	7	2	0	1	7	1	0	0.00
Ferrick	1	1	1	0	0	1	0	1	0	0.00
Reynolds	2	10⅓	7	1	1	4	7	1	0	0.87
Lopat	1	8	9	2	2	0	5	0	0	2.25
Totals	4	37	26	5	3	7	24	4	0	0.73

Philadelphia Phillies

Pitcher	G	IP	H	R	ER	BB	SO	W	L	ERA
Heintzelman	1	7⅔	4	2	1	6	3	0	0	1.17
Roberts	2	11	11	2	2	3	5	0	1	1.64
Konstanty	3	15	9	4	4	4	3	0	1	2.40
Meyer	2	1⅔	4	1	1	0	1	0	1	5.40
Miller	1	⅓	2	2	1	0	0	0	1	27.00
Totals	4	35⅔	30	11	9	13	12	0	4	2.27

1951

COMPOSITE BATTING AVERAGES

New York Yankees

Player-Position	G	AB	R	H	2B	3B	HR	RBI	BA
Brown, ph-3b	5	14	1	5	1	0	0	0	.357
Reynolds, p	2	6	0	2	0	0	0	1	.333
Rizzuto, ss	6	25	5	8	0	0	1	3	.320
Mize, ph-1b	4	7	2	2	1	0	0	1	.286
DiMaggio, cf	6	23	3	6	2	0	1	5	.261
Berra, c	6	23	4	6	1	0	0	0	.261
McDougald, 3b-2b	6	23	2	6	1	0	1	7	.261
Coleman, 2b-pr	5	8	2	2	0	0	0	0	.250
Collins, 1b-rf	6	18	2	4	0	0	1	3	.222
Mantle, rf	2	5	1	1	0	0	0	0	.200
Bauer, lf-rf	6	18	0	3	0	1	0	3	.167
Woodling, ph-lf	6	18	6	3	1	1	1	1	.167
Lopat, p	2	8	0	1	0	0	0	1	.125
Hogue, p	2	0	0	0	0	0	0	0	.000
Morgan, p	1	0	0	0	0	0	0	0	.000
Raschi, p	2	2	0	0	0	0	0	0	.000
Ostrowski, p	1	0	0	0	0	0	0	0	.000
Sain, p	1	1	0	0	0	0	0	0	.000
Kuzava, p	1	0	0	0	0	0	0	0	.000
Hopp, ph	1	0	0	0	0	0	0	0	.000
Martin, pr	1	0	1	0	0	0	0	0	.000
Totals	6	199	29	49	7	2	5	25	.246

New York Giants

Player-Position	G	AB	R	H	2B	3B	HR	RBI	BA
Irvin, lf	6	24	3	11	0	1	0	2	.458
Dark, ss	6	24	5	10	3	0	1	4	.417
Rigney, p	4	4	0	1	0	0	0	0	.250
Lockman, 1b	6	25	1	6	2	0	1	4	.240
Thomson, 3b	6	21	1	5	1	0	0	2	.238
Westrum, c	6	17	1	4	1	0	0	0	.235
Mays, cf	6	22	1	4	0	0	0	1	.182
Thompson, rf	5	14	3	2	0	0	0	0	.143
Stanky, 2b	6	22	3	3	0	0	0	1	.136
Noble, ph-c	2	2	0	0	0	0	0	0	.000
Hartung, rf	2	4	0	0	0	0	0	0	.000
Koslo, p	2	5	0	0	0	0	0	0	.000
Spencer, p	2	0	0	0	0	0	0	0	.000
Jansen, p	3	2	0	0	0	0	0	0	.000
Hearn, p	2	3	0	0	0	0	0	0	.000
Jones, p	2	0	0	0	0	0	0	0	.000
Maglie, p	1	1	0	0	0	0	0	0	.000
Kennedy, p	2	0	0	0	0	0	0	0	.000
Corwin, p	1	0	0	0	0	0	0	0	.000
Konikowski, p	1	0	0	0	0	0	0	0	.000
Yvars, p	1	1	0	0	0	0	0	0	.000
Lohrke, ph	2	2	0	0	0	0	0	0	.000
Williams, ph-pr	2	1	0	0	0	0	0	0	.000
Schenz, pr	1	0	0	0	0	0	0	0	.000
Totals	6	194	18	46	7	1	2	15	.237

COMPOSITE PITCHING AVERAGES

New York Yankees

Pitcher	G	IP	H	R	ER	BB	SO	W	L	ERA
Hogue	2	2⅔	1	0	0	0	0	0	0	0.00
Morgan	1	2	2	0	0	1	3	0	0	0.00
Ostrowski	1	2	1	0	0	1	0	0	0	0.00
Kuzava	1	1	0	0	0	0	0	0	0	0.00
Lopat	2	18	10	2	1	3	4	2	0	0.50
Raschi	2	10⅓	12	7	1	8	4	1	1	0.87
Reynolds	2	15	16	7	7	11	8	1	1	4.20
Sain	1	2	4	2	2	2	2	0	0	9.00
Totals	6	53	46	18	11	25	22	4	2	1.87

New York Giants

Pitcher	G	IP	H	R	ER	BB	SO	W	L	ERA
Corwin	1	1⅔	1	0	0	0	1	0	0	0.00
Konikowski	1	1	1	0	0	0	0	0	0	0.00
Hearn	2	8⅔	5	1	1	8	1	1	0	1.04
Jones	2	4⅓	5	3	1	1	2	0	0	2.06
Koslo	2	15	12	5	5	7	6	1	1	3.00
Kennedy	2	3	3	2	2	1	4	0	0	6.00
Jansen	3	10	8	7	7	4	6	0	2	6.30
Maglie	1	5	8	4	4	2	3	0	1	7.20
Spencer	2	3⅓	6	7	7	3	0	0	0	18.90
Totals	6	52	40	20	27	26	23	2	4	4.67

1952

COMPOSITE BATTING AVERAGES

New York Yankees

Player-Position	G	AB	R	H	2B	3B	HR	RBI	BA
Mize, ph-1b	5	15	3	6	1	0	3	6	.400
Woodling, ph-lf	7	23	4	8	1	1	1	1	.348
Mantle, cf	7	29	5	10	1	1	2	3	.345
Lopat, p	2	3	0	1	0	0	0	1	.333
Noren, lf-ph-rf	4	10	0	3	0	0	0	1	.300
Martin, 2b	7	23	2	5	0	0	1	4	.217
Berra, c	7	28	2	6	1	0	2	3	.214
McDougald, 3b	7	25	5	5	0	0	1	3	.200
Raschi, p	3	6	0	1	0	0	0	0	.167
Rizzuto, ss	7	27	2	4	1	0	0	0	.148
Bauer, rf-ph	7	18	2	1	0	0	0	1	.056
Collins, 1b-pr	6	12	1	0	0	0	0	0	.000
Reynolds, p	4	7	0	0	0	0	0	0	.000
Scarborough, p	1	0	0	0	0	0	0	0	.000
Gorman, p	1	0	0	0	0	0	0	0	.000
Blackwell, p	1	1	0	0	0	0	0	0	.000
Kuzava, p	1	1	0	0	0	0	0	0	.000
Sain, ph-p	2	3	0	0	0	0	0	0	.000
Houk, ph	1	1	0	0	0	0	0	0	.000
Totals	7	232	26	50	5	2	10	24	.216

Brooklyn Dodgers

Player-Position	G	AB	R	H	2B	3B	HR	RBI	BA
Snider, cf	7	29	5	10	2	0	4	8	.345
Reese, ss	7	29	4	10	0	0	1	4	.345
Loes, p	2	3	0	1	0	0	0	0	.333
Shuba, ph-lf	4	10	0	3	1	0	0	0	.300
Cox, 3b	7	27	4	8	2	0	0	0	.296
Campanella, c	7	28	0	6	0	0	0	1	.214
Pafko, lf-rf-ph	7	21	0	4	0	0	0	2	.190
Robinson, 2b	7	23	4	4	0	0	1	2	.174
Furillo, rf	7	23	1	4	2	0	0	0	.174
Holmes, lf	3	1	0	0	0	0	0	0	.000
Morgan, 3b-ph	2	1	0	0	0	0	0	0	.000
Hodges, 1b	7	21	1	0	0	0	0	1	.000
Black, p	3	6	0	0	0	0	0	0	.000
Erskine, p	3	6	1	0	0	0	0	0	.000
Lehman, p	1	0	0	0	0	0	0	0	.000
Roe, p	3	2	0	0	0	0	0	0	.000
Rutherford, p	1	0	0	0	0	0	0	0	.000
Amoros, pr	1	0	0	0	0	0	0	0	.000
Nelson, ph	4	3	0	0	0	0	0	0	.000
Totals	7	233	20	50	7	0	6	18	.215

COMPOSITE PITCHING AVERAGES

New York Yankees

Pitcher	G	IP	H	R	ER	BB	SO	W	L	ERA
Kuzava	1	2⅔	0	0	0	0	2	0	0	0.00
Gorman	1	⅔	1	0	0	0	0	0	0	0.00
Raschi	3	17	12	3	3	8	18	2	0	1.59
Reynolds	4	20⅓	12	4	4	6	18	2	1	1.77
Sain	1	6	6	2	2	3	3	0	1	3.00
Lopat	2	11⅓	14	6	6	4	3	0	1	4.76
Blackwell	1	5	4	4	4	3	4	0	0	7.20
Scarborough	1	1	1	1	1	0	1	0	0	9.00
Totals	7	64	50	20	20	24	49	4	3	2.81

Brooklyn Dodgers

Pitcher	G	IP	H	R	ER	BB	SO	W	L	ERA
Lehman	1	2	2	0	0	1	0	0	0	0.00
Black	3	21⅓	15	6	6	8	9	1	2	2.53
Roe	3	11⅓	9	4	4	6	7	1	0	3.18
Loes	2	10⅓	11	6	5	5	5	0	1	4.35
Erskine	3	18	12	9	9	10	10	1	1	4.50
Rutherford	1	1	1	1	1	1	1	0	0	9.00
Totals	7	64	50	26	25	31	32	3	4	3.52

1953

COMPOSITE BATTING AVERAGES

New York Yankees

Player-Position	G	AB	R	H	2B	3B	HR	RBI	BA
Martin, 2b	6	24	5	12	1	2	2	8	.500
McDonald, p	1	2	0	1	1	0	0	1	.500
Reynolds, p	3	2	0	1	0	0	0	0	.500
Sain, p	2	2	1	1	1	0	0	2	.500
Berra, c	6	21	3	9	1	0	1	4	.429
Ford, p	2	3	0	1	0	0	0	0	.333
Rizzuto, ss	6	19	4	6	1	0	0	0	.316
Woodling, lf	6	20	5	6	0	0	1	3	.300
Bauer, rf	6	23	6	6	1	0	1	1	.261
Mantle, cf	6	24	3	5	0	0	2	7	.208
McDougald, 3b	6	24	2	4	0	1	2	4	.167
Collins, 1b	6	24	4	4	1	0	1	2	.167
Bollweg, ph-1b	3	2	0	0	0	0	0	0	.000
Lopat, p	1	3	0	0	0	0	0	0	.000
Raschi, p	1	2	0	0	0	0	0	0	.000
Gorman, p	1	1	0	0	0	0	0	0	.000
Schallock, p	1	0	0	0	0	0	0	0	.000
Kuzava, p	1	1	0	0	0	0	0	0	.000
Mize, ph	3	3	0	0	0	0	0	0	.000
Noren, ph	2	1	0	0	0	0	0	0	.000
Totals	6	201	33	56	6	4	9	32	.279

Brooklyn Dodgers

Player-Position	G	AB	R	H	2B	3B	HR	RBI	BA
Shuba, ph	2	1	1	1	0	0	1	2	1.000
Podres, p	1	1	0	1	0	0	0	0	1.000
Loes, p	1	3	0	2	0	0	0	0	.667
Williams, ph	3	2	0	1	0	0	0	0	.500
Hodges, 1b	6	22	3	8	0	0	1	1	.364
Furillo, rf	6	24	4	8	2	0	1	4	.333
Snider, cf	6	25	3	8	3	0	1	5	.320
Robinson, lf	6	25	3	8	2	0	0	2	.320
Cox, 3b	6	23	3	7	3	0	1	6	.304
Gilliam, 2b	6	27	4	8	3	0	2	4	.296
Campanella, c	6	22	6	6	0	0	1	2	.273
Erskine, p	3	4	0	1	0	0	0	0	.250
Reese, ss	6	24	0	5	0	1	0	0	.208
Thompson, lf	2	0	0	0	0	0	0	0	.000
Hughes, p	1	1	0	0	0	0	0	0	.000
Labine, p	3	2	0	0	0	0	0	0	.000
Wade, p	2	1	0	0	0	0	0	0	.000
Roe, p	1	3	0	0	0	0	0	0	.000
Meyer, p	1	1	0	0	0	0	0	0	.000
Black, p	1	0	0	0	0	0	0	0	.000
Milliken, p	1	0	0	0	0	0	0	0	.000
Belardi, ph	2	2	0	0	0	0	0	0	.000
Morgan, ph	1	1	0	0	0	0	0	0	.000
Totals	6	213	27	64	13	1	8	26	.300

COMPOSITE PITCHING AVERAGES

New York Yankees

Pitcher	G	IP	H	R	ER	BB	SO	W	L	ERA
Lopat	1	9	9	2	2	4	3	1	0	2.00
Gorman	1	3	4	1	1	0	1	0	0	3.00
Raschi	1	8	9	3	3	3	4	0	1	3.38
Ford	2	8	9	4	4	2	7	0	1	4.50
Schallock	1	2	2	1	1	1	1	0	0	4.50
Sain	2	5⅔	8	3	3	1	1	1	0	4.76
McDonald	1	7⅔	12	6	5	0	3	1	0	5.87
Reynolds	3	8	9	6	6	4	9	1	0	6.75
Kuzava	1	⅔	2	1	1	0	1	0	0	13.50
Totals	6	52	64	27	26	15	30	4	2	4.50

Brooklyn Dodgers

Pitcher	G	IP	H	R	ER	BB	SO	W	L	ERA
Milliken	1	2	2	0	0	1	0	0	0	0.00
Hughes	1	4	3	1	1	1	3	0	0	2.25
Loes	1	8	8	3	3	2	8	1	0	3.38
Podres	1	2⅔	1	5	1	2	0	0	1	3.38
Labine	3	5	10	2	2	1	3	0	2	3.00
Roe	1	8	5	4	4	4	4	0	1	4.50
Erskine	3	14	14	9	9	9	16	1	0	5.79
Meyer	1	4⅓	8	4	3	4	5	0	0	6.23
Black	1	1	1	1	1	0	2	0	0	9.00
Wade	2	2⅔	4	4	4	1	2	0	0	15.43
Totals	6	51⅓	34	33	26	25	43	2	4	4.91

1954

COMPOSITE BATTING AVERAGES

New York Giants

Player-Position	G	AB	R	H	2B	3B	HR	RBI	BA
Rhodes, ph-lf	3	6	2	4	0	0	2	7	.667
Dark, ss	4	17	2	7	0	0	0	0	.412
Mueller, rf	4	18	4	7	0	0	0	1	.389
Thompson, 3b	4	11	6	4	1	0	0	2	.364
Mays, cf	4	14	4	4	1	0	0	3	.286
Westrum, c	4	11	0	3	0	0	0	3	.273
Irvin, lf	4	9	1	2	1	0	0	2	.222
Lockman, 1b	4	18	2	2	0	0	0	0	.111
Williams, 2b	4	11	0	0	0	0	0	1	.000
Maglie, p	1	3	0	0	0	0	0	0	.000
Liddle, p	2	3	0	0	0	0	0	0	.000
Grissom, p	1	1	0	0	0	0	0	0	.000
Antonelli, p	2	3	0	0	0	0	0	1	.000
Gomez, p	1	4	0	0	0	0	0	0	.000
Wilhelm, p	2	1	0	0	0	0	0	0	.000
Totals	4	130	21	33	3	0	2	20	.254

Cleveland Indians

Player-Position	G	AB	R	H	2B	3B	HR	RBI	BA
Wynn, p	1	2	0	1	0	0	0	0	.500
Wertz, 1b	4	16	2	8	2	1	1	3	.500
Glynn, ph-1b	2	2	1	1	1	0	0	0	.500
Rega'do, pr-3b-ph	4	3	0	1	0	0	0	1	.333
Rosen, 3b	3	12	0	3	0	0	0	2	.250
Smith, lf	4	14	2	3	0	0	1	2	.214
Majeski, ph-3b	4	6	1	1	0	0	1	3	.167
Hegan, c	4	13	1	2	1	0	0	0	.154
Westlake, rf	2	7	0	1	0	0	0	0	.143
Avila, 2b	4	15	1	2	0	0	0	0	.133
Doby, cf	4	16	0	2	0	0	0	0	.125
Philley, rf-ph	4	8	0	1	0	0	0	0	.125
Naragon, c	1	0	0	0	0	0	0	0	.000
Grasso, c	1	0	0	0	0	0	0	0	.000
Dente, ss	3	3	1	0	0	0	0	0	.000
Strickland, ss	3	9	0	0	0	0	0	0	.000
Pope, ph-rf	3	3	0	0	0	0	0	0	.000
Mossi, p	3	0	0	0	0	0	0	0	.000
Garcia, p	2	0	0	0	0	0	0	0	.000
Houtteman, p	1	0	0	0	0	0	0	0	.000
Narleski, p	2	0	0	0	0	0	0	0	.000
Newhouser, p	1	0	0	0	0	0	0	0	.000
Lemon, p-ph	3	6	0	0	0	0	0	0	.000
Totals	4	137	9	26	5	1	3	9	.190

COMPOSITE PITCHING AVERAGES

New York Giants

Pitcher	G	IP	H	R	ER	BB	SO	W	L	ERA
Grissom	1	2⅔	1	0	0	3	2	1	0	0.00
Wilhelm	2	2⅓	1	0	0	3	3	0	0	0.00
Antonelli	2	10⅔	8	1	1	7	12	1	0	0.84
Liddle	2	7	5	4	1	1	2	1	0	1.29
Gomez	1	7⅓	4	2	2	3	2	1	0	2.35
Maglie	1	7	7	2	2	2	2	0	0	2.57
Totals	4	37	26	9	6	16	23	4	0	1.46

Cleveland Indians

Pitcher	G	IP	H	R	ER	BB	SO	W	L	ERA
Mossi	3	4	3	0	0	0	1	0	0	0.00
Narleski	2	4	1	1	1	1	2	0	0	2.25
Wynn	1	7	4	3	3	2	5	0	1	3.86
Houtteman	1	2	2	1	1	1	1	0	0	4.50
Garcia	2	5	6	4	3	4	4	0	1	5.40
Lemon	2	13⅓	16	11	10	8	11	0	2	6.75
Newhouser	1	0	1	1	1	1	0	0	0	—
Totals	4	35⅓	33	21	19	17	24	0	4	4.84

1955

Composite Batting Averages

Brooklyn Dodgers

Player-Position	G	AB	R	H	2B	3B	HR	RBI	BA
Amoros, lf-cf	5	12	3	4	0	0	1	3	.333
Kellert, ph	3	3	0	1	0	0	0	0	.333
Hoak, pr-ph-3b	3	3	0	1	0	0	0	0	.333
Snider, cf	7	25	5	8	1	0	4	7	.320
Reese, ss	7	27	5	8	1	0	0	2	.296
Furillo, rf	7	27	4	8	1	0	1	3	.296
Gilliam, lf-2b	7	24	2	7	1	0	0	3	.292
Hodges, 1b	7	24	2	7	0	0	1	5	.292
Campanella, c	7	27	4	7	3	0	2	4	.259
Zimmer, 2b-ph	4	9	0	2	0	0	0	2	.222
J. Robinson, 3b	6	22	5	4	1	1	0	1	.182
Podres, p	2	7	1	1	0	0	0	0	.143
Newcombe, p	1	3	0	0	0	0	0	0	.000
Bessent, p	3	1	0	0	0	0	0	0	.000
Labine, p	4	4	0	0	0	0	0	0	.000
Loes, p	1	1	0	0	0	0	0	0	.000
Spooner, p	2	0	0	0	0	0	0	0	.000
Erskine, p	1	1	0	0	0	0	0	0	.000
Craig, p	1	0	0	0	0	0	0	0	.000
Meyer, p	1	2	0	0	0	0	0	0	.000
Roebuck, p	1	0	0	0	0	0	0	0	.000
Shuba, ph	1	1	0	0	0	0	0	0	.000
Totals	7	223	31	58	8	1	9	30	.260

New York Yankees

Player-Position	G	AB	R	H	2B	3B	HR	RBI	BA
E. Rob'son, ph-1b	4	3	0	2	0	0	0	1	.667
Carey, ph	2	2	0	1	0	1	0	1	.500
Bauer, rf-ph	6	14	1	6	0	0	0	1	.429
Berra, c	7	24	5	10	1	0	1	2	.417
Skowron, 1b-ph	5	12	2	4	2	0	1	3	.333
Martin, 2b	7	25	2	8	1	1	0	4	.320
Rizzuto, ss	7	15	2	4	0	0	0	1	.267
McDougald, 3b	7	27	2	7	0	0	1	1	.259
Mantle, cf-rf-ph	3	10	1	2	0	0	1	1	.200
Howard, lf-rf	7	26	3	5	0	0	1	3	.192
Collins, 1b-rf-ph	5	12	6	2	0	0	2	3	.167
Byrne, p-ph	3	6	0	1	0	0	0	2	.167
Cerv, cf-lf-ph	5	16	1	2	0	0	1	1	.125
Noren, cf-lf	5	16	0	1	0	0	0	1	.063
J. Coleman, ss-pr	3	3	0	0	0	0	0	0	.000
Ford, p	2	6	1	0	0	0	0	0	.000
Grim, p	3	2	0	0	0	0	0	0	.000
Turley, p	3	1	0	0	0	0	0	0	.000
Morgan, p	2	0	0	0	0	0	0	0	.000
Kucks, p	2	0	0	0	0	0	0	0	.000
Sturdivant, p	2	0	0	0	0	0	0	0	.000
Larsen, p	1	2	0	0	0	0	0	0	.000
R. Coleman, p	1	0	0	0	0	0	0	0	.000
Carroll, pr	2	0	0	0	0	0	0	0	.000
Totals	7	222	26	55	4	2	8	25	.248

Composite Pitching Averages

Brooklyn Dodgers

Pitcher	G	IP	H	R	ER	BB	SO	W	L	ERA
Meyer	1	5⅔	4	0	0	2	4	0	0	0.00
Bessent	3	3⅓	3	0	0	1	1	0	0	0.00
Roebuck	1	2	1	0	0	0	0	0	0	0.00
Podres	2	18	15	3	2	4	10	2	0	1.00
Labine	4	9⅓	6	3	3	2	2	1	0	2.89
Craig	1	6	4	2	2	5	4	1	0	3.00
Erskine	1	3	3	3	3	2	3	0	0	9.00
Newcombe	1	5⅔	8	6	6	2	4	0	1	9.53
Loes	1	3⅔	7	4	4	1	5	0	1	9.82
Spooner	2	3⅓	4	5	5	3	6	0	1	13.50
Totals	7	60	55	26	25	22	39	4	3	3.75

New York Yankees

Pitcher	G	IP	H	R	ER	BB	SO	W	L	ERA
Byrne	2	14⅓	8	4	3	8	8	1	1	1.88
Ford	2	17	13	6	4	8	10	2	0	2.12
Grim	3	8⅔	8	4	4	5	8	0	1	4.15
Morgan	2	3⅔	3	2	2	3	1	0	0	4.91
Kucks	2	3	4	2	2	1	1	0	0	6.00
Sturdivant	2	3	5	2	2	2	0	0	0	6.00
Turley	3	5⅓	7	5	5	4	7	0	1	8.44
R. Coleman	1	1	5	1	1	0	1	0	0	9.00
Larsen	1	4	5	5	5	2	2	0	1	11.25
Totals	7	60	58	31	28	33	38	3	4	4.20

1956

Composite Batting Averages

New York Yankees

Player-Position	G	AB	R	H	2B	3B	HR	RBI	BA
McDermott, p	1	1	0	1	0	0	0	0	1.000
Cerv, ph	1	1	0	1	0	0	0	0	1.000
Morgan, p	2	1	1	1	0	0	0	0	1.000
Howard, lf	1	5	1	2	1	0	1	1	.400
Berra, c	7	25	5	9	2	0	3	10	.360
Slaughter, lf	6	20	6	7	0	0	1	4	.350
Larsen, p	2	3	1	1	0	0	0	1	.333
Sturdivant, p	2	3	0	1	0	0	0	0	.333
Martin, 2b-3b	7	27	5	8	0	0	2	3	.296
Bauer, rf	7	32	3	9	0	0	1	3	.281
Mantle, cf	7	24	6	6	1	0	3	4	.250
Collins, ph-1b	6	21	2	5	2	0	0	2	.238
Carey, 3b	7	19	2	3	0	0	0	0	.158
McDougald, ss	7	21	0	3	0	0	0	1	.143
Skowron, 1b-ph	3	10	1	1	0	0	1	4	.100
G. Coleman, 2b	2	2	0	0	0	0	0	0	.000
Turley, p	3	4	0	0	0	0	0	0	.000
Ford, p	2	4	0	0	0	0	0	0	.000
Kucks, p	3	3	0	0	0	0	0	0	.000
Byrne, ph-p	2	1	0	0	0	0	0	0	.000
Siebern, ph	1	1	0	0	0	0	0	0	.000
Wilson, ph	1	1	0	0	0	0	0	0	.000
Totals	7	229	33	56	6	0	12	33	.253

Brooklyn Dodgers

Player-Position	G	AB	R	H	2B	3B	HR	RBI	BA
Bessent, p	2	2	0	1	0	0	0	1	.500
Craig, p	2	2	0	1	0	0	0	0	.500
Snider, cf	7	23	5	7	1	0	1	4	.304
Hodges, 1b	7	23	5	7	2	0	1	8	.304
Robinson, 3b	7	24	5	6	1	0	1	2	.250
Labine, p	2	4	0	1	1	0	0	0	.250
Furillo, rf	7	25	2	6	2	0	0	1	.240
Reese, ss	7	27	3	6	0	1	0	2	.222
Campanella, c	7	22	2	4	1	0	0	3	.182
Gilliam, 2b-lf	7	24	2	2	0	0	0	2	.083
Amoros, lf	6	19	1	1	0	0	0	1	.053
Cimoli, lf	1	0	0	0	0	0	0	0	.000
Maglie, p	2	5	0	0	0	0	0	0	.000
Newcombe, p	2	1	0	0	0	0	0	0	.000
Roebuck, p	3	0	0	0	0	0	0	0	.000
Neal, 2b	1	4	0	0	0	0	0	0	.000
Erskine, p	2	1	0	0	0	0	0	0	.000
Drysdale, p	1	0	0	0	0	0	0	0	.000
Walker, ph	2	2	0	0	0	0	0	0	.000
Mitchell, ph	4	4	0	0	0	0	0	0	.000
Jackson, ph	3	3	0	0	0	0	0	0	.000
Totals	7	215	25	42	8	1	3	24	.195

Composite Pitching Averages

New York Yankees

Pitcher	G	IP	H	R	ER	BB	SO	W	L	ERA
Larsen	2	10⅔	1	4	0	4	7	1	0	0.00
Byrne	1	⅓	1	1	0	0	1	0	0	0.00
Turley	3	11	4	1	1	8	14	0	1	0.82
Kucks	3	11	6	2	1	3	2	1	0	0.82
Sturdivant	2	9⅔	8	3	3	8	9	1	0	2.79
McDermott	1	3	2	2	1	3	3	0	0	3.00
Ford	2	12	14	9	7	2	8	1	1	5.25
Morgan	2	4	6	4	4	4	3	0	1	9.00
Totals	7	61⅔	42	26	17	32	47	4	3	2.48

Brooklyn Dodgers

Pitcher	G	IP	H	R	ER	BB	SO	W	L	ERA
Labine	2	12	8	1	0	3	7	1	0	0.00
Bessent	2	10	8	2	2	3	5	1	0	1.80
Roebuck	3	4⅔	1	1	1	0	5	0	0	2.08
Maglie	2	17	14	5	5	6	15	1	1	2.05
Erskine	3	5	4	3	3	2	2	0	1	5.40
Drysdale	1	2	2	2	2	1	1	0	0	9.00
Craig	2	6	19	8	9	3	4	0	1	12.00
Newcombe	2	4⅔	11	11	11	3	4	0	1	21.21
Total	7	64	67	33	33	21	43	3	4	4.72

1957

Composite Batting Averages

Milwaukee Braves

Player-Position	G	AB	R	H	2B	3B	HR	RBI	BA
Aaron, cf	7	28	5	11	0	1	3	7	.393
Torre, 1b-ph	7	10	2	3	0	0	2	3	.300
Schoendienst, 2b	5	18	0	5	1	0	0	2	.278
Mathews, 3b	7	22	4	5	3	0	1	4	.227
Pafko, rf-ph	6	14	1	3	0	0	0	0	.214
Crandall, c	6	19	1	4	0	0	1	1	.211
Covington, lf	7	24	1	5	1	0	0	1	.208
Adcock, 1b-ph	5	15	1	3	0	0	0	2	.200
Logan, ss	7	27	5	5	1	0	1	2	.185
Rice, c	2	6	0	1	0	0	0	0	.167
Hazle, rf	4	13	2	2	0	0	0	0	.154
Mantilla, pr-2b	4	10	1	0	0	0	0	0	.000
Spahn, p	2	4	0	0	0	0	0	0	.000
Johnson, p	3	1	0	0	0	0	0	0	.000
McMahon, p	3	0	0	0	0	0	0	0	.000
Trowbridge, p	1	0	0	0	0	0	0	0	.000
Buhl, p	2	1	0	0	0	0	0	0	.000
Pizarro, p	1	1	0	0	0	0	0	0	.000
Conley, p	1	0	0	0	0	0	0	0	.000
Burdette, p	3	8	0	0	0	0	0	0	.000
Jones, ph	3	2	0	0	0	0	0	0	.000
DeMerit, pr	1	0	0	0	0	0	0	0	.000
Sawatski, ph	2	2	0	0	0	0	0	0	.000
Totals	7	225	23	47	6	1	8	22	.209

New York Yankees

Player-Position	G	AB	R	H	2B	3B	HR	RBI	BA
Byrne, p	2	2	0	1	0	0	0	0	.500
Coleman, 2b	7	22	2	8	2	0	0	2	.364
Berra, c	7	25	5	8	1	0	1	2	.320
Carey, 3b	2	7	0	2	1	0	0	1	.286
Kubek, lf-3b-cf	7	28	4	8	0	0	2	4	.286
Lumpe, ph-3b	6	14	0	4	0	0	0	2	.286
Howard, 1b-ph	6	11	2	3	0	0	1	3	.273
Mantle, cf-pr	6	19	3	5	0	0	1	2	.263
Bauer, rf	7	31	3	8	2	1	2	6	.258
McDougald, ss	7	24	3	6	0	0	0	2	.250
Slaughter, lf	5	12	2	3	1	0	0	0	.250
Simpson, 1b-ph	5	12	0	1	0	0	0	1	.083
Richardson, pr-2b	2	0	0	0	0	0	0	0	.000
Skowron, 1b-ph	2	4	0	0	0	0	0	0	.000
Collins, 1b-ph	6	5	0	0	0	0	0	0	.000
Ford, p	2	5	0	0	0	0	0	0	.000
Shantz, p	3	1	0	0	0	0	0	0	.000
Ditmar, p	2	1	0	0	0	0	0	0	.000
Grim, p	2	0	0	0	0	0	0	0	.000
Turley, p	3	4	0	0	0	0	0	0	.000
Larsen, p	2	2	1	0	0	0	0	0	.000
Sturdivant, p	2	1	0	0	0	0	0	0	.000
Kucks, p	1	0	0	0	0	0	0	0	.000
Totals	7	230	25	57	7	1	7	25	.248

Composite Pitching Averages

Milwaukee Braves

Pitcher	G	IP	H	R	ER	BB	SO	W	L	ERA
McMahon	3	5	3	0	0	3	5	0	0	0.00
Burdette	3	27	21	2	2	4	13	3	0	0.67
Johnson	3	7	2	1	1	1	8	0	1	1.29
Spahn	2	15⅓	18	8	8	2	2	1	1	4.70
Buhl	2	3⅓	6	5	4	6	4	0	1	10.80
Pizzaro	1	1⅔	3	2	2	2	1	0	0	10.80
Conley	1	1⅔	2	2	2	1	0	0	0	10.80
Trowbridge	1	1	2	5	5	3	1	0	0	45.00
Totals	7	62	57	25	24	22	34	4	3	3.48

New York Yankees

Pitcher	G	IP	H	R	ER	BB	SO	W	L	ERA
Ditmar	2	6	2	0	0	0	2	0	0	0.00
Kucks	1	⅔	1	0	0	1	1	0	0	0.00
Ford	2	16	11	2	2	5	7	1	1	1.13
Turley	3	11⅔	7	3	3	6	12	1	0	2.31
Larsen	2	9⅔	8	5	4	5	6	1	1	3.72
Shantz	3	6⅔	8	5	3	2	7	0	1	4.05
Byrne	2	3⅓	1	2	2	2	1	0	0	5.40
Sturdivant	2	6	6	4	4	1	2	0	0	6.00
Grim	2	2⅓	3	2	2	0	2	0	1	7.71
Totals	7	62⅓	47	23	20	22	40	3	4	2.89

1958

Composite Batting Averages

New York Yankees

Player-Position	G	AB	R	H	2B	3B	HR	RBI	BA
Kucks, p	2	1	0	1	0	0	0	0	1.000
Bauer, rf	7	31	6	10	0	0	4	8	.323
McDougald, 2b	7	28	3	9	2	0	2	4	.321
Skowron, 1b	7	27	3	7	0	0	2	7	.259
Mantle, cf	7	24	4	6	0	1	2	3	.250
Howard, lf-ph	6	18	4	4	0	0	0	2	.222
Berra, c	7	27	3	6	3	0	0	2	.222
Turley, p	4	5	0	1	0	0	0	2	.200
Lumpe, ph-3b-ss	6	12	0	2	0	0	0	0	.167
Siebern, lf	3	8	1	1	0	0	0	0	.125
Carey, 3b	5	12	1	1	0	0	0	0	.083
Kubek, ss	7	21	0	1	0	0	0	1	.048
Richardson, 3b	4	5	0	0	0	0	0	0	.000
Ford, p	3	4	1	0	0	0	0	0	.000
Duren, p	3	3	0	0	0	0	0	0	.000
Maas, p	1	0	0	0	0	0	0	0	.000
Dickson, p	2	0	0	0	0	0	0	0	.000
Monroe, p	1	0	0	0	0	0	0	0	.000
Larsen, p	2	2	0	0	0	0	0	0	.000
Ditmar,p	1	1	0	0	0	0	0	0	.000
Slaughter, ph	4	3	1	0	0	0	0	0	.000
Throneberrry, ph	1	1	0	0	0	0	0	0	.000
Totals	7	233	29	49	5	1	10	29	.210

Milwaukee Braves

Player-Position	G	AB	R	H	2B	3B	HR	RBI	BA
Bruton, ph-cf-pr	7	17	2	7	0	0	1	2	.412
Spahn, p	3	12	0	4	0	0	0	3	.333
Pafko, cf-lf-rf	4	9	0	3	1	0	0	1	.333
Aaron, rf-cf	7	27	3	9	2	0	0	2	.333
Adcock, 1b-ph	4	13	1	4	0	0	0	0	.308
Schoendienst, 2b	7	30	5	9	3	1	0	0	.300
Covington, lf	7	26	2	7	0	0	0	4	.269
Crandall, c	7	25	4	6	0	0	1	3	.240
Torre, ph-1b	7	17	0	3	0	0	0	1	.176
Mathews, 3b	7	25	3	4	2	0	0	3	.160
Logan, ss	7	25	3	3	2	0	0	2	.120
Burdette, p	3	9	1	1	0	0	1	3	.111
Mantilla, ss-pr	4	0	1	0	0	0	0	0	.000
Rush, p	1	2	0	0	0	0	0	0	.000
McMahon, p	3	0	0	0	0	0	0	0	.000
Willey, p	1	0	0	0	0	0	0	0	.000
Pizarro, p	1	0	0	0	0	0	0	0	.000
Wise, ph-pr	2	1	0	0	0	0	0	0	.000
Hanebrink, ph	2	2	0	0	0	0	0	0	.000
Totals	7	240	25	60	10	1	3	24	.250

Composite Pitching Averages

New York Yankees

Pitcher	G	IP	H	R	ER	BB	SO	W	L	ERA
Ditmar	1	3⅔	2	0	0	0	2	0	0	0.00
Larsen	2	9⅓	9	1	1	6	9	1	0	0.96
Duren	3	9⅓	7	2	2	6	14	1	1	1.93
Kucks	2	4⅓	4	1	1	1	0	0	0	2.08
Turley	4	16⅓	10	5	5	7	13	2	1	2.76
Ford	3	15⅓	19	8	7	5	16	0	1	4.11
Dickson	2	4	4	2	2	0	1	0	0	4.50
Monroe	1	1	3	3	3	1	1	0	0	27.00
Maas	1	⅓	2	3	3	1	0	0	0	81.00
Totals	7	63⅔	60	25	24	27	56	4	3	3.39

Milwaukee Braves

Pitcher	G	IP	H	R	ER	BB	SO	W	L	ERA
Wiley	1	1	0	0	0	0	2	0	0	0.00
Spahn	3	28⅔	19	7	7	8	18	2	1	2.20
Rush	1	6	3	2	2	5	2	0	1	3.00
McMahon	3	3⅓	3	2	2	3	5	0	0	5.40
Pizarro	1	1⅔	2	1	1	1	3	0	0	5.40
Burdette	3	22⅓	22	17	14	4	12	1	2	5.64
Totals	7	63	49	29	26	21	42	3	4	3.71

1959

Composite Batting Averages

Los Angeles Dodgers

Player-Position	G	AB	R	H	2B	3B	HR	RBI	BA
Essegian, ph	4	3	2	2	0	0	2	2	.667
Sherry, p-ph	5	4	0	2	0	0	0	0	.500
Podres, p-pr	3	4	1	2	1	0	0	1	.500
Hodges, 1b	6	23	2	9	0	1	1	2	.391
Neal, 2b	6	27	4	10	2	0	2	6	.370
Moon, lf-rf-cf	6	23	3	6	0	0	1	2	.261
Demeter, cf-pr	6	12	2	3	0	0	0	0	.250
Wills, ss	6	20	2	5	0	0	0	1	.250
Furillo, ph-rf	4	4	0	1	0	0	0	2	.250
Gilliam, 3b	6	25	2	6	0	0	0	0	.240
Snider, cf-ph-rf	4	10	1	2	0	0	1	2	.200
Larker, rf-lf	6	16	2	3	0	0	0	0	.188
Roseboro, c	6	21	0	2	0	0	0	1	.095
Zimmer, pr-ss	1	1	0	0	0	0	0	0	.000
Pignatano, c	1	0	0	0	0	0	0	0	.000
Fairly, ph-rf-cf-pr	6	3	0	0	0	0	0	0	.000
Craig, p	2	3	0	0	0	0	0	0	.000
Churn, p	1	0	0	0	0	0	0	0	.000
Labine, p	1	0	0	0	0	0	0	0	.000
Koufax, p	2	2	0	0	0	0	0	0	.000
Klippstein, p	1	0	0	0	0	0	0	0	.000
Drysdale, p	1	2	0	0	0	0	0	0	.000
Williams, p	1	0	0	0	0	0	0	0	.000
Repulski, ph-rf	1	0	0	0	0	0	0	0	.000
Totals	6	203	21	53	3	1	7	19	.261

Chicago White Sox

Player-Position	G	AB	R	H	2B	3B	HR	RBI	BA
Kluszewski, 1b	6	23	5	9	1	0	3	10	.391
Fox, 2b	6	24	4	9	3	0	0	0	.375
Donovan, p	3	3	0	1	0	0	0	0	.333
Aparicio, ss	6	26	1	8	1	0	0	0	.308
Phillips, 3b-rf	3	10	0	3	1	0	0	0	.300
Landis, cf	6	24	6	7	0	0	0	1	.292
Smith, lf-rf	6	20	1	5	3	0	0	1	.250
Shaw, p	2	4	0	1	0	0	0	0	.250
Goodman, 3b-ph	5	13	1	3	0	0	0	1	.231
Lollar, c	6	22	3	5	0	0	1	5	.227
Wynn, p	3	5	0	1	1	0	0	1	.200
Esposito, 3b-pr	2	2	0	0	0	0	0	0	.000
Rivera, rf	5	11	1	0	0	0	0	0	.000
Tor'son, pr-1b-ph	3	1	1	0	0	0	0	0	.000
McAnany, lf-rf	3	5	0	0	0	0	0	0	.000
Staley, p	4	1	0	0	0	0	0	0	.000
Lown, p	3	0	0	0	0	0	0	0	.000
Pierce, p	3	0	0	0	0	0	0	0	.000
Moore, p	1	0	0	0	0	0	0	0	.000
Cash, ph	4	4	0	0	0	0	0	0	.000
Romano, ph	2	1	0	0	0	0	0	0	.000
Totals	6	199	23	52	10	0	4	19	.261

Composite Pitching Averages

Los Angeles Dodgers

Pitcher	G	IP	H	R	ER	BB	SO	W	L	ERA
Williams	1	2	0	0	0	2	1	0	0	0.00
Klippstein	1	2	1	0	0	0	2	0	0	0.00
Labine	1	1	0	0	0	0	1	0	0	0.00
Sherry	4	12⅔	8	1	1	2	5	2	0	0.71
Koufax	2	9	5	1	1	1	7	0	1	1.00
Drysdale	1	7	11	1	1	4	5	1	0	1.29
Podres	2	9⅓	7	5	5	6	4	1	0	4.82
Craig	2	9⅓	15	9	9	5	8	0	1	8.68
Churn	1	⅔	5	6	2	0	0	0	0	27.00
Totals	6	53	52	23	19	20	33	4	2	3.23

Chicago White Sox

Pitcher	G	IP	H	R	ER	BB	SO	W	L	ERA
Lown	3	3⅓	2	0	0	1	3	0	0	0.00
Pierce	3	4	2	0	0	2	3	0	0	0.00
Staley	4	8⅓	8	2	2	0	3	0	1	2.16
Shaw	2	14	17	4	4	2	2	1	1	2.57
Donovan	3	8⅓	4	5	5	3	5	0	1	5.40
Wynn	3	13	19	9	8	4	10	1	1	5.54
Moore	1	1	1	1	1	0	1	0	0	9.00
Totals	6	52	53	21	20	12	27	2	4	3.46

1960

Composite Batting Averages

Pittsburgh Pirates

Player-Position	G	AB	R	H	2B	3B	HR	RBI	BA
Smith, c	3	8	1	3	0	0	1	3	.375
Schofield, ph-ss	3	3	0	1	0	0	0	0	.333
Nelson, 1b-ph	4	9	2	3	0	0	1	2	.333
Law, p	3	6	1	2	1	0	0	1	.333
Haddix, p	2	3	0	1	0	0	0	0	.333
Burgess, c	5	18	2	6	1	0	0	0	.333
Mazeroski, 2b	7	25	4	8	2	0	2	5	.320
Clemente, rf	7	29	1	9	0	0	0	3	.310
Cimoli, lf-ph	7	20	4	5	0	0	0	1	.250
Virdon, cf	7	29	2	7	3	0	0	5	.241
Hoak, 3b	7	23	3	5	2	0	0	3	.217
Groat, ss	7	28	3	6	2	0	0	2	.214
Skinner, lf	2	5	2	1	0	0	0	1	.200
Stuart, 1b	5	20	0	3	0	0	0	0	.150
Oldis, c	2	0	0	0	0	0	0	0	.000
Face, p	4	3	0	0	0	0	0	0	.000
Gibbon, p	2	0	0	0	0	0	0	0	.000
Cheney, p	3	0	0	0	0	0	0	0	.000
Friend, p	3	1	0	0	0	0	0	0	.000
Green, p	3	1	0	0	0	0	0	0	.000
Labine, p	3	0	0	0	0	0	0	0	.000
Witt, p	3	0	0	0	0	0	0	0	.0900
Mizell, p	2	0	0	0	0	0	0	0	.000
Chris'pher, ph-pr	3	0	2	0	0	0	0	0	.000
Baker, ph	3	3	0	0	0	0	0	0	.000
Totals	7	234	27	60	11	0	4	26	.256

New York Yankees

Player-Position	G	AB	R	H	2B	3B	HR	RBI	BA
DeMaestri, pr-ss	4	2	1	1	0	0	0	0	.500
Howard, ph-c	5	13	4	6	1	1	1	4	.462
Blanchard, ph-c	5	11	2	5	2	0	0	2	.455
Lopez, lf-ph	3	7	0	3	0	0	0	0	.429
Mantle, cf	7	25	8	10	1	0	3	11	.400
Skowron, 1b	7	32	7	12	2	0	2	6	.375
Richardson, 2b	7	30	8	11	2	2	1	12	.367
Cerv, ph-lf	4	14	1	5	0	0	0	0	.357
Shantz, p	3	3	0	1	0	0	0	0	.333
Long, ph	3	3	0	1	0	0	0	0	.333
Kubek, ss-lf	7	30	6	10	1	0	0	3	.333
Berra, c-lf-rf-ph	7	22	6	7	0	0	1	8	.318
McDougald, 3b-pr	6	18	4	5	1	0	0	2	.278
Maris, rf	7	30	6	8	1	0	2	2	.267
Turley, p	2	4	0	1	0	0	0	1	.250
Ford, p	2	8	1	2	0	0	0	2	.250
Boyer, 3b-ss	4	12	1	3	2	1	0	1	.250
Ditmar, p	2	0	0	0	0	0	0	0	.000
Coates, p	3	1	0	0	0	0	0	0	.000
Maas, p	1	0	0	0	0	0	0	0	.000
Duren, p	2	0	0	0	0	0	0	0	.000
Terry, p	2	2	0	0	0	0	0	0	.000
Arroyo, p	1	1	0	0	0	0	0	0	.000
Stafford, p	2	1	0	0	0	0	0	0	.000
Grba, pr	1	0	0	0	0	0	0	0	.000
Totals	7	260	55	91	13	4	10	54	.338

Composite Pitching Averages

Pittsburgh Pirates

Pitcher	G	IP	H	R	ER	BB	SO	W	L	ERA
Witt	3	2⅔	5	0	0	2	1	0	0	0.00
Haddix	2	7⅓	2	6	2	2	6	2	0	2.45
Law	3	18⅓	22	7	7	3	8	2	0	3.44
Cheney	3	4	4	2	2	1	6	0	0	4.50
Face	4	10⅓	9	6	6	2	4	0	0	5.23
Gibbon	2	3	4	3	3	1	2	0	0	9.00
Labine	3	4	13	11	6	1	2	0	0	13.50
Friend	3	6	13	10	9	3	7	0	2	13.50
Mizell	2	2⅓	4	4	4	2	1	0	1	15.43
Green	3	4	11	10	10	1	3	0	0	22.50
Totals	7	62	91	55	40	18	40	4	3	7.11

New York Yankees

Pitcher	G	IP	H	R	ER	BB	SO	W	L	ERA
Ford	2	18	11	0	0	2	8	2	0	.0.00
Stafford	2	6	5	1	1	1	2	0	0	1.50
Duren	2	4	2	1	1	1	5	0	0	2.25
Shantz	3	6⅓	4	3	3	1	1	0	0	4.26
Maas	1	2	2	1	1	0	1	0	0	4.50
Turley	1	9⅓	15	6	5	4	0	1	0	4.82
Terry	2	6⅔	7	4	4	1	5	0	2	5.40
Coates	3	6⅓	6	4	4	1	3	0	0	5.08
Arroyo	2	⅔	2	1	1	0	1	0	0	13.50
Ditmar	2	1⅔	6	6	4	1	0	0	2	21.00
Totals	7	61	60	27	24	12	26	3	4	3.54

1961

COMPOSITE BATTING AVERAGES

New York Yankees

Player-Position	G	AB	R	H	2B	3B	HR	RBI	BA
Blanchard, ph-rf	4	10	4	4	1	0	2	3	.400
Richardson, 2b	5	23	2	9	1	0	0	0	.391
Skowron, 1b	5	17	3	6	0	0	1	5	.353
Lopez, rf-ph-pr-lf	4	9	3	3	0	1	1	7	.333
Berra, lf	4	11	2	3	0	0	1	3	.273
Boyer, 3b	5	15	0	4	2	0	0	3	.267
Howard, c	5	20	5	5	3	0	1	1	.250
Kubek, ss	5	22	3	5	0	0	0	1	.227
Mantle, cf	2	6	0	1	0	0	0	0	.167
Maris, cf-rf	5	19	4	2	1	0	1	2	.105
Reed, cf	3	0	0	0	0	0	0	0	.000
Ford, p	2	5	1	0	0	0	0	0	.000
Terry, p	2	3	0	0	0	0	0	0	.000
Arroyo, p	2	0	0	0	0	0	0	0	.000
Stafford, p	1	2	0	0	0	0	0	0	.000
Daley, p	2	1	0	0	0	0	0	1	.000
Coates, p	1	1	0	0	0	0	0	0	.000
Gardner, ph	1	1	0	0	0	0	0	0	.000
Totals	5	165	27	42	8	1	7	26	.255

Cincinnati Reds

Player-Position	G	AB	R	H	2B	3B	HR	RBI	BA
D. Johnson, c	2	4	0	2	0	0	0	0	.500
Edwards, c	3	11	1	4	2	0	0	0	.364
Cardenas, ph	3	3	0	1	1	0	0	0	.333
Post, rf-lf	5	18	3	6	1	0	1	2	.333
Kasko, ss	5	22	1	7	0	0	0	1	.318
Chacon, 2b-ph	4	12	2	3	0	0	0	0	.250
Coleman, 1b	5	20	2	5	0	0	1	2	.250
Robinson, lf-rf	5	15	3	3	2	0	1	4	.200
Blasingame, 2b-pr	3	7	1	1	0	0	0	0	.143
Pinson, cf	5	22	0	2	1	0	0	0	.091
Freese, 3b	5	16	0	1	1	0	0	0	.063
Zimmerman, c	2	0	0	0	0	0	0	0	.000
O'Toole, p	2	3	0	0	0	0	0	0	.000
Brosnan, p	3	0	0	0	0	0	0	0	.000
Jay, p	2	4	0	0	0	0	0	0	.000
Purkey, p	2	3	0	0	0	0	0	0	.000
Henry, p	2	0	0	0	0	0	0	0	.000
Maloney, p	1	0	0	0	0	0	0	0	.000
K. Johnson, p	1	0	0	0	0	0	0	0	.000
Jones, p	1	0	0	0	0	0	0	0	.000
Hunt, p	1	0	0	0	0	0	0	0	.000
Lynch, p	4	3	0	0	0	0	0	0	.000
Gernert, ph	4	4	0	0	0	0	0	0	.000
Bell, ph	3	3	0	0	0	0	0	0	.000
Totals	5	170	13	35	8	0	3	11	.206

COMPOSITE PITCHING AVERAGES

New York Yankees

Pitcher	G	IP	H	R	ER	BB	SO	W	L	ERA
Ford	2	14	6	0	0	1	7	2	0	0.00
Daley	2	7	5	0	0	3	1	0	0	0.00
Coates	1	4	1	0	0	1	2	0	0	0.00
Arroyo	2	4	4	2	1	2	3	1	0	2.25
Stafford	1	6⅔	7	2	2	2	5	0	0	2.70
Terry	2	9⅓	12	7	5	2	7	0	1	4.82
Totals	5	45	35	13	8	8	27	4	1	1.60

Cincinnati Reds

Pitcher	G	IP	H	R	ER	BB	SO	W	L	ERA
Hunt	1	1	0	0	0	1	1	0	0	0.00
K. Johnson	1	⅔	0	0	0	0	0	0	0	0.00
Jones	1	⅔	0	0	0	0	0	0	0	0.00
Purkey	2	11	6	5	2	3	5	0	1	1.64
O'Toole	2	12	11	4	4	7	4	0	2	3.00
Jay	2	9⅔	8	6	6	6	6	1	1	5.59
Brosnan	3	6	9	5	5	4	5	0	0	7.50
Henry	2	2⅓	4	5	5	2	3	0	0	19.29
Maloney	1	⅔	4	2	2	1	1	0	0	27.00
Totals	5	44	42	27	24	24	25	1	4	4.91

1962

COMPOSITE BATTING AVERAGES

New York Yankees

Player-Position	G	AB	R	H	2B	3B	HR	RBI	BA
Tresh, lf	7	28	5	9	1	0	1	4	.321
Boyer, 3b	7	22	2	7	1	0	1	4	.318
Kubek, ss	7	29	2	8	1	0	0	1	.276
Skowron, 1b	6	18	1	4	0	1	0	1	.222
Long, 1b	2	5	0	1	0	0	0	1	.200
Maris, rf	7	23	4	4	1	0	1	5	.174
Richardson, 2b	7	27	3	4	0	0	0	0	.148
Howard, c	6	21	1	3	1	0	0	1	.143
Terry, p	3	8	0	1	0	0	0	0	.125
Mantle, cf	7	25	2	3	1	0	0	0	.120
Berra, c-ph	2	2	0	0	0	0	0	0	.000
Ford, p	3	7	0	0	0	0	0	0	.000
Daley, p	1	0	0	0	0	0	0	0	.000
Stafford, p	1	3	0	0	0	0	0	0	.000
Coates, p	2	0	0	0	0	0	0	0	.000
Bridges, p	2	0	0	0	0	0	0	0	.000
Lopez, ph	2	2	0	0	0	0	0	0	.000
Blanchard, ph	1	1	0	0	0	0	0	0	.000
Totals	7	221	20	44	6	1	3	17	.199

San Francisco Giants

Player-Position	G	AB	R	H	2B	3B	HR	RBI	BA
Sanford, p	3	7	3	3	0	0	0	0	.429
Pagan, ss	7	19	2	7	0	0	1	2	.368
O'Dell, p	3	3	0	1	0	0	0	0	.333
M. Alou, lf-ph-rf	6	12	2	4	1	0	0	1	.333
Haller, c	4	14	1	4	1	0	1	3	.286
Hiller, 2b	7	26	4	7	3	0	1	5	.269
F. Alou, lf-rf	7	26	2	7	1	1	0	5	.269
Mays, cf	7	28	3	7	2	0	0	1	.250
McCovey, 1b-rf-lf	4	15	2	3	0	1	1	1	.200
Cepeda, 1b	5	19	1	3	1	0	0	2	.158
Davenport, 3b	7	22	1	3	1	0	0	1	.136
Kuenn, lf-rf	3	12	1	1	0	0	0	0	.083
Bailey, c-ph	6	14	1	1	0	0	1	2	.071
Orsino, c	1	1	0	0	0	0	0	0	.000
Bowman, pr-ss	2	1	1	0	0	0	0	0	.000
Miller, p	2	0	0	0	0	0	0	0	.000
Larsen, p	3	0	0	0	0	0	0	0	.000
Pierce, p	2	5	0	0	0	0	0	0	.000
Bolin, p	2	0	0	0	0	0	0	0	.000
Marichal, p	1	2	0	0	0	0	0	0	.000
Nieman, ph	1	0	0	0	0	0	0	0	.000
Totals	7	226	21	51	10	2	5	19	.226

COMPOSITE PITCHING AVERAGES

New York Yankees

Pitcher	G	IP	H	R	ER	BB	SO	W	L	ERA
Daley	1	1	1	0	0	1	0	0	0	0.00
Terry	3	25	17	5	5	2	16	2	1	1.80
Stafford	1	9	4	2	2	2	5	1	0	2.00
Ford	3	19⅔	24	9	9	4	12	1	1	4.12
Bridges	2	3⅔	4	3	2	2	3	0	0	4.91
Coates	2	2⅔	1	2	2	1	3	0	1	6.75
Totals	7	61	51	21	20	12	30	4	3	2.95

San Francisco Giants

Pitcher	G	IP	H	R	ER	BB	SO	W	L	ERA
Marichal	1	4	2	0	0	2	4	0	0	0.00
Miller	2	1⅓	1	0	0	2	0	0	0	0.00
Sanford	3	23⅓	16	6	5	8	19	1	2	1.93
Pierce	2	15	8	5	4	2	5	1	1	2.40
Larsen	3	2⅓	1	1	1	2	0	1	0	3.86
O'Dell	2	12⅓	12	6	6	3	9	0	1	4.38
Bolin	2	2⅔	4	2	2	2	2	0	0	6.75
Totals	7	68	44	28	18	21	30	3	4	2.06

1963

COMPOSITE BATTING AVERAGES

Los Angeles Dodgers

Player-Position	G	AB	R	H	2B	3B	HR	RBI	BA
T. Davis, lf	4	15	0	6	0	2	0	2	.400
Skowron, 1b	4	13	2	5	0	0	1	3	.385
F. Howard, rf	3	10	2	3	1	0	1	1	.300
Podres, p	1	4	0	1	0	0	0	0	.250
W. Davis, cf	4	12	2	2	2	0	0	3	.167
Gilliam, 3b	4	13	3	2	0	0	0	0	.154
Tracewski, 2b	4	13	1	2	0	0	0	0	.154
Roseboro, c	4	14	1	2	0	0	1	3	.143
Wills, ss	4	15	1	2	0	0	0	0	.133
Koufax, p	2	6	0	0	0	0	0	0	.000
Perranoski, p	1	0	0	0	0	0	0	0	.000
Drysdale, p	1	1	0	0	0	0	0	0	.000
Fairly, rf-pr	4	1	0	0	0	0	0	0	.000
Totals	4	117	12	25	3	2	3	12	.214

New York Yankees

Player-Position	G	AB	R	H	2B	3B	HR	RBI	BA
Linz, ph	3	3	0	1	0	0	0	0	.333
E. Howard, c	4	15	0	5	0	0	0	1	.333
Lopez, ph-rf	3	8	1	2	2	0	0	0	.250
Richardson, 2b	4	14	0	3	1	0	0	0	.214
Tresh, lf	4	15	1	3	0	0	1	2	.200
Kubek, ss	4	16	1	3	0	0	0	0	.188
Pepitone, 1b	4	13	0	2	0	0	0	0	.154
Mantle, cf	4	15	1	2	0	0	1	1	.133
Boyer, 3b	4	13	0	1	0	0	0	0	.077
Maris, rf	2	5	0	0	0	0	0	0	.000
Ford, p	2	3	0	0	0	0	0	0	.000
Williams, p	1	0	0	0	0	0	0	0	.000
Hamilton, p	1	0	0	0	0	0	0	0	.000
Bright, ph	2	2	0	0	0	0	0	0	.000
Downing, p	1	1	0	0	0	0	0	0	.000
Terry, p	1	0	0	0	0	0	0	0	.000
Reniff, p	3	0	0	0	0	0	0	0	.000
Blanchard, rf	1	3	0	0	0	0	0	0	.000
Bouton, p	1	2	0	0	0	0	0	0	.000
Berra, ph	1	1	0	0	0	0	0	0	.000
Totals	4	129	4	22	3	0	2	4	.171

COMPOSITE PITCHING AVERAGES

Los Angeles Dodgers

Pitcher	G	IP	H	R	ER	BB	SO	W	L	ERA
Perranoski	1	⅔	1	0	0	1	0	0	0	0.00
Drysdale	1	9	3	0	0	1	9	1	0	0.00
Podres	1	8⅓	6	1	1	1	4	1	0	1.08
Koufax	2	18	12	3	3	3	23	2	0	1.50
Totals	4	36	22	4	4	5	37	4	0	1.00

New York Yankees

Pitcher	G	IP	H	R	ER	BB	SO	W	L	ERA
Williams	1	3	1	0	0	0	5	0	0	0.00
Reniff	3	3	0	0	0	1	1	0	0	0.00
Hamilton	1	1	0	0	0	0	1	0	0	0.00
Bouton	1	7	4	1	1	5	4	0	1	1.29
Terry	1	3	3	1	1	1	0	0	0	3.00
Ford	2	12	10	7	6	3	8	0	2	4.50
Downing	1	5	7	3	3	1	6	0	1	5.40
Totals	4	34	23	12	11	11	25	0	4	2.91

1964

COMPOSITE BATTING AVERAGES

St. Louis Cardinals

Player-Position	G	AB	R	H	2B	3B	HR	RBI	BA
Buchek, pr-2b	4	1	1	1	0	0	0	0	1.000
Warwick, ph	5	4	2	3	0	0	0	1	.750
Skinner, ph	4	3	0	2	1	0	0	1	.667
Sadecki, p	2	2	0	1	0	0	0	1	.500
Simmons, p	2	4	0	2	0	0	0	1	.500
McCarver, c	7	23	4	11	1	1	1	5	.478
Brock, lf	7	30	2	9	2	0	1	5	.300
Gibson, p	3	9	1	2	0	0	0	0	.222
K. Boyer, 3b	7	27	5	6	1	0	2	6	.222
Shannon, rf	7	28	6	6	0	0	1	2	.214
Flood, cf	7	30	5	6	0	1	0	3	.200
Maxvill, 2b	7	20	0	4	1	0	0	1	.200
Groat, ss	7	26	3	5	1	1	0	1	.192
White, 1b	7	27	2	3	1	0	0	2	.111
Javier, pr-2b	1	0	1	0	0	0	0	0	.000
Schultz, p	4	1	0	0	0	0	0	0	.000
G. Richardson, p	2	0	0	0	0	0	0	0	.000
Craig, p	2	1	0	0	0	0	0	0	.000
Taylor, p	2	1	0	0	0	0	0	0	.000
Humphreys, p	1	0	0	0	0	0	0	0	.000
James, ph	3	3	0	0	0	0	0	0	.000
Totals	7	240	32	61	8	3	5	29	.254

New York Yankees

Player-Position	G	AB	R	H	2B	3B	HR	RBI	BA
Ford, p	1	1	0	1	0	0	0	1	1.000
B. Richardson, 2b	7	32	3	13	2	0	0	3	.406
Mantle, rf	7	24	8	8	2	0	3	8	.333
Howard, c	7	24	5	7	1	0	0	2	.292
Tresh, lf	7	22	4	6	2	0	2	7	.273
Blanchard, ph	4	4	0	1	1	0	0	0	.250
Linz, ss	7	31	5	7	1	0	2	2	.226
C. Boyer, 3b	7	24	2	5	1	0	1	3	.208
Maris, cf	7	30	4	6	0	0	1	1	.200
Pepitone, 1b	7	26	1	4	1	0	1	5	.154
Bouton, p	2	7	0	1	0	0	0	1	.143
Stottlemyre, p	3	8	0	1	0	0	0	0	.125
Gonzalez, 3b	1	1	0	0	0	0	0	0	.000
Lopez, rf-ph	3	2	0	0	0	0	0	0	.000
Downing, p	3	2	0	0	0	0	0	0	.000
Sheldon, p	2	0	0	0	0	0	0	0	.000
Mikkelsen, p	4	0	0	0	0	0	0	0	.000
Terry, p	1	0	0	0	0	0	0	0	.000
Reniff, p	1	0	0	0	0	0	0	0	.000
Hamilton, p	2	0	0	0	0	0	0	0	.000
Hegan, pr-ph	3	1	1	0	0	0	0	0	.000
Totals	7	239	33	60	11	0	10	33	.251

COMPOSITE PITCHING AVERAGES

St. Louis Cardinals

Pitcher	G	IP	H	R	ER	BB	SO	W	L	ERA
Craig	2	5	2	0	0	3	0	1	0	0.00
Taylor	2	4⅔	0	0	0	1	2	0	0	0.00
Humphreys	1	1	0	0	0	0	1	0	0	0.00
Simmons	2	14⅓	11	4	4	3	8	0	1	2.51
Gibson	3	27	23	11	9	8	31	2	1	3.00
Sadecki	2	6⅓	12	7	6	5	2	1	0	8.53
Schultz	4	4	9	8	8	3	1	0	1	18.00
G. Richardson	2	⅔	3	3	3	2	0	0	0	40.50
Totals	7	63	60	33	30	25	54	4	3	4.29

New York Yankees

Pitcher	G	IP	H	R	ER	BB	SO	W	L	ERA
Sheldon	2	2⅔	0	2	0	2	2	0	0	0.00
Terry	1	2	2	0	0	0	3	0	0	0.00
Reniff	1	⅓	2	0	0	0	0	0	0	0.00
Bouton	2	17⅓	15	4	3	5	7	2	0	1.56
Stottlemyre	3	20	18	8	7	6	12	1	1	3.15
Hamilton	2	2	3	1	1	0	2	0	0	4.50
Mikkelsen	4	4⅔	4	4	3	2	4	0	1	5.79
Downing	3	7⅔	9	8	7	2	5	0	1	8.22
Ford	1	5⅓	8	5	5	1	4	0	1	8.44
Totals	7	62	61	32	26	18	39	3	4	3.77

1965

COMPOSITE BATTING AVERAGES

Los Angeles Dodgers

Player-Position	G	AB	R	H	2B	3B	HR	RBI	BA
Crawford, ph	2	2	0	1	0	0	0	0	.500
Lefebvre, 2b	3	10	2	4	0	0	0	0	.400
Fairly, rf	7	29	7	11	3	0	2	6	.379
Wills, ss	7	30	3	11	3	0	0	3	.367
Osteen, p	3	3	0	1	0	0	0	0	.333
Parker, 1b	7	23	3	7	9	1	1	2	.304
Johnson, lf	7	27	3	8	2	0	2	4	.296
Roseboro, c	7	21	1	6	1	0	0	3	.286
W. Davis, cf	7	26	3	6	0	0	0	0	.231
Gilliam, 3b	7	28	2	6	1	0	0	2	.214
Tracewski, ph-2b	6	17	0	2	0	0	0	0	.118
Koufax, p	3	9	0	1	0	0	0	1	.111
Kennedy, 3b-pr	4	1	0	0	0	0	0	0	.000
Reed, p	2	0	0	0	0	0	0	0	.000
Brewer, p	1	0	0	0	0	0	0	0	.000
Perranoski, p	2	0	0	0	0	0	0	0	.000
Miller, p	2	0	0	0	0	0	0	0	.000
Drysdale, p-ph	3	5	0	0	0	0	0	0	.000
Moon, ph	2	2	0	0	0	0	0	0	.000
LeJohn, ph	1	1	0	0	0	0	0	0	.000
Totals	7	234	24	64	10	1	5	21	.274

Minnesota Twins

Player-Position	G	AB	R	H	2B	3B	HR	RBI	BA
Killebrew, 3b	7	21	2	6	0	0	1	2	.286
Versalles, ss	7	28	3	8	1	1	1	4	.286
Valdespino, lf-ph	5	11	1	3	1	0	0	0	.273
Grant, p	3	8	3	2	1	0	1	3	.250
Nossek, cf-ph	6	20	0	4	0	0	0	0	.200
Quilici, 2b	7	20	2	4	2	0	0	1	.200
Oliva, rf	7	26	2	5	1	0	1	2	.192
Kaat, p	3	6	0	1	0	0	0	2	.167
Hall, cf	2	7	0	1	0	0	0	0	.143
Mincher, 1b	7	23	3	3	0	0	1	1	.130
Allison, lf	5	16	3	2	1	0	1	2	.125
Battey, c	7	25	1	3	0	1	0	2	.120
Zimmerman, c	2	1	0	0	0	0	0	0	.000
Pascual, p	1	1	0	0	0	0	0	0	.000
Merritt, p	2	0	0	0	0	0	0	0	.000
Klippstein, p	2	0	0	0	0	0	0	0	.000
Worthington, p	2	0	0	0	0	0	0	0	0.000
Pleis, p	1	0	0	0	0	0	0	0	.000
Boswell, p	1	0	0	0	0	0	0	0	.000
Perry, p	2	0	0	0	0	0	0	0	.000
Rollins, ph	3	2	0	0	0	0	0	0	.000
Totals	7	215	20	42	7	2	6	19	.195

COMPOSITE PITCHING AVERAGES

Los Angeles Dodgers

Pitcher	G	IP	H	R	ER	BB	SO	W	L	ERA
Miller	2	1⅓	0	0	0	0	0	0	0	0.00
Koufax	3	24	13	2	1	5	29	2	1	0.38
Osteen	2	14	9	2	1	5	4	1	1	0.64
Drysdale	2	11⅔	12	9	5	3	15	1	1	3.86
Brewer	1	2	3	1	1	0	1	0	0	4.50
Perranoski	2	3⅔	3	3	3	4	1	0	0	7.36
Reed	2	3⅓	2	3	3	2	4	0	0	8.10
Totals	7	60	42	20	14	19	54	4	3	2.10

Minnesota Twins

Pitcher	G	IP	H	R	ER	BB	SO	W	L	ERA
Worthington	2	4	2	1	0	2	2	0	0	0.00
Klippstein	2	2⅔	2	0	0	2	3	0	0	0.00
Merritt	2	3⅓	2	1	1	0	1	0	0	2.70
Grant	3	23	22	8	7	2	12	2	1	2.74
Boswell	1	2⅔	3	1	1	2	3	0	0	3.38
Kaat	3	14⅓	18	7	6	2	6	1	2	3.77
Perry	2	4	5	2	2	2	4	0	0	4.50
Pascual	1	5	8	3	3	1	0	0	1	5.40
Pleis	1	1	2	1	1	0	0	0	0	9.00
Totals	7	60	64	24	21	13	31	3	4	2.15

1966

COMPOSITE BATTING AVERAGES

Baltimore Orioles

Player-Position	G	AB	R	H	2B	3B	HR	RBI	BA
Powell, 1b	4	14	1	5	1	0	0	1	.357
F. Robinson, rf	4	14	4	4	0	1	2	3	.286
D. Johnson, 2b	4	14	1	4	1	0	0	1	.286
Aparicio, ss	4	16	0	4	1	0	0	2	.250
B. Robinson, 3b	4	14	2	3	0	0	1	1	.214
Snyder, cf-lf	3	6	1	1	0	0	0	1	.167
Blair, cf	4	6	2	1	0	0	1	1	.167
Etchebarren, c	4	12	2	1	0	0	0	0	.083
Blefary, lf	4	13	0	1	0	0	0	0	.077
McNally, p	2	3	0	0	0	0	0	0	.000
Drabowsky, p	1	2	0	0	0	0	0	0	.000
Palmer, p	1	4	0	0	0	0	0	0	.000
Bunker, p	1	2	0	0	0	0	0	0	.000
Totals	4	120	13	24	3	1	4	10	.200

Los Angeles Dodgers

Player-Position	G	AB	R	H	2B	3B	HR	RBI	BA
Ferrara, ph	1	1	0	1	0	0	0	0	1.000
L. Johnson, rf-lf	4	15	1	4	1	0	0	0	.267
T. Davis, lf-ph	4	8	0	2	0	0	0	0	.250
Parker, 1b	4	13	0	3	2	0	0	0	.231
Kennedy, 3b	2	5	0	1	0	0	0	0	.200
Lefebvre, 2b	4	12	1	2	0	0	1	1	.167
Fairly, ph-rf-1b	3	7	0	1	0	0	0	0	.143
Wills, ss	4	13	0	1	0	0	0	0	.077
Roseboro, c	4	14	0	1	0	0	0	0	.071
W. Davis, cf	4	16	0	1	0	0	0	0	.063
Gilliam, 3b	2	6	0	0	0	0	0	1	.000
Drysdale, p	2	2	0	0	0	0	0	0	.000
Moeller, p	1	0	0	0	0	0	0	0	.000
R. Miller, p	1	0	0	0	0	0	0	0	.000
Perranoski, p	2	0	0	0	0	0	0	0	.000
Koufax, p	1	2	0	0	0	0	0	0	.000
Regan, p	2	0	0	0	0	0	0	0	.000
Brewer, p	1	0	0	0	0	0	0	0	.000
Osteen, p	1	2	0	0	0	0	0	0	.000
Covington, ph	1	1	0	0	0	0	0	0	.000
Barbieri, ph	1	1	0	0	0	0	0	0	.000
Stuart, ph	2	2	0	0	0	0	0	0	.000
Oliver, pr	1	0	0	0	0	0	0	0	.000
Totals	4	120	2	17	3	0	1	2	.142

COMPOSITE PITCHING AVERAGES

Baltimore Orioles

Pitcher	G	IP	H	R	ER	BB	SO	W	L	ERA
Palmer	1	9	4	0	0	3	6	1	0	0.00
Bunker	1	9	6	0	0	1	6	1	0	0.00
Drabowsky	1	6⅔	1	0	0	2	11	1	0	0.00
McNally	2	11⅓	6	2	2	7	5	1	0	1.50
Totals	4	36	17	2	2	13	28	4	0	0.50

Los Angeles Dodgers

Pitcher	G	IP	H	R	ER	BB	SO	W	L	ERA
R. Miller	1	3	2	0	0	2	1	0	0	0.00
Regan	2	1⅔	0	0	0	1	2	0	0	0.00
Brewer	1	1	0	0	0	0	1	0	0	0.00
Osteen	1	7	3	1	1	1	3	0	1	1.29
Koufax	1	6	6	4	1	2	2	0	1	1.50
Drysdale	2	10	8	5	5	3	6	0	2	4.50
Moeller	1	2	1	1	1	1	0	0	0	4.50
Perranoski	2	3⅓	4	2	2	1	2	0	0	5.40
Totals	4	34	24	13	10	11	17	0	4	2.65

1967

Composite Batting Averages

St. Louis Cardinals

Player-Position	G	AB	R	H	2B	3B	HR	RBI	BA
Brock, lf	7	29	8	12	2	1	1	3	.414
Maris, rf	7	26	3	10	1	0	1	7	.385
Javier, 2b	7	25	2	9	3	0	1	4	.360
Shannon, 3b	7	24	3	5	1	0	1	2	.208
Flood, cf	7	28	2	5	1	0	0	3	.179
Maxvill, ss	7	19	1	3	0	1	0	1	.158
McCarver, c	7	24	3	3	1	0	0	2	.125
Cepeda, 1b	7	29	1	3	2	0	0	1	.103
Ro. Gibson, p	3	11	1	1	0	0	1	1	.091
Jaster, p	1	0	0	0	0	0	0	0	.000
Woodeshick, p	1	0	0	0	0	0	0	0	.000
Bressoud, ss	2	0	0	0	0	0	0	0	.000
Hoerner, p	2	0	0	0	0	0	0	0	.000
Washburn, p	2	0	0	0	0	0	0	0	.000
Lamabe, p	3	0	0	0	0	0	0	0	.000
Willis, p	3	0	0	0	0	0	0	0	.000
Carlton, p	1	1	0	0	0	0	0	0	.000
Gagliano, ph	1	1	0	0	0	0	0	0	.000
Spiezio, ph	1	1	0	0	0	0	0	0	.000
Tolan, ph	3	2	1	0	0	0	0	0	.000
Briles, p	2	3	0	0	0	0	0	0	.000
Hughes, p	2	3	0	0	0	0	0	0	.000
Ricketts, ph	3	3	0	0	0	0	0	0	.000
Totals	7	229	25	51	11	2	5	24	.223

Boston Red Sox

Player-Position	G	AB	R	H	2B	3B	HR	RBI	BA
Santiago, p	3	2	1	1	0	0	1	1	.500
Yastrzemski, lf	7	25	4	10	2	0	3	5	.400
Jones, 3b-ph	6	18	2	7	0	0	0	1	.389
Siebern, ph-rf	3	3	0	1	0	0	0	1	.333
Andrews, ph-2b	5	13	2	4	0	0	0	1	.308
Smith, cf	7	24	3	6	1	0	2	3	.250
Scott, 1b	7	26	3	6	1	1	0	0	.231
Petrocelli, ss	7	20	3	4	1	0	2	3	.200
Tartab'l, pr-rf-ph	7	13	1	2	0	0	0	0	.154
Foy, ph-3b	6	15	2	2	1	0	0	1	.133
Adair, 2b-ph	5	16	0	2	0	0	0	1	.125
Howard, c	7	18	0	2	0	0	0	1	.111
Harrelson, rf	4	13	0	1	0	0	0	1	.077
Stange, p	1	0	0	0	0	0	0	0	.000
Stephenson, p	1	0	0	0	0	0	0	0	.000
Brett, p	2	0	0	0	0	0	0	0	.000
Morehead, p	2	0	0	0	0	0	0	0	.000
Wyatt, p	2	0	0	0	0	0	0	0	.000
Bell, p	3	0	0	0	0	0	0	0	.000
Osinski, p	2	0	0	0	0	0	0	0	.000
Ryan, c	1	2	0	0	0	0	0	0	.000
Thomas, ph-rf	2	2	0	0	0	0	0	0	.000
Waslewski, p	2	1	0	0	0	0	0	0	.000
Ru. Gibson, c	2	2	0	0	0	0	0	0	.000
Lonborg, p	3	9	0	0	0	0	0	0	.000
Totals	7	222	21	48	6	1	8	19	.216

Composite Pitching Averages

St. Louis Cardinals

Pitcher	G	IP	H	R	ER	BB	SO	W	L	ERA
Carlton	1	6	3	1	0	2	5	0	1	0.00
Washburn	2	2⅓	1	0	0	1	2	0	0	0.00
Woodeshick	1	1	1	0	0	0	0	0	0	0.00
Jaster	1	⅓	2	0	0	0	0	0	0	0.00
Ro. Gibson	3	27	14	3	3	5	26	3	0	1.00
Briles	2	11	7	2	2	1	4	1	0	1.64
Hughes	2	9	9	6	5	3	7	0	1	5.00
Lamabe	3	2⅔	5	2	2	0	4	0	1	6.75
Willis	3	1	2	4	3	4	1	0	0	27.00
Hoerner	2	⅔	4	3	3	1	0	0	0	40.50
Totals	7	61	48	21	18	17	49	4	3	2.66

Boston Red Sox

Pitcher	G	IP	H	R	ER	BB	SO	W	L	ERA
Morehead	2	3⅓	0	0	0	4	3	0	0	0.00
Stange	1	2	3	1	0	0	0	0	0	0.00
Brett	2	1⅓	0	0	0	1	1	0	0	0.00
Waslewski	2	8⅓	4	2	2	2	7	0	0	2.16
Lonborg	3	24	14	8	7	2	11	2	1	2.63
Wyatt	2	3⅔	1	2	2	3	1	1	0	4.91
Bell	3	5⅓	8	3	3	1	1	0	1	5.06
Santiago	3	9⅓	16	6	6	3	6	0	2	5.59
Osinski	2	1⅓	2	1	1	0	0	0	0	6.75
Stephenson	1	2	3	2	2	1	0	0	0	9.00
Totals	7	61	51	25	23	17	30	3	4	3.39

1968

Composite Batting Averages

Detroit Tigers

Player-Position	G	AB	R	H	2B	3B	HR	RBI	BA
Comer, ph	1	1	0	1	0	0	0	0	1.000
Cash, 1b	7	26	5	10	0	0	1	5	.385
Kaline, rf	7	29	6	11	2	0	2	8	.379
Mathews, ph-3b	2	3	0	1	0	0	0	0	.333
Horton, lf	7	23	6	7	1	1	1	3	.304
Northrup, cf-lf	7	28	4	7	0	1	2	8	.250
Lolich, p	3	12	2	3	0	0	1	2	.250
McAuliffe, 2b	7	27	5	6	0	0	1	3	.222
Stanley, ss-cf	7	28	4	6	0	1	0	0	.214
Wert, 3b	6	17	1	2	0	0	0	2	.118
Freehan, c	7	24	0	2	1	0	0	2	.083
Brown, ph	1	1	0	0	0	0	0	0	.000
Wilson, p	1	1	0	0	0	0	0	0	.000
Price, ph	2	3	0	0	0	0	0	0	.000
Matchick, ph	3	3	0	0	0	0	0	0	.000
McLain, p	3	6	0	0	0	0	0	0	.000
Oyler, ss	4	0	0	0	0	0	0	0	.000
Dobson, p	3	0	0	0	0	0	0	0	.000
Hiller, p	2	0	0	0	0	0	0	0	.000
McMahon, p	2	0	0	0	0	0	0	0	.000
Patterson, p	2	0	0	0	0	0	0	0	.000
Tracewski, 3b-pr	2	0	1	0	0	0	0	0	.000
Lasher, p	1	0	0	0	0	0	0	0	.000
Sparma, p	1	0	0	0	0	0	0	0	.000
Totals	7	231	34	56	4	3	8	33	.242

St. Louis Cardinals

Player-Position	G	AB	R	H	2B	3B	HR	RBI	BA
Ricketts, ph	1	1	0	1	0	0	0	0	1.000
Spiezio, ph	1	1	0	1	0	0	0	0	1.000
Hoerner, p	3	2	0	1	0	0	0	0	.500
Brock, lf	7	28	6	13	3	1	2	5	.464
McCarver, c	7	27	3	9	0	2	1	4	.333
Javier, 2b	7	27	1	9	1	0	0	3	.333
Flood, cf	7	28	4	8	1	0	0	2	.286
Shannon, 3b	7	29	3	8	1	0	1	4	.276
Cepeda, 1b	7	28	2	7	0	0	2	6	.250
Maris, rf-ph	6	19	5	3	1	0	0	1	.158
Gibson, p	3	8	2	1	0	0	1	2	.125
Edwards, ph	1	1	0	0	0	0	0	0	.000
Tolan, ph	1	1	0	0	0	0	0	0	.000
Gagliano, ph	3	3	0	0	0	0	0	0	.000
Washburn, p	2	3	0	0	0	0	0	0	.000
Briles, p	2	4	0	0	0	0	0	0	.000
Davis, p	2	7	0	0	0	0	0	0	.000
Maxvill, ss	7	22	1	0	0	0	0	0	.000
Willis, p	3	0	0	0	0	0	0	0	.000
Carlton, p	2	0	0	0	0	0	0	0	.000
Schofield, pr-ss	2	0	0	0	0	0	0	0	.000
Granger, p	1	0	0	0	0	0	0	0	.000
Hughes, p	1	0	0	0	0	0	0	0	.000
Jaster, p	1	0	0	0	0	0	0	0	.000
Nelson, p	1	0	0	0	0	0	0	0	.000
Totals	7	239	27	61	7	3	7	27	.255

Composite Pitching Averages

Detroit Tigers

Pitcher	G	IP	H	R	ER	BB	SO	W	L	ERA
Patterson	2	3	1	0	0	1	0	0	0	0.00
Lasher	1	2	1	0	0	0	1	0	0	0.00
Lolich	3	27	20	5	5	6	21	3	0	1.67
McLain	3	16⅔	18	8	6	4	13	1	2	3.24
Dobson	3	4⅔	5	2	3	1	0	0	0	3.96
Wilson	1	4⅓	4	3	3	6	3	0	1	6.23
Hiller	2	2	6	4	3	3	1	0	0	13.50
McMahon	2	2	4	3	3	0	1	0	0	13.50
Sparma	1	⅓	2	2	1	0	0	0	0	27.00
Totals	7	62	61	27	23	21	40	4	3	3.34

St. Louis Cardinals

Pitcher	G	IP	H	R	ER	BB	SO	W	L	ERA
Granger	1	2	0	0	0	1	1	0	0	0.00
Nelson	1	1	0	0	0	0	1	0	0	0.00
Hughes	1	⅓	2	0	0	0	0	0	0	0.00
Gibson	3	27	18	5	5	4	35	2	1	1.67
Hoerner	3	4⅔	5	4	2	5	3	0	1	3.86
Briles	2	11⅓	13	7	7	4	7	0	1	5.56
Carlton	2	4	7	3	3	1	3	0	0	6.75
Willis	3	4⅓	2	4	4	4	3	0	0	8.31
Washburn	2	7⅓	7	8	8	7	6	1	1	9.82
Jaster	1	8*	2	3	3	1	0	0	0	—
Totals	7	62	56	34	32	27	59	3	4	4.05

*Pitched to three batters in third inning of sixth game.

1969

Composite Batting Averages

New York Mets

Player-Position	G	AB	R	H	2B	3B	HR	RBI	BA
Weis, 2b	5	11	1	5	0	0	1	3	.455
Swoboda, rf	4	15	1	6	1	0	0	1	.400
Clendenon, 1b	4	14	4	5	1	0	3	4	.357
Boswell, 2b	1	3	1	1	0	0	0	0	.333
Gentry, p	1	3	0	1	1	0	0	2	.333
Kranepool, 1b	1	4	1	1	0	0	1	1	.250
Grote, c	5	19	1	4	2	0	0	1	.211
Harrelson, ss	5	17	1	3	0	0	0	0	.176
Agee, cf	5	18	1	3	0	0	1	1	.167
Jones, lf	5	19	2	3	1	0	0	0	.158
Koosman, p	2	7	0	1	1	0	0	0	.143
Charles, 3b	4	15	1	2	1	0	0	0	.133
Shamsky, ph-rf	3	6	0	0	0	0	0	0	.000
Seaver, p	2	4	0	0	0	0	0	0	.000
Gaspar, ph-rf-pr	3	2	1	0	0	0	0	0	.000
Garrett, 3b	2	1	0	0	0	0	0	0	.000
Dyer, ph	1	1	0	0	0	0	0	0	.000
Taylor, p	2	0	0	0	0	0	0	0	.000
Cardwell, p	1	0	0	0	0	0	0	0	.000
Martin, ph	1	0	0	0	0	0	0	0	.000
Ryan, p	1	0	0	0	0	0	0	0	.000
Totals	5	150	15	35	8	0	6	13	.220

Baltimore Orioles

Player-Position	G	AB	R	H	2B	3B	HR	RBI	BA
Dalrymple, ph	2	2	0	2	0	0	0	0	1.000
Cuellar, p	2	5	0	2	0	0	0	1	.400
Powell, 1b	5	19	0	5	0	0	0	0	.263
Belanger, ss	5	15	2	3	0	0	0	1	.200
McNally, p	2	5	1	1	0	0	1	2	.200
F. Robinson, rf	5	16	2	3	0	0	1	1	.188
Blair, cf	5	20	1	2	0	0	0	0	.100
Buford, lf	5	20	1	2	1	0	1	2	.100
Hendricks, c	3	10	1	1	0	0	0	0	.100
Johnson, 2b	5	16	1	1	0	0	0	0	.063
B. Robinson, 3b	5	19	0	1	0	0	0	2	.053
Etchebarren, c	2	6	0	0	0	0	0	0	.000
Palmer, p	1	2	0	0	0	0	0	0	.000
May, ph	2	1	0	0	0	0	0	0	.000
Motton, ph	1	1	0	0	0	0	0	0	.000
Salmon, pr	2	0	0	0	0	0	0	0	.000
Watt, p	2	0	0	0	0	0	0	0	.000
Hall, p	1	0	0	0	0	0	0	0	.000
Leonhard, p	1	0	0	0	0	0	0	0	.000
Rettenmund, pr	1	0	0	0	0	0	0	0	.000
Richert, p	1	0	0	0	0	0	0	0	.000
Totals	5	157	9	23	1	0	3	9	.146

Composite Pitching Averages

New York Mets

Pitcher	G	IP	H	R	ER	BB	SO	W	L	ERA
Gentry	1	6⅔	3	0	0	5	4	1	0	0.00
Taylor	2	2⅓	0	0	0	1	3	0	0	0.00
Ryan	1	2⅓	1	0	0	2	3	0	0	0.00
Cardwell	1	1	0	0	0	0	0	0	0	0.00
Koosman	2	17⅔	7	4	4	4	9	2	0	2.04
Seaver	2	15	12	5	5	3	9	1	1	3.00
Totals	5	45	23	9	9	15	28	4	1	1.80

Baltimore Orioles

Pitcher	G	IP	H	R	ER	BB	SO	W	L	ERA
Cuellar	2	16	13	2	2	4	13	1	0	1.13
McNally	2	16	11	5	5	5	13	0	1	2.81
Watt	2	3	4	2	1	0	3	0	1	3.00
Leonhard	1	2	1	1	1	1	1	0	0	4.50
Palmer	1	6	5	4	4	4	5	0	1	6.00
Hall	1	0*	1	1	0	1	0	0	1	0.00
Richert	1	0†	0	0	0	0	0	0	0	0.00
Totals	5	43	35	15	13	15	35	1	4	2.72

*Pitched to two batters in tenth inning of fourth game.
†Pitched to one batter in tenth inning of fourth game.

1970

Composite Batting Averages

Baltimore Orioles

Player-Position	G	AB	R	H	2B	3B	HR	RBI	BA
Salmon, ph	1	1	1	1	0	0	0	0	1.000
Blair, rf	5	19	5	9	1	0	0	3	.474
B. Robinson, 3b	5	21	5	9	2	0	2	6	.429
R'tenmund, ph-lf	2	5	2	2	0	0	1	2	.400
Hendricks, c	3	11	1	4	1	0	1	4	.364
Johnson, 2b	5	16	2	5	2	0	0	2	.313
Powell, 1b	5	17	6	5	1	0	2	5	.294
F. Robinson, rf	5	22	5	6	0	0	2	4	.273
Buford, lf	4	15	3	4	0	0	1	1	.267
McNally, p	1	4	1	1	0	0	1	4	.250
Etchebarren, c	2	7	1	1	0	0	0	0	.143
Palmer, p	2	7	1	1	0	0	0	0	.143
Belanger, ss	5	19	0	2	0	0	0	1	.105
Drabowsky, p	2	1	0	0	0	0	0	0	.000
Crowley, ph	1	1	0	0	0	0	0	0	.000
Hall, p	1	1	0	0	0	0	0	0	.000
Cuellar, p	2	4	0	0	0	0	0	0	.000
Lopez, p	1	0	0	0	0	0	0	0	.000
Phoebus, p	1	0	0	0	0	0	0	0	.000
Richert, p	1	0	0	0	0	0	0	0	.000
Watt, p	1	0	0	0	0	0	0	0	.000
Totals	5	171	33	50	7	0	10	32	.292

Cincinnati Reds

Player-Position	G	AB	R	H	2B	3B	HR	RBI	BA
McRae, lf	3	11	1	5	2	0	0	3	.455
May, 1b	5	18	6	7	2	0	2	8	.389
Concepcion, ss	3	9	0	3	0	1	0	3	.333
Cline, ph	3	3	0	1	0	0	0	0	.333
Rose, rf	5	20	2	5	1	0	1	2	.250
Helms, 2b	5	18	1	4	0	0	0	0	.222
Bench, c	5	19	3	4	0	0	1	3	.211
Tolan, cf	5	19	5	4	1	0	1	1	.211
Woodward, ss-ph	4	5	0	1	0	0	0	0	.200
Perez, 3b	5	18	2	1	0	0	0	0	.056
Carroll, p	4	1	0	0	0	0	0	0	.000
Chaney, ss	3	1	0	0	0	0	0	0	.000
Gullett, p	3	1	0	0	0	0	0	0	.000
Corrales, ph	1	1	0	0	0	0	0	0	.000
Merritt, p	1	1	0	0	0	0	0	0	.000
Bravo, ph	4	2	0	0	0	0	0	0	.000
Cloninger, p	2	2	0	0	0	0	0	0	.000
Stewart, ph	2	2	0	0	0	0	0	0	.000
McGlothlin, p	1	2	0	0	0	0	0	0	.000
Nolan, p	2	3	0	0	0	0	0	0	.000
Carbo, lf-ph	4	8	0	0	0	0	0	0	.000
Granger, p	2	0	0	0	0	0	0	0	.000
Wilcox, p	2	0	0	0	0	0	0	0	.000
Washburn, p	1	0	0	0	0	0	0	0	.000
Totals	5	164	20	35	6	1	5	20	.213

Composite Pitching Averages

Baltimore Orioles

Pitcher	G	IP	H	R	ER	BB	SO	W	L	ERA
Hall	1	2⅓	0	0	0	0	0	0	0	0.00
Phoebus	1	1⅔	1	0	0	0	0	1	0	0.00
Lopez	1	⅓	0	0	0	0	0	0	0	0.00
Richert	1	⅓	0	0	0	0	0	0	0	0.00
Drabowsky	2	3⅓	2	1	1	1	1	0	0	2.70
McNally	1	9	9	3	3	2	5	1	0	3.00
Cuellar	2	11⅓	10	7	4	2	5	1	0	3.18
Palmer	2	15⅔	11	8	8	9	9	1	0	4.00
Watt	1	1	2	1	1	1	3	0	1	9.00
Totals	5	45	35	20	17	15	23	4	1	3.40

Cincinnati Reds

Pitcher	G	IP	H	R	ER	BB	SO	W	L	ERA
Carroll	4	9	5	0	0	2	11	1	0	0.00
Gullett	3	6⅔	5	2	1	4	4	0	0	1.35
Cloninger	2	7⅓	10	6	6	5	4	0	1	7.36
Nolan	2	9⅓	9	8	8	3	9	0	1	7.71
McGlothlin	1	4⅓	6	4	4	2	2	0	0	8.31
Wilcox	2	2	3	2	2	0	2	0	1	9.00
Washburn	1	1⅓	2	2	2	2	0	0	0	13.50
Merritt	1	1⅔	3	4	4	1	0	0	1	21.00
Granger	2	1⅓	7	5	5	1	1	0	0	33.75
Totals	5	43	50	33	32	20	33	1	4	6.70

1971

Composite Batting Averages

Pittsburgh Pirates

Player-Position	G	AB	R	H	2B	3B	HR	RBI	BA
May, ph	2	2	0	1	0	0	0	1	.500
Briles, p	1	2	0	1	0	0	0	1	.500
Clemente, rf	7	29	3	12	2	1	2	4	.414
Sanguillen, c	7	29	3	11	1	0	0	0	.379
Dav'illo, ph-lf-cf	3	3	1	1	0	0	0	0	.333
Pagan, 3b	4	15	0	4	2	0	0	2	.267
Robertson, 1b	7	25	4	6	0	0	2	5	.240
Hernandez, ss	7	18	2	4	0	0	0	1	.222
Oliver, ph-cf	5	19	1	4	2	0	0	2	.211
Stargell, lf	7	24	3	5	1	0	0	1	.208
Hebner, 3b	3	12	2	2	0	0	1	3	.167
Cash, 2b	7	30	2	4	1	0	0	1	.133
Clines, cf	3	11	2	1	0	1	0	0	.091
Ellis, p	1	1	0	0	0	0	0	0	.000
Mazeroski, ph	1	1	0	0	0	0	0	0	.000
Sands, ph	1	1	0	0	0	0	0	0	.000
Alley, ss-pr	2	2	0	0	0	0	0	0	.000
Kison, p	2	2	0	0	0	0	0	0	.000
Moose, p	3	2	0	0	0	0	0	0	.000
R. Johnson, p	2	3	0	0	0	0	0	0	.000
Blass, p	2	7	0	0	0	0	0	0	.000
Giusti, p	3	0	0	0	0	0	0	0	.000
Miller, p	3	0	0	0	0	0	0	0	.000
Veale, p	1	0	0	0	0	0	0	0	.000
Walker, p	1	0	0	0	0	0	0	0	.000
Totals	7	238	23	56	9	2	5	21	.235

Baltimore Orioles

Player-Position	G	AB	R	H	2B	3B	HR	RBI	BA
Blair, cf-pr	4	9	2	3	1	0	0	0	.333
B. Robinson, 3b	7	22	2	7	0	0	0	5	.318
F. Robinson, rf	7	25	5	7	0	0	2	2	.280
Hendricks, c	6	19	3	5	1	0	0	1	.263
Buford, lf	6	23	3	6	1	0	2	4	.261
Belanger, ss	7	21	4	5	0	1	0	0	.238
Ret'nd, cf-rf-lf-ph	7	27	3	5	0	0	1	4	.185
D. Johnson, 2b	7	27	1	4	0	0	0	3	.148
Powell, 1b	7	27	1	3	0	0	0	1	.111
Dobson, p	3	2	0	0	0	0	0	0	.000
Etchebarren, c	1	2	0	0	0	0	0	0	.000
Cuellar, p	2	3	0	0	0	0	0	0	.000
McNally, p	4	4	0	0	0	0	0	0	.000
Palmer, p	2	4	0	0	0	0	0	2	.000
Shopay, ph	5	4	0	0	0	0	0	0	.000
Dukes, p	2	0	0	0	0	0	0	0	.000
Watt, p	2	0	0	0	0	0	0	0	.000
Hall, p	1	0	0	0	0	0	0	0	.000
Jackson, p	1	0	0	0	0	0	0	0	.000
Leonhard, p	1	0	0	0	0	0	0	0	.000
Richert, p	1	0	0	0	0	0	0	0	.000
Totals	7	219	24	45	3	1	5	22	.205

Composite Pitching Averages

Pittsburgh Pirates

Pitcher	G	IP	H	R	ER	BB	SO	W	L	ERA
Briles	1	9	2	0	0	2	2	1	0	0.00
Kison	2	6⅓	1	0	0	2	3	1	0	0.00
Giusti	3	5⅓	3	0	0	2	4	0	0	0.00
Blass	2	18	7	2	2	4	13	2	0	1.00
Miller	3	4⅔	7	2	2	1	2	0	1	3.86
Moose	3	9⅔	12	7	7	2	7	0	0	6.52
R. Johnson	2	5	5	5	5	3	3	0	1	9.00
Veale	1	⅔	1	1	1	2	0	0	0	13.50
Ellis	1	2⅓	4	4	4	1	1	0	1	15.43
Walker	1	⅔	3	3	3	1	0	0	0	40.50
Totals	7	61⅔	45	24	24	20	35	4	3	3.50

Baltimore Orioles

Pitcher	G	IP	H	R	ER	BB	SO	W	L	ERA
Dukes	2	4	2	0	0	0	1	0	0	0.00
Hall	1	1	1	0	0	0	0	0	0	0.00
Leonhard	1	1	0	0	0	1	0	0	0	0.00
Jackson	1	⅔	0	0	0	1	0	0	0	0.00
Richert	1	⅔	0	0	0	0	1	0	0	0.00
McNally	4	13⅔	10	7	3	5	12	2	1	1.98
Palmer	2	17	15	5	5	9	15	1	0	2.65
Cuellar	2	14	11	7	6	6	10	0	2	3.86
Watt	2	2⅓	4	1	1	0	2	0	1	3.86
Dobson	3	6⅔	13	3	3	4	6	0	0	4.05
Totals	7	61	56	23	18	26	47	3	4	2.66

1972

Composite Batting Averages

Oakland Athletics

Player-Position	G	AB	R	H	2B	3B	HR	RBI	BA
Mincher, ph	3	1	0	1	0	0	0	1	1.000
Marquez, ph	5	5	0	3	0	0	0	1	.600
Tenace, c-1b	7	23	5	8	1	0	4	9	.348
Green, 2b	7	18	0	6	2	0	0	1	.333
Kubiak, 2b	4	3	0	1	0	0	0	0	.333
Mangual, ph-cf	4	10	1	3	0	0	0	1	.300
Bando, 3b	7	26	2	7	1	0	0	1	.269
Rudi, lf	7	25	1	6	0	0	1	1	.240
Hegan, 1b-ph	6	5	0	1	0	0	0	0	.200
Duncan, ph-c	3	5	0	1	0	0	0	0	.200
Hunter, p	3	5	0	1	0	0	0	1	.200
Campaneris, ss	7	28	1	5	0	0	0	0	.179
Hendrick, cf	5	15	3	2	0	0	0	0	.133
Alou, rf	7	24	0	1	0	0	0	0	.042
Fingers, p	6	1	0	0	0	0	0	0	.000
Blue, p	4	1	0	0	0	0	0	0	.000
Odom, p-pr	4	4	0	0	0	0	0	0	.000
Holtzman, p	3	5	0	0	0	0	0	0	.000
Epstein, 1b	6	16	1	0	0	0	0	0	.000
Lewis, pr	6	0	2	0	0	0	0	0	.000
Hamilton, p	2	0	0	0	0	0	0	0	.000
Horlen, p	1	0	0	0	0	0	0	0	.000
Locker, p	1	0	0	0	0	0	0	0	.000
Totals	7	220	16	46	4	0	5	16	.209

Cincinnati Reds

Player-Position	G	AB	R	H	2B	3B	HR	RBI	BA
McRae, ph-rf	5	9	1	4	1	0	0	2	.444
Perez, 1b	7	23	3	10	2	0	0	2	.435
Co'pcion, ss-pr-ph	6	13	2	4	0	1	0	2	.308
Tolan, cf	7	26	2	7	1	0	0	6	.269
Bench, c	7	23	4	6	1	0	1	1	.261
Uhlaender, ph	4	4	0	1	1	0	0	0	.250
Rose, lf	7	28	3	6	0	0	1	2	.214
Geronimo, rf-cf	7	19	1	3	0	0	0	3	.158
Morgan, 2b	7	24	4	3	2	0	0	1	.125
Menke, 3b	7	24	1	2	0	0	1	2	.083
McGlothlin, p	1	1	0	0	0	0	0	0	.000
Gullett, p	1	2	0	0	0	0	0	0	.000
Grimsley, p	4	2	0	0	0	0	0	0	.000
Hall, p	4	2	0	0	0	0	0	0	.000
Javier, ph	4	2	0	0	0	0	0	0	.000
Nolan, p	2	3	0	0	0	0	0	0	.000
Hague, ph-rf	3	3	0	0	0	0	0	0	.000
Billingham, p	3	5	0	0	0	0	0	0	.000
Chaney, ss-ph	4	7	0	0	0	0	0	0	.000
Foster, pr-rf	2	0	0	0	0	0	0	0	.000
Carroll, p	5	0	0	0	0	0	0	0	.000
Borbon, p	6	0	0	0	0	0	0	0	.000
Totals	7	220	21	46	8	1	3	21	.209

Composite Pitching Averages

Oakland Athletics

Pitcher	G	IP	H	R	ER	BB	SO	W	L	ERA
Locker	1	⅓	1	0	0	0	0	0	0	0.00
Odom	2	11⅓	5	2	2	6	13	0	1	1.50
Fingers	6	10⅓	4	2	2	4	11	1	1	1.74
Holtzman	3	12⅔	11	3	3	3	4	1	0	2.13
Hunter	3	16	12	5	5	6	11	2	0	2.81
Blue	4	8⅔	8	4	4	5	5	0	1	4.15
Horlen	1	1⅓	2	1	1	2	1	0	0	6.75
Hamilton	2	1⅓	3	4	4	1	1	0	0	27.00
Totals	7	62	46	21	21	27	46	4	3	3.05

Cincinnati Reds

Pitcher	G	IP	H	R	ER	BB	SO	W	L	ERA
Billingham	3	13⅔	6	1	0	4	11	1	0	0.00
Hall	4	8⅓	6	0	0	2	7	0	0	0.00
Gullett	1	7	5	1	1	2	4	0	0	1.29
Carroll	5	5⅔	6	1	1	4	3	0	1	1.50
Grimsley	4	7	7	2	2	3	2	2	1	2.57
Nolan	2	10⅔	7	4	4	2	3	0	1	3.38
Borbon	6	7	7	3	3	2	4	0	1	3.86
McGlothlin	1	3	2	4	4	2	3	0	0	12.00
Totals	7	62⅓	46	16	15	21	37	3	4	2.17

1973

Composite Batting Averages

Oakland Athletics

Player-Position	G	AB	R	H	2B	3B	HR	RBI	BA
Holtzman, p	3	3	2	2	2	0	0	0	.067
Bourque, ph-1b	2	2	0	1	0	0	0	0	.500
Rudi, lf	7	27	3	9	2	0	0	4	.333
Fingers, p	6	3	0	1	0	0	0	0	.333
Jackson, cf-rf	7	29	3	9	3	1	1	6	.310
Johnson, ph-1b	6	10	0	3	1	0	0	0	.300
Campaneris, ss	7	31	6	9	0	1	1	3	.290
Bando, 3b	7	26	5	6	1	1	0	1	.231
Alou, rf-ph	7	19	0	3	1	0	0	3	.158
Fosse, c	7	19	0	3	1	0	0	0	.158
Tenace, 1b-c	7	19	0	3	1	0	0	3	.158
De'lillo, cf-ph-1b	6	11	0	1	0	0	0	0	.091
Green, 2b	7	16	0	1	0	0	0	0	.063
Knowles, p	7	0	0	0	0	0	0	0	.000
Lewis, pr	3	0	1	0	0	0	0	0	.000
Pina, p	2	0	0	0	0	0	0	0	.000
Lindblad, p	3	1	0	0	0	0	0	0	.000
Odom, p-pr	3	1	0	0	0	0	0	0	.000
Conigliaro, ph	3	3	0	0	0	0	0	0	.000
Andrews, ph-2b	2	3	0	0	0	0	0	0	.000
Kubiak, 2b	4	3	1	0	0	0	0	0	.000
Blue, p	2	4	0	0	0	0	0	0	.000
Hunter, p	2	5	0	0	0	0	0	0	.000
Mangual, ph-cf	5	6	0	0	0	0	0	0	.000
Totals	7	241	21	51	12	3	2	20	.212

New York Mets

Player-Position	G	AB	R	H	2B	3B	HR	RBI	BA
Boswell, ph	3	3	1	3	0	0	0	0	1.000
Staub, ph-rf	7	26	1	11	2	0	1	6	.423
McGraw, p	5	3	1	1	0	0	0	0	.333
Milner, 1b	7	27	2	8	0	G	0	2	.296
Jones, lf	7	28	5	8	2	0	1	1	.286
Mays, cf-pr-ph	3	7	1	2	0	0	0	1	.286
Grote, c	7	30	2	8	0	0	0	0	.267
Harrelson, ss	7	24	2	6	1	0	0	1	.250
Matlack, p	3	4	0	1	0	0	0	0	.250
Hahn, rf-cf	7	29	2	7	1	1	0	2	.241
Millan, 2b	7	32	3	6	1	1	0	1	.188
Garrett, 3b	7	30	4	5	0	0	2	2	.167
Martinez, pr	2	0	0	0	0	0	0	0	.000
Hodges, ph	1	0	0	0	0	0	0	0	.000
Stone, p	2	0	0	0	0	0	0	0	.000
Parker, p	3	0	0	0	0	0	0	0	.000
Sadecki, p	4	0	0	0	0	0	0	0	.000
Theodore, ph-lf	2	2	0	0	0	0	0	0	.000
Kranepool, ph	4	3	0	0	0	0	0	0	.000
Beauchamp, ph	4	4	0	0	0	0	0	0	.000
Koosman, p	2	4	0	0	0	0	0	0	.000
Seaver, p	2	5	0	0	0	0	0	0	.000
Totals	7	261	24	66	7	2	4	16	.253

Composite Pitching Averages

Oakland Athletics

Pitcher	G	IP	H	R	ER	BB	SO	W	L	ERA
Knowles	7	6⅓	4	1	0	5	5	0	0	0.00
Lindblad	3	3⅓	4	0	0	1	1	1	0	0.00
Pina	2	3	6	2	0	2	0	0	0	0.00
Fingers	6	13⅔	13	5	1	4	8	0	1	0.66
Hunter	2	13⅓	11	3	3	4	6	1	0	2.03
Odom	2	4⅔	5	2	2	2	2	0	0	3.86
Holtzman	3	10⅔	13	5	5	5	6	2	1	4.22
Blue	2	11	10	6	6	3	8	0	1	4.91
Totals	7	66	66	24	17	26	36	4	3	2.32

New York Mets

Pitcher	G	IP	H	R	ER	BB	SO	W	L	ERA
Parker	3	3⅓	2	1	0	2	2	0	1	0.00
Stone	2	3	4	0	0	1	3	0	0	0.00
Sadecki	4	4⅔	5	1	1	1	6	0	0	1.93
Matlack	3	16⅔	10	7	4	5	11	1	2	2.16
Seaver	2	15	13	4	4	3	18	0	1	2.40
McGraw	5	13⅔	8	5	4	9	14	1	0	2.63
Koosman	2	8⅔	9	3	3	7	8	1	0	3.12
Totals	6	65	51	21	16	28	62	3	4	2.22

1974

Composite Batting Averages

Oakland Athletics

Player-Position	G	AB	R	H	2B	3B	HR	RBI	BA
Holt, ph-1b	4	3	0	2	0	0	0	2	.667
C. W'ton, rf-ph-cf-lf	5	7	1	4	0	0	0	0	.571
Holtzman, p	2	4	2	2	1	0	1	1	.500
Campaneris, ss	5	17	1	6	2	0	0	2	.353
Rudi, lf-1b	5	18	1	6	0	0	1	4	.333
Jackson, rf	5	14	3	4	1	0	1	1	.286
Tenace, 1b	5	9	0	2	0	0	0	0	.222
Fosse, c	5	14	1	2	0	0	1	1	.143
Bando, 3b	5	16	3	1	0	0	0	2	.063
North, cf	5	17	3	1	0	0	0	0	.059
Alou, ph	1	1	0	0	0	0	0	0	.000
Mangual, ph	1	1	0	0	0	0	0	0	.000
Fingers, p	4	2	0	0	0	0	0	0	.000
Hunter, p	2	2	0	0	0	0	0	0	.000
Blue, p	2	4	0	0	0	0	0	0	.000
Green, 2b	5	13	1	0	0	0	0	1	.000
H. Washington, pr	3	0	0	0	0	0	0	0	.000
Haney, c	2	0	0	0	0	0	0	0	.000
Maxvill, 2b-pr	2	0	0	0	0	0	0	0	.000
Odom, p	2	0	0	0	0	0	0	0	.000
Totals	5	142	16	30	4	0	4	14	.211

Los Angeles Dodgers

Player-Position	G	AB	R	H	2B	3B	HR	RBI	BA
Messersmith, p	2	4	0	2	0	0	0	0	.500
Paciorek, pr-ph	3	2	1	1	1	0	0	0	.500
Garvey, 1b	5	21	2	8	0	0	0	1	.381
Yeager, c	4	11	0	4	1	0	0	1	.364
Crawford, ph-rf	3	6	1	2	0	0	1	1	.333
Buckner, lf	5	20	1	5	1	0	1	1	.250
Russell, ss	5	18	0	4	0	1	0	2	.222
Wynn, cf	5	16	1	3	1	0	1	2	.188
Cey, 3b	5	17	1	3	0	0	0	0	.176
Ferguson, rf-c	5	16	2	2	0	0	1	2	.125
Lopes, 2b	5	18	2	2	0	0	0	0	.111
Downing, p	1	1	0	0	0	0	0	0	.000
Lacy, ph	1	1	0	0	0	0	0	0	.000
Sutton, p	2	3	0	0	0	0	0	0	.000
Joshua, ph	4	4	0	0	0	0	0	0	.000
Marshall, p	5	0	0	0	0	0	0	0	.000
Auerbach, pr	1	0	0	0	0	0	0	0	.000
Brewer, p	1	0	0	0	0	0	0	0	.000
Hough, p	1	0	0	0	0	0	0	0	.000
Totals	5	158	11	36	4	1	4	10	.228

Composite Pitching Averages

Oakland Athletics

Pitcher	G	IP	H	R	ER	BB	SO	W	L	ERA
Odom	2	1⅓	0	0	0	1	2	1	0	0.00
Hunter	2	7⅔	5	1	1	2	5	1	0	1.17
Holtzman	2	12	13	3	2	4	10	1	0	1.50
Fingers	4	9⅓	8	2	2	2	6	1	0	1.93
Blue	2	13⅔	10	5	5	7	9	0	1	3.29
Totals	5	44	36	11	10	16	32	4	1	2.05

Los Angeles Dodgers

Pitcher	G	IP	H	R	ER	BB	SO	W	L	ERA
Hough	1	2	0	0	0	1	4	0	0	0.00
Brewer	1	⅓	0	0	0	0	1	0	0	0.00
Marshall	5	9	6	1	1	1	10	0	1	1.00
Downing	1	3⅔	4	3	1	4	3	0	1	2.45
Sutton	2	13	9	4	4	3	12	1	0	2.77
Messersmith	2	14	11	8	7	7	12	0	2	4.50
Totals	5	42	30	16	13	16	42	1	4	2.79

1975

Composite Batting Averages

Cincinnati Reds

Player-Position	G	AB	R	H	2B	3B	HR	RBI	BA
McEnaney, p	5	1	0	1	0	0	0	0	1.000
Crowley, ph	2	2	0	1	0	0	0	0	.500
Rose, 3b	7	27	3	10	1	1	0	2	.370
Gullett, p	3	7	1	2	0	0	0	0	.286
Geronimo, cf	7	25	3	7	0	1	2	3	.280
Foster, lf	7	29	1	8	1	0	0	2	.276
Griffey, rf	7	26	4	7	3	1	0	4	.269
Morgan, 2b	7	27	4	7	1	0	0	3	.259
Bench, c	7	29	5	6	2	0	1	4	.207
Concepcion, ss	7	28	3	5	1	0	1	4	.179
Perez, 1b	7	28	4	5	0	0	3	7	.179
Armbrister, ph	4	1	1	0	0	0	0	0	.000
Eastwick, p	5	1	0	0	0	0	0	0	.000
Bonbon, p	3	1	0	0	0	0	0	0	.000
Darcy, p	2	1	0	0	0	0	0	0	.000
Nolan, p	2	1	0	0	0	0	0	0	.000
Norman, p	2	1	0	0	0	0	0	0	.000
Billingham, p	3	2	0	0	0	0	0	0	.000
Chaney, ph	2	2	0	0	0	0	0	0	.000
Driessen, ph	2	2	0	0	0	0	0	0	.000
Rettenmund, ph	3	3	0	0	0	0	0	0	.000
Carroll, p	5	0	0	0	0	0	0	0	.000
Totals	7	244	29	50	9	3	7	29	.242

Boston Red Sox

Player-Position	G	AB	R	H	2B	3B	HR	RBI	BA
Carbon, ph-lf	4	7	3	3	1	0	2	4	.429
Yastrzemski, lf-1b	7	29	7	9	0	0	0	4	.310
Petrocelli, 3b	7	26	3	8	1	0	0	4	.308
Burleson, ss	7	24	1	7	1	0	0	2	.292
Evans, rf	7	24	3	7	1	1	1	5	.292
Lynn, cf	7	25	3	7	1	0	1	5	.280
Doyle, 2b	7	30	3	8	1	1	0	0	.267
Tiant, p	3	8	2	2	0	0	0	0	.250
Fisk, c	7	25	5	6	0	0	2	4	.240
Lee, p	2	6	0	1	0	0	0	0	.167
Beniquez, lf-ph	3	8	0	1	0	0	0	1	.125
Cooper, 1b-ph	5	19	0	1	1	0	0	1	.053
Griffin, ph	1	1	0	0	0	0	0	0	.000
Montgomery, ph	1	1	0	0	0	0	0	0	.000
Cleveland, p	3	2	0	0	0	0	0	0	.000
Miller, lf-ph	3	2	0	0	0	0	0	0	.000
Wise, p	2	2	0	0	0	0	0	0	.000
Moret, p	3	0	0	0	0	0	0	0	.000
Willoughby, p	3	0	0	0	0	0	0	0	.000
Burton, p	2	0	0	0	0	0	0	0	.000
Drago, p	2	0	0	0	0	0	0	0	.000
Pole, p	1	0	0	0	0	0	0	0	.000
Segui, p	1	0	0	0	0	0	0	0	.000
Totals	7	230	30	60	7	2	6	30	.251

Composite Pitching Averages

Cincinnati Reds

Pitcher	G	IP	H	R	ER	BB	SO	W	L	ERA
Billingham	3	9	8	2	1	5	7	0	0	1.00
Eastwick	5	8	6	2	2	3	4	2	0	2.25
McEnaney	5	6⅔	3	2	2	2	5	0	0	2.70
Carroll	5	5⅔	4	2	2	2	3	1	0	3.18
Gullett	3	18⅔	19	9	9	10	15	1	1	4.34
Darcy	2	4	3	2	2	2	1	0	1	4.50
Nolan	2	6	6	4	4	1	2	0	0	6.00
Borbon	3	3	3	3	2	2	1	0	0	6.00
Norman	2	4	8	4	4	3	2	0	1	9.00
Totals	7	65	60	30	28	30	40	4	3	3.88

Boston Red Sox

Pitcher	G	IP	H	R	ER	BB	SO	W	L	ERA
Willoughby	3	6⅓	3	1	0	0	2	0	1	0.00
Moret	3	1⅔	2	0	0	3	1	0	0	0.00
Segui	1	1	0	0	0	0	0	0	0	0.00
Drago	2	4	3	1	1	1	1	0	1	2.25
Lee	2	14⅓	12	5	5	3	7	0	0	3.14
Tiant	3	25	25	10	10	8	12	2	0	3.00
Cleveland	3	6⅔	7	5	5	3	5	0	1	6.75
Wise	2	5⅓	6	5	5	2	2	1	0	8.44
Burton	2	1	1	1	1	3	0	0	1	9.00
Pole	1	0	0	1	1	2	0	0	0	—
Totals	6	65⅓	50	29	26	25	30	3	4	3.96

1976

Composite Batting Averages

Cincinnati Reds

Player-Position	G	AB	R	H	2B	3B	HR	RBI	BA
Bench, c	4	15	4	8	1	1	2	6	.533
Foster, lf	4	14	3	6	1	0	0	4	.429
Concepcion, ss	4	14	1	5	1	1	0	3	.357
Driessen, dh	4	14	4	5	2	0	1	1	.357
Morgan, 2b	4	15	3	5	1	1	1	2	.333
Perez, 1b	4	16	1	5	1	0	0	2	.313
Geronimo, cf	4	13	3	4	2	0	0	1	.308
Rose, 3b	4	16	1	3	1	0	0	1	.188
Griffey, rf	4	17	2	1	0	0	0	1	0.59
McEnaney, p	2	0	0	0	0	0	0	0	.000
Borbon, p	1	0	0	0	0	0	0	0	.000
Billingham, p	1	0	0	0	0	0	0	0	.000
Gullett, p	1	0	0	0	0	0	0	0	.000
Nolan, p	1	0	0	0	0	0	0	0	.000
Norman, p	1	0	0	0	0	0	0	0	.000
Zachry, p	1	0	0	0	0	0	0	0	.000
Totals	4	134	22	42	10	3	4	21	.313

New York Yankees

Player-Position	G	AB	R	H	2B	3B	HR	RBI	BA
Mason, ss	3	1	1	1	0	0	1	1	1.000
Munson, c	4	17	2	9	0	0	0	2	.529
Piniella, dh-rf-ph	4	9	1	3	1	0	0	0	.333
Chambliss, 1b	4	16	1	5	1	0	0	1	.313
Nettles, 3b	4	12	0	3	0	0	0	2	.250
Maddox, rf-dh	2	5	0	1	0	1	0	0	.200
Rivers, cf	4	18	1	3	0	0	0	0	.167
Stanley, ss	4	6	1	1	1	0	0	1	.167
White, lf	4	15	0	2	0	0	0	0	.133
Gamble, ph-rf	3	8	0	1	0	0	0	1	.125
Randolph, 2b	4	14	1	1	0	0	0	0	.071
Hendricks, ph	2	2	0	0	0	0	0	0	.000
Velez, ph	3	3	0	0	0	0	0	0	.000
May, ph-dh	4	9	0	0	0	0	0	0	.000
Tidrow, p	2	0	0	0	0	0	0	0	.000
Lyle, p	2	0	0	0	0	0	0	0	.000
Alexander, p	1	0	0	0	0	0	0	0	.000
Ellis, p	1	0	0	0	0	0	0	0	.000
Figueroa, p	1	0	0	0	0	0	0	0	.000
Hunter, p	1	0	0	0	0	0	0	0	.000
Jackson, p	1	0	0	0	0	0	0	0	.000
Totals	4	135	8	30	3	1	1	8	.222

Composite Pitching Averages

Cincinnati Reds

Pitcher	G	IP	H	R	ER	BB	SO	W	L	ERA
McEnaney	2	4⅔	2	0	0	1	2	0	0	0.00
Billingham	1	2⅔	0	0	0	0	1	1	0	0.00
Borbon	1	1⅔	0	0	0	0	0	0	0	0.00
Gullett	1	7⅓	5	1	1	3	4	1	0	1.23
Nolan	1	6⅔	8	2	2	1	1	1	0	2.70
Zachry	1	6⅔	6	2	2	5	6	1	0	2.70
Norman	1	6⅓	9	3	3	2	2	0	0	4.26
Totals	4	36	30	8	8	12	16	4	0	2.00

New York Yankees

Pitcher	G	IP	H	R	ER	BB	SO	W	L	ERA
Lyle	2	2⅔	1	0	0	0	3	0	0	0.00
Hunter	1	8⅔	10	4	3	4	5	0	1	3.12
Jackson	1	3⅔	4	2	2	0	3	0	0	4.91
Figueroa	1	8	6	5	5	5	2	0	1	5.63
Alexander	1	6	9	5	5	2	1	0	1	7.50
Tidrow	2	2⅓	5	2	2	1	1	0	0	7.71
Ellis	1	3⅓	7	4	4	0	1	0	1	10.80
Totals	4	34⅔	42	22	21	12	16	0	4	5.45

1977

Composite Batting Averages

New York Yankees

Player-Position	G	AB	R	H	2B	3B	HR	RBI	BA
Jackson, rf	6	20	10	9	1	0	5	8	.450
Munson, c	6	25	4	8	2	0	1	3	.320
Chambliss, 1b	6	24	4	7	2	0	1	4	.292
Piniella, lf	6	22	1	6	0	0	0	3	.273
Dent, ss	6	19	0	5	0	0	0	2	.263
Blair, rf-ph	4	4	0	1	0	0	0	1	.250
Rivers, cf	6	27	1	6	2	0	0	1	.222
Nettles, 3b	6	21	1	4	1	0	0	2	.190
Randolph, 2b	6	25	5	4	2	0	1	1	.160
Johnson, ph-c	2	1	0	0	0	0	0	0	.000
Tidrow, p	2	1	0	0	0	0	0	0	.000
Guidry, p	1	2	0	0	0	0	0	0	.000
Gullett, p	2	2	0	0	0	0	0	0	.000
Lyle, p	2	2	0	0	0	0	0	0	.000
White, ph	2	2	0	0	0	0	0	0	.000
Zeber, ph	2	2	0	0	0	0	0	0	.000
Torrez, p	2	6	0	0	0	0	0	0	.000
Clay, p	2	0	0	0	0	0	0	0	.000
Hunter, p	2	0	0	0	0	0	0	0	.000
Stanley, ss	1	0	0	0	0	0	0	0	.000
Totals	6	205	26	50	10	0	8	25	.244

Los Angeles Dodgers

Player-Position	G	AB	R	H	2B	3B	HR	RBI	BA
Rhoden, p	2	2	1	1	1	0	0	0	.500
Lacy, ph-rf	4	7	1	3	0	0	0	2	.429
Garvey, 1b	6	24	5	9	1	1	1	3	.375
Davalillo, ph	3	3	0	1	0	0	0	1	.333
Yeager, c	6	19	2	6	1	0	2	5	.316
Baker, lf	6	24	4	7	0	0	1	5	.292
Smith, rf-cf	6	22	7	6	1	0	3	5	.273
Burke, cf	3	5	0	1	0	0	0	0	.200
Cey, 3b	6	21	2	4	1	0	1	3	.190
Lopes, 2b	6	24	3	4	0	1	1	2	.167
Monday, cf	4	12	0	2	0	0	0	0	.167
Russell, ss	6	26	3	4	0	1	0	2	.154
Goodson, ph	1	1	0	0	0	0	0	0	.000
Grote, c	1	1	0	0	0	0	0	0	.000
Oates, ph-c	1	1	0	0	0	0	0	0	.000
John, p	1	2	0	0	0	0	0	0	.000
Mota, ph	3	3	0	0	0	0	0	0	.000
Hooton, p	2	5	0	0	0	0	0	0	.000
Sutton, p	2	6	0	0	0	0	0	0	.000
Garman, p	2	0	0	0	0	0	0	0	.000
Hough, p	2	0	0	0	0	0	0	0	.000
Rau, p	2	0	0	0	0	0	0	0	.000
Sosa, p	2	0	0	0	0	0	0	0	.000
Landestoy, pr	1	0	0	0	0	0	0	0	.000
Rautzhan, p	1	0	0	0	0	0	0	0	.000
Totals	6	208	28	48	5	3	9	28	.231

Composite Pitching Averages

New York Yankees

Pitcher	G	IP	H	R	ER	BB	SO	W	L	ERA
Lyle	2	4⅔	2	1	1	0	2	1	0	1.93
Guidry	1	9	4	2	2	3	7	1	0	2.00
Clay	2	3⅔	2	1	1	1	0	0	0	2.45
Torrez	2	18	16	7	5	5	15	2	0	2.50
Tidrow	2	3⅔	5	2	2	0	1	0	0	4.91
Gullett	2	12⅔	13	10	9	7	10	0	1	6.39
Hunter	2	4⅓	6	5	5	0	1	0	1	10.38
Totals	6	56	48	28	25	16	36	4	2	4.02

Los Angeles Dodgers

Pitcher	G	IP	H	R	ER	BB	SO	W	L	ERA
Garman	2	4	2	0	0	1	3	0	0	0.00
Rautzhan	1	⅓	0	0	0	2	0	0	0	0.00
Hough	2	5	3	1	1	0	5	0	0	1.80
Rhoden	2	7	4	2	2	1	5	0	1	2.57
Hooton	2	12	8	5	5	2	9	1	1	3.75
Sutton	2	16	17	7	7	1	6	1	0	3.94
John	1	6	9	5	4	3	7	0	1	6.00
Rau	2	2⅓	4	3	3	0	1	0	1	11.57
Sosa	2	2⅓	3	3	3	1	1	0	0	11.57
Totals	6	55	50	26	25	11	37	2	4	4.09

1978

Composite Batting Averages

New York Yankees

Player-Position	G	AB	R	H	2B	3B	HR	RBI	BA
Doyle, 2b	6	16	4	7	1	0	0	2	.438
Dent, ss	6	24	3	10	1	0	0	7	.417
Jackson, dh	6	23	2	9	1	0	2	8	.391
Blair, cf-ph-pr	6	8	2	3	1	0	0	0	.375
White, lf	6	24	9	8	0	0	1	4	.333
Rivers, cf-ph	5	18	2	6	0	0	0	1	.333
Munson, c	6	25	5	8	3	0	0	7	.320
Piniella, rf	6	25	3	7	0	0	0	4	.280
Thomasson, cf-lf	3	4	0	1	0	0	0	0	.250
Stanley, 2b	3	5	0	1	1	0	0	0	.200
Chambliss, 1b	3	11	1	2	0	0	0	0	.182
Spencer, 1b-ph	4	12	3	2	0	0	0	0	.167
Nettles, 3b	6	25	2	4	0	0	0	1	.160
Johnson, ph	2	2	0	0	0	0	0	0	.000
Beattie, p	1	0	0	0	0	0	0	0	.000
Clay, p	1	0	0	0	0	0	0	0	.000
Figueroa, p	2	0	0	0	0	0	0	0	.000
Gossage, p	3	0	0	0	0	0	0	0	.000
Guidry, p	1	0	0	0	0	0	0	0	.000
Heath, c	1	0	0	0	0	0	0	0	.000
Hunter, p	2	0	0	0	0	0	0	0	.000
Johnstone, rf	2	0	0	0	0	0	0	0	.000
Lindblad, p	1	0	0	0	0	0	0	0	.000
Tidrow, p	2	0	0	0	0	0	0	0	.000
Totals	6	222	36	68	8	0	3	34	.306

Los Angeles Dodgers

Player-Position	G	AB	R	H	2B	3B	HR	RBI	BA
Oates, ph-c	1	1	0	1	0	0	0	0	1.000
Ferguson, c	2	4	1	2	2	0	0	0	.500
Russell, ss	6	26	1	11	2	0	0	2	.423
Davalillo, ph-dh	2	3	0	1	0	0	0	0	.333
Lopes, 2b	6	26	7	8	0	0	3	7	.308
Cey, 3b	6	21	2	6	0	0	1	4	.286
Baker, lf	6	21	2	5	0	0	1	1	.238
Yeager, c	5	13	2	3	1	0	0	0	.231
Garvey, 1b	6	24	1	5	1	0	0	0	.208
Smith, rf	6	25	3	5	0	0	1	5	.200
Monday, cf-dh	5	13	2	2	1	0	0	0	.154
Lacy, dh	4	14	0	2	0	0	0	1	.143
North, ph-cf	4	8	2	1	1	0	0	2	.125
Forster, p	3	0	0	0	0	0	0	0	.000
Grote, c	2	0	0	0	0	0	0	0	.000
Hooton, p	2	0	0	0	0	0	0	0	.000
Hough, p	2	0	0	0	0	0	0	0	.000
John, p	2	0	0	0	0	0	0	0	.000
Mota, ph	1	0	0	0	0	0	0	0	.000
Rau, p	1	0	0	0	0	0	0	0	.000
Rautzhan, p	2	0	0	0	0	0	0	0	.000
Sutton, p	2	0	0	0	0	0	0	0	.000
Welch, p	3	0	0	0	0	0	0	0	.000
Totals	6	190	23	52	8	0	6	22	.261

Composite Pitching Averages

New York Yankees

Pitcher	G	IP	H	R	ER	BB	SO	W	L	ERA
Gossage	3	6	1	0	0	1	4	1	0	0.00
Guidry	1	9	8	1	1	7	4	1	0	1.00
Tidrow	2	4⅔	4	1	1	0	5	0	0	1.93
Beattie	1	9	9	2	2	4	8	1	0	2.00
Hunter	2	13	13	6	6	1	5	1	1	4.15
Figueroa	2	6⅔	9	6	6	5	2	0	1	8.10
Clay	1	2⅓	4	4	3	2	2	0	0	11.57
Lindblad	1	2⅓	4	3	3	0	1	0	0	11.57
Totals	6	53	52	23	22	20	31	4	2	3.74

Los Angeles Dodgers

Pitcher	G	IP	H	R	ER	BB	SO	W	L	ERA
Forster	3	4	5	0	0	1	6	0	0	0.00
Rau	1	2	1	0	0	0	3	0	0	0.00
John	2	14⅔	14	8	5	4	6	1	0	3.07
Welch	3	4⅔	4	3	3	2	6	0	1	6.23
Hooton	2	8½	13	7	6	3	6	1	1	6.48
Sutton	2	12	17	10	10	4	8	0	2	7.50
Hough	3	5⅓	10	5	5	2	5	0	0	8.44
Rautzhan	2	2	4	3	3	0	0	0	0	13.50
Totals	6	52⅔	68	36	32	16	40	2	4	5.46

1979

Composite Batting Averages

Pittsburgh Pirates

Player-Position	G	AB	R	H	2B	3B	HR	RBI	BA
Stennett, ph	1	1	0	1	0	0	0	0	1.000
Garner, 2b	7	24	4	12	4	0	0	5	.500
Stargell, 1b	7	30	7	12	4	0	3	7	.400
Madlock, 3b	7	24	2	9	1	0	0	3	.375
Parker, rf	7	29	2	10	3	0	0	4	.345
Moreno, cf	7	33	4	11	2	0	0	3	.333
Foli, ss	7	30	6	10	1	1	0	3	.333
Ott, c	3	12	2	4	1	0	0	3	.333
Milner, lf	3	9	2	3	1	0	0	1	.333
Candelaria, p	2	3	0	1	0	0	0	0	.333
Sanguillen, ph	3	3	0	1	0	0	0	1	.333
B. Robinson, lf-ph	7	19	2	5	1	0	0	2	.263
Lacy, ph	4	4	0	1	0	0	0	0	.250
Nicosia, c	4	16	1	1	0	0	0	0	.063
Alexander, pr-lf	1	0	0	0	0	0	0	0	.000
Kison, p	1	0	0	0	0	0	0	0	.000
D. Robinson, p	4	0	0	0	0	0	0	0	.000
Easler, ph	2	1	0	0	0	0	0	0	.000
Jackson, p	4	1	0	0	0	0	0	0	.000
Romo, p	2	1	0	0	0	0	0	0	.000
Rooker, p	2	2	0	0	0	0	0	0	.000
Tekulve, p	5	2	0	0	0	0	0	0	.000
Blyleven, p	2	3	0	0	0	0	0	0	.000
Bibby, p	2	4	0	0	0	0	0	0	.000
Totals	7	251	32	81	18	1	3	32	.323

Baltimore Orioles

Player-Position	G	AB	R	H	2B	3B	HR	RBI	BA
Stoddard, p	4	1	0	1	0	0	0	1	1.000
Garcia, ss	6	20	4	8	2	1	0	6	.400
Singleton, rf	7	28	1	10	1	0	0	2	.357
Ayala, lf-ph	4	6	1	2	0	0	1	2	.333
Skaggs, c	1	3	1	1	0	0	0	0	.333
Dauer, ph-2b	6	17	2	5	1	0	1	1	.294
Dempsey, c-pr	7	21	3	6	2	0	0	0	.286
Smith, 2b-ph	4	7	1	2	0	0	0	0	.286
Crowley, ph	5	4	0	1	1	0	0	2	.250
Kelly, ph	5	4	0	1	0	0	0	0	.250
Lowenstein, lf-ph	6	13	2	3	1	0	0	3	.231
DeCinces, 3b	7	25	2	5	0	0	1	3	.200
Murray, 1b	7	26	3	4	1	0	1	2	.154
Bumbry, cf-ph	7	21	3	3	0	0	0	1	.143
Roenicke, lf-cf-ph	6	16	1	2	1	0	0	0	.125
D. Martinez, p	2	0	0	0	0	0	0	0	.000
T. Martinez, p	3	0	0	0	0	0	0	0	.000
Stanhouse, p	3	0	0	0	0	0	0	0	.000
Stone, p	1	0	0	0	0	0	0	0	.000
May, ph	2	1	0	0	0	0	0	0	.000
Stewart, p	1	1	0	0	0	0	0	0	.000
McGregor, p	2	4	1	0	0	0	0	0	.000
Palmer, p	2	4	0	0	0	0	0	0	.000
Flanagan, p	3	5	0	0	0	0	0	0	.000
Belanger, ss-pr	5	6	1	0	0	0	0	0	.000
Totals	7	233	26	54	10	1	4	23	.232

Composite Pitching Averages

Pittsburgh Pirates

Pitcher	G	IP	H	R	ER	BB	SO	W	L	ERA
Jackson	4	4⅔	1	0	0	2	2	1	0	0.00
Rooker	2	8⅔	5	1	1	3	4	0	0	1.04
Blyleven	2	10	8	2	2	3	4	1	0	1.80
Bibby	2	10⅓	10	4	3	2	10	0	0	2.61
Tekulve	5	9⅓	4	3	3	3	10	0	1	2.89
Romo	2	4⅔	5	2	2	3	4	0	0	3.86
Candelaria	2	9	14	6	5	2	4	1	1	5.00
D. Robinson	4	5	4	3	3	6	3	1	0	5.40
Kison	1	⅓	3	5	4	2	0	0	1	108.00
Totals	7	62	54	26	22	26	41	4	3	3.19

(NOTE: Pittsburgh individual earned runs do not add up to team total because of rule 10.18(i) applied in Game 3.)

Baltimore Orioles

Pitcher	G	IP	H	R	ER	BB	SO	W	L	ERA
Stewart	1	2⅔	4	0	0	1	0	0	0	0.00
Flanagan	3	15	18	7	5	2	13	1	1	3.00
McGregor	2	17	16	6	6	2	8	1	1	3.18
Palmer	2	15	18	6	6	5	8	0	1	3.60
Stoddard	4	5	6	3	3	1	3	1	0	5.40
T. Martinez	3	1⅓	3	1	1	0	1	0	0	6.75
Stone	1	2	4	2	2	2	2	0	0	9.00
Stanhouse	3	2	6	3	3	3	0	0	1	13.50
D. Martinez	2	2	6	4	4	0	0	0	0	18.00
Totals	7	62	81	32	30	16	35	3	4	4.35

1980

Composite Batting Averages

Philadelphia Phillies

Player-Position	G	AB	R	H	2B	3B	HR	RBI	BA
Unser, ph-cf-lf	3	6	2	3	2	0	0	2	.500
Boone, c	6	17	3	7	2	0	0	4	.412
Schmidt, 3b	6	21	6	8	1	0	2	7	.381
Bowa, ss	6	24	3	9	1	0	0	2	.375
Moreland, dh	3	12	1	4	0	0	0	1	.333
McBride, rf	6	23	3	7	1	0	1	5	.304
Smith, pr-lf-dh	6	19	2	5	1	0	0	1	.263
Rose, 1b	6	23	2	6	1	0	0	1	.261
Maddox, cf	6	22	1	5	2	0	0	1	.227
Trillo, 2b	6	23	4	5	2	0	0	2	.217
Brusstar, p	1	0	0	0	0	0	0	0	.000
Bystrom, p	1	0	0	0	0	0	0	0	.000
Carlton, p	2	0	0	0	0	0	0	0	.000
Christenson, p	1	0	0	0	0	0	0	0	.000
McGraw, p	4	0	0	0	0	0	0	0	.000
Noles, p	1	0	0	0	0	0	0	0	.000
Reed, p	2	0	0	0	0	0	0	0	.000
Ruthven, p	1	0	0	0	0	0	0	0	.000
Saucier, p	1	0	0	0	0	0	0	0	.000
Walk, p	1	0	0	0	0	0	0	0	.000
Gross, ph-lf	4	2	0	0	0	0	0	0	.000
Luzinski, dh-lf	3	9	0	0	0	0	0	0	.000
Totals	6	201	27	59	13	0	3	26	.294

Kansas City Royals

Player-Position	G	AB	R	H	2B	3B	HR	RBI	BA
Otis, cf	6	23	4	11	2	0	3	7	.478
Hurdle, rf	4	12	1	5	1	0	0	0	.417
Aikens, 1b	6	20	5	8	0	1	4	8	.400
G. Brett, 3b	6	24	3	9	2	1	1	3	.375
McRae, dh	6	24	3	9	3	0	0	1	.375
Wathan, ph-rf-c	3	7	1	2	0	0	0	1	.286
Washington, ss	6	22	1	6	0	0	0	2	.273
Cardenal, ph-rf	4	10	0	2	0	0	0	0	.200
Wilson, lf	6	26	3	4	1	0	0	0	.154
Porter, ph-c	5	14	1	2	0	0	0	0	.143
White, 2b	6	25	0	2	0	0	0	0	.080
Chalk, 3b	1	0	1	0	0	0	0	0	.000
Concepcion, pr	3	0	0	0	0	0	0	0	.000
Gale, p	2	0	0	0	0	0	0	0	.000
Gura, p	2	0	0	0	0	0	0	0	.000
LaCock, 1b	1	0	0	0	0	0	0	0	.000
Leonard, p	2	0	0	0	0	0	0	0	.000
Martin, p	3	0	0	0	0	0	0	0	.000
Pattin, p	1	0	0	0	0	0	0	0	.000
Quisenberry, p	6	0	0	0	0	0	0	0	.000
Splittorff, p	1	0	0	0	0	0	0	0	.000
Totals	6	207	23	60	9	2	8	22	.290

Composite Pitching Averages

Philadelphia Phillies

Pitcher	G	IP	H	R	ER	BB	SO	W	L	ERA
Brusstar	1	2⅓	0	0	0	1	0	0	0	0.00
Reed	2	2	2	0	0	0	2	0	0	0.00
Saucier	1	⅔	0	0	0	2	0	0	0	0.00
McGraw	4	7⅔	7	1	1	8	10	1	1	1.17
Noles	1	4⅔	5	1	1	2	6	0	0	1.93
Carlton	2	15	14	5	4	9	17	2	0	2.40
Ruthven	1	9	9	3	3	0	7	0	0	3.00
Bystrom	1	5	10	3	3	1	4	0	0	5.40
Walk	1	7	8	6	6	3	3	1	0	7.71
Christenson	1	⅓	5	4	4	0	0	0	1	108.00
Totals	6	53⅔	60	23	22	26	49	4	2	3.69

Kansas City Royals

Pitcher	G	IP	H	R	ER	BB	SO	W	L	ERA
Pattin	1	1	0	0	0	0	2	0	0	0.00
Gura	2	12⅔	8	4	3	3	4	0	0	2.19
Martin	3	9⅔	11	3	3	3	2	0	0	2.79
Gale	2	6⅓	11	4	3	4	4	0	1	4.26
Quisenberry	6	10⅓	10	6	6	3	0	1	2	5.23
Splittorff	1	1⅔	4	1	1	0	0	0	0	5.40
Leonard	2	10⅔	15	9	8	2	5	1	1	6.75
Totals	6	52	59	27	24	15	17	2	4	4.15

1981

Composite Batting Averages

Los Angeles Dodgers

Player-Position	G	AB	R	H	2B	3B	HR	RBI	BA
Johnstone, ph	3	3	1	2	0	0	1	3	.667
Smith, ph	2	2	0	1	0	0	0	0	.500
Garvey, 1b	6	24	3	10	1	0	0	0	.417
Cey, 3b	6	20	3	7	0	0	1	6	.350
Guerrero, cf-rf	6	21	2	7	1	1	2	7	.333
Yeager, ph-c	6	14	2	4	1	0	2	4	.286
Scioscia, c-ph	3	4	1	1	0	0	0	0	.250
Russell, ss	6	25	1	6	0	0	0	2	.240
Monday, rf-ph	5	13	1	3	1	0	0	0	.231
Lopes, 2b	6	22	6	5	1	0	0	2	.227
L'ndreaux, ph-cf-pr	5	6	1	1	1	0	0	0	.167
Baker, lf	6	24	3	4	0	0	0	1	.167
Forster, p	2	0	0	0	0	0	0	0	.000
Goltz, p	2	0	0	0	0	0	0	0	.000
Niedenfuer, p	2	0	0	0	0	0	0	0	.000
Stewart, p	2	0	0	0	0	0	0	0	.000
Castillo, p	1	0	0	0	0	0	0	0	.000
Welch, p	1	0	0	0	0	0	0	0	.000
Sax, ph-pr-2b	2	1	0	0	0	0	0	0	.000
Howe, p	3	2	0	0	0	0	0	0	.000
Reuss, p	2	3	0	0	0	0	0	0	.000
Valenzuela, p	1	3	0	0	0	0	0	0	.000
Hooton, p	2	4	1	0	0	0	0	0	.000
Th'mas, ph-ss-cf-3b	5	7	2	0	0	0	0	1	.000
Totals	6	198	27	51	6	1	6	26	.258

New York Yankees

Player-Position	G	AB	R	H	2B	3B	HR	RBI	BA
Piniella, rf-ph-lf	6	16	2	7	1	0	0	3	.438
Rodriguez, 3b-pr	4	12	1	5	0	0	0	0	.417
Nettles, 3b	3	10	1	4	1	0	0	0	.400
Jackson, rf	3	12	3	4	1	0	1	1	.333
Gamble, rf-lf-ph	3	6	1	2	0	0	0	1	.333
Watson, 1b	6	22	2	7	1	0	2	7	.318
Milbourne, ss	6	20	2	5	2	0	0	3	.250
Randolph, 2b	6	18	5	4	1	1	2	3	.222
Mumphrey, cf	5	15	2	3	0	0	0	0	.200
Cerone, c	6	21	2	4	1	0	1	3	.190
Winfield, lf-cf	6	22	0	1	0	0	0	1	.045
Davis, p	4	0	0	0	0	0	0	0	.000
LaRoche, p	1	0	0	0	0	0	0	0	.000
Robertson, pr	1	0	0	0	0	0	0	0	.000
Brown, pr-rf-cf-ph	4	1	1	0	0	0	0	0	.000
Foote, ph	1	1	0	0	0	0	0	0	.000
Gossage, p	3	1	0	0	0	0	0	0	.000
May, p	3	1	0	0	0	0	0	0	.000
Righetti, p	1	1	0	0	0	0	0	0	.000
Frazier, p	3	2	0	0	0	0	0	0	.000
John, p	3	2	0	0	0	0	0	0	.000
Reuschel, p	2	2	0	0	0	0	0	0	.000
Murcer, ph	4	3	0	0	0	0	0	0	.000
Guidry, p	2	5	0	0	0	0	0	0	.000
Totals	6	193	22	46	8	1	6	22	.238

Composite Pitching Averages

Los Angeles Dodgers

Pitcher	G	IP	H	R	ER	BB	SO	W	L	ERA
Niedenfuer	2	5	3	2	0	1	0	0	0	0.00
Forster	2	2	1	0	0	3	0	0	0	0.00
Stewart	2	1⅔	1	0	0	2	1	0	0	0.00
Hooton	2	11⅓	8	3	2	9	3	1	1	1.59
Reuss	2	11⅔	10	5	5	3	8	1	1	3.86
Howe	3	7	7	3	3	1	4	1	0	3.86
Valenzuela	1	9	9	4	4	7	6	1	0	4.00
Goltz	2	3⅓	4	2	2	1	2	0	0	5.40
Castillo	1	1	0	1	1	5	0	0	0	9.00
Welch	1	0*	3	2	2	1	0	0	0	—
Totals	6	52	46	22	19	33	24	4	2	3.29

*Pitched to four batters in first inning of fourth game.

New York Yankees

Pitcher	G	IP	H	R	ER	BB	SO	W	L	ERA
Gossage	3	5	2	0	0	2	5	0	0	0.00
LaRoche	1	1	0	0	0	0	2	0	0	0.00
John	3	13	11	1	1	0	8	1	0	0.69
Guidry	2	14	8	3	3	4	15	1	1	1.93
May	3	6⅓	5	2	2	1	5	0	0	2.84
Reuschel	2	3⅔	7	3	2	3	2	0	0	4.91
Righetti	1	2	5	3	3	2	1	0	0	13.50
Frazier	3	3⅔	9	7	7	3	2	0	3	17.18
Davis	4	2⅓	4	8	6	5	4	0	0	23.14
Totals	6	51	51	27	24	20	44	2	4	4.24

1982

Composite Batting Averages

St. Louis Cardinals

Player-Position	G	AB	R	H	2B	3B	HR	RBI	BA
Iorg, dh	5	17	4	9	4	1	0	1	.529
Braun, ph-dh	2	2	0	1	0	0	0	2	.500
Hendrick, rf	7	28	5	9	0	0	0	5	.321
L. Smith, lf-dh	7	28	6	9	4	1	0	1	.321
Oberkfell, 3b	7	24	4	7	1	0	0	1	.292
Porter, c	7	28	1	8	2	0	1	5	.286
Hernandez, 1b	7	27	4	7	2	0	1	8	.259
McGee, cf	6	25	6	6	0	0	2	5	.240
O. Smith, ss	7	24	3	5	0	0	0	1	.208
Green, cf-ph-dh-lf-pr	7	10	3	2	1	1	0	0	.200
Herr, 2b	7	25	2	4	2	0	0	5	.160
Andujar, p	2	0	0	0	0	0	0	0	.000
Bair, p	3	0	0	0	0	0	0	0	.000
Brummer, c	1	0	0	0	0	0	0	0	.000
Forsch, p	2	0	0	0	0	0	0	0	.000
Kaat, p	4	0	0	0	0	0	0	0	.000
Lahti, p	2	0	0	0	0	0	0	0	.000
LaPoint, p	2	0	0	0	0	0	0	0	.000
Ramsey, 3b-pr	3	1	1	0	0	0	0	0	.000
Stuper, p	2	0	0	0	0	0	0	0	.000
Sutter, p	4	0	0	0	0	0	0	0	.000
Tenace, dh-ph	5	6	0	0	0	0	0	0	.000
Totals	7	245	39	67	16	3	4	34	.273

Milwaukee Brewers

Player-Position	G	AB	R	H	2B	3B	HR	RBI	BA
Yount, ss	7	29	6	12	3	0	1	6	.414
Molitor, 3b	7	31	5	11	0	0	0	3	.355
Moore, rf	7	26	3	9	3	0	0	2	.346
Gantner, 2b	7	24	5	8	4	1	0	4	.333
Cooper, 1b	7	28	3	8	1	0	1	6	.286
Money, ph-dh	5	13	4	3	1	0	0	1	.231
Oglivie, lf	7	27	4	6	0	1	1	1	.222
Simmons, c	7	23	2	4	0	0	2	3	.174
Thomas, cf	7	26	0	3	0	0	0	3	.115
Bernard, p	1	0	0	0	0	0	0	0	.000
Caldwell, p	3	0	0	0	0	0	0	0	.000
Edwards, pr-cf	1	0	0	0	0	0	0	0	.000
Haas, p	2	0	0	0	0	0	0	0	.000
Howell, dh	4	11	1	0	0	0	0	0	.000
Ladd, p	1	0	0	0	0	0	0	0	.000
McClure, p	5	0	0	0	0	0	0	0	.000
Medich, p	1	0	0	0	0	0	0	0	.000
Slaton, p	2	0	0	0	0	0	0	0	.000
Sutton, p	2	0	0	0	0	0	0	0	.000
Vuckovich, p	2	0	0	0	0	0	0	0	.000
Yost, c	1	0	0	0	0	0	0	0	.000
Totals		238	33	64	12	2	5	29	.269

Composite Pitching Averages

St. Louis Cardinals

Pitcher	G	IP	H	R	ER	BB	SO	W	L	ERA
Andujar	2	13⅓	10	3	2	1	4	2	0	1.35
LaPoint	2	8⅓	10	6	3	2	3	0	0	3.24
Stuper	2	13	10	5	5	5	5	1	0	3.46
Kaat	4	2⅓	4	1	1	2	2	0	0	3.86
Sutter	4	7⅔	6	4	4	3	6	1	0	4.70
Forsch	2	12⅔	18	10	7	3	4	0	2	4.97
Bair	3	2	2	2	2	2	3	0	1	9.00
Lahti	2	1⅔	4	2	2	1	1	0	0	10.80
Totals	7	61	64	33	23	19	28	4	3	3.39

(NOTE: St. Louis' individual earned runs do not add up to team total because of rule 10.18(i) applied in Game 4.)

Milwaukee Brewers

Pitcher	G	IP	H	R	ER	BB	SO	W	L	ERA
Slaton	2	2⅔	1	0	0	2	1	1	0	0.00
Bernard	1	1	0	0	0	0	1	0	0	0.00
Ladd	1	⅔	1	0	0	2	0	0	0	0.00
Caldwell	3	17⅔	19	4	4	3	6	2	0	2.04
McClure	5	4⅓	5	2	2	3	5	0	2	4.15
Vuckovich	2	14	16	9	7	5	4	0	1	4.50
Haas	2	7⅓	8	7	6	3	4	0	0	7.36
Sutton	2	10⅓	12	11	9	1	5	0	1	7.84
Medich	1	2	5	6	4	1	0	0	0	18.00
Totals	7	60	67	38	32	20	26	3	4	4.80

1983

Composite Batting Averages

Baltimore Orioles

Player-Position	G	AB	R	H	2B	3B	HR	RBI	BA
Ayala, ph	1	1	1	1	0	0	0	1	1.000
Shelby, ph-cf	5	9	1	4	0	0	0	1	.444
Dempsey, c	5	13	3	5	4	0	1	2	.385
Lowenstein, lf	4	13	2	5	1	0	1	1	.385
Dwyer, rf	2	8	3	3	1	0	1	1	.375
Murray, 1b	5	20	2	5	0	0	2	3	.250
Dauer, 2b-3b	5	19	2	4	1	0	0	3	.211
Ripken, ss	5	18	2	3	0	0	0	1	.167
Ford, ph-rf	5	12	1	2	0	0	1	1	.167
Cruz, 3b	5	16	1	2	0	0	0	0	.125
Bumbry, cf	4	11	0	1	1	0	0	1	.091
Landrum, pr-lf-rf	3	0	0	0	0	0	0	0	.000
T. Martinez, p	3	0	0	0	0	0	0	0	.000
Palmer, p	1	0	0	0	0	0	0	0	.000
Flanagan, p	1	1	0	0	0	0	0	0	.000
Sakata, pr-2b	1	1	0	0	0	0	0	0	.000
Singleton, ph	2	1	0	0	0	0	0	1	.000
Davis, p	1	2	0	0	0	0	0	0	.000
Nolan, ph-c	2	2	0	0	0	0	0	0	.000
Stewart, p	3	2	0	0	0	0	0	0	.000
Boddicker, p	1	3	0	0	0	0	0	1	.000
McGregor, p	2	5	0	0	0	0	0	0	.000
Roenicke, ph-lf	3	7	0	0	0	0	0	0	.000
Totals	5	164	18	35	8	0	6	17	.213

Philadelphia Phillies

Player-Position	G	AB	R	H	2B	3B	HR	RBI	BA
Virgil, ph-c	3	2	0	1	0	0	0	1	.500
Diaz, c	5	15	1	5	1	0	0	0	.333
Rose, ph-1b-rf	5	16	1	5	1	0	0	1	.313
Morgan, 2b	5	19	3	5	0	1	2	2	.263
Matthews, lf	5	16	1	4	0	0	1	1	.250
Maddox, ph-cf	4	12	1	3	1	0	1	1	.250
Perez, ph-1b	4	10	0	2	0	0	0	0	.200
Denny, p	2	5	1	1	0	0	0	1	.200
Lefebvre, ph-rf	3	5	0	1	1	0	0	2	.200
DeJesus, ss	5	16	0	2	0	0	0	0	.125
Lezcano, ph-rf	4	8	0	1	0	0	0	0	.125
Schmidt, 3b	5	20	0	1	0	0	0	0	.050
Andersen, p	2	0	0	0	0	0	0	0	.000
Bystrom, p	1	0	0	0	0	0	0	0	.000
Dernier, pr	1	0	1	0	0	0	0	0	.000
Hernandez, p	3	0	0	0	0	0	0	0	.000
Holland, p	2	0	0	0	0	0	0	0	.000
Reed, p	3	0	0	0	0	0	0	0	.000
Samuel, pr-ph	3	1	0	0	0	0	0	0	.000
Hudson, p	2	2	0	0	0	0	0	0	.000
Carlton, p	1	3	0	0	0	0	0	0	.000
Hayes, ph-rf	4	3	0	0	0	0	0	0	.000
G. Gross, cf	2	6	0	0	0	0	0	0	.000
Totals	5	159	9	31	4	1	4	9	.195

Composite Pitching Averages

Baltimore Orioles

Pitcher	G	IP	H	R	ER	BB	SO	W	L	ERA
Boddicker	1	9	3	1	0	0	6	1	0	0.00
Stewart	3	5	2	0	0	2	6	0	0	0.00
Palmer	1	2	2	0	0	1	1	1	0	0.00
McGregor	2	17	9	2	2	2	12	1	1	1.06
T. Martinez	3	3	3	1	1	0	0	0	0	3.00
Flanagan	1	4	6	2	2	1	1	0	0	4.50
Davis	1	5	6	3	3	1	3	1	0	5.40
Totals	5	45	31	9	8	7	29	4	1	1.60

Philadelphia Phillies

Pitcher	G	IP	H	R	ER	BB	SO	W	L	ERA
Hernandez	3	4	0	0	0	1	4	0	0	0.00
Holland	2	3⅔	1	0	0	0	5	0	0	0.00
Bystrom	1	1	0	0	0	0	1	0	0	0.00
Andersen	2	4	4	1	1	0	1	0	0	2.25
Carlton	1	6⅔	5	3	2	3	7	0	1	2.70
Reed	3	3⅓	4	1	1	2	4	0	0	2.70
Denny	2	13	12	5	5	3	9	1	1	3.46
Hudson	2	8⅓	9	8	8	1	6	0	2	8.64
Totals	5	44	35	18	17	10	37	1	4	3.48

1984

Composite Batting Averages

Detroit Tigers

Player-Position	G	AB	R	H	2B	3B	HR	RBI	BA
Trammell, ss	5	20	5	9	1	0	2	6	.450
Gibson, rf	5	18	4	6	0	0	2	7	.333
Herndon, lf-ph	5	15	1	5	0	0	1	3	.333
Castillo, 3b	3	9	2	3	0	0	1	2	.333
Grubb, ph-dh	4	3	0	1	0	0	0	0	.333
Lemon, cf	5	17	1	5	0	0	0	1	.294
Parrish, c	5	18	3	5	1	0	1	2	.278
Whitaker, 2b	5	18	6	5	2	0	0	0	.278
Evans, 1b-3b	5	15	1	1	0	0	0	1	.067
Bair, p	1	0	0	0	0	0	0	0	.000
Hernandez, p	3	0	0	0	0	0	0	0	.000
Lopez, p	2	0	0	0	0	0	0	0	.000
Morris, p	2	0	0	0	0	0	0	0	.000
Petry, p	2	0	0	0	0	0	0	0	.000
Scherrer, p	3	0	0	0	0	0	0	0	.000
Wilcox, p	1	0	0	0	0	0	0	0	.000
Johnson, ph	1	1	0	0	0	0	0	0	.000
Kuntz, ph	2	1	0	0	0	0	0	1	.000
Brookens, ph-3b	3	3	0	0	0	0	0	0	.000
Jones, lf	2	3	0	0	0	0	0	0	.000
Bergman, pr-1b	5	5	0	0	0	0	0	0	.000
Garbey, dh-ph	4	12	0	0	0	0	0	0	.000
Totals	5	158	23	40	4	0	7	23	.253

San Diego Padres

Player-Position	G	AB	R	H	2B	3B	HR	RBI	BA
Bochy, ph	1	1	0	1	0	0	0	0	1.000
Flannery, ph-2b	1	1	0	1	0	0	0	0	1.000
Bevacqua, dh	5	17	4	7	2	0	2	4	.412
Wiggins, 2b	5	22	2	8	1	0	0	1	.364
S'zar, pr-3b-cf-ph	4	3	0	1	0	0	0	0	.333
Templeton, ss	5	19	1	6	1	0	0	0	.316
Gwynn, rf	5	19	1	5	0	0	0	0	.263
Nettles, 3b	5	12	2	3	0	0	0	2	.250
Kennedy, c	5	19	2	4	1	0	1	3	.211
Garvey, 1b	5	20	2	4	2	0	0	2	.200
Martinez, lf	5	17	0	3	0	0	0	0	.176
Brown, cf-lf	5	15	1	1	0	0	0	2	.067
Booker, p	1	0	0	0	0	0	0	0	.000
Dravecky, p	2	0	0	0	0	0	0	0	.000
Gossage, p	2	0	0	0	0	0	0	0	.000
Harris, p	1	0	0	0	0	0	0	0	.000
Hawkins, p	3	0	0	0	0	0	0	0	.000
Lefferts, p	3	0	0	0	0	0	0	0	.000
Lollar, p	1	0	0	0	0	0	0	0	.000
Roenicke, lf-pr	2	0	0	0	0	0	0	0	.000
Show, p	1	0	0	0	0	0	0	0	.000
Thurmond, p	2	0	0	0	0	0	0	0	.000
Whitson, p	1	0	0	0	0	0	0	0	.000
Summers, ph	1	1	0	0	0	0	0	0	.000
Totals	5	166	15	44	7	0	3	14	.265

Composite Pitching Averages

Detroit Tigers

Pitcher	G	IP	H	R	ER	BB	SO	W	L	ERA
Lopez	2	3	1	0	0	1	4	1	0	0.00
Bair	1	⅔	0	0	0	0	1	0	0	0.00
Wilcox	1	6	7	1	1	2	4	1	0	1.50
Hernandez	3	5⅓	4	1	1	0	0	0	0	1.69
Morris	2	18	13	4	4	3	13	2	0	2.00
Scherrer	3	3	5	1	1	0	0	0	0	3.00
Petry	2	8	14	8	8	5	4	0	1	9.00
Totals	5	44	44	15	15	11	26	4	1	3.07

San Diego Padres

Pitcher	G	IP	H	R	ER	BB	SO	W	L	ERA
Lefferts	3	6	2	0	0	1	7	0	0	0.00
Harris	1	5⅓	3	0	0	3	5	0	0	0.00
Dravecky	2	4⅔	3	0	0	1	5	0	0	0.00
Hawkins	3	12	4	1	1	6	4	1	1	0.75
Booker	1	1	0	1	1	4	0	0	0	9.00
Thurmond	2	5⅓	12	6	6	3	2	0	1	10.13
Show	1	2⅔	4	4	3	1	2	0	1	10.13
Gossage	2	2⅔	3	4	4	1	2	0	0	13.50
Lollar	1	1⅔	4	4	4	4	0	0	1	21.60
Whitson	1	⅔	5	3	3	0	0	0	0	40.50
Totals	5	42	40	23	22	24	27	1	4	4.71

1985

Composite Batting Averages

Kansas City Royals

Player-Position	G	AB	R	H	2B	3B	HR	RBI	BA
L. Jones, ph-lf	6	3	0	2	1	1	0	0	.667
Iorg, ph	2	2	0	1	0	0	0	2	.500
Brett, 3b	7	27	5	10	1	0	0	1	.370
Wilson, cf	7	30	2	11	0	1	0	3	.367
Motley, rf-ph	5	11	1	4	0	0	1	3	.364
L. Smith, lf	7	27	4	9	3	0	0	4	.333
Orta, ph	3	3	0	1	0	0	0	0	.333
Balboni, 1b	7	25	2	8	0	0	0	3	.320
Biancalana, ss	7	18	2	5	0	0	0	2	.278
White, 2b	7	28	4	7	3	0	1	6	.250
Sundberg, c	7	24	6	6	2	0	0	1	.250
Sheridan, ph-rf	5	18	0	4	2	0	0	1	.222
Beckwith, p	1	0	0	0	0	0	0	0	.000
Concepcion, pr-ss	3	0	1	0	0	0	0	0	.000
Pryor, 3b	1	0	0	0	0	0	0	0	.000
Quisenberry, p	4	0	0	0	0	0	0	0	.000
Black, p	2	1	0	0	0	0	0	0	.000
McRae, ph	3	1	0	0	0	0	0	0	.000
Wathan, ph-pr	2	1	0	0	0	0	0	0	.000
Leibrandt, p	2	4	0	0	0	0	0	0	.000
Jackson, p	2	6	0	0	0	0	0	0	.000
Saberhagen, p	2	7	1	0	0	0	0	0	.000
Totals	7	236	28	68	12	2	2	26	.288

St. Louis Cardinals

Player-Position	G	AB	R	H	2B	3B	HR	RBI	BA
Landrum, lf	7	25	3	9	2	0	1	1	.360
Pendleton, 3b	7	23	3	6	1	1	0	3	.261
McGee, cf	7	27	2	7	2	0	1	2	.259
Harper, ph	4	4	0	1	0	0	0	1	.250
Clark, 1b	7	25	1	6	2	0	0	4	.240
Herr, 2b	7	26	2	4	2	0	0	0	.154
Cedeno, rf	5	15	1	2	1	0	0	1	.133
Porter, c	5	15	0	2	0	0	0	0	.133
Van Slyke, rf-ph-pr	6	11	0	1	0	0	0	0	.091
O. Smith, ss	7	23	1	2	0	0	0	0	.087
Campbell, p	3	0	0	0	0	0	0	0	.000
Dayley, p	4	0	0	0	0	0	0	0	.000
Forsch, p	2	0	0	0	0	0	0	0	.000
Lahti, p	3	0	0	0	0	0	0	0	.000
Lawless, pr	1	0	0	0	0	0	0	0	.000
Andujar, p	2	1	0	0	0	0	0	0	.000
Braun, ph	1	1	0	0	0	0	0	0	.000
DeJesus, ph	1	1	0	0	0	0	0	0	.000
Horton, p	3	1	0	0	0	0	0	0	.000
Worrell, p	3	1	0	0	0	0	0	0	.000
Jorgensen, ph-lf	2	3	0	0	0	0	0	0	.000
Cox, p	2	4	0	0	0	0	0	0	.000
Nieto, c	2	5	0	0	0	0	0	1	.000
Tudor, p	3	5	0	0	0	0	0	0	.000
Totals	7	216	13	40	10	1	2	13	.185

Composite Pitching Averages

Kansas City Royals

Pitcher	G	IP	H	R	ER	BB	SO	W	L	ERA
Beckwith	1	2	1	0	0	0	3	0	0	0.00
Saberhagen	2	18	11	1	1	1	10	2	0	0.50
Jackson	2	16	9	3	3	5	12	1	1	1.69
Quisenberry	4	4⅓	5	1	1	3	3	1	0	2.08
Leibrandt	2	16⅓	10	5	5	4	10	0	1	2.76
Black	2	5⅓	4	3	3	5	4	0	1	5.06
Totals	7	62	40	13	13	18	42	4	3	1.89

St. Louis Cardinals

Pitcher	G	IP	H	R	ER	BB	SO	W	L	ERA
Dayley	4	6	1	0	0	3	5	1	0	0.00
Cox	2	14	14	2	2	4	13	0	0	1.29
Campbell	3	4	4	1	1	2	5	0	0	2.25
Tudor	3	18	15	6	6	7	14	2	1	3.00
Worrell	3	4⅔	4	2	2	2	6	0	1	3.86
Horton	3	4	4	3	3	5	5	0	0	6.75
Andujar	2	4	10	4	4	4	3	0	1	9.00
Forsch	2	3	6	4	4	1	3	0	1	12.00
Lahti	3	3⅔	10	6	5	0	2	0	0	12.27
Totals	7	61⅓	68	28	27	28	56	3	4	3.96

1986

Composite Batting Averages

New York Mets

Player-Position	G	AB	R	H	2B	3B	HR	RBI	BA
Orosco, p	4	1	0	1	0	0	0	1	1.000
Gooden, p	2	2	1	1	0	0	0	0	.500
Teufel, 2b	3	9	1	4	1	0	1	1	.444
Mazzilli, ph-rf	4	5	2	2	0	0	0	0	.400
Knight, 3b	6	23	4	9	1	0	1	5	.391
Backman, pr-2b	6	18	4	6	0	0	0	1	.333
Dykstra, cf-ph	7	27	4	8	0	0	2	3	.296
Carter, c	7	29	4	8	2	0	2	9	.276
Wilson, lf-cf	7	26	3	7	1	0	0	0	.269
Santana, ss	7	20	3	5	0	0	0	2	.250
Mitchell, ph-lf-dh	5	8	1	2	0	0	0	0	.250
Hernandez, 1b	7	26	1	6	0	0	0	4	.231
Strawberry, rf	7	24	4	5	1	0	1	1	.208
Heep, ph-lf-dh	5	11	0	1	0	0	0	2	.091
Aguilera, p	2	0	0	0	0	0	0	0	.000
Fernandez, p	3	0	0	0	0	0	0	0	.000
McDowell, p	5	0	0	0	0	0	0	0	.000
Sisk, p	1	0	0	0	0	0	0	0	.000
Elster, ss	1	1	0	0	0	0	0	0	.000
Ojeda, p	2	2	0	0	0	0	0	0	.000
Darling, p	3	3	0	0	0	0	0	0	.000
Johnson, 3b-ph-ss	2	5	0	0	0	0	0	0	.000
Totals	7	240	32	65	6	0	7	29	.271

Boston Red Sox

Player-Position	G	AB	R	H	2B	3B	HR	RBI	BA
Barrett, 2b	7	30	1	13	2	0	0	4	.433
Henderson, cf	7	25	6	10	1	1	2	5	.400
Rice, lf	7	27	6	9	1	1	0	0	.333
Evans, rf	7	26	4	8	2	0	2	9	.308
Owen, ss	7	20	2	6	0	0	0	2	.300
Boggs, 3b	7	31	3	9	3	0	0	3	.290
Gedman, c	7	30	1	6	1	0	1	1	.200
Buckner, 1b	7	32	2	6	0	0	0	1	.188
Baylor, dh-ph	4	11	1	2	1	0	0	1	.182
Boyd, p	1	0	0	0	0	0	0	0	.000
Nipper, p	2	0	0	0	0	0	0	0	.000
Sambito, p	2	0	0	0	0	0	0	0	.000
Armas, ph	1	1	0	0	0	0	0	0	.000
Crawford, p	3	1	0	0	0	0	0	0	.000
Romero, pr-ss	3	1	0	0	0	0	0	0	.000
Schiraldi, p	3	1	0	0	0	0	0	0	.000
Stanley, p	5	1	0	0	0	0	0	0	.000
Stapleton, 1b-pr	3	1	0	0	0	0	0	0	.000
Greenwell, ph	4	3	0	0	0	0	0	0	.000
Hurst, p	3	3	0	0	0	0	0	0	.000
Clemens, p	2	4	1	0	0	0	0	0	.000
Totals	7	248	27	69	11	2	5	26	.278

Composite Pitching Averages

New York Mets

Pitcher	G	IP	H	R	ER	BB	SO	W	L	ERA
Orosco	4	5⅔	2	0	0	0	6	0	0	0.00
Sisk	1	⅔	0	0	0	1	1	0	0	0.00
Fernandez	3	6⅔	6	1	1	1	10	0	0	1.35
Darling	3	17⅔	13	4	3	10	12	1	1	1.53
Ojeda	2	13	13	3	3	5	9	1	0	2.08
McDowell	5	7⅓	10	5	4	6	2	1	0	4.91
Gooden	2	9	17	10	8	4	9	0	2	8.00
Aguilera	2	3	8	4	4	1	4	1	0	12.00
Totals	7	63	69	27	23	28	53	4	3	3.29

Boston Red Sox

Pitcher	G	IP	H	R	ER	BB	SO	W	L	ERA
Stanley	5	6⅓	5	0	0	1	4	0	0	0.00
Hurst	3	23	18	5	5	6	17	2	0	1.96
Clemens	2	11⅓	9	5	4	6	11	0	0	3.18
Crawford	3	4⅓	5	3	3	0	4	1	0	6.23
Nipper	2	6⅓	10	5	5	2	2	0	1	7.11
Boyd	1	7	9	6	6	1	3	0	1	7.71
Schiraldi	3	4	7	7	6	3	2	0	2	13.50
Sambito	2	⅓	2	1	1	2	0	0	0	27.00
Totals	7	62⅔	65	32	30	21	43	3	4	4.31

1987

Composite Batting Averages

Minnesota Twins

Player-Position	G	AB	R	H	2B	3B	HR	RBI	BA
Smalley, ph	4	2	0	1	1	0	0	0	.500
Lombardozzi, 2b	6	17	3	7	1	0	1	4	.412
Baylor, dh-ph	5	13	3	5	0	0	1	3	.385
Puckett, cf	7	28	5	10	1	1	0	3	.357
Laudner, c	7	22	4	7	1	0	1	4	.318
Gladden, lf	7	31	3	9	2	1	1	7	.290
Gaetti, 3b	7	27	4	7	2	1	1	4	.259
Hrbek, 1b	7	24	4	5	0	0	1	6	.208
Gagne, ss	7	30	5	6	1	0	1	3	.200
Brunansky, rf	7	25	5	5	0	0	0	2	.200
Newman, pr-2b-ph	4	5	0	1	0	0	0	0	.200
Bush, dh-ph	4	6	1	1	1	0	0	2	.167
Larkin, 1b-ph	5	3	1	0	0	0	0	0	.000
Straker, p	2	2	0	0	0	0	0	0	.000
Blyleven, p	2	1	0	0	0	0	0	0	.000
Davidson, rf-ph	2	1	0	0	0	0	0	0	.000
Viola, p	3	1	0	0	0	0	0	0	.000
Atherton, p	2	0	0	0	0	0	0	0	.000
Berenguer, p	3	0	0	0	0	0	0	0	.000
Butera, c	1	0	0	0	0	0	0	0	.000
Frazier, p	1	0	0	0	0	0	0	0	.000
Niekro, p	1	0	0	0	0	0	0	0	.000
Reardon, p	4	0	0	0	0	0	0	0	.000
Schatzeder, p	3	0	0	0	0	0	0	0	.000
Totals	7	238	38	64	10	3	7	38	.269

St. Louis Cardinals

Player-Position	G	AB	R	H	2B	3B	HR	RBI	BA
Pendleton, dh-ph	3	7	2	3	0	0	0	1	.429
Pena, c-dh	7	22	2	9	1	0	0	4	.409
McGee, cf	7	27	2	10	2	0	0	4	.370
Lindeman, 1b-ph-rf	6	15	3	5	1	0	0	2	.333
Lake, c	3	3	0	1	0	0	0	1	.333
Ford, rf-ph	5	13	1	4	0	0	0	2	.308
Herr, 2b	7	28	2	7	0	0	1	1	.250
Oquendo, rf-3b	7	24	2	6	0	0	0	2	.250
Pagnozzi, dh-ph	2	4	0	1	0	0	0	0	.250
Driessen, 1b	4	13	3	3	2	0	0	1	.231
Smith, ss	7	28	3	6	0	0	0	2	.214
Coleman, lf	7	28	5	4	2	0	0	2	.143
Lawless, 3b	3	10	1	1	0	0	1	3	.100
Cox, p	3	2	0	0	0	0	0	0	.000
Forsch, p	3	2	0	0	0	0	0	0	.000
Morris, rf	1	2	0	0	0	0	0	0	.000
Tudor, p	2	2	0	0	0	0	0	0	.000
Dayley, p	4	1	0	0	0	0	0	0	.000
Mathews, p	1	1	0	0	0	0	0	0	.000
Horton, p	2	0	0	0	0	0	0	0	.000
Johnson, pr	1	0	0	0	0	0	0	0	.000
Magrane, p	2	0	0	0	0	0	0	0	.000
Tunnell, p	2	0	0	0	0	0	0	0	.000
Worrell, p	4	0	0	0	0	0	0	0	.000
Totals	7	232	26	60	8	0	2	25	.259

Composite Pitching Averages

Minnesota Twins

Pitcher	G	IP	H	R	ER	BB	SO	W	L	ERA
Reardon	4	4⅔	5	0	0	0	3	0	0	0.00
Frazier	1	2	1	0	0	0	2	0	0	0.00
Niekro	1	2	1	0	0	1	1	0	0	0.00
Blyleven	2	13	13	5	4	2	12	1	1	2.77
Viola	3	19⅓	17	8	8	3	16	2	1	3.72
Straker	2	9	9	4	4	3	6	0	0	4.00
Schatzeder	3	4⅓	4	3	3	3	3	1	0	6.23
Atherton	2	1⅓	0	1	1	1	0	0	0	6.75
Berenguer	3	4⅓	10	5	5	0	1	0	1	10.38
Totals	7	60	60	26	25	13	44	4	3	3.75

St. Louis Cardinals

Pitcher	G	IP	H	R	ER	BB	SO	W	L	ERA
Worrell	4	7	6	1	1	4	3	0	0	1.29
Dayley	4	4⅔	2	1	1	0	3	0	0	1.93
Tunnell	2	4⅓	4	2	1	2	1	0	0	2.08
Mathews	1	3⅔	2	1	1	2	3	0	0	2.45
Tudor	2	11	15	7	7	3	8	1	1	5.73
Horton	2	3	5	2	2	0	1	0	0	6.00
Cox	3	11⅔	13	10	10	8	9	1	2	7.71
Magrane	2	7⅓	9	7	7	5	5	0	1	8.59
Forsch	3	6⅓	8	7	7	5	3	1	0	9.95
Totals	7	59	64	38	37	29	36	3	4	5.64

1988

COMPOSITE BATTING AVERAGES

Los Angeles Dodgers

Player-Position	G	AB	R	H	2B	3B	HR	RBI	BA
Hershiser, p	2	3	1	3	2	0	0	1	1.000
Gibson, ph	1	1	1	1	0	0	1	2	1.00
Hatcher, lf-rf	5	19	5	7	1	0	2	5	.368
Sax, 2b	5	20	3	6	0	0	0	0	.300
Stubbs, 1b	5	17	3	5	2	0	0	2	.294
Heep, ph-lf-dh	3	8	0	2	1	0	0	0	.250
Marshall, rf	5	13	2	3	0	1	1	3	.231
Shelby, cf	5	18	0	4	1	0	0	1	.222
Scioscia, c	4	14	0	3	0	0	0	1	.214
Dempsey, c	2	5	0	1	1	0	0	1	.200
Griffin, ss	5	16	2	3	0	0	0	0	.188
M. Davis, ph-dh-rf	4	7	3	1	0	0	1	2	.143
Hamilton, 3b	5	19	1	2	0	0	0	0	.105
Belcher, p	2	0	0	0	0	0	0	0	.000
Holton, p	1	0	0	0	0	0	0	0	.000
J. Howell, p	2	0	0	0	0	0	0	0	.000
Leary, p	2	0	0	0	0	0	0	0	.000
Pena, p	2	0	0	0	0	0	0	0	.000
Tudor, p	1	0	0	0	0	0	0	0	.000
Anderson, ph-dh	1	0	0	0	0	0	0	0	.000
Gonzalez, ph-rf-lf	4	2	0	0	0	0	0	0	.000
Woodson, ph-1b	4	4	0	0	0	0	0	1	.000
Totals	5	167	21	41	8	1	5	19	.246

Oakland Athletics

Player-Position	G	AB	R	H	2B	3B	HR	RBI	BA
Javier, pr-lf	3	4	0	2	0	0	0	2	.500
Steinbach, c-dh	3	11	0	4	1	0	0	0	.364
Henderson, cf	5	20	1	6	2	0	0	1	.300
Hubbard, 2b	4	12	2	3	0	0	0	0	.250
Hassey, c-ph	5	8	0	2	0	0	0	1	.250
Phillips, lf-2b	2	4	1	1	0	0	0	0	.250
Parker, lf-dh	4	15	0	3	0	0	0	0	.200
Lansford, 3b	5	18	2	3	0	0	0	1	.167
Polonia, ph-lf	3	9	1	1	0	0	0	0	.111
Weiss, ss	5	16	1	1	0	0	0	0	.063
McGwire, 1b	5	17	1	1	0	0	1	1	.059
Canseco, rf	5	19	1	1	0	0	1	5	.053
Burns, p	1	0	0	0	0	0	0	0	.000
Cadaret, p	3	0	0	0	0	0	0	0	.000
Eckersley, p	2	0	0	0	0	0	0	0	.000
Gallego, pr-2b	1	0	0	0	0	0	0	0	.000
Honeycutt, p	3	0	0	0	0	0	0	0	.000
Nelson, p	3	0	0	0	0	0	0	0	.000
Plunk, p	2	0	0	0	0	0	0	0	.000
Welch, p	1	0	0	0	0	0	0	0	.000
Young, p	1	0	0	0	0	0	0	0	.000
Baylor, ph	1	1	0	0	0	0	0	0	.000
S. Davis, p	2	1	0	0	0	0	0	0	.000
Stewart, p	2	3	1	0	0	0	0	0	.000
Totals	5	158	11	28	3	0	2	11	.177

COMPOSITE PITCHING AVERAGES

Los Angeles Dodgers

Pitcher	G	IP	H	R	ER	BB	SO	W	L	ERA
Pena	2	5	2	0	0	1	7	1	0	0.00
Holton	1	2	0	0	0	0	1	0	0	0.00
Tudor	1	1⅓	0	0	0	0	1	0	0	0.00
Hershiser	2	18	7	2	2	6	17	2	0	1.00
Leary	2	6⅔	6	1	1	2	4	0	0	1.35
J. Howell	2	2⅔	3	1	1	1	2	0	1	3.38
Belcher	2	8⅔	10	7	6	6	10	1	0	6.23
Totals	5	44⅓	28	11	10	17	41	4	1	2.03

Oakland Athletics

Pitcher	G	IP	H	R	ER	BB	SO	W	L	ERA
Honeycutt	3	3⅓	0	0	0	0	5	1	0	0.00
Cadaret	3	2	2	0	0	0	3	0	0	0.00
Plunk	2	1⅔	0	0	0	0	3	0	0	0.00
Young	1	1	1	0	0	0	0	0	0	0.00
Burns	1	⅓	0	0	0	0	0	0	0	0.00
Nelson	3	6⅓	4	1	1	3	3	0	0	1.42
Welch	1	5	6	1	1	3	8	0	0	1.80
Stewart	2	14⅓	12	7	5	5	5	0	1	3.14
Eckersley	2	1⅔	2	2	2	1	2	0	1	10.80
S. Davis	2	8	14	10	10	1	7	0	2	11.25
Totals	5	43⅔	41	21	19	13	36	1	4	3.92

1989

COMPOSITE BATTING AVERAGES

Oakland Athletics

Player-Position	G	AB	R	H	2B	3B	HR	RBI	BA
Blankenship, ph-2b	1	2	1	1	0	0	0	0	.500
R. Henderson, lf	4	19	4	9	1	2	1	3	.474
Lansford, 3b	4	16	5	7	1	0	1	4	.430
Canseco, rf	4	14	5	5	0	0	1	3	.357
Moore, p	2	3	1	1	1	0	0	2	.333
D. Henderson, cf	4	13	6	4	2	0	2	4	.308
McGwire, 1b	4	17	0	5	1	0	0	1	.294
Steinbach, c	4	16	3	4	0	1	1	7	.250
Phillips, 2b-3b-lf	4	17	2	4	1	0	1	3	.235
Parker, dh-ph	3	9	2	2	1	0	1	2	.222
Weiss, ss	4	15	3	2	0	0	1	1	.133
Burns, p	2	0	0	0	0	0	0	0	.000
Eckersley, p	2	0	0	0	0	0	0	0	.000
Honeycutt, p	3	0	0	0	0	0	0	0	.000
Javier, rf	1	0	0	0	0	0	0	0	.000
Nelson, p	2	0	0	0	0	0	0	0	.000
Gallego, 2b-ph-3b	2	1	0	0	0	0	0	0	.000
Phelps, ph	1	1	0	0	0	0	0	0	.000
Stewart, p	2	3	0	0	0	0	0	0	.000
Totals	4	146	32	44	8	3	9	30	.301

San Francisco Giants

Player-Position	G	AB	R	H	2B	3B	HR	RBI	BA
Manwaring, c	1	1	1	1	1	0	0	0	1.000
Litton, ph-2b-3b	2	6	1	3	1	0	1	3	.500
Bathe, ph	2	2	1	1	0	0	1	3	.500
Oberkfell, ph-3b	4	6	1	2	0	0	0	0	.333
Mitchell, lf	4	17	2	5	0	0	1	2	.294
Butler, cf	4	14	1	4	1	0	0	1	.286
Clark, 1b	4	16	2	4	1	0	0	0	.250
Nixon, ph-cf-rf	2	5	1	1	0	0	0	0	.200
Uribe, ss	3	5	1	1	0	0	0	0	.200
Kennedy, c	4	12	1	2	0	0	0	2	.167
Williams, 3b-ss	4	16	1	2	0	0	1	1	.125
Maldonado, rf-ph	4	11	1	1	0	1	0	0	.091
Thompson, 2b-ph	4	11	0	1	0	0	0	2	.091
Bedrosian, p	2	0	0	0	0	0	0	0	.000
Brantley, p	3	0	0	0	0	0	0	0	.000
Downs, p	3	0	0	0	0	0	0	0	.000
Hammaker, p	2	0	0	0	0	0	0	0	.000
Lefferts, p	3	0	0	0	0	0	0	0	.000
Reuschel, p	1	0	0	0	0	0	0	0	.000
Robinson, p	1	0	0	0	0	0	0	0	.000
Garrelts, p	2	1	0	0	0	0	0	0	.000
LaCoss, p	2	1	0	0	0	0	0	0	.000
Sheridan, rf	1	2	0	0	0	0	0	0	.000
Riles, dh-ph	4	8	0	0	0	0	0	0	.000
Totals	4	134	14	28	4	1	4	14	.209

COMPOSITE PITCHING AVERAGES

Oakland Athletics

Pitcher	G	IP	H	R	ER	BB	SO	W	L	ERA
Burns	2	1⅔	1	0	0	1	0	0	0	0.00
Eckersley	2	1⅔	0	0	0	0	0	0	0	0.00
Stewart	2	16	10	3	3	2	14	2	0	1.69
Moore	2	13	9	3	3	3	10	2	0	2.08
Honeycutt	3	2⅔	4	2	2	0	2	0	0	6.75
Nelson	2	1	4	6	6	2	1	0	0	54.00
Totals	4	36	28	14	14	8	27	4	0	3.50

San Francisco Giants

Pitcher	G	IP	H	R	ER	BB	SO	W	L	ERA
Bedrosian	2	2⅔	0	0	0	2	2	0	0	0.00
Lefferts	3	2⅔	2	1	1	2	1	0	0	3.38
Brantley	3	4⅓	5	2	2	3	1	0	0	4.15
LaCoss	2	4⅓	4	3	3	2	4	0	0	6.23
Downs	3	4⅔	3	4	4	2	4	0	0	7.71
Garrelts	2	7⅓	13	9	8	1	8	0	2	9.82
Reuschel	1	4	5	5	5	4	2	0	1	11.25
Hammaker	2	2⅓	8	4	4	0	2	0	0	15.43
Robinson	1	1⅔	4	4	4	1	0	0	1	21.60
Totals	4	34	44	32	31	18	22	0	4	8.21

Index

421